Fourth Edition

ADVANCED DEBATE

READINGS IN THEORY, PRACTICE & TEACHING

Edited by
David A. Thomas
John P. Hart

National Textbook Company
a division of NTC *Publishing Group*

Published by National Textbook Company, a division of NTC Publishing Group.
© 1992 by NTC Publishing Group, 4255 West Touhy Avenue, Lincolnwood
(Chicago), Illinois 60646-1975 U.S.A.

Manufactured in the United States of America.
Library of Congress Catalog Card Number: 91-60323

2 3 4 5 6 7 8 9 BC 9 8 7 6 5 4 3 2 1

To the memory of Daniel M. Rohrer
Colleague, Mentor, Friend

Contents

Part One   **Overview of the Discipline**   **1**

  1   Why Should We Support Debate?   2
      Kent Colbert and Thompson Biggers

  2   Women in High School Debate   8
      J. Cinder Griffin and Holly Jane Raider

  3   Ethics in Academic Debate: A Gaming Perspective   15
      Alfred C. Snider

Part Two   **Advanced Debate Practices**   **31**

  4   Affirmative Case Approaches   33
      Allan J. Lichtman, Daniel M. Rohrer, and Jerome Corsi

  5   A Systematic Approach to Opposing Policy Change   42
      Michael Pfau

  6   A Reevaluation of Negative Division of Duties   50
      Dwaine R. Hemphill

  7   Cross-Examination Reexamined   61
      George Ziegelmueller

  8   Prep Time: Maximizing a Valuable Resource   71
      Gloria Cabada

  9   A Theory of the Turnaround   81
      Walter Ulrich

 10   Value Analysis in Lincoln-Douglas Debate: 87
      The Need for Substance over Form
      Diana Prentice

 11   Impact and Implications of Parliamentary Format on   94
      American Debate
      E. Sam Cox and Kendall R. Phillips

 12   The Use of Empirical Studies in Debate   105
      Tim Lee, Dave Harris, and Craig Dudczak

13   The Role of Causal Argument in Policy Controversies   115
      David Zarefsky

Part Three   Resolutional Considerations   135

14   The Debate Resolution   137
      Allan J. Lichtman, Daniel M. Rohrer, and Jerome Corsi

15   Topicality: Why Not the Best?   141
      James J. Unger

16   On Being Reasonable—The Last Refuge of Scoundrels: 146
      The Scoundrels Strike Back
      Donn W. Parson and John Bart

17   The Affirmative Topicality Burden: Any Reasonable   156
      Example
      Dale A. Herbeck and John P. Katsulas

18   The Counterwarrant as a Negative Strategy: 169
      A Modest Proposal
      James W. Paulsen and Jack Rhodes

Part Four   Decision Rules   179

19   Decision Rules in Policy Debate: Presumption and   180
      the Burden of Proof
      Allan J. Lichtman and Daniel M. Rohrer

20   Presumption in Policy Systems   208
      John P. Hart

21   Presumption in Nonpolicy Debate: A Case for Natural   220
      Presumption Based on Current Nonpolicy Paradigms
      David A. Thomas

Part Five   Models of the Debate Process   243

22   The Stock Issues Paradigm   245
      Walter Ulrich

23   Argument as Hypothesis Testing   252
      David Zarefsky

24   Policy Systems Analysis in Debate   263
      Allan J. Lichtman, Daniel M. Rohrer, and Jerome Corsi

25   Policy Systems Revisited   278
      Allan J. Lichtman, Daniel M. Rohrer, and John P. Hart

Part Six **Judging Stances**   **289**

26 The Debate Judge as Critic of Argument   292
    V. William Balthrop

27 In Search of Tabula Rasa   310
    Walter Ulrich

28 Game Theory: Playing the Same Game—Gaming as   319
    a Unifying Paradigm for Educational Debating
    Alfred C. Snider

29 Application of the Narrative Paradigm in CEDA Debate 329
    Kristine M. Bartanen

30 The Narrative Perspective in Academic Debate: 342
    A Critique
    Robert H. Gass, Jr.

Part Seven **Theoretical Issues in Policy Debate**   **363**

31 A General Theory of the Counterplan   365
    Allan J. Lichtman and Daniel M. Rohrer

32 A Permutation Standard of Competitiveness   377
    Dale A. Herbeck

33 Negative Fiat: Resolving the Ambiguities of "Should"   388
    Roger Solt

34 The Topical Counterplan: A Competitive Policy   413
    Alternative
    Edward M. Panetta and Steven Dolley

35 What Killed Schrodinger's Cat? A Response to Panetta 430
    and Dolley
    David M. Berube

Part Eight **Theoretical Issues in Nonpolicy Debate**   **453**

36 The Role and Function of Affirmative Criteria   456
    Andrew B. Goulet and Michael Bauer

37 It's About Time We Measure   462
    Richard O'Dor

38 Debating Propositions of Value: An Idea Revisited   475
    Ronald J. Matlon

39 Propositions of Fact   491
    John P. Hart and Brian R. McGee

40   Towards a Strategic Focus in Nonpolicy Debate   501
       David J. Shipley

41   The Indivisibility of Value Claims from Policy Positions: 517
       An Argument for Policy in Value Debate
       Dale Herbeck and Kimball Wong

42   Value Implications   528
       Kent Colbert and David A. Thomas

43   Hasty Generalization Revisited   535
       David M. Berube

44   When the Whole Is Greater Than the Sum of the Parts: 549
       The Implications of Holistic Resolutional Focus
       Jeffrey T. Bile

45   Debating Impacts: Intrinsicness Argumentation in   560
       Nonpolicy Debating
       David M. Berube

Appendix A   **Author Directory**   **577**
Appendix B   **Source Notes**   **579**

Part One

Overview of the Discipline

In what sense can debate be called a discipline? There are several senses that come to mind.

First, debate can be considered an academic discipline, studied in the curriculum of such courses as argumentation and debate. In this sense, scholars and theorists conduct research and publicize their findings in the latest advances in debate theory and research.

Second, debate can be considered an extracurricular discipline in the form of a student activity. Like band, athletics, or the student yearbook, debate furnishes an organization and a set of educational goals for students beyond the classroom. In this sense, students and their activities are the focal point for our interest.

Third, as an activity, debate itself incorporates critical thinking and analytical approaches to current issues in society. Debate's routines are disciplined.

In the section that follows, three articles explore the discipline of debate. "Why Should We Support Debate?" is a question Colbert and Biggers ask. Their curiosity echoes that of many school administrators, teachers, parents, and students today. Their answer is optimistic and positive, and their findings should find their way into the rationale of many debate directors as they petition their school administrators for budgetary support.

Griffin and Raider address the issue of white, male dominance of debate, an issue being raised increasingly in the consciousness of educators and directors of many other activities as well. The low participation rates of women and minorities in debate are unsettling. To the extent that the activity discriminates against groups, a flaw in the system exists that must be remedied. This article provides a useful starting point for discussion. Finally, Snider presents a paradigm for addressing ethical questions in the format of the formal academic debate context.

1

Why Should We Support Debate?

Kent Colbert

Thompson Biggers

Training in debate has long been considered a vital part of the educational process. Yet, in this time of financial stress, many forensic directors have been asked to justify expenditures on their programs. We are frequently asked why debate should be funded on our campuses. This may seem curious since debate has a long and honored place in academia. The reaction of many in our field is even more curious. Instead of preparing our arguments in justification, we have often assumed that others understood our importance. Our lack of preparation may be the result of the relative unavailability of materials to build such a defense. While debate may allow a university to develop a reputation for competitive excellence, to recruit outstanding high school students and to be active in community life, its educational benefits for students would seem more immediately relevant grounds for its defense. So, this article presents some supporting material to answer the question, "Why should we support debate?"

The literature suggests that debaters benefit in at least three areas. First, forensic competition improves the students' communication skills. Second, forensics provides a unique educational experience because of the way it promotes depth of study, complex analysis and focused critical thinking. Third, forensics offers excellent pre-professional preparation.

Debate training can significantly improve communication skills. A study by Semlak and Shields concluded that "students with debate experience were significantly better at employing the three communication skills (analysis, delivery, and organization) utilized in this study than students without the experience" (1977, p. 194). Debate training not only improves speaking skills but also helps students in other communication situations. Group discussion and interpersonal skills are also improved. Pollock's research suggests that "persons with oral communication skills honed by varied forensic events were also regarded highly by their colleagues in group discussion activity. Virtually every legislator accorded high ratings in the basic category of interpersonal communication listed forensic experience as a student" (1982, p. 17). Pollock concludes that "indeed a concrete justification of the value of forensics as a co-curricular activity in speech communication may be inferred from these survey results" (p. 17).

Speech educators echo this praise for debate as an educational activity. Pearce's survey concluded, "Attitudes toward forensics by those who teach speech communication in higher institutions are generally favorable" (1974, p. 139). The conclusion seems fairly simple, debate training is an excellent way of improving many communication skills.

The second advantage of debate, mentioned repeatedly, is depth of educational experience. Our goal as communication educators certainly should be to improve the communication abilities of our students. However, we also share the burden with our colleagues in other disciplines to provide an excellent educational experience for our students. Debate does this in two ways: introducing students to the social sciences and improving critical thinking ability.

Debate exposes students to in-depth analysis of many areas in the social sciences. Robinson explains: "[in just six years] high school and college debaters were introduced to such vital and contemporary issues as compulsory arbitration of labor disputes, world government, electoral college reforms, price and wage controls, FEPC, and tariff revision. . . . Study and debate of such topics serves as an introduction to the social sciences for many undergraduates. . . . I suspect that many undergraduates rely on debating for their important contact with social science . . . " (1956, p. 62).

Exposure to the thinking of others on the important issues of our time is valuable, but learning to think critically about these issues is even more important. Ehninger and Brockriede say that critical thinking is grounded in a careful examination and interpretation of relevant facts and values. It should reflect an awareness of options open, of consequences involved, and of the steps required to put the elected alternative into effect.

After reviewing the research on debate and improved critical thinking ability, Keefe, Harte, and Norton concluded, "Many researchers over the past four decades have come to the same general conclusions. Critical thinking ability is significantly improved by courses in argumentation and debate and by debate experience" (1982, pp. 33–34). The importance of critical thinking is best explained by Ehninger and Brockriede:

> The function of debate is to enable men [*sic*] to make collective choices and decisions critically when inferential questions become subjects for dispute.... When collective choices and decisions require personal judgment as well as facts and figures, debate helps insure that these decisions will be made critically.... A critical decision is more 'human,' i.e., rational, than an uncritical one. The ability to arrive at decisions critically is the trait that chiefly distinguishes man [*sic*] from animal (1963, p. 15).

The educational benefits of debate seem to be well documented: improved communication skills; exposure to important social issues of our time; improvement of critical thinking ability. If students benefit from debate, then we should find that debate is excellent pre-professional preparation. Indeed the support is strong for this third advantage.

The data suggesting that forensics is valuable to the pre-law student is overwhelming. McBath reported, "This survey indicated resounding approval of speech participation as a professional foundation and the endorsement of a public speaking and debate requirement" (1961, p. 47). Arnold found that, "of 94 Pennsylvania lawyers ... 62 percent of the respondents with debate experience and 53 percent of the respondents without debate experience believed that debate should be recommended for all pre-legal students" (1974, p. 139). In a study of 98 law school deans, Swanson (1970) found that 69.9 percent would advise pre-law students to take courses in argumentation, and 70.3 percent recommended participation in intercollegiate debate. The support from lawyers and law scholl administrators ranges from strong endorsement of debate for *all* pre-law students to a suggestion that it be *required*. This seems to make a stronger case than even we might propose. The reason for such support may be the professional success of former debaters.

Improved speaking ability seems to be a benefit that helps students when they enter professional life as well. Pollock extends his conclusions to the real world in a study that analyzed the speaking ability of state representatives with and without debate experience:

> In speculating what role the forensic activity plays in the attainment of oral communication success in legislative halls, some positive conclusions can be inferred. For example, the correlation ran high in this survey that the very top debaters and floor speakers in the Florida House of Representatives were also those who had previous experience in scholastic debate or public speaking-type forensic activity (1982, p. 17).

Huseman and Goodman provide testimonials that support this argument from former debaters who have succeeded professionally.

Senator Dick Clark of Iowa stated, "The principal value of debate lies in the development of logical thought processes, and the ability to articulate your positions publicly" (1976, p. 226). Representative Charles E. Bennett of Florida concurred, stating, "Debate not only improves one's ability to speak publicly but improves the thinking process of the debater" (p. 226).

The excellence of debate as pre-professional training is acknowledged by those in business. Center reported, "The results of a recent survey of those responsible for hiring, for a variety of Midwest businesses, listed debating first among 20 other activities and academic specializations that an applicant might present on a resume. Debate was the overwhelming first choice of those responsible for recruiting and hiring for law firms. Moreover, debating was ranked very high by a wide variety of businesses" (1982, p. 5). In a time when many of our students ask us how educational activities will help them get a job, the answer seems to be unequivocal. Debate experience is highly valued by the business world.

The value placed on debate by business is well founded. Former debaters tend to be very successful people. Keele and Matlon (1984) concluded that 90 percent of debaters have attained at least one graduate degree. 30 percent of their sample are university educators while another 15 percent are top ranking corporate executives. Ten percent are now working in the executive or legislative branches of government. They suggest that these ratios do not vary between those who graduated 25 years ago and those who finished within the last five years. It is doubtful that many other activities can boast of so many successful alumni.

It appears that debate develops leadership qualities in individuals. *Freedom and Union* reported that, "A survey of 160 senators, congressmen, governors, Supreme Court justices, and Cabinet members, and other leaders revealed that 100 of the leaders said high school or college debate experience was helpful in their careers, and 90 classified the experience as 'greatly helpful' or 'invaluable.' Of the 60 who did not have debate experience, 26 expressed regret that they had not gone out for the debating team while in high school or college" (1960, p. 6). Those who have become successful believe debate helped them succeed. Their success is recognized by educators, businesses and the debaters themselves. Those who did not have debate experience wish they had. It would seem difficult to imagine stronger support for any educational activity. Perhaps the reason we are asked to defend our activity is our own fault. The evidence is overwhelming, no negative evidence can be found. Have we taken for granted that others realize this? If so it's time we began to be advocates of our profession.

CONCLUSIONS

This paper has attempted to document the chief educational benefits of academic debate. It is clear that the activity is not for everyone. Debate involves countless hours of research, preparation, and practice. However, former participants generally have good things to say about the activity and its results. The late Senator Church of Idaho commented, "As a former debater I know of the tremendous benefits which can be derived from the process of educating oneself to take part in discussions of vital national issues" (Huseman and Goodman, 1976, p. 226). Representative Claude Pepper has stated, "Throughout my public life I have been very grateful for my early experience in formal debates. I believe that encounters are a valuable means of developing in our leaders of the future the ability to express themselves clearly and forcefully on the pressing issues of the times" (Huseman and Goodman, 1976, p. 226).

Former President John F. Kennedy summed it up well:

> I think debating in high school and college a most valuable training whether for politics, the law, business, or for service on community committees such as the PTA and the League of Women Voters. A good debater must not only study material in support of his own case, but he must also, of course, thoroughly analyze the expected arguments of his opponent.... The give and take of debating, the testing of ideas, is essential to democracy. I wish we had a good deal more debating in our institutions than we do now (*Freedom and Union*, 1960, p. 7).

References

Arnold, W. (1974) "Debate and the Lawyer." *Journal of the American Forensic Association* 10: 139.
Center, D. B. (1982). "Debate and the Job Market." *Debate Issues* 15: 4–6.
Ehninger, D. and Brockriede, W. (1963). *Decision by Debate*. New York: Dodd, Mead.
"100 of 160 Leaders Began Careers as Student Debaters." (1960). *Freedom and Union*. 6–7.
Huseman, R. C. and Goodman, D. M. (1976). "Editor's Corner: BYD Congressional Questionnaire." *Journal of the American Forensic Association* 12: 226.
Keefe, C., Harte, T., and Norton, L. (1982). *Introduction to Debate*. New York: Macmillan.
Keele, L. M. and Matlon, R. J. (1984). "A Survey of Participants in the National Debate Tournament, 1947–1980." *Journal of the American Forensic Association* 20: 194–205.
McBath, J. (1961). "Speech and the Legal Profession." *Speech Teacher* 10: 44–47.
Pearce, W. B. (1974). "Attitudes Toward Forensics." *Journal of the American Forensic Association* 10: 139.
Pollock, A. (1982). "The Relationship of a Background in Scholastic Forensics

to Effective Communication in the Legislative Assembly." *Speaker and Gavel* 19: 17.

Robinson, J. (1956). "A Recent Graduate Examines His Forensic Experience." *The Gavel* 38: 62.

Semlak, W. D. and Shields, D. (1977). "The Effect of Debate Training on Students' Participation in the Bicentennial Youth Debates." *Journal of the American Forensic Association* 13: 194–96.

Swanson, D. R. (1970). "Debate as Preparation for Law: Law Deans' Reactions." Paper presented at the annual meeting of the Western Speech Communications Associations.

2

Women in High School Debate

J. Cinder Griffin
Holly Jane Raider

"I don't usually vote for girl debaters because debate really is a boy's activity. I am surprised by your ability to handle these issues."[1]

Given its competitive nature and quest for excellence, scholastic debate serves as a micromodel of the business and academic worlds. Because debaters tend to become business and academic leaders, perceptions of women ingrained through debate experience are translated into society at large. Because of such implications, female representation and treatment in debate takes on added importance. This article addresses several reasons for low rates of female participation in high school debate and offers possible solutions to the problem.[2]

In recent years there has been some effort to identify the factors and consequences of the low participation of women in high school and college debate.[3] Unfortunately, no comprehensive or formal research has been attempted that might explain the causes of this underrepresentation. The factors affecting selection of debate as an activity in general must consider both college and high school debate, as they are interrelated. Because most college debaters were first exposed to the activity in high school, examining participation at the high school level is a necessary first step. It is unlikely that a female who has not experienced some competition and success in the activity while in high school will remain, much less begin, debating in college.

Debate, unlike athletics, does not require physical skills that might restrict the participation of women. Debate's academic orientation ought to appeal to women, for women more so than men, tend to select extracurricular activities that are academic in nature.[4] Based on these assumptions, one would expect proportional representation of the genders in debate. Why then are there four times more men in debate than women?[5]

Several explanations may account for the overall low rate of female participation in debate. At the outset, fewer females enter the activity in high school. Although organizational and procedural tactics used in high school debate may account for low initial rates of participation, a variety of social and structural phenomena, not necessarily caused by the debate community itself, account for the low proportion of female debaters.

Socially inculcated values contributed to low rates of female entry in high school debate. This aspect of gender bias and its relation to debate has been studied by Manchester and Friedly. They conclude, "Males are adhering to sex-role stereotypes and sex-role expectations when they participate in debate because it is perceived by society as a 'masculine' activity. Female debate participants experience more gender-related barriers because they are not adhering to sex-role stereotypes and sex-role expectations."[6] In short, "nice girls" do not compete against or with men, are not assertive, and are not expected to engage in policy discourse. Rather, nice girls should be cheerleaders, join foreign language and art clubs, and sometimes even participate in student government. Although these attitudes have societal origins, there can be no doubt that in debate's competitive atmosphere they are magnified.

While societal sex-role expectations may accouont for low inflow rates of women in the activity, they do not alone explain the disproportionate attrition rate of female debaters. While entry rates for women and men may in some cases be roughly equal, the total number of women who participate for four years is significantly lower than the corresponding number of men. This rate of attrition is due to factors that can be explained largely by an examination of the debate community itself.

Structural barriers endemic to the forensics community dissuade female ninth graders[7] from entering the activity. Recruitment procedures and initial exposure may unintentionally create a first impression of the activity as dominated by men. By and large, male debaters or male debate coaches conduct orientations and discuss the activity with new students for the first time. Most debate coaches are men, reinforcing the perception of prospective debaters that debate is an activity controlled by men.

The disproportionate number of men on most debate teams must influence concerned parents. Especially in this day and age, parents are more likely to let a son go on an overnight debate trip than they are a daughter, particularly when the coach is male and the squad is mostly male. This may be a concern even when the coach is a trusted member of the community.

Once past these first barriers, women who do enter this activity continue to face obstacles that discourage their further participation.[8] The high rate of attrition among women is largely related to their level of success. Motivation to persist in an activity in the face of low success is slight. Given the time and financial commitment involved in debate, if one is not winning, one often quits debating. The difficulty, then, is in determining factors that contribute to the early failure of women debaters.

Even if equal numbers of males and females enter at the novice level, the female perception of women's participation in debate as a whole is not based on the gender proportions of her immediate peer group or cohort. Rather, she looks to the representation of women in all debate divisions. This may be easily understood if one considers traditional structures of novice debate. Often it is the varsity debate team, composed mostly of males, who coach and judge novices. Novices also learn how to debate by watching varsity debates. Thus, the role models will be predominantly the male individuals already involved in the activity and entrenched in its values.

The importance if female role models and mentors cannot be underestimated. There is an intuitive and empirical correlation between the number of female participants and the number of female coaches and judges.[9] Female debaters have few role models to encourage their participation and, consequently, are more likely to drop out than their male counterparts; the result is an unending cycle of female attrition.

Pragmatically, there are certain cost/benefit criteria that high school coaches must consider, given mounting budgetary constraints. Coaches with all-male teams may subconsciously be reluctant to recruit females due to traveling and housing considerations. Thus, even if a female decides to join the team, her travel opportunities may be more limited than those of the males on the team. Once a female has proven herself, the willingness to expend team resources on her increases.

According to research on cross-gender participation in careers dominated by the opposite sex, women are more likely than men to experience low confidence in such situations.[10] Female debaters may lack the self-confidence present in males; their expectations of success are lower and the pressures placed upon them are higher. As a result of socialization, women lack confidence in their public speaking skills. This, coupled with the lack of role models, leads female debaters to view themselves very early in the activity as tokens and outsiders.

This self-perception as token females creates performance pressure.[11] If it is assumed that a female debater is not as competent as her male counterpart, there is additional pressure on the female to overcome the (not necessarily overt) expectation that she will be inadequate. For many people this stress may be so counterproductive that it interferes with their judgment. Ultimately, the predication that the token will be inadequate may become a fulfilled prophecy. Thus, in some situations performance failure is linked to performance pressure and not to the objective validity of the female debater's abilities. This performance pressure does not require explicit expressions of low expectations from the dominant group. Often it is a consequence of simply being unique. [12]

The performance pressure phenomena is more prevalent on select topics in high school debate. For example, it is usually presumed that a female does not have a good grasp of military issues. Therefore, a female debater must debate not only as well as her male counterparts, she must command an even greater level of expertise in this area.

Performance pressure affects selection of events and argument preference as well. In general, women are not encouraged to discuss military and political issues. Women prefer social and theoretical issues, and this is reflected in their choices of debate arguments. On the collegiate level, more women participate in CEDA debate as compared to policy-oriented NDT debate. [13] On the high school level the ratio of male to female participants in individual events activities is nearly one-to-one. Therefore, even if a female is not discouraged from entering debate itself, she may not remain in the activity for long because the argument discourse either does not interest her or she is actively discouraged from becoming fluent in it.

The overall rate of attrition of women in debate and the decision of women not to enter college debate after high school may also be related to noticeable and determinable sexism in the debate community. Our claim of sexism in debate, while not founded in a specific research measure, is founded in our experience as women in the activity and through our interviews with women and men in the activity. High school debate coaches, debaters, tournament brochures and schematics, herald debate as "two-man" debate. How many of us have trophies which depict a model debater: a male orator at a podium? Often, two women debating together are referred to as "the girls." Many female debaters observe that male debaters, when referring to a female competitor's argument, frequently say, "on his argument . . . " Also observed are references to female debaters as "honey" or "dear." Other lingo of the community reinforces gender bias: arguing military issues or confronting the issues directly rather than avoiding them is "manly." A female debater is caught in the middle. If she is not assertive, she will not be an effective debater. But if she is too assertive, she will be deemed bitchy.

The effect of this type of behavior on female attrition is difficult to measure. At the very least, this kind of overt sexism makes debaters uncomfortable. It is offensive and intolerable. Contrary to popular opinion, women do not find it funny, but by the time many females have ended their debating careers, offensive language has become such a part of their daily existence that they may laugh about it. One will never know how many women are intimidated and offended to such a degree that they leave the activity before they develop the self-confidence and level of success necessary to overcome the inherent gender bias against them, a bias contributed to by the "old boy" tactics of the male members of the community.

Solutions to gender bias in debate will not simply appear as the result of a discussion of the issues. Direct reform on issues of language, terminology, and attitude is needed and is immediately attainable.

Given the significance of gender bias on the discussion of arguments, it is logical to assume that resolutions and topics focusing on non-military issues would attract more female participants and encourage them to remain active in debate. This is not to say that all military topics and issues should be phased out; rather, they should be relegated to less dominant position in the overall discourse.

Military issues have come to dominate the activity in a way that overshadows all other concerns. This is not the reality of our society, and it should not be the reality of our debate community. A greater emphasis should be placed upon central issues rather than the often unrealistic large-impact issues. Even when social/economic issues are discussed, they lose presumption to the shorter time frames and cataclysmic impacts of military issue.

We do not underestimate the importance of military issues in society; rather, we feel resolutions of employment and agriculture should not be automatically perverted to military issues. High school debaters ought to argue issues that are more tangible to society at large and more understandable to potential participants. Perhaps this would help train male debaters to discuss issues and ideas more openly and confidently with their female counterparts as well, while slowly socializing women to understand and enjoy discussion of military issues.

Coaches and male participants ought to be more sympathetic to the needs of younger female participants. Concerns of a young woman and her parents about overnight travel and high levels of participation in a traditionally male-dominated activity cannot be ignored. Additionally, it requires a large degree of independence, not traditionally a female characteristic, for a women to enter debate initially. This sense of independence needs to be encouraged and applauded. Women should not be relegated to positions of lesser authority and leadership than their male counterparts. They should be actively encouraged to run for positions such as team captain. Women can discuss arguments after debates and engage in intellectual discourse after a round on the same level as men.

The need to create female role models cannot be overstated. An active effort must be made to increase the percentage of female coaches on all levels, as this would result in direct increases in female participation. This is perhaps the most important, yet most difficult, issue for the community to solve.

Greater incentives should be offered to female debaters to encourage them to remain in the activity. Recruiting females for college debate is not nearly as competitive as the practices used to recruit males. This has a ripple effect on the number of women entering and, consequently, coaching in college.

Socially, it is more accpetable for men to travel on business than women. This makes it even more difficult for a normal, family- and business-oriented female to enter a community that places a premium on extensive travel. Men should accept this fact and offer support to women in this difficult position. While the debate community may not be able to alter social norms on a macro level, it can provide an arena of support to women as opposed to reinforcing existing social biases.

Attracting greater numbers of female coaches is a problem on the high school administrative level as well. While the debate world alone cannot solve the problem, debate coaches and sometimes debaters themselves can influence the selection of new coaches or assistants. This is a useful long-term goal. Statistically speaking, females will continue to select activities other than debate if the selection of male-oriented arguments persists. The community must encourage women to become debate coaches, and it must encourage them to remain in the activity.

At this level, some selection of females over males may prove desirable. All other qualifications being equal, being female should be seen as a further qualification for a debate coaching position. Unlike affirmative action, this is not intended to redress past harms, but to solve future problems. The cycle of male domination will never be broken if female role models are not present and active.

While the debate community may not be able to solve all of the problems related to gender bias in the world, it can most certainly help women develop the independence and self-confidence necessary to combat these problems when they leave debate. Female debaters who have graduated agree that the skills they acquired through debate have been valuable in the real world. More women could benefit from these results if female debaters were better integrated into the debate community at large.

Notes

1. This comment appeared on a ballot received by one of the authors at a large national high school tournament. It was written by a woman who, judging from the other comments on the ballot, had seen a fair, but not large, number of high school debates.
2. This paper deals with those issues influencing the disproportionately low participation rates of women in debate. We do acknowledge the virtual nonexistence of ethnic minority participants in debate, another issue warranting attention.
3. Bibliographical references include: Sheryl A. Friedly and Bruce B. Manchester, "An Examination of Male/Female Judging Decisions in Individual Events," *National Forensics Journal* 5 (Spring 1987); Suzanne Larson and Amy Vreeland, "Gender Issues in Cross Examination Periods of CEDA Debate," *National Forensics Journal* 3 (Spring 1985); Brenda Logue, "CEDA: Male/Female Participation Levels: A Research Report," *CEDA Yearbook* (1987); Shaun P. Martin, *An Analysis of the Participation of Women in Competitive Debate*, Unpublished sociology honors thesis presented to Dartmouth College (June 1988); Holly Jane Raider, *Women in College Debate*, Unpublished sociology thesis presented to Barnard College (May 1989).
4. Marjorie Keeshan Nalder, "The Gender Factor in Selecting Extra-Curricular Activities, "*National Forensics Journal* 3 (Spring 1985): 33–34.
5. See Martin, *Participation of Women in Competitive Debate*, and Raider, *Women in College Debate*, p. 15.
6. Friedly and Manchester, p. 2. It is important to note that this study was specifically concerned with college debate.
7. We have chosen specifically to refer to these students as ninth graders rather than as freshmen for the sake of gender neutrality.
8. Martin, pp. 19–22.
9. Logue. Raider observed that 16.43 percent of the participants at the 1989 NDT were females. 16 percent of the coaches and judges were females.
10. Judith Bridges, "Sex Differences in Occupational Performance Expect-ations," *Psychology of Women Quarterly* 12 (1988): 75–90.
11. Rosabeth Kanter, *Men and Women of the Corporation* (New York: Basic Books, 1977), 208.
12. Logue, p. 24.
13. Martin.

3

Ethics in Academic Debate
A Gaming Perspective

Alfred C. Snider

In his monumental work *An Essay on Man*, Ernst Cassirer has written, "The ethical world is never given; it is forever in the making."[1] Ethics is an extremely important issue in communication in general, and especially important in a competitive activity like academic debate. But, if Cassirer is correct, how should we go about developing guidelines and theories about what constitutes ethical conduct in academic debate? This work will attempt to deal with this issue by establishing a criteria for ethical conduct in academic debate, specifying the major ethical obligations towards each other held by the major participants in the academic debate situation reviewing the major charges of unethical conduct currently observed in academic debate, and finally, indicating how a gaming paradigm as applied to academic debate can advance our understanding of the role ethics play in the debate situation.

This work approaches this topic from the perspective of gaming as a paradigm case for academic debate. Some previous work has laid the foundation for an exploration of ethics through gaming. Gaming is a useful method for understanding communicative behaviors in general.[2] It has also been argued that gaming can be applied to forensics as a useful paradigm case.[3] Two distinct works have attempted to establish that gaming is a viable paradigm for academic debate.[4] Rather than extensively review these previous efforts, this work uses them as a point of departure for an exploration of the role of ethics in academic debate.

THE ETHIC OF HONESTY

Ethics concerns codes of behavior, specifically in the "ought to" or "should" sense of behavior. Duke notes that the ethics of game use is a very important issue.[5] While an issue of importance should be dealt with by strict criteria in the game design process, this is not possible, since many ethical considerations cannot be anticipated during the design process and must be dealt with during the play of the game itself. In attempting to compose an ethical code for the game of debate, the options are either to state a small number of criteria, which lack precision, or to produce a long list of criteria, which restrict the options of the participant. Almost all philosophical disputations that attempt to determine whether a given pattern of behaviors is ethical or not give special attention to the particulars of the situation and the ends which are at issue. While murder is seen as unethical behavior by most individuals, nevertheless these same individuals might find it tolerable if it was committed in self-defense. Once we begin formulating ethical guidelines we are soon lost in a sea of "if . . . then" statements designed to take situational factors and the desirability of certain ends into account.

What is true of general ethical guidelines is also true of ethical guidelines for debate. Recognizing that ethical considerations probably must be dealt with inside a given debate situation, it seems appropriate to opt for the course of generating a small number of generally applicable ethical standards.

Since academic debate is centered within the communication discipline, guidance for establishing ethical standards may be gounded within this field. Karl R. Wallace has examined the various ethics which apply to the teacher of speech and which are grounded within the public character of public utterance in a free society.[6]

Wallace's work is chosen as a starting point for several reasons. First, it represents an attempt to develop ethical guidelines for a competitively oriented, public, persuasion situation, which academic debate certainly is. Second, Wallace attempts to synthesize concepts of ethics from a broad perspective, drawing on the general thinking of western civilization. Third, Wallace's guidelines are united by the ethical thread that I have found so revealing in examining academic debate. These suggested ethical guidelines are presented by Wallace for application to the teaching of speech. It is my intention to demonstrate their relevance to the ethical standard of the game of debate.

Wallace notes four such ethics:

1. During the moment of utterance the communicator is the sole source of argument and information, and thus has an obligation to present this data in an accurate form.

2. The facts and information presented should be done so in a fair manner and without distortion.
3. The communicator should reveal the sources of the information used.
4. The communicator should respect diversity of argument and opinion.

These four ethics seem to apply well to the game of debate. The fourth ethic is important in that a debate could not take place without some regard for the positions of those on the opposite side of the scenario. The first, second, and third ethics seem to have in common a notion of honesty in that communications should be accurate, undistorted, and from a revealed source. These first three imply that the debaters should honestly present their statements. Thus, the major ethical guideline for a debate should be some form of honesty, at least if we are to apply Wallace's ethics to academic debate.

In establishing guidelines for ethics in the game of debate, some lack of precision should be allowed. In other words, all matters coming under the aegis of these criteria may not be ethical matters, but that will have to be discussed within each debate. For example, a debater who misrepresents an opponent's position is perhaps guilty of an ethical offense, but perhaps not so if that debater merely misunderstood a confusing argument offered by an opponent.

The only prescriptive standard of ethics in the game of debate should be *honesty*. Academic debate should not be a forum for lying. This does not mean that when the topic is "RESOLVED: That U.S. military spending should be increased," that only those believing this before the debate can be affirmative debaters. Certainly, persons in this position who are negative debaters would present the best case they could against their personal belief. Rather, it means that those involved should not knowingly deceive others involved. For example, falsehoods (either falsified facts or falsified testimony) should not be entered into the debate; debaters should not knowingly lie about what their colleagues or what they themselves have said during the round, and those keeping time should strive to be accurate and avoid giving additional time to a speaker they favor.

One problem in applying the ethic of honesty is that it may be thought of as assuming that there is a clear definition of truth. While this is a difficulty, it seems that the line is easier to draw between something which might be true and something which is definitely false. For example, describing America's nuclear deterrent as "not strong enough" may or may not be true, but a statement to support such a position which knowingly reports an erroneous number of missiles would be definitely false. Determinations of this type, obviously, must be made within the context of a given situation, but nevertheless the guideline of honesty remains applicable.

One important issue in determining honesty is intention. If a participant makes an innocent and unintentional error in keeping time, this is not an ethical problem. However, if participants intentionally give their partners an extra minute in a rebuttal speech so that their odds of winning are increased, this would clearly be an ethical violation. Determining an individual's intention or motive in a specific situation is difficult, barring telepathy and/or the use of "truth serums" in a debate context.

Because it is difficult to determine intention with absolute accuracy, does this mean that it is impossible to resolve ethical questions? Ethical issues are too important to be swept under the rug simply because such determinations are difficult. It seems that this problem can be resolved in several ways. First, judges and participants may wish to ignore the issue of intention. For example, many judges currently punish debaters for reading falsified evidence even if the debaters did not actually engage in the falsification and even in cases where the debaters had no knowledge that this evidence was tainted. Holding debaters and others responsible for their behaviors and not just for their intentions makes application a great deal easier, even if it does offer some cruel lessons to some unfortunate debaters. But such lessons to the "unintentionally unethical" may help heighten the awareness of ethics as an area worthy of concern as well as prepare students for the real world in which they may often be in a position to profit from the unethical behavior of another by merely acting like they didn't know.

A second resolution to the problem of ethics might be to determine intentionality in a specific debate round, although this might be time consuming. Since the precise nature of ethical concerns is, in Cassirer's words, "forever in the making," this does not seem unreasonable. This sort of application, however, can only take place if the draconian measures utilized by some judges are suspended. For example, some judges contend that if a team raises an ethical charge that they cannot sustain, the team making such a charge should forfeit the decision. While I am totally in disagreement with this position, since I believe that ethical accusations should not be made lightly, I believe such a standard would have to be suspended in cases requiring substantial determination of intention.

As these two solutions show, the issue of showing intent to commit a dishonest act is a thorny one, but it can be handled. Certainly ethical concerns are so vital to a productive debate process that this difficulty should not preclude us from generating some broad criteria for making ethical distinctions in academic debate.

Some may see honesty as inadequate as a single ethical guideline. This terseness of ethical guidance is advocated because if the ethic of honesty can be achieved, other debate practices now seen as unethical may become self-regulating. If debaters and judges are honest about their actions and motives, the situational nature of ethical disputes can be called into play. For example, a judge who is honest about the decision in a round by saying, "The affirmative gave me $10," will certainly find such honest communication motivating others to stop such behavior. If, however, such a pronouncement is tolerated, this would be an indication that such action was within the ethic of the community at large, and thus permissible.

Honesty is the precondition for other ethics-related concepts. My desire is to allow for an open forum for discussion of ethics within gaming, not to compile a long list of what is or is not ethical. It seems to me that achievement of a basic ethic of honesty should allow this forum to exist. For example, if the situation in a debate round is honestly handled, then students can engage in other discussions, such as whether a given move meets a criteria of fairness. One of the purposes discussed within the conceptual map for a game of debate was that this paradigm serves as a contest to determine who did the better job of debating. This standard assumes and implies fairness, but this fairness can only be discussed and decided in the debate if there is honest communication taking place. This situational approach to ethical concerns in academic debate will be elaborated later in this work.

The guideline of honesty may seem broad, but this is because the issue of ethics is broad and touches so many parts of the game of debate. Because ethics is so important, we would like it to be a cut and-dried matter. But because it isn't so easy, we must concentrate on its successful application. In determining the ethical or unethical nature of any occurrence within the game of debate, prescriptive action on ethical grounds should be limited.

Designer-Participant Ethics. By designer in the gaming sense I mean tournament host in the way referred to normally. Designer/ participant ethics would include two elements. First, there should be an accurate exchange of information about the individuals involved and the event planned. Designers should not deceive potential attendees of an event about the opposition, facilities, audiences, or other attractions. The participants, on the other hand, should also convey information honestly about number of attendees, their experience levels, and their identities. Second, there should be an honest effort on the part of designers and attendees to fulfill their obligations. Designers should try to supply promised facilities, meals, etc., while attendees should try to fulfill their obligations by showing up promptly to debate, following tournament rules, etc. In both these examples, it is an honest effort that is required, not a successful result.

Judge-Participant Ethics. After the round begins, the relationship between the judge and the participants is important. Two ethical considerations seem to enter into the judge/participant relationship. First, the participants have an ethical obligation to make an honest presentation of material. Participants should not present knowingly false information to the judge. Second, the judge has an obligation to the participants to explain the reason for a decision after it has been made. This should include relevant issues for awarding the decision.

Designer-Judge Ethics. The designer (tournament host) and the judge form the administrative portion of the game of debate. Three ethical considerations seem to play a part in their interaction. First, they must engage in an honest exchange about judge assignment. The designer, for example, should be honest with the judges about how they are being assigned (randomly, rated by judge ability, geographically, etc.). Conversely, the judges should engage the designer concerning how they would best be assigned (for example, a judge may wish to avoid judging close friends for fear of not being able to make a completely honest decision). Second, the judge should provide to the designer information about the decision once it is made—the correct win/loss designation, points, and reason for decision. Third, since the designer has assigned the judge to specific debates in good faith, the judge should make an attempt to judge the round honestly as an obligation to the designer.

Participant-Participant Ethics. While the simplest of the ethical applications to describe, this set of ethics is perhaps the most important. Two considerations appear here. First, participants should convey to each other an honest description of their position on the topic under debate. Second, the participants should convey to one another as honestly as possible their understanding of the position of the other team on the topic under debate. Participants, in other words, have an obligation to exhibit their true level of understanding of the positions in the debate. While ethics is a very important part of the game of debate it is very much like most of the rest of the activity—it is a consideration to be actively experienced and discovered, not something to be prescribed.

CHARGES OF ETHICAL VIOLATIONS IN MODERN DEBATE

Although not a common complaint in print, it is not uncommon to hear coaches, students, and interested others express concern over certain supposedly unethical practices which take place in academic debate. Comments are often heard that debaters and coaches have lost their values, and that certain competitors will "do anything to win." My purpose here will be to identify ethical concerns, both legitimate and illegitimate. Certainly there are some activities in academic debate that can be indentified as involving unethical practices. In speaking of ethics in debate, it is important to recall the criteria of honesty established. Thus, truly unethical debate practices, at least to me, involve some breach in this ethic of honesty.

The first ethical concern is with evidence. The use of evidence in academic debate is very important to the process in the round and the outcome as represented by the decision. Asserted arguments are not given nearly the weight that evidenced arguments are, while at the same time judges will accept counterintuitive arguments more often if they are accompanied by evidence. Thus, debaters who would manufacture evidence or distort evidence that does exist would stand a far better chance at winning debate rounds.

Concern about evidence is certainly not new in academic debate. In the sixties, for example, as evidence became more prominent, various studies were undertaken to backtrack evidence in order to find out how much of it was real and how much was unethical.[7] Every debater has stories about someone they knew, debated with, or heard about who utilized evidence unethically, but it is rather hard to verify such stories. What is possible to examine, however, is the transcript of the final round of the National Debate Tournament, annually printed in the *Journal of the American Forensic Association*. The complete sources for all evidence are supposedly provided by the teams involved, and the evidence is backtracked and then reported in the footnotes accompanying the transcript. While not wanting to make specific charges, I think it is safe to say that in several instances (1964, 1969, 1970, 1972, 1975 and 1976)[8] some problems have been confronted with the evidence.

If examples can be found in the final round of the National Debate Tournament, and if it is a concern so much on people's minds, there certainly must be a number of instances of such unethical use of evidence that are not reported. Based on experience gained through debating, coaching high school and college debate, cross-checking evidence from debate handbooks, and editing a number of debate handbooks myself, ethical problems in evidence are not uncommon in academic debate.

The second ethical concern deals with the procedures during a debate round. Specifically, it is possible that the honesty criteria can be and at times is violated during a debate. For example, the timekeeping procedures may be dishonestly manipulated. Team members who are entrusted with timing the speech of their partners may find it advantageous to give their colleagues an extra thirty seconds in a rebuttal speech. While often timing problems arise out of simple error (forgetting to announce the time, not watching the clock, using the wrong time limits, etc.), this can be an ethical concern as well.

Another problem that might take place during a round is inaccurate reporting of what has been done in other speeches. For example, a rebuttalist might claim that the other team "had no answer" for a given position, when in fact they did, and thus claim to have won the argument on that basis. Again, while faulty memory and faulty flow charting might be an explanation for this, there is some concern that this may be done on purpose in an attempt to gain the decision.

Another possible ethical violation might involve a team's malicious misrepresentation of its own position. An example illustrates my precise point here. If a negative team asks to see a brief read by an affirmative team, the affirmative may hand over a brief that is *not* the original one read in the debate, but a weak stepsister of the original block. The negative will then attack this brief on the basis of faults on *their* copy, while the judge asking to see the same block at the end of the round would be shown the proper brief. Another example would be a negative debater who, having read a contradictory piece of evidence in a rebuttal speech, denies that any such card was read when questioned about it. Both of these examples, while sounding a bit farfetched, come from my personal experiences as a coach and a judge, so they do have a basis in fact.

A third category of ethical problems involves the judging of the debate. Judges, for example, may willingly vote for the team they actually thought lost the round because of some perverse reason. This might involve benefiting their own team, exacting revenge on a disliked team or coach, or because one team has substantially more reputation than another (a person who did not see the debate would not question the decision since the favorite won). Another example would be a situation where a designer would assign judges to a round because they knew of the biases at work and wanted to aid one team or another, thus attempting to stack the deck. As already indicated, judges should be willing to be open about their motives in judging, a criteria which Wallace has identified as being applicable to *all* public communication.

While these three concerns represent, in my viewpoint, very real and pressing concerns in academic debate, others commenting on debate ethics have gone much farther. Often it is popular to brand any practice one does not care for as "unethical." Some of these supposed ethical violations are considered here.

First, some argue that a coach has a clearly defined ethical role, and should not exceed it. For example, some argue that coaches should not do research, should not aid students in constructing arguments, and should not go over the flowcharts of other teams they have judged. While these may be valid concerns when carried to extremes by any coach, they do not seem to involve an ethical violation.

Second, some argue that anything other than random assignment of judges is unethical. At many tournaments, the designer will rank order judges, and then assign the better judges to those rounds that have the most bearing on the outcome of the tournament competition. Many argue that this is unfair, discriminatory, and leads to rampant elitism. Frankly, I find this hard to view as an ethical violation. If tournament organizers advertised random judge assignment and then proceeded to assign them on the basis of their quality, this would be a violation of honesty, but when the assignment of judges on the basis of perceived quality is announced and communicated to teams and judges, there seems to be little violation of honesty. The reason judges are placed in this manner seems clear to me—debaters and coaches want it that way. These parties want the best possible judge to be put into each round, and certainly this is a greater concern when the round is more important. It is not unusual for judges who dislike being assigned on a "skill" basis (perhaps because of low skill levels, which means judging assignments to lower quality and less important debates) to complain that their teams did not get a good judge in a given round when it was an important or break round. In almost all games, judges are assigned on the basis of their skill levels. For example, the umpires at the World Series are chosen as the *best* umpires during that season, and are rewarded by this assignment. Shouldn't we attempt to skill match for the benefit of all involved? Certainly this is an area of legitimate concern for many, yet it hardly seems an ethical concern.

A final supposed charge of ethics violation involves the use of a new and unfamiliar strategy. Whenever a team comes up with a new way to approach issues so that they have a greater chance of winning, certain parties are bound to claim that this is "unethical." For example, when Lichtman, Garvin, and Corsi proposed the "alternative justification" case,[9] which allowed the affirmative to drop entire action planks of their plan, many responded that this was unethical, probably because they did not know how to answer it yet. One of my favorite personal examples was an affirmative team experiencing its first counterplan. The team members argued that since they didn't know much about counterplans, it was unethical to argue one against them. The response by the negative was that the lack of knowledge on the part of their opponents was hardly an ethical violation on their part. I am sure that every new technique that has emerged, from the independent advantage to the generic disadvantage, has been subjected to this criticism. Rather than being unethical, such practices are merely new, and debaters have not thought out answers to them yet. For example, a certain practice might be unfair (providing a theoretical advantage to one side over the other, thus violating the equal opportunity criteria applied to procedures in the gaming paradigm), while not being unethical. The two concepts, fairness and ethics, are blurred in many instances of this sort of argumentation.

EXPLORING ETHICS THROUGH GAMING

Of all of the criticisms of modern debate, the charge of ethical problems is perhaps the most compelling. Fortunately, gaming offers a very interesting and productive way to study and regulate ethics. Turning to the literature of game theory and game/simulation, we find a lot of attention devoted to ethical issues. This discussion, of course, cannot attempt to communicate the totality of this literature or even the totality of gaming as a paradigm for academic debate to the reader. It is hoped that interested readers will refer to the primary literature to better understand these concepts. While this essay is meant to be an illustration of the possible applications of these concepts, it is hoped that it can be useful to the reader when examined in isolation.

Schelling contends that ethical behavior has a lot in common with gaming.[10] As an example of this, Schelling discusses the implications of dishonesty and how lying can be related to gaming. Schelling reported that children aged ten to twelve years, when questioned about lying, noted that truthfulness was necessary for reciprocity and mutual agreement. "Deceiving others destroys mutual trust." Schelling contends that children find truth socially useful, and that children have freely adopted a rule against lying. Schelling goes on to compare lying to game theory. He notes:

> Lying, after all, is suggestive of game theory. It involves at least two people, a liar and somebody who is lied to; it transmits information, the credibility and veracity of which are important; it influences some choice another is to make that the liar anticipates; the choice to lie or not to lie is part of the liar's choice of strategy; the possibility of a lie presumably occurs to the second party, and may be judged against some a priori expectations; and the payoff configurations are rich in possibilities, since a lie can be told for the good of the victim, the truth can be told to pave the way for a later lie, and a lie can even be told with the intention that it is not to be believed.[11]

Thus, gaming can provide some interesting new perspectives on lyng and the behavior surrounding lying. Several reasons explain ways in which gaming approaches issues of honesty. First, gaming can help in studying the situation surrounding such behavior. For examples, Fletcher notes that in different situations, lying may be permissible. For example, "If a small neighborhood merchant tells a lie to divert some 'protection' racketeers from their victims, no matter how compassionately the lie is told, he has chosen to do evil according to certain intrinsicalist ethics, though it might be considered a lesser evil."[12] Fletcher scorns this, and notes that in some situations, such as this one, "It is not inexcusably evil; it is positively good." This is not to suggest that in certain debate situations lying is good, but it does indicate that any approach to ethics must recognize the "extrinsic" position of Fletcher: that the situation plays an important part in determining the ethical nature of an action.

Schelling has noted that one must evaluate the consequences of an act, including the consequences on the behaviors of others, and one must be personally responsible for evaluating those consequences.[13] Gaming is not an answer to ethical problems, but it does provide a useful way of evaluating situation ethics. As Schelling notes, "It may be too early to credit game theory with much help, but surely there is promise."[14] His summary of Fletcher's position is that in the language of game theory, the situation ethic does not content itself with prescribing individual strategies but requires us to scan the entire matrix, evaluating each outcome, and attending to the preferences of others. "It is not the deed, but its intended (expected) consequences by which morality is to be judged. Ignorance is no excuse; one must think through the consequences and evaluate them; and, if necessary, predicting the behavior of others."

The point seems to be that if all parties adhere to the ethic of honesty, then debate can serve as an open forum to explore the situational nature of ethical questions. Honesty is certainly not the only ethic in the game of debate, but it is a *non-situational* ethic. Other ethics are worthy of exploration, but they do not apply to all situations in a debate round. Through the ethic of honesty we can engage in a situationally specific discussion of ethics. Thus, gaming allows us to better understand the situational nature of ethics.

Gaming also allows us to study how concern for other individuals guides our sense of ethics. One assumption that some have made about competitive games is that players will utilize only those strategies that involve their self interest. Actually, it has become apparent that players develop concerns for other participants, and these concerns can be thought of as a function of ethics. Schelling has noted that some believe that rationality, as exhibited by players, is to be identified with selfishness. Disagreeing with this, he writes:

> This argument, I think, is not usually valid. There is no need to suppose that the payoffs reflect selfish interests. They reflect the player's valuation of the outcomes, and he can surely value them selfishly, altruistically, or in terms of justice or welfare. If a game reflects a lawyer's choice of strategy, the lawyer can be playing to maximize his fee, to get an innocent man acquitted, or to establish a precedent that he believes to be in the interest of justice. He may do this out of fun, pride, or ethical obligation, or to get revenge on an opposing attorney.[15]

Rapoport has also concluded that players are often vitally concerned with the welfare of other players.[16] In summarizing empirical research in this area, he notes that players are often concerned not only with their own payoffs but also with what the co-player gets, sometimes empathizing with him, sometimes, on the contrary, deriving satisfaction from his losses, regardless of what they themselves get. The point here is that gaming recognizes that significant pressures will operate to make players concerned about the welfare of other players. For example, a team clearly winning a round might have a tendency to show mercy on the other team by easing up a bit, a tendency debate coaches live in fear of. Certainly not all will show such concern, but it is hoped that a gaming perspective can continually bring out more and more of such concern.

Gaming is also a useful perspective for investigating how to deter ethical violations. Schelling has stated that gaming can be a very useful tool in examining deterrence as it might arise in capital punishment, international threats of military retaliation, and more generally in the whole realm of rewards and punishments.[17] Various methods can be explored and evaluated in terms of how to increase the motives for ethical behavior on the part of players. His suggestion, which might be considered for application to academic debate, is massive retaliation. Thus, unethical practices could be deterred if massive penalties (such as losing a ballot) were arranged. His hope is that deterrence will be effective, and thus massive retaliation will not be necessary in the vast majority of instances. This is certainly an area where more investigation is warranted in an attempt to relate gaming approaches of deterrence to the control of unethical debate practices.

The conclusion drawn from these points and other issues not covered here must be that gaming and game theory can provide a useful method of understanding and dealing with ethical difficulties. Schelling notes: that substantial area exists for the utilization of game theory and the study of ethics, including ethical problems game theory has already addressed; that the use of game theory can be expanded into the discipline of ethics and philosophy; and finally, that the conduct of a game itself is likely to give rise to new ethical concerns for study.[18] Schelling observes that game theory can study ethics as a constraint on human behavior. Such constraints can come from "religion, ethics, law, instinct, sentiment, taste, the nervous system and other parts of the human body, custom, the physical environment, and the contrivances we equip ourselves with."[19] As well, game theory can be especially helpful in examining constraints that affect "people's expectations about each other, for working out the social-behavioral implications of different ethical systems." Certainly this last ability is one of special import to academic debate. Ethical systems can be examined, according to Schelling, by looking at the interactive implications of ethical systems (how changes in constraints and payoffs make particular rules unnecessary or essential) and by examining the implications of coexistence between two radically different ethics.[20]

There are a number of reasons why the ethics of a game situation matches up well with the ethics of an academic debate situation. Duke, for example, has stated that a game is well suited to handling ethical concerns if it has a neutral, non-manipulative design.[21] Certainly, the game of debate briefly outlined in the works mentioned earlier attempts to meet this criteria, especially by stressing the need for equality of opportunity among players. Schelling has observed that a game is well suited for handling ethical issues if it involves direct consequences of ethical choices.[22] Certainly in academic debate, the possibility of losing a ballot on an ethical issue (such as proven fabrication of evidence) does provide the needed consequences. Valavanis has posited that ethical issues are explored when the welfare of others is interrelated.[23] Certainly in an academic debate, players have the welfare of their partners and the school to think of, as well as the welfare of an opponent against whom they might violate ethical standards in competition.

This does not mean that there will be no ethical problems in the game of debate, nor does it mean that ethical difficulties can be difined outside of actual play. As Duke notes, "New ethical problems may emerge in the *use* of a game."[24] When ethical problems do develop, it is best to let the operator (in this case, the judge) merely observe how ethical disputes are played out in the round. In the best spirit of a liberal education, the debaters should decide by their argument. Duke notes that the "simplest, most straightforward rule is that the operator should blend into the woodwork at the earliest possible moment and let the game proceed with a minimum of operator intervention."[25] Thus, in a debate, ethical disputes are open to argument.

A couple of issues need to be raised in preemption to possible arguments against the position that gaming can operate as a way to approach ethics within academic debate. One would be that ethics is necessarily connected with values, and values are very rarely discussed in a debate context. It seems less than sage to argue that values are *ever* excluded from intellectual concerns. As Bremer notes, intellectual curiosity probably cannot exist without moral concern.[26] Certainly issues such as politics and economics, often discussed in debates, have important ethical components. As Schelling has noted, it is not possible to abstract "ethical man" as separate from "economic man" and "rational man."[27] These concepts are related. Academic debate provides a fertile area for a discussion of ethics, values, and morals.

Another objection may be that not all will be wiling to play the game ethically. Of course this is true. However, the implication must not be that this demonstrates that gaming is a *failure* at studying ethics, but means that gaming is a fertile area for ethical study *because* not all will obey the same set of applied ethical standards. As Schelling notes, when we develop a sort of social contract between players to play the game ethically, we "must take as a premise that not everybody will sign the contract."[28]

Ethical concerns are prevalent in academic debate, both in a discussion of the issues implied by the topics, and by the practices that emerge in academic debates. Gaming provides not an answer, but a feasible methodology for handling the study of such ethical disputes.

CONCLUSION

There are various paradigms that are applied to academic debate. In deciding which paradigm to utilize, we should keep in mind the various intellectual and educational opportunities a paradigm may offer. Ethical concerns are important for communication, education, and competition. A viable paradigm for academic debate should offer a way to understand and teach about ethical concerns. Gaming, as a paradigm for academic debate, does not pretent to offer hard and fast rules for determining what is ethical and what is unethical. It does, however, provide us with a useful perspective on ethics as well as a methodology for increasing our understanding of ethical issues. Cassirer was correct, the ethical world is never a given, but it is always in a state of becoming. The ethic of honesty may well be a standard, but hopefully one that is flexible enough to put debate in the "state of becoming" that Cassirer would approve of. Gaming is one valuable method for aiding us in understanding this never-ending evolution.

Notes

1. Ernst Cassirer, *An Essay on Man* (New Haven: Yale University Press, 1944), 61.
2. Alfred C. Snider, "Gaming as a Form of Human Communication," Paper presented to the World Future Society World Assembly (July 1982).
3. Alfred C. Snider, "Games Without Frontiers: Opportunities for Communication Scholars," *Journal of the American Forensic Association* (accepted for publication).
4. Alfred C. Snider, *The New Debate: A Personal Essay* (Detroit: Privately published, 1981), and *Gaming as a Paradigm for Academic Debate* (Doctoral dissertation, University of Kansas, Lawrence, KS, 1983).
5. Richard Duke, *Gaming: The Future's Language* (New York: John Wiley, 1974), 104.
6. Karl Wallace, "An Ethical Basis of Communication," *The Speech Teacher* 4 (Jan. 1955): 1–9.

7. See, for example, Robert Newman and Keith Sanders, "A Study in the Integrity of Evidence," *Journal of the American Forensic Association* 2 (Jan. 1965): 7–13; and Joy Miller, "More About Integrity and Evidence," *The Rostrum* (April 1967): 8–9.

8. See *Journal of the American Forensic Association*, Summer issue, for each year cited.

9. Allan Lichtman, Charles Garvin, and Jerome Corsi, "The Alternative Justification Affirmative: A New Case Form," *Journal of the American Forensic Association* 10 (Fall 1973): 59–69.

10. T. C. Schelling, "Some Thoughts on the Relevance of Game Theory to the Analysis of Ethical Systems," in Buchler and Nutini, eds., *Game Theory in the Behavioral Sciences* (Pittsburgh: University of Pittsburgh Press, 1969), 46.

11. Schelling, pp. 47–48.

12. Joseph Fletcher, *Situation Ethics: The New Morality* (Philadelphia: Westminster Press, 1966), 64–65.

13. Schelling, pp. 46–47.

14. Schelling, p. 47.

15. Schelling, pp. 56–57.

16. Anatol Rapoport, *Fights, Games and Debates* (Ann Arbor: University of Michigan Press, 1960), 280–90.

17. Schelling, p. 54.

18. Schelling, pp. 53–54.

19. Schelling, pp. 48–49.

20. Schelling, p. 60.

21. Duke, p. 105.

22. Schelling, p. 58.

23. Stefan Valavanis, "The Resolution of Conflicts when Utilities Interact," *Journal of Conflict Resolution* (June 1958): 156–69.

24. Duke, p. 104.

25. Duke, p. 107.

26. Stuart Bremer, *Simulated Worlds: A Computer Model of National Decision-Making* (Princeton: Princeton University Press, 1977), 6.

27. Schelling, p. 51.

28. Schelling, p. 52.

KEY TERMS

critical thinking
attrition
gender
role models
falsification
intentionality

designer-participant ethics
judge-participant ethics
designer-judge ethics
participant-participant ethics
ethical violation

DISCUSSION

1. How could more women and minorities be encouraged to join academic debate?
2. Why should your school support a debate program?
3. Academic debate is a capital-intensive activity: lots of money spent on a relatively small number of people. Respond to an administration that claims funding an organization with more members would give the school more "bang for the buck."
4. You be the judge: A team is challenged by the opposition on an evidence falsification charge. Upon seeing the opposition's photocopy of the original source, the team apologizes, withdraws the evidence from the round, and states that they did not cut the card. What should you do?
5. Compare and contrast the concepts of fairness and ethics.
6. Compare and contrast the concepts of honesty and ethics.

Part Two

Advanced Debate Practices

Noted jazz guitarist George Benson once urged music buffs to attend live concerts because "the proof is in the pudding." Likewise, in debate, what determines the quality of the participant is not so much that person's grasp of theory as it is his or her application of that theory in the actual debate round. Application of theory in the debate environment brings up questions of structures, strategies, and tactics often extrinsic to the positions for which these means are used. We have therefore included this part of the book, focusing on advanced debate in practice, to deal with these concerns. Although the debater is unlikely to quote these articles in the heat of a debate, it is hoped that they may turn out to be very much a part of the debate through usage.

Although many of the articles in this anthology were written for the policy debate setting, we believe the articles in Part Two are applicable to all types of debate. We therefore strongly urge debate practitioners to resist the temptation to skip these articles and turn first to the section they feel is "specifically for them," be it policy or nonpolicy. Instead, consider the practical suggestions discussed here. The use in this section of sources who focus on traditional debate should not be viewed as a preferential statement on the part of the editors as to what type of debate should be practiced. It is our opinion that these articles represent some of the best work in the area at this point in time. We feel that this is a function of the relative newness of publication outlets for alternative forums, as opposed to their inherent quality.

The first essay in the section, by Lichtman, Rohrer, and Corsi, discusses various ways the affirmative case might be constructed as the starting point for analysis in a debate. In practice, this also translates into ways the first affirmative constructive speech should be composed, and the pros and cons of each approach. It should be noted that Lichtman and Rohrer are known as the leading advocates of a policy systems model of debate, and their suggestions here reflect that bias. Michael Pfau details the fundamental elements in analyzing the negative consequences of policy proposals. Dwaine Hemphill discusses the breakdown of the traditional negative division of labor, and the resulting implications for negative approaches.

This group of articles also includes practical considerations of how to perform the skills of debating. Gloria Cabada turns attention to the most effective ways to use the few minutes' preparation time available between the speeches during the debate. By popular consensus, the most underdeveloped portion of the debate is the cross-examination period. George Ziegelmueller provides an insightful summary of past techniques of national debate champions. As constructive speeches have evolved to focus on the pros versus the cons of the affirmative position, rebuttal practice has reflected this emphasis as well. One of the tactics this change has brought increasingly into use is the turnaround. Ulrich proposes standards for the evaluation of this frequently used tactical argument.

Two new formats that have gained increased exposure in both high school and college are Lincoln-Douglas and parliamentary debate. Lincoln-Douglas is already entrenched at the high school level while parliamentary debate may be the next big thing in college debate. Each format has its own unique strategic considerations. Carlin discusses Lincoln-Douglas debate, and Cox and Phillips explore parliamentary debate from a CEDA perspective.

Lee, Harris, and Dudczak weigh in with an article geared towards understanding and evaluating the basic concepts and procedures used in conducting statistical research. Finally, Zarefsky demonstrates how to argue causality in the issues of inherency and plan efficacy.

Shortly after George Benson reiterated the proof cliche, he went on to make the move from being a relatively obscure jazz guitarist to become an international pop superstar. While examination of the chapters in Part Two may not change a debater's performance level from "home-after-the-awards-brunch" to "final-round-participant," it certainly could not hurt. (To understand why this clincher to the Introduction to Part Two is not any stronger, see the chapters on hasty generalization in Part Eight.)

4

Affirmative Case Approaches

Allan J. Lichtman
Daniel M. Rohrer
Jerome Corsi

CASE FORMS

Various forms have been developed for the presentation of affirmative cases. Most familiar are the classical need case and the comparative advantages case. The classical need case derives from the traditional precepts of argumentation theory. Its structure reflects the problem-solution approach to policy analysis, rather than an attempt to compare costs and benefits of competitive policy systems. The problem-solution approach involves a five-state process of analysis: (1) discovery of a supposed difficulty; (2) location and definition of the difficulty; (3) suggestion of the possible solution; (4) development by reasoning of the implication of the suggestion; (5) further observation and experiment leading to its acceptance or rejection. Thus, the need case begins by isolating problems in the *status quo*; it concludes by demonstrating that the affirmative proposal can resolve these problems. Traditional theory requires, however, that the shortcomings in the case must be *significant* and *inherent*. Significance is a highly subjective concept; difficulties that seem extremely grave to an inveterate pessimist may appear trivial to a perennial optimist. Nevertheless, advocates are enjoined to demonstrate the compelling nature of the evils they have identified. To fulfill the burden of inherency, advocates must also show that these problems are fundamental to the present system and cannot be solved by minor modifications of existing policy.

TRADITIONAL NEED CASE

The classical need case requires advocates to identify a significant problem, to demonstrate that this problem is inherent to the status quo, and to prove that the affirmative plan can solve the problem. Affirmative teams may fulfill these burdens by subdividing their presentations into contentions. Baylor University, for example, in the final round of the 1952 National Debate Tournament, defended "a two-fold need; first of all, that inflation presents a permanent threat to our economy; second, in meeting with this threat the present channels are inadequate." Baylor's first contention alleged the existence of a significant problem, while its second contention alleged that the problem was inherent in the present system. A third contention included a specific proposal and an explanation of how that proposal coped with the permanent threat of inflation. These three contentions were developed as a logical sequence so the affirmative was obliged to carry each one of them in order to win the debate.

During the late 1950s, there began a strong trend away from the use of such dependent needs contentions. Instead, teams came to employ parallel case structures built around several distinct arguments for change, each of which fulfilling the burdens of significance and inherency. The progression from significance to inherency, illustrated by the first two contentions of the Baylor case, was incorporated into a single independent contention. A given affirmative case could include more than one such need contention. Thus, Dartmouth College argued in the 1960 College National Championship Debate that: (1) the Supreme Court thwarts national policy; (2) the Supreme Court places the public in legal jeopardy; (3) the Supreme Court creates confusion within the law. Elements of significance and inherency appeared within the substructure of each of these contentions. By proving any one of these arguments Dartmouth could—and did—provide a warrant for changing the present system. (Of course, Dartmouth also had to demonstrate that its proposal could rectify the shortcomings of the present system.)

COMPARATIVE ADVANTAGES CASE

Although the classical need case was dominant through the 1950s, it has since yielded in popularity to the more flexible comparative advantages format. The comparative advantages case turns our attention from the solution of currently insoluble problems to a broader consideration of the ways in which the new policy may be superior to the present system. Advantages of policy change may derive not only from the extent to which an affirmative plan can solve existing problems, but also from the speed of its operation, its cost, or its more beneficial side effects.

The comparative advantages case is not organized quite the same as the classical need case. Generally in a comparative advantages case, the affirmative plan is presented first and the advantages accruing from the plan are then set forth. Traditional theory, however, does not absolve teams from responsibility for significance and inherency even if they advance comparative advantages cases. The affirmative must demonstrate that the advantages generated by its plan are important and cannot be achieved by minor changes in the present system. Following the precedent of parallel or independent affirmative need contentions, advocates generally advance several independent advantages, arguing that any one of them justifies adoption of the affirmative proposal. In theory, it should be immaterial whether the affirmative claims to be solving an existing problem or merely to be generating advantages. Both rhetorical strategies are designed to demonstrate that the gap between the benefits and the costs is far greater for the affirmative team than for the present system. Moreover, there is no fundamental distinction between solving a problem and generating benefits, each process—eliminating costs and obtaining benefits—has precisely the same effects on the calculation of net results. Assuming for a moment that we could neatly quantify costs and benefits, the net result would improve by a magnitude of two, whether a value of two is added to the benefits side of the equation or subtracted from the costs side of the same cost-benefit equation. Thus the significance of any affirmative case should be evaluated according to the extent of its superiority over the *status quo* whether it claims to be eliminating harms or producing advantages.

ALTERNATIVE JUSTIFICATION CASE

The alternative justification affirmative extends the logic of the parallel advantages case. An affirmative team employing this approach explicitly recognizes that a given proposition is sufficiently broad to encompass different policy systems. It offers in a single debate two or more parallel affirmative plans, each of which is a legitimate, if narrow, interpretation of the debating resolution. While the conventional case with parallel advantages defends a single policy system for several independent reasons, the alternative justification affirmative argues for several different policy systems—each with its own advantage or set of advantages. Just as the parallel advantages case can warrant adoption of a policy system on the basis of any one of its advantages, the alternative justification case can warrant adoption of the resolution on the basis of any one of its policy systems. The policy system may have either mutually exclusive alternatives, any one of which could be adopted, or non-contradictory alternatives that could be adopted separately or in combination. For instance, under the aegis of a topic advocating "greater freedom for law enforcement officials in the investigation and prosecution of crime," an affirmative may suggest extension of wire-tapping authority, relaxation of search-and-seizure restrictions, and modifications of the rules governing the interrogation of suspects. The affirmative may begin by arguing that each of these changes is desirable; however, it cautions the judge to realize that if it successfully defends any one of them, it has demonstrated a sense in which the resolution must be adopted.

The alternative justification case rests on the premise that it is not the responsibility of the affirmative to persuade the judge to accept all conceivable interpretations of the debate resolution. To justify affirmation of the debate resolution, a team need only successfully defend one of its many possible meanings. When a team carries one of a series of parallel plans, it has fulfilled its obligation to sustain a proposal whose affirmation logically requires affirmation of the proposition selected for debate.

The alternative justification case reflects policy argument in the real world. Assume, for instance, that a policy advisor argues for the extension of food aid to India. He might argue that the government should adopt any one of three mutually exclusive proposals: direct shipment of food; credits for the purchase of food in the United States; or cash for the purchase of food on the open market. The advisor might also propose a series of alternatives, which could be adopted individually or in combination: shipments of wheat; shipments of seed; and shipments of farm machinery.

CRITERIA CASE

In recent years, the criteria case has become generally accepted as an additional format for the presentation of affirmative analysis. This construct focuses explicitly on the value or goals toward which policy must be directed. The case is designed to demonstrate that the affirmative proposal can do a better job of meeting these goals than the present system. A criteria case would first present the goals being sought, then set forth criteria designed to achieve these goals, and finally attempt to demonstrate that the affirmative plan better fulfills the criteria than the present system. After presenting goals and criteria, however, the criteria case may assume either the structure of the need case or the comparative advantages case. The affirmative may, for example, demonstrate that the present system fails to meet its criteria and then set forth a plan and demonstrate how the plan more closely conforms to the criteria. Alternatively, it may present its proposal immediately after description of the criteria and then attempt to demonstrate that this plan better fulfills the criteria than the existing order.

Theorists recognize that advocates employing the criteria case are not absolved of any of the burdens imposed on advocates using the need or comparative advantages format. They must demonstrate that even if minor modifications were made in the status quo the affirmative plan would still conform better to the criteria of goal fulfillment. Similarly, they must demonstrate the significance of better meeting the goals they identify.

MORAL ISSUES CASE

One variant of the criteria case, which may be termed the moral issues case, is an especially useful format for the presentation of affirmative arguments that do not rest upon the smooth exchange of costs and benefits, but upon absolute rights or moral imperatives. The affirmative using a moral issues case would maintain that certain injustics within the status quo must be rectified regardless of the costs that may be generated. It would reject any attempt to rationalize these injustices through the achievement of countervailing benefits.

While philosophers have asserted that arguments from morality are the most persuasive of arguments, it must be noted that the acceptance of such arguments in modern debate has been rather limited. It may be very difficult to convince a judge that an absolute right or moral imperative is sufficiently compelling to disregard all other possible costs and benefits.

NET BENEFITS CASE

A case structure that conforms to the logic of comparing policy systems would weigh both the benefits and the costs generated by the affirmative proposal. This case form rests on the premise that the affirmative must demonstrate that its policy system yields greater *net benefits* than the present system. New policy cannot be warranted merely by the demonstration that its adoption results in additional benefits: potential cost must be considered. A rational policy maker, for example, would not close down the nation's steel plants to conserve energy. The benefits achieved by saving fuel would be far outweighed by the costs of crippling American industry.

The attempt to evaluate the relative net benefits of competing policy systems must recognize the indispensable unity of such a system. Since all elements of a policy system are connected both horizontally and vertically, a change in one element may affect any other element. Thus all possible outcomes of competing systems, whether intended or not, must be considered in assessing their net benefits.

Questions of both value and probability determine the net benefits of any policy system. Advocates must evaluate the probability or like-lihood of obtaining various outcomes from a policy system and place a value on these outcomes according to the ideology of the system. The gap between the benefits and the cost of a system widens as the probability of achieving desirable outcomes increases and the probability of achieving undesirable outcomes decreases. The gap between costs and benefits narrows as the probability of achieving desirable outcomes decreases and the probability of achieving undesirable outcomes in-creases. Thus the affirmative would attempt to maximize the probability that its plan will produce desired results and minimize the probability that its plan would produce costs. Furthermore, the affirmative would attempt to minimize the probability that the present system would produce desired results and maximize the probability that the present system would produce costly results. The sum of probability times value for all outcomes included in the analysis determines the net benefits of each policy system.

Assume, for example, that an affirmative team proposes adoption of a program of public work for the unemployed. It would, of course, attempt to demonstrate that its plan would be more likely to eliminate the individual suffering and the national economic malaise that accom-panies a high rate of unemployment. The affirmative might argue as well that its plan would promote racial harmony in the United States by decisively demonstrating the government's commitment to resolve a major problem facing minority peoples. But the first affirmative speaker might also weigh the benefits of its plan against such potential costs as the generation of additional inflation and the diversion of federal funds from other worthwhile programs. The speaker might, for example, suggest that the likelihood of stimulating new inflation is low and that inflation is not nearly as harmful as unemployment. He might also try to show that the government would not be likely to cut back needed programs if it guaranteed public jobs to the unemployed.

Affirmative teams using the new case form would not be limited to defending their program from the onslaughts of a negative team. As part of their task of comparing the proposed affirmative policy to the present system or other alternatives served up by a negative team, affirmative speakers could attempt to establish that the policy defended by the negative would engender costs that would not result from adoption of the affirmative plan. An affirmative advocate could argue, for example, that a negative program of job subsidies would produce corruption and lead to the adoption of inefficient business practices.

The traditional burdens of significance and inherency would have a new meaning in a debate that focused on a comparison of the costs and benefits generated by policy systems. This statement should not be construed, however, to mean that the burdens of significance and inherency need not be taken seriously in the context of policy systems debate. On the contrary, these burdens will often be desisive. They must simply be defined and viewed in terms of impact and the likelihood that such impact will occur rather than in terms of whether an entire need, harm, or problem is solved, whether an entire advantage is fulfilled, or whether a single causality has been isolated.

The significance of solving a problem or of generating an advantage is relevant only with respect to the cost involved in achieving such beneficial results. Affirmative proposals that generate significant benefits may produce equally significant costs. Thus the goal of the affirmative team is not merely to maximize the significance of its needs or advantages, but rather to maximize the significance of the difference between the cost and the benefits generated by the proposal as contrasted with that of the negative policy systems.

Moreover, the affirmative need not demonstrate in its initial presentation that its advantages cannot be obtained or its needs met by minor modifications of the present system. The traditional burden of inherency becomes less relevant to policy debate, just as the traditional burden of significance does. Again, policy analysis entails a comparison between the relative net benefits of the alternative policy systems. Since an almost infinite number of alternative policy systems can be produced by minor modification of the status quo it would be impossible for the affirmative to demonstrate that the net benefits of the proposal cannot be obtained through such a modification. Yet the burden is upon both teams, for if the negative proposes minor changes in the present system designed to achieve beneficial results, they may also generate severe costs.

By demonstrating the overall superiority of its proposal with respect to the status quo, the affirmative team provides a rationale for rejecting the present system and adopting its proposal. The negative, of course, is free to argue that a new policy system created through minor changes in the present system is superior to the affirmative plan and should be adopted in its place. Debate would then focus upon a comparison between the benefits and costs of the affirmative policy system and the benefits and costs of the modified present system. This comparison could consider any aspect of either system.

The stipulation that an affirmative team is required only to compare its proposal with the existing order and to alternative policy systems set forth by the opposition, solves one of the most vexing problems of traditional theory. The traditional burden of inherency demands that the affirmative demonstrate that its needs cannot be solved or its advantages produced by minor or nonessential modifications of the status quo. The affirmative need not, however, demonstrate that these results cannot be obtained from any conceivable change in the status quo other than the adoption of the affirmative plan. The distinction between major and minor changes in the existing order is purely subjective. Theorists have failed to set forth objective standards to make a clear distinction between proposed changes based solely on the magnitude or scope of the proposals. However, case development based upon comparison of policy systems focuses the outcome of the debate solely on the net benefits achieved by competing policy systems. This rational approach eliminates artificial distinctions between the types of proposed changes in the status quo. Each policy system is individually compared to the competing systems set forth for defense and examination.

Other work has already demonstrated that issues relating to presumption or prejudgments in policy debate are best resolved in the context of decision rules designed to determine the final outcome of a debate after all arguments have been weighed and evaluated. The use of carefully framed decision rules eliminates the distortion produced by traditional theory and clarifies the rationale for choosing one policy over another.

SUMMARY

This chapter has surveyed a number of affirmative case approaches. Our assumption throughout has been that the ultimate objective of academic debating is to decide upon proposals for policy changes. Viewed from this perspective, we have traced the development of affirmative case strategies from the earlier forms through the latest innovations. We began with the traditional need case. From that point, we progressed through succeeding new stages of case analysis, including the comparative advantage, alternative justification, criteria, moral issues, and finally the net benefits case. Each new stage of affirmative analysis, we believe, represents an attempt to incorporate rational elements into academic debate so that it more closely approximates the methods of decision-making found in the real world of policy deliberation. At the moment, the net benefits approach seems to fit the analogy best.

5

A Systematic Approach to Opposing Policy Change

Michael Pfau

This essay assumes that in a typical debate the advocates of a policy change are the affirmative team. Keep in mind that a negative counterplan is also a proposal for change. All of the strategies and tactics described here apply to the affirmative's attacks on a negative counterplan.

There are two general functions of arguments in opposition to a policy change. First is the process of diminishing affirmative case significance. Straight refutation, countercausality analysis, extra-topicality charges, and support of present system mechanisms, which are designed either to treat the effects of the problem or eradicate it outright—these and additional strategies are all geared toward this basic function. This process continues in the introduction of plan-meet-need or plan-accrue-advantage arguments. If we characterize competitive debate in the terms of the policymaker critic, then the import of negative efforts to diminish affirmative significance becomes apparent. The policymaker tends to evaluate a debate in terms of the following basic equation: *The net need or advantage is greater or less than the net disadvantage*. If we were to expand this simplified equation, it would read as follows:

> Aggregate advantage minus negative minimization minus present system mechanisms to mitigate the harms minus present system mechanisms to promote solvency minus extra-topicality impact minus net play-meet-advantage plus disadvantage turnaround impact is greater or less than net negative disadvantages.

Generally, negative tactics are geared toward diminishing the left side of this equation via all available means. In most rounds, however, the negative fails to reduce the left side of the equation to zero. In the end, some affirmative significance remains in spite of negative efforts.

Thus, the second general function of the negative is to establish a countervailing environment to offset whatever remains of affirmative significance. It is the negative's chance to put something on the right side of the equation to offset net affirmative significance. To achieve this end, the negative strives to establish a counterbalancing value system that is the foundation for truly effective disadvantage argumentation. This concept is developed in some detail later in this essay.

WORKABILITY ARGUMENTS

Workability arguments concern themselves with the mechanics of an affirmative plan. Although now such attacks are categorized under the heading of plan-meet-need or plan-accrue-advantage argumentation, they warrant consideration in their own right. Good workability arguments can be most damaging; mediocre ones are an absolute waste of time.

In considering workability attacks the negative debater should consider some of the following areas. First, look at *mechanical and administrative deficiencies:* Does the affirmative plan provide for sufficient administrative personnel; adequate expertise; a viable revenue source; etc.? Second, *enforcement* must be scrutinized with great care. Utilizing the affirmative plan and the cross-examination periods as vehicles for information, the negative must make an accurate accounting of the means by which the affirmative seeks to secure adequate enforcement. With that information in hand the negative can accurately appraise the viability of possible workability attacks that zero in on affirmative enforcement. Remember also that the extent of enforcement is dependent upon both the total sweep of the affirmative's change and the nature of the affirmative's inherency, which must be circumvented via the plan. Make sure that the enforcement provisions are sufficient to overcome the inherencies (both structural and attitudinal) that are developed in the affirmative case.

Finally, find out whether the affirmative plan has any *precedents*—successful or not. This is an important area for negative research and subsequent argument development. If a particular plan has successful precedents, then the affirmative should be loaded for bear with documented answers to most negative plan attacks. Conversely, if a plan has been tried and has failed, then the negative can turn to a tremendous store of specific information to use in documenting plan attacks. Either way, a consideration of plan precedents is crucial.

SOLVENCY ARGUMENTS

Plan-meet-need (PMN) or plan-meet-advantage (PMA) arguments measure the capability of the affirmative plan to mitigate the harms presented in the debate. Such attacks continue the process of diminishing affirmative significance—thus further reducing the left side of the debate equation. Yet, while most PMNs are designed to diminish affirmative significance, the absolute PMN goes even further. This rare, but potent, argument absolutely precludes affirmative solvency—at any level; it reduces the left side of the debate equation to zero. At this point (barring any turnaround of negative disadvantages) the debate is over.

PMNs come in one of four basic designs. The negative should consider each design as he scrutinizes the affirmative proposal. Each entails a mode of analysis—a way of looking at an affirmative plan.

The first design concerns *alternative causality analysis*. The negative seeks to demonstrate that the affirmative mechanism fails to eradicate important causes of the problem in question. Naturally, if significant causal factors escape the purview of the affirmative plan, then the harm impact will continue to manifest itself in the post-plan environment. Most affirmative analysis is prone to this variant of PMN as a result of oversimplification. The important economic, political, and social problems of our time involve speculative, and multiple causation. Yet, debate procedures mandate the identification of a limited number of causes, which are capable of solution via a relatively simple plan mechanism. Unfortunately, any effort to simplify a complex problem in such a manner is suspect. The negative debater should identify the alternative causal variables and demonstrate the impact of each upon the affirmative harm. Ideally the negative will want to place the affirmative in the position of mitigating only insignificant causal factors—thus failing to produce even modest PMN.

A second design involves the *impact of future causes*. This is a rare, but often telling, mode of PMN analysis. Using this method, the negative argues that the affirmative's causality analysis is shortsighted; that it is limited to the present time frame; that it ignores the emergence of new and significant causal factors in the future. Hence, the affirmative at some future point in time will cease to achieve PMN. The affirmative impact is thus a limited, short-term phenomenon.

Circumvention, the third mode of analysis, invokes maximum real world appeal and is popular with a wide spectrum of judges. Here the negative argues that attitudes and/or structures (often the same one identified in the affirmative inherency analysis) will thwart the affirmative plan. It is a shortsighted affirmative inherency analysis that gives fruition to the circumvention argument in the first place. Affirmatives are too often prone to indictments of present system structures that ignore underlying attitudes. This misperception is simple: It is based on the naive notion that structures exist in a vacuum. This is clearly not the case; it is the presence of attitudes that make possible the emergence and development of structures. In developing the circumvention attack the negative argues that, while the power of fiat might overcome existing structural barriers, the underlying attitudes remain unchanged and will manifest themselves in new ways in the post-plan environment. The net result is the utilization of different structures to undermine the affirmative plan; hence, substantially diminished affirmative PMN.

The negative must accomplish three tasks in developing a good circumvention argument. First, demonstrate the motive. Sometimes this will be provided by the affirmative team. In most cases, however, it is the negative that must offer the analysis and evidence to establish motive. Second, detail the means of circumvention. That is, given the presence of the motive, in what manner will it manifest itself? What mechanisms are operable as channels to thwart the affirmative plan? This step is important and often makes or breaks the circumvention argument. Third, demonstrate the impact of the circumvention on affirmative solvency. The negative constructive speaker who completes each of these tasks has a damaging PMN to launch against an affirmative.

A fourth design is the *PMN-disadvantage.*This amalgamation of two plan attack variants is a potent strategy. Essentially, the PMN-disadvantage is a hybrid; a disadvantage that manifests impact in terms of the affirmative harm criteria. It argues that the affirmative plan exacerbates the very ills which it seeks to eradicate. This mode of attack is most damaging in that it facilitates a comparison of like evils; the standard disadvantage involves a comparison of unlike harms.

When using any of the above PMN arguments, the negative should consider a number of PMN suggestions. First, PMNs do not have to be unique, applicable only to the affirmative plan mechanism. However, this does not give the negative carte blanche to advocate contradictory policy positions with respect to inherency and PMN. PMNs that generically mitigate solvency—of both present system and affirmative alternatives—are obviously applicable to both sectors. A negative team cannot expect to carry mutually exclusive positions in the debate. Thus, while the negative is free to develop an "if . . . then" policy position (ie., the present system can solve; if it can't, then neither can the affirmative plan), it should reasonably expect to carry only one of the two positions. In this instance the PMN takes precedence. If solvency is precluded generically, then present system alternatives will fail.

Second, PMNs should have a perceptible impact on the affirmative case. What is the impact of the PMN on the debate equation? This must be articulated clearly to the judge. Third, PMNs should utilize independent argument construction where possible. The affirmative should be unable to group negative PMNs. Finally, the label of the PMN should reflect its impact. The argument's label is much more important than most debaters realize since it is often the only thing that the judge follows. Hence, the negative should utilize PMN attack labels that reflect the nature of the argument and its impact.

To this point the negative has worked for a common objective: diminishing the left side of the debate equation. Now it is up to the negative to establish a countervailing environment to offset whatever remains of affirmative significance. The negative must provide the most important category of negative argumentation: disadvantages.

DISADVANTAGES

Disadvantages concern the negative impact of an affirmative plan—the consequences of a course of action. Until this point the affirmative is in the most enviable position of being a mythological bearer of gifts—a policymaking Santa Claus—bestowing positive impact oblivious to any other consequences. The disadvantage sector brings the debate back to the real world where the basic principle of scarcity prevails. Scarcity precludes policymaking omnipotence; it presupposes the need to make hard choices. As such, it mandates that there can be no positive impact without negative impact; no benefits without costs; no "free lunch." The negative must develop the most undesirable set of plan consequences possible for a particular affirmative approach.

Two basic assumptions about negative disadvantages must be understood. First, disadvantages entail the same burdens as an affirmative case. They must be significant in extent and severity; and they must be unique to the affirmative proposal. Second, disadvantages often stem from the abandonment of a previously held value position. The negative must think in terms of value hierarchies (continuums that represent diametrically opposed value positions). Fundamental societal values often conflict, and we must elevate some basic values over others regarding specific policy issues at particular points in time. Place the diametrically opposed values on a hierarchy in terms of the following policy questions: Which value does society promote on an a priori basis, *human life or individual freedom?* Relate the value conflict in terms of the existing policy controversies over seat belt usage, abortion, gun control, and others.

Or apply the same process to the value controversy over the right to *security versus individual freedom.* Relate this value conflict in terms of the draft, bail, investigatory agencies, and more. Simply put, policy questions usually involve values in conflict. All affirmative plans alter value hierarchies—affirmative benefits stem from the accelerated promotion of one or more basic values at the expense of others. Sometimes the affirmative takes a value position and argues it outright; usually the mandate is subtle. The negative must be prepared to deal with values—to think in terms of value positions. Movement on a continuum toward a desirable value represents the simultaneous movement away from an equally desirable value. Just as affirmative advantages stem from movement along a value continuum, so do negative disadvantages. In short, any attempt to assign different priorities to basic values produces both good and evil results. The negative must be prepared to deal with the latter.

Disadvantage attacks may stem from one of three basic phenomena. First, some disadvantages are generic to the adoption of the resolution itself, regardless of the specific affirmative approach. In this instance, the basic value presupposition of the resolution serves as the basis for the negative attack. For example, in 1977 the colleges debated the question, "RESOLVE: That the federal government should significantly strengthen the guarantee of consumer product safety required of manufacturers in the U.S." In this case, the value presupposition is that the affirmative approach should involve the federal government in enhancing consumer protection. No matter what particular approach the affirmative chooses, it must embody this essential thrust. Thus, the negative can develop disadvantages that are inherent in the resolution itself, such as centralization.

Second, some disadvantages result from the movement toward solvency and their impact is proportional or inverse depending on the nature of the specific argument. If the evil results from maximum PMN, then the disadvantage gains momentum to that point. If the disadvantage harm stems from the vacuum created from the point of affirmative fiat to maximum PMN, then its impact dissipates during that interim. This latter development is especially effective if the negative can demonstrate that full PMN will never be attained.

Third, other disadvantages stem from the implementation of the affirmative's mechanism per se. The impact of this variant is immediate upon the affirmative fiat. If affirmative harms or solvency are future oriented, then this mode of plan consequence is especially valuable since it enables the negative to compound the harm of the disadvantage. In this instance the affirmative benefit is delayed, but the consequences are immediate. A compounding must be utilized in order to achieve an accurate comparison of policy positions.

STRATEGIC CONSIDERATIONS

We have thus far attempted to offer a process that might assist the negative in acquiring a perspective, or way of thinking. We have suggested specific modes of thought in developing negative observations, workability arguments, PMNs, and disadvantage attacks. Now we must consider strategic considerations—an integral facet of a negative perspective.

Under certain circumstances the negative might develop a uniqueness block. If, for example, the affirmative's change is minimal and its impact is slight, then the potential for damaging negative disadvantages is proportionately reduced. Here the uniquencess block makes sense. The coordinated negative strategy requires the negative to combine generic inherency attacks concerning the viability of existing structures with straight refutation of the affirmative's inherency analysis. This approach calls for the negative to develop a series of existing structures, minor repairs, or conditional counterplans (in any combination) to promote the net result advocated by the affirmative. There are four steps involved in implementing the uniqueness block. First, present an overview concerning the nature of the affirmative's burden. The negative articulates the position that an affirmative approach must represent the most effective means to achieve a particular result; that the negative will offer alternative means to promote the affirmative's objective. The result is an affirmative alternative that is not unique and may not be the most desirable policy position in the debate. Second, delineate the alternative mechanisms. Third, demonstrate efficatiousness. And, fourth, show the desirability of the negative's alternative. This represents a viable strategy under such conditions as noted above.

Another, and most vital, negative strategy involves *tactics to limit plan flexibility*. All too often negative debaters allow affirmative plans to undergo slight modification during the debate round. The consequence is substantial: the emasculation of viable plan attacks. A number of preventive steps must be taken. First, if any feature of the affirmative's plan is unclear, pin it down in the cross-examination periods. Second, if uncertain about some feature of the plan, request to see the affirmative's draft. And third, if the affirmative's plan is intentionally vague, take an overt tactical approach. For example, it has grown increasingly popular to utilize an optimal mix of finance mechanisms. This is designed to preempt negative disadvantages concerning the plan's financing—often the most valid real world attacks. The negative can, and must, pin the affirmative down to a specific formula. It can do so via cross-examination probes designed to ascertain what mix would be utilized in the face of specific economic conditions—present or future. If the affirmative declines to commit itself to a designated mix under specific conditions, then the negative must be prepared to demonstrate what mix would be used according to a consensus of expert opinion of economic policymakers. Either way, the negative can tactically pin down the elusive affirmative and then launch the appropriate plan attacks.

A final strategic consideration involves the use of so-called affirmative guarantees. Here the negative constructive speaker must insure against unreasonable affirmative claims. In short, the negative must not permit the guarantee to become associated with the totality of the affirmative position. Instead, the negative must pin it down to a specific sector.

A perspective, or way of thinking, in approaching the negative is a prerequisite to its success. This chapter has attempted to provide a process, or mode, which might be utilized in an effort to acquire such a perspective. The thought process used to develop various plan attack variants and to devise an effective strategy must be internalized by the second negative. This important first step, coupled with creativity, extensive preparation, and effective application, should result in exciting and effective second negative constructive speeches.

6

A Reevaluation of Negative Division of Duties

Dwaine R. Hemphill

Intercollegiate debate literature abounds with suggestions of possible tactics the negative constructive speaker has at hand in dealing with affirmative cases. Articles and textbooks describe approaches to the varying types of affirmative cases, explain the basics of arguing specific prima facia issues, and explore negative responsibilities in the context of counterplans, direct refutation, and systems analysis (to name a few). The common theoretical basis underpinning this patchwork of first negative options rests with the traditional division of duties between first and second negative speakers. This paper will examine this customary framework, argue for an abandonment of the traditional speaker duty divisions, and examine a few of the practical ramifications of this strategic reordering.

TRADITIONAL FRAMEWORK FOR NEGATIVE STRATEGY

Any coach, judge or debater could easily identify the basic duties of each negative speaker. The division of labor is one of the first concepts the novice debater is introduced to: The first negative attacks the case and the second negative analyzes the plan.[1] All debate textbooks, without exception, echo this basic approach to negative strategy. The division of labor is perpetuated through coaching and the classroom, yet its theoretical basis is rarely explored. The literature unquestionably accepts the undefended assumptions on which this division is based, and only a few articles make more than a simple reference to the fact that this division has its roots in nothing more substantial that tradition.[2]

Freeley notes that first negative deals with affirmative issues, and the plan is "customarily reserved for the second negative constructive."[3] Patterson and Zarefsky also use this traditional division as a guide for beginning debaters while noting that " ... the duties are assigned to specific speeches only by convention; there is no logical or strategic reason for their being assigned in this way."[4] Murphy and Ericson explain that the duty assignments are "merely suggestions" and then go on to present them as the basis for all subsequent tactical negative considerations.[5]

A review of the literature and the relatively few references to the theoretical basis of the traditional division of labor raises several questions. What exactly are the reasons for the seemingly arbitrary statements defining negative speaker responsibilities? Is there a rational basis for instruction that follows customary guidelines? If the division is so important, why is there no theoretical support for it? Is simple tradition enough to use as a basis for all negative tactics that the specification of speaker duties subsumes? And finally, if the theoretical basis is nonexistent, why does the debate community tenaciously maintain its acceptance of what has become a basic tenet of inter-collegiate debate?

In attempting to answer these questions, it becomes apparent that the division of duties is more tactical in nature than strategic. Thomas explained strategy as the term used to describe a concept while tactics are "the specific actions and approaches used ... "[6] A certain division of negative labor is only one possible tactic. Promoting this traditional division as the basic strategy for the negative speakers precludes formulation of a structural framework that allows for new patterns in argumentation.

The origin of the traditional concept of negative speaker duties is a surprisingly simple one. The basis of the case/plan division was explained by James Luck:

> This division of responsibility and labor for the negative grew naturally out of the early affirmative case pattern. Clearly, the plan could not be analyzed until it was presented, and with its presentation delayed to the second affirmative, the analysis likewise would have to be delayed.[7]

The implications of this origin are incredible! Withholding presentation of the specific affirmative policy until second affirmative constructive is a practice that has been completely abandoned in contemporary debate. The focus of debate has become so oriented toward policy systems that any affirmative team that withheld its plan till the second constructive would be subject to understandable cries of "foul" by the opponents. Such a tactic would seriously cripple in-depth comparisons of competing policies. So while advocacy of policy change has evolved to allow defense of specific proposals in the first affirmative speech, the subsequent negative approach has remained relatively unchanged.

The negative division of labor has not remained totally static. Minor modifications have occurred. With the advent of the comparative advantage case, traditional second negative arguments in the realm of plan solvency shifted partially to first negative as advantage accrual arguments. However, the traditional textbook guidelines delineating negative speaker duties remain virtually unchanged.

No text defends this basis of the customary division of labor; it is simply accepted as a convenient ordering of possible areas of negative attack between team members. While I hope it is not a reflection of my limited research capabilities, I have yet to find a defense of the division of duties other than tradition. In a dynamic and academic activity such as ours, unquestioned acceptance of this apparently outmoded approach to negative strategy is unacceptable.

AN ARGUMENT FOR ABANDONMENT OF THE TRADITIONAL FRAMEWORK

Simply pointing out that a strategy is outmoded does not warrant abandonment of that strategy. The questions of its practical and educational benefits to debaters must be considered. When one critically examines the benefits of the traditional division of speaker duties, the conclusions regarding its strategic values are decidedly negative in nature.

To understand this conclusion, it is necessary to discuss the general purpose of any broad-based negative strategy. Patterson and Zarefsky claim that any given negative stance should maximize options and minimize burdens. "The objective is to permit maximum flexibility."[8] The inherent nature of the negative position in relation to the resolution is geared toward strategic flexibility. Affirmative case types include needs, comparative advantage, goals, and alternative justification. A basic specification of negative strategy should allow the option of several approaches to each type of case. The variety of negative tactics and arguments for each case are an ample indication of the importance attached to flexibility. Since the affirmative defines the area for argument, the negative team should have maximun flexibility in dealing with those areas.

Unfortunately, the structural guidelines of the assignment of speaker duties fail to maximize negative flexibility to its optimum level. There are three basic reasons the standard division of labor unduly restricts negative flexibility. The initial problem is that assigning first negatives specific areas to cover restricts their tactical options. When textbooks, coaches, judges, and second negatives reinforce to first negatives that case is their domain, it is easy to realize why the majority of beginning debaters rarely stray from case issues. Presentation of plan attacks in first negative has been considered taboo by many, and the option has received scant attention in scholarly writings. Luck traces this to acceptance of the traditional division of negative labor.[9] First negative flexibility in choice of tactics is clearly discouraged.

The second problem with religious adherence to the ordained duty assignments is that it allows affirmatives to maintain a two-constructive offensive. In any type of debate, it is recognized that there is a psychological presumption attached to being on the offensive.[10] The common affirmative strategy of defending a narrow case area allows them to remain on the offensive. And if the traditional areas of a first negative attack are restrictive, an obvious tactical advantage has been achieved by the advocates of change. Conversely, as Wood noted, "The negative prefers to have the debate judged in the context of negative argument. It wants the critic to be thinking in terms of whether the negative argument is valid, not whether the affirmative case is sound."[11] A valuable tool in shifting the focus to the negative is the plan objection. The presentation of disadvantages allows the negative to choose the areas for clash. Such arguments shift the offensive to the negative and reduce the opportunities for the affirmative to emphasize its own case. When the affirmative is arguing defensively, the negative is more likely to win the decision.

While the assignment of speaker duties does not preclude plan argumentaton by the first negative, such tactics are tacitly discouraged by the divisions. Traditional strategy obviously does not encourage this tactic. This goes beyond the problem of simply reducing negative flexibility. A first negative concentrating solely on affirmative case issues allows the second affirmative speaker to remain on the offensive for ten more minutes. Twenty minutes of affirmative argument construction thus becomes offensive while half of the negative constructive time is, by tradition, defensive in nature. Adherence to a strategy that arbitrarily defines such rules as a guide for negatives obviously provides the affirmative with a tactical advantage.

The third problem is that a traditional division of duties undermines efforts to achieve a consistent and coherent negative position. The advantages of a well thought-out position are clear. The advancement of a clear position provides the judge with a negative framework from which to weigh all arguments in the round. Patterson and Zarefsky explain in detail that such a position encourages selective attacks on vulnerable case areas, maximizes the impact of negative arguments, improves the coordination of team efforts, avoids the pitfalls of point-by-point debating, reduces the likelihood of negative contradictions, and focuses the round toward negative territory. Unfortunately, the authors also note that this "larger view of the negative stance is often neglected in academic debating."[12]

The traditional assignment of speaker duties appears to be partly to blame for the neglect of such a valuable negative tactic. Reliance on the standard negative division of labor has the obvious effect of isolating two distinct areas of attack. Debaters are actively encouraged to consider case and plan as two separate domains. Such a strategy cannot help but to narrow the thinking of each negative speaker. Each works to win on their side of the flow and hopes that the overall position comes together by rebuttals. First negatives risk advancing a position that limits possible plan objections, and second negatives gamely struggle in their rebuttal to extend unfamiliar case arguments as quickly as possible.

This is not as much of a problem with the few more experienced teams. The problem arises with beginning debaters—the very debaters that supposedly require the guidance of specific rules that dictate position responsibilities. To actively train negative debaters to concentrate only on specific assigned issues appears to undermine the entire concept of a comprehensive negative position.

In the interest of maintaining optimum flexibility in selection of negative tactics, the practice of assigning set speaker responsibilities should be abandoned. Explanation of the critical issue areas common to all debates should certainly continue; but determination of which speaker should deal with which issues should be based on strategic considerations such as the topic area, case approaches, team strengths and weaknesses, and amount of advance preparation. To avoid these critical tactical considerations, and to always follow the customary, arbitrary, outmoded, and unbending strategic guidelines smacks of argumentative folly. In a given round, following the traditional assignment of duties may be the most effective tactic. But such rules should not be propagated as the basis for every negative round.

If debate is to be considered a true sport of intellectuals, Willard theorizes that " ... the blame for the most of the pernicious recent developments (in debate) rests squarely with the critics who operationalize the rules of the game in its day-to-day conduct."[13] A less strict adherence to the speaker duty rules would necessitate more communication between the debaters to insure a coordinated attack. Coaches and debaters would have to develop coherent positions by determining topic- as opposed to textbook-oriented speaker/argument assignments. And each debater would need to be familiar with all the issues and evidence related to each case.[14] Such an approach would obviously require more work and thought, and it would just as obviously improve the quality and effectiveness of the negative attack.

PRACTICAL RAMIFICATIONS

A strategy allowing for a more flexible designation of speaker duties has obvious ramifications. With the strict border between case and plan argumentation lessened, the options available to both first and second negatives are increased. While these options are occasionally employed by debaters, little attention has been paid to them in scholarly writing and no theoretical foundation has been advanced in their favor. The following analysis hopes to fill this void.

First Negative Plan Objections

A basic framework that allows plan objections to be advanced in the first negative constructive obviously allows for greater strategic flexibility. Aside from this basic benefit, there are other logical and tactical reasons to support this practice. In the past, these arguments were in the realm of the second negative because the first speaker had no opportunity to examine the specific affirmative policy option. Immediate presentation of the plan in the 1AC allows the negative to directly begin analysis of plan practicality and ramifications. Even if the first negative does not plan on presenting policy objection, his or her examination of the policy should be standard practice in order to critically analyze affirmative solvency claims.

    With the emphasis on policy specifications in academic debate, the opportunities presented by first negative plan attacks cannot be over-emphasized. As Pfau notes, "A comparative weighing of the impact of advantages and disadvantages is at the core of the policymaker decision-making paradigm."[15] Since this is the case, such a comparison should begin immediatley and put the affirmative on the defensive in the 2AC. Luck explains that " . . . immediate introduction of disadvantages would allow immediate comparison of the advantages and disadvantages of the policy systems under consideration."[16] Such a comparison is not always facilitated by holding all plan objections back until the last constructive speech in each round. Dudczak and Semlak recognize this problem in their examination of second negative tactics. They state, "The greatest problem encountered by the second negative in pre-senting disadvantages is the failure to compare the relative importance of the disadvantages to the affirmative advantages or needs."[17]

    In addition to the comparative value of this tactic, first negative disadvantages allow for a fuller development of specific objections. This value has been recognized in traditional negative guidelines. Pfau explained that the strongest attacks should be advanced first by the second negative to ensure time for proper development.[18] The basic concept that no new arguments should be advanced in rebuttals also is based on the recognized need for maximum development and testing of arguments in each round. This concept certainly supports a rationale for first negative presentation of plan objections. It also encourages negatives to develop several tiers of extension briefs, further strengthening their position in the round.

The specific tactics involved with 1NC disadvantages are relatively simple. The degree of argument development depends upon the specific negative approach in his or her rebuttal. In this instance, the attack should be as fully developed as possible in its initial presentation. This reduces the possible need for the 1NR to read a large amount of extension evidence to rebuild the attack.

The second option involves the two-constructive development of a plan objection, where the second negative deals with the 2AC responses. In this instance a superficial second affirmative pays a heavy price for poor allocation of time and analysis, as Muir and Snowball indicate: "Since the argument would not have received a great deal of time in first negative, the unwary second affirmative might only make five or six responses; the 2N would then have time to make ten responses to each 2AC response and could dump more impact evidence as well."[19]

A first negative may develop a skeletal, yet structurally complete, disadvantage that forces a disproportionate amount of time allocation by the second affirmative. Other first negative arguments would receive less-than-usual attention, thereby enhancing prospects for a winning 1NR. The subsequent burden on the poor 1AR provides the negative with an enormous tactical advantage. It is no wonder that more experienced teams are employing this strategy with increasing frequency.

A third option in extending first negative disadvantages is one I have observed and frowned upon. This involves division of the burden for extension between 2NC and 1NR. The second negative covers half of the 2AC answers and leaves the rest for the 1NR. The tactic smacks more of gamesmanship than of an analytical development of a clear position. It disrupts the continuity of the attack, often results in redundancy, and rarely culminates in a coherent and well-explained disadvantage.

Active training of first negatives to deal with plan issues as well as case increases the probability of a well-defined and tactically superior negative position. Some have gone so far as to suggest a complete reversal of negative speaker duties. This is certainly a viable option and should not be ruled out, but a strong second affirmative might be able to effectively neutralize all plan objections presented by the first negative. The most effective tactic appears to be one that incorporates both plan objections and development of a competing system in the first negative.

There are several possible drawbacks to first negative presentation of disadvantages. They may increase confusion in the round and cause flowing problems for both teams and the judge. Many times the disadvantages are poorly developed. And there is the tricky question of determining whether 1AR extensions are new or simply a further development of 2AC responses. But it would seem that most of these problems result more from debater inexperience than from any inherent flaw in the strategy. If anything, these problems indicate a need for a better theoretical framework from which to train young debaters.

The tactical advantages of such a strategy are clear. Negative argument development is enhanced and flexibility is increased. Affirmative time allocation is distorted. And the first negative immediately places his team on an offensive footing that can be fully exploited in the 2NC/1NR block. Such a strategy also forces affirmatives to develop more detailed defenses of their plan, rather than allowing them to rely on abbreviated and clipped 1AR briefs.

Sharing Case Responsibilities

It was noted earlier that many affirmatives hope to gain a tactical, offensive advantage through presentation of a narrow case position in their first speech. Many times an affirmative position is not fully developed until the 2AC. Such tactics pose problems for negatives following the traditional division of labor. The second negative may ignore the new 2AC developments in lieu of previously prepared positions. The first negative rebuttalist is then forced to use precious time to attack the new twists and advantages rather than focusing on his or her original arguments.

A more flexible framework of speaker responsibilities would permit the second negative to allocate a portion of constructive time to new case developments or areas of the original case to which the first negative failed to respond. The tactic of sharing case responsibilities is gaining prominence, and a brief discussion of this practice is warranted.

When a negative team decides to allocate a portion of 2NC for consideration of case issues, they will most likely improve their chances of defeating the affirmative justifications for change. The 2NC has additional time available to analyze specific claims. This speaker is also in a position to view the complete two-constructive development of the case; and he or she is in a position to adapt the negative position in a way unavailable to the first negative. As Pfau explains, the second negative is in the best position to integrate and polish the overall negative approach.[20] Murphy and Ericson point out that the second negative has "the freest hand" in the debate in regard to case issues.[21] While care should be taken to avoid redundancy in arguments, the option of second negative addressing case issues should not be foreclosed by a theoretical framework.

Several case areas are especially suited for second negatives rather than the first negative, the most obvious being the issue of inherency. The largest strategic limitation on negatives who argue inherency is the risk of contradictions. Inherency attacks must be evaluated in the context of plan objections to ensure a consistent position. And second negative, in the role of argument integrator, is in a better tactical positon to examine such considerations. Dudczak and Semlak suggest that minor repair arguments might best be suited for the second negative.[22]

Other options include dividing responsibility for advantages when dealing with a multiple-advantage affirmative case. Case presses in second negative have the potential to be more thought out and analytical because of the amount of preparation time available. Two-constructive development of negative counterplans is another option occasionaly used by experienced teams. And, of course, a total reversal of the traditional duty assignments is a possible tactic.

Whichever tactic is used, the negative team should ideally decide upon it before the 1NC. Second negatives are advised to reserve a portion of their speaking time to account for the developments through the first three constructives. And, depending on the case and issues, it might be best for the second negative to spend his or her entire time on plan objections. My point is that, given the objective of maintaining optimum flexibility for the negative, no strategic framework should ignore this diversity of tactical options.

CONCLUSIONS

The traditional assignment of specific areas of negative speaker duties is outmoded and lacks a contemporary strategic perspective. It has no sound theoretical basis. The division of case and plan responsibilities reduces first negative options, allows affirmatives to launch a two-constructive offensive, undermines a consistent negative position, and encourages narrow thinking by negative team members. In the interest of achieving maximum strategic flexibility in refutation, debaters should be trained in all areas of issue argumentation—not just case or plan. The need for broad-based strategic planning is clear. Coaching for specific speaker positions can focus on the tactical considerations involved with each position. It appears to be a hindrance to coach first negatives along speech content lines that have no basis and are strategically weak.

It may be claimed that such a broad-based negative approach would provide too few guidelines to beginners and only result in confusion. This criticism underestimates the abilities of both student and coach. All the basic tools and issue areas should be covered in the training process. The difference is that the flexible approach defended in this paper emphasizes the integration of these tools into team strategies and team duties—not narrow individual positions. And even if debaters are not exposed to this integrated approach through coaching, they will eventually learn it the hard way at the hands of more experienced negative opponents.

What this paper advocates is not new. Winning teams rarely adhere to the strict division of case and plan duties. It seems that the tactics employed by these teams have outpaced the theoretical position perpetuated by every academic debate text. These debaters are shaping the activity, and we as coaches, judges, and scholars would be remiss if we failed to recognize this evolution. Perhaps it is time we examined the practices of the experienced debate teams and incorporated their winning strategies into a broader theoretical construct of contemporary negative duties.

Notes

1. James Luck, "Restructuring the Negative Attack on Comparative Advantages Cases," in David A. Thomas, ed., *Advanced Debate*, (Lincolnwood: IL: National Textbook Co., 1981), 136.
2. Luck is a notable exception; he advocates a complete reversal of traditional speaker duties.
3. Austin J. Freeley, *Argumentation and Debate*, 5th ed. (Belmont, CA: Wadsworth, 1981), 206.
4. J. W. Patterson and David Zarefsky, *Contemporary Debate* (Boston: Houghton Mifflin, 1983) p. 97.
5. James Murphy and Jon Ericson, *The Debater's Guide* (Indianapolis: Bobbs-Merrill, 1961), 26.
6. David Thomas, "Rebuttal Strategy and Tactics," in *Advanced Debate*, p. 289.
7. Luck, p. 136.
8. Patterson and Zarefsky, p. 230.
9. Luck, p. 139.
10. Roy V. Wood, *Strategic Debate*, 2nd ed. (Lincolnwood, IL: National Textbook Co., 1977) 109.
11. Wood, p. 109.
12. Patterson and Zarefsky, pp. 180–89, *passim*.
13. Charles A. Willard, "The Nature and Implications of the 'Policy Perspective' for the Evaluation of Debate," in *Advanced Debate*, p. 440.
14. Luck, p. 17.
15. Michael Pfau, "A Systematic Approach to Debating the Second Negative," in *Advanced Debate*, p. 199.
16. Luck, p. 139.

17. Craig Dudczak and William Semlak, "Rationale for a Rational Second Negative," in *Advanced Debate*, p. 171.
18. Pfau, p. 197.
19. Star A. Muir and W. David Snowball, *A Conspectus of Theory and Practice in Academic Debate* (Amherst: University of Massachusetts, June 1983), 30.
20. Pfau, p. 190.
21. Murphy and Ericson, p. 78.
22. Dudczak and Semlak, p. 167.

7

Cross-Examination Reexamined

George Ziegelmueller

In 1974, the National Developmental Conference on Forensics recommended that "The NDT Committee should adopt the cross-examination format for the NDT as soon as practicable.... "[1] Obviously, the supporters of cross-examination hoped and believed that it would heighten the educational process and, in the words of the National Developmental Conference, "sharpen the contest among arguments in debate."[2] Today, few debate coaches would seriously oppose continued use of cross-examination in academic debate, although some would question whether the procedure is worth the time it consumes. Like most judges, I have occasionally heard rounds of debate in which the cross-examination was well executed, exciting, and decisive. More often, I have heard cross-examination that was poorly prepared and a waste of time.

PURPOSE AND METHOD OF STUDY

My purpose in this paper is to make some modest suggestions, which may be helpful in teaching students how to engage in more meaningful cross-examination. In order to prepare for this task I studied the texts of the eight final rounds of the National Debate Tournament that have utilized the cross-examination format.[3] These debates provided thirty-two samples of cross-examination for study. In addition to the selected cross-examination samples, I also reviewed debate textbooks, cross-examination textbooks from the field of law, and recent law journal articles.

As one might expect, none of these sources directly provided much new insight. The analysis of NDT transcripts did reveal that topicality and counterplans were particularly important areas for cross-examination, but this fact is not necessarily typical of all debate rounds. The debate textbooks generally provided a list of standard rules and guidelines, and the legal articles, in the words of one critic, tend to "string together examples and suggestions without enabling the reader to understand how they might apply to their own factual situation."[4] Nevertheless, the analysis of the debate transcripts did reveal certain strengths and failures in the application of cross-examination theory, and the study of the texts and articles brought into focus some approaches to cross-examination that have not previously been explicated in reference to academic debate. These findings provide the basis for three general suggestions on how to improve the use of cross-examination in academic debate.

STRATEGIC PERSPECTIVE

First, cross-examination should be studied and developed from a strategic perspective. Such a perspective requires three things: (1) the determination of clear purposes to be achieved during the cross-examination; (2) a plan for achieving those purposes; and (3) the integration of the information gained through cross-examination into the rest of the debate.

The importance of a strategic view is implicit in nearly all of the writings on cross-examination in law, and it is explicity indicated in the titles of numerous works, for instance, *Successful Cross Examination Strategy*[5] and "Psychology and Courtroom Strategy: Cross-Examination."[6] That college debaters sometimes lack this strategic perspective is most apparent in those rounds where the cross-examiner begins with some irrelevant questions about the opposing debater's social life and then proceeds to ask questions that, in effect, only restate the opposition's arguments. While such examples are extreme, they are not necessarily uncommon.

The NDT sample cross-examinations provided no such glaring failures. In almost all cases, the NDT debaters seemed to have a sense of purpose in their questioning, and they generally used an appropriate mix of closed factual questions, open-ended clarification questions, and leading questions to achieve their objectives. Although the NDT debaters sometimes failed to follow up on useful exchanges, this was not generally true. An initial impression that cross-examination was not integral to the overall clash of arguments is created by the fact that there were few specific references to cross-examination in the constructive or rebuttal speeches. However, nearly every cross-examination exchanged produced some data that was used in a later speech, and most exchanges produced three or four vital pieces of information.

Both legal experts and the NDT debates provide some insights into how a strategic perspective can be facilitated. Professor Paul Bergman of the UCLA Law School emphasizes the importance of having an overall theory of the case to guide the selection of questions for cross-examination. He explains:

> The decision as to which, if any, of these factors should be focused on during cross should be based on the cross-examiner's theory of the case. The theory of the case may be thought of as the blueprint upon which the attorney's case is built.[7]

The increasing emphasis within the academic debate community on strategies of argument and on debate paradigms, in general, and policy systems comparisons, in particular, suggests a considerable awareness of this need for "an overall theory of the case." The contribution of Professor Bergman is not so much in the idea of a theory per se, but in his emphasis on the need for that theory to *guide* the cross-examination. He continues:

> The need to tie the factual testimony to the legal elements is for some reason more apparent with direct examination and closing argument than it is with cross-examination. But this should not be so. The fact that different techniques are used on cross than during direct or closing should not mask the basic point that questions asked on cross should be tied into the attorney's blueprint.[8]

How to facilitate the tying of the cross-examination into the debater's overall blueprint is suggested by an examination of the NDT final rounds. These debates indicate that questions relating to disadvantages, topicality, and counterplans were most frequently asked and were most likely to be used in developing constructive and rebuttal arguments. Because these areas of analysis are fairly generic, it is likely that debaters have more experience with them and are better able to anticipate where their partners will use them. Moreover, topicality arguments and counterplans inherently involve case theories, while disadvantages generally incorporate the basic rationale for negative case theories. Thus, the NDT sample debates suggest that it may be easier to utilize a strategic perspective in cross-examination by focusing on topicality, counterplans, or disadvantages.

This is not to suggest that questions on significance, inherency, and solvency were never used by the NDT debaters. Obviously, they were, but not as often or with as much overall impact. Such arguments generally require more specific adaptation to the opposing analyses and, therefore, may not be as easy to use. It is also probably true that current approaches to judging and coaching academic debate view these areas of analysis as less critical to negative case theories.

CROSS-EXAMINATION TOPOI

In addition to developing a strategic perspective, a second way in which instruction in cross-examination could be improved is through the systematic development of what might be called cross-examination topoi for debate. In classical rhetorical theory topoi, or topics, are hunting grounds for arguments or places where one can go to discover arguments. Many of the books and articles in the field of law do little more than provide elaborate lists of standard questions that can be asked of particular kinds of witnesses or in particular kinds of cases—in essence, they are offering a list of cross-examination topoi.[9] While no such published list of standard questions exists for debaters, analysis of the cross-examinations at the National Debate Tournament reveals that debaters do tend to ask similar questions when dealing with the same kind of data or with the same issues. This similarity of approach to questioning suggests that most experienced debaters and coaches probably already have informal checklists of questions, which they mentally refer to in questioning or in teaching cross-examination.

If coaches were to make such checklists more formal and more systematic, they would make it easier for beginning students to approach the process of cross-examination. As long as debaters feel they must confront each debate as if it is a totally new experience, they cannot be expected to engage in consistently productive cross-examination.

Tests of Evidence and Reasoning

At least three different kinds of cross-examination topoi are possible. Both the NDT final debates and the writings of legal experts indicate that one major category of topics can be drawn from the tests of evidence and reasoning. There are numerous legal articles on how to cross-examine in response to particular kinds of evidence, such as expert witnesses or eyewitnesses.[10] The NDT debates also illustrate the applications of standard tests of argument (1978 NDT: Singer questioning Cassanelli, "Well, where have you indicated any other but that one anecdotal example?")[11] and of evidence (1976 NDT Cross questioning Ottoson, "Are those studies controlled for anything? . . . Do they control for other variables? . . . Now are those studies longitudinal or cross-sectional?").[12] Since the tests of evidence and reasoning given in most debate textbooks are often expressed in question form, it would not be difficult to rephrase and refine these tests into usable cross-examination checklists.

Areas of Analysis

A second category of cross-examination topics could be developed relevant to standard substantive areas of analysis, such as topicality, inherency, counterplans, and disadvantages. As the NDT transcripts indicate, negative debaters often find it useful to question the affirmative team regarding its definitions of critical terms before developing their own topicality arguments or offering a counterplan. Affirmative teams, in turn, find cross-examination helpful in setting up responses to disadvantages. From the transcripts one could put together a series of stock questions that could aid affirmatives in developing questions in response to disadvantages: What is the probability of the impact? At what point in time will the disadvantage occur? What is the threshold? and so on.

The questions in this category would probably not need to be directed to any particular subject matter but could focus on analytical requirements specific to the general nature of the issue. Those law journal articles that offer checklists for particular fields of law do exactly this sort of thing. They provide analytical questions directed to the problem area but not specific to the facts of a given case.

Specific Content

A third category of topics for cross-examination might be drawn out of the specific content of a given proposition. Deterrence theory, for example, provided repreated opportunities for content-specific questions during the 1977–78 debate season, just as the Brenner study did in 1978–79 and First Amendment rights did in 1979–80. Once a debate squad developed the first two categories of cross-examination topics, they could be used year after year with only occasional revisions; this latter category of topoi would, however, have to be developed with each new debate proposition.

PRIORITY OF TYPES OF QUESTIONS

The first two suggestions for impoving cross-examination were aimed at helping the student know what to question about; the final suggestion for improvement concerns *how* cross-examination questions are asked. Most works on cross-examination advise students to ask only factual questions to which they know the answer and to avoid open-ended questions and undirected fishing inquiries.[13] While this advice is generally sound, scrutiny of both the NDT cross-examinations and sample cross-examinations offered as models in legal articles and textbooks reveals that, in practice, this advice is often ignored.

The primary rationale underlying the advice to ask only questions with known responses is that such an approach avoids unexpected answers, which can be damaging to the interrogator's cause. As an ideal, this is a wise objective, and for attorneys who have preliminary hearings and depositions available to them, it is a reasonably attainable goal. For the academic debater, however, the avoidance of the unexpected is not so easy. New cases—even new case areas—appear at tournaments throughout the year, including the final rounds of the National Debate Tournament, and in spite of a recommendation from the National Developmental Conference of Forensics, no system of formal discovery has ever been instituted.[14]

In light of these differences between academic debate and the field of law, some more realistic advice needs to be given to students of debate. Professor Bergman of the UCLA Law School has offered a "safety model" for cross-examination, which, with some minor modifications, seems well suited to the academic debate context and which provides clear guidelines on what forms of questions to use and when.[15] The Bergman model does not tell students *never* to ask open-ended questions. Rather, it establishes a priority order of question forms from high safety to low safety, and it even offers specific advice on how to ask low-safety fishing questions with a greater likelihood of success. The degree of risk in asking a question is determined by the possibility of refuting an answer not desired by the cross-examiner.

High-Safety Questions

According to the model, cross-examiners should first consider asking questions from the high-safety category. High-safety questions are ones that can be extrinsically verified; they are questions that are drawn directly from the constructive speeches of the opposition. High-safety questions may point out weaknesses in the support for an argument. "Did you offer any evidence to support that point?" "Was the one example the only empirical evidence cited?" Or, they might point out the failure to clash with a specific part of the case or with specific evidence. "Did you deny the solvency evidence presented in the first affirmative constructive?" Sometimes an opponent will unintentionally say something or read a piece of evidence that contains something that can be useful in providing an argument for the cross-examiner. In such instances the interrogator can safely ask the witness to repeat those statements. All of the preceding types of questions are safe because the judge and the debaters can refer back to earlier statements for verification of answers' accuracy.

Medium-Safety Questions

If productive high-safety questions are not available, the cross-examiner should consider what medium-safety questions are possible. Medium-safety questions are "those where the specific context of the cases furnishes the cross-examiner the *likelihood* of receiving an expected answer."[16] Questions involving facts that are consistent with human experience are relatively safe to ask. While our perception of human experience is not an infallible guide, in most instances, past experience or past perceptions are fairly reliable indicators. In the following cross-examination exchange from the 1797 National Debate Tournament, the cross-examiner relied on past experience as a basis for his cross-examination.

> Cotham: Now, in terms of this energy shortage card, one of the impacts is that things will happen like New York City? That the entire . . . King: Yes, I mean—what I am just suggesting is you are playing with the breakdown of the social system for a period of time. Cotham: OK. Now, what's the last strike which caused an entire breakdown of the social structure? King: The United States has never experienced a general economic strike.[17]

A second category of medium-safe questions consists of requests for information consistent with other information presented earlier by that witness or the witness's partner. While it is possible for a witness to answer in a manner inconsistent with previous statements, to do so would undermine his or her credibility.

A final type of medium-safe questions calls upon the witness to provide information that is generally known but which has not yet been cited in the round. If the witness responds with data different from that expected by the cross-examiner, that information can be refuted with evidence in a following speech. With all medium-safe questions there are restraints operating on the witness that make it likely that the anticipated response will be given.

Low-Safety Questions

As a general rule, low-safety questions should be used only when safer questions cannot be developed or when safer questions fail to explore the theory of the case adequately. In some situations, however, the use of low-safety questions may be unavoidable since failure to fish for leads may mean losing the round automatically. Low-safety questions are less able to control the witness's response, because they tend to be more open-ended. They are asked in the hope of receiving useful information, but without the means of refuting unfavorable responses.

One form of low-safety questions are questions of clarification. Questions aimed at gaining a better understanding of the affirmative plan, the negative's counterplan, or complicated lines of analysis may be essential to avoid misdirected attacks. Nevertheless, these questions are risky, because they involve responses of an unknown nature, afford the opposition additional opportunity to explain its analysis, and make control of time more difficult. One way in which the risk of clarification inquiries can be reduced is to use leading or directed questions. Rather than asking, "How will your plan be enforced?" the negative should attempt to direct the response by asking a leading question such as, "Does your plan rely on civil or criminal suits for enforcement?"

When debaters are faced with an unfamiliar case and lack sufficient evidence of their own, they can probe the conclusions of the opposition and try to show that insufficient factual evidence exists to support those conclusions. Mark Cotham of Northwestern used cross-examination very effectively for this purpose in 1978. Notice how Mark begins his inquiry with fairly closed questions and how he pieces together affirmative data to press his attack.

> Cotham: What is the total cost of the plan? Combs: About $10 billion. Cotham: And that comes from . . . ? Combs: Oh, where did we get that estimate? We looked at different treatment devices; it's our own. Cotham: . . . You indicate that the prime reason right now we do not do this is economic consideration. Now, why should we just accept SC saying, hmmm, sounds like $10 billion to us? Combs: Well, we're pretty reasonable people. *Consumer Reports* says that . . . ozonization of water cost "less that 4 cents per month for a family of four." I think it's closer to $10 billion. Cotham: All right. Now, the solvency in terms of ozonization is never proven, correct? Combs: Oh, no, that's just one example of solvency. . . . Cotham: That's right. It's only one example of cost, unfortunately. Isn't it? Combs: You're right.[18]

Another basic fishing technique, related to the first, is to ask:

> "If what the witness says is true, what other things would also be true?" To phrase it another way, "If A is true, then common human experience tells us that facts B, C and D are likely to be present." The cross-examiner can then fish to see whether facts B, C and D are indeed present. If they are not, then the cross-examiner can argue that fact A is not true.[19]

Mark Cotham used this approach when he tried to demonstrate that: (A) if the affirmative case was topical; then (B) the failure to provide soft water must already be a felony; and (C) felonies can be prosecuted under the present system. If (B) and (C) were not true, then (A) must not be true.

Cotham: Under FWPCA where do you prove that soft water is pollution? Combs: It's not; it's under the Safe Drinking Water Act.... Cotham: So, in other words, we could enforce that as a felony? Combs: No, not now. Cotham: What laws are these felonies under? Combs: You can't do it given the inherencies. Cotham: I know, but I'm afraid the inherencies make the case not topical. Where do you ever indicate that these things are currently felonies under current regulations?... Combs: All drinking water must be effectively treated, if it goes through a treatment process. Cotham: Oh, effective treatment, OK. Right now we do not define effective treatment as soft water, correct? Combs: I don't know, or not.[20]

Low-safety questions may be less desirable to use, but by asking leading questions, probing for insufficiencies in proof, and exploring the validity of corollary conclusions, the risk of fishing questioning can be limited.

CONCLUSION

In conclusion, the art of cross-examination requires some minimal aptitude and intelligence, but like the other arts, it also requires direction, training, and discipline. It is hoped the three suggestions outlined here will make it easier to provide more systematic and useful guidance to students. A strategic perspective based on the theory of the particular case should help direct students to important areas for interrogation. The use of cross-examination topoi can simplify and systematize the search for appropriate questions. And an awareness of the various question forms can make it easier to control the nature and extent of witnesses' responses.

Notes

1. James H. McBath, ed., *Forensics as Communication* (Lincolnwood, IL: National Textbook Co., 1975), 28.
2. Ibid.
3. The texts of these final rounds of the NDT can be found in the Summer issues of the *Journal of the American Forensic Association*, 1976–1983.
4. Paul B. Bergman, "Practical Approach to Cross-Examination," *Criminal Law Bulletin* 15 (Mar./Apr. 1979): 119.
5. Noel C. Stevenson, *Successful Cross Examination Strategy* (Englewood Cliffs: Executive Reports Corp., 1981).
6. Ted M. Warshafsky, "Psychology and Courtroom Strategy: Cross-Examination," *Wisconsin Bar Bulletin* 51 (Aug. 1978) 9–12.
7. Bergman, p. 121.
8. Ibid., p. 122.
9. See for example, Louis E. Schwartz, *Proof, Persuasion, and Cross-Examination*, v. 2 (Englewood Cliffs; Executive Reports Corp., 1973), 1601–2249; and O. J. Weber, "Attacking the Expert Witness," *FIC Quarterly* 31 (Summer 1981): 299–319.

10. See for example, Michael F. Hupy, "Preparation for and Cross-Examination of Identification Witnesses at Trial," *Wisconsin Bar Bulletin* 55 (June 1982): 14–16; and William M. Getzoff, "Direct and Cross-Examination of an Expert," *Trial Lawyer's Guide* 22 (Fall 1978): 267–88.

11. John K. Boaz, ed., "1978 National Debate Tournament Final Debate," *Journal of the American Forensic Association* 15 (Summer 1978): 26.

12. Stanley G. Rives, ed., "1976 National Debate Tournament Final Round," *Journal of the American Forensic Association* 13 (Summer 1976): 7.

13. "Always know answers to questions asked. Never ask questions unless you know what answer will be and that it cannot hurt you. This principle is fundamental. Don't question in hope of favorable answers. Reply might be disastrous." F. Lee Bailey and Henry Rothblatt, *Successful Techniques for Criminal Trials* (Rochester, NY: Lawyers Cooperative Printing Co., 1971), quoted in James M. Copeland, *Cross-Examination in Debate* (Lincolnwood, IL: National Textbook Co., 1981), 18.

14. McBath, p. 32.

15. Bergman, pp. 117–50.

16. Ibid., p. 135.

17. John K. Boaz, ed., "1979 National Debate Tournament Final Debate," *Journal of the American Forensic Association* 16 (Summer 1979): 48.

18. Boaz, "1978 NDT Final Debate," p. 34.

19. Bergman, p. 149.

20. Boaz, "1978 NDT Final Debate," p. 35.

8

Prep Time
Maximizing a Valuable Resource

Gloria Cabada

Articles on debate theory tend to focus on particular arguments or practices, with guidelines for utilizing them in rounds. This article is somewhat different. Rather than discussing an aspect of theory, it presents a practical framework for time use both in and out of debate rounds, which, if consistently followed, will greatly increase a debater's preparation by improving efficiency. Before such a framework can be developed, though, it is essential to understand what is meant by "prep time." Prep time is much more than just the eight or ten minutes of non-speech time allocated to each team in a round. Prep time can include any time from the release of the first pairing of a tournament (or from the moment you begin your van ride to the tournament) until the last debate of the weekend, and any time during the week you may spend preparing for the next competition. This article will focus on efficient time use during and between rounds and will also provide some tips to help your preparation during the year.

There is absolutely no excuse for a debater to be doing nothing at any point during the debate, even if it's not your prep time and you're waiting for the other team to speak. This concept can serve as the foundation for the time-use framework. It is important to realize that any time during a debate when you are neither speaking nor preparing to speak is *free* prep time and should be used as such. Better-prepared teams usually debate better, sound better, and win more than teams that are continuously caught off-guard, waste time searching for misfiled evidence, and don't have partner communication and cooperation.

In-round time-maximization strategies are slightly different for the affirmative and the negative, and thus will be discussed separately, with the affirmative framework first.

The first affirmative constructive has the advantage of being a completely prepared speech, and therefore should be pre-flowed by both affirmative debaters. It is a good idea to have enough detailed pre-flows to get you through the tournament, or to use reusable stickers. By using pre-flows the first affirmative speaker does not have to waste time during the debate to flow the case, and more importantly, the second affirmative speaker can spend the 1AC time organizing case evidence for the 2AC, thinking about potential disadvantages, brainstorming some last-minute topicality responses, or doing anything else that will minimize the amount of actual prep time used before the 2AC.

Both partners can continue these organizational processes while the first negative speaker prepares (free prep time for the affirmative). It is important that the 1AC pre-flows contain all information that may become useful in later speeches and should therefore be easily accessible. For instance, "The third Myers card on solvency also proves topicality," or "The first card is from last week's *New York Times*." Detailed 1AC pre-flows help later speeches sound more eloquent because they make it easy to refer to specific pieces of evidence by source and exact location in the 1AC structure.

Obviously, both partners should flow the first negative constructive, but the 2A should also be writing down responses on her or his flow whenever possible. While this may seem obvious to some, there are many debaters who do not realize how much prep time can be saved by preparing while flowing, or some may be too worried about getting every negative word flowed. Therefore, the 1A should take a very careful flow of the 1NC and listen attentively to evidence in order to double-check the 2A's flow and protect against any missed arguments due to prepping while flowing. During cross-examination, the 1A should ask to see any evidence labeled "turnarounds," links to disadvantages, counterplans, topicality violations, or unclear arguments. While the 2A prepares, the 1A should look through these cards to make sure nothing tricky is going on, checking which way the links on a disadvantage go and making sure any topicality arguments are understood by the 2A. Prep time is a time for partners to communciate such information to prevent embarrassing (and round-losing) contradictions or dropped arguments later on.

The 1A should take a careful, detailed flow of the 2AC, which means that the 2A need not waste valuable prep time writing down blocked responses on her or his flow. After the 2AC, during cross-examination and 2NC prep time, the 1A should take the 2A's flow and *neatly* fill in any arguments that weren't written down before the speech. (Neatness is vital—an illegible flow is useless.) Any prep time taken by the second negative is more free prep time for the affirmative: Flows can be filled in, evidence can be organized for use in rebuttals, and arguments can be discussed to determine 1AR strategy. Considerations for a rebuttal might include such questions as what responses on disadvantages are particularly strong, which evidence read elsewhere may also apply to topicality, and what can be done about the last three arguments on solvency, which were dropped in 2AC. If the 2A unknowingly made contradictory arguments and they are discovered by the affirmative, now is the time to start thinking about a way out. Always think ahead in a debate in order to minimize unpleasant surprises.

Again, both partners should flow the 2NC and 1NR, with the 1A beginning to prepare responses and the 2A acting as the backup flow. 2NC cross-examination is free 1AR prep time, but the 1A should also listen to any questions about arguments such as new links or new disadvantages. The 2A should ask for any relevant evidence, like the 1A did after 1NC, to be looked at while the 1A preps. Leave some time before the 1AR to discuss these cards, if necessary, and certainly to discuss any new twist to be attempted, such as a disco. The 2A should take a careful flow of the 1AR in order to make sure that no crucial argument is dropped, and also to keep track of time allocation. Even if the judge or a timer is keeping time, it is important for partners to time each other and provide accurate time signals, especially in rebuttals. In addition to calling out the time, if this is acceptable to the parties involved, it may be useful to hold up signals where the speaker can easily see them. (You may wish to sit in front of your partner, or place a stopwatch next to her or his flow.) Try different timing systems until you find one that works for you.

After the 1AR, evidence should once again be organized to separate what has been read and which evidence applies to which arguments. Not only will this allow the 2A to quickly find evidence to read in 2AR (if desired), but it will also make filing after the round much easier, and it won't take as long to find a card for the judge.

2NR prep time is a good time for the 2A to go over the flow and discuss strategies for the 2AR. Try to predict which arguments the negative will extend and what implications they will have for the 2AR. It may be useful to write little summaries on the top of the flow of each major issue in order to organize your thoughts. These summaries can serve as the foundation of the 2AR. You may also want to circle certain 2AC responses or 1AC cards that should be extended in order to save prep time.

Another technique that may help in certain rounds (especially in counterplan debates) is to draw a chart that shows how the issues interrelate. For example, you can list the negative policy or policies and then determine how other issues (for instance, the disads) are affected:

"Counterplan X links to disad A, but doesn't get the flips like the aff, and thus the aff is a superior policy; counterplan Y does get the flips to A and captures the aff advantages, but it links to disad B, which the aff prevents." While this technique may seem complicated, it can be extremely effective in providing a holistic perspective on the debate and could result in a very coherent 2AR. Of course, this particular technique may not be applicable to every debate, and it does take some time and requires brainstorming by both partners, but it may be helpful if begun during your free prep time before 2NR.

The 2NR should be flowed carefully by the 1A as backup, and 2AR prep time should be a continuation of whatever process was begun before 2NR. It is essential for both partners to communicate about the choices made by the 2N in order to fully exploit any errors, cover up or outweigh any dangerous arguments. The 1A should flow the 2AR to watch for dropped arguments and time allocation. Again, provide your partner with adequate time signals.

It may seem tedious to some to flow the last two rebuttals (unless you're a 2A), but there are numerous advantages to doing so besides the one discussed above. First, it is good flowing practice, which is essential when you're first starting to debate. Second, you can use the flow to redo your rebuttal at home by referring to 2NR choices and adapting your 1AR accordingly. Third, it provides you with a complete record of your debate for future reference. You now know how that particular team thinks on the negative, which arguments they like to extend, which arguments they may be weak on, and other information that will come in handy next time you debate them. Never throw out a flow—it is a valuable time-maximizing resource and should be treated as such. Instead, label it (with relevant information such as the team, debaters' names, tournament) and save it.

Now for the negative framework. Even if you as a negative debater know what case the affirmative is running, but especially if you don't, it is crucial for at least one of you on the negative to take a detailed flow of the 1AC. Ideally, you will have some information about your opponents before the debate and most of your arguments are organized and ready to go. But, alas, the ideal isn't always realized, and you may have to spend part of the 1AC looking in your files for evidence and writing down responses while trying to flow. This is fine, as long as *someone* is still listening and writing down what is said.

When cross-examining the 1A, the 2N should ask for the plan (and also the case, if necessary, to double-check the flow) and it should be read by both partners. This should avoid unnecessary embarrassment from running inapplicable topicality violations, and it may help in fining links to disads. At the very least, you will know what the affirmative plan is trying to do.

At some point before the end of the debate (a good time is after 2NR), you should copy the plan on the back of your flow for future reference. This practice has several advantages. First, there is no confusion over plan wording when discussing this affirmative with your teammates or when planning a strategy against that case in the future. You or your coach may come up with topicality violations you hadn't thought of in the round. Second, research is facilitated by knowing exactly what the plan intends to do. Links to disads will be easier to find. Third, during the debate itself it may help to have ready access to the plan to make sure that a tricky 2AC or 1AR isn't claiming that the plan does something that is clearly not indicated.

During 1NC prep time, both partners should cooperate when deciding what arguments to run in order to develop a coherent strategy that is understood by both. The 2N can assist by finding relevant evidence for her or his partner, pointing out any interesting CX answers (such as links to disads or solvency problems), and looking over the case flow to determine which advantages may potentially outweigh a disad or other potential problems. The 2N can also begin organizing evidence and arguments to be used in her or his constructive. Both partners can save significant amounts of prep time if certain standard arguments such as topicality, counterplans or disads are pre-flowed (like a 1AC).

During the 1NC, the 2N should flow what hasn't been pre-flowed, and during the presentation of the pre-flowed arguments the 2N can continue organizing evidence for her or his speech. While the 1N is being cross-examined, the 2N should take the 1N's flow and fill in any missing arguments. This not only saves prep time for more important tasks (such as discussing arguments) but is also a lot easier than digging through a pile of blocks or cards to figure out in what order you presented your arguments. Free negative prep time is provided before the 2AC, when the evidence and blocks used in 1NC should be sorted out and discussions begun on how to utilize the negative time block.

The first negative should flow *all* of the 2AC rather than writing out responses for 1NR. After all, the 1N has eleven minutes of free prep time (2NC and CX), and if the 2N will be extending some arguments presented in 1NC (as is becoming more popular) then the 1N *must* take a careful backup flow to compensate for the 2N's prepping during 2AC. As a flexible rule of thumb, the negative should have at least half of the allotted prep time saved for 2NR, so efficient time use is essential during the round.

The 1N should ask for any potentially dangerous cards during CX, including turns and add-ons. These should be examined by the 1N as the 2N preps in order to avoid contradictions or mishandling an argument. Again, both partners must communicate at the outset of 2NC prep time in order to decide who will be extending what in the time block. Also, any new issues should be carefully examined to prevent the introduction of deadly contradictory arguments in the time block. Decisions on which arguments to drop from the round should also begin now, again with careful consultation, to ensure that arguments are jettisoned in such a manner as to prevent them from coming back to haunt the negative in 1AR or 2AR.

Free 1NR prep time begins with the 2NC and ends with the end of CX. Given these eleven minutes to prepare a four-minute speech, there is no reason to use any allotted prep time before the 1NR. The only exception is using a few seconds to consult with the 2N when a question of a potential contradiction exists, or if the 2N fails to address all the necessary issues in 2NC and needs the 1NR to cover some arguments. Under such circumstances it is far preferable to use some prep time to clarify the situation than to speak immediately and possibly jeopardize the team's chances of winning.

Sometimes the 1N may finish preparing her or his rebuttal with several minutes left over. If this happens, the extra time can be spent listening to the 2NC as a check, looking over the flow to make sure there are no holes waiting to be exploited by the 1AR, or even practicing the 1NR. But this is *not* the time to play tic-tac-toe or write a letter. The best and most successful debaters are those who use all the time in a round to their advantage and are constantly thinking ahead in the debate.

The 2N *must* carefully flow the entire 1NR, especially if part of the 2AC was not flowed in order to write out responses for the 2NC. If this happens, chances are that certain 1NR arguments are not easy to follow, and thus, a good flow is crucial to understanding these arguments with the help of the 1N after the rebuttal. A successful 2NR begins with a good flow of 1NR.

The 2N's free prep time is provided by the affirmative's preparation for the 1AR. Unfortunately for the 2N, her or his flow cannot be filled in by the 1N, who has been busily prepping for her or his rebuttal rather than flowing. Therefore, now is the time to quickly go through the flow and fill in any blanks using the evidence read in 2NC, which hopefully has survived in a neat stack up to this point. Decisions about which arguments to extend and which to drop should be made in consultation with the 1N, and several strategies should be discussed by predicting what different strategies may be taken by the 1AR.

Now is the time to begin to decide which arguments are being won by the negative, which can be dropped at no cost, and which must not be lost to win the debate. Potential 1AR discos, hidden turns, or other weapons should be discussed so they don't come by surprise when the 2N has less time to develop a position against them.

The 1N should flow the 1AR as a backup for the 2N, who should

be preparing responses while flowing. The 1N's flow is also important as a means to check the 2NR against dropping or mishandling an
argument. As discussed in the affirmative framework, partners should
time each other to facilitate good time allocation in rebuttals. Also, it is
possible that the 2N will not have enough time to prepare every issue
needed for the 2NR. The 1N can help out by writing out responses on
her or his own flow on any argument with which the 2N needs help and
the 2N can use that flow for that part of the speech. If done legibly and
efficiently, this technique can double a 2N's prep time, since both
partners are preparing the 2NR.

It is essential to allocate some 2NR prep time to discussion. The
amount will vary according to the round, but it may sometimes be
necessary to use a minute or even more to decide what strategy to use in
the 2NR. This may be the speech for which cooperation is most
important, because not only must winning issues be chosen, but options
for the 2AR must be closed.

The 1N should flow the 2NR as a check, and both partners should
flow the 2AR for the same reasons that both should flow the entire
debate when affirmative. Additionally, it may be entertaining to flow the
2AR in order to trace her or his arguments back to constructives and
observe the evolution of issues (or the birth of new arguments). Again,
saving and labeling negative flows of opposing affirmative cases and
plans can greatly maximize preparation time by providing you with a
copy of a case to research, write specific arguments against, and prepare
against traps and tricks that may have caused a loss.

In addition to this set of in-round time-maximizing frameworks,
there are also several practices that can provide you with more
preparation time at tournaments. First of all, when pairings are released
for a round, get one as soon as possible and immediately find your coach
or head to your round (whichever is your squad policy). The point is that
you should start developing a strategy and preparing for the debate as
soon as possible, rather than wandering around, wasting valuable time
and frustrating your partner and coach who are searching for you.

This early preparation will reveal one practical reason why you
should save your flows. If you or anyone on your squad has debated your
opponents, you can look at the flow of the earlier debate and begin
preparing against their positions. For example, if you're affirmative and
you find out that your opponents run a tricky topicality violation that
you've never heard before, you can begin brainstorming responses
against it before the debate even begins. Or, if you're negative, you can
look through your files to find which disads link and which don't, thus
preventing you from looking silly by running inapplicable arguments
and also saving your speech time for running only good, relevant
positions.

If you don't have a flow of your opponents, you can look at earlier pairings (provided it's at least the third round of the tournament) and find and ask the team that debated them on the relevant side or the judge of that debate. These sources may be willing to tell you about the basic arguments made by your opponents. Of course, in order to do this, you need to save all your pairings from the tournament so you can refer to them.

This form of scouting does not provide an unfair advantage to certain squads, because everyone can and should save their flows to learn from them. Debate is, after all, an educational activity, and one should learn from previous mistakes or the mistakes of others. Spontaneity and thinking on one's feet are not destroyed by scouting, since no two rounds ever get debated the same way, and quick thinking shifts toward more knowledgeable and informed argumentation (it is hoped). Scouting, when properly used, does not turn debaters (at least not smart and successful ones) into brief-reading "spewtrons" incapable of independent thought. Such a team will be beaten by an equally well-prepared (through scouting) team that uses its preparation in a creative, intelligent and flexible manner rather than being bound to blocks as an alternative to thinking and working in a round. A debate in which the negative has some knowledge of the affirmative case and has developed a well-thought-out strategy against it, and the affirmative has a good understanding of the negative positions, will be a far superior debate to one in which both sides are knowledgeable about their own arguments only. A well-prepared debate is educational for all involved (even the judge), and depth of argumentation can occur rather than the frantic unprepared negative strategy of running every possible argument to see what gets dropped. If one views debate as an intellectual activity with the goals of teaching research skills, argument development, quick thinking, and informed discussions, then saving one's flows as preparation tools or scouting at a tournament can enhance the educational value of the activity.

Case flows and information obtained from colleagues can be used to create a team list of arguments. A team list consists of the names of teams (including debaters' names) with a brief case outline of their affirmative, a description of their negative positions, and, possibly, even a brief outline of your strategy against that team. By taking this list to tournaments you can have quick access to information about your opponents, saving valuable prep time. Add to your team list as the season progresses, updating the information and developing new strategies that may prove more successful.

After each round it is imperative that you refile all your material. Clumping it together in the back of your files to refile later, or waiting until the next pairing is released to clean up, is a tremendous waste of time. By cleaning up immediately and gathering files together after a round, you minimize the chances that evidence will be misfiled (leading to prep time wasted with frantically looking for it before a speech), it becomes easier to find evidence for the judge, and if you are changing rooms, you can move your evidence as soon as the pairing is released. Even if you think you won't be debating on that same side in the next round, or it's the last round of the day, don't leave your filing for later when you can do it sooner and not lose any of it.

One good way to protect against losing to the same argument twice is to look over your flow immediately after a debate and discuss with your partner any arguments that could have been argued better or on which you were completely unprepared. Then sit and brainstorm some responses and put together a little block against that argument for future reference. This is especially useful on the affirmative against topicality. You can save minutes of future 2AC prep time if you write down your best arguments against a violation the first time you hear it and then save the block. Later, when you are in another debate and the same violation is run, you can add any new responses that come to mind this time around, and have an even better-prepared 2AC.

One way to improve your research and increase your preparation in future debates is to ask your opponents for the cites on particular arguments. By doing so, you can read their affirmative sources and gain a deeper understanding of their case (while perhaps finding some disad links), or improve your impacts to your disads, or strengthen your position in some other way. This is far preferable to trading or copying evidence since you don't take the risk of acquiring shady evidence or miscopying, while you also get to read the original and maybe find better cards. By the same token, you should be willing to provide cites to others. After all, it is an educational activity, and you can't prevent others from finding those cites in an index.

Once the judge has decided your debate, if you believe it is appropriate, it is usually quite helpful to tactfully ask if the judge would be willing to discuss the debate. While some high school judges will not disclose their decision, most are willing to provide a constructive critique of the issues, or give advice on what to argue differently. Not only do you learn how to improve your debating by talking with the judge, but you can also gain some insight into such characteristics as how that judge thinks in evaluating arguments or what preferences she or he may have on delivery styles. Don't be afraid to take notes on particularly helpful suggestions. Next time that judge judges you, it is hoped you will use your knowledge about her or his preferences and any other useful advice to produce a superior debate.

Finally, if you are at a tournament with elimination rounds in which you are not participating, watch and flow as many debates as you can. Take a good flow, even of the plan, and analyze the issues during prep time. Pretend you had to give the next speech. How would you extend topicality, or should you extend it at all? What tension do you see between the various turns to the disads? Where should you start the 2NR? Then compare your strategy to the actual debate and evaluate it. If you can stay to hear the decision and the judges' explanations, do so and think about them. Do you agree or disagree? How would you have voted? These little exercises will improve your ability to analyze arguments and will be useful in preparing for your debates.

The importance of good preparation can't be overemphasized. As Ross Smith has said, "This is your prep time. Your opponents are using it, and you'll never have more" (1987).

9

A Theory of the Turnaround

Walter Ulrich

One of the recent trends in academic debate has been the increased use by affirmative teams of the turnaround. Essentially, this strategy involves an affirmative team arguing that not only will its plan not create a disadvantage, but that its plan will prevent a disadvantage from occurring. The affirmative thus converts a negative disadvantage into an independent reason to vote for the affirmative plan. This strategy is very useful to an advocate, since it shifts the team from a defensive stance to an offensive position, and thus benefits the team logically and psychologically. While in many ways this argument is not new (it is a modification of the "turning the tables" arguments), the increased emphasis on turnarounds has come at a time when the theory behind the practice has not been discussed seriously, either in debate literature or, surprisingly, in most debate rounds. As a consequence, many debaters, when confronted with a turnaround, do not consider its theoretical requirements and instead make arguments in a vacuum. This essay will attempt to explain some of the causes of the increased use of turnarounds, suggest some standards for evaluating turnarounds, and provide guidelines for debating turnarounds.

Increased use of turnarounds has resulted from two characteristics of contemporary debate. The first is the increased use of risk analysis by debaters. Several popular disadvantages argued by negative teams initially claim a very large impact. When the links to the disadvantage are challenged, negatives often argue that even if there is no certainty of a disadvantage, the impact of the disadvantage is so great, that any risk of the plan producing the disadvantage is enough to vote against the case. Since the weight given a disadvantage is calculated by multiplying the harm by the probability of its occurrence, a very improbable disadvantage with a great impact could outweigh many advantages. It is hard to reduce the risk of any disadvantage to zero, but since the initial link between the plan and the disadvantage is often tenuous, the affirmative has another option open to them. The strongest affirmative tactic is to use risk analysis to its advantage by turning the disadvantage and arguing there is as much chance that the plan will be beneficial as that it will be harmful. The affirmative thus might argue that while there is a risk that the plan might melt the polar ice caps, there is also the possibility that the plan, by increasing the world temperature, could save the world from an ice age. By turning around the disadvantage, the affirmative avoids the task of reducing the risk of disadvantage to zero. The negative risk is balanced by the affirmative team's risk, so a judge is likely to view any net risk as insignificant, since its direction is unknown.

Turnarounds have also been used to protect an affirmative against a negative team that argues a large number of poorly developed plan attacks. Negative teams often present many plan attacks and disadvantages in a round, planning to drop the weaker ones in rebuttals. When a disadvantage is turned, however, the negative team is prevented from dropping that disadvantage without giving the affirmative an advantage. Thus the negative team hurts itself by presenting a large number of superficial disadvantages. The more disadvantages the second negative argues, the more potential turnarounds an affirmative can claim. The more turnarounds an affirmative argues, the greater the pressure on the second negative rebuttalist. Thus, use of turnarounds can force a negative team to concentrate on a few good disadvantages.

The increased use of turnarounds has not been without its opponents. Two major arguments are often advanced against the turnaround. First, it is argued that turnarounds violate the prohibition against new arguments in rebuttals. This is only partially true; although the affirmative links to the turnaround are not presented until the first affirmative rebuttal, the negative team's links to the disadvantage are presented in the negative team's constructive speeches. The only question is the final resolution of the link to the disadvantage (or the net impact of the disadvantage), which is an offshoot of a constructive position. It should also be observed that the prohibition against new arguments in rebuttal was designed to aid each advocate (in this case the negative team) by preventing the opposing team from taking a new position in rebuttals. In the case of a turnaround, however, any problem the negative team faces is self imposed; the negative team selected the disadvantages they argued, and they should be responsible for the ultimate outcome of those choices.

A second problem with turnarounds is that they are often not fully developed. Unlike many other arguments, there are only two speeches after a turnaround is introduced in which to explore the nature of the turnaround. Certain negative strategies, such as the use of the counter-plan, cannot be employed against a turnaround. In addition, often the nature of the turnaround is not made clear until the last affirmative speech, preventing the negative team from adequately examining the turnaround.

Others may argue that turnarounds are frequently undeveloped and asserted. While these arguments may have some validity, they are not inherent characteristics of turnarounds. Turnarounds can be well-evidenced and developed, just as alternative responses to plan attacks (attacking links, showing the effect will not occur) can be superficial. Turnarounds, when well developed, can address critical issues in a debate: Does the plan produce the effect, or will it produce an opposite effect? Is the value supported by the negative worthwhile, or is it in fact something to be avoided? The question is not whether turnarounds should be used, but what guidelines should govern their use. Six guidelines are here proposed. Like any other guidelines, these should not be imposed by a judge if the negative team has not pointed out that the turnaround does not meet these guidelines; rather, each require-ment suggests possible negative response to the turnaround.

First, a turnaround must come from a topical provision of a plan. If a turnaround is supposed to be an independent reason to vote for the resolution, it should stem from the resolution, not a plank that could be adopted without the resolution. Just as an extra-topical advantage is thrown out of the debate, an extra-topical turnaround should be ignored in the decision-making process (except, perhaps, to neutralize the initial disadvantage). Thus on the employment topic, a team could not win a debate on a turn of an inflation disadvantage flowing from a plan plank that institutes wage and price controls, since that plan provision is not topical. It is possible, however, that a turnaround based on a non-topical plan provision could be used to defeat another disadvantage to that non-topical provision, but no net advantage should be credited to the affirmative team.

Second, a turnaround should meet all prima facie requirements of a normal advantage. Just as an advantage must provide links and be significant, the turnaround must meet these requirements. In most cases, however, these requirements are met by the second negative.

Third, a turnaround must be inherent to the resolution. While this may seem evident, it is often neglected by negative teams. For example, one common disadvantage argues that an affirmative plan that costs money will result in the reduction of food aid, killing millions of people. Affirmative teams often respond to this disadvantage by attempting to turn it around, arguing that killing millions of people will prevent Malthus (increased deaths due to increased births), saving more lives in the long run. Regardless of the merit of the affirmative argument, it should not become an independent reason for voting for the case; if cuts in food aid are desirable, that program could be cut without adopting the resolution and thus the turnaround is not inherent. This argument does not defeat the disadvantage, however, since the plan may prevent the government from sending food abroad. If Malthus is true, we should cut aid, regardless of whether the plan is adoped; if Malthus is false, we need to reject the plan to keep open the option of sending food aid. The turnaround, like any advantage, must be inherent to the resolution.

Fourth, links to the disadvantage must also apply to the turnaround. There are two instances where this may not be the case. In the first instance, the link may not be constant over a period of time. A plan that harms business confidence in the short term but increases it in the long term will result in a turnaround of a business confidence disadvantage only if the effect of a lack of business confidence will be the same in the future as it is now. This may not be the case if current business conditions have unique characteristics. Decreasing business confidence now may be harmful, while decreasing business confidence in the future may have little effect. In the second instance, the link may not be linear. The affirmative team often assumes that, if doing more of something is bad, doing less of something is good. That is not always the case. It may be that increased spending will result in decreased funding of social programs. That does not mean that decreased spending will result in increased funding of social programs. The excess funds could go into military programs, or they could be used to cut taxes. Just because increased spending is bad does not necessarily imply decreased spending is good; it is possible that any deviation may be harmful.

Fifth, the turnaround must flow from the initial disadvantage. There is a distinction between presenting a new argument in rebuttal and extending an old argument. The second type of argument is considered to be legitimate; the first is generally viewed as unfair. No affirmative team would be allowed to run an entirely new case in rebuttals for example. The question becomes: When is a turnaround a new argument and when is it a legitimate extention? The best guideline would seem to be that a turnaround is a new argument if it could exist without the disadvantage. Responding to a disadvantage with an impact of nuclear war, an affirmative team could not claim that its plan ensured world peace, since they could have claimed that argument as an advantage without the second negative mentioning her or his disadvantage. Without this limitation, any disadvantage that has an impact of saving lives can be turned with a new advantage that has an impact of saving other lives, but which saves those lives in a method that denies the initial link to the disadvantage or argues that the claimed affect of the disadvantage is really desirable. All other turnarounds are new arguments, not extensions of the disadvantage. Thus, the turnaround must be grounded in the negative disadvantage.

The sixth, and final, guideline calls for the affirmative team to give adequate warning to the negative team that a disadvantage has been turned. The turnaround should be claimed in both affirmative rebuttals, and the initial explanation should be adequate enough for the negative to be able to respond to the argument in a critical manner. Failure to do this will undermine the viability of the critical evaluation of policies, since the turnaround would not become clear until it is impossible for it to be critically evaluted by the negative team.

In addition to these theoretical arguments, there are some practical strategies a team should use in debating a turnaround. First, it is vital that turnarounds should not be dropped. Even if a team does not plan to win a specific disadvantage, it should explain why the disadvantage is not turned before responding to other arguments; otherwise the affirmative team would win an advantage by default.

Second, teams need to be alert for affirmative mistakes. Some affirmative teams will argue contradictory turnarounds by attempting to turn both the link to the disadvantage and the impact of the disadvantage. A team may argue both that food aid is bad and that its plan increases food aid. A wise second negative would concede both turns, but argue that, if both turnarounds are true, then the plan, by increasing bad food aid, is undesirable. Some may argue that this is not a legitimate strategy, since the second negative rebuttal position contradicts the second negative constructive position, but since the affirmative team members also contradict themselves, and the affirmative positions are better defended than the initial negative position, a wise policy matter would be to act in the appropriate manner suggested by the best (which in this case would be the affirmative) evidence. In any argument that attempts to discover the truth, it is sometimes required that an advocate admit that he or she was wrong, and then to examine the impact of his or her new view of reality. In this case, the second negative rebuttalist would admit to being in error, but would note that the new information calls for a rejection of the plan.

A third strategy might be built on the fact that often turnarounds do not deny the initial link to a disadvantage. Often policies have multiple effects. It may be that a plan will both save money and cost some money at the same time, or that an economic program will have both good and bad consequences. In turning a disadvantage, however, affirmative teams often do not dispute the initial negative link to the disadvantage. Thus the question becomes whether the affirmative (link or harm) evidence is better than the negative evidence. The turnaround thus develops into a debate within a debate: The second negative should argue that the initial link to the disadvantage is stronger than the link to the turnaround, or that the bad effects of the disadvantage outweigh the good effects, while the affirmative should argue the opposite is true. The initial links and evidence should be weighed against the affirmative evidence.

It may also be wise in some cases to present disadvantages in the first negative speech to give the negative more time to respond to the turnarounds. This is a strategy gaining wider and wider acceptance. Finally, the best way to prevent losing a debate because of a turnaround is to argue disadvantages that are unlikely to be turned around. Be sure you know your disadvantages well and that you have anticipated all possible turnarounds.

It is likely that turnarounds will remain an issue in the debate community for a long time. The amount of success that affirmative teams have had with turnarounds has even caused many negative teams to debate advantages as if they were disadvantages and to try to turn around advantages. This increased use of turnarounds should not continue without an understanding of the requirements of turnarounds. It is hoped the guiedlines suggested in this essay will act as a springboard for further examinations of the turnaround.

10

Value Analysis in Lincoln-Douglas Debate

The Need for Substance over Form

Diana Prentice

Since Lincoln-Douglas debate became a National Forensic League event in 1980, development of theory has often lagged behind practice. The pioneer coaches, debaters, and judges in Lincoln-Douglas were given little direction as to what was expected of them other than a format and a description of the event's purpose that read:

> An orthodox variation of standard debate, Lincoln-Douglas Debate is also known as One-Man Debate and has been utilized often during political campaigns.
>
> Only two speakers are involved, one fulfilling the affirmative responsibilities and the other, the negative. Since students participating in Lincoln-Douglas type debating are usually speaking to an audience, they should be encouraged to develop a direct and communicative delivery. Emphasis is necessarily placed upon the issues involved rather than upon strategy in developing the case. The statement of the topic is a resolution of value rather than of policy. This results in emphasizing logic, theory, and philosophy while eleminating plan arguments (Winfield, 1979, pp. 2–3).

As a result of the paucity of theoretical or practical literature at the time Lincoln-Douglas became a national event, questions still remain regarding the nature of stock issues, the legitimacy of evidence and plans, and the criteria by which Lincoln-Douglas should be judged. Ulrich's 1990 article titled "What Is Lincoln-Douglas Debate and What Should It Be?" appeared in *The Rostrum* eleven years after Winfield's explanation of the event and is but one example of how the activity is still defining itself.

It is the thesis of this essay that the continuing evolution of Lincoln-Douglas debate should take its cues from Winfield's original description and avoid fashioning itself after policy debate. Emphasis should be placed upon values analysis and theory rather than upon debate theory in the form of assigning presumption or identifying stock issues. Form should be of less importance in value debate than it is in policy debate. What should be emphasized in value debate is argumentation which examines the basic values that guide our thinking, our actions, and our policies. The basis for clash and judgment in value debate should be the arrangement of value hierarchies, the rationale for the hierarchies, and a defense of them in light of opponents' arguments not a debater's failure to include all of the stock issues of value debate.

The argument that Lincoln-Douglas debate should eschew adaptations of policy theory is developed by first explaining why policy models fail to apply to value debate and then by offering a three-step approach to value analysis, which should form the basis for argument development.

THE INAPPROPRIATENESS OF POLICY MODELS

Much of the literature on value debate both for CEDA and Lincoln-Douglas borrows from policy theory in describing affirmative and negative burdens (Fryar & Thomas, 1981; Wood & Midgley, 1986; Brownlee, 1987; Matlon, 1987; Thomas, 1987; Mezzera & Giertz, 1989; Bartanen & Frank, 1991); however, there is little agreement as to how to translate presumption, burden of proof, or stock issues into Lincoln-Douglas debate.

On the question of stock issues, for example, value debate theorists provide overlapping, yet distinctive, lists. Fryar and Thomas identify the stock issues as "What are the criteria that apply to the value?" and "Does the resolution meet the criteria?" (p. 21). Mezzera and Giertz claim that there are three "generally accepted stock issues for the affirmative speaker" (p. 65). They are that the affirmative must define the value term, establish the most important value related to the topic, and justify or use arguments to support the value (p. 65). The negative is assigned one stock issue: "to attack the affirmative's value justification" (p. 71). Bartanen and Frank list four stock issues:

1. The issue of definition: How are the issues and values implied in the resolution defined?
2. The issue of criteria: What assumptions can be made about members of the audience and their value system?

3. The issue of significance: Is the problem serious enough to affect members of this audience and their relevant value hierarchies?
4. The issue of comparison: Is this problem more worthy of audience attention than competing problems? (p. 45).

The issue of presumption also fails to offer a universally accepted theory. Matlon notes that while presumption rests with the negative in policy debate, there is no single source of presumption in value debate. He offers three possible sources: against the proposition with popular belief; or with a specific judge's belief (pp. 399–400). Thomas argues for assignment of a "natural presumption" rather than an artificial one that assumes a presumption against the topic. He claims that "audience analysis is the debater's method of determining where presumptions lie, and audience adaptation is the debater's method of influencing audience presumptions, hence, their decision" (p. 450).

Since competing theories of stock issues or presumption could become the focus of debate rather than the values they are intended to illuminate, Lincoln-Douglas argumentation would be better served by ignoring discussions of debate theory and concentrating on presenting debaters with explanations of value theories that would enhance their understanding of the explicit and implicit values in a given topic and would subsequently shape their arguments about them.

Thus, the position espoused in this article regarding the overlay of policy theory on value debate theory is not intended to suggest that Lincoln-Douglas debate should be theory-free. What it does argue is that Lincoln-Douglas practices should be guided by the body of literature regarding values as a means of preserving the intent of Lincoln-Douglas debate to be more oratorical and less inclined to suffer the abuses of policy debate.

The emphasis on theory derived from policy debate models necessitates more concern with the *form* in which cases are structured and refutation organized and the decision rules for judgment rather than the inherent merits of competing value systems. When questions of form are established as criteria for judgment in debate, jargon and tangential arguments about theory can obscure arguments about the values themselves. Four characteristics of value debate further suggest the reasons for rejecting traditional approaches to theory development.

First, Lincoln-Douglas debate, unlike policy or CEDA debate, provides a relatively short period of time for debate—thirty-two minutes. Any time spent arguing about theoretical issues severely limits analysis of the resolution. If the purpose of debate is to teach analysis and argumentation skills, then students are better served by debating questions of substance rather than of form. Lincoln and Douglas managed to debate at great length the questions of slavery and states rights without ever considering the theoretical questions regarding the form their arguments should take. Lincoln-Douglas debaters should do the same.

The multiple types of Lincoln-Douglas topics provide a second basis for rejecting policy models. Generally, policy topics call for a change in a status quo policy. There is usually an agent for change and a direction. Value topics, however, can take one of five forms: (1) quasi-policy topics that imply a specific plan of action; (2) historical or scientific argument that requires assignment of meaning to a phenomena; (3) topics that establish a conflict between or among values; (4) topics that call for a determination of whether or not a value should be assigned to an object, event, person, or act; and (5) quasi-fact topics (Zarefsky, 1987, pp. 389–392). Each type of topic requires a different approach to analysis and argument structure. As Thomas noted, his view of natural presumption works best when the topic is one on which there are "reasonable natural presumptions and divisions of public opinion and values available to both sides" (p. 454). Given that many topics fail to meet that standard, applying any theory of presumption becomes more difficult.

A third basis for rejecting policy models is that the distinction between affirmative and negative responsibilities is not clear-cut since the concept of presumption cannot be applied as in policy debate. Depending on the wording of the topic and the prevailing sentiment of the public or the judge, affirmative and negative stances may actually be the opposite of those assigned by the speaker positions.

The fourth characteristic of value debate, which provides the strongest reason for rejecting an emphasis on theory development, is the purpose for the activity's origin: It is intended as an alternative to policy debate. By emphasizing theory, which is intended to assist in determining decision rules and assisting judges, value debates can put the lay judge at a disadvantage. Lincoln and Douglas debated before the common person; Lincoln-Douglas debaters should also. Furthermore, an emphasis on theory for the purpose of determining winners and losers erodes the purpose of debate as a learning activity. In policy debate, theory is intended to prevent abuse; however, in practice it often leads to abuse or to extended discussions of abuse to the detriment of argument development on the topic itself.

Lincoln-Douglas debate should teach audience analysis, persuasion theory, value theory, and oratorical skills. If theory development becomes the primary emphasis of Lincoln-Douglas literature, then the educational goals originally designed for the activity will be eroded. One thing that should not be forgotten is that Lincoln-Douglas debaters are young people between the ages of fourteen and eighteen. They are not sophisticated professors who have spent years gaining an understanding of the theoretical bases for argumentation and debate. Nor do they really understand the necessity for theory. As a result, theory can become a vehicle for winning debates rather than for clarifying arguments within them. Too much of what is being written about value debate today is being done for purposes of research scholarship rather than pedagogy. It is important to remember for whom and for what purposes the activity exists.

ALTERNATIVE THEORETICAL APPROACHES

If theory is to be taught to Lincoln-Douglas debaters, it should be value and persuasion theory. An understanding of values and persuasion is a prerequisite to debating Lincoln-Douglas topics and to understanding the way in which values operate in the real world.

Since this article was written to make an argument regarding the direction Lincoln-Douglas research and pedagogy should take, this section is not intended to be a textbook of the how-to's of Lincoln-Douglas debate. It does, however, suggest a general direction for gaining an understanding of Lincoln-Douglas debate that centers on the substance of value argumentation rather than on its form.

Values analysis in Lincoln-Douglas debate should take place on three levels: (1) the nature of values and their effect on decision making; (2) the values inherent within a given topic; and (3) the conflict between opposing values presented in a debate. Without a solid understanding of values, the other two levels of analysis, which are essential to debating, are impaired.

Debaters need to read the classic literature on values such as the works of Milton Rokeach (1973). They need to know how values operate in our personal lives and in public policy making. They need to know how values operate in our personal lives and in public policy making. They need to understand the concepts of value hierarchies and the distinction between terminal and instrumental values. Rather than talking about stock issues, Lincoln-Douglas debaters should be concerned with identifying values hierarchies, value conflicts, and the relationship between values, facts, and policies. Based on an examination of value literature, Bill Davis and I (1981) identified five characteristics of values that should be understood by all Lincoln-Douglas debaters:

1. Propositions of value evaluate the external world.
2. Values can be classified (for example, moral, aesthetic, political, pragmatic or terminal versus instrumental).
3. Values are commonly shared by a majority of society.
4. Values cannot be separated from propositions of fact and policy.
5. Values are linked to motivation (pp. 18–20).

Once debaters know what the term *values* means and are acquainted with the five characteristics listed, they are equipped to seek out the values in a given topic. The structure of some topics requires an understanding of the implicit values underlying policy positions, and even topics that identify conflicting values should be explored for related, implicit values.

Case construction for either side should identify the values represented by that side and why those values are desirable. It may be necessary to define value terms as well as provide a rationale for defending a value or value hierarchy. Since value theory tells us that there is a relationship between values, facts, and policies, debaters should select factual evidence and policy examples as well as philosophical positions to support their values.

Within the course of the debate, value positions should be compared and contrasted. Clash should result from conflicts rooted in differing hierarchies, a conflict between a terminal and an instrumental value, a conflict between different categories of values such as an aesthetic value conflicting with a political one, or the emergence of a shift in societal values. Topics that appear to be based in fact or policy can be explored on the basis of the values they represent if debaters work from an understanding of value theory.

SUMMARY

While the original description of Lincoln-Douglas debate appears to be inadequate, reflection after eleven years of experience with the activity suggests that it contains most of what debaters, coaches, and judges need to know. Emphasis *should* be on issues rather than on strategy. Logic, theory, and philosophy should replace plan arguments.

As this article argues, however, the theory emphasized should be that of values and persuasion rather than debate. If Lincoln-Douglas debate is to avoid the overly stylized, theory-driven argumentation of policy debate, then there should be less concern with how to adapt policy theory to Lincoln-Douglas and more on how to develop arguments based on an understanding of value and persuasion theories. Lincoln-Douglas formats and topics preclude imposition of traditional policy standards for judgment such as presumption and stock issues; therefore, practice should be guided by an understanding of the nature of values and persuasion without undue concern for establishing decision rules, which could focus the debate on form as opposed to substantive arguments about values.

References

Bartanen, M. D. and Frank, D. A. (1991). *Debating Values*. Scottsdale, AZ: Gorsuch Scarisbrick, Publishers.

Brownlee, D. (1987). "Approaches to Support and Refutation of Criteria." *CEDA Yearbook* 8: 59–63.

Fryar, M. and Thomas, D. A. (1982). *Student Congress & Lincoln-Douglas Debate*. Lincolnwood, IL: National Textbook Co.

Matlon, R. J. (1987). "Debating Propositions of Value." In Thomas, D. A. and Hart, J., eds., *Advanced Debate: Readings in Theory, Practice & Teaching*, 3rd ed. Lincolnwood, IL: National Textbook Co.

Mezzera, D. and Giertz, J. (1989). *Student Congress & Lincoln-Douglas Debate*, 2nd ed. Lincolnwood, IL: National Textbook Co.

Prentice, D. B. and Davis, B. "An Approach to Analyzing and Debating Lincoln-Douglas Debate Topics." In Pollard, T. and Prentice, D. B., eds., *Lincoln-Douglas Debate: Theory and Practice*. Lawrence, KS: University of Kansas. 17–23.

Rokeach, M. (1973). *The Nature of Values*. New York: Free Press.

Thomas, D. A. (1987). "Presumption in Non-Policy Debate: A Case for Natural Presumption Based on Current Non-Policy Paradigms." In Thomas, D. A. and Hart, J., eds., *Advanced Debate: Readings in Theory, Practice & Teaching*, 3rd ed. Lincolnwood, IL: National Textbook Co.

Ulrich, W. "What Is Lincoln-Douglas Debate and What Should It be?" *The Rostrum* (Dec. 1990): 14–15.

Winfield, D. "From the Executive Secretary." *The Rostrum* (Dec. 1979): 2–3.

Wood, W. and Midgley, J. (1986). *Prima Facie: A Guide to Value Debate*. Dubuque, IA: Kendall/Hunt.

Zarefsky, D. (1987). "Criteria for Evaluating Non-Policy Argument." In Thomas, D. A. and Hart, J., eds. *Advanced Debate: Readings in Theory, Practice & Teaching*, 3rd ed. Lincolnwood, IL: National Textbook Co.

11

Impact and Implications of Parliamentary Format on American Debate

E. Sam Cox

Kendall R. Phillips

Traditional intercollegiate debate has been questioned as to its ability to fulfill educational goals (Cox and Jensen, 1989). Rodden argues that the focus on the tournament system "may be unhealthy" (1985, p. 316). The alternative which Rodden, as well as other writers, offers is public debating (1985; Cox and Jensen, 1989). One form of debate which seems to focus on the public forum is parliamentary debate (Quimby, 1947; Temple and Dunn, 1948; Benn, Boyle and Harris, 1948). British debating has received sporadic consideration in speech communication literature (Rodden, 1985). Much less consideration, however, has been given to American Parliamentary Debate. The American Parliamentary Debate Association provides a good example of parliamentary debate without the cross-cultural problems plaguing discussions of British versus American debating.

REVIEW OF LITERATUTE

Communication scholars have focused primarily on British parliamentary debate. Serval important distinctions have been observed:

Sponsorship. Parliamentary debate is sponsored by debating unions, which are student run and have no faculty supervision. This student body leadership and participation in the debate is proposed as the cause of student enthusiasm for these activities (Temple and Dunn, 1948). However, Rodden explains that "most universities do not have debating unions separate from the university student union ... debates are of second importance at such universities, since the student union has a number of other commitments" (1985, p. 311).

Benn, Boyle and Harris (1948) propose that student sponsorship is superior because "faculty supervision and control tends to focus too much attention on the debaters and not enough on the debate" (469). Other British commentators have agreed with the superfluous nature of debate coaches (Freeth and Cradock, 1949). However, American commentators have argued that "good teaching should be an essential part of debating activities in England and in America" (Lull, 1949, p. 430).

Model. The consensus appears to place British parliamentary debating into a legislative (parliamentary) model focusing on swaying audience opinion. A British debater "becomes an orator, a politician, a leader" (Freeth and Cradock, 1949, p. 427). On the other hand, American debate is based on the legal tradition with emphasis on "careful preparation and at collecting of valid arguments and significant evidence" (Quimby, 1949, p. 159). In addition, Rodden points out differing goals between British parliamentary debate and American debate. The debating unions are seen as "miniature Parliaments" and "the oral counterparts to the student university newspapers." The American debate tradition has "more modest immediate aspirations ... with emphasis on tournaments ... and aimed to improve students' skills to think critically and express ideas cogently" (1985, p. 308). While American forensics is viewed as a laboratory for education (Thomas, 1980), Rodden points out, "the uneven student speaking performances [during British parliamentary debates] ... do support the overall conclusions of several previous touring American debaters that the union's original emphasis on speaker training has been lost" (1985, p. 311).

Audience. The different views of a public audience are noted by Freeth and Cradock.

> The British debater, at home, is surrounded by his audience, who consider themselves a vital and equally important part of the debate, cheering, interrupting, barracking, asking questions. He learns how to put himself in touch with the audience and evoke in it an immediate response.
>
> To us, the American debater, on the other hand, seems desirous of training himself as a junior executive who wishes to give to his senior a severely factual, eminently statistical report ... and thus the audience becomes superfluous, ignored, unwanted, and departs, alas, unmourned. (1949, p. 427).

Temple and Dunn believe that audience participation is "largely responsible for the enthusiasm and interest in [British] debate" (1948,

p. 53). Rodden points out that "British debaters prize audience adaptation highly" (1985, p. 309), and that "the British system sensitizes British debaters to audiences" (p. 305). However, others have noticed problems in attendance of the British union debates (Skorkowsky, 1971; Rodden, 1985).

Resolutions. Two important observations are noted about British resolutions. First, Skorkowsky notes that the British resolution may be interpreted as fact, value or policy (1971). Second, Rodden notes that "British speakers were serious or light, philosophical or trivial, reasoned or banal, depending on the type of debate and the nature and wording of the motion" (1985, p. 309). In addition, earlier discussions of the British aversion to switch-side debating seem to no longer be significant as the British debaters often debate against their convictions (Skorkowsky, 1971).

Impact of the Format. Two important impacts of the format on the specific strategies of debaters are evident. First, the burden of proof lies with neither side in the British debate, but depends on the prevailing audience opinion (Skorkowsky, 1971). Second, this format seems to reduce teamwork between partners (Skorkowsky, 1971; Rodden, 1985).

COMPARISON OF DATA FROM THE AMERICAN PARLIAMENTARY DEBATE ASSOCIATION AND THE CROSS EXAMINATION DEBATE ASSOCIATION

The purpose of this paper is to compare parliamentary debate with traditional American debate (NDT, CEDA) and draw implications and impacts for the more traditional format from the former. This comparison will be based on data from the American Parliamentary Debate Association (APDA) and the Cross Examination Debate Association (CEDA). Seven important factors will be considered in this comparison: geographic participation, sponsorship, procedural differences, resolutions, and decision rendering.

Geographic participation. The American Parliamentary Debate Association has primary concentration in the Northeast (Galvin, 1990). Review of the APDA mailing list for September 1990 reveals that most of the schools are northeastern (Connecticut, District of Columbia, Maine, Maryland, Massachusetts, New Hampshire, New Jersey, New York, Pennsylvania, Rhode Island, Virginia, and Vermont). There are a few notable exceptions (California, Illinois, Missouri, North Carolina, and Ohio). But, 1990 was the first year for Missouri schools to participate and the other states represent only eight of the sixty schools listed. The Cross Examination Debate Association has a broader base of geographical support with more than 300 participating schools in all fifty states.

Sponsorship. The APDA is a student-sponsored organization. While traditional debate is usually housed in communication departments, parliamentary debates are not claimed by any one academic discipline. In addition, parliamentary debate is "the international style of debate" (Gutrick, 1990). This provides for participation in the English-speaking World Championships.

Procedural differences. Parliamentary debate is an off-topic extemporaneous debate with two opposing sides (government and opposition). Like British debate, it is modeled after a house of parliament. It is described as "a rhetorical contest which supposedly takes place in a house of parliament" (taken from *Guidelines of Parliamentary Debate*). Previous literature has indicated that American debate is modeled more on a judicial model with an emphasis on evidence (Quimby, 1949; Rodden, 1985).

The speaker positions in parliamentary debate are prime minister (first government speaker), member of government (second government speaker), leader of the opposition (first opposition speaker), and member of the opposition (second opposition speaker). The speaking times are:

> prime minister (constructive): eight minutes
> leader of opposition (constructive): eight minutes
> member of government (constructive): eight minutes
> member of opposition (constructive): eight minutes
> leader of opposition (rebuttal): four minutes
> prime minister (rebuttal): four minutes

Two important distinctions can be drawn between the APDA format and that used by CEDA. First, the rounds are significantly shorter with only six speeches and no cross-examination. The CEDA format (8–3–5), with eight speeches (four constructives and four rebuttals) and four cross-examinations, provides for much longer debates. The second significant difference lies in speaker responsibilities. While both speakers on a CEDA team give two speeches (a constructive and a rebuttal), the prime minister and leader of opposition are the only speakers in an APDA round giving rebuttals. This seems to place more responsibility on these individual speakers and may account for the criticism that there is little teamwork between parliamentary debate partners.

The final significant area of procedural differences is that of interruptions. In CEDA, interruptions during speaking time are considered inappropriate and impolite, however in APDA interruptions are structured and encouraged. Three forms of interruptions are described in the *Guidelines of Parliamentary Debate*. The first is a point of order.

Points of order are made when house rules are allegedly breached as they might be by new arguments in rebuttals, misconstruing arguments, and speaking overtime. The second interruption is a point of personal privilege, which occurs when a debater feels his character has been insulted or when a previous remark is grossly misinterpreted. These two types of interruptions are answered by the judge (speaker of the house) as either "point well taken" (agreement with the point) or "point not well taken" (disagreement with the point). In either case the debater holding the floor cannot speak in defense of himself or herself. If the point is well taken, the time of the objection is deducted from the speaker's time. If the point is not well taken, the time of the objection is not deducted from the speaker's time. One other form of interruption is heckling. "Both teams, judges, and the audience may heckle the debater at any time (*Guidelines*)." Heckles are defined as "short, witty, and intelligent" (Ibid).

Resolutions. The resolutions for CEDA debate are determined at the beginning of each semester and are national. The resolutions for APDA are different for each round. The CEDA resolution is framed by coaches, while the APDA resolutions are chosen by students. CEDA resolutions define a specific area of controversy to be considered. The affirmative has the right to define terms and form a specific case, and the negative has the opportunity to argue the affirmative's definitions and interpretation. APDA resolutions are more general, and the only parametric argument the negative may present is the link between the government's position and the resolution.

Examples of resolutions debated recently will help clarify the differences. The CEDA topic for fall 1990 is "RESOLVED: That government censorship of public artistic expression in the United States is an undesirable infringement on individual rights." An example of an APDA resolution is drawn from the second round of the University of Chicago's tournament of spring 1990. That resolution was "They want the ocean without the awful roars of its many waves." The CEDA topic certainly calls for the affirmative to show the undesirability of some kind of government censorship of public artistic expression in terms of the infringement on individual rights. While this topic is broad, it does provide a definite limitation on the affirmative case area. The APDA case, however, need only have a link to the quotation/resolution. Subsequently, the government could argue society's desire for freedom without the costs, a policy to provide economic relief to Eastern European countries to allow democracy without excessive economic hardships for these countries, or humankind's attempts to control the environment.

The resolutions of CEDA provide a definite background for research and preparation. The APDA resolutions preclude this type of intense and specific research (particularly since the topic is not known until ten minutes before the debate begins). Also, the APDA resolution prevents the proliferation of generic briefs, which may reduce the amount of unique clash, and emphasizes logic and reasoning, as well as knowledge of current events. As noted above, the government need only have a logical link to the resolution.

There is one other class of jurisdictional arguments the opposition may give to the government interpretation: debatability of the case. The debatability of the case may be argued as specific knowledge (the affirmative example is so small as to preclude general knowledge of the event in question), tautology (circular reasoning), truism (a reasonable proposition that a student could not be expected to opppose), or offensive case (cases that "do not deserve an audience" (*Guidelines*). These arguments focus not on parametric concerns but rather on the appropriateness of the interpretation.

Another interesting feature in the parliamentary interpretation of the resolution allows the government "to define the place and time of the debates, or define the speaker as a certain speaker in a certain situation, faced with a choice" (*Guidelines*). However, when the speaker does so (in first constructive speech only), the participants are limited to the knowledge that existed at the specified time.

Decision rendering. The first important difference under this category is the qualifications of the judges. Traditionally in CEDA judges must be at least college graduates if not coaches or graduate assistants. In APDA, with its student sponsorship, the judges are students as well. Thus, while CEDA offers at least an older evaluator, APDA offers judging by one's peers.

The criteria for decision in APDA rounds, according to *Guidelines*, emphasizes logic, delivery, factual support, and humor. In an attempt to compare the actual decision rendering methods and differences, this paper compares data from a collection of CEDA ballots (from the Central Missouri State University tournament) (Cox & Lyman, 1989) with those of a collection of APDA ballots (from the University of Chicago tournament). The CEDA ballot analysis rendered fifteen subgroups of criticisms (delivery, cross-examination, organization, strength or weakness of arguments, criteria/value, specific case points, offcase/value objections, refutation, evidence, topicality, personal views, judging philosophy, adaptation, specific speaker delineation, and general /or/miscellaneous criticisms). The analysis of APDA yielded twenty-five subgroups of criticism (style, delivery, volume, wording, speed, charisma, specific case points, clarity, definition/interpretation, refutation, sub-stance, structure, evidence, heckles, offending judge/or/audience, humor, APDA format, interpretation, signposting, traditional debate theory, flowing arguments, rebuttal argumentation, personal views and general/or/miscellaneous criticisms). To facilitate discussion of the specific differences, the above factors have beeen classified under four mian headings: presentation, arguments, audience/judge considerations, and procedural.

Presentation

Both groups of ballots discuss presentational critiques. APDA ballots placed about the same emphasis on this factor as CEDA ballots. The APDA ballots discussed style, volume, wording, clarity, speed, and charisma much like the CEDA ballots. In addition, the APDA ballots provided less space for the "Reasons for Decision" section of the ballot, much like the old AFA ballots. The APDA ballot provides more than two-thirds of its space for specific speaker comments, whereas the currently popular CEDA ballot provides a similar rank and numbering device with a large space for general comments and reasons for decision at the bottom. Interestingly, although APDA rounds are already slow by current CEDA standards, the use of rapid delivery (speed) was regularly penalized.

Argumentation

While both CEDA and APDA offer cases and offcase (countercase for APDA), specifically identified points were mentioned more often in CEDA. APDA emphasized the general arguments as opposed to specific subpoints of arguments (some ballots called this substance). Similarly, refutational critiques of CEDA centered more on specific subpoints, while APDA emphasized general arguments. Both sets of critics discussed organization and structure of constructives.

The most striking difference in argumentation analysis was how the critics discussed evidence. While the CEDA critics often discussed specific pieces of evidence, the APDA critics discussed the use of common knowledge, and in fact, one APDA ballot criticized the use specific quotations. The CEDA critics focused comments upon support of a testimonial nature, whereas the APDA critics emphasized different types of support. Discussions of rebuttals seemed similar in both groups.

Audience/Judge Considerations

The area of greatest difference is in the way the judges view themselves. The CEDA critics were more likely to discuss personal judging philosophies, whereas all APDA critics operate under a uniform consensus—the model of a legislative session. APDA critics centered their comments on how well the speakers addressed themselves to the critics as their audience. APDA ballots contained comments about offending the judge, use of humor, and the amount of creativity in heckles. The APDA critics appeared to view themselves as audience members. But experienced CEDA critics view themselves as judges or evaluators of arguments. Ballots from both groups also included statements reflecting the personal views of the critic.

Procedural

Two significant distinctions arise in the area of procedures. First, jurisdictional issues (in CEDA, such issues as topicality/or/prima facie; in APDA, link, or debatability) were more prevalent in CEDA ballots than in APDA ballots. The most prevalent discussion in CEDA ballots was topicality, while the APDA ballots had only two discussions of a truism argument.

The second major distinction is in the critics' discussions of other types of debating (for instance, an APDA ballot criticizing CEDA-style arguments). These criticisms were exclusively on the APDA ballots. The ballots chastised speakers for excessive signposting, using CEDA debate theory, speed, and even carrying a flow pad or legal pad to the podium. The APDA critics seemed aware of the differences between APDA and CEDA and dissuaded the speaker from using the style of the latter.

While distinctions are being drawn between APDA and CEDA, it's important to note that APDA does not use a cross-examination period.

IMPLICATIONS AND IMPACTS OF PARLIAMENTARY DEBATE ON CEDA

In this section we will propose several structural and attitudinal changes that CEDA should adopt from parliamentary debate. The discussion will be divided into six sections: sponsorship, resolutions, argumentation, presentation, decision rendering, and audience/public format.

Sponsorship. The use of forensics as a laboratory exclusively for communication departments has perhaps become disadvantageous. Taking debate from the exclusive control of the communication department might allow for a more interdisciplinary approach. For instance, to what extent do debaters actively interact with professors in all the various disciplines? Current practices often promote isolation and territoriality rather than a healthy cross-discipline approach.

The use of student sponsorship might bring about more support from the non-debating student body. In addition, student sponsorship (with faculty supervision) might prove to be a valuable teaching tool.

Students who are responsible for running tournaments, requesting funds, and public relations might learn many useful skills.

Resolutions. APDA topics may seem at times trivial, however the diverse nature of these topics provides several benefits. First, topics are neither policy, value, or fact. This allows the debaters to experience a variety of criteria and case-building strategies. Also, it excludes debates over the category into which the resolution belongs, and promotes debating the affirmative interpretation, thus increasing clash. Second, APDA topics are not always serious in nature. Perhaps CEDA should consider some topics of a less grave and serious nature as well. Third, the resolutions from APDA tend to support less evidentiary debate and rely more on logic and interpretation. While the resolution is not the whole cause of APDA's logic-oriented approach, it can be seen as a contributing factor.

Argumentation. Argumentation in CEDA seems to rely too heavily on testimonial support. We propose that the use of a variety of support in parliamentary debate is a superior argumentative tool. Simply reading a card with a tag line is often considered sufficient justification for the most counterintuitive of arguments in CEDA. This could cause a deficiency in the use of logic, analysis, and reasoning. The parliamentary debater, on the other hand, is forced to use these skills in debating a resolution. We propose that these are pedagogically valuable tools, which CEDA is neglecting.

In addition, parliamentary debate seems weighted more on the overall reasoning and argumentation than CEDA. With excessive structuring and game playing, CEDA rounds have lost sight of the overall strategy of argumentation. We do not propose that structure is detrimental, however the weight given to minor sub-points at the expense of overall arguments has made CEDA a game. We, further, do not propose intervention by judges in CEDA rounds; however, in the interest of non-intervention, judges are giving every minute sub-point equal weight with every other argument in the round. This not only avoids intervention, it avoids evaluation. The judge in a CEDA round becomes a blackboard on which the debaters write, and the essential evaluative process, in which the critics should be involved, is last.

Presentation. The emphasis on presentation is one which cannot be ignored. Traditional American debate has put a premium on arguments, while parliamentary debate has emphasized presentation. We do not propose abolition of argumentation, or even deemphasizing this important aspect. We claim, however, that the value of presentation in CEDA debate has been neglected. These skills should have equal status with weight of arguments in the decision rendering process.

Decision rendering. The changes listed above can only be facilitated with a shift in decision-rendering philosophy. Increased emphasis on presentation and well analyzed and logically defended arguments can only be achieved if critics consider these factors more heavily.

Among other practices that might be borrowed from parliamentary debate is the inclusion of student judges. This practice would enhance not only the performance of those debating, who would be forced to adapt to the critics, but also the performance of the students given the opportunity to judge these events. Many debaters turned critics would support the idea that an entirely new perspective is gained on the other side of the table.

Audience. We support the conclusions of other writers (Cox & Jensen, 1989; Rodden, 1985) that a public format would greatly facilitate the pedagogical goals of the debate activity. The parliamentary model of the legislative branch could be incorporated into the existing CEDA format. At Central Missouri State University we have used public formats to both improve our students and gain attention and support from the student population. Debate should no longer be an elitist event. If we are to retain our pedagogical goals and increase public awareness of our activity we must be willing to take our skills to the public.

CONCLUSION

This paper has attempted a comparison between American Parliamentary Debate and CEDA. This comparison has shown significant differences in goals and procedures. Finally, we have attempted to draw implications from parliamentary debates for changes in CEDA. While this paper is by no means a comprehensive consideration of this comparison, it is an attempt to show that CEDA can learn and grow from considering some of the aspects of parliamentary debate.

References

APDA Mailing List (1990). Membership mailout, Sept. 1990.

Benn, A. W., Boyle, E., and Harris, K. (1948) "American and British Debating," *Quarterly Journal of Speech* 4: 469–72.

Cox, E. S. and Jensen, S. L. (1989). "Redeeming Part of Debate's Education Mission via Public Formats," in Gronbeck, B., ed., *Spheres of Argument: Proceedings of the Sixth SCA/AFA Conference of Argumentation* (Annandale, VA: Speech Communication Association), 440–45.

Galvin, M. (1990) APDA informational letter, Sept. 19, 1990.

Guidelines of Parliamentary Debate (1990). Membership mailout, Sept. 1990.

Gutrick, A. (1990). University of Chicago Invitational Parliamentary Debate Tournament invitation, pamphlet.

Freeth, D. K. and Cradock, P. (1949). "American Versus British Debating," *Quarterly Journal of Speech* 4: 427–29.

Lull, P. E. (1949). "Some American Replies," *Quarterly Journal of Speech* 4: 429–30.

Quimby, B. (1947). "Can We Learn from Debating the British?" *Quarterly Journal of Speech* 2: 159–61.

Rodden, J. (1985). "British University Debating: A Reappraisal," *Communication Education* 4: 292–307.

Skorkowsky, G. R. (1971). "British University Debating," *Quarterly Journal of Speech* 3: 335–43.

Temple, N. J. and Dunn, D. P. (1984). "British Debating Is Parliamentary," *Quarterly Journal of Speech* 3: 50–53.

Thomas, D.A. (1980). "Sedalia Plus Five: Forensics as a Laboratory," in Rhodes, J. and Newell, S., eds., *Proceedings of the Summer Conference on Argumentation* (Annandale, VA: Speech Communication Association), 246–48.

12

The Use of Empirical Studies in Debate

Tim Lee
Dave Harris
Craig Dudczak

SCIENTIFIC KNOWLEDGE: ITS SCOPE AND LIMITS

Our purpose in this paper is to discuss the use of studies and statistics in the debate context, consider some of the common misapplications of the scientific method to argumentation, and offer some suggestions for what we feel are appropriate strategies for using studies as evidence.

For the sake of making arguments for changes in policy systems, it is necessary to separate the real world from the empirical world. In our everyday existence, we tend to make many choices based on our experiences in the real world. Much of the interaction of phenomena in the real world is irrelevant to our daily course of actions. As individual students and teachers, we are more concerned with the price of gasoline, food, or index cards than we are with an in-depth knowledge of why the monetary policy of the Federal Reserve Board has reduced bank loans one-fourth of 1 percent and, consequently, caused prices to rise.

Not only is our real world experience limited in scope, it is also subjective. What we experience in life reflects human choices made either consciously or unconsciously. Whenever we observe an event, we select what seem to be the most important characteristics of the event. Exposure, attention, perception, and retention of experience are all ultimately selective and subjective. Thus, one person can observe a reasonably simple event and come to entirely different conclusions about its nature than will another.[1] For the purposes of simple decisions concerned with routine daily affairs, real world experience is usually adequate. If we applied the techniques of the scientific method to every choice we had to make, we would be paralyzed into inaction. We can trust our habits, common sense, and adaptive ability to enable us to cope with most of the decisions confronting us daily.

When we move into more complex decisions and judgments—such as the best policy to insure health care for the poor—we need a method of thinking that is more comprehensive and less subjective than our personal real-world experiences. The crucial separation between-world experience and empirical-world experience is that the empirical realm is one in which conclusions and judgments have been scientifically pre-tested and verified. This verification process usually consists of the procedures of the scientific method, with controlled observation of variables that will lead to consistent conclusions. The critical element in thinking empirically about problems and solutions is that *control must be exercised over the variables, the conditions of the test, and the observations made from the test.* Quantitative analysis gives us the assurance of control. The empirical world can extend the knowledge we obtain from our experience of the real world by providing new insight into relationships, discovery of variables, and explanation of phenomena that may otherwise elude our knowledge. The basis for empirical research is always established knowledge—our hypotheses presume the existence of known information.[2]

THE ROLE OF QUANTITATIVE EVIDENCE IN DEBATE

In a practical application for the debater, what happens when the knowledge we have available from experience is inconsistent with the knowledge obtained through scientific verification? Should there be a higher value for commonsense knowledge than the conclusions of quantitative studies? We would not presume that the reliance upon quantitative study is invariably superior to commonsense argument. But with correct research design and application in an argument, quantitative study gives us a superior basis upon which to draw conclusions and a better basis for policy decisions. Evidence that can be verified is preferable to that which cannot.

The normal course of events in a debate round when one team presents a quantitative study is for the other team to respond with a counterstudy or to read a list of generic study indictments. We would like to discuss an informed basis for a team to apply indictments to a specific study. In addition, we suggest some criteria that can be applied when comparing two or more studies.

POTENTIAL AREAS TO INDICT IN QUANTITATIVE EVIDENCE

Hypotheses

The first area a debater should examine when confronted with a quantitative study is an *analysis of the hypothesis*. All studies seek to verify or deny a particular hypothesis or set of hypotheses. The basis of methodological indictment directed toward the hypothesis is to ask the question: "Does the hypothesis identify the problem, the reationship between the relevant variables, and the implication of empirical testing?"[3] We will consider each area separately.

The *statement of the problem* needs to be included in the hypothesis because it determines what parameters of the relevant factors will be considered by the study and what will not be tested. The statement of problem gives a focus to the hypothesis, provides the experimenter with a clearer perspective of what is relevant to his or her effort, and suggests what factors should be excluded. The problem statement can tell the debater the same thing.

The *statement of the relationship between the variables* is as important as the statement of the problem, because it indicates what predicted effects are expected. Verification of a relationship provides the basis for some action, be it application of the findings to particular problems, generation of new tests based upon the results, or rejection of previously assumed knowledge. Failure to verify a relationship, however, cannot be interpreted as proving the opposite of the relationship. When a predicted relationship between variables is not indicated by a study, it may lead to the formulation of a new hypothesis. It is important that the absence of proof not be interpreted as evidence proving the opposite of the stated hypothesis. The null hypothesis, when used properly, can demonstrate that a given relationship between variables does not exist. *The null hypothesis may be used as a negative proof to demonstrate what does not exist, but it does not tell us what does exist.*

As an example, a study which fails to show that smoking causes skin cancer does not show that ozone depletion does. (It does not even prove that smoking and skin cancer are unrelated, merely that the study failed to show such a link.) It would be the responsibility of the advocate supporting the second proposition to provide proof of any relationship between ozone depletion and the incidence of cancer.

Study indictments directed at the formulation of the hypothesis require some previous knowledge of the study. What is most valuable is consideration of the hypothesized relationship between or among variables. If the study cannot predict the expected relationships, its value as evidence is diminished. Without the systematic development of hypotheses prior to an investigation, we have little confidence of accepting the results. Without the hypothesis, we have little prediction with little probability.[5]

The third requirement of the hypothesis is that *the implications of empirical testing need to be stated*. Some relationships may exist that are not measurable by the tools (statistical testing methods) we have available. The debater should be aware that some questions, by their nature, are not subject to empirical methods. Questions of value, often the type surrounding social priorities, are not amenable to empirical methods. A survey may indicate the distribution of attitudes on a given subject, but it does not (and cannot) indicate a necessary superiority of an attitude held by the majority to the alternative positions. That is why scientific research never addresses issues such as what is good, right, or desirable (value judgments), but only what may be cast into operational definitions and measured by statistical methods.

Variables and Operational Definitions

The second category of analysis deals with the definition of variables used in the study. Here the experimenter operationalizes his or her terms by first selecting the relevant variables and then assigning them values in the experiment. The inclusion or exclusion of a given variable as well as the operationalized meaning given to a variable contributes to the conclusions the study produces.

The reason one needs to operationalize terms in an experiment is to provide a consistent meaning for their usage. If we were to hypothesize that hunger reduces motivation for learning, we would have to define what is meant by "hunger" as well as "motivation for learning." It is against these definitions that many of the methodology attacks should be launched. Let us start with hunger. Can a child be said to be hungry if she misses breakfast? An experiment using this definition of hunger might be challenged by other uses of the term. Hunger may be alternatively defined in terms of caloric intake, nutritional value of intake, or time interval between meals. Similar operational variances may be needed for other variables; in this instance, "motivation for learning."

Since different studies may use different operationalizations of variables, it is possible to have studies using similar variables with

seemingly contradictory results. The studies cited may be methodo-
logically correct, but because of different uses of terms operationalized
by the respective studies, they vary in their conclusions. The key to
resolving this discrepancy is tied to the ability of the debaters to *justify
the operational definitions* cited by their sources. Criteria that would help
a debater to justify particular definitions would be general acceptance of
definition, appropriateness to test, and previous use in other similar
studies. These might establish the validity of the operational usage in a
given case.

All tests of operationalization are specifically tied to the subject at
hand. If health is the variable discussed by a study, it would be
strategically wise for the opponent to identify additional criteria of
health beyond those operationalized in the given study. The reason we
recommend an expansion of definition is both to deny an opponent a
narrow definition, which tends to be supported solely by his or her
particular studies, as well as to provide a broader base for policy
comparison. If a team operationalizes a meaning for a given variable
without challenge, then that meaning will probably be accepted for the
course of the debate.

Often a debater will use different studies that operationalize
different variables. This gives different meanings to those variables held
in common, and the different meanings result in a confusion of
concluded relationships. One study may show that when breakfast is
missed, there is no reduction in motivation for learning as measured by
attention span. A second study may show that when caloric intake is
below 1000 calories per day at a weight of 85 pounds, there is an
increased absence from school by a factor of 50 percent compared to a
group receiving 2000 calories per day at 85 pounds.[6] These studies are
not consistent in supporting the notion that hunger affects learning
motivation, but the exact cause and results are blurred by the different
operationalizations of terms.

Blurring of causes and results is of consequence when applied to
the issue of significance. Is it the responsibility of the advocate to
provide the exact level of claimed effects, or is it sufficient that the
advocate simply affirm the existence of a strong relationship to warrant
action? A disparity in the predicted effects due to different operationalizations of variables is not a warrant for rejection of all studies on the
matter. There may be reasons for rejecting one set of definitions, but
not necessarily all sets of definitions. (Later, in the section on application of study conclusions, we will comment on the need for consistency between study mechanisms and plan mechanisms.)

When the studies used by opposing teams rely upon different uses
of terms, it is expected that each side will provide a justification for its
defintions. There is no presumption of definition for the operationali-

zation of terms used in a study.[7] The basis for decision for a given argument, issue, or debate may ultimately depend on the ability of each team to provide an adequate justification for the variables included (or excluded) from a given study.

Data Collection and Significance Level

The third area of study indictment revolves around the collection of data and the use of sampling devices. The statistical measurement of any group can be accurate in terms of proper use of the measuring instrument, yet to generalize the study to a larger population may lead to inaccuracies.

This may occur because the selection procedure reflects an atypical segment of the population. The classic example occurred in 1936 when Alf Landon was predicted to sweep the election against Roosevelt. The sampling technique was to mail ballots to individuals with phone service, which, during the Depression years, was over-represented by people with money and jobs, who were more inclined to vote for Landon. This example represents a problem of applying (extrapolating) the data to a general population. If one were to hypothesize that a majority of people owning telephones during the Depression were inclined to vote for Landon, the data is quite sufficient. It is only when the generalization is extended beyond the bounds of its applicability that the problems begin. In a later section we develop several criteria to be applied to the process of generalizing conclusions from data.

Many statistical tests can be applied to the variables. The choice of the appropriate test is important because its utility is specific to the nature of the variable defined. The results of the various tests will either be significant or not significant. Significance, as applied to statistics, means that the results achieve a level of probability substantial enough to conclude that the *predicted* relationship exists. For various types of tests to be considered valid, the level of significance tells us how strong a relationship needs to be demonstrated before we can reasonably accept the results as being caused by the researcher's experiment, and not by factors such as chance extraneous variables, or sampling error.

Statistical significance is assigned at various levels depending on the nature of the tests applied and the number of variables included. Most researchers use a design that calls for testing the differences in scores produced by an experimental manipulation of the sample, as a "before" and "after" test. Standard statistical tests of the difference in magnitude of differences usually require a confidence level of at least .05 probability or higher, meaning that the *test* can be thought to have produced the difference in scores, and not a random error such as "luck of the draw." The level required for a given test bears a direct relationship to the consequences of the test. As the consequence of the action (or inaction) increases, the level of confidence required tends to decrease. Conversely, as the probability of consequence decreases, the probability (confidence level) requirement tends to increase. The debate over nuclear power plants illustrates this principle. The proponents of nuclear power plants argue that the likelihood of an accident is so small that restraint on construction is unwarranted. On the other hand, the opponents of nuclear power plants maintain that the consequences of a single mishap are so enormous as to warrant at least a moratorium on the construction of new plants.

Similar conflicts often occur in the debate round. One team argues the significance of a consequence, while the other team argues the improbability of a consequence. There is no single solution to resolve the trade-off between the two components. The debater should be aware that the equation for weighing significance of consequence versus the improbability of consequence is determined by the merits of the respective arguments in a given round. Where arguments in support of the respective positions are absent, the criteria applied in evaluation may be entirely arbitrary.[8]

Generalizability

The last category to evaluate the use of quantitative analysis centers around the process of formulating conclusions and generalizing results. To see how this might apply to this discussion we might briefly review the scientific method: First, the experimenter formulates a hypothesis; second, he or she defines variables; and third, he or she gathers data. Assuming that all of the procedures are correctly applied, the study will probably generalize the results from its particular sample to a larger population. In generalizing these results, the experimenter (or the debater) is subject to the greatest potential for error. The variables controlled in the study may be affected by other variables operating in the system to which the results are generalized.

We indicated earlier that there is a general requirement for consistency between study mechanisms and plan mechanisms. A given study, due to its specific hypothesis, operationalization of variables, and methods of gathering and analyzing data, will tend to yield results that are valid within the confines of that study. Another study, with different hypotheses, operationalizations, and treatment of data, could yield substantially different results.

An affirmative team will often cite data from studies to establish significance. The studies cited will presume certain conditions and mechanisms. If the conditions and mechanisms are not approximately the same as those used in the plan, one cannot reasonably infer the same consequences (significant results) will occur when the plan is implemented. An example might illustrate.

Many sources cite the success of health maintenance organizations (HMOs). These HMOs offer certain cost advantages to their subscribers as well as benefits in the quality of care. The success of these HMOs presumes a number of circumstances including location, population density, socioeconomic status of subscribers, and voluntary physician participation. An affirmative seeking to establish mandatory, nationwide HMOs is implementing a plan that differs substantially from the mechanism that currently exists. Success under one set of conditions (voluntary HMO membership) does not imply success under another set (mandatory HMO membership). It would be an affirmative burden of solvency to establish the likelihood of success under the particular mechanism of its plan.

We indicated that the sample selected needs to represent the general population for the results of the study to be extrapolated. If the sample is not representative of the general population, the results of the study will tend to be skewed. This means a disproportionate representation for some groups will occur, while other groups will be under-represented or excluded. Several factors tend to skew results:

1. *Self-Selected Population.* Certain variables tend to be over-represented when the groups for the study are volunteers. Voluntary members may have an interest in the results of the study that tends to bias the results. Also, self-selected groups may possess certain attributes that are not representative of the total population.

2. *Geographic Selection.* The composition of populations in different areas of the country may very. Urban areas tend to have a higher proportion of certain racial and ethnic groups. Certain rural areas (such as the Dakotas) would tend to underrepresent urban population conditions as well as certain racial and ethnic groups. Additionally, certain conditions present in one geographic area may be absent in others. These factors are most relevant to the specific nature of the study and may include factors of climate, pollution, topography, governmental forms, and the like.

3. *Occupational Selection.* Certain occupations may be over- or underrepresentative of the general population. The incidence of cancer, for example, correlates with certain occupations greater than the national average.

Other factors may affect the representation of a given sample group. We advise that the debater question the generalizability of any sample population to a larger group. While the particular problems of generalizability are dependent on the particular study and its development in a given round, it would be the advocate's burden to demonstrate the application of the sample's conclusion.

We normally assume that information which is accessible to others in the same field is more credible than information that is not so available. When information is subjected to the rigorous examination of other experts, we are more confident of accepting the information. This is because the flaws in methodology and analysis that may occur in the research are given a broader scrutiny and are more likely to be discovered. Information that is not subjected to the evaluation of those in a capacity to investigate its validity of methodology and analysis is subject to considerable suspicion. That a given study reaches certain conclusions is irrelevant if withheld from the scrutiny of others in the field. It is primarily for this reason that unpublished studies, private letters, and other such unpublicized information does not gain acceptability. Data may be obtained that may ultimately be acceptable, but no check has been placed upon it.[9]

Several specific components of accessibility include the following:

1. *Freedom to Report.* Information generated by a source with a vested interest in the conclusion is not to be given the same credibility as another source not so constrained. A direct or indirect financial interest is most frequently associated with a vested interest, although other attachments such as political, philosophic, corporate loyalty, and family association may be included.[10]

2. *Standards Availability.* Various standards established by federal, state, and local governments or their agencies as well as standards established by professional organizations serve as one set of measuring rods by which data may be evaluated. That a given standard is established need not imply that it is the best level for a given set of data. Professional standards may reflect an inbred bias in favor of a particular group. By the same token, government standards may reflect the inclusion of external factors, such as politics or cost, that are unrelated to the substance under regulation. Pollution standards for auto emission, for example, would certainly be suspect when presented by auto manufacturers. Federal standards, however, may be influenced by industry lobbying.

3. *Foreign Studies.* Test results acceptable in one country are often at variance with results from another country. Different standards and test procedures may account for variances in test results. Thalidomide was widely marketed in Europe while generally unavailable in the United States. In this instance, the difference in standards appeared to favor the restrictions on the drug.

We would suggest the criterion of consistency when evaluating different sets of standards and data with no apparent basis of selection. Standards that obtain the best results in application to a number of situations would be deemed preferable. One judges the total net effect. Consistency of results may well mean that a given standard in a particular application would not achieve optimum effect. Yet the cumulative impact of the standards would be more desirable than an alternative set of standards overall.

The preceding discussion of quantitative analysis and methodological indictment provides a basis for understanding the implications of the scientific method. When quantitative analysis is applied to the debate round, both the proponent and opponent should be aware of the requirements that accompany the application of statistical methodology. While we do not presume that all studies are flawed and their conclusions are misapplied, the wise student of debate will seek to discover the fallacies of methodology and misapplication. It is hoped that this dicussion has provided some basis for doing both.

Notes

1. For a concise discussion of this phenomenon, see Michael Burgoon, *Approaching Speech Communication* (New York: Holt, Rinehart and Winston, 1974), 152–63.
2. Fred N. Kerlinger, *Foundations of Behavioral Research* (New York: Holt, Rinehart and Winston, 1964), 22.
3. Kerlinger, pp. 20–22.
4. Kerlinger, p. 174.
5. Kerlinger, pp. 27–28.
6. This example is entirely fictitious and *should not be used as evidence in a debate*.
7. Here we refer to presumption in a meaning other than its normal use. We mean that evidence presented by either team has no presumption per se. He who advocates must prove. If one team presented evidence while the other did not, we would assume the superiority of the side supported by evidence. If both sides present evidence (studies or otherwise), neither affirmative nor negative evidence enjoys an advantage because of the respective side of the resolution it happens to be used on.
8. On should not confuse the statistical significance used to demonstrate the *probability of association* with stock issue of significance. When an experimenter concludes that certain relationships between variables are significant, he or she is saying that an association between variables in the research is mathematically probable and is not likely to have been affected by external variables (externalities). This is measured on the level of confidence associated with the test. Put another way, statistical significance refers to the results of an experimental study, whereas "stock issue significance" refers to the advantages and disadvantages of a proposed policy.
9. Robert P. Newman and Dale R. Newman, *Evidence* (New York: Houghton Mifflin, 1969), 166–69.
10. Newman and Newman, p. 166.

13

The Role of
Causal Argument
in Policy Controversies

David Zarefsky

The role that causal arguments play in policy questions is ambiguous, to say the least. Since the time of Hume it has been an accepted axiom that causal connections cannot be observed directly. All one can notice is constant conjunction—a correlation so perfect that it seems invariable.[1] Discovering such a pattern between objects or events leads one to conclude that there must be a necessary connection between them, a connection which is designated as a "causal link."

In some fields of inquiry, it has been held that causation may be established, if not by direct observation then by inference from controlled observation. If we were to compare instances or phenomena which were alike in every respect save one, and found that they behaved differently, we might feel justified in claiming that the difference was caused by the one uncontrolled factor. The procedure, which is at the base of much laboratory research, is one of the five canons for determining causation proposed by John Stuart Mill.[2] Like Mill's other canons, however, it suffers from the defect that Cohen and Nagel explained forty years ago: These methods can only *disestablish*, and cannot establish, causality.[3] One never can be sure that *all* possible sources of variance save one have been controlled. The outcome of a laboratory experiment is a probability statement that the results did not occur by chance. It does not prove that a causal force was present, nor does it enable one with certainty to *identify* the causal force. Of course, depending upon purposes of the inquiry, a probability statement may be all that it is necessary or possible to make.

But inference from controlled observation, even if perfect, will not suit the needs of policy argument, in which the controversy centers on the question, "What should we do?" Such arguments are set in the future, about which one must speculate since no observation or laboratory test is possible. Moreover, the policy advocate, like the historian, differs from the scientist in that he lacks control over his data. He cannot cause a particular sequence of events to recur; he cannot hold factors constant; he cannot induce experimental variation. Even if the scientist could establish causal *laws*, his success would not enable the advocate to make causal *arguments* with the same degree of certainty.

From analysis similar to the foregoing, some have concluded that causal arguments are inappropriate for policy questions. One should identify existing evils, it is claimed, without troubling over the unanswerable question of how or why they came about. One then should imagine an alternative system devoid of these evils. Having two different policy systems before him for comparison, the analyst determines the costs and benefits of each, bypassing altogether the quagmire of causal argument. Nor is anything vital lost by such a procedure, so the argument runs, since it is possible and often desirable to treat the symptoms of a problem without determining its fundamental causes.[4]

This point of view, which would diminish the role of causal arguments in policy questions, is based upon a needlessly limited view of the nature of causal statements and the means of proving them. The inapplicability of the scientist's concept of causation does not render *all* forms of causation inapplicable to policy argument. Moreover, to attempt to diminish the role of causal argument in policy questions would be undesirable. This essay represents an attempt to support these claims.

THE NATURE OF CAUSAL STATEMENTS

At the outset, it may be useful to recognize three distinct types of causal statements, only one of which is addressed by the critique above.

Type I: Application of a Covering Law

In his treatise on historical explanation, Dray described this type of statement as one which explains by "subsuming what is to be explained under a general law," or *covering* a particular case with a general law.[5] Statements of this type are prominent in scientific investigation. If one is asked why a man died, the response might be, "Because his heart, brain, and lungs ceased to function." Such an answer would establish that the case at hand is an instance of the covering law that the cessation of functions by the heart, brain, and lungs leads to death. Or, if asked the cause for malnutrition, one might reply, "Excessive carbohydrates and inadequate protein," thereby demonstrating that the case at hand is subsumed by the covering law that a low-protein, high-carbohydrate diet leads to malnutrition.

Statements of Type I assert physical or material conditions that, in the opinion of the observer, are sufficient to bring about the effect. From the constant conjunction of the antecedent conditions and the effect, we, like Hume, conclude that a causal link is present. We use Type I statements to answer the causal question in contexts in which the question means, "How did the result come about?" and in which the answer is given by citing the conditions that subsume the given case under a covering law.

Type II: Assignment of Responsibility

A second answer to the question of why a man died might be, "Because the suspect shot him." In the example of malnutrition, the answer might be, "Because the government does not fund food-aid programs adequately." An answer of this type disregards natural forces as possible causes, and locates the causal nexus in *people*, who are capable of exerting control over a situation and who are responsible for their acts. As free agents, they may choose either to perpetuate or to change given conditions.[6]

Several philosophers have pointed to the prominence of this sort of causal statement in the writings of historians. After noting the similarity between the historian's use of "cause" and the assignment of blame, Dray concludes, " ... unless we are prepared to hold the agent responsible for what happened, we cannot say that his action *was* the cause."[7] Aron describes causality as, in part, the determination of who is historically responsible: "the man who by his acts sets in motion the event, the origins of which are sought."[8] Walsh refers to a type of causal question that aims "to fix responsibility and to assess the amount of an agent's contribution to a given end."[9]

Implicit in these statements about causality in historical writing is the belief that the causal question takes the form, "Who is to blame?" and is answered by naming the responsible agents. Type II statements also are prominent in the law. Both civil and criminal law generally presume personal responsibility for actions. It should be added that assignment of responsibility need not imply *moral* judgments of praise or censure. It is, rather, the identification of persons who, having the power to choose, made choices that were thought to precipitate the condition or behavior in question.

Type III: Explanation

Yet a third type of causal statement attempts neither to assert the existence of material conditions nor to assign responsibility. Its function is to explain, to provide reasons to justify a belief that a causal connection exists. For Type I statements, the connection between cause and effect is an inferred property of the cause that produces the effect; for Type II statements, the connection is the act-agent relationship;[10] and for Type III statements, it is the force of implication. This force is described by Nowell-Smith as the creation of "a disposition or tendency to behave in a certain way when certain events occur."[11] In the case of the man who died, a Type III answer might be, "These people were ignorant of the basics of nutrition."

Statements of Type III rarely are found in isolation. More commonly, they are used to support *other* statements. They may be offered as grounds for belief of Type I or Type II assertions, or as reasons to establish noncausal claims. For example, one might question the identification of the government as the agent responsible for malnutrition, since, after all, government officials frequently have expressed their interest in solving problems of hunger. The maker of the Type II statement then would need to adduce explanations to justify his original claim. In such a situation, the Type III statement is used to resolve a paradox or solve a puzzle. It explains why a given phenomenon should be considered a cause *in the face of a contrary presumption* created by the government's public statements.

Similarly, one might question the Type I claim that a low-protein, high-carbohydrate diet was the cause of malnutrition, since, after all, many healthy people had the same dietary deficiencies. The maker of the Type I statement then would need to offer justifications. He would offer a Type III statement to justify selection of certain conditions as the true cause and the rejection of other conditions. These two examples illustrate situations in which Type III statements may be most likely to be called into service. For convenience, the first case may be said to illustrate a how-possibly explanation and the second, a why-necessarily explanation.[12]

Of course, Type III statements need not be introduced into a causal argument if the Type I or Type II statement gains immediate adherence. Such a situation seems unlikely, however, if the subject in question is controversial. More likely is the expectation that the scientist would employ a pattern of Type III statements to justify the causal claim he has made with Type I statements, and that the policy advocate would draw upon Type III statements to support causal claims made with statements of Type II.

THE PROOF OF CAUSAL CLAIMS

Type II statements, unlike those of Type I, do not refer to relations even potentially susceptible to empirical verification. Empirical indices of motive or responsibility could be produced, of course, but the constructs themselves are unverifiable. Neither Hume nor Mill appears to have had this type of statement in mind when theorizing about causation. It does not follow, however, that these statements cannot be proved. To see how they are proved, it may be useful to examine how they function in discourse.

When advocate A asserts that the government is to blame for malnutrition, the ascription of responsibility may be accepted without question. If if is challenged, however, A must support the claim by demonstrating that there is a plausible motive for the government to deny food to the hungry, and that the means exist for the satisfaction of this motive. Such demonstrations will require identification of the alleged motives and means, and explanations of why they really are motives and means—in other words, Type III statements. For example, the advocate might claim as the motive that government food programs are beholden to agribusiness, and hence that profit rather than nutrition determines what aid will be provided to the needy. As the means, he might allude to discretion vested in program administrators to determine the components of a food-aid package.

In this example, the function of analyzing motives and means is to provide good reasons for belief that the government is the responsible agent. It might be said, then, that Type II statements are proved through the provision of good reasons.[13] What determines a good reason is not a matter for formal logic, which is impotent to transcend the gap between statements of fact (He *is* heavier than his doctors recommend.) and statements of value (You *ought* to believe that overweight was the cause of death.). What is a good reason is determined contextually; as Nowell-Smith explains, it is a reason that, in the given instance, leaves no further room for the question, "Why did he do that?"[14] In other words, Type II statements are proved rhetorically—by persuading one's auditors that one has reasonable and sufficient ground for belief.[15]

Now, it might be objected that to speak of rhetorical proof is to engage in semantic legerdemain; that rhetorical proofs are not really proofs. They do not manifest the precision or certainty of empirical proofs. To raise such an objection, however, is to elevate one particular *form* of proof so that it becomes the generic *standard*. To treat empirical proof as the only form of proof is to entail the corollary that Perelman and Olbrechts-Tyteca criticize: "that reason is entirely incompetent in those areas which elude calculation and that, when neither experiment nor logical deduction is in a position to furnish the solution of a problem, we can but abandon ourselves to irrational forces, instincts, suggestion, or even violence."[16] If proof is defined extensionally as "the grounds for belief," it should be apparent that the possibilities for intensional definition are far broader than empirical verification.

Like Type II statements, those of Type III require rhetorical proof through the provision of good reasons. One's identification of motive and means, like one's identification of the responsible agent, may be open to challenge. The plausibility of the motive might be challenged by an argument that the persons named did not stand to gain by the act, did not perceive that they stood to gain, or had not acted in a pattern consonant with the alleged motive. The existence of the means might be disputed with an argument that the agent did not have discretion to implement his or her motives, or with an argument that his or her action was effectively neutralized elsewhere. Should any of these challenges be forthcoming, the burden is upon the party who assigned the blame to defend the assignment. The defense is offered by making additional Type III causal statements—by offering reasons that an interlocutor should accept the assignment of responsibility. As in the example above, the interchange would continue either until one party, A, realized the futility of convincing the other, B, that the assignment of responsibility was correct (leading A to abandon the original position or to write off B as a recalcitrant), or until B recognized that further inquiry was unnecessary, that there were satisfactory grounds for accepting the placement of responsibility alleged by A.

In summary, then, just as causal statements come in at least three different types, the means of proving such statements also vary. Whereas Type I statements presumably are susceptible to empirical proof, Type II and Type III statements require rhetorical proof. And these latter types of statements are the ones that are especially applicable to policy controversies. In such situations, the causal question at issue usually is not, "What were the original forces which created this problem?" Such a question may be unanswerable; nor is the answer often necessary. Many are the problems that can be solved without knowledge of their *first* causes.[17] Rather, causal arguments will concern the forces that *sustain* or *perpetuate* conditions once their existence has been discovered.

In a thorough analysis of *stasis*, Hultzén proposed that policy controversies may be characterized by four stock issues, which may be paraphrased as ill, blame, cure, and cost.[18] The first and last involve the discovery and evaluation of conditions. It is with respect to the *blame* and *cure* issues that causal arguments are particularly appropriate—arguments regarding the inherency of a problem and the efficacy of a solution.

CAUSAL ARGUMENT AND INHERENCY

Few concepts in argumentation theory have been as troublesome or as elusive as the nature of inherency; the subject has been examined at length in recent literature.[19] While the goal here is to apply the above analysis of Type II and Type III causal statement to the inherency issue, such an application also may help to bring into sharper focus the nature of inherency itself.

Having addressed the stock issue of ill, the advocate should be prepared to demonstrate the existence of significant evils. Now he or she is ready to raise the causal question which undergirds inherency: *Absent the action contemplated by the proposition, why would presumably good people tolerate evil?* This question does not ask why the proposition has not yet been adopted; rather, it asks why people will tolerate the continued existence of significant harms *unless* the proposition is adopted. To answer the question is to resolve a paradox. In most discussions of inherency, the advocate is advised to answer the question by claiming that there is a structural barrier or structural gap that prevents alleviation of the harms. But, as Strange cogently argues, to offer such advice is to give a non-answer, since all the ambiguities of the term "inherent" simply transfer to the term "structural."[20] An operational answer to the question of what inherency is may be more useful.

First, the advocate mentally should divide the universe of relevant options other than those embodied in the proposition (for convenience, this universe may be designated "Negative-Land") into characteristics that are *essential* to its non-propositional nature and those which merely are *incidental* features—a division, that is, into core and periphery. Of course, no objective standard exists for determining which characteristics compose the core. For some, the core might be thought to consist of laws; for others, administrative structures; for others, decision-making processes. It would seem, however, that all these entities exist *for some reason*. If so, then even more central to Negative-Land than any of these would be *people* who are impelled by *motives*.[21] The first step in analysis of inherency therefore would be to identify the core motives that impel the primary agents of Negative-Land.

To be sure, such identification is fraught with perils. Motives are not observable. Often there are no explicit statements by the agents of what their motives are; as Walsh puts it, "The fact that we cannot question historical personages about their motives . . . makes the task more difficult, by depriving us of a source of evidence."[22] Even when such explicit evidence exists, it may not be useful. It is an open question, for example, whether the preamble to the Employment Act of 1946, committing the United States to maximum employment, production, and purchasing power, is the true core motive of our economic system, in light of the subsequent thirty years' experience. Similar "structural value statements" in existing laws *may* reflect core motives; alternatively, they may be only symbolic statements to reassure a particular constituency.[23] Perhaps the advocate's best advice is to search for a pattern of consistency between word and deed, remembering always that the ultimate test of one's core motive will be his ability to marshal good reasons to support it.

What sorts of core motives might be identified? The following list should be seen as illustrative but certainly not exhaustive.

1. *Actual or perceived self-interest.* The agents stand to gain, or believe that they stand to gain, from behavior that perpetuates the significant evils.

2. *Role definitions.* The social roles occupied by the agents shape their attitudes and behavior in ways that maintain the consistency of the role-definition but which perpetuate the problems.

3. *Role conflicts.* The relevant agents occupy two or more different social roles. When these roles come into conflict, there is a predictable and explainable pattern as to which role will dominate.

4. *Actual or perceived threat to self-concept.* One's view of self as a worthy person is enhanced, or is thought to be enhanced, by a particular course of action that happens also to sustain the problem.

5. *Conflicts in value hierarchies.* The values that would warrant action to remedy the problems have a lower place in the agents' hierarchy than do competing values that warrant perpetuation of the problems.

6. *Jurisdictional concerns.* However great may be the agents' commitment to alleviating problems, they lack the authority to do so, or they are convinced that some other agent is the more appropriate choice to solve the problem.

7. *Perversity.* The presumably good people described in the causal question may not be good, after all. They actively may desire the continuation, or even intensification, of evil conditions, to promote that which is illogical, illegal, or immoral.

To recapitulate, this first step toward answering the question of inherency involves identifying the people and motives at the core of Negative-Land. It should be apparent that this step involves providing an answer to the Type II causal question, "Who is responsible?" and—through the identification of motives—the beginning of an answer to the Type II causal question, "Why do you say so?" The second step of inherency analysis completes this answer: it is to provide reasons to believe that a causal link exists between the core of Negative-Land and the problem that has been identified.

In this second stage, Type III causal claims are made to establish both how-possibly and why-necessarily. For the former purpose, the advocate would maintain that there are means by which the agents can give expression to their core motives. Like the motives themselves, a variety of means may be available, including actual or perceived instructions or mandates to behave in a certain way; unchecked discretion, which permits behavior for which the core motives provide the incentive; the ability to withhold delivery of valuable goods and services if the agents' wishes are not implemented, or the impossibility that the agents' behavior might be detected by others. Any of these types of means would permit acting upon the identified core motives.

The "why-necessarily" part of this step of inherency would seek to establish reasons to believe that *this particular* combination of agents, motives, and means explains the continued existence of a manifest evil. The advocate would search for reasons to believe either that the combination is a sufficient condition for the persistence of the problem, or that altering the combination—changing the core of Negative-Land— is a necessary condition for the alleviation of the problem. These reasons, like all Type III statements, are judged by the standard of good reasons described above—whether they make further inquiry by the interlocutor (or, depending upon the situation, by an impartial judge) unnecessary.

It remains, briefly, to consider why the causal link described here is between the known problem and the *core* of Negative-Land. The reason is simple. Were the agents or motives among the *peripheral features*, they could be changed or removed without a change in the fundamental nature of Negative-Land itself; that is to say, without affirming the proposition. Hence a challenger could reply with ease that the identified problems could be solved without the necessity for running the risks implicit in affirmation.[24]

From the foregoing analysis of inherency, it also should be apparent what will be the focal points of controversy about inherency. They correspond to the two analytical stages.

1. *Is the alleged core truly the core?* If not, of course, the problems could be solved without altering the true core of Negative-Land. In challenging the identification of the core, one might dispute whether the agents named are truly the primary decision makers, in other words, whether they have the power to make choices affecting the persistence or the solution of problems. One might challenge the existence of the motive by arguing that there are no grounds for it or that the agent's behavior is inconsistent with it. Or a challenger

may wish to argue that the alleged motive is merely an incidental consequence of some other, benign disposition.[25] One might argue that, while the identification of motive is accurate, it is offset by counter-motives that would lead the agent to solve rather than to perpetuate the problem. The challenger might argue that the agent lacks the necessary means to perpetuate the problem or that other actors possess the means of control. In response to these and other possible types of challenges, the original advocate must be prepared to present Type III arguments, reasons to believe that the ascription of responsibility is fair and just. Otherwise the original advocate might be guilty of the post hoc, ergo propter hoc fallacy—assuming causality on the basis of sign evidence.

2. *Is the causal relationship valid?* If not, of course, the link between the core—even if identified correctly—and the problem will be broken. In challenging the how-possibly part of this argument, one might claim that the alleged means were not really available to the agents, that they were not available to be used in harmful ways, or that checks against the improper use of the means were operative. With regard to the why-necessarily step, the challenger might cite counterexamples to deny the supposed necessary condition (examples in which the problem had been solved without altering the core) or the supposed sufficient condition (examples in which the problem was absent despite the existence of the core features). Or the challenger might raise traditional objections to causal claims, such as multiple causes, multiple effects, intervening causes, and counteracting causes. As before, the task of the original advocate will be to defend his or her initial Type III statements with *further* Type III statements in an attempt to satisfy the good reasons criterion. It is a pattern of Type II and Type III causal statements, then, that composes the substance of argumentation concerning inherency.

CAUSAL ARGUMENTS AND EFFICACY

The second stock issue for which causal arguments are appropriate is that of cure, the ability of a proposed solution to remedy the problems to which it is addressed. To say the least, it is unwise to *assume* that with the adoption of a plan the problems will disappear. Such an assumption relies upon the belief that the policy advocate has a magic wand enabling him to banish troubles by fiat, a belief that has been criticized soundly, and deservedly, in the literature.[26]

To avoid this pitfall, the advocate must be prepared to demonstrate that the proposal will alter the complex of agent, motive, and means that perpetuates the problem, and that this alteration provides good reasons to believe that the problems will be alleviated. Offering such a proof requires causal statements in much the same pattern as is required by the inherency issue. To begin with, it would be necessary to identify the primary agents of any action envisioned by the proposal, and to establish that *these* agents either lack the core motives perpetuating the problems or else have counter-motives not shared by the agents of Negative-Land. A combination of Type II and Type III statements would be employed to serve this purpose. Then, it would be necessary to claim that *this* combination of people and motives has the means to work its will effectively. In this step, the advocate would offer Type I statements to claim that the chosen means would be efficacious; these claims would be supported by Type III statements providing reasons for belief in the Type I claim. To the degree that any steps in this causal analysis are challenged, the original advocate will need to offer Type III causal claims in their defense.

As was true for the issue of inherency, several approaches to the efficacy issue might satisfy these criteria. Following are several illustrative examples.

1. It may be possible to rearrange institutions in order to separate roles that are in conflict. Dividing one agency that has both advocacy and regulatory responsibilities into two agencies, each with only one of the two roles, would be an example of this approach. Then one could maintain that the new structure lacks the motives for inadequate regulations, which were present in the old, when advocacy always was the triumphant role.

2. It may be possible to deny agents the means by which harmful core motives could be given expression. If agents currently possess discretion which is exercised in harmful ways, one solution may be to replace such a grant of discretion with specific legislative or administrative mandates. Then it might be claimed that, whereas agents might use *discretion* to achieve harmful ends, they would not be inclined to violate specific mandates.

3. It may be possible to change the agents responsible for dealing with a problem. Shifts in jurisdiction from the private to the public sector, from the states to the federal government, or from the executive to the legislative branch all

would be changes of this type. Of course, one must be prepared to prove that the offensive motives that *currently* are manifested by one set of agents, will not be sufficiently flexible as to attach themselves to the *new* agents contemplated by the plan. Otherwise, for instance, it would do little good to advocate federal responsibility for a problem the states have ignored if the federal government, once *it* had the responsibility, would be disposed to ignore the problem as well.

4. It may be possible to claim that offensive motives will disappear as a result of forced compliance with the actions envisioned by the plan. Psychological research has suggested that, in some situations, behavioral change will lead to attitudinal change,[27] and such contemporary events as the enforcement of school desegregation orders in the South would provide examples. Of course, one cannot *assume* that forced compliance will reduce, rather than intensify, the motives at issue. Supporting argument is necessary.

5. It may be possible to propose action which will buy off objectors by outweighing their current motives with positive incentives for compliance. Including what Wilson described as "side payments"—additional benefits to persons other than those for whom a program is designed[28]—may be one form of incentive. Devising an administrative structure such that the self-interest of the objectors is served by compliance is another. Of course, supporting argument would be necessary to demonstrate the effectiveness of the incentives.

Again mirroring the inherency issue, causal analysis of the question of efficacy should suggest the two focal points on which controversy is likely to center. First, has the complex of agent-motive-means really been altered? A challenger might maintain that the current agents are still left with sufficient motives and means to circumvent the solution. Or he might claim that the new agents, far from solving a problems, *themselves* have the motives and means to block effective action. Either of these challenges would need to be anwswered with Type III causal statements that satisfy the good reasons test.

The second focal point for controversy is: Will the alteration of the agent-motives-means complex really solve the problem? This question, of course, is another way of asking whether the causal relationship is valid. As before, this question could be approached with respect to how-possibly and why-necessarily dimensions. Concerning the former, a challenger might assert that the scope of the proposed action is inadequate for the magnitude of the problem, that the proposal omits some necessary grant of jurisdiction or power, or that in some other respect it cannot possibly achieve its intended goals. Concerning the why-necessarily question, the challenger might contend that *additional* agents, motives, or means, not addressed by the proposed action, will remain in sufficiently potent combinations to perpetuate the problem despite the best efforts of the proposed solution.

In sum, causal arguments on the issue of efficacy mirror the pattern identified with regard to inherency. In each case, a combination of causal statements is employed, with additional Type III statements used as necessary to support the original causal claims.

REASONS FOR USING CAUSAL ARGUMENTS

So far it has been established that any perceived inapplicability of causation to policy argument results from the following unwarranted generalization: Because Type I causation may be inapplicable, all causation is inapplicable. Having demonstrated the *possible* use of causal argument, of course, is not necessarily to *recommend* it. "Why should the advocate employ causal arguments?" is the final question for discussion.

First, causal arguments permit control over events through understanding them. Without causal arguments, one would infer directly from the existence of evils that reason exists to change policies, and one would infer directly from the existence of a solution that it will be effective. Inherency-by-inference and efficacy-by-inference both treat the facts as coercive of action. But precisely because policy disputes involve controversial matters, there is seldom a consensually accepted view of the facts. For one advocate, they may indicate the existence of a hopeless quagmire; for another, a temporary irritant.

Moreover, one advocate might infer from the facts that there is a motive blocking solution of the problem; a second advocate might infer that no solution is possible; and a third, that a solution is not worth the cost. Without the use of causal arguments, how can one adjudicate conflicting interpretations of the facts? What reason could be cited to favor one view over another? Indeed, not to insist upon good reasons in response to causal questions is to deny the role of reason in questions of value or policy. The consequences of this denial are explained in Wayne Booth's recent account of the modern dogmas of scientism and irrationalism—the first, a belief that since no good reason can be given for choosing one value or policy over another, one must be indifferent to the decision; the second, a belief that since no good reason can be given, choice is determined by the intensity of passion.[29]

On a more prosaic level, one's ability to solve problems may be impaired by failure to understand the factors that perpetuate them. In the field of social policy, for instance, the administration of President Lyndon Johnson has been criticized for its tendency to "throw dollars after problems." The administration, it has been charged, did not recognize that relative distribution of resources might be more responsible for social problems than was the absolute supply of resources. Accordingly, it was surprised to find that spending money not only did not solve social ills but may have worsened them.[30] If one is "to get beyond estimation and prediction to the problem of control," in Fischer's terms,[31] causal argument is necessary.

It may be argued that causal claims do not permit one to achieve control, since events always have multiple and usually interacting causes. Sometimes they may not. As Cohen and Nagel explain, identification of multiple causes may result from irrelevant variety, a subdivision of causes resulting from unnecessary distinctions.[32] Even where multiple causes do exist, it is worth argument to establish a hierarchy of causes and thereby to determine an order of priorities for action.

Second, causal arguments permit resolution of the paradox mentioned above: the toleration of evil by presumably good people. Without resolving this paradox, the advocate cannot expect the dissipation of whatever forces lead to the toleration of evil as a result of the adoption of the advocate's proposal. If people really are not as good as presumed, their unidentified perverse motives may take effect in ways that will undermine the efficacy of the proposed plan. Alternatively, if people indeed are good, then, without knowledge of why evil is tolerated, the advocate cannot know that his calculus of values will be shared. His proposal might not be perceived as beneficial by those whom it seeks to aid or by the society to which it is accountable. If it is not perceived as beneficial, then efforts may well be made to undermine it.

Third, use of causal arguments is desirable in order to improve the rigor of the advocate's analysis and the fairness of argumentation as a decision-making instrument. In his discussion of the principle that every event has a cause, Hospers suggests that, whether true or false, the causal principal may be a valuable rule.[33] By adopting this rule, the analyst always is stimulated to review his or her data in an attempt to find uniformities or conditions on which events depend. One might ask why it is useful to search for causes, especially if we are not sure that they always can be found. The answer is that to do so is to force oneself to engage in the task of justification, which requires argument, and that this task is valuable because knowledge that meets the test of good reasons is more reliable than that which does not. Searching for causes guards against ceasing analysis prematurely. It increases the chance that one's reading of the circumstances is accurate, that the circumstances have been placed in the proper context, and that there is a presumptive reason for belief in the efficacy of the proposed solution.

Not only does insistence upon causal argument improve the rigor of one's own analysis, but it also improves the fairness of argumentation as a means for decision-making. If one engages in a simple comparison of existing conditions with those imagined to accompany a new proposal, he or she compares one system *as it actually exists* with another *as a theoretical ideal*. Such a double standard produces a pro-affirmative bias, a distortion in the instrument that predisposes one toward the acceptance of new proposals and against the reaffirmation of the existing order. By contrast, to search for causes is to initiate inquiry into why the existing order is as it is, and hence whether its defects can be corrected short of the new proposal. In short, causal arguments direct one toward examination of the *potentialities* of both existing and proposed courses of action.

Finally, and more importantly, to employ causal argument is to provide a basis for one's commitments to policy choices or to systems of belief—to establish grounds for choice that transcend whim, caprice, or the non-reflexive claims of immediacy.[34] Grounding one's commitments in good reasons is valuable precisely to the degree to which one accepts the maxim that the unexamined life is not worth living.

Notes

1. David Hume, *An Enquiry Concerning Human Understanding* (1751), Sections 7 and 8. Many editions exist.
2. See John Stuart Mill, *A System of Logic* (London: Longmans, Green, 1843), Book III, Chapter 5; Book VI, Chapter 2.
3. Morris R. Cohen and Ernest Nagel, *An Introduction to Logic and Scientific Method* (New York: Harcourt, Brace, and World, 1934), 249–67.
4. A representative statement of the comparison of policy systems position may be found in Allan J. Lichtman and Daniel M. Rohrer, "A General Theory of the Counterplan," *Journal of the American Forensic Association* 12 (1975): 72–73. In general, this position holds that policy argument consists of a comparison of competitive responses to a *given* situation. Not all adherents to this point of view, however, would dismiss questions of causality. Cf. Bernard L. Brock, James W. Chesebro, John F. Cragan, and James F. Klumpp, *Public Policy Decision Making: Systems Analysis and Comparative Advantages Debate* (New York: Harper and Row, 1973).
5. William Dray, *Laws and Explanation in History* (London: Oxford University Press, 1957), 1. An early formulation of the covering law approach may be found in Carl G. Hempel, "The Function of General Laws in History," *Journal of Philosophy* 39 (1942): 35–48. For a discussion of the covering law approach to scientific inquiry in communication, see Charles R. Berger, "The Covering Law Model in Communication Inquiry," Paper presented at the Speech Communication Association convention, Houston, TX, Dec. 29, 1975.

6. The notion that causation refers to human intervention in a situation, since only people can make choices, is adapted from R. G. Collingwood, *The Idea of History* (New York: Oxford University Press, 1946).

7. Dray, p. 100.

8. Raymond Aron, *Introduction to the Philosophy of History*, trans. George J. Irwin (1938: rpt. Boston: Beacon Press, 1952), 166.

9. W. H. Walsh, *Philosophy of History: An Introduction*, rev. ed. (New York: Harper and Row, 1968), 198.

10. On the relationship between a person and his acts, see Chaim Perelman and L. Olbrechts-Tyteca, *The New Rhetoric*, trans. John Wilkinson and Purcell Weaver (Notre Dame: University of Notre Dame Press, 1969), 293–305.

11. P. H. Nowell-Smith, *Ethics* (Baltimore: Penguin Books, 1954), 125.

12. Dray describes the first sort of explanation as a how-possibly causal explanation and the second as a why-necessarily explanation. Dray, pp. 164–69. His terminology will be employed here.

13. Cf. Karl R. Wallace, "The Substance of Rhetoric: Good Reasons," *Quarterly Journal of Speech* 49 (1963): 239–49.

14. Nowell-Smith, p. 105

15. The premises for such a proof would consist of what Farrell has described as "social knowledge." See Thomas B. Farrell, "Knowledge, Consensus, and Rhetorical Theory," *Quarterly Journal of Speech* 62 (1976): 1–14. See also Robert L. Scott, "On Viewing Rhetoric as Epistemic: Ten Years Later," *Central States Speech Journal* 27 (1976): 258–66, especially pp. 260–63.

16. Perelman and Olbrechts-Tyteca, p. 3. A similar position is criticized in Wayne C. Booth, *Modern Dogma and the Rhetoric of Assent* (Notre Dame: University of Notre Dame Press, 1974).

17. In "The Meaning of Inherency," Kruger argues that it is not possible to solve problems without eliminating their causes. His conclusion is sound, but not in the sense of eliminating the *antecedent* or *first* cause. A problem or phenomenon may become functionally autonomous long after the antecedent cause has passed from the scene. Instead, the *sustaining* cause should be the focus of attention. Cf. Arthur N. Kruger, "The Meaning of the Inherency," *Gavel* 45 (1963): 46–47, 54; reprinted in *Counterpoint: Debates about Debate* (Metuchen, NJ: Scarecrow Press, 1968), 88–92.

18. Lee Hultzén, "Status in Deliberative Analysis," in *The Rhetorical Idiom*, ed. Donald C. Bryant (1958; rpt. New York: Russell and Russell, 1966), pp. 97–123.

19. See, for example, Kruger, "The Meaning of Inherency"; Robert P. Newman, "The Inherent and Compelling Need," *Journal of the American Forensic Association* 2 (1965): 66–71; David A. Ling and Robert V. Seltzer, "The Role of Attitudinal Inherency in Contemporary Debate," *Journal of the American Forensic Association* 2 (1965): 278–83; Tom Goodnight, Bill Balthrop, and Donn W. Parson, "The Problem of Inherency: Strategy and Substance," *Journal of the American Forensic Association* 10 (1974): 229–40; Allan J. Lichtman and Jerome R. Corsi. "The Alternative-Justification Case Revisited: A Critique of the Problem of Inherency," *Journal of the American Forensic Association* 11 (1975): 145–47; Goodnight, Balthrop, and Parson, "Response to 'A Critique of the Problem of Inherency,'" *Journal of the American Forensic Association* 12 (1975): 46–48; J. Robert Cox, "Attitudinal Inherency; Implications for Policy Debate," *Southern Speech Communication Journal* 40 (1975): 158–68.

20. Kenneth M. Strange III, "Inherency: Motives in Structure," Paper presented at the Central States Speech Association convention, Chicago, April 2, 1976.
21. A corollary of this view is that, ultimately, all inherency is attitudinal in nature, since all valid inherency arguments can be traced back to motives. This assumption is at odds with the point of view implicit in Ling and Seltzer that attitudinal inherency somehow is a special type.
22. Walsh, p. 200. Walsh proceeds to claim that this difficulty does not make it impossible to make informed judgements about motives.
23. The problem of structural value statements embodied in law is discussed in Goodnight, Balthrop, and Parson, "The Problem of Inherency," pp. 230–31. On the symbolic aspects of legislation, see Murray Edelman, *The Symbolic Uses of Politics* (Urbana: University of Illinois Press, 1964).
24. These risks include the risk of unforeseen consequences and the risk of premature commitment to a position. On the question of risk, see Henry W. Johnstone, Jr., "Some Reflections on Argumentation," *Philosophy, Rhetoric, and Argumentation*, eds. Maurice Natanson and Henry W. Johnstone, Jr. (University Park: Pennsylvania State University Press, 1965), 1–9.
25. On this transportation of the means-ends relationship, see Perelman and Olbrechts-Tyteca, pp. 270–78.
26. See the articles by Ling and Seltzer and by Cox cited in note 19.
27. See, for example, Leon Festinger and James M. Carlsmith, "Cognitive Consequences of Forced Compliance," *Journal of Abnormal and Social Psychology* 58 (1959): 203–10; J. Merrill Carlsmith, Barry E. Collins, and Robert L. Helmreich, "Studies in Forced Compliance," *Journal of Personality and Social Psychology* 4 (1966): 1–13. For a general review of research on counterattitudinal advocacy, see Gerald R. Miller and Michael Burgoon, *New Techniques of Persuasion* (New York: Harper and Row, 1973), 50–101.
28. To achieve social change, Wilson believed, might require "giving other people as a condition of acquiescence something that they want. The total package becomes much bigger, and a single change tends to be embedded in a cluster of simultaneous changes." James Q. Wilson, "An Overview of Theories of Planned Change," *Centrally Planned Change*, ed. Robert Morris (New York: National Association of Social Workers, 1964), 22.
29. Booth, especially Chap. 1.
30. For example, it was argued that Medicaid functioned primarily to cause more demand chasing after the same supply of medical care, with the result being an increase in the cost of care generally. See Robert Stevens and Rosemary Stevens, *Welfare Medicine in America: A Case Study of Medicaid* (New York: Free Press, 1974). A similar argument could be advanced that housing programs served primarily to bid up the cost of housing generally.
31. David Hackett Fischer, *Historians' Fallacies: Toward a Logic of Historical Thought* (New York: Harper and Row, 1970), 168.
32. Cohen and Nagel, p. 270.
33. John Hospers, *An Introduction to Philosophical Analysis*, 2nd ed. (Englewood Cliffs: Prentice-Hall, 1967), p. 317.
34. Cf. Maurice Natanson, "The Claims of Immediacy," *Philosophy, Rhetoric, and Argumentation*, eds., Maurice Natanson and Henry W. Johnstone, Jr., (University Press, 1965), 15–16. Natanson believes, however, that immediacy does offer claims susceptible to argument if willingness to risk the self through confrontation is evident.

KEY TERMS

add-on advantage
affirmative
causal arguments
clash
comparative advantage case
constructive
criterion
cross-examination
disadvantage
empirical evidence
evidence
generic arguments
harm
needs case
negative
prep time

prima facie
probability
proof
quantitative
rebuttal
shift
shotgun
solvency
spread
statistical significance
status quo
turnaround
Type I statements
Type II statements
Type III statements
variables

DISCUSSION

1. Can an affirmative win solely with a turnaround (even if they lose or drop case)? Explain.
2. Discuss the pros and cons of waiving a cross-examination period.
3. Are certain types of resolutions or topics more amenable to one affirmative case type than another?
4. You make the call: In a question of policy debate, the 1AR grants out the negative absolute plan meet need, the negative disadvantages, and the negative minor repairs on case (in other words, all negative argumentation). The 1AR argues that the plan meet need takes out case, so the disadvantages apply to the minor repairs. The affirmative would win in this most holistic of turnarounds. 2NR argues that once the affirmative abandons affirmative case, affirmative loses. Presuming the 1AR analysis on the interaction of the takeouts is correct, do you give the affirmative the round? Justify your answer.
5. Discuss the pros and cons of running plan attacks or offcase arguments in the first negative speech.
6. Discuss the pros and cons of the Emory switch, a strategy in two-person debate that calls for the affirmative speakers to switch rebuttals.

7. For which stock issues are causal arguments appropriate? Why?
8. How much of a study's methodological background should a debater be expected to know if pressed in cross-examination?
9. How can the null hypothesis be used in the evaluation of quantitative evidence?
10. How do Type II statements differ from Type I statements?
11. Why should the debater use causal arguments in the round?

Part Three

Resolutional Considerations

There are two levels of decision making in academic debate. First, does advocacy result in affirmation of the proposal? Second, does affirmation of the proposal—the affirmative plan—logically demand affirmation of the resolution as well? This second question, which turns on questions of definition not policy or value, is resoloved by examination of the semantic and structural correspondence between the resolution and the affirmative example. This is the one and only issue in debate that requires a yes/no decision, since it is independent of the process of policy comparison or determining the value hierarchies.

This subject has been a central matter of concern to debate theorists for two decades, and it continues to be the focus in convention papers and journal articles today. The articles included in this section represent some of the earlier foundational theoretical statements on the nature of the debate resolution. They deal with issues that arose in policy resolutional interpretation. More current articles that address the latest controversies in *nonpolicy* resolutional consideration are found in Part Eight.

The Lichtman, Rohrer, and Corsi chapter, "The Debate Resolution," serves as an overview for some of the main lines of development in Part Three. This essay, written in the mid-1970s, includes an argument for expanding the latitude allowed to the affirmative in defining and interpreting the resolution. By the 1980s, many felt that allowing any reasonable definition of the resolution was too delimiting, and gave the affirmative too much leeway in selecting plans to stand as examples of the resolution. Donn Parson presented an influential convention paper that advocated specific standards for determining what reasonability is, a paper which was itself misinterpreted by debaters wishing to impose rigid restrictions on affirmative topical interpretations. Parson and Bart's chapter in this section updates and elaborates on the notion of standards for making reasonable interpretations of the resolution. Unger focuses his article on the debatability to topicality arguments, and begins with the premise that it is an issue like any other issue in the debate. To settle this controversy, he suggests that affirmative teams use not merely reasonable definitions, but the best definitions available.

While best definitions do serve the function of limiting affirmative latitude, Unger's article did not silence the ongoing debate over debate resolutions. From the affirmative side, it seems unfair to allow the negative team to argue that policy deliberations should reside in whether the negative definition is a "better" interpretation of what the resolution implies. Herbeck and Katsulas reiterate that presenting any reasonable example of the resolution is all the burden an affirmative team should shoulder.

Viewed as a logical quandary, the issue of reasonability versus best definitions can be reduced to one's tolerance for ambiguity. How broadly may an affirmative team interpret the resolution and still be legitimate advocates for the resolution? In an article that has proven to be a perennial debate class assignment, James Paulsen and Jack Rhodes suggest that examples of the resolution—the affirmative plan, the negative counterplan—are reasonable to the extent that they provide a reasonable judge with a warrant for adopting the resolution. Thus was born the notion of the counterwarrant, or negative examples of the resolution, to weigh against the affirmative warrant. In this edition, we reprint the original article by Paulsen and Rhodes.

The complexity of the jurisdictional issues has markedly increased over the past couple of decades. Whether one is concerned with the definitions, need to be reasonable, better, or best, or the affirmative's need to defend either the entire resolution or a reasonable example of it, the articles in Part Three illuminate these theoretical controversies. The implications of these controversies continue, however, especially in nonpolicy debating; and the subject of topical interpretations will be taken up again in Part Eight.

14

The Debate Resolution

Allan J. Lichtman
Daniel M. Rohrer
Jerome Corsi

Formal debate focuses the attention of competing advocates upon particular propositions. A proposition is a declarative statement that either must be accepted or rejected at the completion of an argument. Opposing debaters in academic debates attempt to persuade an impartial judge or critic to affirm (the affirmative team) or negate (the negative team) the proposition. An affirmative victory is warranted only if the judge is convinced by the arguments to affirm the resolution; otherwise, a negative victory is mandated.

Traditionally intercollegiate debate resolutions advocate policies or courses of action to be taken by some level of government. For example, in 1910 the national topic for intercollegiate debaters was "RESOLVED: That all railroads engaged in interstate commerce should be operated by companies incorporated by the federal government." In 1974, the national college topic was, "RESOLVED: That the power of the presidency should be significantly curtailed." Resolutions concerning governmental policy are especially fertile sources of debate. Their use enhances the education value, intellectual rigor, and competitive excitement of formal debate.

Policy resolutions require the advocate to perform simultaneously the role of *social scientist, historian, moral critic*, and *rhetorician*. Every good debate displays, in microcosm, a wide range of human intellectual endeavors.

Science demands the formulation and testing of theories or generalizations designed to predict future events. These theories may relatè to any aspect of the real world, including human behavior (in this case we would usually employ the term "social science"). The scientific evaluation of propositions urging courses of action depends upon the anticipated results of those actions; an activity is rationally chosen or rejected on the basis of its expected consequences. Thus, the debater must become a social scientist and use theories or generalizations to predict the outcomes of policies advocated by debate resolutions.

History is especially relevant to public policy debating. The validity of the theories used to predict policy results must be tested against actual experience. A theory that claims to tell us what will happen in the future should be reasonably consistent with what we know has already happened in the past. Therefore, the debater must also assume the role of historian and probe, in detail, various aspects of our past experience.

Debaters cannot limit their approach to debate propositions to that of the social scientist or historian. Analysis of the policy proposal goes beyond making reliable predictions of future events resulting from today's decisions. Debaters must be concerned not only with what is or what will be, but also with *what ought to be*. These value judgments are generally termed ends, goals, or objectives. Statements expressing ends, goals, or objectives are referred to as "normative statements." Thus, the debater must assume the role of *moral critic* and assess the effect of policy actions upon the values that he believes we should strive to attain.

Finally, every debater seeks to persuade an impartial critic of the validity of arguments. No judge, being human, can entirely divorce the analysis of a message from an understanding of the form in which it is presented. Not only must the judge understand the debater's arguments; he or she must also be moved to believe them. Thus, the debater assumes the perceptive role of the *rhetorician*, seeking to present the case as concisely and persuasively as possible.

Debate resolutions usually suggest some change in existing policy. The affirmative team becomes an advocate of change, whereas the negative team has the option of supporting the status quo or suggesting a counterproposal, a policy change that does not involve an affirmation of the debate resolution. In theory, however, debate resolutions could also propose retaining some feature of existing policy. Consider, for example, a resolution maintaining that the United States should retain its criminal penalties against the sale and possession of heroin. In this instance, the affirmative team would be required to support the present system and the negative team would necessarily become an advocate for change.

DEFINING THE RESOLUTION

Formal debate is constrained by the particular resolution. Affirmative teams use the process of policy comparison to lead to the adoption of the debate resolution; negative teams attempt to use this process to lead to its rejection. A policy resolution should be affirmed only if a comparison of policy systems demonstrates that the course of action suggested by the resolution and concretized in the affirmative plan proves to have greater net benefits than all of the suggested alternatives. Using a formal model of policy comparison, this notion is expressed by the following inequality:

$$\text{NB affirmative resolution} >$$
$$\text{NB negative alternative for all suggested alternatives.}$$

The responsibility of the affirmative team is to defend a course of action whose support entails an affirmation of the debate resolution. No affirmative team can win a debate by defending a plan whose defense does not demand an affirmation of the resolution. A debate resolution can best be viewed as a statement of reference that indicates the critieria that legitimate affirmative proposals must satisfy. Individual plans are simply members of the set of all legitimate proposals.

How does one know when affirmation of the resolution is a logical consequence of affirming a particular proposal? The proposal must be a member of the set of legitimate proposals. The outcome of this simple test depends upon the definition of the debate resolution. The process of defining involves articulating the critieria that must be fulfilled so that adoption of a particular plan logically calls for adoption of the resolution. Consider, for example, the resolution advocating that the federal government adopt a program of work for the unemployed. If "unemployed" is defined to mean "individuals out of work and seeking work for more than four weeks," then the affirmation of any federal plan offering specified tasks to individuals who meet the criterion would entail affirmation of the debate proposal itself.

In defining a debate resolution, teams must be limited to objective constructions of the wording of the resolution. Any definition that is reasonably consistent with the grammar and semantics of the debate resolution is legitimate. Since most debate resolutions can be defined in various ways the affirmative definition need only be a reasonable one. It need not be the only reasonable definition or even the definition that most readily springs to mind when scanning a proposition. Any affirmative plan that fulfills the criteria set forth by any reasonable interpretation of a debate resolution is legitimate; for affirmation of that plan would logically entail affirmation of the debate resolution.

In searching for reasonable definitions, teams must examine both the meaning of the individual words (semantics) and the way in which these words are linked together (grammar). Multiple definitions are possible because individual words may have several meanings. Moreover, even if reasonable men could agree that a particular topic has only one definition, different affirmative plans may be consistent with that definition. Consider again the proposition advocating a federal program of work for the unemployed. Even if we stipulate that the only reasonable definition of this topic is the one outlined above, various types of work programs would still fit the criteria established by that definition. No affirmative plan defines a resolution; it can only be one of the proposals whose adoption entails adoption of the resolution. If any single plan actually defined the resolution, then any alternative plan which departed, however slightly, from its provisions would have to be regarded as nontopical. Such a standard would lead to the absurd result that the affirmative and negative teams would both be defending variants of the same resolution.

In brief, to assume that the proposal an affirmative chooses to debate defines the debate resolution is to assume that a part defines the whole. In actuality, any dispute over the legitimacy of a given affirmative plan can be resolved only by determining whether or not the affirmation of that plan entails a reasonable interpretation of the debate resolution.

"SHOULD" PROPOSITIONS

Invariably, debate resolutions state that a particular agent "should" affirm a given policy or course of action. The use of the word "should" in debate propositions is critical to interpreting them. It means that advocates are required only to demonstrate that proposals ought to be, but not necessarily will be, put into effect. Thus affirmative teams need not address the question of whether or not their policy suggestions could feasibly be adopted. Debate pivots on the relative desirability of an affirmative plan irrespective of the political obstacles that may hinder its actual adoption in the real world. The activity of academic debate is based on the recognition that a reasonable person could affirm the wisdom of adopting a particular policy even if he or she knows that under current circumstances it will not be put into effect.

Logically, debate need only be viewed as an effort by both teams to persuade an impartial critic of the wisdom of their policy suggestions. Both teams must, of course, demonstrate the practicality of the policies they defend, but they need not claim that these policies can or will be adopted in the political climate prevailing in the arena of public action.

15

Topicality
Why Not the Best?

James J. Unger

I. THE PROBLEM

In terms of the issue that we broadly label "topicality," evidence of the need for a change seems to abound. With increasing force high school coaches, judges, and students complain of debate topics that are too open ended or unlimited. (Equally pejorative comments occur at the college level.) Indeed, the Wording Committee of the NUEA recently issued an official statement, which declared, "The comment most often heard at the San Antonio meeting was that recent topics have been overly broad." And no wonder, when national resolutions designed to seriously consider safety guarantees on consumer goods have spawned cases dealing with animal traps, ski brakes, or private roads; or a discussion of the problems of the Korean boat people was blithely passed off as a significant change in our forcign trade policies. Undoubtedly, each reader could fill in his or her own distressing and bizarre illustrations of topics gone mad.

It is important to recognize that there are really two problems here. First, affirmatives may often select relatively esoteric or abstruse definitions of what had initially seemed to be simple and direct terms. Second, mischief-seeking affirmatives may be content to employ perfectly conventional definitions, but to apply them in totally unconventional and educationally disruptive ways. It should be stressed that this process of incorrect or unreasonable application of acceptable definitions is equally to be condemned with that of the employment of erroneous definitions itself.

Whatever the nature of the complaint, all can agree upon the evils if fosters. Debaters are forced to spend countless hours of valuable time researching the very latest squirrel cases. Debates themselves often focus upon esoteric issues of little intrinsic value or upon the most wild and mindless of desperate assertions. Competitive tactics are glorified at the expense of educational enrichment. And in the end, all of the participants—coaches, judges, and debaters—are the unquestioned losers.

II. INHERENCY

The present system relies upon three methods of correction for these difficulties. Unfortunately, each is seriously flawed.

(A) Often advanced is the belief that all we need are smaller topics. As the NUEA noted, "There was a clear mandate from delegates to formulate more restrictive debate topic choices for 1981–82. The following resolutions are, accordingly, narrower than those offered last year." Narrower indeed! Already we hear of successful cases focusing upon minimum educational standards for native Hawaiians, or homosexuality, or CPR. Despite the most honest of intent it seems chimerical to believe that any English language statement dealing with important matters of public policy can be at one and the same time sufficiently expansive and educational, creative and constructive, broad and narrow. One must acknowledge that as long as there are dictionaries and debaters, even the most simple of terms may be subjects for forensic obscurantism.

(B) In an effort to impose clarification and limitation, additional statements have been grafted onto the actual topic. (In high school this is the problem area, in college the parameters.) Yet this often serves to only double the difficulty. If one simple sentence seems subject to confusion and dissemblance, how much more so will two or three? (This is especially so in the case of the problem area, which neither poses a problem—it is more properly a plan area—nor offers specific guidance, but is usually framed in more general language than any of the three propositions it covers.)

(C) Certainly most prevalent is the often repeated thesis that the affirmative is bounded in its definitional interpretations by the limits of reasonability. That is, affirmative definitions are acceptable to the extent that they can be adjudged reasonable. The language of reasonableness does surely possess a certain superficial attraction. Unfortunately, closer examination reveals that it is totally ineffective in setting acceptable limits to affirmative definitional abuse. This is so because the word or concept itself is extremely vague and ambiguous. As a court once put it,

"An attempt to give specific meaning to the word 'reasonable' is trying to count what is not number, and measure what is not space." (*Altshuler v. Coburn*, 57 N. W. 836.) In short, one man's reasonability is another's irrationality. Yet this situation is totally at odds with the role we have assigned to this concept. Theoretically, reasonability provides a clear, objective standard to judgment, against which each and every affirmative approach can be compared and weighed. Practically, it is less than useless in offering such guidance. Because the concept itself is so vague and lacking in substance, it often results in a set of individualized, biased, even emotional standards that must vary from judge to judge, debate to debate. Worse still, many judges, conscious of the immense reach of reasonability, are forced to support definitional approaches they intellectually despise simply because the affirmative is able to offer some shred of evidence or analysis sufficient to meet this all-too-broad standard. In short, reasonability as a limitation upon definitional excess is both ineffective and counterproductive.

III. THE PLAN

What then is to be done? The solution, I suggest, lies in the elimination of the current objective standard approach, which requires the affirmative definitions to meet the criterion of reasonability, and the substitution of a comparative definitional model. Here, in order to defeat the topicality of the affirmative approach, the negative must engage in a three step process.

(A) The negative must offer a clear *alternative* definition of terms or a clear alternative standard of application of the affirmative's definitions. (Of course, such a process might apply to one, some, or all of the words in the resolution, the problem area, or parameters.)

(B) The negative must demonstrate the *superiority* of its interpretation to that of the affirmative. This would be accomplished through a two-fold process of comparison between the two competing definitions. First, the relative linguistic and policy support that each approach commands would be assessed. A careful examination of relevant sources of expertise should indicate the strength of each definitional position among the communities of scholars and public policymakers directly affected. This is not simply a matter of stacking up conflicting definitions and their sources. Also to be carefully considered must be the matter of *context*. Definitional superiority would be accorded any approach that placed the words of the proposition in their most relevant and appropriate context. Similar superiority would also lie with a definitional framework that accorded each and every word an independent and relevant meaning. Interpretations that render specific words meaningless or duplicative only defeat the purposes of definitions and should be rejected. Second, the relative forensic support available must also be considered. Obviously the purpose of any resolution is to offer limits to debate. Under this standard each team could explain and defend the range of possible cases of interpretations sanctioned by its definitions. (Issues to be considered here might include which approach better promoted substantial analysis of meaningful questions, which approach made available balanced evidential opportunities, and which approach created more equitable argumentative positions.) Clearly these standards of comparison apply with equal force to the problem area and to the application process of the affirmative.

(C) If under the previous step the negative is able to demonstrate the superiority of its own approach, then it must finally indicate that the affirmative's plan could not be considered acceptable under its own definitions—even if the affirmative had not so initially contended. Once having accomplished all three of these steps, the negative may legitimately claim that for the purposes of this debate the affirmative case no longer meets the proposition as most reasonably therein interpreted, and thus it should be rejected.

The radical nature, in the best sense of that term, of this approach needs to be stressed. It totally eliminates the current emphasis upon a single threshold standard of acceptability, that is, reasonability, and puts in its place a comparative assessment that requires *both* teams to discover the superiority of one of their definitions through a process of comparison and contract. In so doing, it places topicality argumentation on a more rational and equitable level with all other protions of the debate process.

IV. ADVANTAGES

There are numerous reasons supporting the superiority of such an approach. They include:

(A) The superior *educational* concentration upon the use and meaning of words. Both sides would now be forced to examine the proposition, not in an attempt to discover the most esoteric or individualistic of definitions, but rather to uncover and build upon the most central, reasonable, and acceptable approaches. Such linguistic inquiry would be of immense value to all of the students therein engaged.

(B) It would also seem undeniable that the *quality* of argument surrounding topicality would be greatly enhanced. *Both* sides would now be forced to explain and defend specific definitional positions. In contrast to the bombast, irrelevancies, and plastic briefs that too often surround the artificial dispute over the reasonability of the affirmative position, the approach offered here would require both sides to engage in specific, relevant argumentation. Topicality arguments could succeed *only* if they were clearly related to the opposition's actual definitions or applications.

(C) The quality of the substantive public policy arguments would also be substantially improved. By requiring definitions to approximate the "best" standard rather than one that was merely reasonable, the range of possible affirmative cases would be definitely restricted. This could only serve to focus discussion upon a smaller number of policy options at the core of the proposition itself. (Of course this is the very purpose the proposition itself was designed to serve originally.) The subsequent improvement in argumentative sophistication and subject matter education debaters would acquire in a major advantage indeed.

(D) Elementary principles of statutory construction require a delicate balance between legislative intent and the most rational factual outcomes. The goal is consistency and rationality. Such a definitional approach as suggested here would force precisely those goals upon the debaters through the requirement of optimal results.

I would be remiss were I not to briefly consider potential objections to such a proposal. Some might be concerned that too many definitional alternatives might be introduced, thus confusing the debate process. On the contrary, since the negative would now be required to actually explain and defend its specific alternative, one would expect that only carefully thought-through positions would emerge. It might also be argued that unbreakable ties might occur with both positions offering favorable and unfavorable aspects. Yet this poses no real difficulty. The affirmative continues to enjoy definitional presumption. The negative must overthrow that presumption by demonstrating the *superiority* of its own position. If it cannot, then its position will not prevail. Finally, one might see this as a hopeless quest and burden to arrive at the best definition possible. Despite the title of this article, that is not the affirmative obligation. Rather, we are simply seeking the best definition *from among those introduced in the specific round of debate.* When seen in such a light the affirmative's burden is no greater than that of any other issue.

I strongly suggest that a definitional model such as proposed here offers significant educational, linguistic, and subject-matter advantages over the present reasonability standard. On balance, that standard should be rejected. We all deserve the best.

16

On Being Reasonable—The Last Refuge of Scoundrels
The Scoundrels Strike Back

Donn W. Parson
John Bart

In an era of increasingly numerous and creative interpretations of debate topics, and increased negative charges of "unfair," "unreasonable," and "untopical," it was argued that all affirmatives consider themselves reasonable and topical.[1] In response to the creative affirmative invocation of reasonableness: "We are reasonable because we are affirmative"; "Since we are affirmative all we have to be is reasonable"; "To be affirmative is to be reasonable"; "Reasonableness is an affirmative presumption," it seemed that there was at least "reasonable" ambiguity in what constituted reasonableness. There is an interesting parallel in the interpretation of the resolution by debate judges and the interpretation of law by Supreme Court justices; some of the same problems of interpretation and invocation have plagued the Supreme Court.

One of the most difficult acts for any judge, observes Justice Felix Frankfurter, is that of statutory construction. "The intrinsic difficulties of language and the emergence after enactment of situations not anticipated by the most gifted legislative imagination reveal doubts and ambiguities in statutes that compel judicial construction."[2] Frankfurter illustrates the problem by comparing the decision-making process of two twentieth century justices, Oliver Wendell Holmes and Louis Brandeis. For Holmes, "the meaning of a sentence is to be felt rather than proved," and meaning becomes an act of judgment "to determine the felt reasonableness of the chosen construction."[3] Frankfurter comments that Holmes "reached meaning easily"[4] and one might concur that if meaning is to be seen and felt, it might be achieved more easily if one were a visionary. Justice Brandeis, in contrast, determined the meaning of a statute only by exact proof through detailed argument. "More often than either Holmes or Cardozo, Brandeis would invoke the additional weight of some rule of construction."[5] The comparison Frankfurter draws is between the visionary and the rule-governed dialectician. While both determined the meaning of statutes, their methods were far different: The reasonableness of a meaning in one case was felt—in the second case it had to be clearly proven. Fortunately for the twentieth century, both men were giants of jurisprudence.

I. THE JUDGMENT OF TOPICALITY

The construction of meaning, the issue raised by Frankfurter, remains a thorny one in debate adjudication. While numerous recent articles have posited the virtues of a special view of debate or paradigm to judge debate (and some of them are contained in this book), few have addressed the issue of resolving topicality disputes, and especially the problem of what constitutes the reasonable in the area of topicality.

In debate, resolving the topicality issue may pose a unique problem. While older views of the stock issues paradigm for judging debaters treated the stock issues as either/or decisions, more recent views have modified that position. We are much less likely to answer the question "Does the affirmative team have significance?" with a clear yes or no. We are likely to offer similar treatment to other stock issues—in fact to all issues save one: topicality. The issue of topicality still remains a yes/no issue; while medical science and test tube babies may yet destroy the analogy that one cannot be a little bit pregnant, forensic science has yet to rescue the issue of topicality. In fact, this may be about the only issue left in debate calling for a dichotomous judgment.

The argument here is that topicality actually may be a different type of issue. If the Roman concept of stasis were to be revisited, one might find that there are two types of questions to be resolved: substantive and procedural. In the context of debate substantive issues are those arguments growing from the topoi of the resolution (or from the field or fields the resolution may embrace). We need to know how cigarettes affect health, how guns affect users, how educational standards affect student performance, how labor unions affect the economy. These questions can be answered, at least imperfectly, by investigating into the areas of the topic and gathering evidence pertinent to those issues.

The second type of issues, procedural issues, concerns problems of legitimacy of operation within the context known as intercollegiate debate. While there may be several of these procedural issues, the primary one is topicality. Substantive questions, especially as adapted to modern debate, admit to answers of degree, while procedural questions do not. The basic procedural question, does the court have standing in this case, becomes the basis for topicality.[6] If the court does not have standing, the merits of the case are irrelevant. If the affirmative case is not topical, then its benefits are irrelevant. It is not a question of degree, but rather an issue that must be answered yes or no, and it must be answered before the substantive issues can be explored and awarded. Topicality is probably the most difficult issue for judges to decide for precisely this reason: it is an either/or procedural judgment.

In the view of many judges, the difficulty is one of making a probabilistic judgment on an absolute issue. Even if the judgment is viewed as probabilistic, the results are absolute. Austin Freeley probably summarized the feelings of most judges: "Topicality becomes an absolute voting issue if the negative wins this argument."[7] This discomfort leads some judges to resist voting on topicality and many others to demand more solid argument before making such a judgment. In the *NDT Judging Booklet* of 1981, Coulter commented, "as many of you know, I seldom vote on topicality. I will vote on topicality, however, if it is presented in a concise form."[8] One might interpret Coulter's "concise form" as clear standards. Similarly, John Gossett commented: "The affirmative has presumption on topicality. Therefore, the negative must win the topicality argument, not just place doubt in my mind, in order to win the round on that single issue."[9] In other words, a probabilistic judgment is not likely to produce a negative decision.

Such a problem for judges is not at all difficult to understand. Given the all-or-nothing implications of the issue, judges are reluctant to award decisions without clear resolution. With affirmative responses that seem or feel reasonable, and no clear standards for resolution, it is easier to ignore the issue and resolve the debate on substantive issues.

II. THE FUNCTION OF THE DEBATE RESOLUTION

Initially, the resolution provides the debaters with an area of study. The resolution suggests parameters for the affirmative and negative by defining a topic for discussion. As Campbell argues, "The proposition's function is to limit the discussion in a debate to a given problem area."[10] On the 1985–86 college resolution, debaters were to discuss educational policy. On the 1985–86 high school topic, the debaters were to discuss water policy. At this level, the resolution identifies the focal point of the discussion, thus limiting the options of the affirmative and the negative.

The second function of the debate resolution is to divide argumentative ground within the broad area of study. The division of ground must be a fair division that allows both the affirmative and the negative an equal opportunity to win the debate. The nature of any competitive activity necessitates that rules promote fairness and equity between opponents. The focus of a theory of topicality must be upon which criteria can be used to enhance the fair division of ground, thus preserving the integrity of the academic game. One such attempt has been the development of the best definition standard, which will be considered next.

III. THE BEST DEFINITION STANDARD

In response to the growing concern that topics are becoming too broad, James Unger proposed the best definition standard for the evaluation of topicality. He argued that reasonability "itself is so vague that, lacking in substance, it often results in a set of individualized, biased, even emotional standards which must vary from judge to judge, debate to debate."[11] The end result was that the creativity of debaters makes the topic meaningless. As a solution, Unger advocated the best definition approach to topicality.

The best definition approach contains a threefold negative duty. The negative must (a) propose an alternative interpretation of the resolution: (b) demonstrate that the new interpretation is superior; and (c) indicate that the affirmative cannot meet the negative's interpretation of the resolution. While this appears to be a sensible approach to the argument of topicality, it is missing one key element—it fails to reveal how one determines which is the superior interpretation. One can intuit from the article that Unger would like topics to be more limited. As an advantage to his system, he argues, "By requiring definitions to approximate the best standard rather than one which was merely reasonable, the range of possible affirmative cases would be definitely restricted."[12]

This position focuses solely on what makes the affirmative either topical or non-topical. It neglects the topic's implications for the negative. For each limitation that is place upon the affirmative ground there is a concomitant increase in negative ground. For example, on the 1985–86 college topic negative teams have argued that the word "all" should mean "every." The rationale is that if "all" is not synonymous with "every," the affirmative could argue small case areas—perhaps even individual schools—making the number of cases limitless. While the argument that "all" should be the equivalent of "every" seems plausible initially, the result of this interpretation renders the negative ground limitless. The negative could argue any number of small exemptions to the affirmative case; for example, it could exempt the South Dakota schools as different or exempt the Eskimos because they would not like the plan. The point is that moving to more limiting interpretations of affirmative ground has the effect of broadening the negative ground. The implications for the debate round are that the affirmative could never be prepared for all of the squirrel counterplans. The resolution again becomes too broad to be debated, but this time by the negative positions. The argument here is that the definition of terms has implications for the division of ground. Focusing upon affirmative ground often blinds us to its implications for the negative. The evaluation of topicality, therefore, must seek a division that allows teams equal ground.

The best definition standard also suffers from Unger's initial criticism of the reasonability standard. He argues that reasonability would be overly subjective, changing from judge to judge. This problem seems to be magnified by the best definition approach. The method of evaluating which is the superior definition may change from round to round. For example, on the 1985–86 college topic, there are two equally acceptable definitions of "academic standard." One definition states that curriculum is an academic standard while the other states that an academic standard is an evaluation of achievement. Both definitions come from the context of the resolution—education dictionaries; thus, they conform to Unger's criterion for a good definition. These interpretations are mutually exclusive. The judge would have to make an arbitrary choice as to which is superior. Unger anticipates this problem and argues that in such a case, where there are equally good definitions, the critic should side with the affirmative. However, in the example, the two definitions would not be equal. A judge who believes that broader topics are more desirable would be inclined to believe that the curriculum definition is superior. A judge who believes that a topic should be restricted would side with the definition of academic standard as a test. When there are in effect two equal or best definitions, as in the 1985–86 topic, the standard for selection is just as arbitrary as Unger claims the reasonability standard to be. In fact, it may turn out to be more arbitrary because the judge needs to select one interpretation over the other.

IV. THE CRITERIA FOR REASONABILITY

Identifying the problems surrounding the issue of topicality is a much easier task than providing a solution that promotes fairness. The initial version of this essay attacked the concept of reasonability *as invoked*. It argued that such affirmative prayers as "All we need to be is reasonable " needed further scrutiny, that reasonability had consistently been invoked rather than argued. The position in this essay is still that invoked reasonability is a poor way to resolve topicality disputes. However, it argues that there are methods to determine whether an interpretation of the resolution is reasonable. If the critieria of reasonability are used, the concept of reasonability may prove a productive avenue for resolving topicality disputes.

There are several assumptions that must underlie this discussion of topicality. We must begin with the assumption that the resolution is (a) a sentence that is grammatically correct; and (b) a sentence that divides the affirmative and negative ground fairly. The first assumption is based upon the fact that the topic committee takes care in the formulation of the sentence. The second assumption is necessary to preserve the integrity of the activity as a fair event. Following these assumptions, we can begin a discussion of what constitutes reasonability as a test of topicality.

First, a reasonable interpretation of the resolution will provide an *equal amount of argumentative ground to the affirmative and to the negative*, thus preserving equity. The judge will therefore examine the implications of the resolution for both the affirmative and the negative. One of the ways this can be done is through an examination of the cases that would be topical given the affirmative interpretation. For example, on the education topic, one may define a language art as anything that directly deals with language. Language could be defined as communication. While this would make a case regulating the content of school libraries topical, it would also legitimize anything as a language art. For example, signs in school hallways and even the color of walls could be construed as a language art. This would seem an unreasonable interpretation of the resolution because it is difficult to conceive of an affirmative position absent language—and hence outside the scope of the language arts. The focus of topicality is upon ground division rather than upon the affirmative measured against the topic.

Second, while a debate resolution may present terms that are new to the debaters who undertake to research it, the key terms of that resolution will not be new to others—primarily those in fields or disciplines where the terms are commonplace. The argument here is that debaters need to be guided be meanings commonly held by the field where key terms are familiar and commonly used. Herbeck and Katsulas make a similar argument when they comment, "Context is critical to perceiving the meaning of words. Thus, to grasp the meaning of the debate resolution, it is necessary to define words in the relevant context."[13]

While argumentation scholars have argued as to what actually constitutes a field, for our purposes we can roughly equate field with discipline. Terms concerning nuclear weapons would best be interpreted by nuclear physicists; terms concerning economic growth by economists; terms concerning educational policy from educators. Experts in the field of education will commonly use terms like "academic standard" but may not have a unique meaning for the word "significant" or "comprehensive." While these disciplines can provide us with meanings for the key terms in the resolution, they cannot provide meaning for all of the terms in the resolution. As a result, there is a secondary context that operates on the evaluation of topicality—the legal context. The courts rule on words that are common to legislation every day. As a result, words like "regulate," "increase," "rigor," "uniform," and "and/or" gain meaning from a judicial context. These words are policy words defined in the judicial process. The primary focus of this section, however, is upon words that comprise the key words of the resolution, words that are unique to a particular resolution comprising the topic area. Deference to a field for interpretation is common in normal policy making. One has only to trace invitations to testify before congressional committees to realize that terms in key bills are best explained by experts in a particular discipline.

Consider the 1981–82 intercollegiate resolution that called for increased regulation of labor unions. Some enterprising affirmative teams defined labor as to "strive towards a goal"[14] and defined union as "persons associated for common purpose."[15] Thus almost any goal-directed activity of two or more persons in concert became a labor union, broadening the concept to include marriages, debate teams, the Ku Klux Klan, and the CIA. The problem of defining each term separately and then combining them becomes obvious in this example. The fields of labor law and labor economics had used the term "labor union" for nearly a century. Including marriages and the Ku Klux Klan would seem alien to them. The separation of key phrases for definition from a non-field perspective makes the affirmative interpretation of the resolution in this instance unreasonable. This interpretation of labor unions would have placed the resolutional sentence beyond the topic area to be discussed.

A similar example can be drawn from the 1985–86 college topic where debaters have separated the terms "language" and "art" for definitional purposes. Language was defined roughly as communication, and art as that which "pertains to the usage of." As a result, anything which is related to communication becomes a language art. Corporal punishment sends a message to children, as a result it communicates and thus, magically, becomes a language art. The implications of splitting phrases and defining them separately becomes rather clear; to professional educators, in this example, it borders on the absurd.

We can examine the implications of these practices by considering the way these definitions would affect the normal legislative practice of implementation. While a plan can be enacted through fiat, it might be interesting to examine how Congress would treat these examples as a bill. A bill to curtail the power of labor unions would first be examined in the Senate by the Committee on Labor and Human Resources. If the affirmative argued that the Ku Klux Klan was a labor union, such a bill would hardly be assigned to this committee. In other words, normal legislative processes assume bills would be sent to appropriate committees for critical examination and testimony. The point is that common meanings often arise in fields or disciplines where the terms have been commonly used. When debaters ignore the meanings of those fields and create new meanings, ones not recognized by the field where the term is regularly studied, the affirmative team loses the grounds for claiming they are reasonable.

Third, grammatical context provides a criteria for assessing reasonableness. The debate proposition is normally a declarative sentence, complete with subject and verb. Definitions of terms must be consistent with their grammatical use in the propositional sentence. Whether a word is used as a noun or a verb will substantially alter the meaning of the proposition. As Herbeck and Katsulas argue, "the affirmative's definitions must maintain the integrity of the proposition as a grammatical sentence."[16]

Each term within the resolution will have meaning. In David Williams' essay on topicality and reasonableness, he observes:

> The interpretation must preserve a discrete meaning or functioning for each term. The presumption is that the resolution is a well-written sentence and that each word in the sentence is there for a reason, that each word further refines the meaning of the sentence. Hence any interpretation which ignores the existence of one or more terms or which renders two or more terms *redundant* is not a reasonable interpretation because it is not contextual.[17]

Each term then further refines the meaning of the resolution. Words ignored or redundant definitions distort the meaning of the grammatical context. Compbell makes the same point but includes contradictory as well as redundant terms; they are not reasonable in the grammatical context of the proposition.[18]

The function of terms within a grammatical context is to exclude as well as include. Definitions demarcate; they set boundaries. Hence definitions of a proposition must show what is excluded as well as what is included. One reason is that words can be combined into countless numbers of combinations, and each combination produces a different meaning. Jerold Katz argues:

> If we count the number of senses of the lexical items in an ordinary sentence of fifteen or twenty words and compute the total number of possible combinations that could be formed from them when they are paired up in accord with the grammatical relations of the sentence, the number of possible senses usually runs into the hundreds. Since no sentence of a natural language has anywhere near this many senses, and some have none at all, a rather severe form of selection must be going on in the process of producing derived readings.[19]

Grammatical combinations reduce the number of possible meanings of a proposition. Field context further reduces the number of possible meanings of a proposition. While the number of possible meanings will be reduced, there is the necessity that they be reduced in accordance with grammatical rules. Hence grammar provides a meaningful criterion for determining the reasonability of interpretation of a debate resolution.

The purpose of this essay has been to suggest a method by which reasonability can be used to resolve topicality disputes. It has argued that reasonability cannot be invoked or felt, and that the best definition criteria fall short as methods for evaluation topicality. By examining the implications of definitions upon division of affirmative and negative ground; by maintaining the meaning of words commonly accepted in fields where they are commonly used; and by preserving the grammatical integrity of the resolutional sentence, debaters can restore meaning to the traditional concept of reasonability. Unless we are able to acquire the wisdom of Justice Holmes, we are forced to follow the lead of Justice Brandeis, arguing the reasonability of statutes from clearly defined criteria.

Notes

1. Donn W. Parson, "On 'Being Reasonable' The Last Refuge of Scoundrels," in G. Ziegelmueller and J. Rhodes, eds., *Dimensions of Argument: Proceedings of the Second Summer Conference on Argumentation* (Annandale, VA: Speech Communication Association, 1981), 532–43. While the scoundrels in the first article were never named, they did manage to respond. A variety of arguments were constructed by "clever scoundrels" using the article for support. Among positions argued were that the article was a justification for counterwarrants, that topicality was a reverse voting issue, and that topicality was not a voting issue. Only the most creative reading of the first essay could possibly lead to such conclusions—unless the the article was intuited rather than read. It was clear that the scoundrels had indeed struck back.
2. Felix Frankfurter, in Ruggero Aldisert, ed., *The Judicial Process: Readings, Materials and Cases* (St. Paul: West Publishing Co., 1976), 189.

3. *Ibid*.
4. *Ibid*.
5. *Ibid*., p. 191.
6. For a discussion of substantive versus procedural issues, see Donn W. Parson, "The Elusive Search for Evaluative Criteria," Paper presented to the University of Nebraska Symposium on Argumentation, Feb. 1975.
7. Austin Freeley, Judging Philosophy Statement, *National Debate Tournament Judges Booklet*, 1981.
8. Skip Coulter, Judging Philosophy Statement, *National Debate Tournament Judges Booklet*, 1981.
9. John Gossett, Judging Philosophy Statement, *National Debate Tournament Judges Booklet*, 1981.
10. Cole Campbell, *Competitive Debate* (Chapel Hill, NC: Information Research Associates, 1974), 114.
11. James Unger, "Topicality: Why Not the Best?" *The Rostrum* 61 (Oct. 1981): 6.
12. *Ibid*., p. 9.
13. Dale A. Herbeck and John P. Katsulas, "The Affirmative Topicality Burden: Any Resonable Example of the Resolution," *Journal of the American Forensic Association 21* (Winter 1985): 138.
14. *The American College Dictionary* (New York: Random House, 1955), 680.
15. *Ibid*., p. 1325.
16. Herbeck and Katsulas, p. 139.
17. David Williams, ed., *U.S. Trade, Weapons and Assistance Policies: Perspectives and Issues* (Lawrence, KS: Jayhawk Debate Research, 1979), 1–10. Williams' excellent essay focuses specifically on issues of topicality and reasonableness. While he covers several perspectives not discussed here, his development of grammatical context is used in this paper.
18. Campbell, p. 113.
19. Jerold Katz, "The Realm of Meaning," in George Miller, ed., *Communication, Language and Meaning* (New York: Basic Books, 1974), 44.

17

The Affirmative Topicality Burden
Any Reasonable Example

Dale A. Herbeck
John P. Katsulas

The debate resolution is a source of considerable theoretical controversy in published articles, convention papers, and especially in academic debates. Critics argue that traditional concepts of the resolution need to be reformulated because of a multitude of practical problems. The traditional concept of the resolution is held responsible for the decreasing participation in academic debate, the declining quality of argumentation, and the frustrating proliferation of squirrel cases.

One possible solution, most commonly associated with Unger (1981a, 1981b), formulates new standards for ascertaining whether the specific policy proposed by the affirmative is a legitimate interpretation of the resolution. While the traditional standard for determining the topicality of an affirmative case is whether the affirmative's definitions are reasonable, Unger claims that the affirmative must offer a more reasonable definition. Sometimes this line of reasoning extends to require the affirmative to offer the most reasonable definition. According to Unger, this heightened standard of review is justified in order to limit the nature and scope of the debate. Ultimately, Unger claims, this limitation will improve the overall quality of the resulting debate.

We argue that a reasonability standard is a criterion for adjudicating topicality disputes superior to this solution. Unger's advocacy of a more reasonable standard fails to cure the ills he claims are inflicted upon debate by the reasonability standard. Despite the recent barrage of criticism, the reasonability standard continues to be the best standard for the evaluation of topicality arguments.

WHAT MUST THE AFFIRMATIVE DO TO FULFILL THE RESOLUTION?

The Right to Define Terms

Almost all theorists concur that the affirmative reserves the right to define terms (Herbeck and Katsulas, 1982). Freely (1981a) notes that "it is the privilege of the affirmative to stipulate which legitimate definition of term it will use, and the negative must debate on the basis of the definition selected by the affirmative" (p. 46). Musgrave (1945) claims, "The affirmative has the right to make any reasonable definition of each of the terms of the proposition" (p. 13). Snyder (1979) argues, "The affirmative has the right to define terms in the first affirmative speech" (p. 90). Others share in this judgment (Capp and Capp, 1965; Goodnight and Wood, 1983).

While most commentators agree that the affirmative retains the right to define terms, few theorists (Deatherage and Pfau, 1982) provide a comprehensive justification for granting the affirmative such definitional discretion. The affirmative right to define terms is grounded in three considerations. First, since the affirmative initiates the controversy it only seems appropriate to grant them the discretion to define the terms of the discussion. Just as a legislator defines the operating provisions of a bill, and just as a prosecuting attorney defines the charges in a criminal proceeding, the affirmative team presenting an example of the resolution possesses the right to define the terms of the controversy. Second, allowing the negative to define terms is unworkable. If the negative were allowed to define terms, they could always define the affirmative as nontopical and either win the debate on topicality or counterplan with the plan and completely solve the affirmative need. Allowing the negative to define terms would make meaningful debate impossible. Finally, it should be realized that this does not give the affirmative an unfair competitive advantage. Since the affirmative has the right to define their policy, the negative retains the right to define any counterplan that they might initiate.

Affirmative Only Need Be Reasonable

Traditionally, the only limitation on the affirmative right to define terms has been that of reasonability. Williams and Cross (1979) explain the conventional position:

> In order to guard against such definitional liberties, the debate community, following the precedent of the judiciary's reasonable man standard for statute interpretation, usually decides "whether the affirmative definitions of terms are legitimate and acceptable" by way of "the reasonableness of the definitions." Indeed, "the general procedure for testing the topicality of a case involves testing the reasonableness of the definitions" (p. 1–5).

Since most words can be defined in a number of different ways, this deference to reasonability allows the affirmative to select from among any of the reasonable definitions. Lichtman and Rohrer (1979) posit that:

> Since most debate resolutions can be defined in various ways, the affirmative definition need only be a reasonable one. It need not be the only reasonable definition or even the definition that most readily springs to mind when scanning a proposition. Any affirmative plan that fulfills the criteria set forth by any reasonable interpretation of a debate resolution is legitimate (p. 86).

As long as the affirmative presents a reasonable definition, there is no basis for a topicality challenge by the negative team. Smith (1980) ventures so far as to claim, "As long as the affirmative can defend a reasonable definition, alternative definitions are irrelevant" (p. 54).

Thus, to prove that the affirmative case is not topical, the negative needs to demonstrate that the affirmative's definitions are not reasonable. Since the affirmative controls the right to define terms, it is a negative burden to prove that the affirmative's definitions are not reasonable. Absent clear proof that the affirmative's definitions are unreasonable, the affirmative right to define terms mitigates the significance of all counterdefinitions presented by the negative.

To establish that the affirmative definitions are unreasonable, the negative must demonstrate one of two things. The first way to prove that the affirmative's definitions are unreasonable is to prove an absence of field context. The negative must establish that the affirmative is incorrectly importing definitions from one context into another context.

The importance of context in understanding language is a recurrent theme in texts on speech communication, argument, and philosophy (Baird, 1937; Bitzer, 1969; Crocker, 1944, Damer, 1980; Eisenberg and Illardo, 1980; Hayakawa, 1978; Kruger, 1960; Nobles, 1978; Ross, 1977; Toulmin, Reike and Janik, 1979). Context is critical to perceiving the meaning of words. Thus, to grasp the meaning of the debate resolution, it is necessary to define the words in the relevant context. Windes and Hastings (1965) argue that:

> Every proposition possesses a background or history all its own; the proposition did not suddenly happen; it emerged from a complex process of controversy evolution. From the inception of a situation which created basic original concerns through the proposition, this evolutionary development demands the study of the advocate. The advocate must be aware of the evolution, for without the perception and knowledge such a study results in, he would work in an atmosphere of relative ignorance (p. 37).

By demonstrating that the affirmative's definitions ignore the appropriate context, the negative could prove that the affirmative's definitions are unreasonable.

The importance of field context can be illustrated by examining the wording of the high school propositions under the criminal justice problem area. The three resolutions are: "RESOLVED: That the United States should adopt uniform rules governing the criminal investigation procedure of all public law enforcement agencies in the nation;" "RESOLVED: That the United States should establish uniform rules governing the procedure of all civil courts in the nation;" and "RESOLVED: That the United States should establish uniform rules governing the procedure of all criminal courts in the nation." All three resolutions contain the word "procedure." Any standard dictionary defines the word "procedure" as "a particular course of action" (*Webster's*, 1976, p. 1806). Using this definition, the affirmative might mandate the courts to implement a uniform course of action. By this interpretation, virtually any case would be topical if implemented by the courts (Edwards, 1983). Fortunately for the negative team, when considered in the appropriate context the word "procedure" means much more than "a particular course of action." In *State v. Garcia*, (1969), the Court defined "procedure" as:

> . . . related to criminal law and procedure, "substantive law" is that which declares what acts are crimes and prescribes the punishment therefore, while "procedural law" is that which provides or regulates steps by which one who violates a criminal statute is punished (p. 238).

By noting the appropriate context the negative could prove that the affirmative's definitions were unreasonable.

Another way that the negative could prove that the affirmative's definitions are unreasonable is to demonstrate that there is an absence of grammatical context. According to Williams and Cross (1979), this standard "examines both the correctness of the definitions themselves and the correctness of the combination of the discrete definitions of each term" (p. 1–9). In other words, the affirmative's definitions must maintain the integrity of the proposition as a grammatical sentence. Parson (1981) explains, "The debate proposition is normally a declarative sentence, complete with subject, noun, and verb. Definitions of terms must be consistent with their grammatical use in the propositional sentence" (p. 538). Consistent with this is the requirement that the propositions be defined so that each word has meaning.

A clear example of a grammatical misinterpretation occurred under the media resolution debated a few years age. Under that topic, "RESOLVED: That the federal government should significantly strengthen the regulation of mass media communication in the United States," some teams proposed plans legalizing obscenity. This action was topical, they claimed, because "to regulate" meant "to protect" (*Virginia Railroad Company v. System Federation No. 40, Railway Employees Department of the American Federation of Labor et al.*, 1936, p. 650; *The Daniel Ball*, 1870, p. 537; *County of Mobile v. Kimball*, 1880, pp. 696, 697; *Second Employers' Liability Cases*, 1911, p. 47; *U.S. v. Gregg*, 1934, p. 857; *Great Northern Utilities Co. v. Public Utilities Services Commission*, 1930, pp. 298–99). Hence, a plan that protected obscene books and films constituted a regulation of mass media communication. On closer examination this interpretation clearly misconstrues the grammatical integrity of the resolution. In the context of the resolution, the word "regulation" appears as a noun. Accordingly, a regulation in this sense conveys the meaning of a rule or order (*Curry v. Marvin*, 1849, p. 415; *In re Leasing of State Lands*, 1893, p. 988). However, the affirmative advancing this topicality argument utilized the verb meaning "to regulate" in order to derive the interpretation possessed by the noun "regulation." By transposing the meaning of the verb "regulate" for the noun "regulation," these affirmatives destroyed the grammatical context of the resolution. Thus, their use of this particular definition was unreasonable.

Along with grammatical and field context, some theorists also allege that the affirmative must meet the intent of the resolution as embodied in the parameters. Parson (1981), for example, maintains that the parameters "are the most reasonable statement of intent" (p. 538). Hence, parameters "should be the first criterion to decide reasonableness" (p. 538). If the affirmative's definitions conflict with the parameter's interpretation of the resolution, Parson suggests, the affirmative is probably not reasonable.

While the parameters might embody one interpretation of the resolution, they do not deny the reasonableness of the affirmative's definitions. Since the affirmative team only needs to be reasonable, the parameters merely offer one of many possible interpretations of the resolution. There is no rationale for believing that the parameters offer exclusive definitions. Not surprisingly, a minority of the forensic community believe that the parameters are binding on the affirmative. Freeley's (1981b) survey reveals that "only 41 percent of the forensic community think parameters should be universally binding" (p. 7). Rather than imprisoning the affirmative into any one interpretation of the resolution, the parameter merely establishes the reasonability of one interpretation of the resolution. While parameters may be useful in proving that a case is topical, they should not be used to prove that the affirmative's definitions are unreasonable.

IN DEFENSE OF REASONABILITY

Some debate theorists maintain that it is necessary to devise some sort of limitation on the breadth of the resolution. These critics argue that the imposition of more stringent standards for evaluating definitions is necessary in order to place some limits on the topic being debated. As a result, they advocate the use of a standard requiring the affirmative to offer either a more reasonable definition than the negative, or the most reasonable definition of the resolution. Reflecting this sentiment, the National Debate Tournament has adopted a rule that states:

> The standard for the evaluation of topicality at the National Debate Tournament is that definition which obtains (enjoys) superior analytical and evidential support drawn from the (relevant) subject matter area(s) as introduced in the round of debate (*Charter of the National Debate Tournament*, Rule 4, Section E, Subsection 3, Part b).

As a way of combatting the dreaded squirrel case, a growing number of judges endorse the application of more or most reasonable topicality standards.

There are two main lines of argument in support of these new topicality standards. First, the new standards incorporate an indictment of the old standard. They suggest the requirement that the affirmative's use of reasonable definitions to define terms is inadequate. The reasonability standard, according to its critics, is far too subjective, generally too vague, and not sufficiently limiting. Second, proponents argue that a change to a more rigorous standard would foster educational benefits, improvements in the quality of debate, or other advantages.

The criticism of the reasonability standard is really quite simple. Proponents of a more rigorous standard simply argue that mere reasonability is not sufficiently limiting. They argue that reasonability is a vague and confusing construct. For example, Unger (1981b) observes that "one man's reasonability is another man's irrationality" (p. 4). To provide additional support for this statement, critics of reasonability invariably offer a court decision which holds that the term "reasonable" is ambiguous, and hence incapable of precise definition. So, for example, they might cite the *Altschuler v. Coburn* (1984) ("An attempt to give a specific meaning to the word reasonable is trying to count what is not number, and measure what is not space," p. 836), or *Stuyvesant Town Corporation v. Impellitteri* (1952) ("The term reasonable is not subject to exact definition. It may be said to be fitting and proper and characterized by moderation. It is a factual expression not ascertainable by reference to rule, law, or formula," p. 657). Having progressed this far, they suggest that the reasonability standard is unacceptable. Unger (1981a; 1981b) concludes:

> Theoretically, reasonability provides a clear, objective standard of judgment against which each and every affirmative approach can be compared and weighed. Practically, it is less than useless in offering such guidance. Because the concept itself is so vague and lacking in substance it often results in a set of individualized, biased, even emotional standards that must very from judge to judge, debate to debate (p. 6; p. 4).

Because of this, mere reasonability alone is not a sufficient check on the affirmative discretion to define terms. Consequently, the opponents of the reasonability standard argue, a new and more stringent standard must be employed. Thus, they suggest that the affirmative team must offer a more reasonable definition than the negative team, or they might go so far as to conclude that the affirmative must offer the most reasonable definition of the resolution.

But in their haste to transcend mere reasonability, the proponents of more rigorous standards have unjustly indicted the reasonability standard. In their haste to impose judgment, they have overlooked the viability of a standard based on reasonability. First, they totally ignore the possibility for defining reasonability. Accepting for the moment the claim that reasonability is not sufficiently objective or precise enough to assess the topicality of the affirmative case, there is still no justification for totally abandoning the reasonability standard. It is certainly possible to provide some constraints on what is reasonable. If a definition violates the field context or grammatical syntax of the resolution, for example, it does not constitute a reasonable definition.

Second, reasonability is a very common standard of proof in a wide variety of contexts outside of academic debate. Invariably, enterprising negatives select their indictments of the reasonability standard from *Words and Phrases*, or some other legal dictionary or lexicon. But in their haste to gather only the evidence damning the standard, they ignore a plethora of other definitions and explanations that illustrate the viability of a reasonability standard. *Words and Phrases*, for example, offers a myriad of definitions, synonyms, and examples involving reasonability. It identifies laws, judicial proceedings, and other situations in which reasonability is used to arrive at a decision. The sheer quantity of entries and the number of cases involving reasonability should be sufficient proof that the reasonability standard is common, recurrent, and workable. If nothing else, the negative should be able to use these examples to derive standards for proving the affirmative's definitions are unreasonable. Those decisions indicting the reasonability standard represent only a fraction of the total number of entries on the subject.

If there is an argument to be made against reasonability, it lies not in the concept but the application. When debaters flout reasonability with blatantly nontopical cases, or when judges allow affirmatives to slide by with marginal interpretations of the resolution because they "don't vote on topicality," they have cheated the reasonability standard. It is not the standard that causes the fragmentation of the resolution but rather the unwillingness of judges to vote on topicality. Policymakers, courts, and even debate judges all utilize the notion of reasonability in order to resolve other claims besides topicality without any undue problem. It is the way in which the standard is applied with respect to topicality that causes the problem. Any problem with reasonability lies outside of the concept.

Hence, if there were a problem with reasonability, it would not be solved by a more or most reasonable standard. Refining the construct would not change the deficiencies in the application of the construct. Affirmatives would merely develop more lengthy topicality briefs offering a multiplicity of reasons why they are more reasonable than the negative or why their definitions are the most reasonable definitions prossible. Judges who don't vote on topicality will not undergo surprising transformations and start voting on topicality simply because the standard has been changed. Instead, these judges will simply lodge a presumption in favor of the affirmative's definitions and then claim that the negative did not prove that their definitions were more reasonable than the affirmative's or that the negative definition was the most reasonable definition possible.

The second argument against reasonability is that more stringent topicality standards are advantageous. Any number of different advantages are claimed (Unger, 1981a, 1981b). It is argued that more stringent standards would restrict potential affirmative cases, allowing the negative to complete more detailed preparations. This would presumably increase the quality of debate. It is argued that more stringent standards would force debaters to debate the subject that educators selected when they framed the resolution. By avoiding marginal cases debaters would really learn about the topic and not about obscure concerns only peripherally related to the resolution. It is argued that more stringent standards would improve topicality arguments. Topicality arguments would become more than the series of rapidly repeated assertions and counterassertions that plague contemporary debate. Finally, it is argued that more stringent standards would force debaters to study the English language. Instead of being able to hide behind the concept of reasonability, affirmatives would actually have to be able to prove that their cases are topical. They would be forced to learn what the resolution really means. Consistent with this, negatives would be forced to develop arguments to prove that their definitions are better than the affirmatives'. Both sides would be forced to master the language. This list of potential advantages could be extended, but these arguments seem to be the most common and the most substantive.

Unfortunately, all of these claims suffer from the same deficiencies. First, the advantages can be obtained with reasonable definitions. Debaters could achieve exactly the same personal benefits, and the activity could obtain the same quality advantages without a more stringent reasonability standard. Applying a more stringent topicality standard produces no unique advantages.

Second, there is no guarantee that more stringent standards will achieve any of these advantages. The proponents of stronger standards assume that it will be possible to determine, or at least to debate, which definitions are more or most reasonable. This may not be the case. What do you do, for example, if the affirmative claims that their definition should be accepted because it allows for ten different cases and the negative claims that their definition should be accepted because it allows for only one possible case? How is it possible to decide which definition should be preferred? If the critics of reasonability are correct, and if it is difficult to determine which definitions are really reasonable, how can a judge possibly hope to determine which definitions are more or most reasonable? Without some unstated subjective standards it is impossible to compare the reasonability of competing definitions.

Third, application of more stringent topicality standards may actually be disadvantageous. Stringent standards encourage negative teams to devote additional time to considerations far apart from the supposed subject of the debate. Instead of arguing the merits of the affirmative case, the negative is encouraged to devote an extensive amount of time to discussing the matrix in which definitions should be considered. Excessive debate about the rules of debate detracts from the activity. In his critique of the final round of the 1980 National Debate Tournament, Solt (1980) observed that overemphasis on theoretical issues "express[es] the recent tendency of debate to become increasingly esoteric, overly wrapped up in itself, and divorced from real policy concerns" (p. 56). Other have expressed similar reservations (Balthrop, 1982; Olson, 1982; Weiler, 1981). Stringent topicality standards will only exacerbate this trend. While proponents of more stringent topicality standards allege educational benefits, it seems more likely that these stringent standards will diminish the educational value of the activity.

Finally, and perhaps most damaging, the more and most reasonable standards work from the unstated assumption that narrow resolutions are better than broad resolutions. They assume that the best debate occurs when the affirmative team uses one of those few cases that meet these stringent standards. But, as Nadler (1982) has argued, there are equally valid reasons for believing that broader resolutions make for better debates.

Broad topics allow the affirmative flexibility in selecting a case. Such topics encourage the affirmative to investigate the entire problem area. Furthermore, broad topics prevent stagnation. If debate was held on the same few cases round after round, all participants would lose interest. Debates would degenerate into mindless and repetitive brief reading contests. As Nadler (1982) notes, "it seems that broad interpretations of resolutions offer a pragmatic benefit to the debate community as an escape from the boredom that debating a few cases over and over can lead to" (p. 5). A broader topic allows for new ideas, while at the same time encouraging debaters to seek out new case possibilities.

Broader topics encourage and foster critical thinking and analytical skills:

> One of the most valuable educational benefits of academic debate is its ability to teach students good critical thinking and analysis skills. Even those who would not identify this value at the top of the list would probably agree that it is an important element of the activity. There are few situations more challenging to a debater's on-the-spot analytical skills than meeting a case with little or no research on it tucked away in a file box or brief book (Nadler, 1982, pp. 4–5).

Broader topics literally force debaters to think. While debaters might not adapt as much as their coaches or judges might wish, this is certainly not a reason to encourage less thought by narrowing the scope of the resolution through more rigorous topicality standards.

Admittedly there must be some limitation on the subject of the debate, but the subject area established by the resolution and the requirement that the affirmative offer a reasonable definition of terms is more than adequate. There is no need to further reduce this area through the introduction of more stringent standards for evaluating topicality arguments.

CONCLUSION

While we disagree with the arguments advanced by those who reconceptualize the focus and nature of the resolution, we do share some of their concerns. However, neither of the recently proposed solutions adequately redresses these concerns. Changing the focus of the debate or heightening the standards of topicality will not magically remedy all of the evils associated with current debate practices. Reconceptualizing the resolution will not redress these concerns.

There are good reasons for debating examples of the resolution instead of the resolution in its entirety. Traditional debate theory correctly focuses debate on examples of the resolution. Attempting to debate the entirety of any subject in a mere sixty minutes would be folly. Under such circumstances, the resulting test of the resolution is both shallow and narrow. By focusing on examples of the resolution, however, it is possible for debaters to intelligently consider the merits of a specific policy option in considerable detail.

Despite its flaws, the reasonability standard remains the best standard for determining whether the affirmative plan is a legitimate example of the resolution. Theoretically, the standard is premised upon the conviction that the affirmative retains the right to define terms. Under this rule, topicality is not resolved by a comparison of affirmative versus negative definitions. Rather, a negative may prove that an affirmative is not topical only if they demonstrate that the affirmative's definitions are divorced from field or grammatical context. In other words, the question to be asked is whether the affirmative's definitions are reasonable, not whether their definitions are better than the negative's or whether they are the best possible definitions.

While the reasonability standard may not be without fault, it does provide a viable and useful framework for the resolution of topicality arguments. Educationally, the reasonability standard promotes quality debate on the topic. Unlike the most or more reasonable topicality standards, reasonability promotes lively and creative discussion on the topic, rather than a cumbersome exploration of metatheoretical concerns. Overall, the reasonability standard, in theory and practice, emerges as the best standard of topicality.

References

Altschuler v. Coburn, 57 N.W. 836 (Neb. 1894).

Baird, A. C. (1937). *Public Discussion and Debate*. Boston: Ginn.

Balthrop, B. (1982). "Untitled Declamation: Or, Wonderings (Wanderings) of a Rapidly Aging Debate Judge." *1982 Heart of America Final Round Critiques*. Lawrence: University of Kansas Debate Squad.

Bitzer, L. (1969). "The Rhetorical Situation." *Philosophy and Rhetoric* 1: 165–68.

Brock, B. L. (1975). "Perimeters of the Debate Resolution." In R. J. Branham, ed., *The New Debate: Readings in Contemporary Debate Theory*. Washington: Information Research Associates.

Bryant, M. W. (Nov. 1982). *An Examination of Resolutional Focus*. Paper given at the annual meeting of the Speech Communication Association, Louisville.

Capp, G. R. and Capp, T. R. (1965). *Principles of Argumentation and Debate.* Englewood Cliffs: Prentice-Hall.

Charter of the National Debate Tournament, Rule 4, Section E. Subsection 3, Part b.

County of Mobile v. Kimball, 102 U.S. 691 (1880).

Crocker, L. (1944). *Argumentation and Debate.* New York: American Book.

Curry v. Marvin, 2 Fla. 411 (Fla. 1849).

Damer, E. T. (1980). *Attacking Faulty Reasoning.* Belmont: Wadsworth.

The Daniel Ball, 10 Wall. 557 (1870).

Deatherage, L. and Pfau, M. (1982). "Arguing Topicality: Perspectives and Techniques." In R. G. Fawcett, ed., *Debating United States Military Policy: A Preliminary Analysis.* Kansas City: National Federation of State High School Associations. 17–36.

Edwards, R. E. (1983). "Procedure." *Forensic Quarterly 57* (1): 38–39.

Eisenberg, A. and Illardo, J. (1980). *Argument: A Guide to Formal and Informal Debating,* 2nd ed. Englewood Cliffs: Prentice Hall.

Freeley, A. J. (1981a). *Argumentation and Debate,* 5th ed. Belmont: Wadsworth.

Freeley, A. J. (Nov. 1981b). *How Much Should the Words of a Debate Proposition Predetermine the Debate Subject Matter?* Paper given at the annual meeting of the Speech Communication Association, Anaheim, CA.

Goodnight, L. and Wood, R. V. (1983). *Strategic Debate.* Lincolnwood: National Textbook Co.

Goodnight, T., Balthrop, B., and Parson, D. W. (1974). "The Problem of Inherency: Strategy and Substance." *Journal of the American Forensic Association 10*: 229–40.

Great Northern Utilities Co. v. Public Utilities Services Commission, 293 p. 294 (Mont. 1930).

Hayakawa, S. I. (1978). *Language in Thought and Action,* 4th ed. New York: Harcourt, Brace, Jovanovich.

In re Leasing of State Lands, 32 p. 986 (Col. 1983).

In the Matter of Stuyvesant Town Corporation et al., Petitioners, against Vincent R. Impellitteri, et al., Constituting the Board of Estimate of the City of New York, et al., 661 N.Y. Misc. 661 (N.Y. 1952).

Karlen, D., Meisenholder, R., Stevens, G. N., and Vestal, A. D. (1975). *Civil Procedure: Cases and Materials.* St. Paul: West Publishing.

Kruger, A. (1960). *Modern Debate: Its Logic and Strategy.* New York: McGraw-Hill.

Lichtman, A. J. and Rohrer, D. M. (1979). "The Debate Resolution." In D. Thomas, ed., *Advanced Debate.* Lincolnwood: National Textbook Co. 83–88.

Musgrave, G. M. (1945). *Competitive Debate: Rules and Techniques,* 3rd ed. New York: H. W. Wilson.

Nadler, M. K. (Nov. 1982). *Broad Topics: Educational Values Worth Salvaging.* Paper given at the annual meeting of the Speech Communication Association, Louisville.

Nobles, S. (1978). "Analyzing the Proposition." In D. Ehninger and W. Brockreide, *Decision by Debate.* New York: Harper and Row. 151–73.

Olson, C. D. (Nov. 1982). *Pragmatic Considerations of Meta-Argument.* Paper given at the annual meeting of the Speech Communication Association, Louisville.

Panetta, E. (Nov. 1983). *The Resolutional Counterplan: A Gentleman's Agreement.* Paper given at the annual meeting of the Speech Communication Association, Louisville.

Parson, D. W. (1981). "On Being Reasonable: The Last Refuge of Scoundrels." In G. Ziegelmueller and J. Rhodes, eds., *Dimensions of Argument: Proceedings of the Second Summer Conference on Argumentation*. Annandale: Speech Communication Association. 532–43.

Pfau, M. (April 1983). *A Reasonable Approach to Generic Argument*. Paper given at the annual meeting of the Central States Speech Association, Lincoln, NE.

Ross, R. (1977). *Speech Communication: Fundamentals and Practice*, 4th ed. Englewood Cliffs: Prentice-Hall.

Second Employers' Liability Cases, 223 U.S. 1 (1911).

Smith, W. (1980). "Critique of the Final Round of the 1980 National Debate Tournament." *Journal of the American Forensic Association 17*: 54–55.

Snider, A. C. (1979). "Fiat Power and International Organizations. In D. Thomas, ed., *Advanced Debate: Readings in Theory, Practice and Teaching*. Lincolnwood: National Textbook Co. 89–94.

Solt, R. (1980). Critique of the Final Round of the 1980 National Debate Tournament. *Journal of the American Forensic Association 17*: 56–58.

State v. Garcia, 229 So. 2d 236 (Fla. 1969).

Toulmin, S., Reike, R., and Janik, A. (1979). *An Introduction to Reasoning*. New York: Macmillan.

Ulrich, W. (1979). A Prophet Without Honor: A Minority of the 1979 Heart of America Final Round. *1979 Heart of America Final Round and Critiques*. Lawrence: University of Kansas Debate Squad.

Unger, J. J. (1981a). "Topicality: Why Not the Best?" *Rostrum 56*: 3–9.

Unger, J. J. (Nov. 1981b). *The Words of a Debate Proposition and Their Subject Matter: Friends or Foes?* Paper given at the annual meeting of the Speech Communication Association, Anaheim, CA.

United States v. Gregg, 5 F.Supp. 848 (S. D. Tex. 1934).

Virginia Railroad Company v. System Federation No. 40, Railway Employees Department of the American Federation of Labor, 84 F.2d 641 (4th Cir. 1936).

Webster's Third New International Dictionary of the English Language, 3rd ed. (1976). Chicago: Encyclopedia Brittanica.

Weiler, M. (Nov. 1981). *Debate Theory: Delusion and Snare?* Paper given at the annual meeting of the Speech Communication Association, Anaheim, CA.

Williams, D. and Cross, F. (1979). "Approaches to Arguing Topicality." In D. Williams and F. Cross, eds., *U.S. Weapons and Assistance: Policies, Perspectives, and Issues*. Lawrence: Jayhawk Debate Research.

Windes, R. R. and Hastings, A. (1965). *Argumentation and Advocacy*. New York: Random House.

18

The Counterwarrant as a Negative Strategy

A Modest Proposal

James W. Paulsen
Jack Rhodes

The focus of any academic debate, in traditional theory, is the resolution. Goodnight, Balthrop, and Parson observe that a "debate team is arguing for only one goal, ultimately, the adoption of the resolution."[1] In this view of debate, then, the ultimate duty of the judge, regardless of feelings toward the specific policy proposal offered by the affirmative, is to cast a ballot on the general resolution. This has ordinarily been a relatively unimportant distinction, since the affirmative plan embodied the proposition and the contentions and advantages constituted full justification for the resolution.

The sweeping, vast nature of recent resolutions, however, has rendered the concept of plan-as-resolution impractical. Few affirmative teams with narrow cases have the audacity to claim their plan as the only and absolute embodiment of the resolution. Rather, topicality is generally defended with a plea to consider the affirmative cases as but one of many reasonable interpretations of the topic. This relationship of plan to resolution is often made explicit by the common practice of introducing the plan as "an example of the resolution" or as "one of many possible interpretations of this year's topic." The affirmative team in the final rounds of the 1973, 1974, 1975 and 1976 NDTs have used similar language.[2] Even operational definitions are generally not meant to equate resolution with plan:

When the affirmative "operationally defines the resolution in the context of the affirmative plan," this does not actually mean that the plan defines the resolution. Rather it means that the plan represents one of the many proposals that are logically consistent with a reasonable interpretation of the resolution.[3]

The relationship of the proposal to resolution has shifted, and the result of this shift is of immense importance. No longer may the plan be viewed, realistically or charitably, as synonymous with the resolution. Rather, the resolution is seen as the general statement the judge is asked to accept on the basis of the affirmative presentation. The case is a sample from which the affirmative team attempts to infer the characteristics of the resolution as a whole. *The entire affirmative presentation, viewed in macrostructure, may be appropriately seen as an inductive generalization.* Just as principles of induction have been used in the critical examination of the internal strength of a piece of evidence, or the adequacy of facts in support of an argumentative subpoint, so an examination of the characteristics and fallacies of inductive reasoning affords insight into possible new responses to a changed situation.

APPLICATION OF INDUCTION
TO NEGATIVE STRATEGY

The chief pitfall to which students of logic are directed when considering the validity of drawing a broad conclusion from specific instances is that of the hasty generalization. Carney and Scheer summarize:

> The fallacy of hasty generalization is committed when, after observing that a small number, or a special sort, of the members of some group have some property, it is concluded that the whole group has the property. To put it in the language of the statistician, the hasty generalization fallacy occurs when:
> 1. One infers from an insufficiently large or quantitatively unrepresentative sample to the whole population. We can call this the fallacy of the small sample.
> 2. One infers from a peculiarly selected or qualitatively unrepresentative sample to a whole population. We can call this the fallacy of biased statistics.[4]

The second type can be dealt with briefly. It seems that virtually every debate team is guilty of the biased statistics fallacy. Salmon elaborates by describing this fallacy as "basing an inductive generalization upon a sample that is known to be unrepresentative or one that there is good reason to believe may be unrepresentative."[5] It would be naive to suggest that affirmative teams search for the most representative example of the resolution obtainable. Rather, they search for the best case area possible, with the sole intention of winning the round—giving an observer every reason to suspect that the advocate has not chosen the most representative instance available as part of an altruistic search for truth. Although this fact does cast doubt upon the intrinsic validity of narrow cases, the simple charge, "They are biased because they are affirmative," would probably not have much persuasive impact on a judge.

The fallacy of the small sample, however, offers greater potential. Bilsky refers to an inductive leap on the basis of too few examples as "a particularly dangerous form of error."[6] Baird is equally critical, and provides a series of tests useful in determining the validity of generalization from specific instances:

> (1) Are the instances examined sufficient in number to warrant the generalization? (2) Are these instances representative or typical? (3) Are negative instances discoverable? (4) Are the instances actually true or what they appear to be? (5) Does the generalization conform to the requirements of the laws of probability and causation?[7]

Substituting "case area" for "instance" and "resolution" for "generalization," it is possible to draw rough analogies between these tests and current negative approaches to narrow cases. The fourth test— "Are the instances actually true or what they appear to be?"—would translate to denial of the example, or direct refutation of the affirmative case. The fifth—"Does the generalization conform to the laws of probability and causation?" (between example and generalization)— would find its parallel in topicality argumentation. (This analogy is perhaps made clearer by an earlier version of this list, in which Baird termed the fifth test: "Is there any causal connection established?"[8]).

The first three tests, however, find no easy analogy in current debate practice. This fact is of interest since, in his early version, Baird specified that the tests were rank-ordered in importance. How could these tests be translated into arguments for debate? To use the analogy of parliamentary or legislative debate, an advocate trying to win support for a vague, broadly-worded resolution through a single, carefully-selected, and limited example probably would not find his opponents willing to agree to limit themselves to only the example he provides. They would instead draw from other examples that deny the validity of the resolution and would perhaps not even address themselves to the specific example provided by the affirmative advocate. Rather than (or in addition to) denying the specific, therefore, they would offer other specifics. Either strategy should lead the uncommitted legislator, observer, or critic to reject the resolution before the house.

To transfer the analogy to a specific debate round, the negative could elect to ignore the affirmative presentation and attempt to delineate other, more significant areas that would deny the resolution. By so doing, the negative would be demonstrating that negative instances of the resolution are discoverable (Baird's third test); and by providing more than the affirmative, the negative would be showing that the affirmative case is an atypical example of the resolution and that therefore the instances examined by the affirmative are certainly not sufficient in number to warrant the generalization (Baird's first and second tests). For convenience in further discussion, we will refer to a presentation of a negative instance, an example against the resolution, as as counterwarrant.

PRACTICAL APPLICATIONS

We propose that to prove a valid counterwarrant on a resolution, the negative would have to meet two logical requirements: (1) that the area of counterwarrant is a legitimate topical area, that is, a plausible example of the resolution; and (2) the action of the nature suggested by the resolution would be—or in the case of a past example, was—disastrous.

As a hypothetical example, on the consumer product safety topic, an affirmative team might interpret the resolution to mean more sanitary bottle-washing practices in the beverage industry. The negative could choose from a myriad of counterwarrants. They might suggest that past and proposed additions to general manufacturer liability for consumer products have resulted in a very dangerous state of affairs for the insurance industry. They could argue that Consumer Product Safety Commission actions have placed manufacturers in grave financial straits. They might suggest that safety requirements are far too stringent for optimum innovation in pharmaceuticals. They could show that decision of the handgun controversy (in which the CPSC has been embroiled) in the direction indicated by the resolution would lead to massive citizen revolt, and so on ad infinitum. Although none of these arguments would deny the desirability of better bottle-washing, all would suggest that *less*, not *more*, action in the consumer product safety area would be desirable, and that the resolution is thus *generally* a bad idea, regardless of the affirmative's one example to the contrary. Alan Nichols (although he clearly did not favor the approach) described an actual example of a counterwarrant on the 1933–34 Pi Kappa Delta question, "RESOLVED: That the powers of the president of the United States should be substantially increased as a settled policy."

> In one debate, the affirmative supported the increase [of power] granted under the NIRA [National Industrial Recovery Act] as a settled policy. The first negative expanded upon the tremendous burden imposed upon

the president by the appointive power, what a major portion of his time was occupied signing commissions, and so forth. It then suggested transferring the appointive power to a commission, and agreed the president should be clothed with the powers suggested by the affirmative. The negative argued that with such an exchange his powers would be decreased, and hence the affirmative had not proved the proposition. By this preposterous construction they successfully nullified the entire debate.[9]

To put theory into practice and offer counterwarrants in a given round of debate would require a substantial deviation from normal division of labor. The first negative constructive speaker would probably begin with an explanation of and justification for the negative strategy and proceed to give one of several counterwarrants. The second negative could continue with the presentation of counterwarrants and would perhaps assume some of the burden of refuting responses that had been made to first negative arguments.

The second affirmative speaker would have several options. He could extend and expand the significance of the initial problem area presented by the affirmative, debate theoretical issues, refute the counterwarrants, or present additional areas of justification for the resolution (in the manner of presenting independent alternative justifications).

It is very important to note that the negative need not confine itself only to presentation of counterwarrants, at the expense of any analysis of the affirmative case area. Adoption of the counterwarrant position, although it resembles the counterplan in that the negative chooses new ground for argument, need not grant the initial case area. The first negative might choose to engage in traditional refutation, leaving his partner to develop the counterwarrant position. The negative would thus be denying the affirmative example and presenting contrary examples. The combination of the two approaches would be not only compatible but complementary. And the counterwarrant can be reconciled with various paradigms of debate judging.

Should a critic view debate as hypothesis-testing, contrary examples presented by the negative would serve useful purposes. First, the negative would be demonstrating data selection bias by the affirmative. Second, by providing more data, the negative would be moving toward a statistically more probable conclusion. Finally (at least under a scientific hypothesis model), the negative would be demonstrating the impossibility of replication.

A judge using the legislative analogy, viewing his role as that of a policymaker, would require some change in orientation. The current vogue is to present plans as bills, complete with legislative history and intent. The judge, through an affirmative vote, is placed in the position of passing the bill. We do not quarrel with the policy-making analogy in judging as an appropriate *response* to the normal situation occurring in a debate. Ordinarily, by gentleman's agreement, debaters ignore the resolution and discuss the specific policy advanced in the round.

There is a vast difference between using the analogy in situations that seem logically to call for its application, however, and using the word "policymaker" as a yardstick to apply to all debate situations. A negative team advancing a counterwarrant is simply abrogating the gentleman's agreement and discussing the resolution itself. Even when an affirmative speaker argues that, since the resolution is worded as a formal legislative resolution, he will treat it as one, a critic cannot deny the negative's right to conform to reality. Regardless of perceived consequences for the quality of argumentation, then, a judge who wishes to remain an objective critic should find it difficult to self-impose the policy-making paradigm.

A judge preferring the legislative analogy still could cast himself in the role of a legislator—considering not a bill, but a resolution. In the context of a policy-maker considering a resolution, there would be nothing inherently objectionable about an advocate choosing to offer alternative examples. In fact, this action would serve to enhance the quality and the reliability of the ultimate decision. One might look to the Gulf of Tonkin Resolution as an example of the dangers of passing a broadly-worded resolution on the basis of a single example.

PRACTICAL OBJECTIONS

Several practical objections to the use of counterwarrants come immediately to mind. First and most obvious is the fact that extensive use of counterwarrants might well legitimize and even mandate virtual no-clash debate. Certainly, with both teams spending their constructive periods presenting examples and counterexamples, direct refutation could quickly become a lost art. In response, it could be argued that direct clash is still occurring, albeit at the level of the resolution rather than at the level of the specific policy proposal. And the counterwarrant option would certainly not prohibit direct refutation of the affirmative case area. In fact, it might work best (and certainly would be less risky) in combination with case refutation.

A second and related disadvantage of this approach would be a general tendency toward superficial analysis. The same shallowness attributed to alternative justification cases might be magnified with counterwarrants. In response, it might be noted that the current breadth of topics already mandates shallow analysis. On balance, though, the counterwarrant might exacerbate an already bad situation.

The final, and perhaps most serious, objection is that allowing the negative this much flexibility in argument skews the odds far too heavily toward the side that happens to be assigned the negative in a given round. The affirmative must still deal with presumption but has lost the traditional offsetting advantage of choosing the ground.

In short, we do not claim that use of counterwarrants would lead to a better or more enjoyable argumentative experience in general, but only that with a broad resolution and a narrow affirmative case, a negative team might win more rounds. Most likely, the evils attributed to narrow affirmative cases would be magnified: Analysis (if any) would be shallow, confusion would dominate and—most importantly—in the hands of a competent negative team presenting its arguments to a receptive critic, the affirmative would assume a virtually insurmountable burden. Even at its worst, though, this scenario should not serve as an argument against acceptance of the counterwarrant by a judge. Subjective ground rules by individual judges that arbitrarily eliminate any theoretically acceptable approach simply because of some potential for "destruction of debate as we know it" are arguably as great a danger to the integrity of debate as the worst possible results of counterwarrant use.

To assume that widespread acceptance of the counterwarrant would reduce teams to prepared negative scripts and a mandated 4–4 record ignores the dynamics of debate, and the certainty that debaters will respond quickly and creatively to any threat to their competitive success on the affirmative side of the resolution. Several options are available.

The counterwarrant would be dangerous only to an affirmative team using broad definitions and a narrow case area. Should the affirmative choose, they could present a stock case. A broad affirmative case would place the negative at a disadvantage in trying to find countervailing examples of resolutional areas, especially examples of similar or greater importance. The affirmative could further limit the scope of possible counterwarrants by choosing a restrictive and explicit set of definitions (in essence, the exact reversal of current definitional trends). In addition to the normal definitional latitude (anything reasonable) allowed an affirmative, restrictive definitions would enjoy a presumption of their own (since "define" implies "to limit"). The negative, ironically enough, would have to argue that the affirmative definitions were too restrictive and that looser definitions would be more reasonable.

It is possible that a resolution may be couched in terms so general that no affirmative team could offer a broad-spectrum defense of the resolution, even with restrictive definitions. Rather than generate an ad hoc debate theory to deal with poor resolutions, the debate community might simply reword and clarify the resolution—making it feasible for the entire resolution to be reasonably debated. Should there be substance to the fear that a narrow resolution would be boring and repetitive, alternatives are available. These would include more than one resolution during a debate year or several specific resolutions on a general topic from which individual tournaments might choose.

Finally, it is possible that a majority of the debate community prefers and sees educational advantages in the current treatment of the resolution, and the most prefer to see it remain in its current function as a statement of reference rather than as the central object of debate. If so, the proposition could be reworded to eliminate resolutional language and retitled "the general subject area for debate."

In short, we do not advocate the counterwarrant as a major advance in argumentation theory, but as a plausible response to an existing situation. Any negative effects of the strategy reflect mainly on current affirmative approaches, since the counterwarrant is reasonable only given an affirmatively-imposed distinction between plan and resolution. Finally, we would hope that use of the argument would at least kindle interest in the nature and purpose of the resolution, and hopefully lead to a mending of the rift between theory and practice that makes the counterwarrant possible.

Notes

1. Tom Goodnight, Bill Balthrop, and Donn W. Parson, "The Problem of Inherency: Strategy and Substance," *Journal of the American Forensic Association* 10 (Spring, 1974): 234.
2. In the 1969–72 NDTs phrases of this type did not appear. Beginning with the 1973 NDT, remarkably similar language was used: 1973— "will support the national debate proposition, examples of which will be found in the following . . . ;" 1974— "as one illustration of the resolution . . . ;" 1975— " . . . the following example of the resolution . . . ;" 1976— ". . . the national debate proposition, examples of which will be found in the following plan;" 1977— " . . .the national debate proposition, several independent examples of which are found in the following policy proposal . . . ;" 1978— "this year's intercollegiate debate resolution, several examples of which . . . ;"
3. Allan Lichtman, Charles Garvin, and Jerry Corsi, "The Alternative Justification Affirmative: A New Case Form," *Journal of the American Forensic Association* 10 (Fall 1973): 63.
4. James D. Carney and Richard K. Scheer, *Fundamentals of Logic* (New York: Macmillian, 1974), 44.
5. Wesley C. Salmon, *Logic* (Englewood Cliffs: Prentice-Hall, 1973), 85.
6. Manuel Bilsky, *Logic and Effective Argument* (New York: Holt, 1956), 96.
7. A. Craig Baird, *Argumentation, Discussion and Debate* (New York: McGraw-Hill, 1950), 117. Baird's listing is by no means exceptional. For similar categories, see Wayne N. Thompson, *Modern Argumentation and Debate* (New York: Harper and Row, 1971), 123–27; and Richard D. Rieke and Malcolm O. Sillars, *Argumentation and the Decision-Making Process* (New York: Wiley, 1975), 103–8, where specifically applied to tests of evidence.

8. A. Craig Baird, *Public Discussion and Debate* (Boston: Ginn, 1928), 187.
9. Alan Nichols, *Discussion and Debate* (New York: Harcourt, Brace, 1941), 254–55.

KEY TERMS

argumentative ground
best definition
counterwarrant
extra-topical
fallacy of biased statistics

fallacy of the small sample
field context
grammatical context
hasty generalization
inductive generalization

nontopical
reasonability
redundancy
resolution
topicality

DISCUSSION

1. How do Parson's standards for reasonability differ from Unger's standards for best definition?
2. Could you run a counterwarrant against a case that was not a hasty generalization? Explain.
3. Using the 1991–92 high school policy debate topic (RESOLVED: That the federal government should significantly increase social services to homeless individuals in the United States) as an example, would a plan that gives free needles to reduce the spread of AIDS from illegal IV drug use be topical? Justify your answer.
4. Hasty generalizations and counterwarrant theory seem to have found more of a home in questions of nonpolicy than in discussions of policy. What do you think some of the reasons are behind this?
5. Rohrer and others advocate an any-reasonable-definition position while Unger defends a best definition stance. Some debaters argue a better definition position. What would such a position be? How would it differ from other stances? Is there any theoretical justification for such a position?
6. Develop some standards for determining reasonability. What are they? Are they linear or threshold issues?
7. What are the tests for establishing a hasty generalization?

Part Four

Decision Rules

Part Four concerns decision rules. The debate format requires that a third party, be it a critic or a judge, make a yes/no decision at the cessation of advocacy. The three articles in this section describe some decision rules relevant to this process.

Lichtman and Rohrer, in the oldest essay included in this book, differentiate presumption as a decision rule from presumption as an issue in the burden of proof. They advance a risk-based theory of presumption. Hart's original essay critiques the literature of presumption from this perspective. He extends the risk-based concept of presumption to a nonstatic, weighable factor that can change from round to round depending on the amount of risk.

The nature of the nonpolicy resolution has definite and clear implications for the concept of presumption, since policy advocacy always supports a policy change but nonpolicy argumentation does not have this feature as the starting point for assessing presumption. Nonpolicy debate theorists are still searching for a guiding paradigm to govern affirmative and negative responsibilities and stock issues. No matter what paradigm has been proposed for nonpolicy case construction and debate judging to date, Thomas's article analyzes the nature and role of presumption as an issue divorced from the assumptions and constraints of policy theory. In the process, he argues for a new conception of presumption as a natural predisposition of the judge (or audience) towards the resolution for debate, rather than an artificial presumption always residing against the resolution for the purpose of dividing the stock issues and speaker duties between the affirmative and negative side.

19

Decision Rules in Policy Debate

Presumption and Burden of Proof

Allan J. Lichtman
Daniel M. Rohrer

Argumentation theorists long have labored to develop standards governing the conduct of a debate and the assessment of evidence and arguments. Together these guidelines can provide a means for appraising the merits of competing policy proposals. Yet they cannot in themselves warrant a judge's decision. When all the facts are in, the judge still must look for decision rules to tell him which policy system to select. For example, how is he to decide between two systems that prove equally advantageous? Should he always choose the better system no matter how tiny its advantages may be? Or should he consistently favor one type of system, requiring alternatives to be significantly better? Some rule must be imposed to guide this final decision.

Despite their paramount importance, decision rules never have been subject to careful scrutiny by students of argumentation. In fact, the term "decision rule" is not likely to be found in any standard argumentation text. Argumentation theorists have never directly addressed the problem of deciding between policy systems whose merits have already been established. They have only obliquely considered the problem in the context of discussions concerning the concepts of presumption and burden of proof. Traditional understanding of these concepts can be translated into a partial decision rule stating that the present system should be retained unless the superiority of a proposed change is clearly demonstrated. Usually this rule is stated in terms of a presumption against change and a burden of proof imposed on the advocate of change.

This article will suggest that traditional interpretations of presumption and burden of proof do not constitute adequate decision rules. Rather they incorporate serious conceptual and presentational errors that are the source of confusion and misjudgment. In some contexts traditional theory provides no guidance whatever; in other contexts its message is ambiguous or misleading.

The inadequacies of previous work do not stem from minor analytic mistakes. They reflect a fundamental failure to understand the process of evaluating the results of argumentation. Traditional approaches to decision rules through the vehicles of presumption and burden of proof are piecemeal, haphazard, and largely unconscious. This article will criticize existing theories of presumption and burden of proof.

This work will also provide a more direct approach to the shaping of decision rules. It will offer a new conceptual framework for decision rules that addresses such questions as the nature of decision rules, their specific constituents, and the means of evaluating alternative rules.

After establishing this framework, we will attempt to formulate complete and coherent decision rules for the selection of policy. The basis of these rules must be logically sound; they must apply to all types of arguments; and their application must promote the goal of selecting the best policy from among the alternatives.

THE NATURE OF DECISION RULES

Before grappling with traditional theories regarding presumption and burden of proof, it is essential to establish a framework for understanding decision rules. It would not be very fruitful to criticize existing theory from traditional perspectives. Rather its deficiencies can be revealed clearly only after decision rules themselves have been defined and analyzed.

A decision rule tells a judge which policy system to select after an argument has been completed. It operates only after the issues have been evaluated and the merits of each system have been determined. Decision rules are necessary only because the judge is required at the end of a debate to make a yes-no choice between alternative policies. If such a choice were not necessary, he could simply report his evaluation of the competing systems and would not require any rule for deciding between them. But in contexts where a yes-no decision is mandatory, decision rules are inevitable. No matter how the judge chooses to treat alternative policy systems, he is implicitly or explicitly applying some type of decision rule.

Decision rules do more than tell the judge which policy system to select at the end of an argument. They also inform the advocates of their responsibilities. Thus, it is critical that prior to the argument the participants clearly comprehend the decision rule their judge will employ. Without such knowledge neither side would know what conditions it must fulfill in order to win the debate.

To fully guide the choice between competing policies a decision rule must answer three questions:

1. Should a prejudgment be made in favor of the position taken by either side?
2. If so, which side should be favored?
3. How significant an advantage should be necessary to overcome an unfavorable prejudgment or to guarantee victory when neither side is granted a prejudgment in its favor?

The traditional presumption in favor of the status quo answers questions 1 and 2 only for arguments in which an advocate undertakes to defend the present system, and never answers 3 at all. It is thus a fragment of a complete decision rule.

Question 1 determines the most basic characteristic of a decision rule. Its answer decides whether or not either side will be favored in the debate. One important fact should be observed in deciding the issue of preference. A decision rule will exist even when neither side is specially favored. The decision to grant neither side a prejudgment in its favor answers both questions 1 and 2 and thus establishes a partial decision rule; each advocate must satisfy the same requirements to win the debate. The specification of those requirements and the completion of the decision rule, however, require an answer to question 3. One could conclude, for example, that any advantage no matter how slight, is reason to adopt or retain a policy system and that, in the event of a tie, selection should be made on a random basis. Alternatively one could decide that a system should be automatically adopted or retained only if it is sufficiently superior to a competing system to satisfy a particular significance standard. If neither system meets this standard, the decision is made on a random basis.

This second guideline establishes a middle band of inconclusive arguments that must be resolved on a random basis, for example, by flipping a coin. The width of this band depends upon the magnitude of the significance standard. For instance, if an advantage of ten significant units is necessary to adopt or retain policy automatically, the decision rule would read: Use random selection unless either alternative is proved superior by ten units or more. When there is no significance standard, only absolute ties need to be resolved randomly.

If questions 1 and 2 are answered by a prejudgment in favor of either advocate, the weight of that presumption still must be determined before a complete decision rule is formulated. If, for example, the answer to question 2 is that System A should enjoy a prejudgment with respect to System B and the answer to question 3 is that any net advantage that can be demonstrated for System B is sufficient to overcome that prejudgment, the resulting decision rule would read: Select System A unless System B is proven superior to any extent.

If on the other hand, a presumption is granted System A that can be overcome only by an advantage of ten or more significance units, the resulting decision rule would read: Select System A unless System B is proved superior by ten units or more.

Decision rules should be available to guide a judge in every type of argument. This means that clear and consistent rationales must be developed to direct the application of decision rules in different situations. For example, a rule that incorporates a prejudgment of a given weight to the present system is useless alone in the many cases where neither side defends the status quo. Alternately, separate rationales can be developed for different situations. The only requirement is that they be all inclusive.

But the logical coherence of a decision rule is only one of two essential considerations. Once coherent decision rules have been established, they must be evaluated in light of their practical effects on decision making. If a rule results in the selection of inferior policies, or if it has very harmful side effects, it should be rejected. Serious practical disadvantages of this kind can and should warrant the rejection of a decision rule regardless of its logical consistency. Since a decision rule is a general guideline to govern a wide range of situations, it must prove to be useful in selecting the best policy system. Thus, the second essential test of a decision rule must ask: What would be the result if this rule were applied by all decision makers on a regular basis?

It is easy to imagine decision rules that would be rejected on the basis of this second test. For example, consider a decision rule that granted a massive presumption to the decision maker's own self-interest. The rationale would be that each person should advance one's own self-interest at the expense of all others. The decision rules always would give primary consideration to advantages and disadvantages affecting the decision maker, and grant little weight to those that effect the rest of the world. This rule could be applied in a perfectly rational manner and, if applied by only one person, it would always bring to him or her the best results. But if that decision rule were adopted by all persons, the results would be catastrophic. If each person acted only in his or her own short-term self-interest, cooperative human society soon would deteriorate into chaos. Such a disadvantageous decision rule should be rejected.

TRADITIONAL CONCEPTIONS OF PRESUMPTION AND BURDEN OF PROOF

Before developing the concept of decision rules, it will be important to evaluate the traditional theory from which these decision rules evolve and depart because the explications of presumption and burden of proof offered by traditional theorists cannot be translated into complete and coherent decision rules. Rather than offer a summary of traditional theory, which would inevitably fail to do it justice, we will focus on the presentation of presumption and burden of proof by Glen E. Mills in *Reason and Controversy*:

> As a modern rhetorical convention, which is our main concern here, presumption means "a preoccupation of the ground," as Whately so aptly put it. But a presumption in favor of what exists or is believed to be does not imply that the status quo is true or good or desirable. It does imply that the existing situation must stand until sufficient proof is offered to rebut that presumption. . . .
>
> Burden of proof means the risk of the proposition, and it entails on the part of the affirmative the duty to affirm the issues. This is another way of saying that the affirmative has the responsibility to submit a prima facie case. Failure to affirm one contested issue usually means defeat for the prosecution or the plaintiff, especially in a trial before the judge or judges. . . .[1]

This explanation is worthwhile for it tells us what a presumption does. It upholds the present system until a sufficient burden of proof has been met. But Mills's standard statement of traditional theory neither constitutes a complete decision rule nor provides any guidance in a wide variety of contexts.

First, the presumption against change answers questions 1 and 2, but not question 3 in our model of decision rules. It is thus only a fragment of a complete decision rule. Traditional theory does not indicate the extent of the burden established by the presumption against change. Is it so light as to be decisive only in a perfect tie? Or does it demand that a new system achieve a particular degree of superiority over the existing order? If so, how much superiority is required? Is the burden the same in all cases, or does it vary according to circumstances? If so, what are the factors that influence its weight?

Second, the presumption against change is too limited to provide either rules or rationales to guide the selection of poliy when the present system is undefined, inconsistent, or nonexistent. These represent three common situations in which the usual presumption in favor of the present system offers the judge no guidance at all. Consider each of the three situations:

1. No one defends the existing order, and the judge must choose from a selection of new policies. In response to the problem of poverty, for example, an advocate proposes that the federal government adopt a guaranteed annual income for all Americans. Rather than defending existing programs, the opponent offers a program of public work for all of the employable poor combined with in-kind assistance for those who cannot work. In this situation neither program "preoccupies the ground of the present system," and traditional theory offers no means of providing presumption or establishing burden of proof.[2]

2. The advocates are asking the judge to decide between two preexisting programs, one of which must be eliminated. For example, the government is faced with an inflationary economy and finds it necessary to substantially cut federal spending. The decision narrows to a choice between the elimination of an ongoing weapons procurement program or the elimination of the federal food stamp program. Both programs are part of the status quo, and according to traditional theory, both should be granted a prejudgment in their favor. Thus, when the classic trade-off between guns and butter involves the evaluation of existing programs, traditional theory is silent. It provides no means of determining which of two competing status quo programs merits a favorable presumption.

3. A new problem develops and the judge must choose an initial policy in order to deal with it. Consider a few well-known examples in which policymakers had to confront a policy vacuum, where no prior policies preoccupied the ground. The discovery and harnessing of atomic power, for instance, confronted policymakers with a whole new field demanding effective and carefully formulated control, but one in which old systems simply did not exist. The problem was clear and unavoidable. Policies had to be created on short notice and competing alternatives had to be appraised on an equal basis. In the 1960s the advent of the space age confronted policymakers with the task of devising systems of control in an area where policy existed quite literally in a vacuum—outer space. Hedley Bull of the Institute for Strategic Studies observed in 1961:

Nothing should be said on this subject except with the utmost skepticism. The first missile powers contemplate space with the perspective of the first oceanic naval powers, when they contemplated the globe. Their existing legal and political conceptions do not cover it, and their experience provides them only with the analogies. They can have little notion of the problems to which it will give rise, or of the political, strategic, and economic importance it will have for them. It is not even clear what it is, or what the human activities are that will be specially connected with it.[3]

The field of foreign policy also has offered some serious challenges that could not be resolved by falling back on a predetermined course of action when none of the available solutions was obviously the best. The Cuban missile crisis is perhaps the best example of a situation demanding a choice from among a wide variety of possible solutions. What position could possibly have preoccupied the ground in the debate over an appropriate response to the Soviet installation of offensive missiles in Cuba?

In these situations traditional theory provides no guidance for deciding which, if any, of the competing proposals should be granted a favorable presumption. For there is no existing policy that must stand until sufficient contrary proof is offered.

In each of these instances the standard formulation of presumption offers no basis for a decision rule in favor of either side. In example 1, both sides forfeit any claim to the present system's presumption. In 2, each side has an equal claim upon it. And in 3 there is no present system upon which to base a presumption.

The limited applicability of the prevailing view of presumption makes it incomplete as a basis for decision-making in the modern world. The rapid pace of technological change constantly generates new problems requiring original solutions. This proliferation of problems often requires the consideration of policies that advance one goal at the expense of another. Thus, an ever increasing portion of the policy-maker's vital choices do not conform to the traditional present system versus change format.

Not only do traditional conceptions of presumption and burden of proof fail to provide complete and coherent decision rules, they also generate serious confusion, which undermines the ability of policy-makers to identify superior policy systems. A primary purpose of this article is to replace traditional theory with an explanation of final decision making that provides a basis for the formulation of sound decision rules.

PRESUMPTION DISTINGUISHED FROM DECISION RULES

Although in traditional argumentation theory the term *presumption* refers to a prejudgment in favor of the present system, it more generally refers to any type of prejudgment. When applied to decision rules, presumption can identify the policy system or class of systems that is granted a prejudgment in its favor. If the standard necessary to overcome this presumption also is specified, a complete decision rule is found. In itself, however, the assignment of presumption does not constitute the entirety of a decision rule. We also have seen that perfectly coherent decision rules can be found without presumption.

The failure to recognize the proper relationship between presumptions and decision rules has had grave implications for traditional theory. Instead of recognizing the role played by presumption in the shaping of decision rules, traditional theorists have blurred together under the rubric of "presumption" two distinct concepts that apply in different situations. As a consequence of this confusion, traditional theory has insisted upon a very narrow view of the correct assignment of presumption in a decision-making context. Let us first consider the two situations to which the concept has been applied.

In the first case a present policy exists and no argument is advanced to suggest that it should be replaced. In this situation traditional theory says that the system stands because there is a presumption that it should be so " . . . until sufficient proof is offered to rebut that presumption."[4]

The second situation occurs when there is an argument. Then the presumption generally dictates a decision rule that favors the present system, upholding it if argumentation fails to uncover an alternative that is sufficiently superior.

In both cases the present system is retained, and argumentation texts say that in each case the reason is the presumption. The obvious conclusion is that the same decision rule governs both cases. In fact, that is thoroughly untrue and misleading.

In the first case, when no argument takes place, the present system still stands, but it does not do so because of a logical presumption that it should. It stands because it is there, and no attempt is made to change it. In this situation the maintenance of the status quo is a fact that would exist even without the concept of presumption. No decision rule is necessary to support it because no decision takes place. The present system prevails because there is no alternative to it.

The second situation is vastly different. In that case, alternatives are advanced, and thorough argumentation takes place. Unlike the first situation, this does require that a decision be made. A presumption in this situation does fulfill a function. It sustains the present system when the advantages of a new system fail to achieve a required level of significance. It is only in this second case that a decision rule can operate.

The following example may help illustrate this distinction. A presumption that the accused is innocent unless proven guilty beyond reasonable doubt governs criminal trials. But it is false to claim that is the reason most people walk about freely. The fact that people are free is analogous to the first situation described. Their present freedom continues, not because of a decision rule at trial, but because they are never brought to trial. No argument occurs and no decision is necessary. Their freedom continues because it is unchallenged. On the other hand, some persons are brought to trial for crimes. Their cases are analogous to the second situation. An argument occurs, requiring a decision, and, therefore, a decision rule to govern it. The presumption of innocence (with included significance standard) is the decision rule, and it does serve a function, freeing defendants when the evidence of guilt in insufficient. People released at trial retain their freedom precisely because of this presumption.

In the first case, where there is no argument, no decision is necessary. No presumption is necessary to sustain that situation. Yet argumentation texts invariably attribute this maintenance of the present system to the presumption. And worse yet, they compound this error by using the survival of unopposed systems as a basis for imposing a decision rule that favors those systems when they are opposed. Consider the analysis offered by Douglas Ehninger and Wayne Brockriede in *Decision by Debate*, a textbook that is justly acclaimed as an outstanding synthesis of argumentation theory: "Natural presumption reflects things as they are viewed in the world about us. If an argument involves a belief concerning existing institutions, practices, customs, mores, values, or interpretations, the presumption is automatically in favor of that belief simply because the institutions, etc., are thought to exist."[5]

Equally misleading is a variant of traditional theory on presumption and burden of proof outlined by Gary Cronkhite in 1966.[6] Cronkhite argues that presumption does not inhere in the status quo, but is automatically assigned the opponent of anyone advancing a proposition for debate: "The assumption of the burden of proof is inherent in the statement of a proposition. . . . The presumption is unavoidably forfeited by one who states a proposition to the occupant of any other position."[7] Like the advocates of a presumption in favor of the present system, Cronkhite argues that presumption against the initiator of argument "is not artificially assigned," but is the inevitable consequence of the process of argumentation. He claims that if one "does not support his thesis, it will go unsupported. If it is unsupported, the occupant of any other position is hardly obligated to respond with refutation."[8]

Once again, this argument establishes a spurious relationship between the results of nonargument and the specification of decision rules to govern the choice between policy alternatives after debate has occurred.

Moreover, Cronkhite's arguments suffer from an additional deficiency. They misinterpret the results of nonargument when questions of policy choice are at issue. Cronkhite's claim that the opposition need not respond to an unsupported proposition clearly is not universally applicable to policy debate, where the choice is between alternative courses of action. For nonargument may result in the de facto affirmation of the policy proposal advanced by the initiator of discussion. Assume, for example, that one asserts a proposition opposing the repeal of existing legislation outlawing the sale of heroin. In Cronkhite's view an opponent of this position need not respond unless the position is defended: "The other is within his rights to ask, 'Why?', and the . . . party is obligated to respond or fail to prove his case, whereas the [opponent] . . . need do nothing until that obligation is fulfilled."[9] On the contrary, in this instance, the results of nonargument will favor the individual who stated the proposition since the status quo is likely to be maintained.

Even the most modern and thorough attempt to reformulate the concept of presumption fails to make this distinction between the continuation of unopposed policy systems and the use of decision rules to evaluate the final result of an argument. David Zarefsky, of Northwestern University, in a paper presented to the Central States Speech Convention, April 7, 1972, adopts the view advanced by Richard Whately in 1852. It is that the presumption assigns "what in Whately's view is one of the strongest possible arguments—the claim that 'I needn't defend my position until it is attacked.'"[10] This statement, however, is true without the aid of a presumption. No position needs defending "until it is attacked." It is a fact, a law of nature, and not a rule of argument. The present situation is there and will remain if no attempt is made to change it. In accepting this view both Zarefsky and Whately assume the existence of a debate and a judge where neither exists. This confuses the nature and function of a presumption by attributing false qualities to the concept.

This failure to distinguish between a decision rule where there is an argument and the factual result of nonargument, encourages the false belief that the presumption must always favor the present system.

This is a false conclusion because the presumption involved is not the same in each case. Once the distinction between the two situations is made, it becomes clear that a presumption can be granted to new systems. The result in the first case would remain the same. The old system would prevail when no argument was initiated. But when argument occurred, the decision rules could impose a presumption for change rather than against it. The advocate of change could be awarded the decision when ties occur. The key is to realize that these are two different situations, and that the decision rules that govern an argument need not impose the same results that follow nonargument.

The first distinction should now be clear; a presumption is merely one portion of one form of decision rule. Decision rules can exist without presumptions; and the assignment of presumption does not constitute the entirety of decision rules.

BURDEN OF PROOF DISTINGUISHED FROM DECISION RULES

The burden of proof is a concept that can be applied to many situations in which no decision rule operates. Traditionally the phrase "burden of proof" has been used to describe the duty imposed by a decision rule that grants a presumption. In this case it refers to the obligation of showing that a new system is sufficiently superior to warrant a change. But the phrase is also used in a broader sense. "Burden of proof" often is used to describe any obligation to offer evidence and reasoning in support of an argument. Thus the traditional rule that "he who asserts must prove" usually is described as a "burden of proof." The burden in this case does not govern the final balancing of systems, rather it determines the outcome of specific issues within the debate. The burden of proof, therefore, results from the distinct rules of argumentation, one a decision rule, the other a rule governing the evaluation of evidence within.

This distinction has been blurred by the common but misleading practice of using the terms "presumption" and "burden of proof" as if they were interchangeable. It is confusing enough that both the decision rule and the evidence rule mentioned above impose a burden of proof. But the confusion is compounded by the practice of attributing the existence of both rules to the presumption.

This practice has two harmful effects. First, it implies that the two rules are based on the same rationale. They clearly are not. A burden of proof can be imposed by either of two separate and distinct rules: one a decision rule governing the final balancing of competing policies, the other a rule of evidence governing the individual arguments offered within a debate. Second, it creates the false impression that anything that imposes a burden of proof is a presumption and therefore a decision rule. As the the above explanation of the two rules clearly indicates, that is not true either. Yet this confusion has generated a common practice of invoking a presumption in favor of one side or the other on numerous individual issues during the debate.

For example, a presumption is granted against the advocate of change with respect to the specific advantages being claimed for new policy proposals. On the other hand, the advocate of change generally is granted a favorable presumption with regard to disadvantages to new policy proposed by the proponent of the status quo.

At this point it is important to distinguish between decision rules relating to policy and decision rules relating to fact. The questions of policy that are the concern of this work are resolved by a comparision of the benefits of alternative systems. Decision theorists long ago established that the benefits of any policy are a function of both the probability, or the likelihood, that the policy system will achieve certain results and the value of those results. Decision rules convert a particular difference in expected benefits into a yes-no decision in favor of one of the alternatives, Questions of fact are resolved solely by an evaluation of the probable truth of the factual hypothesis that is being considered. Decision rules would be used to convert a particular level of probability into a yes-no decision that the hypothesis is either true or false. For example, civil courts generally will uphold the plaintiff's claim if the probable truth of that claim is greater than 50 percent. Criminal courts, on the other hand, require the state to demonstrate close to a 100 percent probability of guilt before they will render a judgment against the accused.

The application of decision rules to both questions of policy and questions of fact involves a considerable loss of information. For questions of policy, judges covert a statement that System A is X significance units better than System B into a statement that System A should be adopted or retained. For questions of fact they convert a statement that hypothesis A is X percent likely to be true into a statement that hypothesis A is true or false. This loss of information is necessary when a judge must resolve a dispute by making a decision in favor of a particular advocate. It is both unnecessary and drastically misleading to sustain such a loss of information on any of the individual issues that comprise the debate. The evaluation of the advantages of competing policy systems involves the integration of probability and value. If all probabilities are transformed by a decision rule into either one or zero, then wildly inaccurate results can occur.

Assume, for example, that the advocate of change proves that his proposal has a 40 percent chance of saving $100 billion more than the status quo. Thus, the advantage of his policy system over the status quo is 0.4 times the value of saving that amount of money. If, on the other hand, the present system is awarded a presumption of fact on this issue, the 40 percent probability will be converted to 0 percent probability, with the result that the net advantage of the new policy likewise will be zero. Judges who would apply such a presumption would not justify their decision in this way. Rather they would say that the affirmative has failed to prove the advantages of his proposal.

Second, consider that the advocate of change proves a 100 percent probability of saving $100 billion more than the existing order if his policy system is adopted, while the opposition demonstrates a 51 percent probability that, with minor modifications, the present system can achieve this same savings. Clearly, the new system is significantly superior to the modified present system; it has a much greater likelihood of achieving the same desirable result. Yet, if a presumption is granted the negative on the question of the capacities of its minor repairs, the 51 percent probability will be converted to 100 percent probability and the two systems will be considered equal for the purposes of the debate. Again, the judge would not offer these calculations as the basis for his judgment. Rather, he would say that the affirmative has lost the issue of inherency. Mills, for example, in pursuing his hazy analogy between debate and law, indicates that: "Burden of proof means the risk of the proposition, and it entails on the part of the affirmative the duty to affirm the issues. This is another way of saying that the affirmative has the responsibility to submit a prima facie case. Failure to affirm one contested issue usually means defeat for the prosecution or the plaintiff, especially in a trial before a judge or judges."[11]

The foregoing analysis makes clear that advocates do not win or lose the individual issues of fact that arise in the argument. Rather, particular levels of probability are established, which, in combination with assessments of value, yield expected levels of benefits for the policy systems being considered. To convert these probabilities into yes-no decisions would significantly bias these expected benefits and yield incorrect decisions in many instances.

The confused state of current theory also has led judges to grant presumptions to the value judgments of the present system. Recall Ehninger and Brockriede's statement that: "If an argument involves a belief concerning existing institutions, practices, customs, mores, values, or interpretations, the presumption is automatically in favor of that belief. . . ."[12] Glen Mills, in *Reason in Controversy*, corroborates that viewpoint: "Presumption [is] the initial advantage enjoyed by the side that defends existing institutions, prevailing values, or the innocence of the accused."[13]

Yet, the values of a policy system are not susceptible to yes-no decisions to accept or reject them. Rather, the only relevant question is: What is the importance of a given value in relation to other values of the system? Policies can be accepted or rejected, facts can be declared true or false, but values cannot be evaluated on such an either-or basis. A single value obviously cannot be declared true or false like a single allegation of fact. Two values could conceivably be compared as are two policy systems, but except in contrived situations one would not require a decision rule that tells when to accept one and reject the other. Values do not compete with each other in the same fashion as policy systems. Rather the decision maker simply needs to know their importance so that when values are combined with probabilities, accurate judgments of the benefits of competing systems are derived. Certainly, when yes-no decisions are applied to the disputes over value that occur in the course of policy debates, gross inaccuracies will result.

For example, the following argument is entirely plausible under current theory. In advocating a program of public work for the unemployed, an affirmative team claims that "it is a presumption of the present system that we must achieve full employment." But the presumption for full employment is merely a statement of fact and not a decision rule. That presumption merely states the fact that present decision makers generally believe that full employment is a desirable goal. Once actual argument is launched, this presumption carries no argumentative weight. The affirmative team must support its claim regarding the value of full employment with substantive arguments and evidence.

If argumentation over the value of achieving full employment proves equally balanced, with the advantages of full employment exactly offset by its detriments, the presumption of the present system should not operate as a decision rule to break the tie in favor of the affirmative. The equal balance of the evidence shows that full employment is not a worthwhile goal, yet the application of presumption as a decision rule would reverse this evaluation. As a result, the judge may incorrectly choose a policy that promotes full employment but contradicts another goal that is proven equally important by substantive argument.

DECISION RULES AS VALUE JUDGMENTS

In their backdoor approach to decision rules via the concepts of presumption and burden of proof, traditional theorists also distort seriously the evaluative character of such rules. A decision rule is a human convention that imposes a prejudgment about how a decision should be made. Because of the great influence of decision rules on the process of policy selection, the practical effects of a rule should be weighed in determining its desirability. Thus, the process of selecting a decision rule necessitates value judgments prior to the debate. The judge must decide, for instance, whether to favor the present system or new systems, or perhaps show no preference at all. The judge's decision must be based on an analysis of the values that would be served by each choice available. For that reason, any presumption is a prejudgment. The traditional presumption for the present system represents a value judgment that old systems should be preferred to equally good, but new, alternatives. A presumption for change would represent an opposite value judgment. Even a decision rule that granted no preference at all would promote certain values.

The evaluative character of decision rules is blurred in traditional presentation of presumption and burden of proof. Consider, for example, the analysis of Douglas Ehninger and Wayne Brockriede in *Decision by Debate*:

> The technical term for the preoccupation of a piece of argumentative ground is presumption. The party who at the beginning of the debate stands upon the disputed ground . . . is, therefore, said to have the presumption. . . .
>
> Natural presumption reflects things as they are viewed in the world about us. If an argument involves a belief concerning existing institutions, practices, customs, mores, values, or interpretations, the presumption is automatically in favor of that belief simply because the institutions are thought to exist.
>
> Artificial presumption, on the other hand, is the result of ground arbitrarily assigned, a preoccupation by agreement rather than by the present order of things. . . .
>
> The point to bear in mind, however, is that neither natural nor artificial presumption evaluates. The former does not say that a belief about existing institutions, practices, customs, mores, values, or interpretations is intrinsically good or even better than anything that might be substituted for it. Presumption merely recognizes that the belief now stands on the ground that any alternative belief would have to occupy. Nor does the artificial presumption of innocence mean that an accused man is more apt to be innocent than guilty, or that the judge thinks him innocent, or that most men brought to trial are not guilty. Here the presumption is only a man-made convention, invoked so that an order may be established and debate proceed. The accused must be placed on some piece of ground to begin with; and American legal tradition assumes that the interests of justice and expediency will best be served if he is assigned the ground of "innocence."[14]

The major thrust of this passage is the claim that presumption merely describes and does not evaluate. This claim cannot be sustained after careful analysis. The problem stems primarily from the failure to make the distinction between presumption as a decision rule and as a description of the results of nonargument. But this text does come closer to that distinction than others. The concept of natural presumption as a descriptive one is very close to the concept that the present system stands if unattacked. Artificial presumption, on the other hand, is a human convention that is essentially the decision rule operating whenever debate occurs. The flaw in this presentation is that these two concepts both still are treated as presumptions, and, therefore, as decision rules.

Whenever presumption functions as the basis of decision rules, it necessarily reflects value judgments. Ehninger and Brockriede's effort to deny this point is betrayed by the very example they use. They write of the artificial presumption of innocence in a criminal trial as a nonevaluative convention. Yet five lines later they note that this presumption reflects the American legal system's value judgments that will best serve the interests of justice and expediency.[15] The presumption of innocence represents an evaluation which finds that an individual accused of crime is entitled to the same freedom and respect due an innocent member of the community. This presumption does not evaluate the guilt or innocence of the accused, but it does reflect a value judgment about the way an accused person should be treated.

Even the so-called "natural presumption" must reflect values whenever it is used as the basis of a decision rule. No law of nature forces argumentation theorists to impose a decision rule favoring an idea or institution simply because it exists. Any such rule is a man-made convention reflecting the explicit value judgment that change must be justified by a sufficient advantage. This appraisal may be based upon tradition, upon fear of the consequences of change, or upon a belief in the wisdom of the present system. But it involves a conscious act of the human will based upon evaluation. It is not a humble submission to natural law.

Thus decision rules are chosen on the basis of their practical effects and the values that those effects serve. Yet, because of the confusion between the results of nonargument and the rationale for decision rules, traditional theorists generally have failed to analyze decision rules on this basis.

Rules that govern the final selection of policy systems should not be viewed through the perspective of traditional theory on presumption and burden of proof. These theories not only ignore important issues that are involved in the shaping of decision rules, they also create considerable confusion and in a variety of ways distort the process of decision making.

To correct these deficiencies we have adopted a direct approach to the shaping of decision rules. We have constructed a general model of decision rules that clearly indicates their nature and content and establishes standards for evaluating alternative rules. The elaboration of a model for decision rules is a prerequisite to the formulation of specific rules which will best govern the process of policy selection. This additional task now merits our attention.

BEYOND PRESUMPTION AND BURDEN OF PROOF

New Rules for Policy Decisions

The judge or critic of an argument concerning questions of policy can play one of two very different roles. First, the judge can serve merely as an evaluator, providing assessments of the merits of alternative policy systems. Second, the judge can serve as an actual decision maker, deciding which policies are to be adopted or retained. In this second role, the judge requires some type of decision rule to guide policy choices.

Recall that to guide fully the choices between competing policies, a decision rule must answer three questions:

1. Should a prejudgment (presumption) be made in favor of the position taken by either side?
2. If so, which side should be favored?
3. How significant an advantage should be necessary to overcome an unfavorable prejudgment or to guarantee victory when neither side is granted a prejudgment in its favor?

Types of Decision Rules

In order to find appropriate rules, we must examine various types of decision rules and select one based on its logical and practical merits. This examination will discuss decision rules based upon: judge discretion; random tie breaking; and presumption against change. Following this discussion, we shall examine how to apply a decision rule to a debate.

Judge discretion

This category is actually the absence of any decision rule. It leaves the final choice to the discretion of the judge on a case-by-case basis with no particular guidelines to follow. This discretionary power can involve either total control or limited control.

Total Discretion. Total discretion grants the judge not only the power to decide when and to whom to grant a presumption, but also the significance standard the other side must meet to overcome that presumption. This total control is a poor type of decision rule for two reasons. First, since each of these decisions is made by the judge on an arbitrary case-by-case basis, no debaters would ever know their responsibilities during the debate. The advocates would be at a loss to know what they had to do. Second, it would destroy the fundamental purpose of the debate. The judge could always select policies on the basis of personal preference. In short, the outcome of the debate would have little to do with the arguments or evidence presented, and the debate process generally would not lead to the selection of the best available policy system.

Limited Discretion. The power of the judge to select a system arbitrarily could be limited only to debates where the merits of competing systems are equally balanced. The judge would be subject to a rule calling for the adoption of any superior system. The judge's discretion would include only the ability to choose the means of breaking a tie, and would not extend to control over the standard of significance necessary to overcome a presumption. This would mean that the judge could choose between tied systems on any basis ranging from dice rolling to personal preference.

This decision rule also has significant disadvantages. First, granting the judge power to resolve ties would provide an incentive to declare all close debates a tie and decide the argument on the basis of personal preference or self-interest. Second, this rule leaves the advocates uncertain of their responsibility since they have no way of knowing in advance what criteria will be employed to resolve tied debates. Third, the arbitrary resolution of ties could erode confidence in the decision-making process, particularly if judges used their discretionary powers to promote their own interests.

Random tie breaking
This type of decision rule says the judge should always adopt the superior policy no matter how small its advantage may be, and that when a tie occurs some form of random selection (that is, coin flipping) should be used to choose a policy.

This completes our analysis of a decision rule that enforces no presumption and breaks ties at random. In the course of that analysis, we have found no logical flaws in the formulation or application of this rule. But we have found two potentially serious disadvantages that would result if this rule were universally adopted by decision makers. In short, we have found that random tie breaking is bad. There should be a presumption. Perhaps more importantly, we have found that presumption should impose a decision rule against change rather than for it, in order to maintain a high quality of argumentation.

The preceding analysis, however, need not establish the sole basis for the shaping of decision rules in argumentation. Perhaps additional rationales could be found to guide us further in formulating meaningful rules for various situations. To this end, let us examine reasons that have been offered to support the traditional presumption against change.

Presumption against change

Argumentation texts and debate tradition have developed a number of possible rationales on which to base a decision rule that operates to favor the present system and thus to oppose change. Let us now turn to an examination and critique of these rationales in the hope that one will prove adequate and give us an additional basis for applying the necessary decision rule against change. Perhaps this rationale will apply as well when neither advocate defends the present system, or when both advocates defend different aspects of the status quo.

Tradition. As a basis for a decision rule against change, a presumption traditionally has been granted to existing institutions. However, tradition is an essentially meaningless reason for the choice. It provides no sensible rationale to determine who should get the presumption in cases where two competing proposals both differ from the present system, and offers no basis for determining responsibilities in a variety of cases. It blindly asserts that there should be a presumption and goes no further.

Precedent. It can be argued that existing policies should be preferred to new ones because they were evaluated at the time of their adoption and found desirable. Essentially, the rationale is that we should respect the opinions of our predecessors. This argument suffers at least two severe shortcomings. First, it relies on the tenuous assumption that past decisions were made on a purely rational basis. In fact, many existing systems in government and society at large did not represent the best solutions, even at the time of their adoption. Often they were sloppy political compromises arrived at by competing groups and did not achieve all they could for any group. In some cases, only a narrow special interest group influenced the decision, and the resulting system is far from the best in the public's viewpoint. But, regardless of the specific circumstances of adoption, there is no assurance that past decisions will reflect the wisest available solution to a problem.

Changeover. It can be argued that, when two systems show equal benefits, the old one should be retained because of the costs involved in the very process of change. The effort required to make a change may be costly, and even afterwards there may be efficiency costs due to unfamiliarity with the new system's operation on the part of those who run it. While such costs do occur, to use them as the basis of a presumption also will lead to the error of double-counting. Many types of disadvantages to a new proposal can be considered costs of change. The advocate would never know in a given debate which costs were not considered in the costs of formulation of the presumption and can be debated without double-counting. If a new system will be costly to implement and operate, these facts should be empirically established by its opponents.

Preoccupation of the Ground. This rationale argues that a presumption against change is imposed by the nature of argumentation. It assumes that all arguments necessarily must pit a present system against a new one. Any argument is a dispute over a piece of ground on which the existing system stands, and which the new system seeks to occupy. The traditional basis for this highly restrictive analogy is provided by Ehninger and Brockriede. Noting that presumption is the technical term for preoccupation of the ground, they explain:

> Every debate which ever has or ever will take place concerns, if not an actual, at least a figurative piece of gound. One of the disputants preoccupies—figuratively stands upon—an idea, interpretation, or value that the other thinks he should not be occupying. Indeed, unless some actual or figurative piece of ground is pre-occupied, there can be no debate. There is no established order or pattern of relationships that may be challenged. The situation is chaotic or formless and hence not subject to reordering. There is nothing to argue about, no matter concerning which the parties can disagree.[16]

The essence of this argument is that, without a present system and a presumption in its favor, there is only chaos in which no sensible debate can take place. Indeed, they assert that, without preoccupied ground, "there is nothing to argue about, no matter concerning which the parties can disagree."[17] This assertion clearly is untrue. We already have identified three situations in which the notion of preoccupied ground is irrelvant.

1. No one defends the existing order, and the judge must choose from a selection of new policies.
2. The advocates are asking the judge to decide between two existing programs, one of which must be eliminated.
3. A new problem develops and the judge must choose an initial policy to deal with it.

Thus, the notion of preoccupied ground is robbed of its meaning and function when no present system has a clear claim to the ground. Preoccupied ground is useless as a basis for decision rules whenever the gound is unoccupied or nonexistent.

The traditional reasons we have examined thus far for a decision rule against new proposals have failed to give us the rationale necessary to guide the formulation and use of that rule. But now, at last, we come to an understanding of the hazards of change that not only supports the existence of a rule against change but also gives us a set of criteria we can use to determine whether we should assign a presumption in various kinds of situations and what standard of significance is necessary to overcome it.

The Risk of Uncertainty. A decision rule should grant presumption to existing policy systems because we can predict the effects of such systems more reliably than those of proposed but currently nonexistent policy systems. The greater uncertainty regarding the impact of new policy systems suggests that we should be more wary of change than of stability.

Any change we introduce in the complex system of a modern society will have far-reaching effects that will be difficult to predict. The vast number of variables a single program might change is a strong reason to suspect any prediction, since many vital effects may remain unpredicted. The problem is intensified by the fact that empirical evidence indicates that changes in complex systems operate in a manner which is not only complex, but also counterintuitive. For example, Jay Forrester of M.I.T. conducted a thorough study of the effects of programs undertaken to improve urban life. The results, published in 1969 in *Urban Dynamics*, indicate that these programs, obviously intended to improve urban living conditions, touch off a chain of complex interactions that bring about counterproductive results that would not be intuitively expected. He notes that the failures of urban programs:

> demonstrate the counterintuitive nature of complex social systems by showing that intuitively sensible policies can affect adversely the very problems they are designed to alleviate. Commonly in complex systems a vicious cycle develops in which the action erroneously assumed to be corrective makes the problem worse, and the worsening calls forth even more of the presumed remedial action, which only further aggravates the situation.[18]

What this clearly indicates is that the direct and indirect effects of a change in our complex social system are extremely difficult, perhaps impossible, to predict. Any change is going to bring with it certain unanticipated results.

The continued operation of the existing policy may also yield unexpected consequences. But evaluations of the present system have one inherent advantage in their attempt to assess the total impact of the system. The past consequences of an existing system can be analyzed and used to predict the future impact of the system. In the case of a nonexisting system such empirical information obviously is not available, and predictions will be more conjectural. Hence, evaluations of new policy systems are more uncertain than evaluations of the existing order.

The greater uncertainty surrounding new proposals is a reason for a presumption *against* those systems because the unpredicted effects of a system are more likely to lower rather than raise its expected benefits. Any complex system is designed to work toward a desirable goal. Results that are not anticipated are virtually certain to have the effect of diverting it from its goals, thus reducing its beneficial effects. This is precisely the case in all Forrester's examples. The unforeseen is always a monkey wrench tossed into the machinery. Chances are high that it will hinder rather than aid the system's operation. This interference not only will divert the new system from its goals, but, through widespread effects, similarly may interfere with other systems, disrupting their operation and efforts to achieve desirable ends. Unforeseen side effects, therefore, are most likely to keep the new system from meeting its needs, and generate disadvantages by interfering with other systems.[19]

The reason for this likelihood of harmful results is inherent in the nature of complex organized systems. These systems depend on delicate and intricate structures designed for cooperative efforts. There is no reason to expect that an unanticipated change in a system will fortuitously serve to promote its goals. Only a few of the virtually infinite variety of unpredicted changes are likely to fulfill the specific requirements necessary for the management of any highly organized policy system. Such changes are much more likely to upset the delicate coordination of a policy system, and thereby undermine its effectiveness.

At this point one crucial observation must be made. The rationale we have uncovered calls for a presumption against uncertainty because of the risks it inherently imposes. This does *not necessarily* warrant a prejudgment against new systems. It is conceivable that our knowledge of an old system would be less reliable than what we know of a new one. If that were the case, the presumption against uncertainty would call for a decision rule favoring the new system over the old one. The crucial element in this rationale is its indictment of uncertainty and not necessarily of change.

Thus, we have established a rationale for a decision rule in favor of one side in the debate. In most cases, this uncertainty rationale will operate in favor of existing systems. But that conclusion can be subjected to debate and changed. In order to permit constructive debate over the assignment and weight of the presumption, and to provide judges with the criteria they need to apply it properly, we now must carefully delineate the manner in which the uncertainty rationale should operate within a debate.

DECISION RULE AND HOW TO USE IT

Debate should begin with a decision rule in favor of existing systems. The reason is that new systems generally involve greater uncertainty than preexisting systems. And that uncertainty carries a high risk of harmful consequences.

This decision rule, however, should always be subject to argumentation within the debate. The advocate of change should be free to argue that a new system is entitled to a presumption in its favor, a reversal of the presumption traditionally granted. The advocate can win this argument if the maintenance of the present system involves greater uncertainty than adoption of a new one. Similarly, the advocate should be free to dispute the standard of significance necessary to overcome a presumption. For example, the negative might argue that the advocate of change must show an extremely significant advantage because it introduces grave uncertainties about the effects that might follow. In order for debate on these issues to be possible, both advocates and judges must understand how and why a decision rule is imposed, and when it is used.

Assigning a Decision Rule

The basis of a decision rule should be the level of uncertainty surrounding the policies that are debated. Policies including little or no uncertainty should be favored over those with highly uncertain consequences. The judge must apply this principle to decide which system should be awarded a presumption, and to measure the standard of significance needed to overturn the presumption. First, determine which of the two systems entails the greater risk as a result of uncertainty, introducing a presumption against that system. Seond, determine the degree of risk imposed by the uncertainty. The higher the risk, the higher the level of significance required in an alternative system's advantages before a change is warranted.

Both these determinations are essential before a sensible decision rule can operate. Obviously, a presumption cannot be utilized until after the judge decides whether it will be imposed, and which side it will operate against. But, even after it is assigned, a presumption remains useless until a standard of significance is attached to it.

No presumption can operate as a decision rule until the judge determines the level of significance necessary to overturn that presumption. For example, if one advocate holds the presumption and the other establishes a moderate advantage for his proposal, the judge cannot decide whether that is enough to warrant a change. What level of advantage is required to overcome the presumption? The presumption can be assigned a mere feather's weight, toppling as soon as the affirmative shows any perceptible advantage. Or, it can impose a heavy burden of significance upholding the present system until a large advantage to change is demonstrated.

This kind of variation in the presumption's weight actually exists in the decision rules applied by the courts in differing types of trials. In civil court, the defendant's presumption generally is overturned by a mere preponderance of evidence; if the plaintiff establishes a greater than 50 percent probability for the allegations, he is awarded the judgment. No particular degree of superiority is demanded. In contrast, the criminal courts require a heavy presumption in favor of the defendant's innocence. The prosecution loses unless its evidence proves the defendant guilty beyond a reasonable doubt.

These twin tasks of assigning the presumption and setting a level of significance necessary to overturn it compel the judge to examine the level of uncertainty in our knowledge of each system, and to determine the seriousness of the risk that uncertainty imposes. It is on that basis that the decision rule is determined. A system involving greater risks must demonstrate superiority to a larger extent than a low-risk system. Five factors are relevant to these critical assessments:

The Extent of Change. The level of uncertainty entailed by a new program will vary with the number and degree of the changes it is likely to create. The more a policy departs from precedent, the less reliable are predictions about its behavior because existing policy systems are less useful as models to foresee its consequences.

The Importance of the Affected Systems. The degree of danger posed by uncertainty depends on the importance and sensitivity of the things that are most likely to be affected by change. A high degree of uncertainty is tolerable in areas of little importance. For example, it might be hard to predict how people would react if the Pentagon began using pink stationery, but it would not matter a great deal. However, a change in nuclear weapons policy could be extremely dangerous; even a small degree of uncertainty would be very serious. The risk of uncertainty will impose varying degrees of danger in different problem areas. The standard of significance should rise or drop with the degree of danger risked. [20]

The State of the Present System. One factor that can lessen the undesirable aspects of uncertainty is the state of the present system. It is conceivable that existing systems could be so bad that alternatives with uncertain consequences might be comparatively less risky than the status quo. When the foreseeable consequences of the present system are catastrophic, it increases the likelihood that any change at all will be a good one. Uncertainty is not a risk when there is nothing to lose. Therefore, the state of the present system is important in assessing the dangers of uncertainty.

The Reversibility of the Change. In 1969 the National Academy of Sciences Panel on Technology Assessment indicated that: "The reversibility of an action should be counted as a major benefit; its irreversibility, a major cost." [21] The value of reversibility is intimately related to the problem of unforeseen consequences. The reason for placing such a high premium on reversibility is that policies can be reversed to cope with a serious unforeseen result. For example, if the unexpected consequence of a new system were to introduce deadly poisons into our drinking water, it would be unfortunate if that policy system proved irreversible. Thus, policies that govern sensitive matters should be chosen for their reversibility.

The Quality of Available Analytic Tools. Excellent analytic tools can sharply reduce the dangers of uncertainty involved in adopting a new system. Predictions based on shallow sporadic information and poor comparisons obviously are unreliable. They are highly uncertain, and reliance on them therefore imposes high risks. But when a prediction is the result of thorough information studied in complete analytic models that have been proved reliable in the past, the likelihood of inaccurate prediction is reduced drastically. Conclusions based on complete data, where there are reliable computer models and other closely similar systems that can be studied, are most likely to be accurate.

Having appraised these five factors, the judge should be able to determine on the basis of the oral advocacy in the debate the level of uncertainty attached to each proposal and the seriousness of the risk that uncertainty carries in each case. On that basis the judge should be able to assign a presumption and assess its weight.

Obviously, when the presumption is debated in this manner, the debaters never can know during the argument precisely what its weight will be, or even which side will enjoy the presumption. This uncertainty, however, is inherent to any issue that is subject to argumentation. The advocates can never know how the issue will be evaluated by the judge and what its effect on the outcome of the debate will be. The important fact is that under the decision rule formulated in this essay, advocates will know at the outset of the debate precisely what their responsibilities will be if the presumption is either argued or ignored.

Past precedent, prior policy, and predictive models can serve as guidelines for weighing the potential outcome of uncertainty. Debaters need not find an exact precedent for every new policy they propose. Rather, a limited number of precedents could form a scale for approximately weighing the unpredicted effects of policy systems. Previous policy changes could be arranged in rank order on a scale, with those involving least risk on one end and those involving the most risk at the other. Each policy change then would be assigned a weight corresponding to the substantive importance of the level of risk it entails. For the scale to be most accurate each point should correspond not to a single past policy, but to a number of past policies involving the same degree of risk. Weighting then would be based upon the actual impact of the unpredicted effects of these policies.

Recall that the five factors previously outlined can at least form the basis for determining that one policy involves more or less risk than another. Thus, a new policy suggestion could be placed upon the scale above past precedents that involved less risk and below past precedents that involved more risk. The substantive weight for the risks of unpredicted effects of this policy could be approximated as an average of the weights of the two past precedents that form its boundaries on the scale.

Once this basis for the assignment and use of presumption is understood, the participants not only will know their responsibilities, but will be able to subject them to debate. Each debate that occurs thereafter should serve to clarify those responsibilities and in some cases to alter them.

Because more is likely to be known about existing systems than nonexisting systems, argument should begin with the presumption that change involves greater uncertainty than does the present system. Therefore, when no advocate specifically debates the presumption, the decision rule should favor the present system. But when an advocate for change substantiates that the present system is more uncertain, the presumption shifts in favor of the affirmative's proposed change. The decisive factor in assigning the presumption is the accuracy with which a proposal's effects can be predicted, and the probable impact of unknown effects. The weight of that presumption then depends on the risk imposed by the less dangerous alternative. Although the present system enjoys the presumption at the start of the debate, there are exceptions to that general rule that can shift the presumption by argument within the debate. Those arguments should focus upon the five criteria we have just examined. [22]

Summary—A Rationale for Use of Decision Rules

The quest for a rationale to guide the application of decision rules has been doubly rewarded. Two distinct rationales have been found, each supporting a presumption against change and a consequent decision rule in favor of existing systems. Taken together, these rationales can guide a judge's decision in virtually every situation.

Rationale No. 1 indicates that there should be a presumption against whichever policy system entails more *uncertain consequences*. The specific assignment of this presumption and its weight of risk or significance can be determined in any debate by arguments based on the five criteria previously outlined. If, however, the issue is not debated by either side, a feather's weight presumption is granted to the present system over any proposed change. This rule stems from the judgment that the adoption of new policy generally involves more uncertainty than the maintenance of the existing order, and that the substantive importance of this uncertainty is impossible to predetermine.

One might object, however, that there is a danger of double-counting the uncertainty argument, weighing it both as a plan disadvantage and as a reason for increasing the standard of significance that the affirmative case must achieve. This problem is resolved by the realization that, unlike changeover costs, the uncertainty issue is clearly identifiable. Any statements about the problem of uncertainty can simply be regarded as pertaining to the assignment or weight of the presumption.

In some cases, the uncertainty rationale alone provides insufficient guidance for the decision maker. In these situations Rationale No. 2 is employed. Recall that for important practical reasons there should be a feather's weight presumption against whichever advocate is in a position to expand the debate by enumerating new alternatives to his opponent's proposals. Proliferation of proposals and deterioration of debate both were seen as undesirable. Specifically, the present system should be granted a presumption over suggested changes. And an initial affirmative proposal should be granted a presumption over subsequent counterproposals.

CONCLUSION

Implicitly or explicitly all decision makers must apply some rule for deciding between competing policies whose merits already have been established. This article contends that fully articulated decision rules are superior to the adaptation of traditional presumption and burden of proof rules as a guide to final decision making.

The article establishes a conceptual model of decision rules and develops rationales to govern the use of decision rules in any specific situation. These rules help assure that the process of argumentation results in the selection of the best policy from among available alternatives. They also delineate responsibilities of advocates and lend direction and coherence to policy disputes.

Notes

1. Glen E. Mills, *Reason in Controversy* (Boston: Allyn & Bacon, 1964), 25–28.
2. In academic debate, for example, a presumption generally would be granted the initial proponent of new policy; and the advocate who responds to such a proposal with a second new alternative, rather than a defense of the status quo, generally is assigned the burden of proof. But this is an arbitrary convention not grounded in the precepts of traditional theory.
3. Hedley Bull, *The Control of the Arms Race* (New York, 1965), 175.
4. Mills, p. 25.

5. Douglas Ehninger and Wayne Brockriede, *Decision by Debate* (New York: Dodd, Mead, 1963), 83.
6. Gary Cronkhite, "The Locus of Presumption," *Central States Speech Journal* 17 (Nov. 1966): 270–76.
7. Ibid.
8. Ibid.
9. Ibid.
10. David Zarefsky, "A Reformulation of the Concept of Presumption," paper presented at the Central States Speech Association Convention, Chicago, April 7, 1972, p. 3.
11. Mills, p. 27.
12. Ehninger and Brockriede, p. 83.
13. Mills, p. 26.
14. Ehninger, and Brockriede, p. 83–84.
15. Ibid.
16. Ehninger and Brockriede, p. 83.
17. Ibid.
18. Jay W. Forrester, *Urban Dynamics* (Boston, 1969), 70.
19. For information concerning how finely balanced complex organizations must be, see Robert Dubin, "Stability of Human Organizations," in Mason Haire, *Modern Organization Theory* (New York, 1959); and Sherman Krupp, *Patterns in Organization Analysis* (New York, 1961), Chapter 6.
20. David Braybrooke and Charles E. Lindblom, *A Strategy of Decision* (New York, 1970), 48–51.
21. National Academy of Sciences, *Technology: Processes of Assessment and Choice* (Committee on Science and Astronautics: U.S. House of Representatives, July 1969), 39.
22. For additional readings, see Gary Cronkhite, "The Locus of Presumption," *Central States Speech Journal* (Nov. 1966); Brock, Bernard, Cragan, and Klumpp, *Public Policy Decision-Making: Systems Analysis and Comparative Advantages Debate* (New York, 1973); Kenneth M. Strange, "A Reconstruction of Presumption," paper presented at the Speech Communicatoin Association Convention, New York, Nov. 9, 1973; James J. Unger, "A Reformulation of Burden of Proof," paper presented at the Speech Communication Association Convention, New York, Nov. 9, 1973.

20

Presumption in Policy Systems

John P. Hart

One may not view the worlds of fashion and academic debate as having much in common. One thing the two communities do share is that, in both, styles seem to come and go quickly. The goals-criteria case has gone the way of the Nehru jacket. Perhaps the nature of debate and the intellect of the individual it attracts results in our total immersion in an idea and then disregarding it as we become enchanted with something new. The issues of the Malthusian nightmare, the effects of business confidence in investment, and the trade-off of one social program for another are still as relevant to the world today as when they were the focus of plan disadvantages in the debate community a few years ago. This preoccupation with the new has extended itself to a proliferation of world views, so-called "paradigms," of how one judges a debate. However, some ideas, like fashion's proverbial blue blazer, will always be timely.

The Lichtman-Rohrer essays of the early 1970s served to define policy system debate.[1] Although in the eighties, newer perspectives have flourished, whether one is a critic, evaluator, blank slate, or just plain judge, most ballots in a debate round are still ultimately cast for the superior policy option. "A General Theory of the Counterplan," is still required reading for many debate classes while other literature from this time period is now often associated with the label "dinosaur" or "dark ages."

Today few remember that the Lichtman-Rohrer series of articles on policy systems started with their response to Zarefsky's stance on presumption.[2] (Presumption here refers specifically to a system that is granted a prejudgment in its favor, as opposed to the more general definition of any type of prejudgment). Lichtman and Rohrer later advanced a theory of presumption based on the amount of uncertainty over the outcome of the implementation or maintenance of a policy.[3] It is not the purpose of this essay to defend a policy systems paradigm of debate. The paradigm itself has been adequately defended elsewhere. This essay is concerned with the advocacy of a nonstatic or linear concept of presumption as an applied decision rule once the merits of competing policies have been weighed. This examination will consist of three parts: a review of the concept of presumption; a theory of nonstatic presumption; and the implications of this theory.

REVIEW OF LITERATURE

Whately introduced the concept of presumption to argumentation.[4] He used the analogy from law that the accused is presumed innocent until proven guilty. His position is that presumption is the "preoccupation of ground" that favors existing institutions. His basis for this position is that change is not an automatic good and therefore those advocating change must justify it. Contemporary theorists such as Cronkhite, Lichtman, and Rohrer have attempted to distance themselves from Whately. Cronkhite argues that Whately's arguments have lead to the incorrect idea that the status quo is the locus of presumption, while Lichtman and Rohrer have objected to the preoccupation of ground idea on the basis that it is based on a scenario of nonargument.[5]

Presumption is a decision rule. Decision rules are necessitated by the requirement of making a yes or no decision after the cessation of advocacy. Lichtman and Rohrer noted that a decision rule must answer the following three questions:

1. Should a presumption be granted in favor of the position taken by either side?
2. If so, which side should receive the favorable presumption?
3. How significant should the net advantage be to overcome presumption or when neither side has presumption?[6]

Ehninger and Brockriede use the survival of the unopposed system as the basis for imposing presumption in favor of a system when it is opposed.[7] They also grant presumption to values of the present system. They claim presumption to be descriptive rather than evaluative. Presumption is used as the technical term for the preoccupation of ground. This view is rather simplistic. In their first situation— presumption granted to the unopposed system—where there is no argument, no presumption is necessary. In their second case, the values of a policy are not susceptible to a yes-no decision to accept or reject. In their third case, presumption necessarily reflects value judgments. In the final case, the notion of preoccupied ground is irrelevant when the existing order is not defended, when a trade-off between existing programs occurs, or when a new problem area develops.

Mills offers a definition of presumption based on Whately's concept of "a preoccupation of the ground."[8] Presumption upholds the status quo until a sufficient burden of truth has been met. He extends this presumption to the value judgments of the present system. In most cases his defense is based on an analogy between debate and law. Mills' theory does not indicate the extent of the burden established by the presumption against change nor provide a rationale to guide decision-making when the status quo is undefined, inconsistent, or nonexistent. The widely used Freeley text uses the same view as Mills, even in its latest edition, and suffers from the same deficiencies.[9]

Cronkhite argues that presumption is not in favor of the status quo, but is automatically assigned to the opponent of anyone advancing a proposition for debate.[10] He argues that presumption against the initiator of argument is the inevitable consequence of the process of argumentation. This argument establishes a spurious relationship between the results of nonargument and the specification of decision rules to govern the choice between policy alternatives after the debate has occurred. In addition, Cronkhite's claim that the opposition need not respond to an unsupported proposition clearly is not universally applicable to debating questions of policy, where the choice is between alternative courses of action. We do not choose between one position or nothing. We choose between competing policies.

Zarefsky indicts traditional debate theory's view of presumption and advances a reformulation of that concept.[11] He examines the dichotomy between change and stability, advances an analogy of scientific hypothesis testing, and concludes presumption is not in favor of the status quo but lies against the resolution. Lichtman and Rohrer note the need for the reformulation of the concept of presumption in argumentation theory and argue that Zarefsky's attempt is lucid but unworkable.[12] They argue three flaws in Zarefsky's position: (1) An absence of a clear rationale for presumption and the functions which it serves; (2) reliance upon the "fallacious and inappropriate" analogy of hypothesis testing; and (3) logistic disadvantages to the approach as used in the debate process. While confirming their analysis to Zarefsky's position, Lichtman and Rohrer do not offer a position of their own.

Although an early example of policy systems debate, Brock, Chesebro, Cragan, and Klumpp's concept of presumption is not the same as Lichtman and Rohrer's view of the term.[13] Brock, et al, claim that change is inevitable and that the question is not whether we should change, but what we should change to. Presumption, according to this concept, favors present policies because of changeover costs, not because policies are presumed correct. In this view, presumption does not carry much weight and therefore "does not necessarily require an overwhelming case to overturn it." This definition blurs the distinction between presumption and disadvantages. If the policy would be costly to implement this should be proven in the disadvantages. To count this argument both in presumption and disadvantages would be to count the same argument twice.

The Lichtman and Rohrer essay on presumption, included elsewhere in this volume, contains perhaps the most comprehensive examination of presumption to date.[14] The essay critiques previous efforts at defining presumption, delineates the distinction between presumption and burden of proof, and advances a theory of presumption based on the risk of uncertainty. This risk establishes that assessments of the more known policy are more reliable than the less known policy because the former's counterintuitive effects are more likely to be anticipated. Application of this decision rule depends on the following factors: the extent of the change; the importance of the affected systems; the state of the present system; the reversibility of the change; the quantity and quality of available information; and the quality of available analytic tools.[15]

"The Logic of Policy Dispute," a summary of Lichtman and Rohrer's decade-long work in this area, briefly explains how a policy systems view would affect each issue in debate including presumption.[16] In attempting to provide a capsule summary of their work, they were unable to note many of the fine distinctions that separate policy systems from other world views. This essay can serve as an introduction to this view, but a fuller understanding of the ideas referred to here can be gained by referring to the earlier works this essay so briefly summarizes.

Balthrop's provocative essay was the first to recognize the argumentative implications of the risk-based theory of presumption.[17] However, his view was not favorable as he argued that risk-based presumption would destroy the concept of burden of proof. Balthrop's view fails to distinguish between presumption as an issue in burden of proof and presumption as a decision rule. While he indicts the risk-based theory of presumption he neglects to offer an alternative.

The section of Goodnight's 1980 Summer Argumentation Conference paper dealing with presumption and academic debate looks at presumption in terms of the positions and values in which the debate judge believes[18] Goodnight's position should be understood as a relatively narrow application of presumption. It has to do with presumption as a factor in the evaluation of individual issues, not as a decision rule to be used after the merits of various arguments have been evaluated. Although this perspective may be useful for judge adaptation, it would seem to lead away from advocacy of what Perelman would call the "universal audience" to particular audiences.

Hynes critiqued Goodnight's essay at the same conference.[19] On the issue of presumption in academic debate, Hynes noted that the thrust of Goodnight's position—the consideration of an audience's holding of a liberal or conservative presumption—is more relevant to the area of public argument than to academic debate. Hynes reasoned that the debate judge is supposed to be objective and that debaters attempt to improve advocacy skills as opposed to actually changing attitudes.

Strange holds that prescriptions for presumption are arbitrary.[20] He endorses Cronkhite's position on the burden of proof on initiated claims. Strange states that risk should be considered as a substantive rather than procedural issue. In the case of a tie, coin tossing or automatic negative balloting are considered less arbitrary prescriptive standards. Given that risk is based on the amount of uncertainty—the unknown—Strange's position that unforeseen consequences can be advanced as known disadvantages seems problematic at the least. As for Strange's solution, three problems would probably result: (1) It provides an incentive to declare all close debates a tie; (2) it leaves advocates uncertain of their argumentative responsibilities; and (3) it could erode confidence in the decision-making process, given the lack of specific prescription in a form where a yes-no decision is required at the cessation of advocacy.

Willard states presumption is the conventional standard of proof in the field.[21] He claims an actor must take the perspective of a given field to understand the conventional practices of that field. His essay focuses on presumption as a burden-of-proof issue as opposed to presumption as a decision rule once individual arguments have been adjudicated.

Sanders argues from Whately that presumption is automatically in favor of the status quo, although he notes that contemporary alternative views exist.[22] He argues that counterplans lose presumption because the negative has granted that there is a need for change. Objections to Whately's original theory are applicable to Sanders as well. His position on counterplans is acceptable only if one believes counterplanning requires the negative to grant the affirmative harm, as opposed to merely advocating a superior alternative policy.

Patterson and Zarefsky maintain that presumption indicates which side will be presumed correct in the absence of argument to the contrary. They state that "presumption ought to rest against the resolution in order to assure that the resolution receives a thorough and rigorous test."[23] Despite this conclusion, they explicitly recognize that propositions may affirm present systems or values. Where presumption would lie in this case, given their above prescription, is unclear.

Lee and Lee's thesis is that the emotive dimensions of presumption preclude a wholly satisfactory descriptive or prescriptive treatment of the term's meaning. They define "emotive" as being the ability of a term to note an affective response.[24] This position is based on two arguments: (1) Presumption is not subject to empirical explication; and (2) presumption cannot be explained by prescriptive analysis. Lee and Lee's essay is of limited direct use to debaters since it focuses on presumption as a burden-of-proof issue in the evaluation of individual arguments that have been adjudicated. Their paper does contain an interesting critique of Patterson and Zarefsky.

Rowland believes that there is no reason to grant presumption to either team absent argument in the debate.[25] He allocates no argumentative weight to presumption except as a tie breaker. He argues the policy-oriented risk view of presumption is inadequate because major policy changes can have unexpected benefits as well as costs. Rowland claims that if change is risky, the negative should be able to prove it in a disadvantage. He argues that presumption should be used in the event of an exact tie. In this case, Rowland would award the debate to the negative. He offers no analysis why other than it is a "stipulated standard" that could just as easily be awarded to the affirmative.

Lichtman and Rohrer argue that, although the unforeseen consequences of a policy can be positive, they are almost always negative. They also note that it is tautological to expect unforeseen consequences to be advanced as foreseen disadvantages, and to do so would amount to double-counting the same argument. Rowland's granting of presumption to the negative by "stipulated standard" seems to realize Lichtman and Rohrer's worst fears that functional-type paradigms lead to totally subjective judging standards.

Michael Pfau, David Thomas, and Walter Ulrich, in their recent textbook take a policy systems perspective of debate tha subscribes to the risk-based view of presumption. They implicitly accept the non-static theory of this essay when they suggest that there are situations when the affirmative can claim presumption.[26]

In summary, it appears a risk-based concept of presumption is the most superior explanation. Alternate world views fail to meet the decision rule criteria cited at the start of this section and fail to distinguish between presumption as an issue in burden of proof and presumption as a decision rule. Automatically assigning presumption to the status quo fails to answer the third question (How significant should the net advantage be to overcome presumption?) and therefore is not an adequate decision rule. (The same goes for arguing that the affirmative has the burden of proof.) Automatic presumption against change offers no decision rule when the status quo is undefined, inconsistent, or nonexistent. Lichtman and Rohrer offered the following as examples of the above:

1. Neither team defends the existing order.
2. One of two competing systems in the present system must be eliminated.
3. An initial policy must be developed for an area where there has been no prior action.[27]

They concluded that presumption should be awarded to a system when "it runs a lower risk of harmful unforeseen consequences."[28]

Having weighed these six factors (the extent of change, the system's importance, the present state, change reversibility, available information, analytic tools) in the debate, the judge can determine the level of uncertainty in each policy and consequently the seriousness of risk in that uncertainty, resulting in a presumption for one of the policies, in some cases, even the status quo.

THEORY OF NON-STATIC PRESUMPTION

Although the view of presumption as the result of risk analysis was quickly accepted by many, the implications of the theory remained largely unnoticed, especially in practice. One of these implications is that, insofar as the amount of uncertainty can be different for different policies, the amount of presumption should be different as well. Consequently, because the amount of presumption varies from debate to debate, the amount of benefit the more uncertain system needs to overcome presumption varies accordingly. Once risk analysis theory is subscribed to, presumption must be viewed as linear or non-static— varying from debate to debate. Non-static presumption would hold that as the amount of uncertainty, and therefore risk, of a system increases, the presumption against that system increases on a linear basis.

Presumption can therefore be more than the feather's weight impact it has been given traditionally in debate rounds. If the uncertainty and its consequent risk in a system is great, presumption is great. Absent any threshold on this linearity, presumption in some situations in and of itself could outweigh a tangible advantage. For example, under a proposition calling for the increased development of space, the affirmative could advocate a specific extension of the space program, such as the addition of a Halley's comet probe or an educational satellite for the Third World. The negative could respond with counterplans such as a Marcusean-type revolution or a world government. The affirmative could argue that the uncertainties from the adaptation of such systems in and of themselves—regardless of disadvantages—outweigh the possibility of the system's advantages, regardless of the outcome concerning the viability of the counterplan's advantages and disadvantages versus the affirmative system.

Like other theories of Lichtman and Rohrer, some of the strengths of a theory of non-static presumption lie in that it is real world, or at least has applications and foundations outside the realm of debate literature. The grounding of a risk-oriented theory of presumption has been documented in the original series of Lichtman-Rohrer articles. The non-static presumption has real world extensions as well. For example, take the college football player who decides to turn professional. He may have to choose between playing in the World Football League or the National Football League. The former will often offer more money while the latter offers a more certain future. This is clearly a balancing of advantage versus uncertainty. In this case the staus quo, in the guise of the N.F.L., has presumption. That many players choose to play in the league with the more certain future as opposed to the league with the larger salaries indicates that in policy decisions there are situations where uncertainty or presumption can outweigh a tangible advantage.

DISCUSSION

Since this theory of non-static presumption is the direct extension of risk-based presumption, it should not be surprising that many of the objections against the latter would form the basis for possible criticisms against the former. And as with the case of risk-based presumption, these objections do not hold against non-static presumption when they are examined.

As with Lichtman and Rohrer's risk-based presumption, presumption does not make clear how judges or debaters are to balance the six factors cited earlier to determine the amount of presumption. Certainly it would seem problematic to some that we can weigh the unknown. However, that the concept is difficult to provide impact for is not a reason to reject the concept of a non-static presumption. Certainly the difficulty of weighing such qualitative concepts as democracy, human rights, freedom, and non-technological mindsets, have not prevented these issues from being advocated in forums requiring a yes or no decision. Lichtman and Rohrer note specific ways that past precedent, prior policy, and predictive models can serve as guidelines in weighing the unpredicted effects of policy systems.[29] These could be used to infer the amount of presumption against a given system.

Any change in a system, including evolution of the status quo, is likely to bring about unanticipated effects. This brings about two questions: Are these effects usually detrimental? And is the continuation of the status quo more certain than an alternate policy? The answer to both these questions is "yes." Policy systems are designed with a specific objective in mind and any unanticipated outcomes are most likely to be counter to that objective. Empirical evidence indicates that changes in complex systems are therefore often counterintuitive, as interferences not only disrupt the relevant system, but chain off to affect other systems as well.[30] Certainly the state of no change can also bring about unforeseen consequences. However the status quo has the advantage of being able to utilize historical evidence of its past consequences to predict future ones. The alternate system is hypothetical and therefore usually lacks this empirical data. Therefore uncertainty in alternate systems is usually greater than the status quo and this risk is detrimental.

Although non-static presumption and plan disadvantages share the concept of linearity, the distinctin between the two positions needs to be drawn. First, presumption is a decision rule, that is, a procedural issue, and a disadvantage is a substantive issue. Disadvantages are one of the elements that are weighed in a debate, while presumption provides us with a way of balancing those and other weights in order to determine the yes or no answer that the debate ballot and policy making require. Second, disadvantages describe known, direct effects of a policy while presumption concerns . self with the unforeseen side effects of that policy. It would seem tautological that we cannot predict, through disadvantages, the unforeseen. Presumption allows us a way to factor in the risk of uncertainty. To the extent that any possible consequence can be advanced as a disadvantage to a policy, that consequence is no longer unexpected and is out of the realm of presumption. In addition, to count such a consequence as both a disadvantage and a factor in presumption would be to engage in double-counting, doubling the impact of an argument by counting it twice. Presumption, then, is not to be confused with disadvantages.

Finally, non-static presumption should not be viewed as a device to reduce the advocacy of plan disadvantages. Although some might argue that this approach would encourage negatives to stop researching plan objections and simply argue "big changes are bad," the affirmative can return to Lichtman-Rohrer's factoring criteria already cited, and argue that the state of the opposing policy limits presumption, given the absence of disadvantages.

A theory of non-static presumption does not destroy presumption's role of breaking a tie in debate. In weighing presumption against a tangible advantage, it is possible that the advantage of the alternate system can equal the amount of presumption against it. However, a risk-based concept of presumption could still assign the feather's weight against the team that seized the initiative to expand the scope of the discussion. Proliferation of proposals in a debate round can lead to a deterioration in the quality of debate. The more policy options advocated in the fixed format of a debate round necessarily results in a more superficial examination of those policies. Therefore, in situations where the advantage of one side equals the presumption of the other, presumption would be granted to the present system over suggested changes, and to an affirmative proposal over subsequent counter-proposals.

None of the above discussion should be taken to imply that a system of increased judge intervention in the debate round is advocated. Debaters should advance the concept of presumption in the round. Each team could seek to demonstrate that its policy can better cope with uncertainty or that the risk of uncertainty is small. If neither side addresses the issue of presumption, they run the risk of the judge voting for the policy system that is more advantageous, no matter how insignificant that advantage might be (a common charge levied against policy systems debate theory as utilized in practice).

From the above analysis we can see that the concept of non-static presumption arises naturally out of the view of presumption through risk analysis already accepted by much of the debate community, and that the concept of non-static presumption is a viable decision rule to utilize in the debate forum. Presumption as a decision rule has fallen into disrepute in the decade since Lichtman and Rohrer introduced the concept of risk-based presumption. Since that time affirmative cases have continued to become more focused and narrower, making it more difficult for negative teams to advance applicable plan disadvantages. Those who argue that the policy systems model has resulted in an affirmative bias should contemplate if this is inherent within the model or if it is the result of using a model's guidelines for substantive issues without the accompanying procedural guidelines. The concept of non-static, linear presumption would be an important decision rule in examining affirmative cases that change much but claim little.

Notes

1. Although written earlier, these works first appeared under the titles: "The Role of the Criteria Case in the Conceptual Framework of Academic Debate," in Donald R. Terry, ed., *Modern Debate Case Techniques* (Lincolnwood, IL; National Textbook, 1970), 20–61; "Presumption and Burden of Proof: A Reevaluation," *Issues 7* (Feb. 1974.): 1–3 +; "Competitive Policy Proposals: A Systems Theory," *Issues 8* (March 1975): 1–3 +. (The *Issues* articles later appeared in revised forms, along with additional Lichtman-Rohrer articles in David A. Thomas, ed., *Advanced*

Debate (Lincolnwood; IL: National Textbook, 1979, rev. ed.); "A General Theory of the Counterplan," *Journal of the American Forensic Association* 12 (Fall 1975): 70–79.

2. "Critique of Zarefsky on Presumption," in James I. Luck, ed., *Proceedings: National Conference on Argumentation* (Texas Christian University, 1973), 38–45.
3. "Beyond Presumption." (See note 14.)
4. Richard Whately, *Elements of Rhetoric*, ed. Douglas Ehninger (Carbondale: Southern Illinois University Press, 1963), 112–32.
5. Gary Cronkhite, "The Locus of Presumption," *Central States Speech Journal* 17 (Nov. 1966): 270–76; Lichtman and Rohrer, "Presumption," 1–3.
6. Lichtman and Robrer, "Presumption," 2–3.
7. Douglas Ehninger and Wayne Brockriede, *Decision by Debate* (New York: Dodd, Mead, 1963), 83.
8. Glen E. Mills, *Reason in Controversy* (Boston: Allyn & Bacon, 1964), 25–28.
9. Austin J. Freeley, *Argumentation and Debate*, 6th ed. (Belmont, CA: Wadsworth, 1986), 38–43.
10. Cronkhite, "Presumption," 270–76.
11. David Zarefsky, "A Reformulation of the Concept of Presumption." Paper presented at the Central States Speech Association Convention, Chicago, April 7, 1972.
12. Allan J. Lichtman and Daniel M. Rohrer, "Critique of Zarefsky on Presumption," in James I. Luck, ed., *Proceedings: National Conference on Argumentation* (Texas Christian University, 1973), 38–45.
13. Bernard L. Brock, James W. Chesebro, John F. Cragan, and James F. Klumpp, *Public Policy Decision Making: Systems Analysis and Comparative Advantages Debate* (New York: Harper and Row, 1973), 153–56.
14. This essay appeared originally as: Allan J. Lichtman and Daniel M. Rohrer, "Beyond Presumption and Burden of Proof: New Rules for Policy Decisions," *Issues 8* (Dec. 1974): 1–3, 8–16; and Allan J. Lichtman and Daniel M. Rohrer, "Presumption and Burden of Proof: A Reevaluation," *Issues 7* (Feb. 1974): 1–3, 10–16.
15. "Beyond Presumption," pp. 13–14, contains criteria 1–4, and 6. "The Logic of Policy Dispute," *Journal of the American Forensic Association* 16 (Spring 1980): 244, adds criterion 5. "Policy Dispute" is the published version of their 1979 SCA Convention paper, "Policy Systems Debate: A Reaffirmation."
16. Bill Balthrop, "Citizen, Legislator, and Bureaucrat as Evaluators of 'Competing Policy Systems.'" Paper presented at the convention of the Speech Communication Association, San Francisco, Dec. 1976. Reprinted in David A. Thomas ed. *Advanced Debate* (Lincolnwood, IL: National Textbook, 1979), 405–6.
17. Lichtman and Rohrer, "Policy Dispute," p. 244.
18. G. Thomas Goodnight, "The Liberal and Conservative Presumptions: On Political Philosophy and the Foundation of Public Argument," *Proceedings of the [First] Summer Conference for Argumentation*, eds. Jack Rhodes and Sara Newell (Washington, DC: Speech Communication Association, 1980), 304–37.
19. Thomas J. Hynes, Jr., "Liberal and Conservative Presumptions in Public Argument: A Critique," *Proceedings of the [First] Summer Conference on*

Argumentation, ed. by Jack Rhodes and Sara Newell (Washington, DC: Speech Communication Association, 1980), 338–47.

20. Kenneth M. Strange, "An Advocacy Paradigm of Debate." Paper presented at the Speech Communication Association Convention, Anaheim, Nov. 13, 1981. Dowling also indicts the assignment of universal presumptions. As for Lichtman and Rohrer's risk-based theory, Dowling notes that it is based on "buying" other "complementary assumptions" and notes he chose not to do so, without offering any rationale. In addition, his analysis confuses presumption as a decision rule and presumption as an issue in determining the burden of proof. See Ralph Dowling, "Debate as Game, Educational Tool, and Argument: An Evaluation of Theory and Rules,"*JAFA* 17, (Spring 1981): 234–41.

21. Charles Arthur Willard, *Argumentation and the Social Grounds of Knowledge* (University of Alabama Press, 1983), 127–33.

22. Gerald H. Sanders, *Introduction to Contemporary Academic Debate*, 2nd ed. (Prospect Heights, IL: Waveland Press, 1983), 69–70, 114.

23. J. W. Patterson and David Zarefsky, *Contemporary Debate* (Boston: Houghton Mifflin, 1983), 28.

24. Ronald Lee and Karen King Lee, "Reconsidering Whately's Folly: An Emotive Treatment of Presumption." Paper presented at the Central States Speech Association Annual Convention, 1984.

25. Robert Rowland, "The Debate Judge as Debate Judge: A Functional Paradigm for Evaluating Debates," *Journal of the American Forensic Association* 20 (Spring 1984): 183–93.

26. Michael Pfau, David A. Thomas, and Walter Ulrich, *An Introduction to Debate* (working title), Glenview, IL: Scott, Foresman (in press), Chapter 12: Negative Strategies and Tactics.

27. "Presumption and Burden of Proof," 2–3.

28. "Presumption and Burden of Proof," p. 12.

29. See note 15 above.

30. See, for example, Robert Dubin, "Stability of Human Organizations," in Mason Haire, ed., *Modern Organization Theory* (New York, 1959); Sherman Krupp, *Patterns in Organizational Analysis* (New York, 1961), Chapter 6.

21

Presumption in Nonpolicy Debate

A Case for Natural Presumption Based on Current Nonpolicy Paradigms

David A. Thomas

It has now been more than a decade since the Cross Examination Debate Association CEDA began using nonpolicy resolutions, and almost as long since Lincoln-Douglas debate was adopted by the National Forensic League (NFL) as a national tournament event (in 1980). By the rules initially promulgated by the NFL, Lincoln-Douglas debate was to use value topics exclusively, and debaters were instructed not to use the stock issues of policy debate for their analysis. Along with other theorists, I have grappled with the problem of reformulating concepts such as the constituents of a prima facie case, burden of proof, nature of proof, and presumption into some new version for use in nonpolicy debates.

To a substantial degree, I mistakenly aimed my initial theorizing at a target audience that did not exist: I assumed people would be debating about values and value resolutions. That has rarely been the case in terms of the resolutions chosen, or of the debaters' aproach to the resolutions. The list of CEDA topics since 1971 includes a preponderance of quasi-policy topics as well as a significant number of outright policy topics. (*CEDA Yearbook 1985,* p. 67.) This fact permitted Rowland (1983) and Dudczak (1983), among others, to argue that

CEDA's so-called value resolutions imply policy dimensions, and by inference, ultimately reduce value disagreements to policy disputes, which must be resolved by traditional policy stock issues. While policies are related to value contexts, it is not true that every nonpolicy resolution must be translated into a policy proposal before it can be debated.

In this article, I want to focus once more on the subject of presumption in nonpolicy debate. I will review the approaches used in nonpolicy paradigms. My synthesis will show some common themes among them, so that they will seem more compatible with each other in terms of presumption. If I succeed in this effort, there may be some changes in the ways debaters analyze and argue in nonpolicy debates. There will also be incentive to rethink the assignment of an artificial presumption as a decision rule for judging close rounds.

A TIED NONPOLICY DEBATE SHOULD BE JUDGED AS A TIE

Why must a nonpolicy debate always result in a win or lose decision? My first argument is that there is no good reason why this conventional rule needs to exist. If a nonpolicy debate results in a tie in the eyes of the judge, it is irrational and unfair to give the debate to the negative. A tied debate, like any other tied competition, should result in the award of a tie decision to the contestants.

The first answer that usually comes to mind when that question is asked is "presumption." I intend to analyze why presumption does not require this result in any current nonpolicy debate paradigms. For the time being, imagine for the sake of my argument that presumption does not require that a tied nonpolicy debate be anything other than a tied debate. The rule that requires that ties be given to the negative is an artificial rule that is not necessary in nonpolicy debate.

If presumption is not the reason for awarding a victory to one team or the other in the event of an actual tie in a nonpolicy debate, then what theoretical or practical reason is there? My argument is that there is none. A tied debate should result in a tie decision being awarded to the two teams. A case can be made for adopting a new rule in nonpolicy debates to allow judges to award ties in tied decisions. It would be feasible to implement this proposed rule in tournaments. I have written another paper to build this case, but space does not permit including it here.

As we proceed to the more important parts of my arguments, please grant me fiat power at this point, and judge my subsequent arguments on their merits. Assume for the remainder of my argumentation that it is not necessary to break ties in debate. For now, consider the subject of presumption in nonpolicy debates divorced from its present application as a tie breaker in tied debates.

WHAT IS PRESUMPTION IN
A NONPOLICY DEBATE?

The real substance of this article is to explain what presumption is in nonpolicy argument, and to analyze its role in the leading paradigms for nonpolicy debating. I hold with Whately, as explained by Sproule (1976), that presumption is a psychological predisposition held by the audience or decision maker in nonpolicy debate. Presumption is a natural, complex, multipolar aggregate of beliefs, attitudes, and values held by the audience or decision maker. Therefore, in nonpolicy debate, audience analysis is the debater's method of determining where presumptions lie, and audience adaptation is the debater's method of influencing audience presumptions, hence, their decisions.

Rybacki and Rybacki (1986) divide presumption into artificial and natural presumption. Artificial presumption, they say, is a convention employed to determine who wins an argument. Their example is the situation currently prevailing in academic debate, in which hypothesis testing, for instance, stipulates that presumption must always be in opposition to the debate resolution.

Natural presumption, on the other hand, is derived from observing argumentative practices in the "natural world." Rybacki and Rybacki wrote: "The importance of determining where presumption lies is emphasized when we consider that natural presumption resides in whatever point of view the audience of argumentation may hold" (p. 18). Their example is the familiar public controversy over abortion, where there are groups like NOW that favor free choice for women, and other groups that are predisposed to legal protection of the right to life for the fetus. What are some of the multiple values stemming from the abortion controversy?

Pro-choice groups argue that the fetus is a part of a woman's body, and that women should have control over their own bodies. Pro-life groups argue that life begins at conception, and a fetus is an independent person with its own life. By this premise, a woman's right to her own body does not extend to aborting the life of a fetus.

Pro-choice groups argue that legalized abortions are necessary for the health and safety of women, since illegal abortions are much more dangerous than abortions done properly in hospitals. Pro-life groups argue that all abortions ought to be illegal, and that laws ought to be enforced to prevent illegal abortions—thus, eliminating dangerous risks.

Pro-choice groups argue that all children born into the world ought to be wanted by their parents. Pro-life groups argue that there are no unwanted children, since adoption agencies exist to place "unwanted" babies into homes. Pro-choice groups argue that women must not be forced to bear children conceived as a result of crimes like rape or incest. Pro-life groups argue that it is possible to allow for exceptions to an absolute ban on abortions for such instances of crimes, which victimize women, or for cases in which bearing a child poses a serious risk to the life of the mother.

And so on.

As a mere man, I am torn between these two value constellations that exist in the society of which I am a part. I am predisposed to believe major elements of both of them. I have attitudes, beliefs, and values compatible with both sides. It becomes important for me to choose between them only when arguments are put to me that necessitate my choice, such as a public issue over a right-to-life referendum or a debate. My resulting choice stems in large measure from the arguments put to me in the situation, not from any initial artificial presumption against the resolution, however the resolution may be phrased. Thus, I have presumptions both for and against abortion, as does society. It matters little whether an abortion resolution is phrased as "abortion is moral" or "abortion is immoral" in terms of presuming what has to be proved to me, or to society.

Natural presumption is what the audience presumes to be true. Presumption in its rightful role is a concept of the predisposition to believe on the part of the audience or decision maker in a debate. I am gratified to read opinions in agreement with mine from generally recognized CEDA sources. Michael Bartanen, for example, wrote in *The Forensic* (1981), "Presumption, or the audience's predispositions with regard to particular beliefs or values, are [sic] fundamentally important in all argumentative situations."

In our 1981 Alta conference report, Maridell Fryar and I elaborated upon this definition, basing much of our analysis on Sproule's (1976) explanation of Whately's evolving views on presumption. Apparently, during his writing career, Whately shifted from his earlier legalistic "preoccupation of the ground" interpretation, to a later psychological view of presumption, a view based on prevailing opinion and deference to credible sources. Since, in the matters people debate about in nonpolicy arenas, many values and credible sources are in conflict, presumption cannot be awarded in advance of a debate. Fryar and I argued that presumption must be appropriated by the debaters based on the arguments they bring to bear in the debate (*Student Congress and Lincoln Douglas Debate [1981]*, p. 33). It follows that the most effective arguments are those most successful in tapping those values and beliefs to which the audience or decision maker is presumptively committed.

Zeuschner and Hill also bought into Sproule's version of Whately in their article in *The Philosophy and Practice of CEDA* (*1981*, p. 24): "A judge may agree in principle with the affirmative side of a psychological presumption argument, but the negative side may fulfill Sproule's criteria to a fuller degree. Thus both sides would carry a burden of proof until the issue is won. . . . That decision may not come until late in the debate." Indeed, as I have suggested, *that decision may never come during the debate, so that a tie could be the final result.* Whatever the final result, in this approach presumption is not a decision rule dictating a vote for the negative side, or for the affirmative either. Instead, it is a predisposition by the audience or judge to which the debater must respond.

Take, for instance, the resolution, "That communism is superior to capitalism." In the typical debate, the predisposition of the judge would probably be to oppose it. If I were the judge, such would be my predisposition. This, as far as it goes, is consistent with the traditional rule that presumption is for the negative, or against the resolution, which amounts to the same thing. However, suppose the resolution were stated in the opposite direction, "That capitalism is superior to communism." It would still be a nonpolicy debate resolution. Viewing presumption as a predisposition to believe, we would anticipate that most judges or audiences (in the United States) would be predisposed in favor of this resolution. Obviously, this requires the negative to analyze the judge's or audience's presumptions to see how to make a persuasive case for communism over capitalism, reversing traditional presumptive roles.

That such a case *can* be written and argued successfully, there is no doubt. In policy debate, there have been and still are plans, and counterplans, to surrender to Russia, to encourage Marcusean revolutions, to abolish schools, and so on. In nonpolicy debate, similarly unpopular positions contrary to some strongly held beliefs and values *can be* drawn up and argued. (That is probably not a good practice in nonpolicy debate. Ideally, topic selection procedures ought to avoid placing either side in nonpolicy debate into the position of having to resort to extremely radical or reactionary positions.)

Presumption is not an artificial function of the negative side of a nonpolicy resolution. Presumption is not a property of the resolution itself. To impose presumption in this way is thoughtless and artificial dogma. In nonpolicy debate, presumption is best thought of as an audience's or decision maker's natural predisposition to believe.

There are indications that this view of presumption is gaining acceptance in the nonpolicy debate community, but there has been resistance to it. Podgurski attempted to answer this position specifically. In the *CEDA Yearbook 1983*, Podgurski responded to Fryar and me simultaneously with his response to Matlon (p. 37): "This position of presumption as a function of audience analysis contains the same inadequacies as the legislative paradigm," he wrote. However, our analysis had nothing to do with the legislative paradigm, which is a policy resolution paradigm. Our analysis focused on nonpolicy resolution. Podgurski went on (p. 37):

> At the very least, it ignores the context of competitive value debate as a man-made convention. If, for example, prevailing opinion were aligned with the resolution, as was likely the case during the 1978–79 CEDA resolution (That human rights in U.S. foreign policy is desirable), assigning presumption to the affirmative at the start of the debate would at best render the first affirmative speech virtually meaningless and at worst place an unreasonable burden on the negative team.

Podgurski's argument here is directed more towards Matlon's article (1983) than ours. We did not give nearly as much play to the "prevailing public opinion" view of presumption as Matlon did. In dealing with the notion of prevailing public opinion, Matlon limited his discussion to the shortcomings of public opinion polls. Matlon made his case *against* the practical usefulness of public opinion polls as evidence in a debate. No one denies that there are many difficulties involved in measuring relevant public values. Many others have also commented on this problem, including Ulrich in his discussion of the "Philosophical Systems as Paradigms for Academic Debate" (1983, p. 22): "It is often difficult to evaluate precisely what are the dominant American values, especially since America contains many diverse cultures." Indeed, in our Alta paper, Fryar and I also included a set of indictments against public opinion polls as evidence for presumption in value debates (1981, p. 522).

Even so, none of these pragmatic difficulties with polling techniques deny the theoretical validity underpinning a view of presumption as an audience or decision maker's natural predispositions. They merely point the way for further research to set out guidelines for argumentation based on natural presumption, similar to the task that confronted the debate community when it became necessary to increase its understanding of quantitative empirical evidence (studies) in weighing costs benefits in the policy systems paradigm.

If one accepts Podgurski's assumption that prevailing opinion *was* naturally aligned with the human rights resolution, he was correct in warning about the unfair distribution of burdens of proof; but the same increase in the negative's workload he described would have been true with or without an artificial presumption arbitrarily bestowed on the negative. Any unfairly worded resolution skews most of the credible evidence to one side.

If the debate resolution were "That incest between fathers and their daughters is morally unjustified," it would not help the negative much to know that Podgurski and others would assign an initial artificial presumption against the resolution to them. The negative would still have to prove its arguments against what the prevailing opinion believes is moral. The negative would still swim upstream against a torrent of affirmative evidence cards drawn from credible sources, all of whom condemn incest.

What audience, or decision maker, would give credence to any arguments or sources that assert the morality of incest? Would a judge vote against any affirmative who asserted the obvious? Debate judges who are slavish in adherence to an artificial presumption rule might spend time after the debate poring over the affirmative's evidence cards. No other audience in the world would spend ten seconds in making up their minds.

The artificial presumption rule, in situations involving undebatable resolutions such as the incest example above, encourages bad practices. If offers the only hope for the negative to win the debate on the basis of a "tie-goes-to-the-negative" decision rule. If the negative can hopelessly confuse the issues through some of the strategems and practices currently in vogue, they can lead the judge to vote negative. I have in mind here the so-called mindless spread, and/or contorted linguistic daisy chains passed off as topicality arguments, as examples of what goes for nonpolicy debating in some instances. I also have in mind the use of quotes knowingly taken from scandal sheets or hate literature, and representing them as credible evidence. Disguising the true nature of the source is no less a distortion of evidence than changing the content of the evidence. Far from being exercises in critical thinking, these varieties of arguing boil down to survival measures by negative debaters whose cause would be doomed without the existence of artificial presumption.

The problem is at least partly attributable to the rule that grants artificial presumption to the negative. Eliminate the artificial presumption and audiences would check their perception of both sides' arguments against their own natural presumptions. The only way shysters ever win is by exploiting some decision rule like artificial presumption. The simplest solution is to devise more debatable resolutions, for which there are reasonable natural presumptions and divisions of public opinion and values available to both sides.

What about Podgurski's warning about what would happen if the affirmative side enjoyed presumption in arguing over the human rights topic? The resolution proved to be debatable. The problems Podgurski warned about hardly ever came up. In Podgurski's example about the human rights topic, there were conflicting public opinions about Carter's human rights program, as well as about our country's dichotomous human rights/sovereign self-interest values in foreign policy. Natural presumptions existed for significant aspects of both sides of the resolution. Since both sides enjoyed some measure of natural presumption, both sides had some measure of the burden to overcome their opponents' positions and some opportunity to reinforce the favorable positions held within our pluralistic society.

This concludes my discussion of the need to eliminate the artificial presumption rule in nonpolicy debate and to rely instead on the notion of natural presumption. I have tried to show that artificial presumption is unnecessary in properly worded resolutions, and that it is unfair and counterproductive in some instances.

PARADIGMS BASED ON NATURAL PRESUMPTION BEST SUITED FOR NONPOLICY DEBATE

In this section, I will examine some of the leading nonpolicy paradigms for debate. My purpose is to show the relationship between each one and the concept of natural presumption. I begin with the policymaking paradigm and concede the usefulness of an artificial presumption based on cost-benefit analysis as a decision rule, but only in policy debates. It is ruled out of consideration in nonpolicy debates.

Hypothesis testing is the second paradigm I shall discuss. I shall challenge Zarefsky's insistence that hypothesis testing requires an artificial presumption to be against the resolution. The hypothesis testing paradigm is no worse off for relying on natural presumption.

Third, we shall discuss the issues-agenda model. We shall discover that it already relies on natural presumption. In my discussion of this paradigm, I will elaborate further on the nature of public opinions, attitudes, and values regarding nonpolicy resolutions. Fourth, I will also discuss Fisher's narrative paradigm, which is even more deeply rooted in a theory of natural presumption than any of the other paradigms.

The Policymaking Paradigm

In the early 1970s, Litchman and Rohrer began their series of articles on policy systems analysis, also known as the policymaking paradigm, as a response to Zarefsky's reformulation of presumption. They, like Zarefsky, attacked the previous traditional conception of presumption as discussed in the debate textbooks of the day.

According to Lichtman and Rohrer's paradigm, all policy debate is a comparison between alternative policies based on cost-benefit analysis. Presumption is an eventual product of the judge's determination of which policy position advocated by the two sides in a debate entails the least risks. Presumption, according to Lichtman and Rohrer, is not a decision rule in the traditional sense in which it was discussed in the debate textbooks of the time, nor is it a decision rule according to Zarefsky's reformulation. Lichtman and Rohrer denied that there should be any initial presumption for the negative side, or against resolution.

This edition of *Advanced Debate* includes a new article by John P. Hart, which provides a defense of Lichtman and Rohrer's concept of presumption as a dynamic decision rule based on the comparative risks of competing policy proposals. To facilitate our discussion, let us foreclose further consideration of the legislative paradigm at this point. For our purposes, let us stipulate that presumption based on the least risk serves us well as a decision rule in policy debate.

The purpose of this article is to discuss presumption in nonpolicy resolutions. If it is not necessary to extrapolate a nonpolicy resolution to entail specific policy consequences, as Rowland (1983) and others urge us to do, then it is sufficient to note here that presumption—as a decision rule based on least risk of policy change—does not extend to nonpolicy debates. Michael Bartanen (1981, p. 17) said, "*The* presumption [against the resolution] certainly would not exist in value debate unless a quasi-policy is debated. Presumption, therefore, may have a considerably different function in value debate and have important implications regarding the specific wording of the resolution to be debated."

Absent a specific comparison of policy options, nonpolicy debates need not be decided on the basis of an artificial presumption based on the hypothetical risks entailed in potentially relevant policies. Nonpolicy resolutions, by definition, take no action. A decision maker confronted with a quasi-policy resolution such as, "That compulsory national service for all qualified U.S. citizens is desirable," may find it helpful to consider the consequences of this resolution as if it were translated into a specific proposal; but nothing in the resolution locks the decision maker into a presumption based on cost benefit analysis of the risks of any *potential* policy proposal. This compulsory national service resolution is not a policy, but an example of a value judgment about the desirability of the idea of compulsory national service generally. It is more useful to consider presumption to be the predispositions of the audience or decision maker vis-a-vis this value judgment. Exploration of the consequences of a specific, but nonbinding, possible proposal serves as only one form of evidence among the rest of the evidence and arguments in the debate.

Hypothesis Testing

According to Ulrich (1986, p. 80), hypothesis testing is a popular paradigm for nonpolicy debates, more popular than it is for policy debates. Outside of Patterson and Zarefsky's textbook, *Contemporary Debate* (1983), the best statement of hypothesis testing is Zarefsky's article which appears in this edition of *Advanced Debate*.

In the first CEDA handbook published, Vasilius (1980) proposed the applicability of Zarefsky's hypothesis testing paradigm to nonpolicy debate. Along with many others, I concur that this paradigm is applicable to nonpolicy debate and that it offers many advantages for such activities as debate analysis and case construction.

In hypothesis testing, a key premise is that presumption always rests against the resolution for debate. Zarefsky suggests two reasons for this premise: that argumentation is analogous with scientific methods of determining knowledge, and that presumption should be stipulated to be against the resolution. I will address both of these reasons.

Zarefsky's explanation of this premise is that artificial presumption is analogous to the scientist's institutional skepticism towards the experimental hypothesis being tested. The hypothesis testing model is based on the laudable desire to add argumentative rigor to the advocacy of claims, similar to the rigorous standards employed in the scientific testing of experimental hypothesis.

In the scientific analogy, an experimental hypothesis is held to be a tentative prediction of the empirical relationship between one independent variable and another. The purpose of the experiment, according to this analogy, is to test the probable truth of the hypothesized link between variables. Positive results of the experimental test cannot prove the hypothesis is true, only that the proposed link cannot be rejected as false. Negative results of the experimental test mean that the hypothesis can be rejected as invalid.

By this analogy, the affirmative likens the debate resolution to a hypothesis to be tested for its probable truth. Artificial presumption represents the same tentativeness towards the resolution's validity. The affirmative who successfully tests the predicted hypothesis (via argumentation) merely establishes that the resolution cannot be rejected based on the arguments. The negative tries to reduce the probable truth of the affirmative hypothesis (by which Zarefsky means the resolution), to increase the chance of rejecting the hypothesis. Thus, by analogy, presumption is always against the resolution.

In my opinion, hypothesis testing works best when the nature of the argument is most closely analogous to the knids of statement a scientist calls a hypothesis. For example, a resolution of fact is an empirical statement, which can be shown by argument to be probably true or not. Also, the kinds of arguments necessary to establish causal links between proposed policies and their outcomes are directly related to hypothesis testing principles. For this reason, as Corsi pointed out (1983, p. 168), hypothesis testing can make a valuable contribution to our understanding of how to evaluate the alleged causal links between proposed policies and their advantages or disadvantages (and their offspring, turnarounds).

The analogy that a debate resolution is like a scientific hypothesis has frequently been attacked as a false analogy, since public argument is not scientific, nor are arguers constrained by professional standards to meet high standards of reliability and validity. Two articles, one by Corsi (1983) and the other by Hollihan (1983), repeated the analysis of why debate cannot be held to scientific standards. Personally, I find such critiques persuasive. I agree with their analysis of why debate is not analogous to the scientific laboratory.

The insistence that an artificial presumption always rests against the debate resolution is at the root of some unwanted byproducts of the present application of the paradigm. Among the unwanted byproducts of artificial presumption is the proliferation of unwarranted and inconsistent alternative hypotheses cranked out by negative teams who claim no responsibility for supporting anything they say. An artificial presumption against the resolution is translated by some to mean that only the affirmative has any obligation to prove anything regarding the resolution.

In practice, this means that the affirmative not only has the burden to prove its own case, but also to disprove the unsupported assertions made by the negative. Since so much nonpolicy argumentation is circumstantial rather than material, negating the opponent's speculative interpretations is logically impossible. Faced with the burden of disproving ghostly shadows of negative assertions, affirmative arguments must also enter the Twilight Zone of speciousness. If the affirmative drops any of the negative's hypothetical arguments, potentially sound or not, artificial presumption rules that the affirmative has therefore lost them. But covering specious arguments with equally specious replies regains the lost ground for the affirmative.

Looking at this process overall, it seems to me that the end result is the substitution of specious arguments and counterarguments for more substantive debate over the issues. Artificial presumption provides the driving force for a Gresham's law of arguments: the bad drives out the good. As the debaters often claim these days, debate is thereby destroyed.

Zarefsky's answer to all such criticisms is consistent, and also cryptic. The hypothesis testing paradigm is based on an analogy, but it is not meant to be a literal analogy. Zarefsky seeks to import higher standards for testing argument into public arenas analogous to the high standards in use in scientific laboratories—but it is not meant that the *same* standards are to be employed. It can be seen that Zarefsky's rationale for applying artificial presumption as a decision rule for non-policy debate rests on a figurative analogy. As is widely recognized, a figurative analogy is the weakest form of logical proof.

It is not necessary to impose artificial presumption against the resolution in order to achieve greater rigor and discipline in debate. In his article, "The Role of Causal Argument in Policy Controversies," reprinted in this edition of *Advanced Debate*, Zarefsky described the rhetorical standards for judging the causal arguments made for the existence of some policies and the denial of other policies. In discussing this subject, Zarefsky explained the logical and rhetorical requirements for establishing causal arguments in issues that are essentially motivational and evaluative. This article is an excellent contribution to our understanding of how to make arguments in rhetorical and political areanas conform to a higher level of rigor, analogous to the rigor achieved in the scientific laboratory. What I do not find in this article is a satisfactory rationale for why presumption must always be laid against the resolution.

Even in factual arguments, the analogy between hypothesis testing principles and an artificial presumption for the debate resolution is stretched. In my opinion, hypothesis testing fits the burden-of-proof rule (He who asserts must prove.) on the micro level of individual contentions; but no satisfactory rationale is suggested why it should apply only to the affirmative side at the macro or resolutional level. By my reasoning, then, a negative team that proposes a counterplan in a policy debate is vulnerable to the same demands to prove its hypothesis as the affirmative is to prove its plan.

In a debate over a factual resolution, if the negative team asserts a contradictory factual argument to the affirmative, then I would expect the negative to be bound to the same burden to prove their assertion. A factual resolution might be, "RESOLVED: That Kristin shot J. R." If the negative argued that this resolution is wrong, and then made a series of unsupported accusations that Jock did it, Miss Ellie did it, Sue Ellen did it, Brother Bobby did it, or Howdy Doody did it, I would not expect the affirmative to have to disprove each of these alternative accusations, unless the negative shows some reason for making these charges.

Fortunately, it is not necessary to grant an artificial presumption against the resolution for the hypothesis testing paradigm to be useful in nonpolicy debate. It is merely an artificial decision rule. Presumption could be regarded as the psychological presuppositions of the audience or decision maker towards the arguments and sources used by the advocates of both sides, and the application of the paradigm would not be essentially altered for the purpose of making rigorous rhetorical arguments.

Hypothesis testing would be modified by my proposal in that it would no longer insist on granting an artificial presumption against the resolution.

Apart from stating that the rationale for hypothesis testing is a figurative analogy between a debate resolution and a scientist's lab, Zarefsky also states that establishing presumption against the resolution is a stipulation. This, I believe, is ultimately the only effective rationale for its acceptance. Zarefsky stipulated the rule, and the forensics community, finding the rule comfortably familiar in its resemblance to the traditional textbook rules of the 1960s, uncritically accepted it.

Zarefsky's stipulation of presumption, like the original analogy between debate presumption and the legal presumption of innocence for the accused, might have also originated in the courtroom forum. In a court, a lawyer may offer to stipulate certain evidence to be true in order to avoid having to introduce it into the proceedings. The only reason a stipulation is ever accepted is because it is self-evident, or for some other admissible reason. The stipulation itself is not evidence. It is never automatically accepted, especially if the other side challenges it. Otherwise, prosecutors would request the court to stipulate the existence of material evidence in rape or conspiracy cases all day long. No defense attorney would ever agree to such a stipulation. It would violate the defendant's right to due process and result in miscarriages of justice.

Why should a stipulation that artificial presumption acts as a decision rule favoring the negative in a tied debate ever be accepted by the nonpolicy debate community? I submit that it should not be. Natural presumption is certainly not always against a value resolution in public argumentation. It is not even always against a factual resolution in public argumentation. So why should it be stipulated to be so? It is not necessary for presumption to be against the resolution. It can be unfair, with bad consequences for debate. A better stipulation would be to agree that, in the event of a tied nonpolicy debate, the judge should award a tie decision.

The Issue-Agenda Model

Michael Bartanen and David Frank (1983) proposed a new model for arguing value debates, which they named the Issue-Agenda model. Their original article is reprinted in this edition of *Advanced Debate*. Their purpose was to focus debate on the discrepancies between public values and issues at the grassroots level, and the policies that emerge at the institutional level. They did not wish to reduce the issues to a formal cost-benefit analysis, such as occurs at the institutional level. Neither did they wish to ignore public concerns and conduct the debate over values in a philosophical vacuum.

The issues-agenda model views argument as situational. In this model, based upon Cobb and Elder's 1972 book, *Participation in American Politics*, some public argumentative community serves as the setting for the argumentation over the issues involved in the resolution. Key to this concept is that the debating takes place in the systemic level before the issue reaches formal policy comparison methods at the institutional level. In other words, issues are generated and delineated by conflicts at the citizenry level before they become formalized for decisions at the legislative level. The issues-agenda model views the resolution as "a statement urging the acceptance of some value or belief as a part of the systemic agenda. The audience (debate judge) performs the role of gatekeeper, determining whether the issue contained in the resolution will be considered a part of the systemic agenda," (Bartanen and Frank, p. 5).

With regard to presumption, Bartanen and Frank take a position that appears to be compatible with the views I have expressed in this article. One of their four basic assumptions about the issues-agenda model deals with presumption. They say:

> The issue-agenda model is audience centered. Arguments are advanced to achieve some action or change of belief by an audience. This process necessarily begins with the arguer making some assumptions about the audience and the values the audience holds. While individual values differ widely, generally held sets of values exist which may guide the arguer in the process of structuring appropriate appeals.... These audience assumptions become criteria by which subsequent arguments about the relative importance of issues may be weighed (pp. 6–7).

In terms of conflicting values, the authors write:

> Problems, therefore, must be considered in light of competing issues and values. If an arguer advances a position that privacy is more important than any other constitutional right, she must be prepared to defend this statement in light of other competing rights, such as freedom of the press and equal protection of the laws.... Comparison of competing values is crucial to the issue-agenda model of debate (pp. 7–8).

Bartanen and Frank's issues-agenda model is obscure on the nature of public opinions and social values related to the kinds of issues we want to debate. Social or community values in natural settings are intersubjective. Otherwise, political and social agreements could never be achieved. Yet they are also complex and multidimensional. To say that there are intersubjective values within a community toward which we may direct persuasive appeals, of upon which we may base our estimates of presumption, is not to say that communities share only consistent and coherent value structures. It is a dangerous oversimplification to search for a super value to provide a surefire defense of a nonpolicy resolution, just as it is a delusion to claim a single, isolated causal inherency within a policy debate. Within ourselves as individuals, and within our social communities, we hold numerous value structures simultaneously. These may be unrelated and may even be contradictory.

Martin Rein said (1976, p. 158), "In principle, ethical issues may be logically isolated down to a single first premise that deals with intrinsic values, and which is therefore not subject to further debate; but in practice men always pursue many ends." As individuals, and as collective communities, we are committed to numerous value judgments. Value hierarchies are possible, but they are not often stable and they are never really permanent. Inevitably, changing circumstances create new contexts for decision in which new value hierarchies must be arranged. Abraham Kaplan explained this internal value flux with regard to personal decision making (1963, p. 35):

> No man . . . can serve two masters. If we are not bothered it is because we have fragmented our lives, institutionally and individually, to accommodate both. We look to practicality in business and politics, and to the realm of the ideal in religion and morality. As businessman, scientist, politician, I have one responsibility; as father, husband, citizen, another. It is all a question of the role I am to play.

The same fragmentation of value hierarchies pertains in U.S. society, which is nothing if not pluralistic. Rein continued (p. 158):

> Even our first principles become subject to further analysis when we subscribe to a number of first principles that are mutually contradictory, and this plurality of goals raises the basic problem of goal conflict and goal priorities . . . . The main problems of the development of policy involve these contradictions in goals.

Kaplan (p. 5) also commented on the fragmentation of values and value systems in the United States: "America is so multiple, so varied and vast, that only the deviant is truly representative. On the morals of politics, there are not two parties but hundreds, differing by region and religion, caste and class, ethnic origin and personal destination."

Values within the larger society are identifiable and measurable, even though they are intangible and largely in continual flux. The intersubjective value agreements on which debaters seek to find rock-solid social consensus are termed by Lane and Sears (1964) as "unimodal," a term that means relatively unified mass responses to certain recurring, permanent features of life. The context for public opinion on most controversial public issues does not, and cannot, produce unimodality. By a variety of public opinion techniques, Lane and Sears explained (pp. 7–10):

> We can determine which position is modal within the population; i.e., which opinion is held by the most people.... If there is only one mode, as in the case of opinions toward universal suffrage, the issue cannot be described as highly controversial. However, sometimes public opinion is bimodal; that is, there are two very popular, and opposed, positions. And sometimes there are several modal positions [as in] the case of federal aid to education.... Unimodal values do not usually generate debate, being uncontroversial.

Debaters might believe at first glance that bimodal values would be ideal subjects for debate; but this assumption, too, would most probably be in error. Edelman (1964, p. 176) wrote, "When, on the issues that arouse men emotionally, there is bimodal value structuring, threat and insecurity are maximized. Those who hold the other value are the enemy ... [and] responses are chiefly to threat perceptions." Examples of bimodal value structures are those represented by extremist positions, and we do not ordinarily subject ourselves and our student debaters to seasons of debating extremist questions. Among other reasons, extremist evidence is usually available only from extremist sources. When a group feels threatened and it sees those who disagree as the enemy, then the weapons it uses in its struggle are no-holds-barred.

Edelman sees multimodal values, rather than unimodal values, as the opposite of bimodal values. He wrote (p. 175), "A multimodal scattering of values is the opposite extreme. In this situation a very large part of the population is likely to see merit in both sides of the argument; to be ambivalent and at the same time feel free to explore the possibilities of alternative courses of action."

It should be clearly seen that, in the issues-agenda model, public opinions and attitudes on nonpolicy resolutions (such as whether providing military support to nondemocratic governments is justified, whether higher education has sacrificed quality for institutional survival, or whether continued membership in the United Nations is beneficial to the United States), are not unimodal, foundational public values. Debaters can expect the public to have mixed feelings, to see merit in both sides, and to be open to change, just like themselves. Moreover, on nonpolicy issues, the public will be open to further change once the debate of the present moment is replaced by a new debate later.

In this situation, there can be no singular, simple unimodal presumption against the resolution. There are numerous audience values, both pro and con, both to sustain one's cause and to resist it. If one of the purposes of the issues-agenda model is to simulate realistic public argument in natural settings, then one of its assumptions must be that presumption consists of multimodal values within the audience, or within the decision maker. How, then, can presumption be cited as a decision rule for awarding a tied decision (not an unlikely outcome in the uncertainties and vagaries of any public issues-agenda forum), to the negative?

The Narrative Paradigm

As this article is written (January 1986), the narrative paradigm exists only as a proposal for use in nonpolicy debate. Based on journal articles by Walter Fisher (1984, 1985), Thomas Hollihan, Patricia Riley, and Kevin T. Baaske (1985) and Kristine Bartanen (1985) have each presented proposals to adapt Fisher's narrative paradigm to nonpolicy debate. K. Bartanen's paper is reprinted in this edition of *Advanced Debate*.

My comments here stem more from the Hollihan and Bartanen articles than they do from Fisher's. Much as I regard these sources, the fact is that at the moment, they represent the *only* debate articles on the subject of which I am aware. In terms of nonpolicy debate, the articles by K. Bartanen and by Hollihan, Riley, and Baaske may or may not survive in the long haul as the definitive or foundational articles on this topic. Only time will tell.

Fisher's original articles in *Communication Monographs* are concerned with rhetorical theory in general, not with debate theory. Moreover, Fisher's own discussion is ambiguous with regard to what actually constitutes the narrative paradigm. He claims that narration is a perspective, not a paradigm; and he refers to his theory as a "meta-paradigm," with broad applicability to all varieties of rhetorical forms and genres. Yet he also uses the term, "narrative paradigm," in the title of one of the articles, and at numerous places throughout his discussion.

The narrative paradigm is a truly innovative approach to rhetorical theory. According to Fisher, the traditional model for the analysis and criticism of rhetoric has been a rationalistic world view. The traditional rationalistic world view features reasoning, analysis, and argumentation as the heart of the deliberative decision-making process. It awards status to informed discussion and debate.

Fisher's innovative new idea is that, instead of this rationalistic framework for viewing rhetoric, a more accurate model of rhetoric is narrative storytelling. People think—and more importantly, they feel, imagine, and find their motives to believe and act—in terms of dramatic events, myths, histories, and personal encounters. Society is shaped by stories. Stories, in turn, form the basis for new intersubjective community agreements. Rhetoric that matters, then, is that which primarily employs dramatic, mythic, personal narrations, not merely rhetoric limited to the rationalistic world view.

Many debaters and coaches have felt frustration through the years in attempting to develop arguments and cases that deal adequately with values. Fisher's narrative paradigm can be an important new theory that offers great hope for accomplishing success in their endeavors.

As applied to nonpolicy debate by Kristine Bartanen (1985), the logic of narrative would employ the concepts of narrative probability (internal coherence, logical ordering) and narrative fidelity (stories must ring true to the listener) as stock issues (p. 4). Case construction could use any of several dramatic forms; K. Bartanen suggests the Burkeian pentad as a possible starting point. Negative refutation of a narrative case could utilize a challenge strategy (directly attacking the narrative probability of fidelity a challenge strategy (directly attacking the narrative case); a redefinition strategy (a particularly inviting approach of reinterpreting the important meanings to be derived from the narrative); or a reconstruction strategy (the negative tells its own story, which is better than the affirmative's story) (pp. 4–6).

In this new narrative paradigm for nonpolicy debate, K. Bartanen sees these theoretical implications: "Both stories may be true, while not necessarily being the truth. . . . A judge, from the narrative perspective, chooses at the conclusion of a round the better story" (p. 8). Although most of these concepts of rhetoric as narration are very novel and unfamiliar to debaters, Fisher's theory is proving to be extremely provocative. The parallels with value debating, at least, are insightful. As Bartanen concludes, "This alternative paradigm suggests to debaters who wish to debate values and criteria more effectively that they build a narrative that embodies their chosen value(s) by clearly, coherently, and consistently linking story elements" (p. 10).

Based on just this much development of the narrative paradigm, it can be seen at once that presumption as a decision rule in nonpolicy debate is dead. The narrative paradigm is heavily audience oriented. It is impossible to attach presumption as a decison rule to one story in preference to another story, when the object of the debate is to present two competing stories, both of which may be true. But by the same token, the paradigm also facilitates the notion of presumption as audience predispositions and values. As Hollihan and his co-authors said (1985, p. 818):

> This new perspective of debate also requires a different understanding of the concept of presumption. The notion of presumption has already undergone many changes. In fact, the traditional conception of presumption . . . seems to have almost disappeared from contemporary debates, as most critics will accept any argument supported by evidence as worthy of warranting a belief. Critics seeking to develop a narrative understanding will proceed differently, however, for they will be determining whether arguments hang together as stories and evaluating them in terms of their own cultural beliefs, values, and experiences. Narrative

critics might well be more cynical of all stories and probably will not presume any argument to have merit until it is woven into the fabric of a story which is sufficient to convince them.

Or they might also well be more or less tolerant of all stories. Or critics might well presume that conflicting stories have equal merit in them, to the extent that the stories from either the affirmative or the negative story tellers engage the judge's imagination and motivate the judge to action.

As Hollihan, et. al. continued, "The primary difference in debate from this perspective is that human values, human emotions, and human experience will play a much larger role in the argumentative process" (p. 820). This statement is a strong endorsement of the application of natural presumption, and a rationale for repealing the rule of artificial presumption against the affirmative in a nonpolicy debate using the narrative paradigm.

One problem with the narrative paradigm is to determine what counts as argument, evidence, and refutation. Some of the strongest features of good stories are mythical, fictional, and dramatic elements. Current debate rules regard fabrication of evidence as the most serious violation of debate ethics. Will the narrative paradigm restrict debaters to the use of stories certifiable as true, that is, historical and factual accounts found in reliable journalistic and professional literature? Such a standard of evidence would seem to dilute the real power and utility of the narrative paradigm. The most evocative story to arouse and motivate an audience's commitment might be a classical myth like the Oedipus story, a modern drama like *Death of a Salesman,* or a great novel like *The Great Gatsby*—each of which Fisher referred to in his articles.

A logical extension of the basic principles underlying the narrative paradigm might be that debaters should be allowed to create their own reconstructed visions of reality, such as fiction, poetry, or drama. Perhaps the most educationally sound approach would be to reformulate evidence rules concerning what to allow debaters to introduce into evidence. Doing so might encourage added advantages for debate, one of which would be an increased level of community interest in hearing the debaters.

The narrative paradigm might be vulnerable to the charge of pandering to an individual judge's subjective biases, since different judges may be moved in different ways by the same narratives. This problem is not unique to the narrative paradigm; debate judges now differ in their interpretation and evaluation of such elements as evidence, reasoning, analysis, and organization. Otherwise all judging panels would render unanimous decisions. It is just that the standards for evaluation narrative qualities—narrative probability and narrative fidelity—seem to be ever so much more subjective than their corresponding judgment rules in policy debate.

It seems safe to conclude, however, that the narrative paradigm does not provide any theoretical or practical basis to award an artificial presumption to either side of the resolution. To be true to the dramatic assumptions underlying the narrative paradigm, presumption must always be an intensely audience-bound, open-ended concept. Earning a judge's decision in nonpolicy debate set in the narrative mold, then, must finally hinge on the qualities of the stories told, together with the skills of the narrators in capturing the audience's values, emotions, and experiences. It probably also involves the unknown dimension of the auditor's right-brain aptitudes and sensitivities to the paradigm's apparently nonrational devices used as rhetoric and argument by the debater-as-storyteller. The judge is moved to identify himself or herself consubstantially (to tie in Kenneth Burke's contribution to the paradigm) with the stories of *both sides*. In the event, an artificial presumption for the negative's story, or against the affirmative's story, would be unwarranted by the paradigm. Only a theory of natural presumption is appropriate for the narrative paradigm.

CONCLUSION

In my analysis, I have argued that there is no need for an artificial presumption against a nonpolicy resolution. This article has made a case for nonpolicy debate to turn away from an artificial presumption rule to renewed reliance on the judgment of the audience or decision maker, which is the reality of a natural presumption theory.

A view of natural presumption is superior to an artificial presumption in nonpolicy debate. Artificial presumption is an unnecessary rule, and it can produce bad results in debate. I have analyzed some of the leading paradigms for nonpolicy debate, and I have attempted to show that natural presumption is appropriate to each of them. My analysis included the hypothesis testing model, the issues-agenda model, and the narrative paradigm. It might be interesting in the future to perform a similar analysis of other nonpolicy paradigms, to see whether natural presumption also applies to the games perspective or the judicial paradigm, for instance.

References

Bartanen, K. (Nov. 1985). "Application of the Narrative Paradigm in CEDA Debate." Paper presented at the Speech Communication Association, Denver, CO. References in the present article are the original paper.

Bartanen, M. D. (1981). "The Criteria for a Good CEDA Resolution." *Forensic 67* (Fall): 16–19.

Bartanen, M. D. (1982). "The Role of Values in Policy Controversies." In D. Brownlee, ed., *CEDA Yearbook 1982.* 19–24, 31.

Bartanen, M. D. and D. Frank (1983). "Creating Procedural Distinctions Between Value and Policy Debate: The Issues-Agenda Model." *Forensic 69,* I (Fall): 1–9. References in the present article are to the original source.

Brownlee, D. (1985). "Topics Selected for Debate by CEDA 1971–1985." In Brownlee, D., ed., CEDA *Yearbook 1985.* 67.

Cobb, R. and C. Elder (1975). *Participation in American Politics.* Baltimore: Johns Hopkins Press. Cited in Bartanen, "Creating Procedural Distinctions."

Corsi, J. R. (1983). "Zarefsky's Theory of Debate as Hypothesis Testing: A Critical Re-examination." *Journal of the American Forensic Association 19,* 3 (Winter): 158–70.

Dudczak, C. A. (1983). "Value Argumentation in a Competitive Setting: An Inhibition to Ordinary Language Use." In D. Zarefsky, M. O. Sillars, and J. Rhodes, eds. *Argument in Transition: Proceedings of the Third Summer Conference on Argumentation.* Annandale, VA: Speech Communication Association. 837–44.

Edelman, M. (1964). *The Symbolic Uses of Politics.* Urbana: University of Illinois Press.

Fisher, W. R. (1984). "Narration as a Human Communication Paradigm: The Case of Public Moral Argument." *Communication Monographs 51,* 1 (March): 1–22.

Fisher, W. R. (1985). "The Narrative Paradigm: An Elaboration." *Communication Monographs 52,* 4 (Dec.): 347–67.

Fryar, M. and D. A. Thomas (1981). *Student Congress and Lincoln-Douglas Debate.* Lincolnwood, IL: National Textbook.

Hart, J. P. (1992). "Presumption in Policy Systems," in D. A. Thomas and J. P. Hart, eds., *Advanced Debate: Readings in Theory, Practice, and Teaching.* Lincolnwood, IL: National Textbook.

Hollihan, T. A. (1983). "Conditional Arguments and the Hypothesis Testing Paradigm: A Negative Rebuttal." *Journal of the American Forensic Association 19,* 3 (Winter): 186–90.

Hollihan, T. A., P. Riley, and K. T. Baaske (1985). "The Art of Storytelling: An Argument for the Narrative Perspective in Academic Debate." In Cox, J. R., M. O. Sillars, and G. B. Walker, eds. *Argument and Social Practice: Proceedings of the Fourth SCA/AFA Conference on Argumentation.* Annandale, VA: Speech Communication Association. 807–26.

Kaplan, A. (1963). *American Ethics and Public Policy.* New York: Oxford University Press, a Galaxy Book, printed with corrections.

Lane, R. E. and D. O. Sears (1964). *Public Opinion.* Englewood Cliffs: Prentice-Hall.

Lichtman, A. J. and D. M. Rohrer (1974). "Decision Rules in Policy Debate: Presumption and Burden of Proof. *Debate Issues* (Feb. and Dec.). In D. A. Thomas and J. P. Hart, eds., *Advanced Debate: Readings in Theory, Practice, and Teaching.* Lincolnwood, IL.: National Textbook.

Lichtman, A. J., D. M. Rohrer, and J. Corsi (1979). "Policy Systems Analysis in Debate". In D. A. Thomas and J. P. Hart, eds., *Advanced Debate: Readings in Theory, Practice, and Teaching.* Lincolnwood, IL.: National Textbook.

Matlon, R. J. (1978). "Debating Propositions of Value." *Journal of the American Forensic Association 14* (Spring): 194–204.

Matlon, R. J. (1981). "Propositions of Value: An Inquiry into Issue Analysis and the Locus of Presumption." In G. Ziegelmueller and J. Rhodes, eds., *Dimensions of Argument: Proceedings of the Second Summer Conference on Argumentation*. Annandale, VA.: Speech Communication Association. 494–512.

Patterson, J. W. and D. Zarefsky (1983). *Contemporary Debate*. Boston: Houghton Mifflin.

Podgurski, D. (1983). "Presumption in the Value Proposition Realm." In D. Brownlee, ed. *Perspectives on Non-Policy Argument*. CEDA. 34–39.

Rein, M. (1976). *Social Science and Public Policy*. New York: Penguin.

Rowland, R. (1983). "The Philosophical Presuppositions of Value Debate." In D. Zarefsky, M. O. Sillars, and J. Rhodes, eds. *Argument in Transition: Proceedings of the Third Summer Conference on Argumentation*. Annandale, VA.: Speech Communication Association. 822–37.

Rybacki, K. C. and D. J. Rybacki (1986). *Advocacy and Opposition: An Introduction to Argumentation*. Englewood Cliffs: Prentice-Hall.

Sproule, J. M. (1976). "The Psychological Burden of Proof: On the Evolutionary Development of Richard Whately's Theory of Presumption. *Communication Monographs 43* (June): 115–20.

Thomas, D. A. (Nov. 1982). "Presumption in Value Debate: Notes Toward a New Theory." Paper presented to the Speech Communication Association, Louisville, KY.

Thomas, D. A. and M. Fryar (1981). "Value Resolutions, Presumption, and Stock Issues." In G. Ziegelmueller and J. Rhodes, eds. *Dimensions of Argument: Proceedings of the Second Summer Conference on Argumentation*. Annandale, VA.: Speech Communication Association. 513–31.

Ulrich, W. (1983). Philosophical Systems as Paradigms for Value Debate." In D. Brownlee, ed. *CEDA Yearbook 1983*. 22–28.

Ulrich, W. (1986). *Judging Academic Debate*. Lincolnwood, IL.: National Textbook.

Vasilius, J. (1980). "Presumption, Presumption, Wherefore Art Thou Presumption?" In D. Brownlee, ed. *Perspectives on Non-Policy Argument*. CEDA. 33–42.

Zarefsky, D. (1977). "The Role of Causal Argument in Policy Controversies." *Journal of the American Forensic Association 13* (Spring): 179–91.

Zarefsky, D. (1979). "Argument as Hypothesis-Testing." In D. A. Thomas and J. P. Hart, eds., *Advanced Debate: Readings in Theory, Practice, and Teaching*. Lincolnwood, IL.: National Textbook. Page references in the present article are to this 1979 source.

Zarefsky, D. and B. Henderson (1983). "Hypothesis-Testing in Theory and Practice (Response to Hollihan)." *Journal of the American Forensic Association 19* (Winter): 179–85.

Zeuschner, R. and C. A. Hill (1981). "Psychological Presumption: Its Place in Value Topic Debate." In D. Brownlee, ed. *Contributions on the Philosophy and Practice of CEDA*. CEDA. 20–24.

KEY TERMS

artificial presumption
burden of proof
decision rule
natural presumption
nonstatic presumption

presumption
risk
risk-based presumption
uncertainty

DISCUSSION

1. Would Lichtman and Rohrer agree with Thomas' position on presumption? Why?
2. Can the affirmative ever win on presumption? Give examples to illustrate your position.
3. Compare and contrast the stock issues, hypothesis testing, and policy systems view of the concept of presumption.
4. Should presumption be a debatable issue in the round, or is it something that should be left up to the judge to decide after the round?
5. How would a judge vote in the event of a tie in a nonpolicy debate?
6. Describe a specific example where a judge could vote affirmative on presumption.
7. In policy systems debate, what is the difference between presumption and an uncertainty disadvantage?

Part Five

Models of the Debate Process

A generation ago, theory concerning the resolution of questions of policy was akin to the state of nonpolicy theory in the 1970s. Stock issues were grounded in tradition rather than theory. The Second Edition of this anthology (1979) placed models such as hypothesis testing and policy making as "new ideas" on the "green growing edge" of debate. In fact, the editor referred to hypothesis testing as a "cloud on the horizon, no bigger than a man's hand." Today, Ulrich notes, the policy making model is the dominant world view in debate. Hypothesis testing, a lucid but controversial paradigm, has also found wide use not only in questions of policy but also in questions of nonpolicy propositions as well. This development has not only legitimized Zarefsky's belief in the worth of the "hypo-testing" perspective, but perhaps also Lichtman and Rohrer's statement as to where that perspective is most applicable.

Part Five includes Ulrich's summary of the stock issues of debate, the seminal Zarefsky article on hypothesis testing, and a Lichtman, Rohrer, and Corsi article on policy systems analysis. The latter article focuses on policy questions, but its discussion of the relationship between policies and values should be of interest to the nonpolicy debate practitioners as well.

There has been an explosion of analysis and criticism in the area of paradigms since the various models of debate appeared over a decade ago. Lichtman, Rohrer, and Hart discuss recent developments in debate theory from a policy systems perspective.

Whether one views debate as the testing of a hypothesis, a comparison of competing policy alternatives, or one of the newer "exotic" paradigms, he or she should realize that not everyone in the debate community shares that particular terministic screen. We have previously compared the status of paradigms and models of debate with "a patchwork quilt" rather than "a seamless blanket." The same diversity of ideas still characterizes the mosaic of debate theories today. The difference is that today, the various candidates for paradigm preeminence, vying to serve as the ground against which all the other alternatives must stand as figures, all boast stronger credentials and more coherent rationales year by year. We strongly suggest that readers not only familarize themselves with the readings here that support their own preferred stance, but also examine all paradigms to understand their colleagues, their critics, and their opponents. Habermas argued that critical thinking solves for the tragedy of ideology. It is hoped a healthy discussion of the presuppositions underlying debate theory in the debate laboratory can accomplish the same result.

22

The Stock Issues Paradigm

Walter Ulrich

Until the late 1960s, there was general consensus among debate theorists about the way argument should be evaluated. This paradigm has been called the stock issues paradigm. This paradigm was almost universally accepted by debate theorists. One observer noted:

> In glancing through the indices of current texts dealing, in whole or in part, with preparation for deliberative speaking, one will usually find page references to "stock issues." No formal treatment of debate, for example, is considered complete without a set of such issues in one guise or another; the number may vary from two to seven or more, but it seems that the debaters cannot get along without these standard approaches to the analysis of a proposition.[1]

This view of argument suggests that there are certain responsibilities that any advocate of a change in policy must face. The advocate must address four stock issues before the change can be said to be justified. These issues are :

1. Is there a need for a change? (need)
2. Can the present system solve the problem? (inherency)
3. Will the proposed policy solve the problem? (solvency)
4. Will the proposed policy produce undesirable side effects? (desirability)

Some theorists add a fifth stock issue: topicality (the policy must meet the requirements imposed by the resolution), but it is frequently left out of the discussion, perhaps because it is a requirement that has little applicability outside the debate community and the stock issues model is frequently used in other contexts. According to the stock issues paradigm, an advocate of a change must demonstrate that the answer to all four of these questions supports the desirability of the new policy. On the other hand, if the answer to questions one or three is no, or if the answer to either of the other two questions is yes, then the policy advocated should not be adopted. For the stock issues judge, then, the focus of the debate will be on these four stock issues.

Harpine[2] suggests that there are a number of justifications for the stock issues model. It provides guidance for the debater and judge. It may reflect the way decisions are reached in the real world. Its approach may "correspond to the inherent logical obligations of the advocate of change."[3] Nadeau argues:

> What is a *stock* issue? In his preparation for deliberative speaking (as well as for forensic and epideictic occasions), man long ago discovered that certain question[s] occurred so frequently that an orderly listing of them provided a convenient pattern for analysis as well as a guide to the proper phrasing of specific issues related directly to a particular proposal. . . . A stock issue, then, is a *possible* issue, general in its phrasing, which may or may not become an actual and specific issue in the discussion of a definite proposition.[4]

The paradigm thus provides useful guidelines for the participants in the activity. The utility of these specific guidelines will be discussed in the next sections.

AN ANALYSIS OF
THE INDIVIDUAL STOCK ISSUES

Harm. The first stock issue examines the need for a change. Before we adopt a new policy, there should be a reason why we are dissatisfied with existing policies. Thus an advocate for a new policy needs to demonstrate that the present system (or status quo) contains some problems that need to tbe addressed. An advocate of gun control, for example, would argue that under current conditions many people die in gun accidents. This would suggest that there is a problem that we should be concerned with. The nature of the harm or need that the advocate isolates would vary depending on the type of policy being advocated. Sometimes an advocate can point to a large number of deaths (for example, if an advocate is addressing the issue of pollution or smoking). In other cases, the harms may be less serious, such as the loss of a small amount of money. Sometimes the need will be philosophical in nature (for example, if the harm is to individual freedom or privacy), while in other situations the harm may take the form of a risk of an undesirable condition resulting from current programs (as would be the case if an advocate were concerned about the risk of nuclear war or a nuclear accident). Whatever the nature of the problem, it is vital that the advocate isolate the existence of a harm, or else an audience would have no reason to be concerned about any change in policy.

This stock issue really has two components. First, it assigns presumption to the present system. Second, it imposes the burden of *significance* on the affirmative team. Both of these components are the subject of some controversy. The first component of the stock issue of harm is the requirement that the affirmative demonstrate that there is a harm. The assumption of this component is that we do not change for the sake of change; we change current structures only if there is a reason to do so. The affirmative team must demonstrate that there is a problem before they can win.

This view of debate can be traced back to the works of Richard Whately, who argued that "there is a presumption in favor of every *existing* institution."[5] Thus the affirmative team (which is seeking to change current structures) must overcome this presumption by demonstrating a problem with the present system; if there is no harm, we should stay with the present system (or status quo). The defenders of this view of presumption note that the present system is a known: We know how it works and we know its bad side effects. On the other hand, any change will have the risk of producing unknown disadvantages and hence should be adopted with caution (and, the argument goes, we are more likely to know about the known problems with the present system than the problems of a new policy). In addition, the present system will exist if there is no debate; thus the affirmative should be required to justify a change, not the negative.

The second component of the harm stock issue is even more controversial. For many stock issues judges, not only must the affirmative team demonstrate a harm; they must demonstrate a significant harm. Significance thus becomes a voting issue.

The basis for this interpretation of the stock issues model is unclear. Some justify it by drawing an analogy to law, where an individual accused of a crime must be proved guilty beyond a reasonable doubt, although in civil cases (which are probably closer to academic debate) a much lower standard exists, and almost any evidence can overcome a presumption. In other cases, this call for a demonstration of significant harm may be used to impose a judge's conservative political views on debate.

Inherency. Once an advocate has demonstrated that some harm exists, the advocate should provide some reason the present system cannot solve the problem that has been isolated. This requirement is called the requirement of inherency. In order for an advocate to demonstrate why a new program should be adopted, it is important, for the stock issues judge, to understand why existing programs cannot solve the problem. The problem must be tied in some way to the existing ways of doing things. An inherent problem is one that is inevitably tied to current policies; the only way the problem can be solved is to alter the fundamental way we do things. To meet the requirement of inherency the advocate must demonstrate that the problem cannot be solved given existing laws, regulations, and attitudes.

The requirement that an advocate demonstrate inherency is justified for several reasons.[11] First, inherency is justified because without knowing why a problem exists, we do not know whether a new policy will help solve the problem. Before we attempt to develop new policies, we need to know why old policies fail. If we do not do this, then our new policies may have the same flaws as the old policies. If the cause of poor health care is a lack of doctors, for example, reducing the costs of health care will do nothing to solve the problem because the policy would not address the root cause of the poor health care. Before we attempt to develop a remedy to a problem, then, it would be wise to know the cause of the problem so that we can direct our remedy at the problem.

Inherency is also justified because of presumption. Presumption is the assumption that, in the absence of evidence to the contrary, a certain view should be supported. In a court of law, it is argued, a person is presumed innocent until proven guilty. The stock issues paradigm suggests that a similar presumption exists when we debate policies; the present system should be presumed innocent (or desirable) until it is shown to be guilty (or undesirable). The assumption is made that, when addressing an issue of public policy, we should attempt to work within existing structures before we attempt to try out a new policy. Thus if there is a problem with the welfare system, we should attempt to solve the problem with minor modifications of the existing system, and only when those modifications are shown to be inadequate should we try to make a major change in the way we attack the problem. The presumption is that we should use existing policies to solve a problem unless we know these policies cannot solve the problem. Only then do we seek out new ways of eliminating the problem.

Finally, inherency is justified in order to demonstrate that the problem being discussed is a permanent one. Many problems are so temporary that they may vanish even if no action is taken. If that is the case, then there is no reason for us to act since the problems can be solved with no effort. On the other hand, some policies are so inherent to existing structures that they are likely to continue, and thus action is justified. By discovering the cause of the problem, we can discover if the problem is likely to continue. This permits us to decide if the problem is worthy of action.

Solvency. The third stock issue is solvency. It is not enough to suggest that existing programs cannot solve the problems being debated;

an advocate must be able to prove that a new policy will avoid the pitfalls of the existing policies while eliminating the problem. Many times an advocate will emphasize the harm of current programs, but then fail to provide a constructive solution to these policies. A politician may argue that current rates of unemployment and inflation are harmful, but offer no specific program to remedy these problems or, if such a program is proposed, offer no reasons why we shuold expect that the policy would solve the problem. This is obviously an unwise tactic. If no potential solution to the problem is defended, the discussion of the problem has accomplished very little. In addition, if the new program does not solve the problem isolated, there is no reason to adopt that program. If an advocate argues gun control is justified because of the large number of accidents involving firearms, yet all the advocate supports is a system of gun registration, it is arguable that the policy would do nothing about the problem (since the same individuals would continue to possess guns) so the policy should be rejected. Unless a policy has some positive effect on the problem it is designed to eliminate, there is no reason to adopt that policy.

Desirability. The final stock issue is that of desirability. An advocate must prove that the policy being advocated has no serious disadvantages. While no policy can be expected to be perfect, it is important that the policy not create more problems than it eliminates. If a policymaker eliminates one problem only to create a new, more serious problem, the effort has been in vain. For example, we may be able to solve all crime in a city by arresting all individuals who live within the city limits, but it would be unwise to adopt such a policy because the infringement of individual rights that such a policy would entail would be much greater than the benefits of reducing crime. The advocate of a policy thus should be able to demonstrate that the negative side effects of the policy advocated would not outweigh the positive effects of that policy. This characteristic of the stock issues paradigm has received relatively little criticism; in fact most paradigms include a similar feature.

Justification Arguments. Many judges that use the stock issues paradigm require that affirmative teams *justify* all terms in the resolution. For example, if the resolution calls for the federal government to establish and enforce regulations to control air pollution, the affirmative team would need to justify federal (as opposed to state, local, or international) action—*both* the establishment *and* the enforcement of regulations—as well as the regulations themselves. In the absence of such a justification, the negative team would win. While this requirement is not part of the stock issues structure, it is a part of the paradigm for many judges.

THE PRIMA FACIE CASE

One feature of the stock issues paradigm that deserves special emphasis is that of the prima facie case. Many stock issues judges require that an affirmative team present a prima facie case in the first affirmative. The nature of a prima facie case is somewhat unclear. Definitions of the prima facie case usually emphasize one of two concepts or a combination of the two. The first approach suggests that a prima facie case is one that a reasonable person would believe justifies the resolution. The idea is that, after the end of the first affirmative speech, a reasonable person would support the resolution. There are two problems with this definition of the prima facie case. First, it is unclear how one operationalizes the concept "reasonable person." In law, the term is very ambiguous, and different people might reach different conclusions about what a reasonable person would think about an argument. Given the ambiguity in the term, it is frequently of only limited use in guiding the debater.

The best view of the stock issues paradigm would view the stock issues as potential topoi for the negative team. When confronted by an affirmative case, the stock issues paradigm identifies potential areas to look at in order to seek weaknesses in the case. While the affirmative team needs to respond to these arguments when they are made, it does seem unreasonable for a judge to expect the affirmative team to anticipate all potential negative attacks and to respond to them in a single speech.

CONCLUSION

The stock issues paradigm has been very influential in the past half century. It is probably the most dominant paradigm among high school judges. It has set the agenda for the paradigm debates in the past decade and a half. Even if a theorist disagrees with the paradigm, the theorist will have to at least address the major components of the stock issues model. The discussion of many of the newer patterns will frequently follow the agenda set up by the stock issues model: What does the new paradigm say about inherency? Presumption? Justification arguments? Many of the newer paradigms have begun as reactions against the stock issues paradigm (which is why attacks on it are easy to find) and attempt to address its weaknesses. Certainly the stock issues model has the advantage of simplicity; even strong proponents of alternative paradigms would use the stock issues paradigm to explain debate to a naive observer. The problems with the application of the paradigm to more complex debate situations, however, have resulted in the introduction of numerous other debate paradigms that will be examined in the following chapters.

Notes

1. Ray Nadeau, "Hermogenes on Stock Issues in Deliberative Speaking," *Speech Monographs* 25 (1958): 59.
2. William D. Harpine, "The Theoretical Base of Stock Issues," *Forensic* (Fall 1984): 6–13. This article is generally critical of the stock issues approach to judging, except perhaps for its pedagogical value.
3. Harpine, p. 9.
4. Quoted in Harpine, p. 11.
5. Richard Whately, *Elements of Rhetoric* (Carbondale: Southern Illinois University Press, 1963), 114 (emphasis in original). This is a reprint of the seventh edition (1846).
6. See Arthur N. Kruger, "The Underlying Assumptions of Policy Questions: II. Indictment of the Status Quo," *Speaker and Gavel* 2 (Jan. 1965): 60–62; Arthur N. Kruger, "The Underlying Assumptions of Policy Questions: III. Inherent Evil," *Speaker and Gavel* 2 (March 1965): 79–82; Charles W. LaGrave, "Inherency: An Historical View," in *Advanced Debate*, ed. David Thomas (Lincolnwood, IL: National Textbook Co.), 53; Walter Ulrich, "The Role of Inherency in the Final Round of the National Debate Tournament, 1949–1975," unpublished master's thesis, University of Houston, 1975, chapter 2; and William L. Benoit, "The Nature and Function of Inherency in Policy Argumentation," *Speaker and Gavel* 19 (1982): 55–63.

23

Argument as Hypothesis Testing

David Zarefsky

THE HYPOTHESIS-TESTING PARADIGM

In the latter part of the nineteenth century, the pragmatist philosopher Charles Sanders Peirce described four ways of answering the question, "How do we know what we know?"[1] After discussing tenacity, authority, and the priori method as epistemological instruments, Peirce indicated his preference for verification—the method of science. The value of this method, he wrote, was that perception would be unaffected by quirks of the perceiver; science was a method "by which our beliefs may be caused by nothing human, but by some external permanency—by something upon which our thinking has no effect."[2] Since the scientific method is impersonal, it always can be replicated, and the process by which results are obtained can be specified. As a consequence, scientific knowledge is reliable knowledge.

Certainly Peirce was not alone in asserting the primacy of science as a means of gaining knowledge. Within the last few centuries, empiricism has come to share a preferred position with logical deduction among epistemological methods. Both verification and deduction seem to offer the promise of certainty, to yield knowledge which can be labeled *truth*. And the difference between what could be called *knowledge* and that which could be identified only as *belief* goes back to Plato's time.[3]

But if the only way to obtain knowledge is through science, large domains of human interaction must operate without benefit of knowledge: all things that cannot be observed, all value judgments, all predictions about the future, all suggestions for action, and so forth. Without being able to *know* anything with respect to these topics, we have no grounds for justifying one position over another. We either must be indifferent to the choice among values or judgments or else believe that the choice must be made on the basis of intensity of commitment to a position, or some other nonrational grounds.[4] Drawing the same conclusion in the form of a rhetorical question, Perelman asks whether we must conclude "that reason in entirely incompetent in those areas which elude calculation and that, where neither experiment nor logical deduction is in a position to furnish the solution to a problem, we can but abandon ourselves to irrational forces, instincts, suggestion, or even violence."[5]

The alternative to accepting this dreary state of affairs is to reformulate the notions of *truth* and *reliable knowledge*. In such a reformulation, science is valued not for what it *is* but for what it *does*. According to this view, science is valuable not primarily because it is empirical but because it yields knowledge that is reliable and consistent. The task then becomes one of inquiring whether a similar epistemological instrument exists in the nonempirical realm.

A growing number of scholars has suggested that rhetoric functions in just such a way. Rejecting the premise that rhetoric is a means of adornment for truths previously discovered, these writers suggest that rhetoric is a means of creating truth. As Carroll Arnold explains, "Manipulating symbolic devices for the purpose of gaining someone else's assent is essential to the very process of coming to know. . . . Rhetorical activity thus becomes not persuasion alone but an activity of ideational discovery."[6] A notion such as this may seem hard to reconcile with the traditional view that rhetoric, focused on appearances and probabilities, is antithetical to the discovery of certainty and truth. But rhetorical truth differs in two major respects from scientific truth. First, it exists within a particular context. It is bound by time, and, hence, as Scott says, "It can be the result of a process of interaction at a given moment."[7] By contrast, scientific truth is thought to be tenseless, knowledge that exists for all time. Second, rhetorical truth is obtained by consensual validation—it is the assent of an audience that gives to a proposition the status of knowledge. If *agreement* is the criterion for rhetorical knowledge, it follows that rhetoric yields not objective knowledge but "social knowledge"—that is, propositions that are accepted as true by a particular community of society.[8]

What has been suggested so far is that rhetoric is the counterpart of science. Science generates knowledge about matters of fact whereas rhetoric generates knowledge about the uncertain and contingent. Yet the matter is not so simple. To claim that science and rhetoric are distinct (even if analogous) is to assert a difference between fact, which can be observed, and value, which cannot. Increasingly, however, this distinction is being called into question. In his seminal work on revolutions in scientific thought, Thomas Kuhn has observed that scientific belief includes "an arbitrary element compounded of personal and historical accident."[9] As a result, facts are not immutable and independent of the perceiver. Instead, one's context or world-view affects what one observes and declares to be fact. As Kuhn puts it, "scientists see new and different things when looking with familiar instruments in places they have looked before."[10] What gives a perception the status of "fact," then, is that a very wide and durable consensus exists as to its truth. The difference between fact and value is one of degree rather than kind: Statements of fact, like those of value, are proved by consensual validation.

What follows from Kuhn's analysis is that science and rhetoric are not distinct modes of knowledge. Instead, scientific knowledge is of a special type because—except in times of scientific revolution—it commends a *broad* and *stable* consensus of adherence. But it, too, depends on consensus, and rhetoric, in Richard Rieke's phrase, "is inextricably involved in the generation of knowledge; not merely *a* way of knowing, but involved in all ways of knowing."[11]

Particularly if rhetoric is seen as ubiquitous, but even if it is not, the notion that rhetoric serves as a way of knowing may seem somewhat discomforting. Throughout history, rhetoric has been viewed with suspicion, often identified with sophistry and deception. If whatever an audience may be induced to believe is granted the status of knowledge, the meaning of "to know" would seem debased, to say the least. Booth illustrates the possibilities: "Charles Manson will be confirmed by the assent of his witches, Hitler by his SS troops, every Christian sect by its hundreds or millions of adherents, and indeed evey political and religious program by its ability to present witnesses." Despairing of such possibilities, Booth asks, "Am I not now forced to accept any piece of silliness that any fanatic wants to advance, provided only that he can get somebody to assent to it and that it cannot be clearly refuted with particular disproofs?"[12]

To answer Booth's question in the negative, one must demonstrate that a counterpart exists in rhetoric to the rigor of scientific procedure: the assumption of the null hypothesis, the revelation of one's method, or the advance determination of needed levels of significance. Such a counterpart is not always found in rhetorical transactions—people may be persuaded to accept the unreasonable—but it is present when rhetoric is approached from the perspective of argumentation. The National Developmental Conference on Forensics defined the argumentative perspective as one that focuses on the processes by which people give reasons to justify their attributes, beliefs, values, and actions.[13] Rieke elaborates on this definition by referring to "instances in communication when people give reasons to justify their claims, and others interact critically with them to test those reasons in relation to competing claims."[14] In such a situation one knows (or imagines) that an interlocutor will be present to probe the weaknesses in his claims and to present counterclaims; one's interlocutor, moreover, is assumed to be at least as intelligent and skilled as oneself. This knowledge serves as a disincentive to the presentation of sophistical arguments or specious appeals, and as a strong incentive to the presentation of the most tenable claims one can develop—claims that are so strong they will warrant the adherence of even such a talented interlocutor.

Moreover, the audience of argumentation withholds its assent from a proposition unless and until it survives the test served up by the interlocutor. Another way in which to make this statement is to say that a presumption is stipulated to lie against the proposition in dispute, and the overturning of that presumption is a necessary condition for the affirmation of the proposition. It is this stipulation of the presumption that introduces rigor into the argumentative exchange in order to avoid the acceptance of a false claim.[15] When a rhetorical transaction is characterized by the presence of this rigor, one may feel comfortable in giving to its outcome the same status of knowledge that he would grant to the results of scientific investigation.

A recapitulation of the ideas developed to this point now seems in order. The argumentative perspective enables rhetoric to function in a manner analogous to science or analytic philosophy, yielding reliable knowledge about topic these methods cannot address. (If Kuhn's point of view is correct, rhetoric is at the base of both scientific and non-scientific knowledge.) To extend the analogy, the argumentative encounter is the counterpart of the scientific procedure or the logical deduction. The proposition being argued is the counterpart of the scientist's or philosopher's hypothesis, and placing presumption against the proposition is the means of providing for a rigorous test of the proposition. Finally, the judge of argument is the counterpart of the scientist; his goal is to test the hypothesis to determine whether it is probably true. By "probably true," it is not meant that the proposition's truth-value is enternal and unchanging, but that, in the situation at hand, the judge has good reason to assent to the proposition.[16]

Two corollaries of this position should be noted briefly. First, argumentation is seen as an essential human activity; it is not a set of strategies or techniques for the presentation of truth, which has been obtained by other means. Indeed, Johnstone has argued that what makes us human is precisely this exercise of judgment in generating and accounting for conclusions, and inviting others to do so. Only such an activity introduces "opacity" into experience, transcending the realm of immediacy.[17] Second, the participants in argument always are one step removed from action. They are, in Ehninger's phrase, imprisoned in the world of words.[18] The process of argumentation leads to belief but not necessarily to action. Commitment to the proposition does not *adopt* it; the judge merely declares that he believes a statement to be probably true. Of course, action sometimes is incipient in belief. Even so, the choice of specific action and the mechanics of implementation lie beyond the process of argument. A commitment to action, in other words, includes both argumentative and nonargumentative components.

IMPLICATIONS FOR CURRENT FORENSIC PRACTICE

Forensics should offer laboratory experience in developing the argumentative perspective on communication. When the hypothesis-testing paradigm is applied to current forensic practice, several theoretical implications result. Six of these implications will be considered briefly.

(1) The wording of the proposition receives increased importance; the specifics of the plan to implement the resolution are of less importance. For the terms of this paradigm, nothing is being *adopted*, so the mechanics of the plan are of relatively trivial significance. The function of a plan is to illustrate the principles embodied in the proposition, thereby focusing the argument upon those principles. But all debate about the plan itself is conditional, or hypothetical, in nature. Consequently, it may not always be necessary to present a plan—the principles of the proposition may be self-evident. If a plan is presented, it need not have the specificity of a piece of legislation, since it is not being submitted for adoption. Should some difficulty be discovered in one of the plan's peripheral features, the plan could be amended, so long as the amended version still embodied the principles implicit in the proposition.

By contrast, the wording of the proposition is of central importance, since the proposition is the hypothesis being put to the test. Any different statement of a proposition assumes the character of an alternate hypothesis. In order for proposition X to withstand the challenge that alternate hypothesis Y could account equally well for the phenomena being discussed, a *specific* defense must be made for proposition X—not just for "a change" or even for a direction in which change should proceed. Hence the genre of justification arguments is of special significance. For example, the proposition that the federal government should establish, finance, and administer programs to control air and water pollution fails if reason cannot be given for each of the three indicated actions, for action by the federal government, and for controls over both air and water pollution. To do less might call for an alternate proposition, but not the specific one at hand.[19] Or, as Trapp summarizes, the key question for the judge is, "Does the affirmative case provide sufficient reason to affirm or justify all of the terms of the resolution?"[20]

(2) Presumption is placed against the specific proposition being debated. This procedure, as described above, assures a rigorous test of the proposition. It differs significantly from the traditional approach, in which presumption is thought to lie naturally with the present system because of the risks inherent in change. The hypothesis tester regards presumption as stipulated rather than natural. Moreover, he recognizes that there are risks in both change and stability and that neither change nor stability is a complete characterization of the normal state of affairs.

One might ask why rigor is served by placing presumption always *against* the proposition; indeed, it might seem that to do so is to fail to test rigorously the arguments advanced by the negative. But the negative is not proposing a thesis for adherence; its aim is only to negate. Rejecting the proposition does not preclude taking any other position. An alternate hypothesis may be proposed for testing, the original hypothesis may be refined and then reexamined, and further study may be undertaken. By contrast, to affirm the proposition is to make a personal commitment that it is probably true. Since rejection involves fewer risks than does acceptance, it is appropriate to locate presumption against the resolution. Such reasoning is analogous to that by which the scientist presumes the null hypothesis. Mueller, Schuessler, and Costner explain that "false rejection of the null hypothesis will lead to action that will not in itself provide a corrective for a wrong decision."[21]

It might seem that the hypothesis tester's placement of presumption involves a distinction without a difference, since it still rests initially with the negative. But the difference is that the negative cannot lose the presumption, except by concession or by advocacy of the proposition. As a consequence, hassles over the differences between major and minor repairs, or between repairs and counterplans, are avoided. So long as the negative opposes the proposition, it retains presumption.

(3) "Fiat power" is but a figure of speech. In recent years, there has been much discussion of the role of first power in argument, especially as a device to overcome attitudinal barriers to the solution of a problem.[22] According to one point of view, debate involves the "willing suspension of disbelief" so that, for the duration, the judge is regarded as if he were a decision maker with the power to implement a decision. Much argument may ensue, therefore, about advantages

deriving from a *guarantee* of action or from the presence of a clear mandate. In response, it has been argued that such advantages are bogus because they derive from the existence of the fiat power rather than from the substantive merits of the proposition.

According to the hypotheses-testing paradigm, all such dispute is rendered moot. Fiat power is not treated as if it were real, because argument remains in the world of words and nothing is adopted. To speak of fiat power is only to talk, in a shorthand way, about what might be imagined to be the consequences if action contemplated by the proposition were taken. Assuming, *for the purposes of argument*, that actions were taken is a convenient way to consider their effects and implications. But it is a far different assumption to imagine that actions *actually* were taken.

(4) Case development emphasizes the generic defense of the proposition, and inherency becomes especially important. It would be a weak affirmative case that reported the facts (such as the number of deaths from highway accidents), *assumed* that the facts were coercive of action, and conveniently offered the proposition as an appropriate solution. The negative might respond to such a case with a long list of alternative possibilities for action that might be equally good. Since these options are analogous to alternate hypotheses, they would defeat the proposition unless the affirmative could undermine each of them individually—a difficult task, especially when time is limited. Instead, the affirmative should take as its point of departure not "the facts" but the proof requirements of the proposition. The principles implicit in the proposition would be defended; this defense then could envelop a large array of nonpropositional alternatives. On the proposition calling for a guaranteed annual income, for example, discretionary programs might be indicted on the grounds that they are necessarily arbitrary in their administration. Any discretionary program the negative might introduce (unless it could be shown specifically to be an exception) would fall prey to this indictment, whereas any nondiscretionary alternative, by definition, would incorporate the guarantee called for in the proposition. The generic defense of the proposition, which may be strategically the wisest choice in any case, becomes a necessity within the hypothesis-testing paradigm.

Similarly, inherency becomes a crucial consideration. Some answer must be offered to the causal question, "Absent the action envisioned by the proposition, why would presumably good people tolerate evil?" It will not do to report "the facts" and then to *infer*, without analysis, the existence of some causal force that would be removed if the action stated in the proposition were taken. The reason is that there are other, equally plausible, inferences that can be made from the same data. For example, policymakers simply may not yet perceive a situation as a problem. Or they may have determined that the problem cannot be solved. Or they may have concluded that, on balance, solving the problem would bring about far worse consequences than the evils that would be removed. Each of these inferences, because it offers a different interpretation of reality, stands as an alternate hypothesis that must be defeated in order to provide a unique defense of the proposition. To defeat the alternatives, the affirmative will need to answer the causal question at the base of the analysis of inherency.[23]

(5) Counterplans are by nature conditional. Just as the affimation of the proposition does not lead automatically to the adoption of a a plan, so the rejection of the proposition does not constitute endorsement of some alternative. The function of the counterplan is to argue by example that the specific proposition under consideration has not been justified. How can proposition X be said to be warranted if alternative proposition Y accounts for the data equally well? The counterplan, then, is merely the justification argument in a different form. And, like the justification argument, it always contains an implicit conditional: *If* it is necessary to take some action to deal with a problem, then the action contemplated by the proposition has not been shown to be warranted. As a consequence, to present a counterplan is not necessarily to concede that there *is* a need for a change. Nor—as explained above—does the presentation of a counterplan constitute a surrender of presumption (unless, of course, the counterplan affirms the proposition). And, since arguments about both the plan and the counterplan are conditional, the counterplan need not be presented with the specificity appropriate to legislation. All that is necessary is to claim that action based on principles incompatible with the principles of the proposition would be an equally appropriate way to deal with a given problem.

(6) Finally, the hypothesis-testing model directs that the judge make a yes-or-on decision, rather than a this-versus-that decision. His choice is not similar to the one he faces when he votes for candidates for public office and must answer the question, "Which shall I choose, X or Y?" Rather, his choice is similar to the one he faces when deciding whether to support a tax increase in his school district: "Shall I choose X, yes or no?" Only one hypothesis is being tested—the hypothesis that takes the form of the proposition at hand. To affirm the proposition is to commit oneself to its probable truth. To reject the proposition, however, is not necessarily to make any commitments with respect to alternatives. The decision to reject X need not imply the affirmation of Y. Instead, the choice is between the central principles of the proposition and the universe of nonpropositional alternatives.

Other examples could be cited, but these six should illustrate the implications for current forensic practice of a point of view that regards argumentation as hypothesis testing for the purpose of determining probable truth.

THE CHOICE AMONG PARADIGMS

Until the last ten or fifteen yeas, argumentation theory was relatively monolithic. The underlying assumption was that reasonable citizens use argument to decide whether or not to change—whether to reaffirm a commitment to the present order or to proclaim a new one. So widespread was the agreement on this basic paradigm that it was not recognized as only *one* among a number of possible paradigms. As theoretical controversies developed—over such questions as the meaning of presumption and burden of proof, the concept of inherency, and case focus and principles of case contruction—these controversies were seen as separate and independent issues. Often, discussion did not advance beyond initial statements and subsequent repetitions of thesis and antithesis, with further development stifled by the fact that the disputants began with fundamentally different assumptions.

Now forensics is in a period much like that which Kuhn described as paradigm shift.[24] The old rules seem blurred, fundamental assumptions are reexamined, and competing paradigms are vying for consensus within the field. How to choose among these paradigms is a crucial question, since, as has been demonstrated here, one's choice of a paradigm may dictate his opinion about many theoretical disputes. Yet the choice among paradigms is a particularly vexing one because each resists attack except on its own terms. Nothing is gained, for exmaple, by attacking the policy-comparison paradigm for its uselessness in facilitating hypothesis testing. Advocates of the policy-comparison paradigm would reply, and rightly so, that the attack involved the fallacy of irrelevant function—attacking a paradigm for failing to achieve what it was not designed to achieve in the first place.

Arguments about paradigms belong to that class of philosophical arguments for which, as Johnstone finds, only *ad hominem* argumentation is a suitable response.[25] That is to say, one defeats an argument for a particular paradigm only by showing that it undermines its own purpose. That task may be very difficult, however, since each paradigm seems internally consistent. Furthermore, many of the problems that might be noted disappear when one realizes that the analogies on which the paradigm is built—argument as science, the judge as legislator, debate as incrementalism, and so on—are figurative rather than literal.

In the absence of appropriate *ad hominem* arguments, other bases for choice among paradigms suggest themselves. One could argue for a particular paradigm on the basis of its practical consequences. This approach may be fruitful. But it also may be dangerously misleading if arguments are based upon the *misuse* of a paradigm rather than upon its intrinsic characteristics. And it may put the cart before the horse, defending one paradigm or another on the basis of its suitability to a particular contest format, forgetting that the contest format is a contrivance to respond to theoretical and pedagogical needs rather than the other way around.

One might argue for a paradigm on the basis of its breadth of utility—noting, for instance, that the hypothesis-testing paradigm applies to all argumentation rather than only to controversies of policy. But such a claim presumes that types of argumentative encounters are more alike than different, a claim which is possible but which has not been much investigated. In the last analysis, we may be forced paradoxically, to choose a paradigm for reason giving on the basis of intuition.

Precisely because argumentation is a generative, or architectonic, process, users differ as to its purposes and product. Hence there exist various paradigms of the process of argument. Since stipulation of a paradigm involves choices and affects one's position in many other controversies, we should be aware of the profound significance lurking behind a seeming tautology when, in an early essay, Ehninger observed that "debate is what we say it is."[26]

Notes

1. Charles Sanders Peirce, "The Fixation of Belief," *Popular Science Monthly* 12 (1877): 1–15.
2. Peirce, p. 11.
3. Plato, *Gorgias*, 454.
4. These two options are considered at length in Wayne C. Booth, *Modern Dogma and the Rhetoric of Assent* (Notre Dame: University of Notre Dame Press, 1974), especially pp. 12–24. The first option is labeled by Booth as "scientism"; the second, as "irrationalism." See also the report of the National Developmental Project on Rhetoric, *The Prospect of Rhetoric*, eds. Lloyd F. Bitzer and Edwin Black (Englewood Cliffs: Prentice-Hall, 1971), 239.
5. Chaim Perelman and L. Olbrechts-Tyteca. *The New Rhetoric*, trans. John Wilkinson and Purcell Weaver (Notre Dame: University of Notre Dame Press, 1969), 3.
6. Carrol C. Arnold, "*Inventio and Promuntistio* in a New Rhetoric," paper presented at the Cental States Speech Association convention, Chicago, April 6, 1972, p. 4. Similar statements can be found in Robert L. Scott, "On Viewing Rhetoric as Epistemic," *Central States Speech Journal* 18 (1967): 9–17; Perelman and Olbrechts-Tyteca, p. 32; Booth, p. 106; Susanne K. Langer, *Philosophy in a New Key—The Uses of Argument* (Cambridge: Cambridge University Press, 1958), 248; Douglas Ehninger, "A Synoptic View of Systems of Western Rhetoric," *Quarterly Journal of Speech* 61 (1975): 452–53.
7. Scott, p. 13.
8. On the nature of "social knowlege," see Thomas B. Farrell, "Knowledge, Consensus, and Rhetorical Theory," *Quarterly Journal of Speech* 62 (1976): 1–14.
9. Thomas S. Kuhn, *The Structure of Scientific Revolutions*, 2nd. ed. (Chicago: University of Chicago Press, 1970), 4.

10. Kuhn, p. 111.
11. Richard D. Rieke, "Rhetorical Perspectives in Modern Epistemology," paper presented at the Speech Communication Association convention, Chicago, Dec. 28, 1974, p. 1.
12. Booth, p. 106.
13. *Forensics as Communication: The Argumentative Perspective*, ed. James H. McBath (Lincolnwood; IL: National Textbook Co., 1975) 11.
14. Rieke, p. 2. Rieke's model for such an instance is "communication among philosophers." There is a strong similarity between this model and Perelman's view of the "universal audience." See Perelman and Olbrechts-Tyteca, pp. 31–35.
15. A fuller explanation of this idea may be found in Daved Zarefsky, "A Reformulation of the Concept of Presumption," paper presented at the Central States Speech Association covention, Chicago, April 6, 1972. On the function of presumption in inducing rigor, see also Robert A. Trapp, "Non-Policy Debate in Search of an Audience," paper presented at the Western Speech Communication Association convention, San Francisco, Nov. 24, 1976, p. 7.
16. "Good reasons" are those which are psychologically compelling in that they render further inquiry unnecessary and superfluous. See Karl R. Wallace, "The Substance of Rhetoric: Good Reasons," *Quarterly Journal of Speech* 49 (1963): 239–49.
17. Henry W. Johnstone, Jr., "Some Reflections on Argumentation," *Philosophy, Rhetoric, and Argumentation*, eds. Maurice Natanson and Henry W. Johnstone, Jr. (University Park: Pennsylvania State University Press, 1965), 3.
18. Cf. Douglas Ehninger, "Argument as Method: Its Nature, Its Limitations, and Its Uses," *Speech Monographs* 37 (1970): 107.
19. This example is developed in Zarefsky, "A Reformulation of the Concept of Presumption," p. 9.
20. Trapp, pp. 9–10.
21. John H. Mueller, Karl F. Schuessler, and Herbert L. Costner, *Statistical Reasoning in Sociology*, 2nd ed. (Boston: Houghton-Mifflin, 1970), 400; cited in Bill Henderson, "Debate as a Paradigm for Demonstrating Truth Through Hypothesis-Testing," paper presented at the Speech Communication Association convention, Chicago, Dec. 29, 1974, p. 5.
22. In this regard, see especially David A. Ling and Robert V. Seltzer, "The Role of Attitudinal Inherency in Contemporary Debate," *Journal of the American Forensic Association* 7 (1971): 278–83; and J. Robert Cox, "Attitudinal Inherency: Implications for Policy Debate," *Southern Speech Communication Journal* 40 (1975): 158–68.
23. This sort of inherency analysis is described more fully in David Zarefsky, "The Role of Causal Argument in Policy Controversies," *Journal of the American Forensic Association*, in press.
24. See especially Kuhn, pp. 84–86.
25. Henry W. Johnstone, Jr., *Philosophy and Argument* (University Park: Pennsylvania State University Press, 1959), 73–92. Johnstone does not use ad hominem to refer to personal attack.
26. Douglas Ehninger, "Debating as Critical Deliberation," *Southern Speech Journal* 24 (1958): 30.

24

Policy Systems Analysis in Debate

Allan J. Lichtman
Daniel M. Rohrer
Jerome Corsi

The responsibility of affirmative debaters can be quickly and simply stated: They must convince an impartial critic to support or affirm the debate resolution. For propositions of policy, affirmative teams are required to formulate proposals whose affirmation logically entails affirmation of the resolution. Such proposals constitute what we shall term "policy systems."

Debate pivots on the comparison of policy systems. Affirmative teams seek to demonstrate that their policy systems are superior to the alternative systems defended by the negative teams. This chapter will explore the nature of policy systems. Policy systems have definite functions and structures, which must be thoroughly understood by advocates if they are to construct coherent and persuasive cases.

Contemporary policy systems analysis has recently been subjected to telling criticism by skeptical scholars. Critics have suggested, for example, that the rhetoric of systems analysis is often used to mask shallow, unoriginal thinking to create an aura of scientific rigor and authority. They have also noted that the policy science tends to overlook soft variables—factors that cannot be quantified or numerically measured but which, nonetheless, play an important role in the assessment of alternative decisions. In addition, critics have warned that policy systems analysis pays scant attention to the processes and procedures that guide individual and collective action as well as the ultimate outcomes that people seek to achieve. Instead, they insist, this mode of thinking rivets our attention to the selection of a means of advancing fixed, well-defined objectives.

In attempting to explain debate as a comparison of policy systems, we are not content merely to invoke the genie of systems analysis and decision theory. We will describe in detail the nature of policy systems and their relevance to argumentation theory and practice. We will endeavor to show that the analysis of policy systems does not squeeze out of debate a consideration of soft variables, that it includes a focus on process as well as final results, and that it allows an open confrontation with questions of value. We intend to advance a flexible model of policy systems analysis that clarifies the options available to advocates and broadens rather than narrows the vistas of traditional argumentation.

POLICY SYSTEMS

The Policy Hierarchy: From Abstract Goals to Concrete Actions

A policy system comes into being whenever poeple organize themselves, marshal their resources, and elaborate procedures in pursuit of common objectives. Such a system is a complex, multifaceted entity consisting of goals or objectives, a set of means designed to achieve these goals, and a code of checks and balances designed to ensure that emphasis on one means will not unduly impair the operations of the other means. Most often, policy systems that are subjects for debate involve particular areas of concern. Hence, systems underlying compulsory arbitration of labor disputes, wage and price controls, executive control of foreign policy, and guaranteed annual income invite discussion in relatively limited arenas of human endeavor. But policy systems are also conceived on a much grander scale. Thus, we talk of the American system of government, the American way of life, and the Judeo-Christian tradition. At a very high level of abstraction, these systems express and organize all the ideas that give form and substance to our society. These are broadly encompassing systems that articulate, in hierachical or pyramid fashion, the specific policy systems that humans employ to carry on their daily affairs. The complete hierarchical form of policy systems includes both the ultimate ends of human endeavor (abstract values) and the everyday activities of ordinary men and women in accordance with those values.

The concept of the policy hierarchy has intrigued thinkers from ancient Greek philosophers to present-day existentialists. The ideas of Aristotle offer an excellent starting point for understanding the hierarchical structure of policy systems. Aristotle suggests that the controlling purpose of human thought and action is happiness. Happiness he defines a priori as the good life. Subsequent philosophers have criticized the precise prescriptions of Aristotle, but they generally have recognized the necessity for establishing some a priori foundation for human striving, a final end or purpose that is accepted for its own sake and not based on any other proposition. This ultimate goal forms the apex of the policy hierarchy, the source of all the other objectives that people consider worthwhile.

It is apparent that the abstract, ultimate goal of the policy hierarchy as posited by Aristotle does not provide us with very much information. The concept of happiness is intended to be only a starting point that integrates those principles which form the mainsprings of human activity and belief. In order to make sense of these principles, further definitions must be proposed. Happiness must be broken down into its constituent principles—for instance, security, freedom, economic well-being, dignity, humanitarianism, justice, beauty, and knowledge. But these principles in themselves are vague and require additional elaboration. The hierarchy must unfold to still lower levels, transforming highly abstract ideas into more definite and concrete propositions. This process of differentiating and specifying the actual, tangible parts of more abstract goals and principles is almost infinite. The process of refinement is bounded only by the limits of human capacity. As the hierarchy becomes more specialized, it exposes concrete programs of action that can be subjected to more logical and empirical analysis. From the lofty realm of the philosopher, the policy hierarchy leads to the more earthly domain of the economist, the engineer, and the technician. From the most general concepts, policy systems evolve that are specific enough to direct the conduct of our lives.

Let us again turn to Aristotle for an illustration of the manner in which the hierarchy of goals translates itself into practical action in its lower tiers. Aristotle considers the security of the city state to be an essential component of happiness. Security is gained in part when the city is able to protect itself from outside attacks. Protection of the city demands fortifications, armed troops, and naval vessels. Each of these elements, in turn, must be implemented practically. Fortifications, for example, require stout city walls, outposts, and sentries. City walls must be built and maintained. Construction of the walls requires levying taxes, recruiting engineers, and employing manual laborers. As the paradigm develops, Aristotle reduces the idealistic philosophical principle to the meanest tasks of our daily lives. His paradigm for security might be diagrammed as in Figure 1.

In a similar way, all other elements of security might be diagrammed as might the other constituents of happiness.

Structurally, the policy hierarchy is built upon the principles of

Figure 1

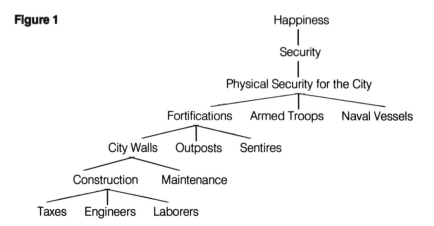

vertical and horizontal linkage. Vertical linkage establishes sets of ends-means relationships. Beginning with happiness, the ultimate end, notions such as security, freedom, economic well-being, and justice are defined to that end. Each means of happiness, in turn, becomes an end in itself, whose means then become the ends that demand additional implementation. Thus, the hierarchy is organized into a vertical chain of logically dependent concepts in which the means at one level serve as ends for subsequent levels.

Horizontal linkage is the structural principle that interrelates the interactions among means at any level in the hierarchy. It must be understood that seldom, if ever, is it possible to implement an end by a single mechanism; goal achievement requires the joint functioning of a number of means. Physical security for the city is thus attained when fortification, armed troops, and naval vessels are simultaneously obtained. Logically, means have the potential both to complement and contradict each other. While fortifications, armed troops, and naval vessesl are complementary means of defending the city, they must compete for the available resources of the city—money, manpower, technology, and physical materials, to mention only a few. Over-emphasis of one means may contradict the development of others. Through the principle of horizontal linkage, however, means are harmonized and balanced, thereby preventing their contradiction of one another. The model in Figure 2 illustrates the structural principles of vertical and horizontal linkage.

Harmonizing and balancing potentially contradictory means is not an easy matter. In the same vein, goals conflict with one another and compete for available resources. Often multiple goals as well as multiple means cannot be maximized simultaneously. At some point, emphasis upon one goal or mean may work to the detriment of another. Military defense, for example, rests in part on manpower and in part on

Figure 2

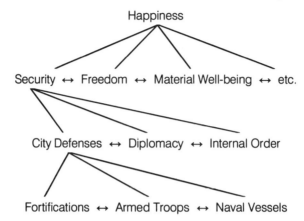

weaponry. Suppose that in seeking to increase the size of his army, a rather dull-witted dictator elects to draft as combat soldiers large numbers of scientists and technicians engaged in weapons development. To the joy of his enemies, the dictator's emphasis on building a large army contradicts the goal of weapon development and procurement. Therefore, it is necessary to trade off costs in one area for benefits in another.

The notion of trade-off (or compromise) underlies virtually every human decision. In the real order, policy systems reflect compromise, the product of trade-offs made by people as they decide what must be relinquished in one area in order to make gains in another. There are no limitations to the trade-offs that may occur in a policy system. Alteration in any one element of the system may produce disturbances in any other element. Moreover, some constituents of policy systems can be especially significant in the degree of change. Relatively small changes of these strategic items may produce trigger effects that profoundly influence other aspects of the policy system.

Components of a Policy System

For purposes of analysis, we divide policy systems into three components: ideology, structure, and checks and balances. *Ideology* describes the core values of a policy system, values that are not themselves dependent upon any logically prior values. Ideology gives direction and purpose to policy systems by stating and defining their final ends or objectives. Rarely is the ideology of a policy system explicitly set forth in a clear statement of principles. Yet ideology undeniably exists. Generally, it is necessary to infer the ideology of a policy system from history and tradition and from concrete programs and policies.

The *structure* of a policy system consists of all subsequent ends-means relationships that are required to implement the ideology. The description of Aristotle's paradigm of happiness through security, with its pyramid of horizontal and vertical linkages, illustrates this concept.

Checks and balances are designed to prevent harmful contradictions within the system while preserving flexibility to adapt to shifting circumstances. Emphasis on what appears to be a high-priority program may contradict other desirable programs to such an extent that the margin between the costs and the benefits begins to narrow. In a well-regulated policy system, potential contradictions are harmonized in a manner that maximizes outcome by increasing benefits and decreasing costs.

Checks and balances involve grants of power and limitations on the use of power. Grants of power enable a policy system to place emphasis on particular means to achieve its objectives. Limitations of power are designed to preserve the integrity of all ends and means.

Checks and balances are not confined to the formal discussions and decrees of political decision makers. They may also be more spontaneous. Customs, mores, public opinion, and informal agreements often serve as the basis for regulating policy systems. Whereas debaters are frequently in a position to propose alterations in the formal system of checks and balances created by legislation (executive orders and judicial decisions), they generally have little control over the informal system. An affirmative team might propose, for example, that police power be limited through prohibition of stop-and-frisk searches unless police officers have probable cause to believe that a felony has been committed. But the affirmative team cannot guarantee that individual police officers will not attempt to circumvent the law and continue the practice of stop and frisk.

Dynamic Systems: Adapting to Environmental Forces

Policy systems do not exist in isolation. They operate in the context of a dynamic environment. Systems analysts recognize the existence of both closed systems and open systems. *Closed systems* are self-contained; except for occasional disruptions, they operate without respect to the environment. A submarine, for example, during its submerged period would be considered a closed system. *Open systems*, on the other hand, engage in a process of mutual exchange with an environment of external forces. All living organisms, for example, are open systems. They are dependent upon aspects of their environment, and, in turn, their activities affect the nature of their environment. Realistically, all policy systems are open systems. They draw resources from the environment, process and transform them, and, in turn, release the products of this transformation back to the environment. Environmental forces may also generate changes in the policy system, altering anything from their ideology to the structure of subsequent ends and means or the existing network of checks and balances. Moreover, the environment of a system may contain potentially hostile forces that must be resisted if the system is to develop and survive. Thus, the world of policy systems is one of continuous opportunity and challenge.

The environment of a policy system may be partitioned into the following categories: natural forces, ideas, attitudes, resources (personal and material), and other organized systems. *Natural forces* are influences arising from nonhuman activity such as disease, climate, floods, and earthquakes. *Ideas* may be considered as models employed by people for organizing and explaining experience. They include, for example, scientific principles, systems of logic and ethics, and economic and psychological theories. *Attitudes* incorporate our emotional reaction to the world. They include such feelings as love and hate, anger and fear and may be directed at both individuals and groups. *Resources* include any factors that if incorporated by the system, advance its growth and development. Resources may encompass land, energy, minerals, and trained personnel.

Other organized systems take many forms. They may be competitors, cooperators, or neutrals. Competing systems rival each other for resources, prestige, and power. In the nineteenth century, for instance, European nations competed for spheres of economic and political influence in Asia and Africa. Cooperating systems, on the other hand, coordinate their activities in the hopes of achieving mutual benefits. During World War II, for example, the United States, Britain, and Russia joined with other allied nations to defeat the Axis armies. Neutral systems exert no perceptible influence on each other. For example, the activities of a small African nation may have no effect on the formulation of policy in the state of Alaska.

The status of external systems is not fixed. Depending upon the time period and the nature of the policies being considered, a given outside system may fall into any one of the categories. Nations may compete at one time but cooperate at a later time. Two hundred years ago, the United States and Great Britain were at war; today they are NATO allies.

Environmental elements, on all levels, are in a constant state of flux, with different elements exhibiting various degrees of flexibility. Environmental elements are salient to a policy system when they serve as materials for its enrichment, barriers to its goal fulfillment, or influences on its ideology, structure, or regulators. A surviving system must constantly adapt to changes in its environment, or it will not survive.

It should be emphasized that policy analysis pivots on the distinction between a policy system and its environment. The policy system includes factors that are under the direct control of the policymaker; all other factors are part of the environment. Policymakers can postulate change in the ideology of a system; they can alter its structure; or readjust its checks and balances. However, policymakers cannot directly control natural forces, resources, ideas, attitudes, or external systems. These factors can be influenced only indirectly through changes in the policy system itself.

Even for "should" propositions, which exclude discussions of political feasibility, advocates still must consider the effect of the environment on the adoption of new policy. A policy, for example, may be ineffectual or counterproductive if it outstrips available resources, runs counter to prevailing ideas or attitudes, or provokes the hostility of competing systems. Thus, advocates in academic debate need to consider the influence of environmental factors in analyzing the practicality or workability of the plan proposed for adoption.

THE AFFIRMATIVE POLICY SYSTEM

Whenever debate propositions advocate changes in the status quo, affirmative teams must propose alterations in the existing policy sysyems. Proposed policy changes may be aimed at any of the components of the hierarchy and may be as extensive as time and imagination permit. The alterations proposed by the affirmative, *combined with continuing features of the status quo*, constitute the new affirmative policy system.

Affirmative Approaches to Core Values of the System

Ideology

Affirmative teams may justify new policy either by referring to existing ideology or by proposing revisions in the present ideology.

By rejecting the ideology of the present system, the affirmative team can justify the adoption of proposals consistent with the debate resolution. Changes in ideology may require changes in the structure of policy systems. According to the principle of vertical linkage, all means within a policy system are motivated and justified by the ideology of the system. If changes in ideology entail affirmation of the debate resolution, the affirmative team has discharged its fundamental obligation in the debate.

Debate at the level of ideology does not absolve the affirmative team of its requirement to present a specific proposal, which embodies the policy implications of the affirmative team's more abstract ideological arguments. Without a concrete proposal, it would be impossible to determine whether or not the affirmative team has warranted adoption of the resolution.

However, attempts to alter the ideology that underlies existing policy are rare because they do not permit advocates to challenge the status quo on a comparative basis. The core values of the present system constitute what scientists and social scientists term "axioms," propositions that are assumed to be true rather than proven. In a value conflict, comparison is problematic. Unless the affirmative team accepts these axioms, it cannot establish a logically common ground for arguing the superiority of its proposal. By rejecting one or more of the core values of the status quo, the affirmative team establishes an alternative system of logic. Logic has different meanings when it is refracted through different perspectives; there is no way to argue that one perspective is superior to another, since all logical systems are based on nonrational assumptions (axioms).

Suppose, for example, one accepts a religious view of the universe and decides to enter a life of prayer, meditation, and retreat. That person could not be convinced on nontheological grounds that, instead of praying, he or she should be studying mathematics. Another person accepts a physical view of the universe and decides to be a scientist. For that person, the study of mathematics takes priority over theology. Neither studying mathematics nor praying is superior to the other, except within its own context, unless a yet higher commonly shared value can be found to serve as a criterion. Thus, a debate between two teams that embrace different core values could easily become less argument-bound and more sophistic, like an oratory contest in which each side plays upon the emotions of the audience for acceptance of its own world view.

In an affirmative case that depends on the acceptance of new social axioms in place of the old, persuasion is made difficult. An affirmative case that challenges the core values of the present system could be readily devised under the debate proposition "RESOLVED: That executive control of American foreign policy should be significantly curtailed." Proposing a philosophy that would require all worldly decisions to conform to Roman Catholic principles, the affirmative could argue that the pope should make all important foreign policy decisions for the United States and that the role of the president should be simply to enforce the judgment reached. Indeed, while such a proposal *implements* the new core value, it clearly has a long way to go to justify it to the debate judge, especially when the negative team stands on the traditional core values of pragmatic and nonsectarian politics.

A more fruitful avenue for debate, however, is provided by the ambiguity that characterizes the core values of a complex society like that of the United States. According to one view, the United States has a mission to extend democracy throughout the world and to intervene to defend it where it exists. But according to another view, our country is responsible only for itself and should keep its hands off other countries. In actuality, there is no clear consensus on the ideology that guides national decisions. This ambiguity opens the door for the affirmative to aruge that policy systems of the status quo are based on a *misunderstanding* of the core values that underlie the policy hierarchy. The affirmative could propose a set of core values that represent the moral and historical traditions of the United States. Given this premise of clarification, the affirmative could attempt to demonstrate that these values imply substantial changes in actual policies and programs. In seeking to curtail American foreign policy commitments, for example, an affirmative team might argue that particular commitments are derived from the belief that the United States has a responsibility to protect freedom across the globe. The affirmative might argue instead that we must allow other nations to determine their own destinies independent of our influence. This change in objectives would require substantial changes in our foreign policy commitments.

By clarifying the relationship between means and ends in policy choice, the analysis of policy systems paves the way for direct clashes over the ideology that implicitly or explicitly guides all human decisions. A thoughtful explanation and exploration of core values through the process of argumentation and debate may at times appear remote and ethereal to hard-headed decision makers. Yet, considerations of the ends that people seek are especially important for a society experiencing rapid technological change. Unless we maintain a firm grip on our own destiny, we may find that our technology has begun to define our values for us.

Structures, checks, and balances

In general, however, affirmative teams will not choose to engage in argumentation at the level of abstract values. Rather, they are likely to focus their attention on lower tiers of the policy hierarchy, concentrating on relatively concrete values. Debate can take place on a comparatively equal basis, since these lower values are all logically derived from the same ideology of the policy system. Naval vessels or armed troops, for example, may be valued because they are a means of securing the physical safety of the city-state. The affirmative team could attempt to demonstrate that core values could be better achieved by altering the priority among derived values at a particular stratum of the policy hierarchy. Since derived values have their own sets of means, changes in derived values will necessarily dictate changes at the levels of implementation of the policy hierarchy. These changes would be expressed in the proposal advanced by the affirmative team.

Affirmative plans generally entail alterations in the checks and balances of policy systems; either new powers are granted or new limitations are placed on existing powers. Changes in checks and balances necessarily require changes in structure. New means may be added or existing means eliminated. For example, industry's growth in America has inevitably led to greater concentrations of air and water pollution. Therefore, it became necessary to limit industry's power in order to reduce the problems of pollution. The limitations on industry's power involved in pollution control have required the creation of regulatory agencies, the elaboration of procedures of monitoring pollution, and the development of appropriate enforcement mechanisms— all of which are structured additions in the policy system to maintain minimal air and water quality standards.

The changes in the policy systems incorporated in affirmative plans are justified on the grounds that they better fulfill the criteria set forth in the ideology of the system. New policy is warranted if it has greater net benefits than the existing order. The principle of horizontal linkage indicates that alterations in the checks and balances of a policy system generate trade-offs in which likely costs are exchanged for likely benefits. The net benefits of alternative policy systems are measured both by the likelihood of possible policy outcomes and by the values ascribed to these outcomes by the ideology of the policy system. The extent to which outcomes are to be regarded as costly or beneficial is determined by this ideology. In determining costs and benefits, advocates must keep in mind that means cannot be considered in isolation. Changes in one aspect of the system can generate further changes in other aspects of the system. All these interrelated changes must be considered in the process of evaluating the net benefits of the new policy.

Integrating the Soft Variables into Systems Analysis

In evaluating policy alternatives, analysts generally assume that costs in one area can always be exchanged for benefits in another. For example, national leaders may be willing to exchange the costs entailed lin reducing the armed forces in order to reap the benefits produced by a reduction in the taxes. For each policy alternative, the differences between benefits and costs are calculated and the policy that maximizes the difference is selected.

It is possible, however, that the ideology of a policy system may not always accommodate the smooth exchange of benefits and costs. Certain costs may be regarded as flatly unacceptable regardless of the concomitant benefits. Some philosophers have argued for the recognition of fundamental rights that should be given absolute priority over all other interests. Such rights might include certian political values, such as the right to vote, the right of self-expression, or the right to have children. Philosophers have also maintained that there are *moral imperatives* that must not be transgressed regardless of the likely benefits. Such moral structures might include the commandments against murder or sacrilege.

Thus, important constraints may be imposed on the process of policy comparison. Boundaries may be drawn that cannot be crossed regardless of the interests that may be served. Within these boundaries cost-benefit analysis may take place.

It is important for policy advocates to investigate the constraints that could be imposed on cost benefit analysis. As George Orwell's nightmare vision of 1984 reminds us, if we continue exchanging freedom and liberty for material benefits, we may unwittingly create a society in which the human spirit is snuffed out, and regimented men must march to the regular beat of a superficially benevolent dictatorship. Free and open debate is the proper means of provoking society to understand the choices it confronts.

Calculations of costs and benefits must consider not only the final outcomes of policy decisions but also the process by which those outcomes are produced. The ideology of a policy system might ascribe significance to individual and collective action independent of the final products generated by these activities. The democratic process, for example, is valued for its own sake irrespective of its implications for the formation and implementation of public policy. Changes in process as well as changes in end states may be regarded as costs or benefits to be weighed in evaluation of policy.

The Comparison of Policy Options

The following section of this chapter incorporates the insights of the policy sciences into a new framework for analyzing debate propositions that advocate courses of action.

Disputes over questions of policy are subject to different standards of judgment than are disputes over questions of fact. Factual disputes pivot solely on the issues of probability, whereas policy disputes are concerned primarily with the issues of probability and value. Each advocate in a factual dispute seeks to demonstrate that his factual claim is more probable or likely to be true than the claims of his opponent. This applies to both propositions offering factual statements that refer to the past and factual statements that refer to the future. This concept in analyzing propositions is based on the theory that we cannot be absolutely certain of the truth value of statements referring to the real world.

For purposes of this discussion, probability will be defined as the degree of likelihood that any statement claiming to describe the past or predict the future is true. In quantitative terms, the value of a probability varies between 0 and 100 percent. A probability of 0 percent corresponds to the belief that a statement is certainly false; a probability of 100 percent corresponds to the belief that a statement is certainly true. Intermediate probabilities correspond to the intermediate degrees of belief in the truth of a given statement. The stronger our belief in the truth of a statement, the closer its probability will approach 100 percent. Consider three illustrations from the realm of prediction. The claim that a tossed coin has a 50 percent probability of turning up heads corresponds to a belief that a statement predicting heads on a particular toss has equal likelihood of being true or false. Alternatively, the claim that the Philadelphia Phillies have a 1 percent chance of winning the pennant coresponds to the belief that a statement predicting victory for the Phillies is far more likely to be false than true. Finally, the claim that adoption of a public works program has a 90 percent chance of eliminating long-term unemployment corresponds to the belief that a statement predicting this result is significantly more likely to be true than false.

Theorists have stipulated that the benefits of any policy system are a function of both the probability that the system will achieve certian results and the value or worth of those results. A rational decision maker seeks policy that provides the greatest probability of obtaining the most highly valued consequences. Debaters and judges must attempt to determine both the probabilities and the values of possible policy outcomes.

It is essential to realize that advocates need not guarantee any particular outcome of a policy system in order to warrant adoption or retention of that policy. Focusing our attention for the moment upon a single consequence of a policy decision, the worth or utility of that policy equals the probability that the desired outcome will indeed be achieved times the value of that outcome (Utility = P × V). The utility of any policy outcome increases as both the probability and the value of desired results increase. For example, if a new policy offers a 50 percent chance of eliminating American inflation, the utility of that policy (with respect only to this outcome) is 0.5 times the value of eliminating inflation. Only the most foolhardy decision maker would reject the new policy because its proponents have not proven that it will eliminate inflation. To determine the net benefits or expected utility of a policy system when multiple outcomes are considered, policymakers simply sum up for all anticipated results the product of the probabilities and values.

Decisions in academic debate should be based on a comparison of the net benefits or utility of policy systems proposed by the affirmative and negative teams. One policy will obviously be preferred over another if it has a higher probability of achieving more favored outcomes and lower probabilities of achieving less favored ones. Debate over propositions of policy can be viewed as an attempt to select the best policy action from a range of alternatives. This process necessarily involves a comparison of two or more policy systems to determine their relative merits. A policy proposition can be tested only by comparing it to alternative policies. A course of action is affirmed only if it is better than all other possibilities and rejected only if it is not as good as at least one other possibility.

Inevitably, the rejection of one policy or course of action means the adoption of another policy or course of action. Even doing nothing (or suspending judgment) about a particular situation is a form of action. Because of this, a policymaker cannot suspend the flow of time while he or she deliberates over the preferred course of action. Within the confines of an academic debate, a judge must make a choice because his or her decision must reflect the selection of the better of the two policy options the advocates have presented in that debate.

No one can decide how to spend time, energy, and resources without a knowledge of possible alternatives. To cite an example, you would not decide to watch a movie unless you felt that watching that movie was preferable to alternatives such as reading, playing cards, or sleeping. Similarly, on the level of national policy, a government would not decide to adopt a system of socialized medicine, for example, unless it believed that this was a better way to achieve health care than an alternative system, such as subsidizing private insurance plans.

The contention that evaluation of policy propositions inherently involves comparative judgments is a fundamental precept of contemporary decision theory. The verbal statement that policy choice demands the comparison of alternative policy systems has been formalized by the following simple inequality equation: $NB^a > NB^n$. This equation means that policy a is chosen only if the net benefits (NB) of policy a are greater than those of any perceived alternative (n) to policy a. All policy decisions, then, are based on an inequality equation that necessarily includes at least two alternative policies. Policy analysts generally strive to express the net benefits of policy systems in numerical terms by quantifying both the value of policy outcomes and the probabilites that these outcomes will be achieved. Whenever possible, debaters should also strive to express their value judgments and factual predictions as precisely as possible.

It is not recommended, however, that debate be filled with the algebraic expressions and computer output typically found at research seminars. One of the prime benefits of debate as training for the real world lies precisely in its requirement that advanced knowledge and analysis be communicated intelligibly, efficiently, and persuasively to a receptive but nontechnical audience. This task is of critical importance in the real-world policy formulation, since technically trained analysts must present their views to audiences such as congressmen, mayors, and administrators, who, in turn, are ultimately responsible to voters. Debate presents the opportunity for orienting fairly advanced policy-analytical thinking to nontechnical evaluators (debate judges) under the pressure of time. It is unmatched by doing purely analytical work in solitude. However, debaters must make their own analytical habits rigorous enough so that they will be informed and capable of communicating the best information to decision makers that the current state of knowledge permits.

SUMMARY

In conclusion, we have described the nature of policy systems analysis as it relates to academic debate theories and practices. In this endeavor, we have suggested a model of a systems hierarchy consisting of a pyramid with an ultimate abstract goal at its apex, supported by a descending arrangement of derived goals, structure, and checks and balances. These components are linked together both horizontally and vertically.

We pointed out how a system is located within an ever-changing evironment, to which it must adapt itself (or be adapted from without) in order to survive. The environment consists of natural forces, ideas, attitudes, resources, and other systems.

In academic debate, affirmative justification for the resolution may be achieved by approaching the relevant policy system at any level. Affirmative case construction may emphasize alteration of the core values of the system. This may be accomplished either by replacing them with new core values or by clarifying ambiguities among pluralistic core values in order to rearrange their assigned priorities. Going beyond this method, affirmative case construction may bypass core values of the system and focus instead on its structures and its code of checks and balances. We indicated that, while systems analysis is a useful tool for considering policy proposals, it should not be applied mechanically, without regard for relevant unmeasurable soft factors.

Finally, we explained the process of comparing policy systems in debate. While we uphold quantitative measures comparing the relative utility of alternative systems, we recognize the important role of rhetoric in presenting these arguments to decision makers who may be non-technical judges and lay audiences.

25

Policy Systems Revisited

Allan J. Lichtman
Daniel M. Rohrer
John P. Hart

The last decade has witnessed an explosion of articles on debate theory, particularly in the area of models of the debate process. In less than a generation, we have gone from one, to three, to a plethora of paradigms. Too easily the choice of an appropriate paradigm for academic debate can be attributed to differences of taste or disposition. Recently, however, Rowland has proposed five standards for evaluating the worth of competing paradigms:

1. Clarity and internal consistency
2. Competitive fairness
3. Accurate reflection of the policy environment
4. Encouragement of clash
5. Adaptability to the current form of debate[1]

Rowland's formulation omits the overriding criterion that a proposed model should conform to the logical requirements of upholding resolutions of policy in a competitive format requiring a yes-no decision at the conclusion of advocacy. Questions of policy present unique concerns, the major one of which is the ability of a paradigm to affirm or negate any resolution of policy. Any paradigm, moreover, is not invariant with respect to the wording of resolutions or the form of the debate process. Adjustments would be necessary, for example, if advocacy were directed to matters of fact, not policy, or if the debate format permitted "no-verdict" decisions.

Within the context of policy resolutions and prevailing debate practice the policy-making model remains the only legitimate paradigm

for debate. In not only informs advocates and judges of their responsibilities, but offers standards capable of resolving virtually every contro-
verted issue of debate theory. We feel that our criticisms of traditional
theory and hypothesis testing have stood the test of time and will not be
repeated here.[2] This paper will reaffirm the primacy of policy systems
debate by responding to recent indictments made by Rowland, Ulrich
and Balthrop, while showing how the theory can settle disputes over
matters such as counterwarrants and permutation standards. It should
be noted that Lichtman and Rohrer certainly did not have such
strategies in mind when the principles of policy-systems debate were
first set forth in an article written fifteen years ago.

In his last-word commentary for a recent *JAFA* forum on paradigms of debate, Rowland charges that the "policy-making paradigm . . .
has become so vague as to be all things to all people."[3] In particular,
Rowland claims that the Lichtman-Rohrer version of policy debate is
inconsistent on the requirement for quantitative comparison of costs
and benefits, and irresolute on whether or not negative teams may
legitimately advance multiple policy options.[4]

Rowland's first objection simply misconstrues our explication of
policy comparison, thus conjuring contradictions of his own imagining.
Rowland claims that in their recent work, Lichtman and Rohrer
sanctioned "special attention to qualitative or value-related harms,"
blurring the earlier position that "no interest" ever be given "absolute
priority over other interests."[5] Yet in 1970 Lichtman and Rohrer
recognized that advocates may argue for the resolution of policy comparison not by the smooth exchange of costs and benefits, but according
to an overriding moral value given absolute priority over other considerations.[6] This strategy, available to either affirmative or negative
advocates, does not obviate the requirement for policy comparison, but
discloses only the option for contending that examination of costs and
benefits should take place within the boundaries set by certain value
priorities. Indeed, the principle of boundary conditions is well recognized in contemporary forms of systems analysis. The call for value
priority is scarcely equivalent either to the conventional wisdom that
requires an affirmative decision on each of several stock issues or to
the hypothesis testing model that gives special priority to all nonresolutional alternatives.

Neither is the policy-making model ambiguous regarding the
legitimacy of presenting multiple policy options. Again, our position has
been consistent for more than a decade. The logic of the policy-making
paradigm explicitly sanctions either the affirmative or the negative
proposing for consideration more than a single policy system. Central to
the paradigm is the thesis that affirmation of a single policy system may
logically entail affirmation of the resolution, irrespective of the dis-

position of other resolutional systems. Indeed, in an article published in 1973 Lichtman, Garvin, and Corsi elaborated this insight into a new affirmative option dubbed the alternative justification case.[7]

Although Rowland seems surprised by the caution that alternative options not contradict one another, the rationale for this warning is simple. The defense of contradictory positions is self-defeating for the advocate, since the arguments and evidence deployed in defending one position will undermine the credibility of the other contradictory position. Although Zarefsky is correct is noting that one of two contradictory claims may be true, this observation is of little help to the advocate whose own arguments simultaneously undermine both of his or her positions.

Finally, our sanctioning of multiple policy options for negative advocates, does not, as Rowland charges, collapse the policy-making model into a version of the hypothesis-tesing paradigm. Unlike hypothesis testing, the policy model does not automatically grant a favorable presumption to whatever counterplan is proposed for debate.[8] The policy-making model discourages the presentation of counterproposals designed to consume affirmative speaking time by not automatically granting those counterplans presumption. Unlike hypothesis testing, moreover, it requires that each negative counterplan be presented in sufficient detail to permit comparison with affirmative policy systems. The hypothesis testers reject the necessity for anything more elaborate than a brief outline of alternatives to the hypothesis expressed by the debate resolution. Indeed, it was an early indictment of these flaws in the hypothesis-tesing model which may have suggested that Lichtman and Rohrer's formulation of policy systems debate forbade multiple policy options by negative advocates.[9]

Another cardinal principle of the policy-making paradigm is symmetry between the options available to affirmative and negative teams disputing policy statements phrased. Negative teams, like their affirmative counterparts, can defend multiple policy options. Affirmation of any competitive alternative as superior to the affirmative plan (assuming there is a single plan offered in the debate) entails rejection of the debate resolution. Again, there is no inconsistency between our position now and that taken in the alternative justification article of 1973. "So, too," observed Lichtman, Garvin, and Corsi, "the negative should be able to propose alternative counterplans to policy suggestions offered by the affirmative team."[10]

Perelman and Olbrechts-Tyteca demonstrated that advocates can address at least three audiences: themselves, their particular listeners, and a universal audience incorporating our best notions of reasonableness and rationality.[11] Argument addressed to the universal audience grounds this analysis of debate as a comparison of policy systems.

Without the universal audience, debate would be a purely manipulative practice, unbounded by standards of ethics or rationality. The first and second audiences of any given debate—the advocates and the judge— are free to apply whatever standards for judgment happen to suit them at the time. Consideration of the universal audience, however, means that theory should be fashioned to reflect the logic of disputing policy questions.

Our recommendation that debate follow a process of policy comparison is not sustained by any analogy to role models of policymakers in the political system (which is Balthrop's core objection to our position).[12] Rather, our analysis is founded solely on the logic of defending resolutions of policy in a format requiring a yes-or-no decision after the cessation of advocacy. Thus the status of the judge as an arbiter of policy choice and of debaters as advocates for competing policy systems is inherent in the kinds of resolutions that debaters consider and the type of decision that judges must render. Balthrop's recent attempt to subsume our position fails to address this crucial distinction.[13]

Any attempt to depart from the logic of the debate process either begs the question of what should guide debaters and judges or imposes arbitrary and artificial standards that reflect the idiosyncrasies of particular theorists. Even the most adroit and thoughtful critics of the policy model fail to escape the horns of this dilemma in their efforts to present alternative theory. Balthrop, for example, after an insightful investigation of debate as policy analysis, can offer no more illuminating criterion for the guidance of judges and debaters than the venerable suggestion that judges should function as critic, awarding decisions to whomever has done "the better job of debating."[14] Similarly, those proposing a hypothesis-testing model for debate reveal their personal preferences for a symmetry between debate and science, but do not respond to the special requirements of disputing resolutions of *policy*.

From Rowland and Balthrop's idiosyncratic positions we move to a model at the other end of the spectrum. This view of the debate process that has recently gained popularity is the so-called tabula rasa approach. Ulrich's view of the debate judge as a clean slate uncontaminated by any prior knowledge incorporates a trivial truth about advocacy while missing a much more profound one.[15] Ulrich originally sought to create a paradigm for debate by denying the possibility of agreeing on a paradigm independent of the arguments made in individual rounds of debate. Although Ulrich is, of course, correct that all matters are open to dispute both in the debate forum and elsewhere, he neglects the critical need for theorists to probe the logical requirements of policy discourse and develop guidelines that can clarify the responsibilities of judges and debaters. The wheel need not be reinvented in every debate. Ulrich's approach, moreover, encourages the most frivolous kinds of arguments as well as shallow spread attacks since judges must give equal credence to every substantive and theoretical claim made by competing advocates. "Shazam—and that defeats the case," if unanswered, would be sufficient grounds for a negative victory according to the logic of Ulrich's nonparadigm. Ulrich offers the reservation that positions must have reasons. How is the judge to determine what is sufficient reasoning without intervening in the round?

The above remarks should not be taken to mean that we disagree with much of which Rowland, Balthrop, and Ulrich have to say. We find that all three offer reasoned responses to recent theoretical and practical trends in academic debate. We agree with Rowland that the debate format has theoretical implications. We agree with Balthrop that the judge determines the superior policy by critiquing the arguments relevant to each. And we agree with Ulrich that the evaluator of competing policies should strive to be objective. We feel all three of these theorists are grounded in the policy-making model of debate. They appear to be not so much concerned with whether debate should be viewed as a comparison of policies, as differing over the role of the critic-judge in comparing those policies. However, there have been recent theoretical developments that are not based on the policy systems model. We would now like to address these issues.

A new variant of hypothesis testing that has emerged in recent years is the counterwarrant. This variant of the justification argument has stirred heated controversy in recent years. As indicated by Paulsen and Rhodes in a 1979 *JAFA* article, the counterwarrant negative position argues against adopting a resolution by showing that examples of the resolution distinct from the affirmative plan would produce undesirable results.[16] Theorists have argued inconclusively over the legitimacy of counterwarrants, offering equally arbitrary notions of how to construe debate resolutions and how to interpret the effect of the counterwarrant strategy.[17] Analysis of the counterwarrant strategy by the logical tools of the policy-making paradigm recasts the terms of this debate. Such analysis shows that, like justification challenges, counterwarrants are a disguised form of counterplan, albeit one not considered in Lichtman and Rohrer's general theory of the counterplan, published in 1975.

The error made by Paulsen and Rhodes in their analysis of counterwarrants is a fundamental one, little different from that made by the hypothesis testers in their attempt to fashion a general paradigm for debate. For Paulsen and Rhodes a debate resolution is akin to an empirical generalization about a class of items (for example, the mean per capita for residents of the United States is $8,000 per year). Like an empirical generalization, moreover, a resolution is most accurately affirmed inductively through scrutiny of a sufficiently large number of representative examples. In this view the affirmative plan constitutes but a sample of one, the import of which can be overcome by the presentation of counterexamples that together constitute both a broader and move representative sample than the affirmative plan alone.[18]

Unfortunately for proponents of the counterwarrant theory, policy resolutions are not empirical generalizations sustained by inductive inference. A resolution's relationship to a particular affirmative plan is, in fact, deductive rather than inductive. It can be readily shown, for instance, that for certain classes of resolutions—namely those calling for adoption of a particular kind of program or policy—affirmation of any single realization of the resolution logically entails affirmation of the resolution irrespective of the evaluation of any other instances. Consider, for example, the resolution that "the federal government should adopt a program of public work for the unemployed." In this instance, affirmation of any one such program would entail affirmation of the resolution, irrespective of the disposition of any other programs. A favorable verdict, for instance, on a program of repair, maintenance, and service work would mandate adoption of the resolution whether or not advocacy also sustains the efficacy of a program of heavy construction or one of digging and refilling ditches. The negative, in this case, could endlessly propose counterwarrants without advancing its goal of opposing affirmation of the debate resolution.

For another class of debate resolutions—those proposing a quantitative change (either an increase or a decrease) in one or more policy variables, acceptance of a single policy system need not logically entail affirmation of the debate resolution. Consider, for example, the resolution that "Congress should decrease the powers of the president in foreign affairs." Assume, for instance, that the affirmative demonstrates that Congress ought to prohibit the president from appointing the head of the National Security Council without the advice and consent of the Senate. While adoption of this plan may result in a small curtailment of presidential powers, it does not compel affirmation of the debate resolution irrespective of the disposition of other proposals relative to the power of the president in foreign affairs. For negative advocates may be able to demonstrate that the government should adopt other desirable plans (for instance, repeal of the war powers act) that expand rather than decrease presidential power in foreign affairs. On balance, the result of plan and counterplan adoption might be to increase rather than decrease the power of the presidency in foreign affairs. In this instance, the result of debate will have been to warrant rejection rather than affirmation of the resolution. What is relevant to debate over such quantitative resolutions is not, as Paulsen and Rhodes imply, the demonstration that additional examples of the resolution ought to be rejected. Rather, a negative team could compel rejection of the resolution by advocating the adoption of proposals that cut in the opposite direction of the increase or decrease called for in the resolution. We term this negative strategy the "anti-resolutional counterplan." For the counterplan competes not against the affirmative proposal, but against the quantitative change called for in the resolution.

Mayer advocates a similar concept, called the "counterresolutional counterplan."[19] His position differs from ours in theory in that he views the counterresolution as an extension of counterwarrants while our position is in opposition to counterwarrants. (This is probably due to Mayer's view that counterwarrants are part of the policy-systems model, which has been disputed here.) His use of the theory in practice, given his examples, seems limited to banning the affirmative plan in order to make generic disadvantages unique. Our examination below indicates that a ban is not necessary for policy comparison.

Inadvertently, Paulsen and Rhodes give the game away in the explication of their most important example. They argue that an affirmative team might interpret the consumer product safety topic "to mean more sanitary bottlewashing practices in the beverage industry." In turn, "the negative could choose from a myriad of counterwarrants," including for instance, arguments that "manufacturer liability for consumer products has resulted in a very dangerous state of affairs in the insurance industry," that "safety requirements are far too stringent for optimum innovation in pharmaceuticals," or that new gun control regulations would provoke a "citizen revolt." They argue that "although none of these arguments would deny the desirability of better bottle washing, all would suggest that *less* not *more* action in the consumer product safety area would be desirable, and that the resolution is thus *generally* a bad idea, regardless of the affirmative's example to the contrary."[20] The key here is that only by showing that less action in the consumer product safety area is desirable do the affirmative counterwarrants cut against adoption of the resolution in the face of the affirmative example. If, for instance, all the counterwarrants were akin to the arguments that more gun control is undesirable, then the negative would not have warranted rejection of the resolution. The examination of the resolution would have shown only that it ought not to be affirmed in realms other than bottle washing. Such demonstration is irrelevant to the disposition of the debate. If the affirmative could show that consumer product safety requirements should be expanded to the area of bottle washing and the negative has not demonstrated any realm in which such requirements should be curtailed, then the policy-making judge is mandated to affirm the debate resolution. The conclusion that we ought to expand consumer product safety regulations would be unchanged even if the negative could point to a dozen areas other than bottle washing in which consumer product safety requirements ought not to be expanded.

The new anti-resolutional counterplans suggested in the foregoing analysis must satisfy four criteria to be dispositive of the outcome of a round of debate.

1. Anti-resolutional counterplans must propose a quantitative change in the policy variables cited in the resolution.
2. Such change must be opposite in direction to the change proposed in the resolution.
3. Adoption of the counterplan must yield an additive advantage over the status quo as modified by the affirmative proposal (otherwise the rational policy-maker would opt for the affirmative plan alone).
4. On balance, the quantitative change in the policy variables resulting from adoption of one or more anti-resolutional counterplans must be greater in magnitude than the quantitative change realized by the affirmative proposal.

If adoption of both the affirmative plan and the negative's counter proposals still result in net change in the direction set forth in the resolution, then the resolution will be affirmed at the conclusion of advocacy. Consider, for example, the resolution that "law enforcement officials be given greater freedom in the prosecution of crime." An affirmative case calling for repeal of the exclusionary rule, the Miranda warnings, and the right of indigent defendants to professional representation would not be offset in its capacity to warrant adoption of the resolution by the simultaneous adoption of a plan curtailing strip searches of defendants arrested on misdemeanor charges. For the net result of policy adoption would still be an expansion of the freedom of law enforcement officials in the prosecution of crime. Thus when debating quantitative resolutions, affirmative teams have a positive incentive to offer proposals that involve changes of considerable magnitude in the policy variables being considered. They offer narrow-gauged cases at the peril of being defeated by the anti-resolutional counterplan.

The anti-resolutional counterplan has implications for another recent innovation in debate theory, the permutation standard of counterplan competitiveness.[21] In the view of debate as a comparison of policies, the implications of the compared policies on the question of topicality must be considered, as the ballot ultimately requires a yes-no decision on the resolution.[22] Therefore, although elements of two policies may be fused to determine their competitiveness, the judge must decide which one of those policies is superior. If the permutation of the affirmative plan and elements of the negative counterplan is the superior policy option but cuts against the resolution, then the permutation has topicality implications because the affirmative permutation is not advocating the resolution. Using the example used in

Herbeck's essay on competitiveness, found elsewhere in this volume, if an affirmative permutes elements of a negative's ban (x) counterplan, creating a fusion that bans everything but the affirmative plan, how would deciding in favor of this policy result in a net increase in the exploration or development of outer space, which is what the resolution in question called for?

Finally, we would note that, although Herbeck's interest in putting limits on counterplanning is of value, perhaps competitiveness standards is not where we should be looking. We note that Herbeck does not specifically indict our decade-old criteria for competitiveness, reprinted elsewhere in this volume. We feel the questions he raised may be effectively answered through the application of those standards (we also feel that other competitiveness standards such as redundancy, philosophical, and existential are subsumed by our original criteria of mutually exclusive and net benefits).

Permutation is not the only counterplanning issue discussed recently that would be resolved by a closer examination of our original works. Recent essays by Gass and Ulrich, concerning agents of change, included elsewhere in the volume, are examples of this. Our position on the ability of counterplans to fiat is extremely clear. As the "Logic of Policy Dispute" noted:

> An individual or governmental unit reasonably can be asked to reject a particular policy if an alternative yields greater net benefits. If, however, a counterplan must be adopted by another individual or unit of government, the initial decision-maker must consider the probability that the counterplan will be accepted. [23]

Imre Lakatos, the philosopher of science, offers two criteria for evaluating the durability of scientific theory. First, have adherents avoided making ad hoc changes in the core principles of the theory? Second, can the theory explain new facts that come to light only after its formulation? [24] On both these grounds, we would suggest that policy-systems debate has withstood the test of time. As we have tried to show by reference to papers published a decade and more ago, the basic principles of policy systems debate have remained intact. Moreover, as we have tried to show with respect to functional paradigms, tabula rasa judging, counterwarrants. and permutations, this paradigm can continue to resolve controversies that have risen long after its initial development. The burden of proof, we would suggest, is on those who would attempt to point debate in new directions.

Notes

1. Robert C. Rowland, "Standards for Paradigm Evaluation," *JAFA* 18 (Winter 1981): 137–40.
2. See for example, Allan J. Lichtman, Daniel M. Rohrer, "Critique on Zarefsky on Presumption," in James I. Luck, ed., *Proceedings National Conference on Argumentation* (Texas Christian University, 1973), 38–45.
3. Robert C. Rowland, "The Primacy of Standards for Paradigm Evaluation: A Rejoinder," *JAFA* 18 (Winter 1982): 156.
4. Rowland, "Rejoinder," pp. 156–57.
5. Rowland, "Rejoinder," pp. 156–57.
6. Allan J. Lichtman and Daniel M. Rohrer, "The Role of the Criteria Case in the Conceptual Framework of Academic Dabate," in Donald R. Terry, ed., *Modern Debate Case Techniques* (Lincolnwood; IL: National Textbook, 1970), 21–22.
7. Allan J. Lichtman, Charles Garvin, and Jerry Corsi, "The Alternative Justification Affirmative: A New Case Form," *JAFA* 10 (Fall 1973): 59–69.
8. Lichtman, Garvin, and Corsi, p. 68.
9. Lichtman and Rohrer, "Critique."
10. Lichtman, Garvin, and Corsi, p. 62.
11. C. Perelman and L. Olbrechts-Tyteca, *The New Rhetoric*, trans. John Wilkinsen and Purcell Weaver (Notre Dame: University of Notre Dame Press, 1969), 13–47.
12. V. William Balthrop, "Citizen, Legislator, and Bureaucrat as Evaluators of 'Competing Policy Systems,'" in David A. Thomas, ed., *Advanced Debate* (Lincolnwood, IL: National Textbook, 1979), 404.
13. V. William Balthrop, "The Debate Judge as 'Critic of Argument': Toward a Transcendent Perspective," *JAFA* (Summer 1983): 2.
14. Balthrop, "Evaluators," p. 417.
15. Walter Ulrich, "Tabula Rasa as an Approach to the Judging of Debates," paper presented at the Annual Meeting of the Speech Communication Association, Minneapolis, Nov. 1978.
16. James W. Paulsen and Jack Rhodes, "The Counter-Warrant as a Negative Strategy: A Modest Proposal," *JAFA* 15 (Spring 1979): 203–10.
17. See, for example: Patricia M. Ganer, "Counter-Warrants: An Idea Whose Time Has Not Yet Come," in G. Zeigelmueller and J. Rhodes, eds., *Dimensions of Argument: Proceedings of the Second Summer Argumentation Conference* (Annandale, VA: Speech Communication Association), 476–84; Marjorie Keeshan and Walter Ulrich, "A Critique of the Counter-Warrant as a Negative Strategy," *JAFA* 16 (Winter 1980): 199–203.
18. Paulsen and Rhodes, p. 207.
19. Michael E. Mayer, "Extending Counter-Warrants: The Counter-Resolutional Counterplan," *JAFA* 12 (Fall 1982): 122–27.
20. Paulsen and Rhodes, pp. 207–8.
21. Dale A. Herbeck, "A Permutation Standard of Competitiveness," *JAFA* 22 (Summer 1985): 12–19.
22. Although Herbeck seems to advocate this position, few debaters advocating this theory seem to consider it. See Herbeck, "Permutation," pp. 15–16.
23. Allan J. Lichtman and Daniel M. Rohrer, "The Logic of Policy Dispute," *JAFA* 16 (Spring 1980): 240–41.

24. Imre Lakatos, "Falsification and the Methodology of Scientific Research Programmers," in I. Lakatos and A. Musgrave, eds., *Criticism and the Growth of Knowledge* (Cambridge: Cambridge University Press, 1970), 173–74.

KEY TERMS

anti-resolutional counterplans
harm
hypothesis testing
inherency
plan meet need

policy making
prima facie
significance
solvency
stock issues

DISCUSSION

1. Compare and contrast each of the major paradigms.
2. Does policy systems theory have any relevance in examining questions of nonpolicy? Explain.
3. What are the stock issues in the stock issues paradigm?
4. Compare and contrast how hypothesis testing and policy system theory view inherency.
5. How would Lichtman, et al., translate soft variables into quantifiable elements for use in cost/benefit analysis?
6. Would Lichtman, et al., believe that the affirmative example becomes the resolution? Why? What are the implications of this for nonpolicy debate?
7. Would Lichtman, et al., believe that the affirmative plan inductively proves the resolution? Why? What are the implications of this for nonpolicy debate?

Part Six

Judging Stances

Whether one views debate as a dialectic in search of a truth or an exercise in rhetorical skills, a third party still makes a yes/no decision at the end of the round. Part Six displays some of the most influential views in this area of thought. To many, the separation between these essays and Part Five, "Models of the Debate Process," is artificial, given that all of the views contained in these sections are considered paradigms. Accepting for the monent the use of the term "paradigms" to describe these models, we believe that one reason for the paradigm controversy that abounds is that these paradigms operate at different levels. Critic-of-argument and tabula rasa, for instance, are differing views of the *judge's* role in the debate process.

Part Six begins with Balthrop's award-winning critic-of-argument essay. This view has gained strength in the debate laboratory over the past decade. From this perspective, debate is a rhetorical activity for evaluation by a critic trained in the skills of argumentation. It should not be mistakenly assumed that this stance is a throwback to elocution or oratory contests, in which debates hinged on delivery or logical fallacies. Balthrop sees rhetoric as integral to political decision making, and criticism to be both an intellectual and a social necessity.

Walter Ulrich's tabula rasa judging stance starts from the premise that debate is a setting for debaters to make their arguments to a totally impartial judge. The tabula rasa judge demands that debaters prove their own arguments, and disprove those of their opponents, without assuming any givens. All issues must be decided by debating them in the round. According to this judging stance, the judge's neutrality is such that he or she is not permitted to intervene. This means that the judge may not classify certain arguments as stupid, or certain pieces of evidence as being irrelevant, simply because he or she thinks they self-evidently are stupid and irrelevant. Anything presented as an argument is taken as an argument, unless specifically refuted by the opposing debaters.

The tabula rasa judge attempts to be a blank slate at the beginning of each debate, and never to make a subjective or biased judgment that is not derived from direct statements of the debaters. The tabula rasa judging stance is the preferred position of many experienced and committed debate coaches. However, it is not universally accepted.

Snider, in an essay written especially for this edition, advocates that debate be viewed as a game, an academic game to be sure, but a game with appropriate rules and regulations that recognize both the parameters and the limits of the debate format. Debate is, after all, a simulation undertaken by students under the supervision of trained educators for the purpose of teaching certain specific humanistic skills— reasoning, communicating, arguing, criticizing, refuting, making conclusions and leading the listeners to make decisions.

The narrative paradigm is an approach to rhetorical theory introduced by Walter Fisher of the University of Southern California in the mid-1980s. A few of us—to include *one* of the co-editors of this book—saw this as a brilliant and stunning new creative innovation in understanding how people construe the world, and how people communicate. The narrative paradigm has proven to be a genuinely new perspective, which has generated much scholarship and criticism in areas such as religious rhetoric and political communication.

Some debate theorists see the potential for application of the narrative paradigm to academic debate as well. In the Third Edition, we included the article by Kristine Bartanen to introduce the concept to readers of this book. We bestowed the title of "cloud on the horizon, no bigger than a man's hand," to the narrative paradigm. The narrative paradigm has not succeeded in taking the debate community by storm yet, but it remains a threat to do so.

To some, its chief drawback remains its ambiguity. They are open to the idea but want more information before committing to it. What are the stock issues for the affirmative to prove, or the negative to refute, about a narrative? These and other basic questions are still seeking answers that can be reduced to practical application in a debate.

The most threatening aspect of the narrative paradigm to many is precisely its irreducible subjectivity, which invites—even demands— judge intervention in the round. The final determination of whose story to select among the competing stories being told rests in the sole discretion of the person behind the ballot. Stories are grasped, not proved. Even the most critical listeners respond to stories, but few analyze them. Proponents point out that, conversely, policy systems analysis is also inherently subjective in the areas of greatest import to making judgments—in evaluating source credibility of conflicting experts, in weighing the value of intangibles such as the psychological and emotional harms of circumstances, or even the relative comparative importance of arguments such as the quality of life versus life as an absolute value. To prize objectivity over subjectivity is itself a subjective choice. A preference for logic is just a preference, but is in and of itself not a *logical* choice. To rule out all nonempirical, intuitive judgments from consideration is itself an arbitrary judgment contrary to accepted practice in the real world analogs of the debate activity. Decisions in the courtroom, the legislative hall, and the negotiating table, to mention a few benchmarks for the debate laboratory to simulate, all rest ultimately on subjective cognitive processes, no matter how quantitative the evidence is.

Still the narrative approach will not go away. Debaters are beginning to talk narrative talk. At least one affirmative case based totally upon the narrative paradigm was heard by one of the co-editors in the elimination rounds at the 1991 CEDA national tournament. Narrative concepts, such as character, peripeteia, narrative fidelity and narrative plausibility, are being heard from time to time even in policy debates. If for no other reason, we think a second look at the narrative paradigm is warranted by increased debater interest in it.

We have concluded that this is still an early date in the career of the narrative paradigm. *Advanced Debate* is not the place to bury or coronate it. In time, narrative debate may become the next big idea, like hypothesis testing; or it may go the way of alternative justification cases and other new ideas that never went far. This is not a decision for us to make, it is, rather, for coaches, debaters, and theorists—our natural constituency—to decide through practice and through continued thoughtful discussions.

We have, accordingly, reprinted K. Bartanen's original piece, along with an aggressive critique by Gass.

26

The Debate Judge as Critic of Argument

V. William Balthrop

Despite the most earnest desires of participants, the role of the judge in intercollegiate debate has assumed increased importance in recent years. Rather than seeing the fulfillment of Cross and Matlon's 1978 prophecy that "our current concern over judging philosophies [may become] irrelevant,"[1] more contemporary explorations conclude that the "choice among [judging] paradigms is now the dominant theoretical issue in debate."[2] It makes a difference, such scholars argue, whether a judge evaluates a debate from the paradigm of policy making, hypothesis testing, tabula rasa, game theory, or some other as yet unidentified formulation; and, further, the assumptions undergirding these paradigms have pragmatic implications for debaters seeking to devise the most instrumental argumentative strategies.

Regardless of specific differences, each of these paradigms seems to share the fundamental assumption that the essential attributes of debate, or the overriding purpose of the activity, provide the most appropriate criteria by which to evaluate any given round. In somewhat stronger language, Rowland claimed that "not only do debate paradigms provide the standards by which judges evaluate debates, but paradigms actually determine what the judge perceives."[3] Thus, if debate is a comparison of competing policy systems, the judge functions as a decision-maker evaluating the justifications advanced for specific policies, one of which must be selected. Accepting that the debate pivots on this comparison, however, Lichtman, Rohrer and Corsi would impose the logic of policy analysis on all debates.[4] Similarly, to describe the resolution as an hypothesis to be tested is to cast the judge into the role of scientist or philosopher, and Zarefsky would impose the "counterpart of the scientific procedure or the logical deduction" as the appropriate decision criteria.[5]

This essay seeks to explore an alternative perspective, that of the *critic of argument*, which transcends any individual paradigm and provides a general orientation for many judges that encourages an emic approach, thus allowing evaluative criteria to emerge from each debate, while also permitting each judge to rely upon his or her own areas of expertise to make sense of what happens in the debate. It is this latter characteristic, the conscious involvement of the judge in a dialogue with the debate, which most clearly distinguishes the critic of argument from tabula rasa. A brief review of what it means to adopt the critical stance will be followed by a consideration of how a critic of argument might function during a debate, a response to some objections made to this perspective and, finally, some speculation about the implications of this judging perspective on debate practices.

THE *CRITIC* OF ARGUMENT

The idea of critic-judge is certainly not novel; indeed, this image seems to have predominated during the history of intercollegiate debate. Traditional interpretations of this image, however, seem to focus upon a judge explaining why one team's delivery skills exceeded those of another or why losing one stock issue meant loss of the debate. Even now, whether making decisions according to the criteria of policy-making or hypothesis-testing paradigms, the judge still functions as a critic to the extent that one makes statements about *why* one policy position is superior to another or *why* the probable truthfulness of the resolution has been demonstrated. To explain *why* in contemporary debate is to have made an evaluation as to which team did the better job of debating, regardless of the criteria used to reach that decision.[6] Evaluation implies further that one has apprehended the event and has made some sense of the positions advanced. That one has, in other words, understood what happened in the debate. Understanding in this sense means far more than merely comprehending the symbols used to transmit descriptions of policy options and to foreshadow their success or failure. Rather, it also includes an awareness and examination of the modes of thought that lead to the attribution of particular meanings. One can listen to a debate and conclude that one team was superior; but to go a step further and be aware consciously of the ways that meaning and importance were attached to specific issues and positions is to impose a certain distance between the observer—the judge, and the event—the debate. This distance, however, serves not to separate the critic and event, but rather permits reflexivity to govern the dialogue dialectic which exists between them. It is here, I would argue, that the judge has adopted the critical stance and entered into the critical, or hermeneutic, circle.[7]

The hermeneutic circle represents that process of relationship existing between the individual and his or her attempts to understand some phenomenon, and is predicated upon the dialectical tension between the particular and the whole, between the unfamiliar and the familiar. As one progresses through the circle, never to escape from its force, the critic arrives at a point where his or her interpretation has been internalized through the act of understanding such that it helps now to form the basis for preconceptions brought to bear upon the next interaction. The following diagram taken from Murray's *Modern Critical Theory*, may help explain the process.[8]

The Judge as Critic of Argument

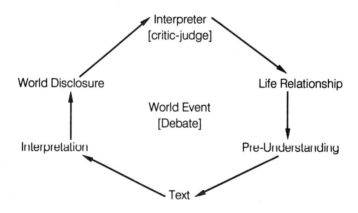

In this sequence, the interpreter, or critic-judge, forms the horizon, or that "range of vision that includes everything that can be seen from particular vantage point,"[9] for each interpretation. The potentialities for each interaction rest, to a significant degree, upon the skills, attitudes, sensitivities, and interestedness of the critic. The critic and the phenomenon, however, do not just exist in isolation or even conjoined only through their immediate context. Rather, they exist in a life relationship with one another through their mutual participation within a given community. As Murray noted, "the author who speaks [the debater] and the critic who interprets must in some sense belong to the same world, the same linguistic community."[10] By this view, the critic-judge and the debaters stand together in history, bound by their participation within the forensic community as well as their physical proximity. As members of that community, they share certain beliefs, values and orientations, which permit them to address one another with greater possibilities for understanding. Moreover, these participants in community also share responsibility for its practices and ethical judgments. It is the joint membership between debaters and judges within this community that forms the basis of their understanding for each debate. Each event can be understood only within the context of debate as an activity and, on a somewhat more particularized level, as a debate within an individual topic area. Inevitably, despite the best attempts to exclude such factors, the set of experiences and beliefs each participant holds has fundamental importance for the ways reality is perceived, interpreted and constructed. A judge's predispositions may lead to granting greater persuasive presumption to rights arguments, for instance, whereas another may adopt the view expressed in one conversation: "If nobody dies, nobody cries." Rather than seeking to ignore or to exclude such factors, the critical stance acknowledges their presence and seeks to bring that presence into conscious awareness. In this way, the judge explores how such influences affect perceptions and consequent evaluations flowing from them. The debate critic cannot understand any specific debate without a pre-understanding of procedures, of the obligations of participants, of the terminology, and, increasingly, of the substance included within the topic. Also included within this perceptual structure—as indicated by Rowland's comment cited previously—is each individual's approach to judging, for it is through this filter that the judge begins to make some sense of the debate and to arrive at the decision as to who did the better job of debating and why.

The judge who enters a debate and imposes a particular mode or method of decision-making ethically seems to use this pre-understanding in a dogmatic fashion. To one who imposes the criteria for understanding mandated by the logic of policy dispute, for example, the negative tactic of presenting a number of hypothetical arguments (many of which may contradict) will, literally, make no sense. The paradigm does not allow for such behavior within the purview of a coherent, consistent policy system.

The judge who imposes his or her standard upon the round regardless of the arguments presented is imposing an interpretation upon the debate that does not do justice to the text of the debate or to its voice in the dialectic. On the other hand, the judge who enters into the debate, also operating from a particular paradigm, and who realizes that the event itself does not quite square with his or her preconceptions must then search for other explanations or interpretations to account for this behavior.

It is at this point that the critic has entered into a relationship with the text, or linguistic characteristics of the debate, as exemplified in issues, arguments, evidence and so on. And from this interaction, in which the critic relies upon pre-understanding as a way to begin the dialectic while simultaneously relying upon the text question and testing that pre-understanding, the critic is able to arrive at an interpretation of the debate, a statement about what the debate means and why one team performed better.

One should note that adoption of the critical stance and the interpretation resulting from it does not mean that one is precluded from functioning *as if* he or she were a tester of hypothesis or an evaluator of competing policies or skill in gamesmanship. Rather, any of these may be appropriate for any particular debate. In many debates, however, such paradigms become uneasy masters. In rounds where both teams seek an alternative paradigm to that preferred by the judge, the switch may be relatively simple and most judges seem willing and able to accommodate. In others, where one team argues for one paradigm and the other for a different one, it seems that to evaluate the debate from either stance, without consideration of the arguments presented for and against, imposes the worst sort of subjectivity upon the debate. Even in those instances where the judge listens to the counterargument, so long as he or she remains wedded to the preeminence of his or her own preferred paradigm, that bias is likely to influence the perception of argumentative strength, leading to an acceptance of those arguments consonant with that paradigm.

Instead of this scenario, however, it appears that most judges seek to transcend thes individualized views and to switch gears, as it were, arriving at a position where they consider arguments advanced for each perspective and *then*, based upon a concentration on better arguments as they emerge within the debate, select the appropriate criteria from whichever paradigm is argued most persuasively, even at the expense of personal favorites. The judge has, it would seem, adopted the critical stance and resolved the dispute according to standards emerging as appropriate to the debate. This essay simply argues for this transcendent perspective as the basis for pre-understanding rather than as a "refuge when one's own personal choice is rendered moot."[11]

Adoption of the critical stance as a judging perspective means, also, that the judge participates actively in the debate process. One of the most frequent objections to the tabula rasa approach is that it seems to fly in the face of intuition,[12] that it seems impossible for any person to be objective and not filter events through his or her perceptual screens. Even the most outspoken advocate of this view seems to acknowledge the legitimacy of this concern, yet he still strives for a sense of critical isolation. Ulrich, for instance, has written that:

One certainly should be aware of their own biases an idiosyncraticies [sic]. It may be impossible to eliminate those biases totally. That does not mean, however, that a judge should not attempt to minimize those biases by developing a critical stance that minimizes his/her influence on the debate. Rather than having biases and actively injecting them into a debate round, a tabula rasa judge admits biases and attempts to keep them from affecting his/her decision unless necessary.[13]

Such goals, however admirable, seem doomed to failure. The most charitable scenario involves the judge absorbing material from the debate and then, at the end of the round, attempting to attribute meaning to the arguments presented. Nevertheless, at some point in time—either at the end of the debate or, more likely, during the presentation of arguments themselves—the judge is involved in interpretation, placing these positions into a schema such that the importance of *some* evidence and *some* arguments can be identified relative to others. It is here, at the point of interpretation, that the judge engages in the hermeneutical process. It is here that an awareness of the rules of debate *as that judge understands them*, of the content area of the debate *as that judge understands it*, of various judging paradigms *as that judge understands them*, all combine to influence the interpretation *by that judge* as to which team did the better job of debating. The judge cannot withdraw from participating with the debaters in the creation of meaning, though it is a different kind of participation; and rather than admitting one's biases and seeking to keep them from affecting one's decision, a better perspective seems to be that which tests one's biases against the debate itself and seeks to understand how they affect the decision.

Even after the critic-judge has reached an interpretation of the debate, the responsibilities of the critic and participation in the circle are not yet complete for, as Murray argues, "The final purpose of hermeneutic criticism is to carry out the meaning of the work as an event which reveals, communicates and sets up a world."[14] The world which is set up in this instance is that of the debate as explained by the critic-judge. The importance of this act is not only that it serves as a check upon the individual critic's subjectivity—as will be discussed in the following section—but that it enters into the critic's horizon as well as into the tradition of the debate community. In this regard it functions as an influence upon not only the individual critic but also upon the community; and, as a consequence of their being trapped within the circle, judges now enter into new relations with new debate acts.

The strength of adopting the critical stance as an alternative to any single paradigm is that it provides an orientation toward interpretation that permits the use of *any* paradigm so long as it is appropriate to the individual debate while avoiding the necessity of imposing a paradigm upon an act for which it is inappropriate. The importance of this seems even clearer in contemporary debate practice than in rhetorical criticism from which this perspective is borrowed. After all, it is a common axiom that debate practice precedes theory and, interestingly, this is perhaps nowhere more pronounced than in the development of judging paradigms. Recognition of the inappropriateness of traditional standards for evaluating debates conducted along the comparative advantage format, along with other reasons, hastened emergence of the policy-making paradigm. That judging paradigm arose inductively from the characteristics typical of many debates. Subsequently, the failure of policy-making to explain strategies evolving in the 1970s led to formulation of the hypothesis-testing paradigm. And it is the failure of *this* paradigm to offer appropriate explanations and, ultimately, criteria for the evaluation of *all* debates that led to the development of other judging approaches. To force all debates to fit into any of these individual molds is to impose a rigidity and stultification of thought that would deny much that is commendable in contemporary debate; to seek to impose any one specific mode or method of judging upon all debates is to deny the forces that give each mode of interpretation its birth and legitimacy. The critic of argument, as a transcending perspective, permits the advantages of each individual method to emerge as an aid in evaluation when appropriate without incurring the disadvantages of any individual method in those cirumstances where it does not fit.

THE CRITIC OF *ARGUMENT*

If the judge does not adopt the critical stance and eschews the strait-jackets of policy analysis, the rigors of scientific procedure and the isolation of tabula rasa, upon what bases are decisions made? They are made, I would submit, upon the essential quality of debate: upon the strength of arguments. Debate is, from my point of view, a laboratory or game simulation designed to teach students an understanding of argument and to provide opportunity for developing skill in its use. This rationale cannot, of course, be claimed to have any objective validity or truth, for such absolutes are generally unknowable. Such views do, however, achieve a kind of truth through the intersubjective agreement of members within a particular community, and this view of debate was presented clearly in the definitional statement of the National Developmental Conference on Forensics in 1975 and has received continued support since.[15] Standards for evaluating debates on the basis of argument quality are thus derived intrinsically from the activity itself and, upon this basis, provide the possibility for transcending differences between paradigms and between the immediate contexts which make one more appropriate than another.

To focus upon argument is not without its difficulties, however. One scholar has argued that this imposes a judge's view of logic upon the debate;[16] another claimed that the issues in argumentation theory bear no relationship to issues in debate;[17] and another expressed concern that until one knows what argument is, one cannot structure debate on argumentation theory.[18] These criticisms deserve answers, to be sure, but none constitutes either a necessary or sufficient reason for abandoning concentration upon argument.

Perhaps the most important of these objections is that which claims the critic-of-argument perspective imposes an individual judge's view of logic upon the debate. This claim seems to rest upon two apparent flaws: (1) that the question of judge subjectivity is more apparent here than in other approaches; and (2) that standards for argument evaluation rest upon models of formal validity. The answer to each of these can be found within the view that sees debate as a field. Fields, according to Willard, constitute "systems of thought, shared standards for communication and—quite by definition—shared meanings or ways of looking at and explaining phenomena."[19] Most theorists grant that adopting an argumentative perspective means to focus upon the *reasons* given in support of a particular claim. Burleson's comments seem representative; "For an argument to be made, it is not enough for a claim or assertion to be put forward; there must also be reasons given for believing it. An argument is composed of a claim and a statement or set of statements, *adduced in its support*. This proposition defines argument as reason-giving discourse."[20] Within the field of argument and its sub-field of debate, one can find refuge in certain relatively traditional measures to evaluate such reasons: the recognized expertise and motivations of sources within the content area; the internal and external consistency of evidence used in support of positions; the extent to which sources and evidence present the rationale linking data and claim; and the extent to which counter explanations and arguments can be accounted for. In each instance, however, the emphasis rests upon the reasons given in support of any claim. One must also recognize that no absolute, identifiable formula exists for evaluating any given argument such as a test for logical or formal validity; rather, the strength or persuasiveness of any argument in any given debate will emerge only through the interactions of the debaters themselves.

The concept of field also permits a response to the allegation that a critic-of-argument perspective is overly subjective in that it places too much emphasis upon the judge's own creation and interpretation of what happens in the debate. An illustration of two different views toward judging, both acknowledging deficiencies in evidence and both reaching the same decision, can be found in the critiques of the final round of the 1981 National Debate Tournament. In that debate, the

University of Pittsburgh argued that concealment of nuclear weapons delivery systems may lead to preemptive strikes.[21] Ralph Carbone expressed his concerns and reactions thus:

> The card is not very good. What "forces"; "being considered" by whom? What does "relatively invulnerable" mean, or caves are "likely to be" the dominant modes of protection? How am I to evaluate phrases like "may make a preemptive strike more attractive"? I guess I'm a bit old fashioned, but I really expect that when evidence is used to support an argument that it is going to be more on point and defensible. But, *that's me making arguments which are not made by any one in the round and so although I could have voted on an evidence challenge in this instance, I cannot and will not inject myself into the round.*[22]

Alternatively, Balthrop's critique considers another of Pittsburgh's arguments—that all nations must participate in collective action to reduce the risk of accidental war to gain any solvency[23]—and notes explicity that:

> [the] evidence seems unreasonably conclusionary and counterintuitive. No explanation is provided in the evidence, nor in subsequent speeches, as to why all nations must engage in collective effort.... Further, the incentives to accept safeguards outlined in 1AC have been challenged but not, at this moment in the dialectic, defeated. The expectation is that subsequent affirmative speeches will retain this position.[24]

An interpretation, and with it, certain expectations, has been made early in the debate that the negative argument willl not counter the strength of an affirmative position. But, as the critic continues the dialogue with the debate as it occurs, that interpretation changes such that Balthrop noted, "as the rebuttals progress and repeated negative demands that the evidence is absolute are met only with assertions—without supporting explanation—that 100 percent is not needed, the Larus evidence, and this argument, acquire a preeminence lacking at first presentation."[25]

Both judges noted deficiencies in evidence and were remarkably similar in their assessments, indicating at least some intuitive consensus on standards for argument evaluation that exist within the field or community. The one, however, expressed a reluctance to weigh such objections without comment from the opposing team, for to do so would be to make an argument for them. The other critique, also aware of evidentiary shortcomings, appeared to opt for a different stance, acknowledging that argument's weakness but considering this in evaluating the importance of that argument *relative to* its dialectical response. Both judges recognize intuitively that quality of argument and evidence are important in contemporary debate and that some standards for evaluating these exist within the community, but one seeks an objectivity *vis-a-vis* the debate whereas the other seeks to be aware of that quality when making relative comparisons and to bring that factor into conscious awareness so as to remain cognizant of its influence in the interpretive process.

Few right or wrong decisions, if any, exist in intercollegiate debate, but there do exist relatively better or worse decisions. Two judges may arrive at different conclusions without having thrust upon either the epithet of "bad judge." More important than voting affirmative or negative seem to be the reasons, or justifications, given for each interpretation. Certainly, to the extent that two people observing the same event reach different interpretations, subjectivity occurs. Even in the more formulary worlds of policy analysis and scientific investigation, subjectivity rears its head in assigning probabilities of occurrence, values of outcomes, and even questions to be investigated. But to acknowledge critical subjectivity does not weaken the intellectual value of the perspective. What is important is that *some* checks exist that keep subjective interpretations bound to the event and to the community's, or field's, standards of appropriateness.

The first check on rampant subjectivity rests in an attempt to conduct the dialogue with the debate itself with as much faithfulness as possible to the text—the linguistic utterances of the debaters. Indeed, it is the effort to describe accurately the events within the debate that leads the tabula rasa judge in a futile search for objectivity. Objectivity is a radically different construct than open-mindedness or objectification, both of which seem to require critical distance and reflexivity.[26] Instead of seeking an objective interpretation, the critic of argument seeks to moor his or her interpretation in the event while admitting and coping with the individualized meaning which results. The critic-judge is able to demonstrate the extent of that mooring through an ability to describe the debate in terms of issues, evidence and responses. But an ability to *describe* the debate does not equate to an ability to *interpret* the debate, to explain what it means and to make a decision accounting for the different interrelationships among arguments and for differences in their importance. To be sure, those interpretations and the explanations given in support of them must be rooted in the debate's text, but they acquire meaning only through the interpretive process of the critic-judge. Further, emic approaches to evaluation also require concentration upon the debate itself as the source for an appropriate method of interpretation.[27]

A second check on excessive subjectivity, although related integrally to the critic's mooring in text, results in the ultimate purpose of hermeneutic criticism, the production of the critique that posits the judge's statement of "how the debate was." That is, through discussions with debaters, coaches, and other judges; through ballot writing; and even through critiques of final rounds at such tournaments as the National Debate Tournaments and Heart of America, the critic-judge must share his or her interpretation with other members of the community. It is through this interaction that existing standards and values in the field are reaffirmed or challenged, and through this process, as the critic opens her or his own interpretation to criticism, a never-ending hermeneutic circle is perpetuated and expanded to include others. Participation in this hermeneutic process establishes the intersubjectively agreed upon standards for debate and, more specifically, for quality argument, evidence, and even critiques.

Acceptance of field-bounded procedures, practices and standards and adherence to that field's form of rationality accounts, I believe, for the intuitive consensus that seems to underlie the evaluation of argument within the debate community and for Cross and Matlon's observation that "the majority of judges in the academic debate community view debates with extraordinary consensus regardless of their stated judging philosophies."[28] The grounding of debate judges in the values of the community generates the intuitive consensus that seems to characterize debates as events and to provide criteria for the evaluation of argument. The sharing of this intuition among members of the debate community, and with it the values emphasizing concentration upon what happens in the round and evaluating arguments upon criteria generated in the round regardless of personal paradigmatic prejudices, seems to account for the agreement noted by Cross and Matlon.

In addition to the allegation that the critic-of-argument perspective imposes a judge's view of logic on the round, the two other objections to this approach rest upon concerns about the relation between debate and argumentation theory. At the same time, such views tend to ignore relatively broad-based areas of agreement in both debate and argumentation. Debate may still provide an excellent format for teaching and practicing many of argumentation's essential qualities.

Similarly, to discount the relationship between argument and debate because one is not certain what argument may be at the moment or what it may become—product, process, procedure, or social construct?—ignores the necessity of acting, teaching, and learning in an imperfect world. Refusal to teach, even through simulation, public policy analysis, physics, urban planning, or even argument, because uncertainty exists in some areas or because final answers cannot be given, seems to fly in the face of reason. One must proceed as best one can using the state of the art as it is understood at any moment, all the while recognizing the tentative nature of knowledge. It seems better, I would submit, to teach argument even with its present limitations than to deny knowledge and skills to students until scholars have sorted out the thorniest of theoretical issues. Once such issues are resolved, they can then be incorporated into teaching practice. To delay is also to run the risk that each resolution will only generate further uncertainties and questions.

IMPLICATIONS FOR DEBATE

Adoption of the critic-of-argument perspective does not seem, in and of itself, to have any serious implications for most theoretical issues in debate. Such questions as presumption, topicality, emphasis upon plan versus inherency, whether disadvantages should be specified to the affirmative plan or generic to the resolution seem little affected by this approach to judging other than to focus attention on how these are debated in the rounds. Indeed, most theoretical issues, as well as those categorized by some as unassailable—such as topicality as a voting issue, ethical considerations, and debate format[29]—would seem to be influenced more by the consensus within the debate community. If the community has reached significant agreement on these issues, and if that agreement is free from attack, then it would appear that both debaters and judges, as members of the community, would reflect those values in their behavior. If, however, disagreement exists within the community over such issues—such as whether topicality is always a voting issue or whether counterplans must be nontopical—then such issues are likely to receive more discussion in debates because such issues are themselves now open for debate. At the same time, if practice does precede theory, it is equally probable that attacks upon widely accepted communal standards, generated for strategic reasons, may well bring those practices into question. In either instance, it is still through the activity of debate itself that many of the theoretical positions of the community are examined and resolved. Thus, each debate depends upon the standards of the community and upon the stability of those standards as guides for appropriate conduct.

The main consequence for current debate practice as a result of employing a critical perspective would seem to be a greater emphasis upon evaluating quality of argument and in recognizing the role of the judge as a creator of meaning for each debate. The judge as critic assumes an active role in the debate process on the basis of his or her expertise or knowledge of practices and standards within the community. Such a view assumes that judges are able to evaluate the adequacy of reasons presented in a debate and that they will do so. At the same time, a burden rests upon the judge to justify *why* such reasons are treated as adequate or inadequate and to explain how this influenced the interpretation of the round.

The effect of this discretionary license will, no doubt, be criticized on the grounds that "arguments that may appear to be weak or fallacious at face value can be defended against these charges when an attack is made on the argument. A team should have the opportunity to defend its position against these attacks, and this cannot be done if the judge decides, after the debate, that an argument is inadequate."[30]

Perhaps so, although such a statement seems to beg the question of whether, given those standards, one could ever question the adequacy of an argument, since it could always be claimed that "if that attack were made, it could be defended against."

Nevertheless, arguments are and must be evaluated in terms of their adequacy, and such evaluation occurs through two types of judgment, each of which makes qualitative evaluations of arguments within the context of a dialectic. On the one hand, an evaluation of an argument's adequacy is made within the context of the dialectic of the debate itself, in relation to the argument's importance to others in the debate. The fact that weak arguments are unrefuted does not ipso facto make them sufficiently important in overall context of the debate to warrant their becoming a voting issue. Even when the advocates make such a claim, however, the critic need not accept such a claim unquestionably. When the critic rejects such a claim, he or she assumes the responsibility to justify such a decision, and it is here that one may rely upon the second type of dialectic relationship, which explores the individual argument within the broader context of communal standards. Even where the critic-judge grants a special status to an argument within the more limited context of the debate, he or she may still place it within the broader dialectic as he or she presents the critique.

The importance of any given argument, then, is derived through its dialectic relationship with other arguments in the debate and with standards and practices accepted by the community at large. It seems likely that the critic is thus engaged in two related yet distinct decisions. The first is that, relative to other issues in the debate, the critic may accept that an argument functions as if it were a voting issue and render a decision as to who did the better job of debating in this limited context. The second decision, also expressed in the critique, is that according to the community's standards, this argument would not, in most circumstances, function as a voting issue. Only through the inclusion of each of these can the education goals of increasing understanding and skill in the use of argument be made compatible with the competitive aspects of contemporary debate.

Closely related to the question of adequate arguments, and indeed perhaps a standard for evaluating relative importance, is this perspective's implication on the use of evidence and on the number of responses made to arguments. Evidence, or support for the claim, is usually crucial in contemporary debate and acceptance of the critic-of-argument approach may enhance that importance. By emphasizing the giving of reasons as the essential quality of argument, evidence that provides those reasons in support of claims will inevitably receive greater credibility than a number of pieces of evidence, each presenting only the conclusion of someone's reasoning process. It is, in crudest terms, a preference for quality of evidence over quantity.

The main justification presented for using conclusionary evidence is that the reasons given are so technical that they cannot be evaluated without considerable expertise in that particular content field or, (the usually related reason that the source of the evidence is so qualified that this source's testimony should be accepted. These justifications are certainly legitimate, although they are heard infrequently in most debate rounds. If the credibility of the evidence does indeed rest upon these premises, let them be presented explicitly as reasons why the evidence should be accepted in the absence of explanations more specific to the substantive issues. Every piece of evidence is not the same as every other, and the critic-of-argument perspective appears to reward those debaters who are concerned with explanation rather than conclusion, with source qualification and quality rather than quantity.

As evidence is not equal, neither are responses to arguments. Perhaps the most notable wrinkle to emerge in debate practice during the late 1970s and early 1980s is the number of answers presented in first affirmative rebuttal to disadvantages. This is, no doubt, a logical extension of the spread, but thirty-seven answers to one disadvantage, as heard in one debate, does seem to mark a qualitative shift in rebuttal tactics. The judge operating as a critic of argument will not necessarily be opposed to spread debate, and adoption of the perspective will not, by itself, spell doom for the fast-talking debater. Nevertheless, an emphasis upon quality of argument may shift debaters from the strategy of putting out a number of tagline answers toward one that presents fewer individual responses but which gives greater explanation as to why those responses either take-out or turnaround the disadvantage. The 1AR may present just as many words as before, but the focus is now on providing deeper explanation. This emphasis on quality of reasons is not limited to first affirmative rebuttals and should extend to all speeches.

Questions do, naturally, arise about what constitutes good reasons and to what extent debaters should be pushed in their quest to present quality argumentation. Inevitably, answers to such questions must rest upon the subjectivity and discretion of each individual critic. The danger does exist than any given critic will impose an interpretation upon arguments and evidence that assumes a reality quite unlike that envisioned by the text or by the debaters themselves. These dangers appear to be of degree rather than of essence, however, for no judge can avoid the unique values and thought processes which she or he brings to the interpretation of a debate. At the same time, however, that subjectivity can be kept within certain bounds by mooring one's interaction in the debate's text and by testing one's interpretation though the world disclosure of critiques and the subsequent interpretation of those critiques by other members of the community.

THE CRITIC OF ARGUMENT AS PLURALIST

Acceptance of the critic-of-argument perspective places culmination of the critical process in the resulting critique. It is, after all, only through the critique that the judge can reveal his or her construction of reality, can indicate the extent of the dialogue with the debate text, can demonstrate knowledge and skill in the use of a community's standards, and can make a case for the quality of the arrived-at interpretation. Equally important, it is only through the critique that one can generate the kind of interaction from other critics within the community that allows both individual and communal standards to be tested. And, finally, it is only through this testing that individual and communal knowledge can be broadened and deepened.

Accepting this perspective also promotes a kind of critical pluralism, one which grants the legitimacy of any given method or paradigm according to its own claims of appropriateness and internal logic rather than giving one a superordinate position to the exclusion of others. Two critics, each approaching a debate from this perspective, may adopt different individual paradigms to construct their interpretations based upon their unique interactions with the round and upon the questions they choose to ask. Each may, also, present clear and consistent explanations about the debate that indicate the appropriateness and plausibility of respective interpretations; and each interpretation may in turn resist being absorbed into the paradigmatic mold of the other, regardless of how much distortion occurs. Yet each also may constitute an equally valid approach toward understanding this particular debate. What is important is the justification advanced by each for the interpretation offered and the case that can be constructed for each interpretation's appropriateness according to the debate's text and the community's standards. Such variety does not constitute relativism but rather the capabilities of two individual minds at work on an event, both grounded in the intrinsic qualities of the event and in communal values. Both constitute approaches to understanding that complement and strengthen, rather than denounce, the other.

As a transcendent perspective, this approach does not deny any paradigm the possibility of critical merit in specific instances while it grants a flexibility to judges which more limited end more formulary methods for interpretation might prevent. It recognizes the unique function of the debate judge, which is, after all, to make a determination as to which team did the better job of debating—of constructing, analyzing, presenting and responding to arguments—and draws the criteria for making such determinations from the essential attributes of the activity itself. This view also offers an approach that sees the fulfillment of the process not in merely rendering a decision—yes, the affirmative has a superior policy; no, the resolution did not emerge from tests as being probably true—but in producing a critique of an event that will, one hopes, increase the understanding and skill in the use of argument for debaters, for judges, and for the entire community.

Notes

1. John D. Cross and Ronald J. Matlon, "An Analysis of Judging Philosophies in Academic Debate," *Journal of the American Forensic Association* 15 (Fall 1978): 123.
2. Robert C. Rowland, "Standards for Paradigm Evaluation," *Journal of the American Forensic Association* 18 (Winter 1982): 133. See also David Zarefsky, "The Perils of Assessing Paradigms," *ibid.*, 141.
3. Rowland, p. 133.
4. Allan J. Lichtman, Daniel M. Rohrer, and Jerome Corsi, "Policy Systems Analysis in Debate," in *Advanced Debate: Readings in Theory, Practice and Teaching*, ed. David A. Thomas (Lincolnwood, IL: National Textbook Co., 1979), 375–90; Lichtman and Rohrer, "The Logic of Policy Dispute," *Journal of the American Forensic Association* 17 (Spring 1980): 236–47; and Lichtman and Rohrer, "Policy Dispute and Paradigm Evaluation: A Response to Rowland," *Journal of the American Forensic Association* 18 (Winter 1982): 145–50.
5. David Zarefsky, "Argument as Hypothesis-Testing," in *Advanced Debate*, p. 430.
6. Lichtman and Rohrer envision that those who depart from the logic of poilcy dispute in evaluating debate are left with nothing more helpful than "the venerable suggestion that judges should function as a 'critic,' awarding decisions to whomever has done 'the better job of debating.'" See "Logic of Policy Dispute," p. 247. Within that essay, they appear to adopt a critical perspective even though it is focused through the lens of policy analysis. They hold that "through appropriate evidence and reasoning, advocates seek estimates of probabilities and values that are as precise as possible, given limitations of information, time, and analytic technique.... *The very purpose of oral advocacy in a round of debate is to convince a critic that a debater's assessment of probability and value is more plausible than that of an opponent.*" Logic of Policy Disputed," pp. 238–39. Emphasis added.
7. V. William Balthrop, "Argumentation and the Critical Stance: A Methodological Perspective," in *Advances in Argumentation Theory and Research*, eds. J. Robert Cox and Charles Arthur Willard (Carbondale: Southern Illinois University Press, 1982). This essay presents an extended discussion of the critical stance and its application to argumentation. This perspective is influenced heavily by the works of Hans-Georg Gadamer. See especially *Truth and Method*, trans. G. Barden and J. Cumming (New York: Seabury Press, 1975); *Philosophical Hermeneutics*, ed. and trans. D. E. Linge (Berkeley: University of California Press, 1976); and *Dialogue and Dialectic: Eight Hermeneutical Studies on Plato*, trans. P. C. Smith (New Haven: Yale University Press, 1980). Other works that present lucid accounts of the hermeneutic process are the following: Josef Bleicher, *Contemporary Hermeneutics: Hermeneutics as Method, Philosophy and Critique* (London: Routledge and Kegan Paul, 1980); Michael Murray,

Modern Critical Theory: A Phenomenological Introduction (The Hague: Martinus Nijhoff, 1975); and Richard E. Palmer, *Hermeneutics: Interpretation Theory in Schleiermacher, Dilthey, Heidegger, and Gadamer* (Evanston, IL: Northwestern University Press, 1969).

8. Murray, p. 82.
9. Gadamer, *Truth and Method*, p. 269.
10. Murray, p. 73.
11. V. William Balthrop, "First Judge Critique," *Journal of the American Forensic Association,* 18 (Summer 1981), p. 48.
12. Many critics of this approach have raised this point: Ralph E. Dowling, "Debate as Game, Educational Tool, and Argument: An Evaluation of Theory and Rules," *Journal of the American Forensic Association* 17 (Spring 1981): 234–41; Robert C. Rowland, "Substance or Procedure: Misapplication of the *Tabula Rasa* Approach," paper presented at the Speech Communication Association Convention, Anaheim, CA, Nov. 1981; and A. C. Snider, *The New Debate: A Personal Essay*, unpublished manuscript, 1981.
13. Walter Ulrich, "In Search of *Tabula Rasa*," paper presented at the Speech Communication Association, Anaheim, CA, Nov. 1981, p. 12.
14. Murray, p. 83.
15. National Developmental Conference on Forensics, "Definitional Statement," in *Forensics as Communication: The Argumentative Perspective*, ed. James H. McBath (Lincolnwood, IL: National Textbook Co., 1975), 11. Also see Rowland, "Standards for Paradigm Evaluation"; Dowling; and Snider.
16. Snider, p. 26.
17. *Ibid.* Snider also cites Rowland (1980), although no more explicit reference is provided.
18. Zarefsky, "The Perils of Assessing Paradigms," p. 142.
19. Charles Arthur Willard, "Some Questions about Toulmin's View of Argument Fields," in *Proceedings of the Summer Conference on Argumentation*, eds. J. Rhodes and S. Newell (Salt Lake City: Speech Communicaton Association, 1980), 387.
20. Brant R. Burleson, "On the Analysis and Criticism of Arguments: Some Theoretical and Methodological Considerations," *Journal of the American Forensic Association* 15 (Winter 1979): 141.
21. John K. Boaz, ed., "1981 National Debate Tournament Final Debate," *Journal of the American Forensic Association* 18 (Summer 1981): 36
22. Ralph Carbone, "Second Judge Critique," *Journal of the American Forensic Association* 18 (Summer 1981): 51. Emphasis added.
23. Boaz, p. 25.
24. Balthrop, "First Judge Critique," p. 49.
25. Ibid.
26. Ulrich argues that this search for objectivity permeates other critical endeavors as well: "This goal of objectivity can be found in other fields of argument. In rhetorical criticism, we tell our students that there is no one, best way of examining a speech; rather students should be aware of a variety of ways of looking at a rhetorical action. The critical stance should evolve out of the discourse; it should not be imposed a priori on the discourse by the critic." ("In Search of *Tabula Rasa*, p. 12.) Ulrich then cites Karlyn Kohrs Campbell, *Critiques of Contemporary Rhetoric* (Belmont: Wadsworth, 1972) in support of his position. Campbell certainly supports the inductive, or emic, approach to criticism but does

not appear to share Ulrich's goal of objectivity: "The critic asks his reader to see a discourse as he sees it, to understand and judge it as he does. In other words, criticism is never wholly impartial and objective. In all cases it is to some extent evaluative, judgmental, and subjective." (p. 1.)

27. A distinction is being made between *paradigm* and *perspective* similar to that described by David Hoy existing between *method* and *methodology*: "A discussion of *method* involves discussion of how to read a book or debate about the merits of different 'approaches.' A discussion of methodology, on the other hand, must be more abstract and philosophical; it belongs at the level of the theory of knowledge and understanding." Hoy, *The Critical Circle* (Berkeley: University of California Press, 1978), 102. Paradigm is equated with a method, or mode, of investigation whereas perspective is analogous to methodology. Within a given methodology or perspective, a critic may employ any number of methods or paradigms depending upon their appropriateness.

28. Cross and Matlon, p. 123.

29. See Rowland, "Substance or Procedure."

30. Ulrich, "In Search of *Tabula Rasa*," p. 8.

27

In Search of Tabula Rasa

Walter Ulrich

There are at least three ways to approach the study of argumentation and debate. The first approach takes the point of view of an arguer and attempts to determine what arguments will help achieve the arguer's goals. The second approach views argument from outside the argumentative situation and attempts to describe what goes on when people engage in argument. The final approach attempts to view argument from the perspective of an individual who evaluates the arguments advanced by advocates in an argument. While all three approaches to argument are interrelated, they each call for a set of perspectives that differ in critical ways. The first approach to argument attempts to discover what arguments are effective; it is directed toward those individuals engaged in the daily activity of arguing. The second approach to argument is directed toward the study of argument in the abstract. The third aproach is helpful for those who seek to observe argument and to utilize argument to assist them in reaching a decision. In law, for example, the counterparts would be individuals instructing a lawyer about how to argue; a sociologist describing the nature of a legal system; and a judge attempting to decide how he or she should decide a specific legal case.

In academic debate, there has been an increased emphasis on the third approach to the study of argument. This emphasis has resulted in an increased concern about the proper role of the judge in a debate round. Given the importance of the judge to the success of the debate activity, this emphasis has been desirable. Not only will an understanding of the way that argument should be judged promote the educational value of debate, but it will also enable us to understand how to evaluate debate outside the academic debate setting.

In order to understand any individual's method of reacting to argument, it is necessary to understand the nature of a judging philosophy. To label a judge as a hypothesis tester, a policy maker, or a stock issues judge is helpful, but it oversimplifies a more complex description of any judging philosophy. Any individual brings into argument several conceptions of the way argument should be resolved. In a sense, each judge's philosophy consists not of one single view of argument, but rather it consists of a theory of argument containing several independent levels of belief.

The first level includes all the values that a judge brings into a round, including such ideas as the value of life, liberty, economic growth, or pollution prevention. The second level includes a judge's view toward the mechanical rules used to evaluate these arguments (such things as a dropped argument should be ignored by the judge, or the requirement that the first affirmative rebuttalist must cover the case). The third level would consist of the judge's view of intra-paradigm issues. This would include the judge's view of the nature of the various philosophies of debate (for example, would a policy maker consider more than two sets of policies?). The fourth level would be the paradigm that the judge prefers to utilize, other factors being equal. A fifth level would be the judge's standard for paradigm evaluation. This would include the standards utilized by a judge in selecting a judging paradigm.[1] There are probably an infinite number of levels beyond these five levels of a judging philosophy (standard for evaluating standards; standards for evaluating standards for standards, etc.), but as a practical matter, the first five levels of a judge's philosophy are the most relevant for academic debate.

While every judge has certain preconceived notions about the proper characteristics of each level of a judge's philosophy, one current issue is the extent to which a judge should impose his or her bias on the participants in a debate round. There are three potential ways that rules can be imposed upon a debate. The first way would be for an external agency to impose rules on the judges. For example, the AFA could require that all judges be hypothesis testers, or that specific standards of evaluating argument be utilized by judges. Fortunately, except for issues involving the ethics of evidence, these rules have not been advocated or implemented, due in part to our commitment as scholars to the principles of academic freedom.

The second way to impose rules on debate is for a judge to impose his or her views on the debaters. This judge would evaluate the debate using his or her standard for correct argumentation and would cast out arguments not meeting the standard whether or not the other team argues against the position discarded. The third way to impose rules on debates is for the judge to utilize those rules that the debaters agree to in a debate round or, when the rules are in dispute, to utilize the rule that is best defended.

While this approach to judging has been called the tabula rasa approach,[2] it should be noted that this does not mean that the judge is a blank slate. The judge obviously must bring in certain preconceptions about argument into any round; tabula rasa means that the judge should be open to argument on all issues and should impose his or her view of argument on the round only when necessary. If there is no theoretical argument, the judge would utilize his or her theoretical system. If there is a theoretical dispute, however, the judge would enter the round only if there was a response by the other team, and then the judge would enter using standards drawn from the next higher level (for example, if there were a dispute about what paradigm to use, the judge would resolve the issue based upon his or her view of how paradigm should be resolved).

Tabula rasa is not a judging paradigm; it is an approach to judging that emphasizes the desirability of having debate rules evolved from each individual debate instead of being imposed upon a round externally by the judge. This does not mean that the judge is freed of the responsibility of developing standards for evaluating argument when there is no theoretical argumentation in the round.[3] In addition, there may be a few instances when theory may not be debatable, such as when a rule is imposed upon the judge from the outside (the AFA code of ethics, for example), or when one team has no opportunity to respond to an argument (such as when the last speaker introduces a new position into the round). The judge would also have to set up standards for when an argument warrants consideration and when an argument has not been developed enough to warrant altering a judging standard.[4] While all of these issues are critical ones, the emphasis of tabula rasa in the majority of the rounds is to emphasize the need for individual debaters to develop standards for the evaluation of argument.

THE JUSTIFICATION OF TABULA RASA

There are three reasons why the tabula rasa approach to the evaluating of argument is desirable. First, the tabula rasa approach encourages the development of perspectives for the evaluation of argument. There is a great value in encouraging the development of a diversity of viewpoints about argument. Any history of knowledge would include a large number of viewpoints that at one time were thought to be true, but which turned out to be invalid, as well as theories that were thought to be invalid which, upon reflection, turned out to be superior to the theories they replaced. Science, for example, can grow only by encouraging the development of new theories that, while they may seem initially to be weak, have the opportunity to prove themselves in the marketplace of ideas. While we should not set standards for argument too low, if we reject any argument that does not meet existing standards for argument, we risk grave consequences:

> With standards set higher, no one satisfying the criterion of rationality would be inclined to try out the new theory, to articulate it in ways which showed its fruitfulness or displayed its accuracy and scope. I doubt that science would survive. What from one viewpoint may seem the looseness and imperfection of choice criteria conceived as rules may, when the same criteria are seen as values, appear an indispensable means of spreading the risk which the introduction or support of novelty always entails.[5]

To force one view of argument upon participants in a round may prevent the development of other ways of looking at argument. This diversity of viewpoints is one of the desirable aspects of debate. To argue that there is only one way to argue (or to evaluate argument) and to ignore all other existing and potential paradigms would deprive students of a wider understanding of argument, just as an introduction to ethics course that taught only one approach to ethics would be viewed with skepticism. Robert Nozick argues:

> There are various philosophical views, mutually incompatible, which cannot be dismissed or simply rejected. Philosophy's output is the basketful of these admissible views, all together. One delimiting strategy would be to modify and shave these views, capturing what is true in each, to make them compatible parts of one new view. While I know of no reason in principle why this cannot be done, neither has anyone yet done it satisfactorily. . . . some views can be rejected, and the admissible ones remaining will differ in merits and adequacy. . . . Even when one view is clearly best, though, we do not keep only this first-ranked view, rejecting all the others.[6]

Encouraging debaters to argue theory in a round (which obviously cannot be done if the judge is rigid about theoretical issues) would expose debaters to a greater number of theories, as well as encourage them to develop modifications of existing theories,[7] and may even enable critics to discover needed modifications in their own theories of argument.

A second justification of the tabula rasa approach to argumentation is that it promotes educationally sound goals. By requiring that debaters be able to defend argumentation theory, we require that they understand argument. If we impose one standard of argument on students, they may very well conform to that standard, but they have no reason to learn why that standard exists. Debaters may be taught that affirmative cases must be topical or inherent, but they have no incentive to learn why we have these requirements if the judge will impose these requirements on the debaters whether or not the justification for those requirements is explained by the teams. By requiring that they be able to defend these positions, we insure both that they be familiar with the requirements of an advocate and that they know the reasons behind these requirements. To teach a technique without requiring that it be defended does a student a disservice:

> The 'normal' scientist . . . has been badly taught. He has been taught in a dogmatic spirit: he is a victim of indoctrination. He has learned a technique which can be applied without asking for the reason why. . . .[8]

In addition, by requiring that debaters discover weaknesses in argument and explain those weaknesses before we reject an argument, we help train them to argue effectively. When they are confronted with weak arguments in real world argument, they will not have a judge who will disregard the weak argument without response to the argument. By forcing arguments to be evaluated by the arguers, not by the judge, we encourage a deeper knowledge of argument.

The final justification of the tabula rasa approach to judging is that it is consistent with the adversary system. Argument can take place in many forums; in academic debate we choose to use an advocacy forum. This places certain constraints on each participant in the argument:

> The philosophy of adjudication that is expressed in "the adversary system" is, speaking generally, a philosophy that insists on keeping distinct the function of the advocate, on the one hand, from that of the judge, or that of the judge and jury, on the other. The decision of the case is for the judge, or for the judge and the jury. The decision must be as objective and free from bias as it possibly can.[9]

The judge has a role in the debate distinct from that of the participants. The judge does not enter into the dispute to take a side in the argument and assist one participant in arguing for or against a position, but rather the judge should remain external to the deliberation.[10] To be sure, the judge must enter the deliberation to decide which of the two conflicting arguments is superior, but it is not the role of the judge to ignore arguments that are not refuted. The validity of an argument should not be tested in isolation; rather the only determination of the validity of an argument should be based upon the defense of the argument. Many arguments that may appear to be weak or fallacious at face value can be defended against these charges when an attack is made on the argument. A team should have the opportunity to defend its position against these attacks, and this cannot be done if the judge decides, after the debate, that an argument is inadequate. The judge in this instance becomes an opponent, not a disinterested observer. In addition, the opponents of the team are rewarded even though they were confronted with a weak argument and were unable to think of anything wrong with it. If one wants to reward good argument, one should equally penalize a team that does not know what is wrong with a bad argument, which in this case would be both teams.

ATTACKS ON THE TABULA RASA
APPROACH TO JUDGING

While the tabula rasa approach to judging has gained a moderate amount of support in recent years, it has not been without its critics.[11] Two objections are raised with a great deal of frequency. The first objection is that the tabula rasa approach encourages a use of the spread; presumably a prima facie evil. Dowling, for example, argues:

> The prescribed adherence to dropped/unrefuted arguments is fair, but it does nothing to insure that those who argue well are rewarded. Critics are forced to reward those who give scant attention to the core issues of a controversy in order to refute *all* arguments in a spread, regardless of their quality of relevance.[12]

In a modification of Gresham's law, the argument is advanced that bad arguments will drive out good arguments, and debaters will emphasize the quantity of arguments instead of developing a few arguments in depth.

There are several problems with this position. First, to blame the tabula rasa approach to judging for the spread seems unjustified. The trend toward the spread was well under way in the late 1960s, while the tabula rasa approach to judging did not gain large acceptance until the early to mid-1970s. In addition, there is no logical connection between tabula rasa and spread debate; indeed, the reverse may be true. If a team knows that all of their arguments will be accepted at face value, they can confidently consolidate issues in rebuttals without worrying that the judge may not like the one or two issues that they select to defend. On the other hand, if the judge will ignore arguments that do not meet his or her standards for argument, a team may be tempted to defend multiple positions in the hope that the judge will find one of them acceptable.

In addition, the most potent argument against the spread can be advanced in any debate round judged by a tabula rasa judge. A team confronted with an excessive spread could always argue that the spread is an undesirable debate strategy, and that the other team should be penalized with a loss for introducing the spread into the debate. The debate would then revolve around whether or not the spread is undesirable, whether the effect of the spread is serious enough to justify a loss, and whether or not the spread in this specific round was excessive. Rather than having a judge impose his or her view on the debaters, however, these issues would all be brought out in the open.[13] Even short of this position, both teams have the opportunity to set standards for the evaluation of argument within a round, and this could include the minimum amount of development or support required for the judge to accept an argument. My only argument is that this should not be imposed by an external agent.

The objection that the tabula rasa approach encourages the spread assumes that a judge is the best individual to screen out bad arguments. As previously argued, the only way to know whether or not an argument is bad is to see it developed and defended. How many times has a judge voted against a team on an argument never made by the other team? That hardly promotes our educational objectives, yet the judge may think that his or her objection to the case was an honest one. Only by refraining from entering into the debate until the last minute can impartiality be insured. In addition, the process of debating will screen out bad arguments. Certainly, other factors being equal, teams would rather present thirty good arguments instead of thirty bad arguments. Cooter and Kornhauser note that in law, even without judges, the litigation process will move toward a better legal system through natural evolution (although it will never reach the optimum state).[14] There is no reason to believe students will run bad arguments instead of good arguments simply because the judge is tabula rasa.

The final criticism of tabula rasa is that it is internally inconsistent. It is argued that, if judges are indeed biased, merely telling them to be tabula rasa will not decrease those biases:

> How can we trust the same idiosyncratic judge to evaluate the outcome of those arguments that are argued by both teams through the rebuttals? Surely some individual standards must be applied before the critic can determine which side of these arguments is superior and whether a given argument is a "voting issue."[15]

While this criticism has a great deal of validity if the tabula rasa approach was to be imposed upon a judge externally, it loses much of its force when tabula rasa is adopted internally as an approach to judging. The issue facing each judge is, what is the best approach to judging that I can utilize? In answering that question, one certainly should be aware of his or her own biases and idiosyncrasies. It may be impossible to eliminate those biases totally. That does not mean, however, that a judge should not attempt to minimize those biases by developing a critical stance that minimizes his or her influence on the debate. Rather than having biases and actively injecting them into a debate round, a tabula rasa judge admits biases and attempts to keep them from affecting his or her decision unless necessary. In short, while a tabula rasa approach does not guarantee fairness, it is a desirable condition for fairness.

This goal of objectivity can be found in other fields of argument. In rhetorical criticism, we tell our students that there is no one best way of examining a speech; rather students should be aware of a variety of ways of looking at a rhetorical action. The critical stance should evolve out of the discourse, it should not be imposed a priori on the discourse by the critic.[16] The issue is what type of critic we want for argument. The most desirable type of critic is one with an open mind, an individual that will accept arguers as his or her equal and will give their arguments the same respect that he or she hopes they will give his or her decision. This involves accepting all arguments at face value (and nothing more) until they are responded to, and to give the advocate a chance to defend his or her point of view. Argument should be a discussion among equals with open minds. To ignore arguments just because they do not seem reasonable without allowing their advocate a chance to defend them against an attack seems to undermine the whole purpose of testing ideas in an open forum.

Notes

1. See Robert C. Rowland, "Standards for Paradigm Evaluation," *Journal of the American Forensic Association* 18 (Winter 1982): 133–40.
2. Walter Ulrich, "Tabula Rasa as an Approach to the Judging of Debate," paper presented at the Speech Communication Association Convention, Minneapolis, Nov. 4, 1978.
3. Ulrich, pp. 13–15. For a more detailed development of a judging philosophy consistent with many of the assumptions of tabula rasa, see Ken Strange, "An Advocacy Paradigm of Debate," paper presented at the Speech Communication Association Convention, Anaheim, Nov. 1981.
4. This standard in academic debate, however, should probably be set fairly low (for example, to require that some reason be given, but with low standards for the acceptability of the reason).
5. Thomas S. Kuhn, *The Essential Tension* (Chicago: University of Chicago Press, 1977), 332.
6. Robert Nozick, *Philosophical Explanations* (Cambridge: Harvard University Press, 1981), quoted in *Alasdair* MacIntyre, "Pluralistic Philosophy," *New York Times Book Review*, Sept. 20, 1981, p. 34.
7. Merely having a variety of judging philosophies does not guarantee that a student is exposed to all viewpoints. There are relatively few hypothesis testers, but since we allow debate theory to be debated, more students are exposed to this theory than are actually judged by hypothesis testers.
8. K. R. Popper, "Normal Science and Its Dangers," in *Criticism and the Growth of Knowledge*, Imre Lakatos and Alan Musgrave, eds. (New York: Cambridge University Press, 1980), 53.
9. Lon L. Fuller, "The Adversary System," in *Talks on American Law*, ed. Harold J. Berman (New York: Vintage Books, 1971), 34.
10. Bill Henderson, "Debate as a Paradigm for Demonstrating Truth Through Hypothesis Testing," in *Advanced Debate: Readings in Theory, Practice, and Teaching*, 2nd ed., David Thomas, ed. (Lincolnwood, IL: National Textbook Co., 1979), 420.
11. See for example, Ralph E. Dowling, "Debate as Game, Educational Tool, and Argument: An Evaluation of Theory and Rules," *Journal of the American Forensic Association* 17 (Spring 1981): 234–41.

12. Ibid., p. 235.
13. See Lane Bearden and Walter Ulrich, "Bad Theory as a Voting Issue," unpublished paper, University of Alabama, 1981.
14. Robert Cooter and Lewis Kornhauser, "Can Litigation Improve the Law Without the Help of Judges?" *Journal of Legal Studies* 9 (Jan. 1980): 139–64.
15. Dowling, p. 236.
16. Karlyn Kohrs Campbell, *Critiques of Contemporary Rhetoric* (Belmont, CA: Wadsworth, 1972), 22.

28

Game Theory
Playing the Same Game— Gaming as a Unifying Paradigm for Educational Debating

Alfred C. Snider

Paradigms for educational debating have come into being in an attempt to organize, determine, and present criteria for deciding questions of debate theory and practice. Although much of debate theory has been discussed in particular, the discussion often needs to rise above particular concerns and become a comparison of macro views of the debate process.

This is a time of evolution and change in academic debate, and thus an appropriate time for paradigmatic discussions by forensic participants and educators. Paradigms provide the macroscopic view within which various discussions of debate theory, inside and outside of the actual debate, can be resolved. These unifying theoretical attempts are especially warranted given that educational debate in America is at a crossroads. With widening gulfs between nonpolicy (Cross Examination Debate Association), policy (National Debate Tournament), high school (National Forensics League and National Federation), parliamentary, and Lincoln-Douglas formats, theoretical approaches that might unite differing formats could be of great value. After all, how valuable can a paradigm for debate be if it only applies to one or two of the many formats for educational debate?

One entry into the paradigm discussion is the concept of gaming. Although it is difficult to determine how widely accepted gaming is as a debate paradigm, it does seem clear that interest in this paradigm is growing. The judging philosophy books compiled by the National Debate Tournament (Ulrich, 1987; Ulrich, 1988a) indicate that more judges are taking this perspective into policy debate rounds with them. In 1988, thirteen judges at the NDT identified themselves with the gaming concept.

Another indication of influence is that criticisms of gaming have now emerged in the literature (Katsulas and Herbeck, 1987; Katsulas, Herbeck, and Panetta, 1987) as well as a defense against these criticisms (Snider, 1987). The gaming paradigm literature has discussed gaming as a useful way to understand common communicative behavior (Snider, 1982a), as well as a useful way to analyze and understand competitive forensics (Snider, 1984a). Two distinct works have attempted to spell out in some detail the application of gaming to educational debating (Snider, 1981; Snider, 1982a).

In CEDA debate, for example, a number of paradigmatic proposals have been made, but these paradigms have not been applied to policy debate. Even in CEDA debate these paradigms have not made their way into the actual argumentative debate components themselves (Walker, 1989).

The heightened interest and emerging criticism of gaming, and assumptions made by those who have not studied the actual paradigmatic proposals, has led to some misunderstandings. Ulrich (1988b, p. 145) has noted, "The games paradigm is perhaps the most misunderstood paradigm. To many observers, the games paradigm implies a nonserious approach to debate whereby debates are won by cheap shots rather than analysis."

The purpose of this essay will be to introduce the essentials of gaming as a paradigm for any current debate format. Rather than just repeat explanations that exist elsewhere, this essay will attempt to highlight those portions of gaming that would be most explanatory to an audience that is already somewhat familiar with educational debate in some or all of its current formats.

GAMING AND OTHER PARADIGMS

The gaming aspects of educational debate become clear if you imagine yourself describing a debate to someone who has never seen one. An educational debate has many components (opposing sides, judges and audiences who designate winners and losers, points assigned as quality ratings, time limits during which competition takes place, strategic moves that must be countered, an array of matches set up in succession, and much more) that prove an obvious point—modern debates are very much like educational games. The scholarly literature on games also supports a high congruence between what games are and what educational debates are (Avedon and Sutton-Smith, 1971; Snider, 1981).

Educational debate already possesses the characteristics of a game, thus no one needs to be persuaded to change debate so that it fits gaming. This is important to understand before comparing gaming to other paradigms. Most of the educational debate paradigms (policy making, hypothesis testing, critic of argument, narrative, philosophical system, ideology, issues and agendas, etc.) take some portion of discourse and then try and make academic debate fit the model suggested by that outside discourse. In other words, most of the paradigms are "external-prescriptive," in that they require debate to be modeled after some outside phenomenon. Gaming, on the other hand, is an "internal-descriptive" paradigm because it uses the characteristics already internal to educational debate to describe it.

A superior paradigm should apply easily and without coercion (Snider, 1982a, pp. 232–33). In a simplified taxonomy, we can designate an "old" and a "new" debate to draw the distinction noticed by Walker—the distinction between what the debate rounds actually contain (new debate) and what paradigmatic theorists write about what the debates should contain (old debate). The old debate is a fantasy about debate rounds as bouts of hypothesis testing, policy making, narration, or ideology. The new debate exists in all debate rounds that actually take place, and without guidance from paradigmatic theoreticians. In this new debate, students use various theoretical concepts as ploys within the game setting to win the game. The old debate can be thought of as our current set of theories, whereas the new debate can be thought of as the practices students and judges actually engage in. The old debate is dead, and the paradigms of the old debate have become nothing more than available strategies in the new debate. Snider states (p. 233), "My contention is that these issues of theory and practice need to be united. Specifically, the contention is that gaming can serve as a viable theory which will fit the practice satisfactorily."

Student debaters already see debate as a game, and in an attempt to win they use whatever strategies or concepts they think will work. They only wish to make the proper move in order to win. They borrow these from various debate formats and from various theoretical constructs. The new debate recognizes debate's inherent gaming nature. The existing paradigms are alternative strategies within the game, but they are not useful paradigmatic models. Gaming recognizes that these existing approaches need to be subsumed and sorted out and not regarded as mutually exclusive. Gaming unifies all of these paradigms within one comprehensive perspective.

DESIGN, CONSTRUCTION, AND USE OF
THE GAME OF DEBATE

The steps that have been followed in mapping out a game of debate have been those of Richard Duke. Duke began his work by concentrating on gaming as a technique for urban planning (Duke, 1964). Since then he has written extensively on the broader application of the gaming concept (Duke, 1972; 1979; 1980a; 1980b). The following summary of a game of debate involves the five steps outlined by Duke.

Game Design and Debate Design

The first step in the game design phase is to generate a conceptual map of the game. A conceptual map is a mental blueprint of the game (Duke, 1974, p. 63). It is essential that, through this process, basic game objectives be specified.

Considering my observations of how debaters argue about the worth of the debate process and the game goals already in the literature (Snider, 1988), the three most commonly cited game objectives are: to provide an educational experience for the participants, to provide for a fair contest, and to discuss important issues. Different judges may indicate different purposes. Steve Dolley (1987) indicates that for him the goals of the game of debate are self-actualization, enjoyment, and personal realization of truth.

The rest of the conceptual map can easily be drawn up by anyone familiar with academic debate as an oral discussion of differing points of view in a set context (Snider, 1982a, pp. 148–155).

The second step in the game design process is to define the message of the game, indicating which communications are part of the game and which are not. In the game of debate, as suggested by Duke (1974, p. 86), the message of the game includes the messages acted out, flow charts, and related texts. The message acted out includes speeches, cross-examinations, and the reactions of the judges. Flow charts are an important part of most games and certainly are one of the most important communicative components of debate. In the terminology of Duke (1974, pp. 47–48), the completed flow chart is a blueprint of the actual game run that took place. It is a graphic representation of the various elements of the game, with linear pointers going from concept to concept to illustrate flows, linkages, and impacts. Related texts would consist of evidence, prepared briefs, and notes used by the debaters as well as the ballots of the judges and the pairings and results the tournament may produce.

Game Construction and Debate Construction

The game construction phase involves designation of the processing order, models used in the game, and the nature of inputs and outputs.

The models used in the game are the factors manipulated by the participants and then utilized by the judge to make a decision. Duke (1974, p. 97) notes that three kinds of models are generally found in a game: accounting systems, simulations, and heuristics. Accounting systems are representations of some real world value at an acceptable level of detail for use in the context of a game. These would correspond to the values and impacts discussed in the debate. Simulations are models that indicate speculation about some complex process. Given the values existing in accounting systems, simulations allow debaters to explain how their arguments influence these accounting systems. Simulations are intended to predict, and would be the counterparts of what we know as links in current debate arguments. Heuristics are concepts that aid the participant in discovering through the game process. In this sense heuristics in the game of debate would be composed of what we currently call the theoretical issues in the debate. Thus, the models used in a game, as defined by Duke, are all found in the game of debate.

The last step in the game construction phase is to define the inputs and outputs of the game. The inputs would be the speeches and cross-examinations of the debate, and the outputs would be the decisions of the judges, ballots and critiques, tournament results, and seasonal records.

Putting the Game into Use and Staging Debates

Two important factors in putting any educational game of debate into use would be how to disseminate the game and the ethics of game use.

For the game of debate, dissemination would involve team identification with specific schools, debate leagues and associations, phasing through tournaments and seasons, and the rotation of topics.

The ethics of game use is an important issue in the ultimate success of any game (Duke, 1974, p. 104) Snider (1984b) has indicated that the ethical standards of Karl Wallace (1955) can be applied to academic debate to create a nonsituational ethic of honesty.

Game Components and Debate Components

Game components include roles, rules and procedures, mechanics of play, and the specification of the scenario of the game. Duke (1974, p. 121) indicates that in a game there are gamed roles, pseudo roles, and simulated roles. Gamed roles for debate would include the debaters and the judges. Pseudo roles are played by participants who are not formally involved in the game message, such as coaches and tournament administrators. Simulated roles are not represented by players, but in the mechanics of play through judge interaction. These simulated roles in CEDA debate, for example, are composed of criteria and decision rules. A number of the old paradigms may be found here acting as decision rules.

Next come rules and procedures. Rules are those guidelines that are not open to change during the debate, such as time limits and the wording of the topic. Procedures are more flexible, being the items of debate and argument theory that debaters introduce into the debate. Through an application of heuristics, the debaters can argue these procedures based on how they influence the goals of the game itself, which were discussed earlier.

The next component consists of the mechanics of play. In the game of debate the times for speeches and cross-examinations are set, and then these debate rounds are phased into tournaments and seasons.

The final component is the scenario of the game. CEDA debate, for example, has a topic that changes each semester. Duke (1974, p. 134) indicates what many debaters and coaches already know, that a poorly constructed and specified scenario is a common reason for game failure.

Techniques for Games and Techniques for Debates

The first technique involves the nature of participant interaction. In any game, there can be cooperation, competition, or cross-pressuring. The game of debate would appear to emphasize cross-pressuring, where students cooperate with partner and coach in order to compete against opponents. Duke (1974, p. 141) believes such a combination is optimal.

The second technique involves the critique. A critique of a game involves making the implication of participants' choices evident to them. In CEDA debates, for example, the critique usually comes in written form and is received sometime after the debate (often a day or so), although some judges do provide immediate verbal critiques. The gaming literature indicates that an effective critique must not be a delayed written message directed at the players, but a multilogue in which players and judges become involved. As Duke (1974, p. 143) observes, a successful critique will be a rough and tumble session during which people are committed to what they have done. They will "pursue with diligence any ambiguities, errors, or undocumented postures which seem invalid to them." Since there is not just one perspective in the discussion, but "multiple roles addressing the same problem from different perspectives, a critique can develop exceedingly sharp discussions about the character of a . . . system." The best critique, then, would be an immediate multilogue.

The third area of technique includes alterations to enrich the educational impact of the game (Duke, 1974, p. 150). These involve the use of tipping points, crisis management, and cross-specification. All three of these techniques are prominent in debates. A tipping point is some idea that emerges during the debate as central to the decision. Perceptive debaters anticipate the tipping point arguments and then avoid or utilize them. Crisis management is a talent called on when the unexpected occurs in the debate round, and debaters must improvise an argumentative strategy on the spot. Cross-specification involves the recognition by a player at a given moment during the game that various ideas in the debate have implications for each other, as ideas are seen as mutually exclusive, contradictory, correlative, or irrelevant in relation to each other. Cross-specification may be the essence of good debating.

JUDGING A DEBATE AS A GAME

In any game, the judges should be honest, hardworking, and knowledgeable. However, some additional characteristics would seem to be a natural outgrowth of accepting gaming as a paradigm for educational debate.

First, gaming calls for a suspension of needless fantasy. A debate is an educational, co-curricular contest, and it is not exclusively an exercise in policy-making, story-telling, hypothesis testing, or ideological conflict. These concepts now become simulated roles. Gaming does not eliminate these discussions, it merely locates them in their proper format.

Second, gaming calls for an application of rules and procedures by the judge. The rules are specified and are not open to discussion during the debate. Procedures are common practices that can still be called into question and debated. In determining which competing procedures should be utilized, the judge should select those that best meet the purposes of the debate activity as discussed by the debaters. This may not be attractive to those judges who currently offer the debaters a list of inviolable mandates in their judging philosophies (Snider, 1989).

Third, the game of debate would call for the judge to award the decision to the team that scores best in various accounting systems as discussed in terms of simulations. Style and organization are essential in aiding the communication of these arguments, but the reasoning component remains primary.

Fourth, the game of debate draws from the gaming literature a concept of ethics a judge may wish to apply (Snider 1984b). Honesty should be a central issue if the dispute is to involve ethical questions.

Fifth, the gaming nature of debate calls for a distinctive approach to critiquing the debate. The reasons for the decision in the debate are the most critical points in the entire process. When the students are confronted by the judge's interpretation of events, the consequences of their actions are made clear to them. Each completed critique implies an integrity of perspective to the knowledge acquired and provides a starting point for the education of the next debate. Duke (1974, pp. 63–64) verifies this notion of how game runs should educate. It is a basic axiom of communication that for feedback to be effective, it needs to be specific and immediate. This may not be attractive to those who believe decisions by judges should not be immediately disclosed or should be disclosed only through written ballots. This issue is certainly one worthy of elaboration, and deserves an active discussion.

ADVANTAGES OF GAMING

Three central arguments seem to recommend gaming as a paradigm for educational debate.

Gaming fits current educational debate. Most paradigms either call for taking some outside model and imposing it on the debate, or they take merely part of the debate process and grant it primary importance. Those essential elements of debate not explained by these paradigms (competition, iteration, changing sides, or the role of the judge) are simply ignored. No paradigm has quite the conceptual fit that gaming has demonstrated (Snider 1981; Snider 1982a).

Gaming can improve theory and practice. A cross-fertilization between debate and gaming can provide us with new insights into how we can improve debate as an educational activity (Snider, 1982b, pp. 327–328). For example, insights into the gamed nature of speed of play, differing competitive pressures, the role of critiques, and ethics may help us improve the activity. We also may come to realize that the true value of educational debate is its ability to become a gestalt communication mode (Snider, 1984a). Gaming also offers unique opportunities to formulate theoretical approaches for new and evolving formats in ways more appropriate than borrowing concepts from other debate formats. By viewing theory as gamed procedures, gaming provides a framework within which these ideas can be discussed, and a decision criteria for the selection of competing procedures based on the perceived purposes of the activity.

Gaming can provide a unifying theoretical perspective. Debate formats in America are changing. It is hard to imagine policy-making applying as a paradigm for CEDA, or nonpolicy debate, just as it is hard to imagine the narrative paradigm as applying to NDT, or policy, debate. Gaming is a paradigm that applies to all of the existing debate formats. The other paradigms tend to isolate formats from each other by making them dependent on mutually exclusive theoretical concepts. Gaming tends to operate in a new relationship with the old paradigms, in that it subsumes them rather than calling for their rejection.

We are all playing the same game, but our procedures are flexible. Recognition of gaming as a paradigm for various formats would allow coach, theorist, and student to move from one debate format to another with more ease.

References

Avedon, Elliot and Sutton-Smith, Brian (1971), *The Study of Games* (New York: Wiley and Sons).

Dolley, Steve (1987), in *National Debate Tournament Booklet of Judges*, ed. Walter Ulrich (Nashville: American Forensic Association).

Duke, Richard (1964), *Gaming Simulation in Urban Research* (East Lansing: Michigan State University).

Duke, Richard (1972) "Gaming-Simulation: A New Communicative Form," in *Proceedings of the Third International Gaming Conference* (Birmingham, England: International Gaming Conference).

Duke, Richard (1974), Gaming: The Future's Language (New York: Wiley and Sons).

Duke, Richard (1979) "Nine Steps to Game Design," paper presented to the International Simulation and Gaming Association Convention, Leeuwarden, Netherlands, Aug.

Duke, Richard (1980a), "Format for the Game—Logic or Intuition?" *Simulation and Games* (March): 27–34.

Duke, Richard (1980b), "A Paradigm for Game Design," *Simulation and Games* (Sept.): 374–77.

Katsulas, John and Herbeck, Dale (1987), "In Defense of Policy Debate: An Argument Against Utopian Fiat," paper presented to the Eastern Communication Association Convention, Syracuse, NY, May.

Katsulas, John; Herbeck, Dale; and Panetta, Edward (1987), "Fiating Utopia: A Negative View of the Emergence of World Order Counterplans and Future Gaming in Policy Debate," *Journal of the American Forensic Association* (Fall): 95–111.

Snider, Alfred (1981), The New Debate: A Personal Essay (Detroit: privately published). Copies may be obtained from the author: University of Vermont, Burlington, VT 05405.

Snider, Alfred (1982a), "Gaming as a Form of Human Communication," paper presented to the World Future Society World Assembly, Washington, DC, July. Copies may be obtained from the author.

Snider, Alfred (1982b), *Gaming as a Paradigm for Academic Debate* (Lawrence: unpublished doctoral dissertation, University of Kansas). Copies may be obtained from the author.

Snider, Alfred (1984a), "Games Without Frontiers: A Design for Communication Scholars and Forensic Educators," *Journal of the American Forensic Association* (Winter): 162–70.

Snider, Alfred (1984b), "Ethics in Academic Debate: A Gaming Perspective," *National Forensic Journal* (Fall): 119–34.

Snider, Alfred (1987), "Fantasy and Reality Revisited: Gaming, Fiat Power, and Anti-Utopianism," *Journal of the American Forensic Association* (Fall): 119-30.

Snider, Alfred (1989), "Tabula Rasa: What's Wrong with Most Judging Philosophies," in *Starmakers* 51: ii.

Ulrich, Walter (1987), ed., *National Debate Tournament Booklet of Judges* (Nashville: American Forensic Association).

Ulrich, Walter (1988a), ed., *National Debate Tournament Booklet of Judges* (Nashville: American Forensic Association). See specifically the judging philosophies of: Steven Anderson, Sue Balter, David Berube, Jeff Bile, David Boman, Ralph Carbone, Steve Dolley, Jeff Leon, Laura Rollins, Alfred Snider, Roger Solt, Fred Sternhagen, and Melissa Wade.

Walker, Gregg (1989), "The Counterplan as Argument in Non-Policy Debate," *Argumentation and Advocacy* (Winter): 178–91.

Wallace, Karl (1955), "An Ethical Basis of Communication," *The Speech Teacher* (Jan.).

29

Application of the Narrative Paradigm in CEDA Debate

Kristine M. Bartanen

Both comments outside of rounds and behavior during rounds suggest that many CEDA debaters have difficulty debating about competing criteria or values. They seem to seek some kind of formula to apply and, or course, to quote; a formula analogous to the childhood game of "scissors cut paper, paper covers rock, rock crushes scissors"; a formula which would allow them to *prove* in a given case that value position A is superior to value position B.

Unfortunately, in terms of quick resolution of the difficulty of debating values, no such formula exists. I do not think that advising debaters, as Gaske and Young suggest, to "test the value and its accompanying end-states against the competing value and its subsequent policies by *finding their order in a predetermined hierarchy*" (my emphasis) is a useful remedy (1984, p. 27).[1] Sillars and Ganer note that "hierarchies do not appear to typify societal thinking in general" and go on to offer the example that the hierarchy developed by Rokeach in the late 1960s is not replicated by audiences of the late '70s and early '80s (1982, pp. 188, 190). Clash of predetermined hierarchies in a debate round—such as between Rokeach's (1973) and Maslow's (1943)—generally does not tell us why one hierarchy is more fitting than another. MacIntyre offers an appropriate description from the realm of philosophical debate:

> It is precisely because there is in our society no established way of deciding between [normative and evaluative] claims that moral argument appears to be necessarily interminable. From our rival conclusions we can argue back to our rival premises; but when we do arrive at our premises; argument ceases and the invocation of one premise against another becomes a matter of pure assertion and counter-assertion (1981, p. 8).

Many debates seem to parallel MacIntyre's description; the affirmative asserts one value position and the negative asserts another. As critics, we are left to choose, somehow, one version of looking at the world over the other. But we do choose. The relevant questions are: How? And is that choice merely irrational?

Walter Fisher's observation in "Narration as a Communication Paradigm" that "the world is a set of stories which must be chosen among" (1984, p. 8) suggests that there might be helpful advice for CEDA debaters and judges faced with "our version versus their version" in a better understanding of the narrative paradigm. Fisher's contention is that the narrative paradigm allows us to see how choices between stories are made and to see that those choices are rational. Given that the narrative paradigm finds a society's values in its stories (MacIntyre, p. 174) and views all stories as advice for good living, it is especially fitting to consider value debate within a narrative perspective. In this paper, I will compare the narrative and traditional paradigms,[2] explain the stock issues of the narrative paradigm, and then offer both practical and theoretical applications of the narrative paradigm to value debate.

COMPARISONS OF THE PARADIGMS

The traditional perspective from which human communication is viewed, which Fisher (1984) labels the rational world paradigm, is based upon five assumptions:

1. that humans are rational beings
2. that they make decisions and communicate through arguments
3. that argument rules differ from situation to situation, from field to field
4. that rationality is determined by knowledge of subject matter, argumentative ability, and skill in employing the rules of advocacy in given fields
5. that the world is a set of logical puzzles, which can be solved through application of argumentative analysis and reason

Rationality, or argumentative competence, must be learned; consequently, says Fisher, "an historic mission of education in the West has been to generate a consciousness of national community and to instruct citizens in at least rudiments of logic and rhetoric" (1984, p. 4). Academic debate, certainly, is a central vehicle of that educational mission. Forensics educators seek to aid their students in becoming competent members of the rational world community.

The narrative paradigm does not deny that educational mission. Rather, it adds to the picture of humans as rational beings the characterization that "man is in his actions and practice, as well as his fictions, essentially a storytelling animal" (MacIntyre, p. 201). The narrative paradigm, as an alternative to the rational world paradigm, "insists that human communication should be viewed as historical as well as situational, as stories competing with other stories constituted by good reasons, as being rational when they satisfy the demands of narrative probabilty and narrative fidelity, and as inevitably moral inducements" (Fisher, 1984, p. 2). The narrative paradigm not only allows nonargumentative discourse to be considered rational, but asks that arguments be considered in terms of the criteria for good stories. As Fisher stresses, "narrative rationality does not negate traditional rationality. It holds that traditional rationality is only relevant in specialized fields and *even in those arenas narrative rationality is meaningful and useful*" (my emphasis) (1984, p. 33). Taking up Fisher's challenge, we can ask: What meaning and use can be gained from adding to our picture of debaters as arguers the scenario of debaters as storytellers?

STOCK ISSUES OF THE NARRATIVE PARADIGM

In order to see useful applications of the narrative paradigm, we need to consider, first, what constitutes a good story. The stock issues of the narrative paradigm have already been introduced but deserve greater clarification. Good stories are those that pass the tests of narrative probability and narrative fidelity. Narrative probability demands that stories be coherent, that their parts be orderly and logically related in such a way as to make the events they recount and account for comprehensible. Bennett and Feldman present this standard as a question: "Could it have happened that way?" (1981, p. 33) Narrrative fidelity demands that stories "ring true," (Fisher, 1984, p. 8) that the narrative correspond with known facts, qualities, conditions, or events. Bennett and Feldman express this standard via the question: "Did it happen that way?" (1981, p. 33) Both questions can be decided rationally.

The logic[3] of this rationality is comprised of three operations. First, the central action of the story must be located. Second, inferences must be constructed about the relationship of elements surrounding the central action; the action must be interpreted in context. Third, the network of inferences must be tested for internal consistency and descriptive completeness (1981, p. 41).

APPLICATIONS OF THE NARRATIVE PARADIGM

Application of the logic of narrative to the debate setting has implications for traditional issues and practices.

Case Construction

Identification of central action. This first step of analysis demands that debaters locate the key behavior in the resolution and in the affirmative and negative cases as they are presented. Such analysis has at least three implications. First, primary focus on the central action of the conveyed narratives should encourage debaters to focus directly on the subject matter of debate, rather than on meta-debate discussions of, for example, what is or is not appropriate in CEDA versus NDT debate. Second, focus on the central action of the conveyed narratives provides solid bases for topicality challenges; if the central action of the affirmative story is not within the central action of the resolution, the negative has grounds for dispute. Third, focus on the central action of the conveyed narratives reinforces the growing recognition that values must be debated in the context of the actions which embody them.[4] Value debate, within this context, is a rhetorical activity.[5]

Interpretation of central action. Bennett and Feldman offer the Burkean pentad as a tool for conducting this level of analysis. Debaters would identify the act, scene, agent, agency, and purpose through which the central action is developed in order to generate an interpretation of that action. The linkage of these elements into a narrative would be the means of justifying the judgmental terms of the resolution, terms such as "desirable," "justified," or "detrimental." Bennett and Feldman advocate use of the Burkean framework, arguing that "the appeal of Burke's scheme is that it actually specifies the structure of the frames we apply to social interpretation.... The basic element of scene, act, agent, agency, and purpose seem to operate as supercategories into which multiple connections among symbols can be collapsed, and through which quick access to alternative symbolizations can be obtained" (1981, p. 62). Debaters, however, need not be constrained by this particular model of narrative; other conceptions of basic elements of storytelling could be made to serve the same interpretive purpose.[6]

Evaluating the Interpretation of Central Action

Examination of the completeness of the narrative elements presented, and of the relationships between the elements presented in support of a particular interpretation, is the means by which listeners choose between competing stories. Given the limited timeframe of an academic debate, debaters necessarily relate only some portions of a much larger narrative. A hasty generalization challenge is an argument that suggests the given narrative is incomplete. A value objection/implication or disadvantage argument reveals an untold portion of the story.[7] Inconsistencies in the relationships between story elements also weaken narrative interpretations, as do alternative relationships to those presented by a given team. Here debaters would employ causality, alternate causality, and other challenges to narrative links. If using the Burkean scheme, debaters would examine various ratios for consistency, pointing to what may seem to be reasonable connections in isolation but which do not make sense when combined into an overall pattern or case.

Issues and Strategies

I have thus far discussed the logic of narrative in general terms applicable either to affirmative or negative cases. In all debates, the affirmative would need to complete steps one and two of the above analysis in order to present a prima facie case; they need to present a coherent, complete, and consistent story. The negative would have three options. They could employ a challenge strategy, pointing to structural incompleteness or inconsistency in affirmative analysis. As Bennett and Feldman summarize in legal terms, they could "choose to show merely that there are missing elements in the prosecution case or that the definitions of various scenes, acts, actors, agents, or purposes do not all support the same interpretation . . . " (1981, p. 94). A second option would be a redefinition strategy, one in which the negative redefines "particular elements in the story to show that a different meaning emerges when slight changes are made in the interpretation of the evidence" (1981, p. 94). The third strategy, labeled reconstruction, puts the negative in the position of telling its own story; in this approach, as in the counterplan approach of policy debate, the negative would be subject to affirmative burdens; the negative would have to present a clear, complete, and consistent narrative.

A brief and admittedly simple example from the fall 1985 CEDA topic may be helpful at this point. Most affirmative debaters identified the central action of the resolution as U.S. media coverage of terrorism. In interpreting that action, they asked us to compare two scenarios, such as the following:

Scenario I
Agent: U.S. media
Scene: in the absence of significant restrictions
Purpose: in their efforts to get and publish a story

| Agency: | interfere with crisis resolution, reveal intelligence information |
| Act: | endanger lives of hostages. |

versus

Scenario II

Agent:	U.S. media
Scene:	under conditions of significant government restriction
Purpose:	in their efforts to get and publish a story
Agency:	are precluded from interference or revelation
Act:	do not endanger lives of hostages.

Based on the value of saving life, Scenario II was presented as preferable and, thus, the resolution presented as justified.

Negative arguments were presented that illustrate each of the narrative options. Arguments that challenged the affirmative interpretation, for example, included: (1) reconsiderations of scene (significant restrictions, either self-imposed or governmental, already exist); (2) reconsiderations of purpose (journalists are not irresponsible fools when they pursue or publish a story); or (3) questions of narrative fidelity (has the scenario of endangered lives ever occurred?). A sample argument that redefined, so as to generate a differing interpretation of the elements, set forth the following scenario:

Agent:	U.S. media
Scene:	in the absence of significant restrictions
Purpose:	in an effort to get and publish a story
Agency:	gain information about crisis resolution, intelligence operations
Act:	serve as a watchdog on government actions.

A reconstructive negative approach, in this case one which relocated the central action of the resolution, offered the following scenario for comparison to those offered by the affirmative:

Agent:	U.S. government
Agency:	by imposing significant restrictions on the press
Purpose:	in order to control coverage of terrorist activities
Scene:	in the absence of clear restraints on such power
Act:	endangers First Amendment freedoms.

Choice of particular strategies by the negative would depend upon two factors: the strength of the affirmative case and the particular debate paradigm in use in the round. Within a legal or hypothesis-testing paradigm, or in instances where presumption is clearly against the resolution, the negative could defeat the affirmative narrative simply by employing challenge or redefinition strategies. Within a policy-making paradigm, where two courses of action must be weighed; or an issues-agenda paradigm, where the importance of competing issues must be compared; it would behoove the negative to have a competing story in the round and, thus, the reconstruction strategy would seem most appropriate. Of course, once a negative presents its version, the affirmative should bring into play challenge and redefinition strategies to weaken that narrative in the minds of the adjudicators.

The above discussion assumes a rather global narrative approach to a debate round. While a debate case following the Burkean pentad may seem unlikely at the present moment, I think that debaters will be well served to recognize the elements of their traditional analysis to which a narrative perspective readily applies. CEDA resolutions, at least since 1975, have asked debates to interpret past or current world events. Such interpretation requires constructing narratives about those events. Furthermore, intensification of values within a system (Sillars and Ganer, 1982, p. 189); value redistribution, value rescaling, value re-employment, and value restandardization (Rescher, 1973, pp. 14–16); capitalization upon values (Fisher, 1981, p. 1016); establishment of salience and significance (M. Bartanen and Frank, 1983, pp. 6–7); and definition of terms demand that debaters relate stories about their world. At the very least, debaters can employ a narrative perspective reflexively, by examining their own cases and analysis: What values are embedded in the way we tell this story? Are those values consistent with what we offer as criteria in the round? Are those values ones which coincide with those held by the audience? What are the audience's values? How can we structure our narrative so as to induce the value perspective we think characterizes the action embodied in the resolution?

Evidence

Greater understanding of the narrative paradigm should strengthen debaters' use of evidence. As discussed above, the standard of narrative probability examines the structural relationships of items presented within a case. Assessment of narrative fidelity, however, requires examination of the documentary or empirical evidence. The standards of the narrative paradigm, then, certainly reinforce the admonition voiced recently by M. Bartanen and Frank that the CEDA debaters need to be concerned about the discovery of evidence (1983, p. 2). However, it is clear that evidence alone is not enough. Debaters need to understand the evidence in terms of its historical context and in terms of the narrative they are building in a given round. While written for the legal context, Bennett and Feldman's summary comments are fitting here:

> Despite the greater reliance on documentation in legal cases than in some other story-construction settings, several considerations argue for the dominance of story structure over the facts in legal judgment. First, the story structure is the means of organizing, testing, and placing an interpretation on the facts. Second, ... equally well documented definitions can be offered by each side for the same structural element in a story. In the end, it is the fit of the symbolized element into the larger structure, and not the pure documentation for the element itself, that dictates final judgment. Third, alternative definitions are available for virtually any fact or bit of evidence. Once again, the key issue is how the chosen definition fits within the competing accounts of the incident. Finally, evidence is most powerful when it is used rhetorically to suggest a missing link in a case or to support a redefinition of a key element in the opposition case. That is, evidence is most often at the service of evolving cases, not the other way around [1981, p. 114].

Thus, as the authors suggest earlier, "adequately documented but poorly structured accounts will be rejected because they do not withstand careful scrutiny within a story framework. Similarly, a well-constructed story may sway judgments even when evidence is in short supply" (1981, p. 68). Understanding better the stock issues of the narrative paradigm may help coaches and debaters deal with the losses of rounds where, "We documented everything, and they hardly read any cards!"

Function of Debate

Viewing debate from a narrative perspective also has some theoretical implications concerning the function of debate. Perceived as narrators, debaters present competing stories relevant to the topic area. They recount ideas of others and events of the past and try to account for those ideas and events. Interwoven, necessarily, are their own experiences and perceptions. The competing narratives provide advice about how the audience or judge should perceive and evaluate past and future events and actions. The stories relate competing truths about the human condition (Fisher, 1984, p. 6).

Both stories may be true, while not necessarily being *the* truth. This is not to say that debaters may lie; stories presented in the debate context should not be fictions. It is a recognition that "stories ... are capsule versions of reality. They pick up an incident and set it down in another social context. In this transition, the data can be selected, the historical frame can be specified, the situational factors can be redefined, and 'missing observations' can be implied" (Bennett and Feldman, 1981, p. 37). Just as competing debaters may present good definitions of a concept in a round, neither of which is necessarily the best definition of the concept in life, and the judge must choose the better definition in terms of the rationale presented to her, so a judge, from the narrative perspective, chooses at the conclusion of a round the better story. An affirmative vote means that judge chooses the resolutional story.[8] The judge chooses *a* truth, not necessarily *the* truth. Debate is a truth-seeking activity, then, only as individual rounds become part of the Burkean "unending conversation" that is itself a narrative search for truth (Fisher, 1984, pp. 6–7).

Judging

Fisher contends that narrative rationality, the ability to judge between stories, is a capacity all persons acquire through natural socialization (1984, pp. 9–10). This viewpoint has several implications for judges and judging. One has already been addressed, that being the judge's choice of the better story at the conclusion of a round. A second implication is embedded in the criterion of narrative fidelity; if a judge compares the story or stories presented in the round with stories he knows to be true, then the idea of a tabula rasa critic is nonsensical. The narrative paradigm expects judges to compare stories objectively, but in order to compare, the judge must bring with her into the round relevant prior experience and knowledge. Like Balthrop's critic of argument, the judge must "rely upon his or her own areas of expertise to make sense of what happens in the debate" (1983, p. 2).

A third implication regarding judging lies in the inherent awareness of narrativity among listeners. Not all judges are equally competent in the knowledge of issues and understanding of argumentative procedures that the rational world paradigm demands. We can expect this noncompetence to be increasingly true as more specialized and jargon-laden theories become part of CEDA debating. Yet Brydon is not alone in advocating an open system for the judging of CEDA debates (1984, p. 86); many coaches advocate use of more real or lay judges.[9] Brydon's question—"How would we expect real audiences to react to a given debate?"(1984, p. 87) finds an answer in the narrative paradigm. We would expect them to use narrative criteria to make a decision. Bennett and Feldman write: " . . . audience members understand that the accounts must be regarded either as true or as probably false, and in the end, they must commit themselves to either believing or not believing them" (1981, p. 113). They go on to suggest that "the gravity of the courtroom situation and the consequences of the verdict must have some impact on the way jurors listen to cases. We expect, however, that these factors weigh in favor of a more rigorous application of story evaluation routines rather than an increased reliance on such superficial indicators as whether the storyteller had an honest face or a firm voice" (1981, p. 113). Granting that debate tournaments have less impact than jury verdicts, would we not expect the same tendency toward more rigorous application of story evaluation techniques to occur in debate rounds where lay judges know that students try seriously to win their points and that decisions rendered may keep teams in or out of competition for awards?

Finally, the narrative paradigm's recognition that stories are chosen among rationally means that the decisions rendered by real, lay, or even IE judges may be considered no less valuable than those rendered by the rational world paradigm's elites.

A New Metaphor

Lakoff and Johnson, in *Metaphors We Live By*, suggest that "the most fundamental values in a culture will be coherent with the metaphorical structure of the most fundamental concepts in the culture" (1980, p. 22). We might paraphrase this comment to say that values are embodied in the metaphors we use in telling stories about ourselves and our world. Given the predominance of the metaphor "argument is war" in our culture (Lakoff and Johnson, 1980, p. 4), the centrality of argument within the rational world paradigm means that this paradigm highlights competition, winning and losing, and battling over concepts of cooperation and tolerance of multiple world views. The act of adding to our characterization of debaters as arguers the description of debaters as storytellers is an action that highlights the ability of one story to prevail over another at a given time without brutality being wrought upon the competing narrators. While the narrative metaphor is not a new one to our culture, it is a relatively novel perspective for the world of academic debate. Lakoff and Johnson observe that "new metaphors have the power to create a new reality. This can begin to happen when we start to comprehend our experience in terms of a metaphor, and it becomes a deeper reality when we begin to act in terms of it. If a new metaphor enters the conceptual system that we base our actions on, it will alter that conceptual system and the perceptions and actions that the system gives rise to" (1980, p. 145). Viewing participants in forensics as persons with alternate stories to tell, as opposed to only opponents with whom to do battle, should be a positive complement to the various actions the debate community is undertaking to promote ethical behavior among its members.

CONCLUSION

Arguments heard in debates may not necessarily differ markedly when considered from a narrative as opposed to rational world perspective. Such should be the case, given that the narrative paradigm subsumes both the logic of reasons and the logic of good reasons. The narrative paradigm, however, adds factors for consideration—narrative probability and narrative fidelity—that can strengthen our understanding of case construction, analysis of issues, debate strategies and burdens, and use of evidence. Furthermore, the narrative paradigm raises additional insights regarding the function of debate, the nature of judges and judging, and competitor attitudes. This alternative paradigm suggests to debaters who wish to debate values and criteria more effectively that they build a narrative which embodies their chosen values by clearly, coherently, and consistently linking story elements.

I have noted already that helping students become more competent within the rational world paradigm is a central focus of our educational system, and of educational forensics in particular. To the extent that the general population is less competent than college debaters in their capacity to participate within that paradigm, which means that discourse is likely to be judged by narrative standards, and to the extent that none of us is competent in the argument skills of all fields, which means that we make decisions in those areas based on criteria of probability and fidelity, it makes sense that we become more conscious of narrative rationality. Considering its application to value debate is one effort in that direction.

Notes

1. Debaters could, of course, develop a hierarchy among themselves in the round and then test the competing values and end-states, but given the time constraints and competitiveness of the situation, this seems unlikely.
2. Paradigm, as used here, refers to frameworks for viewing human communication in general, not to frameworks for academic debate. Hypothesis-testing, policy-making, stock issues, and other debate paradigms are models subsumed by the rational world and narrative paradigms. As Fisher emphasizes in his elaboration of the narrative paradigm, it is a "metaparadigm" not to be misconstrued by considering it "as a representation of practices that characterize inquiry in a specific discipline . . . " (1985, p. 347).
3. "Logic" is used here in the sense employed by Fisher, meaning "a systematic set of procedures designed to aid in the analysis and assessment of elements of reasoning in rhetorical interaction" (1978, p. 377).
4. See for example, M. Bartanen and Frank, 1983; Jones and Crawford, 1984; and Young and Gaske, 1984.

5. See Fisher, 1981: "Rhetoric deals with values in context of proposed actions, as they are embedded in decisions regarding human conduct" (p. 1015).
6. Lakoff and Johnson, for example, discuss "participants" and "parts" ("episodes" and "states"), "stages," "causal connections" among the parts, and "plans" meant to achieve a "goal" or a set of goals as the elements of a story (1980, p. 173).
7. That value objections or disadvantages need to pass the test of narrative probability would mean that they would have to be plausible rather than speculative, which would mitigate Dempsey's (1984) concern with these types of arguments.
8. This decision rule does not require the judge to support personally either the affirmative or negative value (see Ulrich, 1984, pp. 2–3).
9. Resolutions 31–33 passed by the National Developmental Conference on Forensics in September 1984 address this issue of a wider judging pool (see Parson, 1984, p. 46).

Resources

Balthrop, V. W. (1983). "The Debate Judge as 'Critic of Argument': Toward a Transcendent Perspective." *The Journal of the American Forensic Association* 20: 1–15.

Bartanen, M. D. and Frank, D. A. (1983). *The Forensic* 69: 1–9.

Bennett, W. L. (1975). "Political Scenarios and the Nature of Politics." *Philosophy and Rhetoric* 8: 23–42.

Bennett, W. L. and Feldman, M. S. (1981). *Reconstructing Reality in the Courtroom*. Rutgers.

Brydon, S. R. (1984). "Judging CEDA Debate: A Systems Perspective." In D. Brownlee, ed. *CEDA Yearbook 1984*. Cross Examination Debate Association.

Dempsey, R. (1984). "Theoretical Illegitimacy of Speculative Value Objections." In D. Brownlee, ed. *CEDA Yearbook 1984*. Cross Examination Debate Association.

Fisher, W. R. (1985). "The Narrative Paradigm: An Elaboration." *Communication Monographs* 52: 347–67.

Fisher, W. R. (1984). "Narration as a Human Communication Paradigm: The Case of Public Moral Argument." *Communication Monographs* 51: 1–22.

Fisher, W. R. (1981). "Debating Value Propositions: A Game for Dialecticians." In G. Ziegelmueller and J. Rhodes, eds. *Dimensions of Argument: Proceedings of the Second Summer Conference on Argumentation*. Speech Communication Association.

Fisher, W. R. (1978). "Toward a Logic of Good Reasons." *Quarterly Journal of Speech* 64: 376–84.

Jones, M. A. and Crawford, S. W. (1984). "Justification of Values in Terms of Action: Rationale for a Modified Policy-Making Paradigm in Value Debate." In D. Brownlee, ed. *CEDA Yearbook 1984*. Cross Examination Debate Association.

Lakoff, G. and Johnson, M. (1980). *Metaphors We Live By*. University of Chicago Press.

MacIntyre, A. (1981). *After Virtue*. University of Notre Dame Press.

Maslow, A. H. (1943). "A Theory of Motivation." *Psychological Review* 50: 370–96.

Parson, D., ed. (1984). *American Forensics in Perspective.* Speech Communication Association.

Rescher, N. (1973). "The Study of Value Change." In E. Lazlo and J. B. Wilbur, eds., *Value Theory in Philosophy and Social Science.* Gordon and Breach.

Rokeach, M. (1970). *The Nature of Human Values.* Free Press.

Sillars, M. O. and Ganer, P. (1982). "Values and Beliefs: A Systematic Basis for Argumentation." In J. R. Cox and C. A. Willard, eds., *Advances in Argumentation Theory and Research.* Southern Illinois University Press.

Ulrich, W. (1984). "The Nature of the Topic in Value Debate." In D. Brownlee, ed., *CEDA Yearbook 1984.* Cross Examination Debate Association.

Young, G. W. and Gaske, P. C. (1984). "On *Prima Facie* Value Argumentation: The Policy Implications Affirmative." In D. Brownlee, ed., *CEDA Yearbook 1984.* Cross Examination Debate Association.

30

The Narrative Perspective in Academic Debate

A Critique

Robert H. Gass, Jr.

That disputes involving debate paradigms have occupied the center stage of the debate literature for the last half dozen years is evident in Rowland's (1982) comment that "the choice among competing paradigms is now the dominant theoretical issue in academic debate" (p. 133). Today, the controversy over debate paradigms continues to loom large, but the focus of that discussion has recently shifted with the arrival of Hollihan, Baaske, and Riley's "narrative perspective" (Hollihan, 1985; Hollihan, Baaske, and Riley, 1987a; Hollihan, Baaske, and Riley, 1987b; Hollihan and Riley, 1987). Their approach, which represents an ambitious effort to apply Walter Fisher's narrative paradigm to academic debate (see Fisher, 1978, 1980, 1984, 1985a, 1985b; Fisher and Filloy, 1982), is intended not as another contender to be added to the list of existing debate paradigms, but rather as a "transcendent exemplar model" for academic debate (Hollihan et al, 1985). The authors eschew the label "debate paradigm," not only because they feel that term has been misused or misapplied in relation to current models of academic debate, but also because they wish to avoid a whole host of theoretical, substantive, and stylistic assumptions that have come to be associated with the term "debate paradigm" (Hollihan et al, 1985, Hollihan et al, 1987b).

Like Fisher, Hollihan and his coauthors disdain an elitist conception of argument, believing that such a conception fosters a tyranny of experts. And, like Fisher, Hollihan and his co-authors advance a view of argument that champions the native abilities of ordinary people to test and evaluate the quality of reasons in the stories they hear.

Though the narrative perspective has much to recommend it, most notably the prospect of achieving a rapprochement between academic debate and marketplace argument, I believer that in its present form the approach possesses several liabilities. My purpose is to offer a critique of the narrative perspective as it relates to NDT debate[1] and to suggest that an alternative expert model would better satisfy the goals of the activity while simultaneously remedying the primary shortcomings of NDT debate.

Much of the attraction of Fisher's narrative perspective stems from its near universality as a critical/analytical tool for understanding human communication. Whereas traditional rationality is limited to specialized fields (Fisher, 1984, p. 5), narrative rationality enjoys unlimited scope (Fisher, 1984, p. 10). As Fisher emphasizes, "There is no genre, including technical communication, that is not an episode in the story of life" (1985a, p. 347). Elsewhere, he stresses that "narration is the context for interpreting and assessing all communication" (Fisher, 1987, p. 193). Much like Kenneth Burke's dramatism (Burke, 1941, 1950), narration lays claim to a major portion of the symbolic landscape and, like dramatism, achieves its scope by operating at a high level of abstration, or as what Leonard Hawes has labeled a "Type I" theory (1975).

LACK OF PRECISION WITHIN THE NARRATIVE PERSPECTIVE

To admit that principles of narration provide insight into a wide variety of human communicative phenomena is not to say, however, that narration functions as a superior pedagogical model for academic debate. Indeed, I believe the high level of abstraction at which the theory operates serves as a liability insofar as its applicability to academic debate is concerned. Stated simply, the theory suffers from over-generality. The principles of narration are too broad or vague to be of practical benefit in an *applied, competitive* communication context such as academic debate.

A common characteristic of global theories, like Burke's dramatism or Fisher's narrative paradigm, is that they tend to achieve their scope at the expense of precision. That is, high generality in a theory often necessitates low precision. As Reynolds (1979) explains:

> Usually, these two characteristics are negatively correlated; a very precise theory is applicable to a few specific situations, and a less precise theory is applicable to a wider range of situations. (p. 133)

Similarly, Siebold, Cantrill, and Meyers have cautioned that "grand theories ... are often too general to permit precise communicative influence predictions" (1985, p. 553). I believe the generality of the narrative perspective as it relates to academic debate functions as a liability because the theory is unable to provide specific guidance on a number of theoretical issues that are important in debate rounds. This indictment hinges on a central assumption; that a debate theory should precisely specify the elements of its application. Before proceeding further, I would like to develop a justification for this requirement. Otherwise, the preceding indictment could be dismissed as "question begging," in that it faults the narrative perspective for failing to do that which it neither needs, nor intends, to do.

Must a debate theory be precise? Whether generality or precision is deemed more desirable in a theory depends, of course, on what one seeks to *do* with the theory. Pure theories, or theories which are largely speculative in nature, can often afford the luxury of imprecision because their primary aim is to explain, understand, or interpret phenomena. Typically, such theories operate after the fact, in other words, they attempt to explain events or phenomena after they have taken place. Imprecision may be an asset for pure or speculative theories because it serves to broaden their scope. The narrative perspective, when used as a critical tool in the analysis and explanation of symbolic acts, functions in this manner.

Applied theories, or theories that are pragmatic in nature, can rarely afford the luxury of imprecision because their primary aim is to regulate or govern phenomena, typically as the phenomena are taking place. An applied or pragmatic theory cannot sacrifice precision for scope, lest the theory's reach exceed its grasp. All debate theories fall into this second category inasmuch as they attempt to *do something*; they attempt to regulate the activity of debate. The narrative perspective is no exception. Though the theory may operate at a different level than other debate models, it is still an *applied* theory; its aim is to regulate, govern, and dictate *debate practice*. Precision is therefore essential if debaters and judges are to know how and when they are adhering to the guidelines of the theory. It is not enough for an applied theory to provide a philosophical orientation and a few guiding principles, since an applied theory must do more than explain; it must *perform*. Hence, an applied theory should also include an "instruction manual" to ensure proper use of the theory.

A second reason for desiring precision in a debate theory is related to the *competitive* nature of academic debate. In any formal competitive activity in which there are winners and losers, it is essential that the rules of the game be clearly articulated. Uncertainty or ambiguity surrounding the rules and procedures will tend to breed frustration and confusion. Imagine, for example, a game of chess being played in which the rules for castling were so vague as to allow for several possible interpretations. It is not difficult to imagine the conflict that would develop when one player shouted "Checkmate!" only to hear the other respond, "Not at all, I'm about to castle." As with all formal competitive activities, then, the rules governing a debate theory must be sufficiently precise to allow the debaters to ascertain *how* the theory functions in relation to particular arguments, and judges must to able to evaluate specific arguments in accordance with the theory. In sum, those who use and rely on the theory must be able to understand how it applies in the particular case, not just in the general case. In the absence of specific rules and prohibitions, debaters would not know when their arguments modeled the theory and, in the absence of clear-cut guidelines, judges would not know whether their decisions reflected the theory or not.

Precision, then, is a desirable feature in all theories, though it is not always attainable in grand theories or pure theories, which seek primarily explanation and understanding. For applied theories, especially those applied theories that seek to govern and regulate formal competitive activities, precision may be regarded as a desideratum.

Is the narrative perspective espoused by Hollihan, Baaske, and Riley imprecise? Decidedly so. First, the theory is imprecise in specifying *which* theoretical issues common to current debate practice are applicable to the narrative perspective. The authors themselves have acknowledged the applicability of one theoretical issue, presumption, and the inapplicability of another, conditional argumentation (Hollihan et al., 1987b).[2] However, it is far from clear that this list is exhaustive.

No mention is made, for example, of the role, if any, that counterplans would play in the narrative perspective. Yet, it would seem that the concept of offering an alternative to an opponent's proposal is not limited to prevailing debate models. Counterplans could conceivably function within the narrative perspective in the form of rival or incompatible stories. The issue is more complicated than this, however. Presuming for the moment that counterplans or rival stories were deemed applicable, would the concept referred to as "competitiveness" also apply (see Lichtman and Rohrer, 1987)? That is, would a determination of whether a rival story offered by the negative was truly incompatible with the story offered by the affirmative be required? Further complicating the picture, if such things as counterplans or their narrative equivalents were applicable, could the affirmative permute the negative team's story by weaving together the compatible elements of both stories (see Herbeck, 1983)? Given the prevalence of counterplans in current debate practice, it would seem important to know which of these theoretical constructs, if any, bore relevance to the narrative approach. In its present state of development, however, the theory provides no clear-cut answers.

Second, the narrative perspective is imprecise in specifying *how* theoretical issues would be resolved. Within the narrative perspective, only two standards for evaluating arguments are provided; "narrative probability" and "narrative fidelity" (Fisher 1984, p. 8; Hollihan et. al, 1987b, p. 187). While these standards provide general guidelines for argument evaluation, it is impossible to predict how these two standards would be employed in resolving the kinds of theoretical issues mentioned above. How, for example, would the standards of narrative probability and narrative fidelity be employed in resolving a dispute over the issue of counterplan competitiveness? Current debate models rely on one or more relatively precise criteria (for example, mutual exclusivity, net benefits, redundancy, and philosophical competitiveness) in making such a determination (see, for example, Lichtman and Rohrer, 1987; Lictman, Rohrer, and Hart, 1987). Yet, it is difficult to ascertain which, if any, of the prevailing criteria most closely conform with the requirements of narrative probability and fidelity, or how the standards of narrative probability and fidelity would be used to test the incompatibility of a rival story.

Regardless of the level at which the narrative perspective is claimed to operate, it is safe to predict that debaters and judges would ponder whether the theory allowed for the possibility of counterplans or rival stories, or whether the theory limited negative teams to a defense of the status quo. At present, the theory is silent on this score. And, if counterplans or rival stories were permitted, debaters would need to know when and under what circumstances, as well as how such issues as the competitiveness or incompatibility of rival stories would be evaluated. At present, the standards of narrative probability and fidelity appear to offer no guidance on these concerns.

Of course, the issue of counterplan competitiveness represents only one of many knotty theoretical concerns found in contemporary debate rounds. Even the role of basic stock issues is unclear within the narrative perspective. Moreover, one can legitimately inquire as to what role, if any, a variety of other theoretical issues such as fiat power, decision rules, turn-arounds, or alternative agent counterplans would play in the narrative perspective. Which of these would remain issues and which would become nonissues? How would those theoretical issues that survived translation into the narrative perspective be argued and evaluated? Because the intricacies of the theory have yet to be spelled out, the narrative perspective would invite considerable ad hoc guessing on the part of debaters and judges as they sought to determine which features of prevailing debate theory were applicable and which were not, and how those features which were applicable were to be resolved according to the overly general standards of narrative probability and fidelity.

For the narrative perspective to function as a workable exemplar model for debate, its proponents must articulate more precisely which prevailing theoretical practices would be regarded as applicable or inapplicable, which as sound and or unsound. The process of articulating and elaborating the narrative perspective is thus far from complete. A number of important theoretical issues remain open questions insofar as Hollihan, Baaske, and Riley's approach is concerned.

In contrast to the above situation, current debate models do provide relatively clear-cut answers to specific theoretical concerns. Debaters and judges share a fairly clear understanding of which theoretical practices are allowed or disallowed under the policy-making and hypothesis-testing paradigms, for example. Such clarity is desirable in that it ensures consistent application of the prevailing debate models from round to round. Owing to its lack of precision, however, the narrative perspective would invite considerable variability in its application. An argument upheld by a judge in one debate could be disallowed by the judge of the next debate. Such variety in argument evaluation, it could be argued, might prove beneficial for the activity, but this would be the case only if the variations in argument evaluation remained within the tenets of the theory. As it now stands, the vagaries of the theory could easily lead to misunderstandings over what kinds of arguments fell within the purview of the theory and how those arguments were to be evaluated. The theory's lack of precision, then, might invite inconsistency in its application.

LOW ARGUMENT EVALUATION STANDARDS WITHIN THE NARRATIVE PERSPECTIVE

A second major weakness of Hollihan, Baaske, and Riley's new exemplar model is that it establishes an unnecessarily low standard for argument and for argument evaluation. In championing the common man or woman as the measure of argument acceptability, the narrative perspective fails to maximize the intellectual potential of academic debate. Hollihan and his co-authors stress that the current elitist conception of debate devalues the abilities of ordinary persons to comprehend complex policy issues. "An elitist ideology," they note, "presumes that the man or woman off the street is too uninformed, uninterested, unintelligent, or biased to play an important policy making role" (1987b, p. 185). As a result, "debaters are not taught how to . . . value the opinions of such audiences" (1987b, p. 185). By contrast, the narrative perspective "celebrates the ability, wisdom, and judgment of the public" (1987b, p. 187). Like Fisher, Hollihan and his co-authors evince the view that "the public [is] capable of evaluating complex issues and that individuals reason by testing the quality of the stories they hear" (1987b, p. 187).

Within the narrative perspective, the words "common man or woman" and "layperson" clearly function as god terms, and the words "expert" or "elite" as devil terms. This romanticized portrait of the ordinary citizen is open to serious challenge, however, as is their assumption that the use of a layperson standard for judging debates is superior to that of an expert or elite standard. The notion that the "man or woman off the street" is capable of successfully understanding and evaluating complex policy issues, and that debaters in making arguments, and judges in evaluating them, should therefore gear their reasoning to ordinary citizens can be assailed on two grounds. First, the assumption that lay audiences attend to, let alone understand, complex policy issues appears to be somewhat fanciful. Second, even if lay audiences occasionally do succeed in this regard, academic debate should employ a higher standard of argumentative excellence than is accepted by the norm. Each of these points will be taken up in turn.

In extolling the virtues of the citizenry, Hollihan, Baaske, and Riley commit a significant error; they neglect to provide actual data to support their claims. But for a single reference to a selected case offered by Fisher, no evidence is presented in support of the view that laypersons can and do carefully scrutinize complex public policy issues. No factual or empirical support is offered on behalf of their assertion that ordinary persons successfully employ the standards of narrative probability and narrative fidelity to test the coherence of stories presented for their assent. Merely *hoping* that ordinary persons do so is not sufficient. Prior to asking the debate community to embrace their new exemplar model, Hollihan, Baaske, and Riley should provide evidence establishing that public audiences can distinguish the better cause from the worse, the stronger story from the weaker; that they do so by utilizing narrative tests of reasoning; and that their ability to do so constitutes the rule rather than the exception. At present, the authors' notions regarding the wisdom and judgment of the citizenry apear to constitute little more than wishful thinking.

While it is not my intention to malign the intelligence of the general public, I feel it only fair to note that there is a good deal of evidence pointing to a contrary conclusion than that reached by Hollihan, Baaske, and Riley. Millions of Americans are woefully ignorant of public policy issues that have been on the forefront of the political scene for years (Weissberg, 1976). To illustrate, five out of six persons in one recent survey ("Genetic Engineering Mystery," 1987) either had never heard of "genetic engineering" or said they did not understand the moral and political issues well enough to take a firm position on the issue. By their own admission, then, most Americans are ill-equipped to judge or interpret stories about this issue. Another recent survey ("Newsmakers," 1988) revealed that three out of four Americans questioned could not locate the Persian Gulf on a map, while one in four failed to find the Pacific Ocean! To the extent that knowing *where the story takes place* is important, these Americans would have difficulty evaluating the significance of events taking place in the Middle East.

A knowledge and awareness of the key characters would also seem to be an important ingredient in the evaluation of a story, yet millions of Americans are woefully ignorant of the leading players in national and international dramas; 55 percent of Americans, for example, had not heard of or read about Robert Bork's nomination to the Supreme Court, which had taken place one month beforehand; fully 63 percent of the public did not know which two countries had engaged in the SALT Talks (Sanoff, Solarzano, Moore, Kalb, and Budiansky, 1987, p. 88). Clearly, the general public does not appear to pay serious attention to the above stories. That the above examples of public inattention or disinterest are typical is reflected in Thomas Dye and L. Harmon Ziegler's conclusion that:

> Many people simply have no opinion about political issues that are the subject of heated debate in the mass media. No more than a third of the public recognizes legislative proposals that have been the center of public debate for months, and sometimes years. Further, even among that third, few could describe the proposal accurately or in detail, and fewer still could describe the intricacies and alternatives available to policy makers. (1978, p. 162)

Perhaps the man or woman off the street *can* understand and evaluate complex policy issues, as Hollihan, Baaske, and Riley suggest, but he or she does not appear interested enough to *want* to do so. As Phillip Converse explains, "For many people, politics does not compete in interest with sports, local gossip, or television dramas" (1963, p. 213).

Even more to the point, there is evidence that the average person is not adept at identifying inconsistent or contradictory evidence (Dresser, 1963; Harte, 1971). Nor can the results of these investigations be dismissed for relying on traditional rational standards, since the types of arguments and evidence employed were much more akin to marketplace reasoning than to formal logic. These findings are noteworthy, because they cast doubt on the assumption that laypersons utilize the narrative probability standard to assess argumentative coherence as Hollihan, Baaske, and Riley suggest they do (1987b, p. 188).

A significant shortcoming of the narrative perspective, then, involves its potentially misplaced confidence in the ability of the common man or woman to understand and evaluate complex policy issues. The preceding suggests that ordinary citizens often fail to carefully scrutinize the quality of the reasons in the stories they hear. In fact, they often fail to attend to the stories altogether. Before making further demands for wholesale changes in the debate activity, Hollihan, Baaske, and Riley should provide corroborating evidence for the underlying precepts of their exemplar model.

Even if public audiences do, on occasion, attend to complex policy issues with a thoughtful ear, the reliance on a "layperson" standard of argument in academic debate rounds would establish an unnecessarily low standard for argument quality. There is little intellectual merit in requiring that debaters gear their arguments to an average level of intelligence or understanding when they can appeal to a higher degree of intelligence and understanding instead. In short, academic debate should hold to higher intellectual aspirations than are required for convincing lay audiences. In direct contrast to Hollihan, Baaske, and Riley's exemplar model, I would recommend that academic debate serve as the training ground for students who will one day enter the professional ranks of society, to become the very experts and elites the authors disdain. Accordingly, I believe debaters should learn to argue before expert or professional audiences. NDT debaters do not represent the norm among college students, they represent some of the brightest young minds in the country. They are far more likely to pursue professional careers in law, politics, business, and education than their peers (Matlon and Keele, 1984), and therefore have a correspondingly greater need to learn how to argue before highly professional, highly specialized audiences.

While Hollihan and his coauthors maintain that there are already "technocrats to spare" (1987b, p. 186) among the decision-making bodies of society, I would submit that there is already an abundance of used car and door-to-door salespersons as well! To reorient debate toward a narrative standard of argument would therefore be to squander its potential as an intellectual activity. If, as Hollihan, Baaske, and Riley maintain, "debaters already understand how to construct and test stories" (1987b, p. 187), it makes little sense to provide debaters with additional formalized training in that which they already know how to do. If the ability to reason narratively is intuitive or innate, then the activity of NDT debate has little that is unique or special to offer debaters.

The present models for the activity, and especially the expert approach that I endorse, do impart a special purpose and meaning to NDT debate. What academic debate does well—and what few or no other activities succeed in doing nearly as well—is to teach students to reason according to traditional rational standards, to conduct in-depth research, to engage in the complex analysis of issues, and to practice focused critical thinking (Colbert and Biggers, 1987; Colbert, 1987). Even with all its limitations, academic debate succeeds admirably in training students to become expert advocates and decision makers in professional fields. Thus, while I believe the existing models can be improved upon, I disagree with the nature of the improvements recommended by the advocates of narration.

In faulting academic debate for relying on an expert standard of judging and proposing a public audience standard instead, I believe the advocates of narration have misanalyzed both the nature of the problem and its solution. The real problem, I believe, is that judges *have not behaved enough like experts* in evaluating debate rounds. Here, I depart from a defense of present day debate practices. The solution to many of the problems confronting NDT debate, I would submit, is for judges to behave *more like real-world experts* in evaluating arguments.

I believe Hollihan and his co-authors are mistaken when they claim that the present models of debate "encourages policy debaters to emulate the behaviors of highly trained, technically skilled public policy advocates" (1987b, p. 184). I frankly suspect that few, if any, real-world experts could understand what transpires in many debate rounds, largely due to the excessive speed, the overreliance on labels or taglines, the prevalence of low-quality evidence and sources, and an emphasis on unrealistic scenarios. All of the preceding may appear to duplicate the complaints made by Hollihan, Baaske, and Riley about NDT debate. The important point, though, is that the preceding problems inhibit not only laypersons' ability to comprehend debate rounds, but *experts as well*. When Hollihan and his co-authors criticize debate because it cannot be appreciated by "faculty colleagues, university administrators, community leaders, or even alumni if they graduated more than ten years ago" (1987b, p. 186), they appeal to an *expert standard* themselves. The groups they mention are highly educated, highly trained specialists in their respective fields, not public audiences. While I acknowledge that reforms are needed in debate, then, I believe the reforms should begin with a concerted effort to make debate more intelligible or sensible to experts and professional audiences.

My recommendation is that debate should employ a higher standard of argumentative excellence than that which is presently found in many debates or than that entailed in the narrative perspective. Specifically, I would suggest that debaters and judges adopt as their role model an expert criterion, based upon what recognized experts in the fields of the debate topics would regard as reasonable claims, plausible grounds, and warranted inferences. Hollihan, Baaske, and Riley complain that real-world audiences would find the links to many disadvantages incredulous. For me, however, the more important point is that real-world *experts* would probably reject the plausibility of such links as well. How actual experts would react to links is a better indicator of argument quality, since experts can bring greater knowledge to bear in testing the speciousness of links.

In advocating that judges behave more like expert auditors when evaluating arguments, I agree with Hollihan, Baaske, and Riley that the prevailing norm of complete nonintervention is responsible for many of the problems in debate. Judges should intervene, I believe, but as experts on the subject of argument and as experts on the subject matter of the resolution. My approach is not at odds with Balthrop's (1983) notion of the debate judge as critic of argument or Rowland's view of the "debate judge as debate judge" (1984), in that it recognizes and champions the judge's qualifications as an expert in the field of argumentation. In addition, however, I would recommend that judges behave as experts within the domain of the topic when evaluating arguments. Judges would thus need to immerse themselves in the literature on the debate topic, just as they now expect debaters to do. This additional requirement admittedly places a greater responsibility on judges to stay well read and well informed about events relating to the topic. To the extent that the possession of greater knowledge serves as an asset in decision-making, judges willing to do the hard work of keeping abreast of the topic would find themselves in a better position to carefully evaluate arguments and evidence than would judges relying on the narrative perspective.

Using one of the examples cited by Hollihan and Riley (1987), I believe the superiority of relying on an expert standard, rather than the narrative perspective, in evaluating arguments is made clear. They cite the example of a debater arguing "that homosexuals should be killed (in response to an AIDS epidemic argument)" (p. 402) as an instance of an argument that would not receive serious consideration in the real world. While neither experts nor laypersons have called for such extreme measures, the latter have displayed far more reactionary attitudes than the former. Many members of the general public initially accepted the argument that AIDS was God's punishment of homosexuals, and many persist in the belief that quarantines and other drastic measures are needed to stem the epidemic (Adler, Greenberg, Hager, McKillop, and Namuth, 1985; Gostin, 1986; Petit, 1986). Experts, on the other hand, such as the surgeon general and researchers for the Centers for Disease Control, have denounced such extreme measures as ineffective and threatening to fundamental civil liberties (Adler et al, 1985; Center for Disease Control, 1986; Gostin, 1986; "Straight Talk on AIDS," 1986). Whereas the public reacted out of fear or panic (Gostin, 1986, p. 3), the experts reacted on the basis of facts and information. As this example illustrates, a judge employing the narrative perspective would be more inclined to react as the public did—*reflexively*, while a judge employing an expert standard would be more inclined to react as experts did— *reflectively*.

A reliance on an expert criterion in debate rounds—one which simultaneously recognizes the judge as an expert on argument, *and* as one who is well versed on the topic for debate—establishes a higher standard of argumentative excellence than does the narrative perspective. As the above example illustrates, emotions often play a greater role in shaping public attitudes than do reasons. Hollihan, Baaske, and Riley (1987b) criticize debate for being without passion and "free of the tainting influence of human emotion" (p. 186), yet emotional excess can be equally undesirable. Mobs brim with passion. I believe that reliance on an expert standard establishes a more desirable mix of reason and emotion than does the narrative perspective. While emotion should not be excluded entirely from debate rounds, it should remain the servant, and reason its master.

RISK OF EXCESSIVE JUDGE INTERVENTION WITHIN THE NARRATIVE PERSPECTIVE

A third major criticism addresses the degree of judge intervention contemplated by the narrative perspective. While I am sympathetic to Hollihan and his co-authors' charge that the prevailing emphasis on complete nonintervention has hampered the educational goals of the activity (Hollihan et al, 1985; Hollihan et al, 1987b), there is also danger in allowing the pendulum to swing too far in the opposite direction. The tabula rasa approach gained popularity, after all, in response to a felt need by many at the time that some judges were intruding too much upon the debate process (Ulrich, 1981; Ulrich, 1982; Ulrich, 1984). That the prospect of judge intervention looms large within the narrative perspective is evident in Hollihan et al's statement that:

> The principle of judge noninvolvement in the debate process would most certainly dissipate as judges would be called upon to have a very different conception of their role. . . . Critics would of course bring their beliefs and knowledge from past experience, their values, and passions with them into the argumentative encounter. (1985, p. 819)

In seeking to replace the principle of nonintervention with a principle of almost unlimited intervention, however, the advocates of narration may err in embracing an equally unappealing extreme. What Hollihan, Baaske, and Riley romantically refer to as the judge's "beliefs," "knowledge," "values," and "passions," could be dispassionately labeled as "biases," "stereotypes," "prejudices," and "dogma." And, though the authors do take the trouble to note that they are not advocating *unlimited* intervention (Hollihan et al, 1985, p. 819; Hollihan et al, 1987b, p. 190), there is no clear indication as to *where* or *how* they would draw the line. In "The Art of Storytelling" (1985), Hollihan, Riley, and Baaske offer the following disclaimer:

> This new principle of judge involvement should not be taken as a license for unlimited intervention into the debate, however, but rather, judges should seek to serve in an intersubjective role engaged in a dialogue with the texts of the stories (p. 819).

What is difficult to determine, though, is *how* the last clause of this statement acts as a stricture against unlimited intervention, since any and all intrusions could be defended on the grounds that the judge was merely seeking to serve "in an intersubjective role engaged in a dialogue with the texts of the stories." The distinction between which kinds of intervention would be allowed, and which not, and under what circumstances, appears fuzzy at best.

Given a principle of nearly unlimited judge intervention, two situations could arise that would threaten the integrity of the debate process. First, some judges might refuse to accept arguments that failed to ring true with their belief systems, despite compelling evidence to the contrary. Second, other judges might accept arguments that struck sympathetic chords within their belief systems, even when those arguments were not accompanied by adequate evidence. The fact that the narrative perspective relies on a layperson standard for argument evaluation tends to increase the likelihood that both to these situations would occur.

A clear example of the first danger can be found in the public paranoia surrounding the AIDS crisis, mentioned earlier. Despite an overwhelming *and* well-reported consensus of scientific and medical evidence to the contrary (Gostin, 1986; Centers for Disease Control, 1986; Padian, 1986; Petit, 1986; "AIDS Risk Found Low," 1985; "Straight Talk on AIDS," 1986), the public persists in believing that AIDS can be casually transmitted (Adler et al, 1985; Gallup Report, 1987; Petit, 1986; "Straight Talk on AIDS," 1986). Fisher comments that "the people have a natural tendency to prefer the true and the just" (1984, p. 9), but this natural tendency has not manifested itself where AIDS is concerned. Parents have lobbied to keep children who have tested positive for HTLV antibodies from attending public schools, and neighborhoods have organized in an effort to exclude home health care hospices for dying AIDS victims. Thus far it has been the courts, acting in the role of experts or elites, that have protected the constitutional rights of AIDS sufferers.

An example of the second danger, that of accepting an argument that was not adequately supported, is provided by Rowland:

> ...a narrative can be effective and yet false. The many accusations of blood libel against the Jewish people over a course of centuries illustrate

how demonstrably false stories may be believed by large groups of people (1987, p. 269).

The two concerns highlighted here—the prospect that judges employing a narrative perspective might reject arguments despite compelling evidence or accept arguments without sufficient evidence—point up a significant shortcoming in Hollihan, Baaske, and Riley's exemplar model. Indeed, if the narrative perspective contains an Achilles heel, it is in the fact that true stories sometimes ring false, and false stories sometimes ring true. To a debater, there is no experience more frustrating than to learn upon the conclusion of a debate that he or she has been debating a "third team" in the person of the judge seated in the back of the room, a team whose arguments were kept secret from him or her during the debate, and whose objections were made known only after the ballot was completed.

One may legitimately ask why the expert perspective I have advocated would not be subject to the same attendant risks regarding excessive judge intervention. Admittedly, a judge who was a loose cannon could manage to find some pretext for intervening under any debate model. The narrative perspective, however, substantially increases the likelihood of such intervention taking place for two distinct reasons. First, the narrative perspective, and the narrative perspective alone, endorses the legitimacy of *conscious intrusions* upon the debate based upon the *emotions or feelings* of the judge. True, an expert judge's feelings might unconsciously influence his or her evaluation of the issues. Conscious forays into the debate, however, would be authorized only on the basis of specific knowledge and facts possessed by the judge. A judge might intervene, for instance, because he or she knew, based on his or her reading of the literature, that one side was overclaiming or misrepresenting the position of a given author. An expert judge *would not* intervene simply because he or she disagreed with the particular author's views, as a narrative judge might, but because he or she knew one side was overstating the author's conclusions. Debaters would thus be spared the judge's passions more often under an expert than a narrative perspective.

Second, the standards of narrative probability and narrative fidelity are incapable of serving as correctives in situations involving excessive judge intervention. These standards operate *within* a given judge's belief system, they do not serve as external checks on whether the judge's belief system corresponds with reality. Hollihan, Baaske, and Riley (1987b) wrongly suggest that narrative fidelity "is similar to a test of external consistency" (p. 187). However, narrative fidelity only tests new information in relation to other information *already believed to be true by the individual*, not whether the information already believed to be true *is consistent with reality*. That the narrative approach masquerades what is really a test of the internal consistency of the individual's belief system with what is claimed to be an external test of the validity of a story is evident in the following except:

> ... audiences test narrative fidelity by asking themselves how well the stories ring true with their own experiences. ... How similar is this story to other stories already experienced and believed to be true? Stories that are consistent with previous stories are assumed to possess greater truth than those which contradict stories which we have previously come to know and accept (Hollihan et al, 1987b, p. 187).

The standard of narrative fidelity, then, involves little more than the application of traditional consistency theory or psychologic to the metaphor of storytelling. Unlike narration, the expert perspective I have described would be subject to external verification. In the case of a judge who claimed one side had overstated or misinterpreted the position of a particular author, the actual works of the author could be consulted as an external check on the validity of the judge's or the debaters' interpretation. Published reviews of the author's works could also be consulted to determine which parties' interpretation of the author's position was most accurate. A judge might also intervene if he or she knew a quoted source was unqualified or that a quoted source's views were at odds with the consensus of expert opinion on an issue. Again, such intrusions by the judge would be subject to external verification by reference to the original published sources.

In comparison to an expert approach, then, the narrative perspective uniquely enhances the risk of judge intervention by relying on standards that exist only in the mind of the judge and, hence, are not subject to external checks. There is little merit in replacing existing models of debate, which the proponents of narration criticize for allowing too little intervention, with an alternative model that encourages too much intervention. The expert standard I have proposed would strike a harmonious balance between these two extremes by authorizing judge intervention over issues relating to the quality of sources, the accuracy with which sources' positions were represented, and the credibility of sources' positions as measured against the known consensus of expert opinion. An expert standard thus would allow for limited intervention in select situations, but would not encourage nearly unlimited intervention as would the narrative perspective.

While I remain unconvinced that the narrative perspective offers the best approach for reforming academic debate, I do agree with Hollihan, Baaske, and Riley that certain changes are in order, especially with respect to the style of NDT debate as it now exists. My suggestion is that many of their criticisms could be redressed through the expert approach I have described. Following, then, are several suggestions for improving the quality and integrity of argumentation in debate rounds within an expert model.

Were judges to impose three basic requirements on the style of presenting arguments in debate rounds, I believe much of the non-communicative behavior that passes for argumentation could be eliminated. First, arguments and evidence would have to be *intelligible* in order to be counted. If a debater garbled his or her speech or read evidence unintelligibly, an expert judge would discount the argument entirely. Evidence that could not be heard or understood would not be called for at the end of a debate. I frankly believe this practice is already commonplace on the national circuit. Such a requirement is clearly consistent with an expert standard of judging, since real-world experts would be loathe to accept arguments they could not hear or understand.

Second, expert judges would demand that debaters speak in complete sentences rather than in labels, tag lines, or pidgin English. Just as students writing essay exams are customarily expected to write in complete sentences, supplying a subject and predicate for each complete thought or idea, debaters would be required to speak in complete sentences for each argument made. Just as an essay exam is, at least in part, a test of writing ability, so too would debate tournaments be regarded, at least in part, as tests of speaking ability. Again, this requirement is consistent with an expert standard of judging. In the real world, experts do demand that advocates communicate their ideas clearly and cogently.

Third, expert judges would not give consideration to utterances that failed to meet the minimum requirements for a wholly contained argument, such as the presence of a claim, data or grounds, and a clearly perceived warrant. The problem with the use of tag lines is that while a claim has been stated and, perhaps, some semblance of grounds, the *relationship* between the data and the grounds remains unexplained. In short, the warrant authorizing movement from the grounds to the claim is missing and may not be clearly perceived by the opponent or the judge. Expert judges, because they are also experts in the field of argument, would encourage debaters to recognize the importance of the warrant-building or warrant-establishing process in argumentation.

The acceptance and incorporation of the above three requirements into the expert judging standard I have endorsed would go a long way toward allaying many of the concerns involving speed and shallow analysis raised by Hollihan, Baaske, and Riley. Debaters would still speak rapidly, but they would speak intelligibly, and in complete sentences, and would present completed arguments. In my experience, debaters who regularly win top speaker awards at national tournaments already meet these requirements. These are the kinds of debaters we are proud to parade before fellow colleagues, university administrators, community leaders, and debate alumni. Considerable improvement in the quality of communication in debate rounds is thus possible without embracing the narrative approach.

CONCLUSION

History has a way of repeating itself in the debate activity as in other walks of life. The fact is that early in the history of the debate activity the narrative perspective, or something closely resembling it, was tried and found wanting. The advent of present day "elitist" models to which Hollihan, Baaske, and Riley object is a comparatively recent phenomenon and reflects, in large part, the result of decades of dissatisfaction with previous judging practices. A reliance on lay judges and a common man or woman standard of judging was at one time the rule rather than the exception in intercollegiate debate, and was also the source of considerable pulling of hair and gnashing of teeth on the part of coaches and debaters frustrated with the process. For example, in bemoaning the scarcity of faculty judges, R. O. Hollister noted as early as 1917 that "students cannot be long dissatisfied with the judging in contests without losing their heart in such contests" (p. 235). Lew Sarett echoed similar sentiments in that same year, commenting that:

> ... the fact remains that, because of a vast amount of inexpert or incompetent judging there is much dissatisfaction with our present system. Most of us are willing to try out at least any new system which promises to improve the quality of judging (1917, pp. 134–135).

Somewhat later, a survey of high school debate coaches revealed that of thirty possible judges, high school coaches ranked "college debate coaches" first and "housewives" last. "The most common criticism ... directed towards judges who lack[ed] knowledge of debate itself," the survey noted, was that such judges "[were] prejudiced concerning the question for debate or [were] influenced by their own opinion" (Williams, 1958, p. 9). Still later, Robert Schrum noted in an article appearing in the *Rostrum*:

> It is difficult to understand the continuing practice of using as judges laymen who are likely to be consistently fallible because they lack sufficient knowledge of even the fundamental principles of debate. . . . The problem with typical lay judges—mothers, bus drivers, and teachers with free time on Saturday—is that they often do not understand or adhere to even the simplest rules of debate. . . . Incompetent decisions . . . undermine the accuracy of a tournament and confuse and discourage debaters. Such decisions should not be tolerated in an activity that holds forth the promise of intellectual training in a context characterized by understandable and usable rules applied by critic-judges who know at least as much as the debaters (1968), pp. 6–7).

Continued calls like these for improvements in judging eventually gave rise to the prevailing models that now dominate debate. While obviously incorporating some differences, the narrative perspective can thus be viewed not so much as an advancement in the method for judging debates, but rather, as a return to a past method that was wisely discarded.

The history of efforts to reform debate is a tale of vessels laden with lofty goals. Hollihan, Baaske, and Riley have set out on an ambitious voyage, but have yet to prove their vessel is seaworthy. The criticisms raised in this essay point out several leaks and holes in the narrative perspective which require shoring up if their model is to survive. At present, the narrative perspective seems aptly suited for public audience debates, and perhaps CEDA debate, but appears less well-suited to NDT competition. Academic debate is clearly in need of some reform, but the expert approach I have championed would accomplish more good with far less harm to the present activity than the narrative perspective. Those who are intent on taking a voyage, then, would be better advised to book passage on the expert model.

References

Adler, J., Greenberg, N. F., Hager, M., Mckillop, P., Namuth, T. (1985). "The AIDS Conflict." *Newsweek* (Sept. 23): 18–24.

"A Dose of Straight Talk on AIDS" (1986). *U.S. News & World Report* (Nov. 3): 8.

Balthrop, V. W. (1983). "The Debate Judge as 'Critic of Argument': Toward a Transcendent Perspective." *Journal of the American Forensic Association* 20: 1–15.

Bennett, W. (1986). "Differing Figures." *Wilson Library Bulletin* 60: 34.

Burke, K. (1941). *The Philosophy of Literary Form*. Baton Rouge: Louisiana State University Press.

Burke, K. (1945). *A Grammar of Motives*. Englewood Cliffs: Prentice-Hall.

Centers for Disease Control (1986). *AIDS Recommendations and Guidelines*. Washington, DC: U.S. Public Health Service.

Colbert, K. R. (1987). "The Effects of CEDA and NDT Debate Training on Critical Thinking Ability." *Journal of the American Forensic Association* 23: 194–201.

Colbert, K. R. and Biggers, T. (1987). "Why Should We Support Debate?" In D. A. Thomas and J. Hart, eds. *Advanced Debate: Readings in Theory, Practice, and Teaching*. Lincolnwood, IL: National Textbook Co. 2–6.

Converse, P. E. (1964). "The Nature of Belief Systems in Mass Publics." In D. E. Apter, ed. *Ideology and Discontent*. New York: Free Press. 213–30.

Dye, T. R. (1978). *The Irony of Democracy: An Uncommon Introduction to American Politics*. 4th ed. North Scituate, MA: Duxbury Press.

Dye, T. R. (1985). *Politics in States and Communities*. 5th ed. Englewood Cliffs: Prentice-Hall.

Fisher, W. R. (1978). "Toward a Logic of Good Reasons." *Quarterly Journal of Speech* 62: 1–14.

Fisher, W. R. (1980). "Rationality and the Logic of Good Reasons." *Philosophy and Rhetoric* 13: 121–30.

Fisher, W. R. (1984). "Narration as a Human Communication Paradigm: The Case of Public Moral Argument." *Communication Monographs* 51: 1–22.

Fisher, W. R. (1985a). "The Narrative Paradigm: An Elaboration." *Communication Monographs* 52: 347–67.

Fisher, W. R. (1985b). "The Narrative Paradigm: In the Beginning." *Journal of Communication* 35: 74–89.

Fisher, W. R. (1987). *Human Communication as Narration: Toward a Philosophy of Reason, Value, and Action*. Columbia: University of South Carolina Press.

Fisher, W. R. and Filloy, R. A. (1982). "Argument in Drama and Literature: An Exploration." In J. R. Cox and C. A. Willard, eds. *Advances in Argumentation Theory and Research*. Carbondale: Southern Illinois University Press. 343–62.

Gallup Report (1987). "Avoiding Suspected AIDS Victims." *The Gallup Report* (June): 9.

"Genetic Engineering Mystery" (1987). *The Los Angeles Times* (Sept. 28): pt. 2, p. 3.

Gostin, L. (1986). "Acquired Immune Deficiency Syndrome: A Review of Science, Health Policy, and Law." In M. D. Witt, ed. *AIDS and Patient Management: Legal, Ethical, and Social Issues*. Owing Mills, MD: National Health Publication. 3–24.

Greenstein, F. J. (1963). *The American Party System and the American People*. Englewood Cliffs: Prentice-Hall.

Hawes, L. C. (1975). *Pragmatics of Analoguing Theory and Model Construction in Communication*. Reading, MA: Addison-Wesley.

Herbeck, D. A. (1983). "A Permutation Standard of Competitiveness." *Journal of the American Forensic Association* 22: 12–19.

Hollihan, T. A., Baaske, K. T., and Riley, P. (1985). "The Art of Storytellng: An Argument for a Narrative Perspective in Academic Debate." In J. R. Cox, M. O. Sillars, and G. B. Walker, eds. *Argument and Social Practice: Proceedings of the Fourth SCA/AFA Conference on Argumentation*. Annandale, VA: Speech Communication Association. 807–26.

Hollihan, T. A., Baaske, K. T., and Riley, P. (1987a). *Debaters as Storytellers: The Narrative Perspective in Academic Debate*. Paper presented at the Joint Central States Speech Association and Southern States Speech Association Convention, St. Louis.

Hollihan, T. A., Baaske, K. T., and Riley, P. (1987b). "Debaters as Storytellers: The Narrative Perspective in Academic Debate." *Journal of the American Forensic Association* 23: 184–93.

Hollihan, T. A. and Riley, P. (1987). "Academic Debate and Democracy: A Clash of Ideologies." In J. W. Wenzel, ed. *Argument and Critical Practice: Proceedings of the Fifth SCA/AFA Conference on Argumentation*. Annandale, VA: Speech Communication Association. 399–404.

Hollister, R. O. (1917). "Faculty Judging." *Quarterly Journal of Public Speaking* 3: 235–41.

Jacobs, H. C. (1985). "A Shamefully Illiterate Society." *Vital Speeches of the Day* 51: 446–48.

Lichtman, A. J. and Rohrer, D. M. (1987). "A General Theory of the Counterplan." In D. A. Thomas and J. Hart, eds. *Advanced Debate: Readings in Theory, Practice, and Teaching*. 3rd ed. Lincolnwood, IL: National Textbook. 243–53.

Lichtman, A. J., Rohrer, D. M., and Hart, J. (1987). "Policy Systems Revisited." In D. A. Thomas and J. Hart, eds. *Advanced Debate: Readings in Theory,*

Practice, and Teaching. 3rd ed. Lincolnwood, IL: National Textbook. 231–40.

Matlon, R. L. and Keele, L. M. (1984). "A Survey of Participants in the National Debate Tournament." *Journal of the American Forensic Association* 20: 194–205.

McGraw, Jr., H. W. (1987). "Adult Functional Illiteracy: What to Do About It." *Personnel* 64: 38–42.

Newsmakers (1988). *The Los Angeles Times* (July 28), part 1, p. 2.

Petit, C. (1986). "California to Vote on AIDS Proposition." *Science* 234: 277–78.

Reynolds, P. D. (1971). *A Primer in Theory Construction*. Indianapolis: Bobbs-Merrill.

Rowland, R. C. (1982). "Standards for Paradigm Evaluation." *Journal of the American Forensic Association* 18: 133–40.

Rowland, R. C. (1984). "The Debate Judge as Debate Judge: A Functional Paradigm for Evaluating Debates." *Journal of the American Forensic Association* 22: 125–34.

Rowland, R. C. (1986). "The Relationship Between Realism and Debatability in Policy Advocacy." *Journal of the American Forensic Association* 22: 125–34.

Rowland, R. C. (1987). "Narrative: Mode of Discourse or Paradigm?" *Communication Monographs* 54: 264–75.

Sanoff, A. P., et al. (1987). "What Americans Should Know." *U.S. News & World Report* (Sept. 28): 86–94.

Sarett, L. R. (1917). "The Expert Judge of Debate." *The Quarterly Journal of Public Speaking* 3: 135–39.

Schrum, R. M. (1968). "Do Judges Know when Debaters Win or Lose?" *The Rostrum* (Jan.): 6–7.

Ulrich, W. R. (1981). *In Search of Tabula Rasa*. Paper presented at the Annual Meeting of the Speech Communication Association, Anaheim.

Ulrich, W. R. (1982). "Flexibility in Paradigm Evaluation." *Journal of the American Forensic Association* 78: 115–53.

Ulrich, W. R. (1984). "Debate as Dialectic: A Defense of the Tabula Rasa Approach to Judging." *Journal of the American Forensic Association* 21: 89–93.

Weissberg, R. (1976). *Public Opinion and Popular Government*. Englewood Cliffs: Prentice-Hall.

Williams, D. (1958). "Attitudes of High School Coaches Toward the Judging of Debate Tournaments." *The Rostrum* (Nov.): 7–9.

Notes

1. My comments in this essay are directed toward NDT debate practice, although they may have applicability for CEDA debate as well. My choice in focusing on NDT debate was influenced by two concerns. First, I see the goals of NDT debate as being different from those of CEDA debate, or from those of large, public audience debates. Hence, I'm more inclined to accept the applicability of the narrative perspective to the latter two forums than to NDT debate. Second, the bulk of Hollihan, Baaske, and Riley's criticisms are directed specifically at NDT debate practice, especially the evils they associate with the policy-making, hypothesis-testing, and tabula rasa models of NDT debate. My focus thus reflects, in large part, the focus of their own published articles and essays.

2. With respect to conditional arguments, one may legitimately question whether Hollihan, Riley, and Baaske's proscription against such argu-

ments inheres within the narrative perspective itself, or within their particular brand of narration. Real-world advocates often do change their stories. For example, defense lawyers frequently enter changes in their clients' pleas, from "guilty" to "not guilty," and vice versa. Presidential hopefuls often lambaste rival candidates during their party's primaries, but pledge full support to their party's nominee at the national convention. Furthermore, Zarefsky's hypothesis-testing paradigm offers a coherent, self-contained story on behalf of conditional arguments; *if* the debate resolution is viewed as a hypothesis, then any number of alternative hypotheses may be legitimately entertained. Conditional arguments are thus consistent with the hypothesis-testing story.

KEY TERMS

critic of argument

game theory

narrative paradigm

pluralism

tabula rasa

DISCUSSION

1. What explanatory powers do you think are unique to the narrative paradigm? Why?
2. Compare and contrast each of the major paradigms.
3. What do you think Lichtman, et al. (Part Five), would say concerning Snider's game theory paradigm?
4. Why is the paradigm discussion in this book divided into two sections? Is each paradigm in the proper section?
5. Why do you think the narrative paradigm has found little use in academic debate rounds?
6. Do you see any scenarios where Ulrich would allow judge intervention?
7. Could one hypothesis-test a narrative?

Part Seven

Theoretical Issues in Policy Debate

It is commonly considered that there are three kinds of debate propositions: questions of fact, questions of value, and questions of policy. Questions of fact concern ontology of existence. Questions of value focus on intrinsic worth. Questions of policy ask if the net benefits of a system indicate that an action should be taken. Part Seven of this book concerns itself primarily with questions of policy.

Kenneth Burke argues that choice is often tragic. With this in mind, Part Seven focuses on alternative policy proposals. The trend by negative teams to emphasize negative consequences of the affirmative position has resulted in the increasing use of the counterplan when debating questions of policy. The counterplan is often used to offer a superior option to the affirmative proposal; or sometimes, as seen in some recent tournaments, just to insure the uniqueness of the negative's disadvantages.

Included in this volume is Lichtman and Rohrer's seminal article, "A General Theory of the Counterplan." The subsequent proliferation of counterplans has caused theorists to search for possible avenues of limitation. Perhaps the most successful of these essays is Herbeck's "Permutation Standard of Competitiveness."

Competitiveness and studies are not the only issues in the restriction of counterplanning. Another concern is the counterplan that offers an alternative agent of change to the one specified in the resolution. This brings into play the issue of fiat, that magic moment when, in order to focus the debate on the desirability of the resolution rather than on the implementation, we consider the affirmative proposal as if it already exists. Roger Solt's thoughtful overview on questions regarding fiat power has been reprinted here.

Due to the bidirectional nature of the past few policy topics, the once heretical notion of topical counterplans has become a potential counterplan option. Noting the trend away from debate resolutions that practically write an affirmative plan, and toward vague topics that do not restrict the affirmative to supporting a specific direction of policy change, Panetta and Dolley, longtime advocates of this option, present the case for the innovation. In concept, their position says that the affirmative plan, not the resolution wording, defines the topic. The topical counterplan is a negative proposal for change in the opposite direction from the affirmative's plan—topical by virtue of being a proposal to change the present system, but not topical by virtue of being competitive with the affirmative plan. Berube argues against it. While the logic of the topical counterplan may be evident when considering vague resolutions, the problem does not lie in inflexible debate theory, which more or less defines the negative out of the round. The problem lies in improperly worded debate resolutions that offer maximum flexibility to the affirmative, and maximum rigidity to the negative.

31

A General Theory of the Counterplan

Allan J. Lichtman

Daniel M. Rohrer

Increasingly, the practice of academic debate is being integrated with modern methods of policy analysis.[1] Debaters and coaches now employ such sophisticated behavioral concepts as systems models, statistical inference and cost-benefit analysis.[2] Unfortunately, formal debate theory tends to lag behind the actual practice of competitive debate. More effort is required to synthesize traditional argumentation theory and the techniques developed by contemporary scholarship for the analysis of public policy.

This article uses concepts drawn from decision theory to establish criteria for identifying competitive policy proposals—that is, policy suggestions that rival each other to the extent that acceptance of one is tantamount to rejection of the other. This formulation has obvious relevance to formal debate where an affirmative advocate is charged with upholding a particular policy position and a negative advocate may defend the present system or propose a counterproposal or counterplan. But the relevance of this study extends beyond the boundaries of formal debate to all variants of policy dispute.[3]

Traditional theory approaches the problem of recognizing competitive policy suggestions through its analysis of the counterplan response to proposals for changing the status quo. Paradoxically, standards set forth by theorists wedded to traditional concepts of argumentation may serve both to confuse the conscientious advocate and to restrict unreasonably the scope of argumentation. This article establishes new criteria for competitive policy proposals that derive from a model of academic debate based upon contemporary techniques of policy analysis rather than the traditional problem-solution approach. These criteria assist in clarifying counterplan theory, serve to reconcile debate practice and theory, and help reveal the full scope and power of the counterplan as a tactic of argumentation.

TRADITIONAL THEORY

Traditional theory of the counterplan is based upon the old problem-solution approach to policy analysis. According to Brock et al, the problem-solution approach entails a five-stage process of analysis:

> (1) (Discovery of) a felt difficulty; (2) location and definition of the difficulty; (3) suggestion of possible solution; (4) development by reasoning of the bearings of the suggestion; (5) further observation and experiment leading to its acceptance or rejection.[4]

In this view an advocate advancing a counterplan assumes the validity of the problems cited by the affirmative presentation. But rather than admit that the affirmative plan offers an optimal solution to these problems, the negative debater argues for the adoption of a counter-proposal that differs from both the present system and the debate resolution. In defending a counterplan the negative must contend that it provides a better solution to the problems under indictment than does the affirmative proposal. In fact, the negative virtually is required to admit the affirmative need or problem and to restrict its argumentation to other areas of the affirmative case. Consider the presentation of Douglas Ehninger and Wayne Brockriede, two of the nation's most respected authorities on debate theory:

> ... The negative may present a counterplan. If he employs this kind of case, he can admit that serious problems inherent in the present policy demand a change of some sort, but argue that his counterplan would be superior. . . .
> When a counterplan is advanced, the need issue drops out of the controversy and issues are raised in the other two stock issues. Which of the two proposals is more practicable? Which of the proposals entails the fewest serious disadvantages?
> ... The affirmative selects the ground of argumentation in the stock issues of need and remedy, and the negative adapts his arguments to those the affirmative has initiated. Only in the disadvantages stock issue may the negative select the terrain by initiating the arguments. . . .[5]

This exegesis of the counterplan was useful so long as policy analysis was dominated by the problem-solution approach and argumentation by the corresponding stock issues of need, practicality, and disadvantages. But it provides little assistance for the practicing debater or the real-world advocate in an era when policy analysis is increasingly based upon the new insights of decision theory and debaters increasingly confront such formats as the comparative advantages or criteria cases in which there is no clear dividing line between the traditional stock issues.[6] Moreover, conventional theory needlessly restricts the set of permissible counterplans to those that provide superior solutions to the problems set forth in the affirmative case. A clearer and more cogent theory of the counterplan can be developed through a model of argumentation that incorporates both modern methods of policy evaluation and the contemporary practice of academic debate.

DEBATE AS A COMPARISON OF POLICY SYSTEMS

Counterplan theory exemplifies the most fundamental defect of the traditional approach to argumentation. It rivets our attention upon particular problems and their solution, rather than enabling us to envision the full range of alternative policy actions and providing criteria for choosing among them. Both the logic of comparative advantages and contemporary decision theory indicate that policy argument is an attempt to select the best policy from the range of available options. Indeed, the comparative advantages format, routinely employed by practicing debaters, focuses argument upon cost-benefit analysis in which a balance is made between all aspects of the affirmative plan and the policies defended by the negative. Affirmative teams must support policies that entail affirmation of the debate resolution; negative teams are free to support any nonresolutional alternative.[7]

This process of policy argument inherently requires a comparison of two or more policy systems to determine their relative merits. Decision theory posits that a policy proposal (which, unlike proposals of fact or value, requires action to be taken) can be tested only by comparision to alternative policies. A course of action is affirmed because it is better than all other possibilities or rejected because it is not as good as at least one other possibility. Inevitably, the rejection of one policy or course of action means the adoption of another policy or course of action. Even doing nothing or suspending judgment is a form of action and thus a policy. Negative teams cannot merely adopt the position sometimes known as straight refutation a simple denial of arguments raised by the affirmative team. In order for comparison to take place it must defend one or more alternatives to the policy system advocated by the affirmative. A judge cannot decide whether or not to adopt a given policy system without knowledge of other options.

The insight that actions or policies must be evaluated on a comparative basis is formalized by Riker and Ordeshook in their standard treatise on deductive theories of politics:

> A person adopts one alternative rather than another if he believes that the net benefits of the chosen activity exceed the net benefits of any alternative activity. Thus, if we let B denote the benefits of an activity and C its costs, and if we identify alternatives by subscripts, then alternative i is preferred to alternative k if $Bi - Ci > Bk - Ck$ and alternative i is chosen if this inequality is satisfied for all perceived alternatives to i. . . . This condition is frequently simplified incorrectly by asserting that an activity is chosen if the chooser believes that the benefits of the activity exceed its costs . . . $Bi > Ci$. Observe, however, that there may be other activities for which the discrepancy between costs and benefits is greater, in which case these alternative activities are preferred and i is not chosen.[8]

Debate propositions generally propose alterations in the status quo or present system that can be concretized in various ways. The combination of the altered and unaltered features of the present system constitute the new affirmative policy system. Affirmative teams seek to demonstrate that the future operation of their policy system promises greater net benefits than the future operation of negative alternatives: the status quo, the status quo with repairs, or counterproposals that do not fulfill the debate resolution. Returning to the formal model of Riker and Ordeshook where B denotes the benefits of a policy and C the costs, an affirmative team attempts to demonstrate that $Ba - Ca > Bn - Cn$.[9]

Decision theory stipulates that the net benefits of any policy system $(B - C)$ are a function of both the probability that the system will achieve results and the value placed upon those results. A rational decision maker seeks policy that provides the greatest chance of obtaining the most desirable consequences. This precept is stated succinctly by Victor A. Thompson of the University of Illinois:

> It is generally accepted that in the empirical world we never have certainty . . . we either have probabilities or no knowledge at all. Thus, between an alternative and each consequence is a number expressing the probability (P) of the consequence occurring. . . . Our utility yardstick comes next and includes our goal. With this yardstick we choose the alternative that, considering the probabilities, gives us the best ratio of plus values to minus values, or of accomplishment to cost, which means the same thing.[10]

Thus, policy disputes pivot upon the two issues of prediction and evaluation. The best policy is chosen on the basis of attempts both to determine the probabilities of possible policy outcomes and to assess the value of those results. Once the focus of analysis is shifted from the comparison of problem-solutions to the comparison of alternative policy systems, it is possible to understand the substantive deficiencies of traditional theory and to formulate sound criteria for the identification of competitive and noncompetitive counterplans.

COMPETITIVE AND NONCOMPETITIVE COUNTERPLANS

Legitimate counterplans must not fulfill the affirmative resolution, but they must be genuinely competitive with the affirmative plan. Adoption of a counerplan must be tantamount to rejecting the policy system offered by the affirmative team and hence rejecting the debate resolution as well. A counterplan may yield greater net benefits than an affirmative plan without providing reasons for rejecting the affirmative plan. This occurs whenever it is possible to adopt both plans and achieve greater net benefits than would derive from the adoption of the counterplan alone. In formal terms, a counterplan is not competitive with an affirmative plan whenever $Ba - Ca + Bc - Cc > Bc - Cc$. In debate jargon, this formula expresses the argument that adoption of the affirmative plan generates an additive advantage over adoption of the counterplan alone.

Assume, for example, that a negative team responds to an affirmative case proposing the elimination of criminal penalties for possession of marijuana with a counterproposal of comprehensive health insurance. Even if the program of health insurance has greater expected utility than the decriminalization of marijuana use, the affirmative can argue that adoption of the counterplan does not preclude adoption of the affirmative plan or render it undesirable (that is, $Bm - Cm + Bi - Ci > Bi - Ci$). Thus, the negative has not fulfilled its responsibility of opposing the debate proposition; at best it has merely justified adoption of both the policy system fulfilling the resolution and an additional noncompetitive alternative.

Traditional theory suggests that a legitimate counterplan is one that proposes an alternative solution to the particular problems cited by an affirmative case. If the negative solution proves more practical and entails less serious disadvantages, both the affirmative plan and the debate proposition should be rejected. Not only may this criterion generate confusion, but it also fails to rule out all noncompetitive counterplans and excludes important categories of genuinely competitive counterproposals.

It is logically possible that a negative policy system can prove to be a superior means of achieving affirmative goals without warranting the rejection of the affirmative policy system. The best way to secure common goals may be the simultaneous adoption of both the debate proposition and the negative counterplan. Assume, for example, that an affirmative team proposes a program of public work in order to combat long-term unemployment. The negative team demonstrates that, because significant numbers of unemployed Americans will reject public employment, a counterplan of job creation subsidies to business is a better way of handling the problem. In this instance, however, more careful analysis might reveal that unemployment is dealt with most effectively through the adoption of both the affirmative public work program and the negative program of business subsidies. In our formula, $Bw - Cw < Bs - Cs$, but $Bw - Cw + Bs - Cs > Bs - Cs$.

The key to a new theory of the counterplan is the demonstration that a counterplan is not competitive with an affirmative plan if simultaneous adoption of the plan and counterplan yields greater net benefits than adoption of the counterplan alone: $Ba - Ca + Bc - Cc > Bc - Cc$. To identify competitive counterplans it is necessary only to specify the conditions under which this inequality does not hold. Fortunately, these conditions can be stated precisely.

A counterplan is competitive with an affirmative plan if it satisfies either of two criteria. These criteria shift the defining characteristics of competitive counterplans to the negative policy system itself and away from the problem it seeks to resolve. This shift in the definition of a legitimate counterplan means that an advocate may claim advantages in any area, as long as the counterplan is a genuine rival of the affirmative proposal. Moreover, in attempting to demonstrate the greater net benefits of the counterplan, the negative is perfectly free to criticize any aspect of the affirmative case, including its indictments of the status quo. By supporting a counterplan the negative argues in effect that the present system plus suggested counteralterations are superior to the present system plus the alterations suggested by the affirmative. Any aspect of the comparison between counterplan and the affirmative plan is subject to argumentation in the debate.

First, a counterplan is competitive with an affirmative plan if the two proposals are mutually exclusive. Clearly, if it is impossible for the counterplan and the affirmative plan to exist simultaneously, then adoption of the counterplan means rejection of the affirmative plan. If two policy systems cannot coexist, a decision maker must choose between them. The inequality $Ba - Ca + Bc - Cc < Ba - Ca$ obviously cannot hold if $Ba - Ca + Bc - Cc$ does not exist. A counterplan can fulfill this criterion of mutual exclusivity without tacitly conceding affirmative criticisms of the existing order, and without even dealing with the problem areas of the affirmative case.

Assume, for instance, that an affirmative advocate proposes that all American troops be withdrawn from Europe in order to reduce our balance of payments deficit. The opposition might offer a counterplan proposing that America's European forces be supplied with chemical and biological weapons in order to provide a genuinely credible deterrent against Soviet aggression. This counterproposal is not designed to cope with the balance of payments problem that concerns the affirmative. But it still competes with the affirmative plan because the affirmative and negative proposals cannot coexist. The United States cannot simultaneously strengthen and eliminate its European troops. Thus, the decision maker is forced to choose between the affirmative proposal and the negative counterproposal. The negative would support its counterplan by arguing that the advantages of establishing a credible deterrent outweigh the advantages achieved by the affirmative attempt to reduce the balance of payments deficit. The negative would not be obliged to concede the significance of the inflation problem cited by the affirmative. On the contrary, it would be in the negative's best interest to minimize this problem to create a more favorable comparison between the counterplan and the plan.[11]

A counterplan also is competitive with an affirmative plan if simultaneous adoption of both, although possible, is less desirable than adoption of the counterplan alone (that is, $Ba - Ca + Bc - Cc > Bc - Cc$, the converse of the inequality identifying noncompetitive counterplans). In this instance, if the counterplan proves superior to the affirmative plan (that is, $Bc - Cc > Ba - Ca$), then only the counterplan should be adopted, and the affirmative plan discarded. Again, to fulfill this second criterion, a counterplan need not concede any asepct of the affirmative analysis nor even deal with the problem areas identified by the affirmative.

Assume in this case that the affirmative proposes a program of national health insurance costing approximately $20 billion. The negative responds with a counterplan calling for the procurement of a new weapons system involving similar costs. The affirmative might reasonably argue that, since adoption of the weapons procurement program does not preclude adoption of national health insurance, it is not a competitive counterplan. The negative could respond, however, that the simultaneous adoption of both programs is less desirable than the adoption of just the weapons procurement program (that is, $Bi - Ci + Bw - Cw < Bw - Cw$). It might argue that, whereas the economy could withstand the expenditures entailed by either program, the expenditures resulting from the adoption of both programs would lead to runaway inflation and economic collapse. Thus, if the negative could prove that its weapons procurement program has greater expected utility than the affirmative program of health insurance, it would warrant rejection of the affirmative plan. Again, in seeking to minimize the advantages flowing from the affirmative plan, it can attack the affirmative need as well as question the practicality of the affirmative plan and propose plan disadvantages.

Some may fear that this second criterion will unduly tempt negative teams to concoct counterplans that permit them to ignore the affirmative case. Yet for the negative to succeed in this strategy, they have the very difficult task of proving that the counterplan alone is more desirable than the counterplan and the affirmative plan taken together.

Even when both proposals entail substantial expenditures, it does not necessarily follow that, if highly desirable, they should not both be adopted. After all, cuts could be made in less desirable programs. In addition, the negative has a strong incentive to clash with the affirmative proposal in order to minimize its benefits and maximize its costs. The affirmative has a similar incentive to clash with the negative counterplan. In cases where the affirmative spends large sums for a relatively small net advantage, it is perfectly legitimate for the negative to use the counterplan strategy to propose alternative expenditures.

Indeed, the formulation of both criteria serves as a check on the irresponsible use of a counterplan strategy; they identify for judges and advocates illegitimate counterplans that are not genuinely competitive with affirmative proposals.

These criteria only define the acceptability or legitimacy of a counterplan. They are not necessarily dispositive of the outcome of a debate. If the affirmative team can show that simultaneous adoption of its plan and a counterplan is possible and more desirable than adoption of the counterplan alone, it has established sufficient reason for not rejecting its proposal regardless of the net benefits of the counterplan. If however, the negative can demonstrate that simultaneous adoption of the two plans is either impossible or less desirable than adoption of the counterplan alone, it simply has restored the normal comparative process. The debate then pivots upon a comparison of each individual proposal. Only if adoption of the counterplan alone proves superior to adoption of the affirmative plan alone is the negative team assured of its victory.

Traditional paradigms of argumentation, however, do not encompass the type of advocacy that may result from the presentation of a competitive counterplan that does not address the affirmative problem area. The conventional wisdom essentially recognizes two forms of argumentation. First, there is the situation in which one advocate advances a new policy system and the opposition defends the status quo. Second, there is the situation in which both teams recognize problems in the status quo and offer alternative means of coping with these problems. If however, competitive policy proposals deal with distinct areas of concern, then advocates would be simultaneously arguing for new policy and defending the present system.

In this instance, the debate would pivot on a comparison of the present system plus affirmative alterations and the present system plus the alterations suggested by the counterplan, The operative comparison would be first, affirmative plan versus aspects of the present system unaltered by the counterplan, and, second, counterplan versus aspects of the present system unaltered by the affirmative plan. In developing these comparisons, of course, advocates must consider the ways in which the affirmative plan and counterplan interact with ostensibly unaltered features of the status quo. Adoption of the counterplan may undermine the ability of the existing order to achieve the goals sought by the affirmative plan, whereas adoption of the affirmative plan may undermine the ability of the existing order to achieve the goals sought by the counterplan. Moreover, adoption of these plans may undermine the ability of the status quo to achieve goals not explicitly considered by either the affirmative or negative case. This latter type of interaction would be expressed as plan disadvantages, which may be directed against both affirmative and negative proposals.

Assume, once again, that an affirmative proposal of national health insurance is opposed by a competitive counterplan (criterion 2) advocating adoption of a new weapons system. In seeking to minimize the expected utility of the affirmative plan, the negative advocate would assume the traditional role of the negative arguing that the status quo could achieve affirmative goals, that the affirmative plan could not achieve these goals, and that the plan would produce significant disadvantages. In maximizing the expected utility of its counterplan, the negative then would assume the role of the traditional affirmative, arguing that adoption of the new weapons system would yield significant advantages that cannot be realized under the status quo. The affirmative now would assume the role of the traditional negative, arguing that the advantages of the counterplan can be obtained without the new weapons system, that the weapons system would not even achieve these advantages, and that it would generate serious disadvantages. A reasonable decision maker would opt for whichever plan proved to have greater utility vis-à-vis the present system.

Debate becomes even more complex when a counterplan partly overlaps the affirmative problem area. In this instance the operative comparisons are affirmative plan versus present system plus relevant aspects of the counterplan, and counterplan versus present system plus relevant aspects of the affirmaitve plan. In addition to the roles described in the previous paragraph, when plans do not overlap, debaters also would assume the roles of advocates in a conventional counterplan debate. Each debater would attempt to demonstrate that, in areas of overlap, his or her suggestions offer a superior means of coping with existing problems.

CONCLUSION

This new theory of the counterplan generates criteria for legitimate counterplans that clearly can guide advocates through every argumentative situation. A negative team offering a counterplan must be prepared to demonstrate either that the affirmative and negative plans are mutually exclusive or that adoption of both plans is less desirable than adoption of the counterplan alone. Similarly, an affirmative seeking to argue that a counterplan is not competitive must demonstrate both that the affirmative plan and the counterplan can coexist and that adoption of the affirmative plan and counterplan is superior to adoption of the counterplan alone. Of course, if the affirmative believes that a negative counterplan is not competitive, they must explicitly discuss this issue and not expect the judge to invent the argument for them.

The theory also enhances the strategic value of the counterplan approach to negative argumentation. Since negative teams must no longer concede the affirmative need, or address the same problem areas as the affirmative case, they can draw upon a much richer storehouse of potential counterplans. Freed from the artificial constraints of traditional theory, debaters can far more creatively design competitive alternatives to affirmative policy systems. So long as they are indeed competitive, the adoption of negative counterplans can be justified by any aspect of their comparison with the affirmative proposal. Thus, the new theory provides advocates far greater latitude in the type of argumentation they may employ in support of a counterplan. They need not regard as sacrosanct affirmative indictments of the existing order, and can attack the affirmative case at every level of analysis.[12]

The types of policy comparisons made possible by our revision of traditional counterplan theory brings this theory into closer correspondence with policymaking in the real world. Diverse varieties of decision makers frequently are obliged to choose between competing policy systems designed to achieve different objectives. In each instance, the policies are competitive because they satisfy one of the two criteria set forth above. Government officials continually must choose between gearing fiscal and monetary policy to the reduction of inflation or unemployment. Legislators must regularly decide between different types of programs (perhaps as distinct as a program for the procurement of a new missile system and a program of comprehensive health insurance) that cannot all be funded within reasonable budget guidelines. And each day, every one of us must choose between spending our time on such ranges of activities as attending a concert or social gathering, reading, working, sleeping, and eating.

The importance of defining the characteristics of rival policy systems extends to every forum in which policy alternatives are evaluated. It is essential that advocates and policymakers be able to distinguish between competitive and noncompetitive policy systems. First, if advocates do not comprehend the proper critieria for identifying competitive policy systems, they may mistakenly exclude from consideration important policy alternatives. Second, cognizance of these criteria helps decision makers to avoid the adoption of contradictory or redundant policy systems. Third, knowledge of the critieria avoids useless argumentation over policy systems that are not genuinely competitive. It is extremely important to conserve the limited time and energy that decision makers can devote to the evaluation of policy.

This attempt to formulate a new thery of the counterplan based upon a systems model of policy dispute has important implications both for academic debate and the actual formulation of policy. It clarifies untapped potential of the counterplan for competitive debate, and provides a rational basis for assessing the legitimacy of counterplans. It thus helps decision makers to discover for each situation the full range of policy alternatives, to avoid meaningless arguments, and to insure that the process of argumentation produces the best possible policy choices.

Notes

1. Bernard Brock et al., *Public Policy Decision Making: Systems Analysis and Comparative Advantages Debate* (New York: Harper and Row, 1973), 3.
2. Allan J. Lichtman and Daniel M. Rohrer, "Presumption and Burden of Proof: A Reevaluation," *Issues* 7 (Feb. 1974); "Beyond Presumption and Burden of Proof: New Rules for Policy Decision," *Issues* 8 (Fall 1974).
3. Formal debate is distinguished by the fact that competing advocates are charged with the responsibility to affirm or negate a particular debate resolution. In this type of argumentation, negative counterplans must, of course, lie outside the boundaries of the debate resolution.
4. Brock, p. 3.
5. Douglas Ehninger and Wayne Brockriede, *Decision by Debate* (New York: Dodd Mead, 1963), 243–44. See also, Roger E. Nebergall, "The Negative Counterplan," *The Speech Teacher* 6 (Sept. 1957): 217–20; Wayne N. Thompson, "The Effect of a Counterplan upon the Burden of Proof," *Central States Speech Journal* 13 (1962): 247–50; Glen E. Mills, *Reason in Controversy* (Boston: Allyn and Bacon, 1964), 69, 178; Austin J. Freely, *Argumentation and Debate*, 3rd ed.(Belmont, CA: Wadsworth, 1971), 236–39; Roy V. Wood, *Strategic Debate* (Lincolnwood, IL: National Textbook Co., 1968), 28–30, 121–24; C. William Colburn, *Strategies for Educational Debate* (Boston: Holbrook, 1972), 157–59; Arthur N. Kruger, *Modern Debate* (New York: McGraw-Hill, 1960), 38–40, 55–56, 140, 366.
6. For examples of such formats see: L. Dean Fadely, "The Validity of the Comparative Advantages Case," *Journal of the American Forensic Association* 4 (Winter 1967): 28–35; Bernard L. Brock, "The Comparative Advantages Case," *The Speech Teacher* 16 (March 1967): 118–23; James W. Chesebro, "The Comparative Advantages Case," *Journal of the American Forensic Association* 4 (Winter 1968): 57–63; David Zarefsky, "The 'Traditional Case'–'Comparative Advantage Case' Dichotomy: Another Look," *Journal of the American Forensic Association* 4 (Winter 1969): 12–20; John F. Cragan and Donald C. Shields, "The 'Comparative Advantage Negative,'" *Journal of the American Forensic Association* 5

(Spring 1970): 85–91; David A. Thomas, "Response to Cragan and Shields: Alternative Formats for Negative Approaches to Comparative Advantage Cases," *Journal of the American Forensic Association* 7 (Spring 1972): 201–6; Allan J. Lichtman and Daniel M. Rohrer, "Role of the Criteria Case in the Conceptual Framework of Academic Debate," parts 1–5, *Issues* 3 (Jan.-May 1970), reprinted in Donald R. Terry, ed., *Modern Debate Case Techniques* (Lincolnwood, IL: National Textbook Co., 1970), 20–61; Clark D. Kimball, "Is There a Rationale Criteria Case?" *Issues* 4 (Oct. 1970): 11–16, reprinted in *Modern Debate Case Techniques*, 62–78; James W. Chesebro, "Beyond the Orthodox: The Criteria Case," *Journal of the American Forensic Association* 7 (Winter 1971): 298–315; David A. Thomas, "The Criteria Case," *Issues* 4 (May 1971): 1–2; John D. Lewinski, Bruce R. Metzler, and Peter L. Settle, "The Goal Case Affirmative," *Journal of the American Forensic Association* 9 (Spring 1973): 458–63; Allan J. Lichtman, Charles Garvin, and Jerome Corsi, "The Alternative-Justification Affirmative," *Journal of the American Forensic Association* 10 (Fall 1973): 59–69.

7. A discussion of the controversial question of whether a negative team may, in a single debate, defend multiple alternatives is beyond the scope of this article. None of our arguments depend upon the response to this question.

8. William H. Riker and Peter C. Ordeshook, *An Introduction to Positive Political Theory* (Englewood Cliffs: Prentice-Hall, 1973), 46–47.

9. A critic might suggest that, if we view the resolution as a normative statement simply to be affirmed or denied, it might be possibe to reject it on its merits without the comparison of policy alternatives. Yet as Riker and Ordeshook's formal model clearly demonstrates, the problem with this contention is that so long as the normative statement is, in effect, a call for action (as every policy proposition must be) the decision to accept or reject the statement can only be based upon a comparison of the net benefits of the proposition with the net benefits of possible alternatives. It is not adequate to examine in isolation the net benefits of the affirmative plan itself.

10. Victor A. Thompson, "Decision Theory, Pure and Applied," *General Learning Press* (1971). See also, Kurt W. Back, "Decisions under Uncertainty," *The American Behavioral Scientist* 4 (Feb. 1961); Howard Raiffa, *Decision Analysis* (Reading, MA: Addison-Wesley, 1968); R. Duncan Luce and Howard Raiffa, *Games and Decisions* (New York: Wiley, 1957).

11. In a debate where the negative does not advocate a counterplan, traditional theory would permit the negative to argue as a disadvantage that withdrawal of our European forces would undermine our deterrent against Soviet agression. The crucial difference, of course, is that the disadvantage would be argued with respect to the status quo rather than with respect to the situation prevailing after adoption of the counterplan.

12. This does not, of course, imply that we advocate the presentation of trivial counterplans; under our theory negative teams would still have to shoulder normal burdens of proof.

32

A Permutation Standard of Competitiveness

Dale A. Herbeck

Debate theory has traditionally lagged behind debate practice. This discrepancy between theory and practice is conspicuously evident with respect to counterplans, in particular, the requirement that counterplans be competitive. While most of the writing on competitiveness makes the iusse appear simple and straightforward, in practice, debates involving competitiveness are usually the opposite. This article attempts to redress this disparity: It offers a brief summary of some of the existing theory and practice, develops a general critique of present practice, and proposes a new criterion for assessing whether counterplans are competitive.

THE THEORY AND PRACTICE OF COMPETITIVENESS

In his seminal work on argumentation, Ehninger claimed that argument was limited by its bilaterality:

> Arguments, of necessity, thus are limited because only such causes or parts of causes as are mutually exclusive can statiate, and causes or parts of causes which are mutually exclusive pose choice situations of such a nature that unless judgment is reserved, it is necessary to endorse one of the alternatives and to reject the other (1970, p. 106; 1966, p. 182).

Absent a pair of mutually exclusive alternatives, argument is distinctly impossible. Thus, the key question is how to determine when it is that two policies or ideas are mutually exclusive. That is, when is the adoption of one tantamount to the rejection of the other. Until it can be proved that such a condition exists, argumentation is impossible.

By applying this argument standard to the debate context it is possible to ascertain the theoretical premise underlying the competitiveness debate. In academic debate, the affirmative plan is the basis of argument. Although some have argued that the debate should focus on the resolution (Paulsen and Rhodes, 1980), there are good reasons for believing that the proper focus of debate is the plan (Herbeck and Katsulas, 1985). A brief review of the literature supports this position. As Goodnight and Wood (1983) note, "It is not the affirmative's responsibility to persuade the judge to accept all interpretations of the resolution; it is their responsibility only to defend one possible meaning" (p. 69). Ulrich (1979) observes that the resolution "serves as a guideline for the participants in the debate. It divides potential argumentative ground between the two teams" (p. 2). Herbeck and Katsulas (1985) note, "The resolution exists to establish common argumentative ground. The resolution itself is not the subject of debate" (p. 134).

Since the debate focuses on the plan, to be a persuasive strategy the counterplan must constitute a reason to reject the plan. Thus, the counterplan must compete with the plan. Consequently, adoption of the counterplan must entail rejection of the plan. A counterplan that did not compete with the plan would not even meet the minimum threshold condition for argumentation. As a result, the importance of counterplan competitiveness cannot be overstated. Until the counterplan is proved to be competitive, there is no need for argumentation over its merits.

Despite the importance of the burden, traditional debate texts treat competitiveness in only the most cursory fashion (see, for example, Freeley, 1981; Sanders, 1983; Ziegelmueller and Dause, 1975; Patterson and Zarefsky, 1983). They generally claim that a counterplan must meet the entirety of the affirmative advantage in addition to offering some sort of additional advantage. This seems to suggest implicitly that a counterplan is competitive if it meets the affirmative need, or phrased differently, if the counterplan could substitute for the affirmative plan.

Contemporary theorists have afforded the negative considerably more flexibility in demonstrating competitiveness. These theorists have suggested that the negative need not solve the affirmative need in its entirety so long as the negative defends an alternative that constitutes a reason to reject the affirmative plan. In their seminal work on counterplans, Lichtman and Rohrer (1975, 1979) argue that a counterplan that does not meet the affirmative need can still be competitive with the affirmative plan so long as it satisfies one of two conditions. The first standard of competitiveness developed by Lichtman and Rohrer is "mutual exclusivity." A counterplan is mutually exclusive when it is impossible to adopt both the plan and the counterplan simultaneously. The second standard of competitiveness developed by Lichtman and Rohrer is net benefits. They theorize that this standard should be employed in a situation where, although it is possible to adopt both the plan and the counterplan, it would be better to adopt only the counterplan. Thus, even if it is possible to do both the plan and the counterplan, the counterplan might still be competitive with the plan if it could be demonstrated that adoption of the counterplan alone is superior to the adoption of the plan and the counterplan together.

Given the comparative simplicity of the theoretical literature, one might suspect that the actual debates involving competitiveness would focus on a few central issues. An analysis of the existing treatment of competitiveness in debate texts and articles would lead one to the conclusion that most arguments over competitiveness would focus on whether the counterplan needed to meet the entirety of the affirmative need, whether the counterplan was mutually exclusive with the plan, or whether the adoption of the counterplan alone was net beneficial. But even the most cursory exposure to contemporary debate practice would prove that nothing could be further from the truth. As most debaters and judges would surely agree, most debates over competitiveness focus on a much different set of issues. There is a wide disparity between the theory and the practice surrounding competitiveness.

A CRITIQUE OF COMPETITIVENESS STANDARDS

Despite the diversity among these different standards of competitiveness, it can be argued that all suffer from the same two critical deficiencies. First and foremost, they are all based on extremely simplistic bilateral comparisions of the two proposed policies. Invariably they look only at the plan as compared to the counterplan. None of the standards looks at the different ways in which the plan and the counterplan might be rearranged to form a third policy containing the best features of both the policies being debated. Rather, they are based only on static comparisons of potentially dynamic and interactive systems.

Several examples will serve to illustrate this point. One graphic example is the funding diversion counterplan. This counterplan bans the implementation of the affirmative plan and diverts the affirmative funding to some other project. One popular alternative is biomedical research. By diverting the plan's resources the negative suggests that it would be possible to achieve greater benefits than would be produced by the adoption of the plan. Invariably the negative's first competitiveness argument is that it is impossible to implement the counterplan and fund the alternative mandate while implementing the affirmative plan. Consequently, the negative concludes, it is impossible to do both the plan and the counterplan and, hence, the two policies are competitive since they are mutually exclusive.

Unfortunately the negative never considers what would happen if the topical features of the plan were merged with the operative provisions of the counterplan. In other words, the negative never considers the possibility of funding both mandates at the same time. Since this would be possible (although not necessarily desirable), the plan and the counterplan are not mutually exclusive. But, because the common standards of competitiveness are based on a simple comparison of the plan and the counterplan, they are unable to account for possible combinations of the plan and the counterplan.

This bias toward static comparisons also obfuscates debates over the appropriate agent of action. So, for example, on the intercollegiate topic making the producers of hazardous waste legally responsible for injury resulting from disposal of that waste, a frequent negative counterplan mandated that the federal government assume responsibility for injuries instead of the producer. The negative defended this counterplan as being competitive because two parties cannot be legally responsible for the same waste and because it is better for the government to assume responsibility than for the government and the industry to share responsibility for the waste. But these arguments suffer from exactly the same deficiency described in the study counterplan example. It would be possible to structure a proposal drawing on the affirmative plan that included features of the counterplan. One could, for example, devise a system in which the producers of the waste were legally responsible, with the government having responsibility only as a last resort. Thus, the two policies are not mutually exclusive. In fact, it is very possible that the best hazardous waste disposal policy would merge the topical features of the plan with nontopical components from the counterplan.

Any number of examples could be used to prove this point. Because the traditional standards of competitiveness assume that the only question to be resolved is whether the counterplan is competitive with the plan, they do not consider whether the counterplan would be competitive with combinations of the plan and the counterplan. As a result of this bias, they fail to consider the possibility that the optimal policy might be a combination of the plan and the counterplan.

The second problem with traditional competitiveness standards is that they do not address the relevant issue. The purpose of a counterplan should be to offer an alternative to the plan. The fact that there are other desirable courses of action does not necessarily mean that the plan should be rejected. It merely means that there are other policies which should also be adopted. The counterplan only necessitates rejection of the plan when it is competitive with the plan. Frequently, competitiveness standards do not assist in making this judgment. In the words of Branham (1979), "For all its importance, competitiveness is generally debated and determined by reference to conventional rules for which the logical bases have been forgotten or unexplained" (p. 61).

In many debates the competitiveness arguments do not prove that the counterplan is competitive with the plan. Instead, in these debates the competitiveness standards amount to little more than a series of labels distinguishing the plan from the counterplan. The negative issues between two and ten such labels, proclaims that any single label is sufficient to prove the counterplan to be competitive with the plan, and then proceeds to the advantages produced by the counterplan.

While this problem might be attributed to the deficiencies of the debaters, if seems more realistic to argue that the problem lies with the standards themselves. Rather than constituting reasons why the counterplan should be adopted, the usual competitiveness standards amount to little more than a comparison of two different systems. When the negative argues that the plan and counterplan are redundant because they solve the same problem, that the plan and the counterplan are based on inconsistent philosophical premises, or that the counterplan is a substitute for the plan, they are merely comparing the plan to the counterplan. The fact that two systems differ does not mean that they are competitive.

Instead of testing competitiveness, existing standards generally test little more than the relative abilities of debaters to sift through long lists of generally irrelevant distinctions. Because they encourage breadth of analysis while at the same time allowing negatives to defend noncompetitive counterplans, these standards accentuate practices that detract from the reasoned evaluation of the plan. At the same time they offer the judge little guidance in determining which of the two policies advocated should be preferred.

To truly prove that the counterplan constitutes a reason to reject the plan, the negative should have to prove that it would be better to adopt the counterplan than to adopt the best combination of the plan and the counterplan. Only after satisfying this rigid standard has the negative really proved that the counterplan is competitive and thus constitutes a reason to reject the plan. The existing standards of competitiveness simply do not guarantee such a rigorous analysis. Thus, to guarantee such rigor it seems that a variant of the permutation standard of competitiveness tentatively suggested by Louis Kaplow should be utilized when evaluating a counterplan.

Before progressing it seems necessary to note that the permutation standard developed here goes well beyond Kaplow's argument. Kaplow

(1981) proposed using permutations to ascertain "whether the counterplan posed a choice concerning the merits of the resolution or merely demonstrated another area of policy, in addition to the resolution, warranting attention" (p. 218). The method proposed in this article uses permutations both as a competitiveness standard and as a method for evaluating policy systems. Thus, the permutation standard is very different from the notion of permutation that is suggested by Kaplow.

THE PERMUTATION STANDARD OF COMPETITIVENESS

As the name suggests, this standard of competitiveness suggests that the relevant comparison is not between the plan and the counterplan. Instead, the permutation standard suggests that the relevant comparison is between the optimal combination of the plan plus the counterplan versus the counterplan alone. To achieve this result the standard bifurcates the competitiveness issue into two separate analytical steps.

In the first step the plan and the counterplan are permuted. In the statistical sense permutations are nothing more than arrangements of different objects (Pfaffenberger and Patterson, 1977; Hays, 1981). Thus, the first step would involve working through the possible arrangements of the plan and the counterplan. The possible permutations would be constrained only by topicality (the topical mandate could not be permuted out of the affirmative plan) and possibility (it might prove impossible to adopt certain features of the plan and the counterplan at the same time). Once the permutations were completed, it would be possible to select the single optimal arrangement of the two policies.

The second step would involve selecting between the two policies. This process would be no different than the comparison that takes place under current competitiveness standards. The only substantive differences in the resulting comparison would be that the debate would focus on the optimal permutation of the plan and the counterplan versus the counterplan alone.

In essence, the permutation would subsume the other competitiveness standards. The mutual exclusivity standard would automatically be included in the permutation process. If two policies were truly mutually exclusive, then it would be impossible to permute the policies into a distinct policy. And if the policies were competitive by a net benefits standard, then the permutation standard would configure the policies so that this fact could be more easily ascertained. Many of the other standards would be subsumed because by permuting the plan with the counterplan, it would be possible to ascertain exactly which segments within the plan detracted from the desirability of the counterplan. This would in turn facilitate the determination of whether the permutation or the counterplan should be adopted.

More importantly, use of the permutation standard would transform many of the concerns traditionally associated with competitiveness into more manageable and constructive arguments. Instead of arguing that the plan and the counterplan are redundant or that adopting both would squander resources, the permutation standard would transform these arguments into disadvantages against the permutation. They would no longer merely distinguish between the plan and the counterplan, instead they would become independent disadvantages. Thus, the permutation standard would transfer the focus of discussion from differences between policies to an evaluation of the competing policies.

An example helps to conceptualize the nature of the permutation standard. Consider the intercollegiate topic that dealt with the exploration or development of outer space. On that topic many affirmative teams deployed satellites for the benefit of people on earth. Against such a case, the negative frequently proposed a counterplan banning all satellites. As an advantage to the counterplan, the negative claimed that the military would use such satellites to implement a warfighting doctrine.

In considering such a counterplan, the permutation standard would ask first if it is possible to permute the plan and the counterplan. In this case a permutation comes readily to mind. Why not adopt the plan and gain the civilian benefits and then ban the military use of satellites? This permutation, at first glance, would seem to gain both the case and the counterplan advantage. Having completed the permutation, the second step would be to compare the two competing policy systems. During this step the affirmative would defend the permutation while the negative would try to prove that only the counterplan should be adopted. Thus, the affirmative would argue for an exclusively civilian system while the negative would argue for no satellite system. In arguing for the counterplan the negative might attempt to develop a disadvantage which claimed that the military would still be able to use the civilian satellites for military applications.

As the example illustrates, adoption of such a standard of competitiveness would produce a more rigorous comparison of the competing policies. This would be true for a number of different reasons. First, such a standard would greatly simplify the debate over competitiveness. It would reduce the multiplicity of theoretical arguments to a single, simple comparison. Instead of arguing over the different levels of competitiveness, the debaters would argue over the possible arrangements of the plan and the counterplan. The permutation standard would clarify the debate over competitiveness while transforming other issues often subsumed within competitiveness into viable negative arguments. Branham (1979) has identified conceptual benefits to considering counterplan competitiveness arguments as disadvantages.

Second, such a standard would enhance substantive policy comparisons. The permutation standard would compare the optimal arrangement of the plan and the counterplan against the counterplan. Thus, instead of choosing between the plan and the counterplan, the judge would have the choice between the counterplan alone and the optimal combination of the plan and the counterplan. Since the counterplan would presumably embody the optimal alternative to the plan, the resulting combination of provisions would guarantee that the best policies were compared. It would be possible to transcend the static comparisons frequently associated with competitiveness arguments.

POSSIBLE OBJECTIONS TO THE
PERMUTATION STANDARD

Although the permutations standard may facilitate considerations of competitiveness, such a standard is not totally without adverse consequences. Several potential objections come readily to mind. First, it might to be argued that such a standard would be prone to abuse. Rather than using permutations as a means to determine competitiveness, enterprising negatives might simply append the permutation standard to their already burgeoning list of competitiveness arguments. Practice seems to support the claim the debaters will take any theoretical position to its logical extreme.

While abuse is a possibility, it seems an unlikely result of adherence to a permutation standard. By its very nature, the permutation standard subsumes all other possible standards. Its use would minimize and even destroy the alternative competitiveness standards employed in debate. Given the nature of permutations, the permutation process itself would render alternative competitiveness standards useless. Consequently, there would be little incentive for debaters to append a permutations argument to their already lengthy list of competitiveness arguments.

Second, it might be argued that the permutation standard would lead to direct intervention by the judge in resolving the debate. Because the standard allows for the consideration of the plan, the counterplan, and the permutations of these two policies, it might seem that such a standard would require the judge to intervene to derive the optimal permutation of the different alternatives. While such an outcome might result, it is not the intent of the standard. It is the responsibility of the debaters within a given debate to formulate and compare the different permutations. In particular, the affirmative must clearly specify the particular permutation that it plans to defend in its initial answers to the counterplan. The standard is not intended, nor should it be used, to justify judge intervention. As with other issues, it is the job of the debaters to develop arguments and to consider the implications of those arguments. The permutation would not demand nor enhance judge intervention in the decision-making process.

Third, it might be argued that the permutation standard is illegitimate because it allows the affirmative to change its plan during the debate. Consistent with this objection, Hingstman (1984) has gone so far as to suggest that permutations are a form of hypothesis-testing. Since the standard allows the affirmative to advocate certain features of the counterplan as if they were part of the plan, it might seem that the only way for the affirmative to effectuate such features would be for the affirmative to amend the plan to include the desirable features of the counterplan. Such a practice, the argument would continue, is unacceptable since it would grant the affirmative the implicit power to modify or amend the plan within the debate.

While the concern underlying this objection has merit, the argument is based on a distorted conception of the permutation standard. When the plan and the counterplan are permuted to form the optimal policy, neither policy is materially changed. Rather, the permutation process merely determines which parts of the counterplan constitute valid reasons to reject the plan. More simply put, the permutation standard determines the focus of the debate. Features of the counterplan that are permuted with the plan are not actually added to the plan in the form of modifications or amendments, rather they are dismissed from the debate. Since they do not constitute a reason for rejecting the plan they are no longer relevant to the argument.

Finally, it might be argued that a permutation standard would not really solve the problem at all. Rather, it might be postulated that the permutation standard would simply change bad competitiveness arguments into bad plan arguments. For example, if a plan and counterplan are competitive because they both use the same scarce resources, then utilization of a permutation standard would change this competitiveness argument into a potential disadvantage. Instead of arguing that adoption of both is not possible because both require the same scarce resources, the negative would simply formulate a disadvantage arguing that adoption of the plan is bad because it precludes adoption of another more advantageous alternative.

While such transformation may be possible in some instances, it will not be possible in all instances. Many competitiveness arguments which function only to describe differences between the plan and the counterplan cannot be restructured into other arguments. For example, it would be impossible to transform an argument postulating that the counterplan is competitive with the plan because it enforces against adoption of the plan into a disadvantage against the adoption of the plan. Those that can be restructured, moreover, can be more easily evaluated in the context of disadvantages than as competitiveness arguments. Moreover, these arguments should be considered for what they are, reasons to reject the plan, and not reasons to support alternatives to the plan. Arguments that claim that the counterplan is competitive because of limited resources could easily be transformed into disadvantages claiming that the adoption of the plan would drain resources from other more beneficial areas.

Furthermore, even if the permutation standard did force such arguments in the back door, the result would still be superior to present practice. Instead of having myriad arguments intended to prove competitiveness, the result of employing the permutation standard would be a lengthy list of possible objections to the plan. The result would be to channel the argument into a detailed consideration of the affirmative plan, instead of a confusing and unenlightening discussion of the differences between the systems.

CONCLUSION

The permutation standard of competitiveness offers a viable alternative to the theoretical abyss surrounding the competitiveness of counterplans. While utilization of the permutation standard is not without consequence, using the standard would eliminate many of the problems associated with current competitiveness standards. The standard would allow for a comparison of the optimal arrangement of policies. So too, the standard would resolve the problems associated with the current morass of competitiveness standards. It would focus the debate on the optimal combination of the plan and the counterplan. In the process, the permutation standard would simplify competitiveness arguments, facilitate and encourage substantive policy comparisons, and eliminate noncompetitive counterplans.

References

Branham, R. J. (1979). "The Counterplan as Disadvantage." *Speaker and Gavel* 16: 61–66.
Ehninger, D. (1970). "Argument as Method: Its Nature, Its Limitations, and Its Uses." *Speech Monographs* 37: 101–10.

Ehninger, D. (1966). "Debate as Method: Limitations and Values." *The Speech Teacher* 15: 180–85.

Freeley, A. J. (1981). *Argumentation and Debate*. 5th ed. Belmont, CA: Wadsworth.

Goodnight, L. and Wood, R. V. (1983). *Strategic Debate*. Lincolnwood, IL: National Textbook Co.

Hays, W. L. (1981). *Statistics*. 3rd ed. New York: Holt, Rinehart & Winston.

Herbeck, D. A. and Katsulas, J. P. (1985). "The Affirmative Topicality Burden: Any Reasonable Example of the Resolution." *Journal of the American Forensic Association* 21: 133–49.

Hingstman, D. (1984). "The Relationship Between Debate Paradigms and Political Argument." Paper given at the annual meeting of the Speech Communication Association, Chicago, Nov.

Kaplow, L. (1981). "Rethinking Counterplans: A Reconciliation with Debate Theory." *Journal of the American Forensic Association* 16: 215–26.

Lichtman, A. J. and Rohrer, D. M. (1979). "A General Theory of the Counterplan." In D. Thomas, ed. *Advanced Debate*. Lincolnwood, IL: National Textbook Co.

Lichtman, A. J. and Rohrer, D. M. (1975). "A General Theory of the Counterplan." *Journal of the American Forensic Association* 12: 70–79.

Patterson, J. W. and Zarefsky, D. (1983). *Contemporary Debate*. Boston: Houghton-Mifflin.

Paulsen, J. W. and Rhodes, J. (1980). "The Counterwarrant as a Negative Strategy." *Journal of the American Forensic Association* 15: 205–10.

Pfaffenberger, R. C. and Patterson, J. W. (1977). *Statistical Methods*. Homewood: Irwin.

Sanders, G. (1983). *Introduction to Contemporary Academic Debate*. 2nd ed. Prospect Heights: Waveland.

Ulrich, W. (1979). "A Prophet Without Honor: A Minority View of the 1979 Heart of America Final Round." *1979 Heart of America Final Round Critiques*. Lawrence: University of Kansas Debate Squad.

Ziegelmueller, G. and Dause, C. A. (1975). *Argumentation: Inquiry and Advocacy*. Englewood Cliffs: Prentice-Hall.

33

Negative Fiat

Resolving the Ambiguities of "Should"

Roger Solt

The concept of "fiat" has long provided a source of both amusement and embarrassment to those contemplating debate theory. It has been branded an immoral and irrational strategy by some and has generated innumerable low-level witticisms pertaining to magic wands and Italian sports cars. The tendency to treat fiat as a reality rather than merely a figure of speech was at its peak in the mid-1970s, when fiat was often argued to be nondemocratic because it circumvented the normal decision-making process. It was even argued that the use of fiat would destroy business confidence because business people would be completely boggled by the apparently miraculous intervention of fiat into the normal workings of the political and economic system.

During the 1970s, the major controversies involving fiat related to the fiating of affirmative plans. Affirmative fiat still generates some controversies. Is fiat time-bound? Is fiat continuing? Does it assume some level of attitude change? Does fiat permit specification of implementational procedures? Does it allow or require specification of an agent or method of adoption? Does it extend to extra-topical provisions designed to preempt disadvantages? Can it be conditional? Such questions have remained in currency throughout this decade without producing any theoretical consensus. Although sometimes troubling, these remaining ambiguities of affirmative fiat are peripheral to most debates. What does seem to have emerged is a fair degree of consensus regarding to basic nature of affirmative fiat.

Fiat is not an artificial intervention into the normal political process; rather, it is the assumption, for the sake of argument, that such a normal process has been employed, and the affirmative plan has come into being. Fiat is merely another way of expressing the idea that something should rather than necessarily will be done. The view has sometimes been expressed that fiat is unnecessary, and perhaps the term itself is unfortunate. Nonetheless, some logical equivalent to the idea of fiat is necessarily implicit in any proposition of policy. To consider whether something should be done involves both the temporary suspension of concern for whether it would be done and an examination purely in terms of desirability.

There is currently consensus that such a minimalist concept of affirmative fiat is both necessary and legitimate. There is clearly, however, no such consensus where negative fiat is concerned. With the rise to prominence of the counterplan as a negative strategy, it is negative rather than affirmative fiat that is increasingly contentious. While affirmative fiat is a necessary consequence of the resolution's wording, negative fiat is definitely more problematic. If affirmative fiat involves imagining that the affirmative plan were adopted, negative fiat is the act of imagining alternatives to the affirmative. While the resolution usually places some constraints relating to realism on the affirmative, the nonresolution places no such constraints on the negative. Consequently, the potential (and actual) abuses of negative fiat could fill a forensic wax museum.

Negative fiat has on occasion been extended both to private institutions and to foreign governments. Such an extension of negative fiat suggests the following potential counterplans. In a debate over pollution control, the negative could argue that the government should not establish stricter standards because industry *should* voluntarily control its emissions. Or in a debate over defense policy, the negative could argue that the U.S. should not build a new weapon system because the Soviet Union *should* unilaterally disarm. Intuitively, these two examples seem highly abusive, but they are not really very different than counterplans that have actually been run. The central premise of the labor union topic was clearly that unions could on occasion misuse their power. Yet counterplans were popular under that topic which assumed that fiat could occur at the level of the union itself. In effect the counterplan assumed away the basic premise of the topic by dictating that unions *should* go forth and sin no more. And if the Soviet disarmament counterplan seems unacceptable, it is hard to see why it is more acceptable to imagine that all the nations of the world lay down their weapons, forget cultural differences and national animosities, and form a peaceful (but appropriately decentralized) world government—a counterplan that has been run with some degree of frequency.

Not only are the actual and potential abuses of private sector and international fiat disturbing; many in debate have been concerned about the rise to prominence of such arguably utopian (and certainly generic) transtopical counterplans as anarchy and socialism. Such counterplans have been widely employed and frequently successful negative strategies. They have also launched a spate of speculation into the appropriate range of negative fiat. The argument has been made, drawing on Branham's (1979) view of counterplan as disadvantage, that there should be no negative fiat. Other approaches have emerged (Perkins' "realm of discourse" standard being perhaps the most notable), which while somewhat less restrictive than the no-negative-fiat position still dramatically curtail the scope of the counterplan option.

My position in this article is that while some limits on negative fiat are needed, theoretical solutions that effectively gut the counterplan option are excessive; they are radical surgery on the body of debate argument, when a relatively minor change in argumentative diet might be a sufficient cure for the dyspepsia of negative fiat abuse. The approach recommended here is to search for a middle ground, one that can minimize abusive counterplans while at the same time preserving the counterplan as a viable negative option. In the process of doing so, I hope to suggest a new, more pluralistic paradigm of debate argument.

The general viewpoint from which this article derives is that academic debate is a dialectical competition. Debate theory must also be dialectical, balancing a plurality of interests—intellectual, competitive, and educational. Previous paradigms tend to be one-sided, to view debate almost solely as a mode of intellectual inquiry or almost solely as a game. The reality is that academic debate is (and should be) both. The pluralistic view of debate theory would seek to strike a balance between the competing values and interests. Thus, in the case of negative fiat, a balance must ultimately be struck between the value of political realism on one hand and the value of speculative intellectual inquiry on the other.

I will begin with a consideration of the primary justifications for placing limits on negative fiat. Having concluded that some limits on negative fiat are necessary, I will then consider the leading alternative approaches for limiting fiat. I will consider the no-negative-fiat position associated with Branham's (1979) concept of counterplan as disadvantage and will conclude that some scope for negative fiat is desirable. I will then consider two alternative standards by which fiat might be limited: Perkins' (1989) concept of the "realm of discourse" and Ulrich's (1979, 1981) view of fiat as limited to the resolution's agent. Finding none of these options fully acceptable, I conclude by offering three independent but it is hoped complementary suggestions of my own for how the scope of negative fiat might best be defined.

THE CASE FOR LIMITS

Before considering the arguments in favor of limiting negative fiat, it would probably be helpful to clearly enumerate and distinguish between the major types of counterplans argued in recent years. The following list may not be exhaustive, but it does distinguish twelve different types of counterplans, all of which have possessed some measure of popularity over the past decade.

The first type of counterplan employs foreign fiat. A good example of this type of counterplan arose on the 1988–89 intercollegiate topic, pertaining to U.S. policy toward Africa. In response to an argument that the U.S. should act to correct some evil in Africa, the negative has argued as a counterplan that the Organization of African Unity should instead take action to deal with the problem. Counterplans on the space topic argued that the European Space Agency, rather than the United States, should undertake a certain aspect of space development. Both of these counterplans acted through groups of nations of which the United States is not a member. Despite this international flavor, foreign fiat through a group of non-U.S. nations seems no different in principle than fiat through a single non-U.S. nation. This suggests the heretofore apocryphal counterplan mentioned earlier: That in response to an argument for increases in U.S. defense efforts, the negative might advocate as a counterplan that the Soviet Union should voluntarily disarm.

The second type of counterplan involves fiat through an international organization of which the United States is a member. Counterplans employing the UN or the OAS have been popular on a number of topics.

The third type of counterplan involves fiat through private self-interested institutions within the United States. On the topic calling for increased government regulation of mass media, self-regulation by the media themselves was suggested as a counterplan. Similarly, on the topic calling for government curtailment of the powers of labor unions, a counterplan was run with some frequency calling for unions to reform their own practices.

The fourth type of counterplan involves fiat through private institutions ostensibly dedicated to serving the public interest. The basic example is the counterplan that called for private foundations rather than the government to deal with some problem.

The fifth type of counterplan has called for fundamental changes in the basic structures of U.S. government. Socialism, libertarianism, anarchy, authoritarianism, bioregionalism, and world government are all examples.

The sixth counterplan variety has called for radical reforms specific to the problem area suggested by the topic. Most recent topics have generated at least one such counterplan: isolationism, disarmament and surrender on the military commitments topic, abolition of labor unions, abolition of the space program, government responsibility for hazardous wastes, deschooling and privatization on the education topic. Type five counterplans (those changing basic government forms) have been run recurrently on a number of topics. In contrast, the type six counterplan generally has been applied only to a single topic, the exception being some of the military posture counterplans that have reappeared on several foreign policy topics.

The seventh type of counterplan involves action (usually similar to that called for by the affirmative) by a level of government other than that employed in the resolution. Since a majority of recent resolutions have called for federal action, counterplans at the state and local level have proven the most popular.

The eighth type are process counterplans. Rather than directly denying the desirability of the affirmative policy, they have argued for a different process than the affirmative employs to decide on the best policy. The study counterplan was the grandfather of this genre, but it has had many descendants: referendums, negotiations, planning and prioritization, and consultation being among the most prominent.

Ninth are exceptions counterplans. They have arisen on topics employing the term "all." For example, on the topic calling for the elimination of all U.S. military intervention in the Western Hemisphere, a popular counterplan called for the elimination of all but humanitarian interventions. On the topic that called for stricter standards in all U.S. schools, a variety of counterplans argued to exempt certain types of schools.

Tenth is the offset counterplan. This has appeared on topics employing terms such as "increase" or "decrease." For example, the space topic called for an increase in exploration or development of outer space. In contrast to a plan calling for a new remote surveillance satellite, the negative might urge a counterplan to adopt the new satellite but ban SDI, claiming that these two policies taken together would be a net decrease in space development.

The eleventh type of counterplan is one that simply aims to reduce the affirmative advantage. Such counterplans, which have largely replaced the traditional minor repair, are now frequently applied directly to the affirmative case, in effect as an inherency argument.

The twelfth type of counterplan is one intended to make disadvantages unique. It has become increasingly popular for the second negative to counterplan out affirmative uniqueness answers to disadvantages. One example is U.S. credibility disadvantages on the NATO topic. Counterplans designed to make such disadvantages unique ranged from reneging on the INF deal to firing the current Secretary of Defense.

Undoubtedly, there are counterplans that fall beyond the boundaries of these twelve categories and some counterplans that combine
categories, but I believe these classes cover both the most prominent
and the most controversial types of counterplans. Many of these types of
counterplans are controversial—and they are controversial for a variety
of reasons. The uniqueness-generating counterplan is controversial
because it so often appears in second negative; the advantage-reducing
counterplan is rarely attacked on theoretical grounds, but is frequently
criticized because it is so often blithely asserted without analytical or
evidential substance. The offset counterplan is highly controversial but
mainly on grounds of competitiveness rather than negative fiat. With
many of these counterplans, however, the primary controversy relates to
the propriety of their use of fiat. The first five types of counterplans
have been particularly controversial in this regard. And perhaps because
of their popularity, it is the government form counterplans (type five)
which have probably created the greatest furor. Especially with the rise
of permutations, most counterplans are somewhat vulnerable on competition grounds. Nonetheless, given a consistent, additive disadvantage,
many such counterplans have been able to prove themselves competitive
by net benefits. Thus, there has been an increasing interest in looking
beyond competition as a means of dealing with these counterplans. One
prominent approach has been to seek to place limits on the scope of
negative fiat.

In evaluating the different proposals for limiting negative fiat, it
seems essential to consider the varying reasons offered for why negative
fiat should be limited. How fiat should be limited is critically related to
the rationale for why it should be limited. There are at least four major
reasons offered for why restrictions are needed. First is the so-called
utopianism of many counterplans. Second is the slippery slope of abuse
potential present in the concept. Third is the overly generic (especially
trans-topical) nature of many counterplans. Fourth and finally, there is
the sense of non sequitur that many counterplans seen to produce. I
wish to consider each of these in some detail.

The first objection, utopianism, is launched primarily against the
generic change of government form counterplans such as socialism,
anarchy, and world government. I find this objection the least compelling reason for limiting negative fiat. First, it seems very difficult to
define the utopian. Each of these forms of government has advocates
who believe in its viability. They may not believe in the immediate
political practicality of such reforms, but they clearly don't believe them
to be utopian. All policies, affirmative or negative, fall on a continuum
of political practicality, and there is certainly no clear dividing line
between utopian and non-utopian policies. Second, what is considered
utopian depends critically on time and place. Most of the world's

population lives under a government or with an economic system that could be labeled either authoritarian or socialist. None of these alternatives may be very likely in contemporary America, but certainly there are circumstances, such as an ecological crisis or serious depression, under which one or more might be seriously considered. In such a situation an informed understanding of the benefits and drawbacks of such alterr ative government forms might well be crucial. Even one firmly opposed to such radical alternatives might feel they should be debated in order to expose their weaknesses. Third, if one takes seriously the claim that debate should involve a broadly philosophical inquiry into questions of public policy, that is, should attack fundamental assumptions and consider basic alternatives, then it seems inappropriate to rule certain positions out of order simply because of their radical nature.

While it is not clear that utopianism is an adequate ground or criterion for limiting negative fiat, it does seem clear that the extreme abuse potential present in limitless fiat provides a rationale for setting some limits. Even those who find government form counterplans acceptable might balk at some other types of counterplan. I believe that the first four types of counterplans listed above (foreign, international, and the two private sector types) illustrate this type of abuse potential. But even they do not exhaust the limits to which negative fiat could be carried. It might be possible to generate counterplans based on individual fiat: Rather than stricter sentencing, a counterplan might say that individual criminals *should* morally reform themselves. At the farthest extreme one could even imagine metaphysical fiat: The negative might argue that the laws of nature *should* be different. The affirmative is, at least at first glance, limited to proposing policies that fall within the resolution; in contrast, there is almost no limit on what falls outside the resolution. Surely some of the counterplans suggested above would go beyond the scope of what almost anyone could consider either fair or intellectually illuminating to debate. Debatability and intellectual coherence require that some limits be placed on negative fiat.

The third reason for limiting negative fiat is to avoid overly generic counterplans, especially those that recur on topic after topic. There is both a practical and a more theoretical reason for wishing to provide such a limit. Practically speaking, it seems educationally undesirable to encourage debaters to sepecialize so much on an individual argument, running it year after year until in effect they become "professional" anarchists or authoritarians. A more theoretical rationale derives from the consideration of the discussion-directing function of the topic. The notion that the resolution directs discussion has been held to apply primarily to the affirmative, but if this purpose is to be accomplished it seems clear that it must in some sense bind the negative as well. If the negative can with impunity raise a set of issues unrelated to the ostensible subject of the resolution—for example, shifting from a debate over old age policy to one concerning world government or anarchy— the purpose of the resolution in directing discussion to a different specific subject area each year has been frustrated.

The fourth and final concern is difficult to precisely formulate, but it seems to go to the heart of the negative fiat issue. If often seems that the counterplan as a response to the affirmative plan constitutes a kind of argumentative non sequitur. To respond to an argument for strengthening NATO with the argument that the Soviet Union should disarm simply seems nongermane; it seems irrelevant given the basic germs of the discussion. Similarly, an argument that corporations shouldn't pollute seems beside the point in the context of a discussion of public policy toward the environment. Similarly, the alleged merits of anarchy or world government do not seem germane to a discussion of social security reform. This is true even if these alternatives are competitive, as in fact they often seem to be. (Action by government and the abolition of government really do seem mutually exclusive.) Thus, competition is not in itself a sufficient means for excluding this type of counterplan. The point seems to be that every discussion operates within a certain implicit frame of reference (or, as Perkins puts it, a "realm of discourse"). To avoid this sense of non sequitur, what is needed is to find some way of discovering or defining that implicit frame of reference for debate.

THE CASE FOR COUNTERPLAN AS COUNTERPLAN

Given the conclusion that some limits on negative fiat are essential, the question then arises as to just what those limits should be. The most draconian limit proposed is that there should be no negative fiat at all. The argument that there should be no negative fiat is one which has been frequently made in intercollegiate debate over the past few years. The theoretical basis for the no-negative-fiat position is found in Branham's (1979) view of counterplan as disadvantage. The crux of Branham's position, as I understand it, is that one of the primary costs of adopting any policy is that one forgoes the opportunity to obtain the benefits of other competitive policies (Branham, 1989). These opportunity costs can be accrued either because the first policy physically excludes the second, because it undercuts its benefits, or because it makes it politically less feasible to adopt. The degree to which the opportunity cost is a relevant one, however, depends upon the degree to which the counterplan was a politically realistic option to begin with. The abolition of all government in the United States may well be competitive with a policy requiring consumer math to be taught in U.S. public schools, but since anarchy has no realistic chance of coming into being at present, and since a consumer math program would have no discernible effect on the likelihood of anarchy being adopted, then the benefits of anarchy are an irrelevant cost in considering the adoption of consumer math.

Branham's discussion is very illuminating in explaining how a counterplan (taking the term in his somewhat idiosyncratic sense) does function as a disadvantage. It also seems to be a very sensible way to evaluating the costs of an individual policy considered in isolation. While his theory does considerable justice to the counterplan conceived of as a disadvantage, it is my contention that it fails to do justice to the counterplan conceived of as a counterplan. That is, Branham's framework is not appropriate for a situation in which two or more policies are being directly compared in terms of their desirability.

What is at issue here is clearly a question of terminology, but it is an important one. I believe that Branham uses the term "counterplan" in a rather different sense than is customary. As commonly envisioned, a counterplan is a negative plan (that is, the negative team has designed and specified its details), which is offered to the judge as an alternative possessing coequal status with the affirmative plan. (That is, the counterplan, like the plan, is to be assessed purely in terms of its desirability, rather than in terms of its political practicality.) The judge is assumed to have as much ability to either adopt or endorse the counterplan as he or she has to adopt the plan.

What Branham calls a "counterplan" is merely an alternative open to the status quo. To have any impact as a disadvantage, there must be at least some likelihood that this alternative will come into being absent the affirmative plan. Furthermore, this is not an alternative designed by the negative team (hence not a plan in the normal debate sense); nor is there any real incentive for the negative to designate specific features (such as funding or enforcement) of this policy unless it can be shown that those precise features would be adopted absent the affirmatve. Indeed, the very language of "counterplan" seems irrelevant to this type of argument. Arguments of this type are advanced frequently simply as disadvantages (for instance, the affirmative plan prevents socialism) with none of the language or theory of the counterplan being invoked.

In essence, Branham's position shifts the focus of the debate from a normative comparison between two (or more) co-equal policies to a comparison of the world with the affirmative plan to the world without it (that is, the status quo as it would predictably evolve). Such a shift might be desirable; nonetheless, it is important to realize that a genuine shift has occurred. In traditional debate, the counterplan has not functioned solely (or perhaps even primarily) as a disadvantage; it has often served as an inherency argument, as argument that the plan (or resolution) is not the best solution to a problem. The essential function of the counterplan is often to reduce affirmative significance to the point where some disadvantage (linked to the plan but avoided by the counterplan) is sufficient to outweigh. This primary role of the counterplan in academic debate is essentially nullified if the counterplan is viewed exclusively as a disadvantage.

While Branham's construct provides a good way of understanding and evaluating a certain important type of disadvantage (that is, disadvantages relating to the opportunity costs associated with forgoing other policies or rendering them less valuable), it is not a good way of evaluating counterplans. In fact, I believe that the no-negative-fiat or counterplan as disadvantage positions effectively destroy the counterplan as a negative strategy. Certainly it seriously undercuts any of the more radical counterplan varieties—the various forms of international fiat, the radical change of government form counterplans, and the relatively radical counterplans that contemplate fundamental changes in core institutions unique to the particular topic. In none of these cases is the likelihood really very great that such a counterplan would occur absent the plan; thus, the plan will provide a minimal disadvantage link at best (and in the case of very small affirmative plans, the link will be even more miniscule.) Similarly, process counterplans that rely for their advantage on some relatively unusual decision-making process are unlikely to have impact as disadvantages precisely because they advocate a departure from normal means. Likewise, exception counterplans are unlikely to meet this test, since it will be rare that the negative can show any likelihood that the counterplan with the negative's exact exception would be adopted absent the affirmative. Finally, even the most common types of counterplan, harm-reducing and uniqueness-enhancing, are unlikely to function well solely as disadvantages since they would require specific tradeoff evidence, which will often be unavailable. If might be argued that this simply proves that these are not very good arguments. My response would be that it shows that they are not arguments that can be well linked as disadvantages. As counterplans—that is, policies considered on their own merits—they may well have substantial intellectual merit. Certainly they have considerable strategic significance given the current competitive balance of contemporary debate.

I believe that the no-negative-fiat position that has emerged (at least historically) out of the counterplan-as-disadvantage theory would mean the end of the counterplan as we have known it. How tragic this occurrence would be depends, of course, on how intellectually and competitively valuable one believes the counterplan to be. I personally see four major values associated with the counterplan as counterplan and hence with negative fiat.

First, the counterplan best fulfills the intellectual/analytical function of debate. The primary purpose of a policy debate should be to find the best policy. There are clearly some policy debates that would focus on the narrower question of whether one policy is better than the status quo. A Congressional floor debate parallels this narrower situation. But it is also important that there be forums which consider more fundamental, even if less realistic, alternatives. After all, political realities are fleeting. In 1928, how politically likely was the New Deal? In 1975, what were the political probabilities of the Reagan revolution? Those involved in academic debate are far from the centers of political power. It therefore seems more useful, especially for undergraduates, to consider the broad directions in which society should move rather than what policies have immediate political practicality. The abolition of negative fiat, I believe, rules out such an inquiry. It would tie debaters to the realm of policies that are currently realistic, offering essentially no options for the consideration of alternatives outside of the political mainstream. The result is likely to be intellectual tunnel vision, discourse conducted exclusively within the narrow confines of present political realities. It should be noted further that it is not only so-called "utopian" government form counterplans that the prohibition of negative fiat would preclude. Such radical but topic-specific counterplans as deschooling (for which there is no more realistic chance at present than there is for socialism) raise fundamental questions of public policy that could not realistically be raised in the absence of negative fiat. If the search is really to find the best policy, then alternatives from beyond the political mainstream should be allowed.

A second basic argument for negative fiat relates to the role of the counterplan in providing competitive equity. Two major developments in debate over the past twenty years were the demise of the stock issues emphasis and the popularity of extremely expansive topics. The result has been that on most topics the affirmative possesses an extremely wide range of choice and the most minimal burdens in terms of significance. Significance, inherency, and solvency are rarely winning arguments for the negative in themselves. To win a debate on its policy merits usually requires the negative to win either a disadvantage or a counterplan. In such an argumentative world, disadvantage-ducking has become a prime affirmative strategy. Moreover, the type of case least prone to disadvantages is likely to be a fringe interpretation with very low significance. Pushed to its extreme, the result can be topic trivialization— affirmatives have every incentive to select the most petty and insignificant examples of the resolution.

The generic counterplan emerged in large part as a strategy for countering expansive topics and trivial affirmatives. Rather than being limited to the narrow corner of the topic selected by the affirmative, the counterplan refocused debate on larger issues. Given fiat, a generic counterplan will probably link as well to a small affirmative as a large one. But if the counterplan must be run solely as a disadvantage, the same problems that arise in linking any disadvantage to obscure, small-significance affirmatives would apply. Thus, in a world without negative fiat it seems fairly clear that there would be added incentives toward trivial affirmatives.

The rise of the counterplan has helped to restore side equity to debate, as several factors suggest. In the mid-1970s, before the popularization of the counterplan, affirmatives had a decided competitive advantage. To choose negative in an elimination round was almost unheard of. While I know of no data on the subject of the percentage of affirmative wins, my distinct impression (based upon attendance at from ten to fifteen NDT tournaments a year for the past sixteen years) is that negatives are winning far more often. Certainly far more teams select the negative in elimination rounds than was once the case. Other factors are clearly involved in the revitalization of the negative, but the very popularity of the counterplan as a strategy would suggest that it has played an important role.

A final fairness/equity consideration speaking in favor of negative fiat is the simple consideration of reciprocity. The affirmative is allowed to design in detail a policy and offer it for consideration on its own merits, regardless of its political practicality. Thus, there seems to be at least some equity interest in allowing the negative to design its own policy and advocate it on its own merits.

A third major argument is that the equivalent of negative fiat exists in most forums other than academic debate which consider these types of policy questions. As maintained above, the actual decision of whether to vote for or against a bill may reflect a relatively rare instance in which the focus would be exclusively on one policy, and a no-negative-fiat situation would prevail. But even in Congress, at an earlier stage in the decision process, the equivalent of negative fiat would exist. An administration drug bill, for example, would probably be countered by an alternative bill sponsored by members of the opposing party. In fact, there might be several bills being considered in the same set of hearings. Arguments relating to political feasibility might still be raised to some degree even at this stage of the policy process. But surely the primary focus of discussion would (or at least should) be normative—that is, which really is the better bill. A member of Congress who was too exclusively preoccupied with politics would be blameworthy in the eyes of most citizens. Presumably, the ideal Congressional committee would attempt first to discover the optimal policy and then search for means to make it politically feasible. Only after considerable efforts of persuasion should second-best policies be endorsed.

In scholarly forums where policy issues are argued, the emphasis tends to be even more normative and less political. A sholar who offered one policy proposal would almost certainly compare his or her suggestion to other competitive policies that have been proposed. Given the situation, arguments might arise about comparative political feasibility, but argument would more often center on the actual merits of the policies, not their immediate practicality.

A fourth consideration favoring negative fiat relates to the role of the judge as decision maker. I believe that the judge should not assume any particular role, be it member of Congress or social scientist, in evaluating the debate. Rather, the judge should reflect the perspective of an ideally impartial, informed, and eclectic viewpoint. Most consistent with this view of the judge seems to be a view of fiat simply as an act of intellectual endorsement. If intellectual endorsement is all that occurs at the end of the debate, there is no real reason why the judge should be precluded from endorsing options outside the political mainstream—if they are competitive with the affirmative.

For those who still envision the judge as playing the role of an actual decision maker, and therefore think of fiat as a power, a relatively expansive view of negative fiat still seems to be justified. As the policy making perspective has evolved, the judge is generally imagined to act with the full powers of the agent specified in the resolution, most commonly the federal government. Assuming the judge to have such powers, she or he could adopt by fiat any competing policy within the realm of federal authority.

PREVIOUS APPROACHES TO LIMITING FIAT

The consensus of the debate community is, I believe, that negative fiat in some form or another is desirable. Nonetheless, there appear to be compelling reasons for placing some limits on negative fiat. This section of the article will examine two previous attempts to define the reasonable scope of negative fiat.

The first standard for limiting negative fiat is Dallas Perkins' (1989) concept of the "realm of discourse." Perkins' position suggests that negative fiat should be allowed only for policies at least as politically feasible as the affirmative (that is, enjoying at least as great a likelihood of passage). Any other counterplans would not enjoy fiat and would be forced to function simply as disadvantages.

Perkins' position represents, I believe, a major theoretical advance. Its great merit is that it recognizes that argument does function within a realm of discourse—that it operates within certain implicit limits as to the proper scope of argument. I believe, therefore, that the concept of a realm of discourse is an extremely fruitful one and one that provides considerable illumination to the issue of negative fiat. My quarrel is not with what I believe to be Perkins' most basic insight—that determining an appropriate realm of discourse is the proper route to limiting negative fiat. It is rather with the exact limits of the realm of discourse which he defends.

My basic indictment of Perkins' approach may well be what he considers its greatest strength: that, in effect, it guts the counterplan as a negative option. Because I believe it would eliminate most of the major types of counterplans run in recent years (and seriously compromise those that remained), most of the indictments leveled against the no-negative-fiat position would also apply, albeit with somewhat muted forced, to Perkins' approach.

The following factors militate against the extreme limit provided by the comparative political feasibility standard. First, it is not a standard observed in most non-debate policy advocacy settings. Real world advocates are not limited to proposing policies as politically feasible as those advanced by their opponents. If advocates felt strongly enough about a given option, they might still devote most of their time and energy to arguing its merits, even if the hope of adoption seemed slim. Surely there are occasions on which even politically shortsighted members of Congress propose alternative policies despite their relatively slim chance of passage. If advocate A proposed mandatory seat belt laws and advocate B proposed mandatory air bags, the air bag proposal would (in most settings, especially those of an academic or theoretical sort) probably be considered germane and relevant even if its political practicality were somewhat less than the initial seat belt proposal. In most situations, certain policies (such as anarchy) are excluded because of their lack of political practicality. Perkins' approach would successfully exclude these types of counterplans, but it would also exclude many counterplans that, while less politically likely than the initial plan, are still intuitively relevant.

Second, Perkins' approach is inconsistent with the most common views of the role of the judge. If the judge is assumed to have the powers of the resolutional agent, she or he would have the ability to adopt alternatives even if they were less politically likely. If the power of the judge is merely the power of intellectual endorsement, she or he clearly has the ability to intellectually affirm an approach that is more marginal politically.

Third, the political feasibility standard would eliminate most of the popular generic counterplans run in recent years. Except as a response to the most radical of affirmatives, alternative government form counter-plans would clearly be excluded. Further, systemic but topic-specific counterplans such as deschooling or disarmament) would also be excluded. So would most process counterplans. Even the exception counterplan might not fare well under this approach since to carve out a narrow exception to a general policy might be less politically feasible than a more all-encompassing policy. Many would fail to mourn the demise of the generic counterplan. It is my perception, however, that these counterplans (especially those geared to specific topics) have raised interesting intellectual issues and that in many, if not all, instances, they have introduced into debate ideas worthy of consideration.

A fourth problem is that Perkins' standard would rule out innovative solutions. If advocates were generally limited to politically likely options, new ideas would rarely be raised. The result would be an even more stultified political discourse than presently prevails.

Fifth, advocacy may influence probability of adoption. Radical ideas eventually reach the political agenda by being advocated and gradually accepted. If such ideas were never entertained on their own merits until political practicality was established, the political agenda would never change.

Sixth, the political feasibility standard is difficult to debate. Most public policy argument is normative—it concerns the desirability of policies, not the probability of their adoption. It is an attempt to persuade, not an attempt to predict political outcomes. Except for policies under immediate consideration, there may be little if any evidence about probability of adoption. Political feasibility turns on many imponderables: Who is the bill's key sponsor? How many political debts can he or she call in? How will the media react? How much money will go into the lobbying effort? How many phone calls will the president make? Will the president's credibility be up or down at the time of the plan's consideration? Not only are these issues intangible; they also seem less than scintillating subjects for debate. Obviously, some policies are orders of magnitude more politically feasible than others, but in other cases, the political prospects of a policy would be pure guesswork. How does one compare the probability that the Supreme Court would reverse a 9–0 decision with the probability of world government?

Seventh, the political feasibility standard encounters the topic trivialization problem with a vengeance. To undercut counterplan ground, the affirmative would have a large incentive to argue for the smallest possible topical deviation from the status quo. Bills on the verge of passage and court cases already on appeal would become prime affirmative territory. If negatives could advocate nothing more radical than the affirmative, affirmatives would almost certainly come to inhabit almost exclusively the dead bull's eye of the absolute political center. One need not be a subscriber to *World Marxist Review* to find that prospect unappealing.

The eighth and final argument is that a long-term normative focus is more important for debaters than is short-term political realism. Political realities are transitory, and debaters have no short-term influence on policy anyway. It seems more intellectually valuable for debaters to acquire a general understanding of the range of policy alternatives, both radical and mainstream, proposed for dealing with a given problem than it is for them to acquire an intricate knowledge of the politics of the present Congress.

A second standard for limiting negative fiat has been proposed by Walter Ulrich (1979, 1981). His suggestion is that negative fiat should be limited to acts that could be undertaken by the agent specified in the resolution. The basic argument is that in considering, for example, a federal resolution, the judge is assuming the role of a federal decision maker (or perhaps the federal government in general). A decision maker occupying that institutional role would not simultaneously occupy an institutional role at another level of government; hence, there would be no fiat power at those alternative levels.

I believe that Ulrich's standard is the best proposed thus far—indeed, it is fairly close to the domestic public actor standard I will suggest below. Ulrich's standard, however, posits a very narrow policy making view of the debate process. It assumes that the judge actually adopts the role of a federal decision maker, or whatever the topical agent may be. I have already indicted the idea that the judge should assume such a critical perspective. Many who consider questions of public policy are not actual decision makers, and for such non-decision makers, a question such as the comparative desirability of state versus federal action (which Ulrich's approach would exclude) might well arise.

THREE NEW ALTERNATIVES

In this section, I wish to discuss three suggestions of my own for limiting the scope of negative fiat. The first of these is that fiat should be limited to domestic public actors. This is a limitation in accord with the implicit framework of NDT and high school policy debate. Over the past twenty years, every topic except one at the high school or college level has called for action by some agent of the United States government. (Even on apparently agentless topics, there has been an implicit U.S. governmental agent.) These debate topics have embodied liberal and conservative values; they have addressed both domestic and foreign policies; they have allowed both state and federal actions. They have varied in innumerable ways, but with one exception they have shared a common perspective: They have raised questions of United States public policy.

This suggests to me that U.S. public policy is the implicit frame of reference (or realm of discourse) for this type of debate. If foreign or private action were considered an appropriate subject for discussion in this forum, it seems likely that at least occasionally such a position would be assigned to the affirmative. Since this has not occurred, it seems clear that such approaches are not considered relevant or appropriate by the debate community. In the mid-1970s there was one high school topic that called for action by an international organization. This experiment has not been repeated, suggesting that such an approach did not prove to be highly successful. Thus, despite this exception, it seems safe to say that U.S. public policy is the focus of academic policy debate as it occurs in the United States.

This restriction makes sense in light of the widely held perception that debate is most useful as an adjunct to democratic decision-making. If debate is seen as part of the democratic process, then it makes sense for debate to consider only alternatives that are subject to democratic influence. While the responsiveness and rationality of government actors is highly imperfect, U.S. governmental actors are ultimately accountable to the public and must therefore be at least somewhat attentive to public argument. Foreign governments clearly have no such accountability to the U.S. public and very minimal incentives to be attentive to argument within American media. Similarly, private actors are accountable to shareholders and customers, not to the public at large; hence, their susceptibility to reasoned argument appealing to a disinterested concept of the public good is limited.

This limitation of the realm of discourse to U.S. public policy corresponds to the argumentative practice found in most non-debate forums. Arguments about U.S. foreign policy almost always take the rest of the world as a given. To respond to a proposal to strengthen NATO with a proposal for Soviet disarmament seems inappropriate because alleged Soviet militarism is one of the essential preconditions of the discussion. To imagine it away is to abolish the framework within which the discussion is to proceed. The debate over ballistic missile defense has not been shaped by the argument that the Soviet Union should disarm (while there are activists who argue for U.S. disarmament as an alternative to a military buildup). Nor to my knowledge has the argument that business should take the initiative to control its own pollution ever been a major force in the acid rain debate. As this example suggests, debates concerning the regulation of business have to take the reality of present business practices as a given in order to be intelligible. Self-regulation is sometimes suggested, but it carries impact as an argument only if it can be shown to be practically feasible. To say that self-regulation is preferable would almost never, in and of itself, be considered an adequate response. (It is almost by definition preferable, as is a peaceful world in which strong defense would be unnecessary.) Thus, my primary conclusion is that when a question of U.S. public policy is raised in almost any argumentative forum, it is likely to be considered appropriate to juxtapose alternative U.S. public policies, but it is very unlikely that policies involving non-U.S. or non-governmental actors would be considered, absent arguments about their likelihood. The limitation to domestic public actors seems to correspond to an implicit limitation already observed in public policy argument.

The U.S. public actor standard provides a clear, relatively unequivocal limit and avoids the slippery slope of highly abusive modes of negative fiat (such as foreign, private, individual or metaphysical). It would, in principle, rule out the first four types of counterplan mentioned earlier. Some examples of the fifth type of counterplan (that is, world government and world anarchy) would also be eliminated, though other utopian counterplans would be permitted provided they were limited to actions which could be undertaken by the U.S. government.

This approach assumes that fiat is simply an act of intellectual endorsement, and it assumes an ideally generalized rather than a specifically role-governed perspective by the judge. It closely parallels the Ulrich standard, but it differs in two ways. First, Ulrich's standard seems to assume that the judge takes the actual role of the resolutional agent; when in fact this limitation is one observed in almost all discourse in which Americans are likely to engage pertaining to the topics considered in policy debate. A second distinction is that the public domestic actor standard would probably allow counterplans at another level of the U.S. government. The legitimacy of such counterplans strikes me as a close call. One of the basic assumptions of many calls for federal action is that the states have had authority in a certain area and failed to act; thus, arguably, state action as it will predictably evolve should be taken as one of the givens of the discussion. On the other hand, normative discussion over the desirability of state versus federal action is common in American public policy discourse. At any rate, the domestic public actor standard would by definition allow counterplans at alternative levels of the U.S. government—the availability of such a large literature comparing the effectiveness of different levels of government seems to make this a relevant debate, although one that has become rather tedious.

The case for eliminating exclusively foreign fiat and fiat through private self-interested institutions (types one and three) is, I believe, relatively clear. It is the more mixed types of counterplans, international counterplans with U.S. participation (type two) and fiat through private public interest institutions that require more consideration. The domestic public actor standard would clearly eliminate both. It thus seems appropriate to examine both these types of counterplans specifically.

A defense of international fiat could proceed as follows. Americans are citizens of the United States, but they are also citizens of the world. They can attempt to persuade their own domestic institutions, but they can also attempt to persuade international institutions; thus, arguments for what global institutions *should* do is also appropriate and important. This analysis, however, seems to assume that such international institutions are fundamentally autonomous, rather than embodying the various national interests of their member countries. International organizations derive their powers from and are ultimately accountable to individual governments. A prerequisite of changing the policy of an international organization would be to first change the policy of enough non-American governments to permit the counterplan. Thus, such a counterplan involves foreign fiat once again, albeit at one remove. As suggested above, there are very few argument situations in which an argument about what a foreign government should do that are considered germane to a discussion about what the U.S. government should do.

The argument for fiat through private foundations is that they too serve the public interest and therefore should be attentive to the types of public policy argument debate employs. But while such entities may have a quasi-public purpose, they are not ultimately accountable to the public. Possessing their own purposes and priorities, they exist largely beyond the scope of public influence; hence, argument is unlikely to center on what they should do relative to what government should do.

Furthermore, allowing fiat through this type of institution raises the spectre of a slippery slope by assuming that it is the institutional purpose of the entity that determines whether it is an appropriate agent for fiat. But unions, for example, are ostensibly dedicated to the interests of their members. By this logic, counterplans where unions took action to aid their own membership would have been legitimate on the labor topic. Foreign fiat would become legitimate by this standard provided that it could be shown that such a counterplan was consistent with the interests of that nation's citizens. Such arguments, I have suggested, destroy the implicit framework of debate; moreover, they are not a mode of argument employed in any forum of public policy discourse. Similarly, the argument that the government should not act because some private, charitable actor should (rather than that it will) is rarely if ever encountered in such discourse. Finally, a prerequisite for changing the scope of policies of private philanthropic organizations is persuasion of the individuals or firms that endow those organizations. Once again, either private or individual fiat would have to be implicit in such a counterplan.

Some limit on the scope of negative fiat is necessary, and the domestic public actor standard marks a relatively clear dividing line in the continuum of possible counterplans. If it excludes some types of counterplans that some would want to defend, it clearly justifies many counterplans placed at risk by other standards. Given some of the current draconian proposals to limit counterplan ground, it provides a reasonably moderate constraint.

It is not, however, totally satisfactory. It still leaves room for relatively free play for most of the so-called "utopian" counterplans. While I do not object to their utopianism per se, I do find their highly generic, trans-topical character to be troubling. In addition, they often raise, in the most violent form, the sense of argumentative non sequitur. To suggest that we should not teach consumer math because we should dissolve the government is not an argument that I have ever seen in a public forum.

It is because of these lingering problems that I offer a second potential limit for negative fiat: that counterplans should be constrained by the relevant policy literature.

This policy context standard would not rule out generic government form or process counterplans, but it would require that in order for the negative to run the counterplan, they be able to offer evidence that these policies have been proposed as relevant to the problem the resolution considers. Thus, for example, on the retirement security topic, socialism would probably be an acceptable counterplan (a good deal of literature isolates capitalism as the root cause of retirement insecurity), but anarchy probably would not. (I have never seen anarchy defended as a solution to the problems of the aged.) A negotiation counterplan (calling on all interested parties to negotiate a solution to the affirmative harm area) would be acceptable on an environmental topic (environmental policy being a major area where negotiation has been employed) but would not probably be considered germane to questions of old age security.

I see a number of benefits to this approach. First, it places a relatively clear and objective limit on negative fiat. Field context is a familiar and empirically functional standard of topicality analysis. Policy context is considered to be a good standard for determining what a topic means in order to place limits on affirmative case selection. Similarly, it seems appropriate that policy context define the range of alternatives considered germane to a discussion of a certain policy area.

Second, this approach maximizes the discussion-directing function of the resolution. A major reason for having a resolution is to direct discussion to a certain area of public policy. The policy context standard requires that negative argument also be grounded in positions actually found in the problem area the resolution addresses. The notion that the resolution should also in some sense bind the negative will seem counterintuitive to some, but if the negative can readily shift debate from the ground to which the resolution directed the affirmative, its discussion-directing function will have been largely vitiated.

Third, the policy context standard limits trans-topical counter-plans. A counterplan such as socialism could still be run on many topics (socialist writers tend to blame all the ills of mankind on capitalism), but most other generic counterplans would be limited on many topics.

Fourth, I believe this standard may best answer the sense of argu-mentative non sequitur that many generic counterplans have created. What better way to prove a policy germane than to show that authors publishing in the topic's policy literature have considered it so? Alternatively, if no source regards the policy as relevant to the problem area of the topic, such a policy is almost certainly an argumentative non sequitur; no one evaluating arguments on this topic would be likely to consider it relevant.

This standard could (and I think should) operate in conjunction with the U.S. public actor standard discussed above. Together, they should offer a reasonable, though clearly not overly limiting, standard for negative fiat.

Nonetheless, the policy context standard does raise a number of troubling problems. First, it can be argued that debate is not the real world and hence that real world standards of argument are irrelevant to debate's purposes. Debaters should not be bound by what has been advanced in the published literature surrounding the topic. This objection rests on what I believe to be a false dichotomy between debate and the real world. As Snider (1982) has pointed out, the debaters and judges are all real, and a real debate is going on; that is, a real policy argument is taking place. A debate before Congress is no more or less real than a debate in a university classroom. If debate is regarded as a real public policy argument, then the same standards that an intelligent individual would apply in evaluating such arguments in other settings would also apply to debate. Admittedly, academic debate has its unique attributes, but as an example of public policy discourse, I see no good reason why its argumentative standards should depart radically from the logic of policy discourse in general. And, as I have contended, one of the basic facts about policy discourse is that it always operates within an implicit frame of reference or set of argumentative assumptions. Given this premise, the published literature seems to be the most objective source of inferences for that implicit frame of reference in terms of a specific policy debate.

A second objection is essentially the opposite of the first: that this standard provides no meaningful limits on the scope of fiat. A detailed computer search, it is argued, could turn up some source that would link a given counterplan to almost any topic. Obviously, for one for whom the allegedly utopian counterplans are an anathema, the prospect that this standard might allow them to flourish is a major mark in its disfavor. How limiting this standard would prove in practice is an open question. I suspect that many counterplans really have so little to do with many topics that no literature search, no matter how rigorous, would turn up evidence linking the two. Nor is it clear that negative debaters would have the competitive incentive to devote immense amounts of time to conducting such a search. At the very least, the successful effort to find evidence linking the generic counterplan to the problem area of the topic should serve to make the counterplan more germane and make for a better, more topic-focused debate. Finally, if there really is a body of literature proposing a certain generic counterplan as a means of addressing the issues the topic raises, then the counterplan does seem to be germane and to dismiss it out of hand seems intolerant and anti-intellectual.

A third problem is the question of whether this standard justifies requiring specific link evidence for disadvantages. I don't believe that it does. The question of disadvantage links involves a factual question: Will X cause Y? Certainly specific evidence helps to establish such a link, but there may be other methods of analysis or logical inference that can produce some probability that the link is true. Moreover, the non-specific link is likely to be assessed as less probable than the specific one. The germaneness of a counterplan is a different kind of question. It is a question of whether the counterplan is an appropriate policy alternative to consider in relation to a given subject. The policy context standard imposes the minimal test that at least some published source must have considered the counterplan to be a germane alternative. Not only is this a minimal test of relevance; it is probably the only one available.

There is another, related, answer to this objection. The question of disadvantage links is almost purely a question of the logic of policy discourse—that is, it is a question of substantive policy analysis. Standards of fairness have nothing to do with empirical questions of factual linkage. Negative fiat, on the other hand, is a more mixed kind of construct—both substantive and procedural/fairness considerations seem to be involved. The logic of the subject matter is unclear in terms of the proper scope of negative fiat—"should" remains an ambiguous term. There are compelling fairness grounds for limiting negative fiat—the potential abusiveness of nongermane counterplan—thus, the fact that there is a fairness component makes the counterplan fiat issue distinct from the question of disadvantage links.

Finally, disadvantage links are probabilistic; whether fiat is extended to a certain counterplan is a threshold question, more analogous to topicality. A disadvantage without a specific link is likely to be assigned a low probability. Once the right of fiat is extended to a counterplan, however, the lack of specific link evidence in no way compromises its impact. Relevance is a threshold, all or nothing, issue; thus, it seems legitimate to have somewhat higher standards of proof than is the case with probabilistic questions such as the magnitude of a disadvantage link.

A fourth problem concerns the scope of the relevant policy literature. Most topics seem to implicate a fairly distcrete policy literature. It does not seem too difficult to determine the basic scope of the literature on U.S. policy toward Africa, but certainly some ambiguity will continue to exist on the exact scope of the relevant literature. This raises some practical problems in applying this standard.

Another problem of scope relates to counterplans directed toward affirmative harms that are tangential to the topic. The appropriate standard here would seem to be that if the affirmative introduces a harm issue into the debate, it should be liable to counterplans derived from the literature surrounding that harm area. Thus, if the affirmative claims to avert a nuclear war, the negative should be able to argue for counterplans that lower the nuclear war risk.

A trend that has recently developed is the proliferation of counterplans intended to minimize affirmative case harms or to make disadvantages unique. If a counterplan fulfills such an obviously specific and limited purpose, it should probably be judged to be germane—its relevance being intuitively obvious—even if there is no field-contextual support for such a counterplan. Or, putting it another way, if such minor repair-type counterplans have solvency evidence then they would by definition meet the test of germaneness to the issue they address. Lacking such evidence, they usually will have no impact anyway. But if a repair is so clearly addressed to a particular harm that it requires no documentation, then its germaneness should be equally intuitive and it should presumably be allowed. This reasoning would apply only to these narrow categories of analytical counterplans.

Probably the more fundamental indictment, however, is that the policy context standard will not eliminate very many counterplans. I believe that it could have impact on some to the overly generic, trans-topical counterplans that are the most controversial. Nonetheless, I think that this is fundamentally a minimalist constraint. I believe that the balance of equities favors a relative degree of openness in terms of what counterplans should be permitted. The two standard articulated here should eliminate truly abusive counterplans; it is certainly my intention that the negative have a wide range of options remaining.

While the two standards I have just articulated are acceptable ways of limiting negative fiat, there is a third very different approach, which is in fact superior. The two standards just suggested are an attempt to strike a middle ground in the counterplan fiat debate. But it may be that debate does not need new theories so much as it does ways of avoiding theoretical disputes altogether. Many theory disputes (for instance, broad versus narrow interpretation of topics or conditionality) arise out of concerns over fairness and the particularities of the current debate format. The fiat problem arises from the ambiguities of topic wording and the lack of a specific context in which the debate is assumed to occur. Issues such as these are esoteric and have little relevance to the world beyond contest debate. Some theories may be better than others (although better and worse in this context may amount to nothing more than different tastes where debate argument is concerned), but best of all might be to resolve such issues in a non-theoretical fashion.

One way of doing this would be to clarify topic wording. Where negative fiat is concerned, there are several ways in which this could be accomplished. One way would be to write caveats into resolutions, indicating the appropriate range of alternatives. If only the status quo is considered relevant, the topic could read "RESOLVED: That policy X is preferable to the present system." If the intention were to avoid change of government counterplans, topics could be written, "assuming present basic government structures, X should be done." A second approach would be to write a kind of negative resolution. The resolution could contain two sentences, one indicating the scope of affirmative choices, the other the scope of negative choices. Such a negative resolution might state that "policy alternatives germane to this resolution are those that operate within present basic government structures and which could be adopted by domestic public actors."

There are two benefits of a topic-based solution relative to any theoretical construct. The first is that theory debate is avoided. The topic itself sets the appropriate limits of negative fiat. Second, the range of comparisons permitted could change from topic to topic. Perhaps there are topics where radical and systemic alternatives should be considered. But not every resolution operates within such a context of utopian speculation. Anarchy and socialism may well be worth debating, but not every year and on every topic. I have argued throughout this article that "should" is an inherently ambiguous term. It is possible to draw inferences and set standards for its meaning, but it seems far simpler just to clarify what it does mean in terms of a given topic. Why persist in ambiguity if it can be avoided? I am certainly opposed to efforts to legislate questions of substantive theory (although for individual tournaments to experiment with theory guidelines strikes me as productive). But setting limits on the scope of discussion is something that resolutions already attempt to accomplish. Most other argument situations have a relatively clear, if implicit, framework of assumptions. For the debate resolution to define some relevant parameters of discussion (parameters binding on the negative as well as the affirmative) does not seem fundamentally different from mandating that the affirmative defend an example of the resolution. The contexts of purpose and policy that guide discussions outside of academic debate are less clearly present in the debate context. It thus seems reasonable that the debate community should define some of those contextual assumptions for the purposes of a particular topic.

CONCLUSION

The perception that certain counterplans are overly generic, overly utopian, and operate outside the realm of normal policy discourse is producing a backlash against the counterplan option in general. Disenchantment with particular counterplans should not, however, be allowed to generate standards that would effectively vitiate the counterplan option altogether. The approach proposed here suggests that in the area of negative fiat, as in many theoretical issues, there is a viable middle ground in which competing values may be balanced. For those beginning to tire of the theory wars, the pursuit of such a middle ground, derived from a pluralistic paradigm, may offer the best hope of achieving commonly accepted standards for how to evaluate debates. At least such an approach offers the hope of widening somewhat the zone of theory consensus and of leading to the awareness that our theoretical controversies are mainly differences of emphasis rather than of principle.

References

Branham, R. (1979). "The Counterplan as Disadvantage." *Speaker and Gavel* 16: 61–66.

Branham, R. (1989). "Roads Not Taken: Counterplans and Opportunity Costs." *Argumentation and Advocacy* (in press).

Isaacson, T. and Branham, R. (1980). "Policy Fiat: Theoretical Battleground of the Eighties." *Speaker and Gavel* 17: 84–91.

Perkins, D. (1989). Counterplans and Paradigms." *Argumentation and Advocacy* 25.

Snider, A. C. (1982). *Fantasy as Reality: Fiat Power in Academic Debate.* Paper given at the annual meeting of the Central States Speech Association Convention, Milwaukee.

Ulrich, W. (1979). *The Agent in Argument: Toward a Theory of Fiat.* Paper given at the annual meeting of the Central States Speech Association Convention, St. Louis.

Ulrich, W. (1981). *The Judge as an Agent of Action: Limitations on Fiat Power.* Paper given at the annual meeting of the Speech Communication Association, Anaheim.

34

The Topical Counterplan
A Competitive Policy Alternative

Edward M. Panetta and Steven Dolley

Allan J. Lichtman and Daniel M. Rohrer's essay, "A General Theory of the Counterplan" (1975), remains the standard treatment of counterplan burdens and theory in competitive policy debate. Our position is that their treatment of counterplans represents a starting point and not the culmination of the policy systems approach (Corsi, 1986).

One of the requirements of a legitimate counterplan that Lichtman and Rohrer detail is that it must not fulfill the affirmative resolution (1975, p. 74). This particular requirement is based upon the convention that the affirmative must support the resolution while the negative calls for rejection of the resolution. The traditionally accepted belief is that resolutional advocacy is the focus of academic debate (Paulsen and Rhodes, 1979, p. 705).[1]

We argue in this essay that the negative should have the option of presenting a topical counterplan. Given the evolution of policy advocacy during the years since the publication of Lichtman and Rohrer's essay, adherence to the convention that a counterplan must be nontopical seems unwarranted.

The topical counterplan enhances the quality of policy debate. We believe that the topical counterplan promotes the educational value of debate while maintaining ground for both the negative and affirmative teams. Given the assumptions of a policy systems approach, there is little justification for maintaining the application of the topicality convention to a negative counterplan.

In many NDT-style debates the focus of argumentation is on the particular policy forwarded by the affirmative and not the resolution.

"Ordinarily by gentleman's agreement debates ignore the resolution and discuss the specific policy advanced in the round" (Paulsen and Rhodes, 1979, pp. 208–09). The shift towards policy discussion creates the need for reexamination of theory in order to explain the practices of today's intercollegiate debate. The present rules assume a discussion of the resolution; the practice of debate often focuses on particular examples of the resolution forwarded by the affirmative.

The topical counterplan is a theoretical advance that reduces the schism between theory and practice. The topical counterplan is premised on the assumption that policy comparison, and not the testing of the validity of the resolution, is and should be the accepted practice in debate. This essay will outline the traditional arguments against topical counterplans, respond to these arguments, and provide a rationale for the topical counterplan.

TRADITIONAL POSITIONS ON COUNTERPLAN TOPICALITY

One could object to a topical counterplan by asserting that the function of the activity is the discussion of the resolution. Viewed from this perspective, the affirmative would claim that acceptance of the resolution in any form should result in an affirmative victory. A necessary starting point for discussion of this view is a delineation of its assumptions about the logical structure of the resolutions. An examination of the relationship between the resolution and the affirmative plan will follow, and the function of each when the resolution is assumed to be the focus of debate will be detailed.

The claim that we "debate the resolution" assumes that the resolution is a propositional statement, which the affirmative defends as true and the negative rejects as untrue (or, more accurately, rejects as not adequately proven true) (Patterson and Zarefsky 1983). By presenting a specific policy proposal in the form of a plan, the affirmative attempts to prove the resolution true by documenting the desirability of a specific topical instance. Under this view, the plan would be what logician Irving M. Copi defined as a *substitution instance*.

> Any singular proposition is a substitution instance of a propositional function, the result of substituting an individual variable into the propositional function. Ordinarily, a propositional function will have some true substitution instances and some false substitution instances (Copi, 1961, p. 305).

In this logical construct, a plan must be topical to be a substitution instance. To be a *true* substitution instance, a plan must be topical and satisfy the requirements of the ubiquitous resolutional term "should." In other words, if a topical plan ought to be adopted, it is a true substitution instance. A false substitution instance would be a topical plan that ought not be adopted. Under a resolution calling for increased safety regulation on motor vehicles, for example, a plan mandating air bags in all autos would, by virtue of its topicality, be a substitution instance. If proven desirable, the proposal would be a true substitution instance. A plan calling for food aid to starving Ethiopians would not be a substitution instance at all, either true or false, since it it not topical.

It is important to note that the resolution as a concept—what Copi calls "the propositional function"—carries no intrinsic truth value standing alone. It is neither true nor false, absent a specific substitution instance. It is merely a structure that actual, specific cases of affirmative advocacy must follow to be topical. The desirability of the specific plan is then debated, and the results of this dispute used to ascertain the truth of the plan as a substitution instance: Is the resolution's "should" term true, given this plan's net benefits? For example, the statement "the object is green" is neither true nor false standing alone. What object is referred to? Some are green, and some are not. Substituting "my lawn" for "the object" creates the statement "my lawn is green," a claim that is either true or false and can be readily verified by observation.

To summarize, the resolution is an abstract logical construct, carrying no intrinsic truth value. Only the introduction of a specific substitution instance, in the form of a topical affirmative plan, turns the resolution into a propositional statement that can be disputed. If desirable, the plan is a true substitution instance.

From the perspective of hypothesis testing, and indeed any paradigm which demands that counterplans be nontopical, testing the truth of the resolution is assumed to be a process of inductive argument, and the discovery of false substitution instances a denial of the resolution's truth. This claim rests on a further hidden assumption about the logical structure of the resolution.

Formal logic recognizes the importance of *quantifiers*, which are defined as "symbols indicating a quantum of objects taken into account in a sentence" (Marciszewski, 1981, p. 303). In the age-old example, the proposition "all swans are white," the word "all" is the quantifier. The scope of this proposition extends to every swan, making it a universally quantified proposition. The discovery of a single black swan would disprove this statement, which is an inductive generalization based on all swans encountered thus far.

Academic debate theory has not thus far directly addressed the question of resolutional quantification. Counterwarrant theory (Paulsen and Rhodes, 1979) assumes that all debate resolutions are universally quantified propositional statements, refutable by the discovery of counterinstances. For some resolutions, this is true. The topic "RE-SOLVED: That all automobiles should be destroyed" is untrue if it can be satisfactorily proven that even a single autombile, any one, should not be destroyed.

The issue of resolutional quantification is most frequently addressed indirectly in current debate in the form of the exception counterplan. Against a resolution containing a universally quantified term, negative teams will frequently argue that topical action should be taken for all parts of the term except a specific subset. The reasons why this subset should be exempted are then developed and defended. The college topic requiring educational standards for all U.S. public elementary and secondary schools is a recent example. Negative teams frequently contended that schools for the developmentally disabled, gifted, Native Americans, or culturally distinct regions should be free from the affirmative mandates, either to accommodate the special needs of the students in them, or to respect the autonomy of the peoples who operate and attend such schools. Since the resolution required affirmative plans to include *all* public elementary and secondary schools, affirmative teams were often left only with the options of defeating such counterplans on their merits, or explaining why the schools in question did not in fact fall into the category that plans were topically required to cover. As a result, these negative strategies were frequently successful by capitalizing on the universal quantification of the 1985–86 resolution.

Not every resolution is universally quantified. Many are existentially quantified. George F. Kneller distinguishes the two types by explaining that "the universal quantifier (X) can be translated, 'for all X.' The existential quantifier (X) can be translated, 'there is an X'" (1966, p. 29). An example of an existentially quantified proposition would be the topic "RESOLVED: we should eat at a restaurant." If at least one restaurant exists at which we should eat, the resolution is true. The existence of many other undesirable dining establishments, including the unsanitary and dangerous Green Cafe, does not disprove the truth of the resolution,[2] for "every existential proposition may be interpreted as asserting that *at least one individual exists*" (Simco and James, 1976, p. 119). False substitution instances do not disprove the existential propositional statement if at least one true substitution instance exists. Proving the truth of an existentially quantified resolution by demonstrating a true substitution instance is a deductive argument, which eliminates the question of inductive overgeneralization.

Sometimes propositional statements suffer from suppressed quantification, "a form of ambiguity where . . . we do not know whether the word or sentence refers to all members of the class or only some" (Angeles, 1981, p. 233). The 1982–1983 college resolution called for prohibition of all U.S. military intervention into the internal affairs of "any foreign nation or nations in the Western Hemisphere." Much confusion and dispute surrounded the term "any." As used in the resolution, did the word "any" mean that U.S. military intervention could be used in *no* foreign nation in the Western Hemispher? Or did it permit affirmatives to select one single nation, "any nation," and consider the merits of banning intervention there—say, in Nicaragua or in Guatemala? Because of the ambiguity of "any," the quantification of the resolution was unclear. In such instances analysis must focus on determining the quantification of the proposition, because there is no other way of knowing whether single true substitution instances can prove the proposition. Advocates must be careful to avoid quantifier shift fallacy, "the fallacy of confusing universal and particular [existential] qualities in an argument of inference" (Angeles, 1981, p. 233).

Implications of resolutional quantification for counterwarrant and hasty generalization argumentation against existentially quantified resolutions are obvious. Existentially quantified propositional statements, being deductive in argumentative structure, are not susceptible to the discovery of alternate instances, because such instances are irrelevant. Nor can there be hasty overgeneralization, because no generalization need be made to prove the argument true. The effects on the acceptability of topical counterplans are, unfortunately, neither as clear nor as directional.

It might be argued that considerations of resolutional quantification prove the illegitimacy of topical counterplans. In an existentially quantified proposition, any true substitution instance, apparently including a topical counterplan, would deductively prove the resolution true. Consider again the resolution on safety regulation of motor vehicles, and the affirmative plan mandating installation of air bags in autos. A negative team might counterplan with mandatory seat belt use laws. The counterplan might claim to save almost all the same people from death and injury in accidents that the air bag proposal would protect. Perhaps the net benefits competition of the seat belt counterplan would be avoiding financial stress in the auto industry (air bags are costly) and preventing a trade war with Japan (air bag regulations are perceived to be a non-tariff barrier to auto imports).

Of course, all of these claims can be disputed in direct clash with the counterplan. Under traditional theory, the affirmative could also object to the counterplan as topical. We suggest that, since the counterplan disproves the desirability of the affirmative plan, it shows that the plan is not a true substitution instance. Since a competitive alternative to the plan has been proven to be more desirable than either the plan alone or the plan and counterplan together, the affirmative plan does not prove the resolution true, even by deduction.

Those opposed to topical counterplans will be quick to respond that, even though the plan may not be a true substitution instance, the counterplan is, by virtue of its topicality and desirability. On a purely logical level, this is correct. However, this turns the usual accusation of groundstealing on its head. Opponents of topical counterplans claim that such strategies steal ground from the affirmative, which has a claim to all action within the scope of the resolution. The common response, and one with which we concur, is that the counterplan's competitiveness burden precludes such usurpation. A topical counterplan steals no ground the affirmative can defend, since the counterplan competes with the action the affirmative team advocates in their plan. To reject this position is to allow affirmative advocates of any resolution to defend simultaneously "X" and "not X." In fact, in nondirectional resolutions, such distorted logic would give affirmatives the overwhelming advantage of being able to defend direct opposites. On the topic "RESOLVED: That the U.S. should significantly change its nuclear weapons policy," both banning the MX missile and building 500 more such weapons would be topical. Is it truly fair, or intelligent policy analysis, to allow either of two opposites to justify an affirmative concurrence?

This clearly places negative advocates in a no-win situation. Their arguments for rejection of the affirmative plan can be turned around by the affirmative into justifications for a different topical proposal, even though that proposal is incompatible with the original plan. Directional resolutions would avoid some of the more extreme instances of abuse, but not all of them. Fundamental burdens of advocacy would become meaningless if both a proposal *and* its refutation (in the form of a competitive, desirable alternative) mandate a ballot for the advocates of the original proposal.

More traditional issues regarding division of ground will be considered momentarily. For now, we merely contend that we have little choice from a fairness and logic perspective but to view topicality as a unilateral burden of the affirmative team, and irrelevant to counterplans, once the initial topicality of the affirmative proposal is established. Ignoring the topicality of counterplans does not moot the issue of topicality for both teams. Requiring that affirmative plans be topical is still vital for jurisdictional and pragmatic reasons, many of which are discussed by Madsen and Louden (1988). Otherwise, sensible debate cannot take place—either on any specific plan, or indeed on entire resolutions.

Perhaps academic debate should seek another way of disputing policy propositions. It is possible that a broad general resolution, which the affirmative operationalizes in the form of a specific plan, creates too much confusion regarding the burdens and nature of proof. Nevertheless, the affirmative plan is a fact of life in contemporary academic debate. If an affirmative team presents a plan, they shoulder advocacy burdens as a result. For reasons of fairness and logical analysis, these burdens must include substantive clash with competitive alternative policies, whether topical or not. To require less is to permit affirmative teams to be logically inconsistent and to win debates by means of usurpation rather than refutation.

This, in fact, is more consistent with the gradual trend in current debate. Based upon our conception of resolution, we draw several conclusions concerning propositional advocacy. As mentioned previously, the common practice in academic debate is the discussion of policy and not the resolution. From a policymaking perspective, the affirmative is expected to defend an example, not necessarily the entire set of examples contained within a resolution. Thus, an answer to the objection of the affirmatives' need to defend the resolution is that the practice in debate demands policy comparison.

Most debate resolutions are so broad that affirming them in their entirety is of little value. The imposition of an arbitrary set of standards on a general statement to assess its validity has very little real world application for the student. If one discusses the merits of the resolution, there is no way to determine if it (the resolution) is true or false, for debate resolutions are policy propositions that call for judgments of both value and probability. Additionally, the policy permutations inherent in a debate resolution are too numerous to be effectively discussed in a competitive policy debate. As such, the more specific the policy question, the more thoroughly its desirability is assessed. Hence, debating specific plans is preferable to debating general resolutions.

Perhaps the strongest argument in support of the resolution serving as the basis of discussion is that it divides the ground between the affirmative and the negative teams (Patterson and Zarefsky, 1983). There are two problems with this claim. First, once the affirmative chooses its policy for discussion, a shift in emphasis back to resolutional discussion seems unwarranted. The rationale behind the divided ground argument seems to be that a subject area should have limits. If the affirmative forwarded a nonresolutional alternative, the unique substantive limits of a resolution would be lost, implying decreased opportunity for preparation and a lower quality of analysis. By allowing the negative to venture into the topic area for a policy alternative to present against the affirmative, the problem area for discussion would in no way be expanded and the substantive limits of the problem area would remain intact. There is no reason why the affirmative should be shielded from discussion of the substantive issues of the problem area.

A second argument against the resolution as dividing ground position is that it assumes there is a direction to the resolution. Recent topics at both the high school and collegiate level have provided demonstrative evidence that there need not be direction to a resolution.

The 1987–1988 high school debate resolution, for instance, merely calls for a United States government policy to increase political stabililty in Latin America. The affirmative is allowed the option of establishing either philosophically conservative or liberal policies. Some affirmative plans on this topic have eliminated aid to the Nicaraguan rebels, while others have dramatically increased such aid; and some encourage and others discourage massive economic development; and some encourage and others discourage nuclear weapons proliferation. A negative team could advocate the exact opposite of the affirmative plan proposed in any of these examples. Assuming traditional debate theory, however, they could lose the debate on topicality despite the fact that they presented a policy option which was opposite to that presented by the affirmative.

A recent example of dual directionality of resolution at the collegiate level can be found in the aforementioned educational standards topic. Affirmative teams during the course of that season advocated greater instruction in sex education and creationism. Other teams ran cases proposing that education in these areas be eliminated. Better selection of topics is not an answer to the issue of dual directionality in resolutions, for the simple reason that the framers cannot anticipate before the season begins the numerous (and sometimes devious) ways in which the directional term in the topic can be construed to include its opposite. Without the *certainty* of directionality, there is very little reason to support the position that the resolution should serve as a dividing mark between teams.

In debate, an affirmative alternative and the resolution are no longer regarded as synonomous. The breadth and lack of direction in debate topics disproves the assumption that an example and the topic are one. The nondirectionality of resolutions also reduces the ground from which the negative may select in formulating its policy. A negative's ground can be greatly diminished when a topic lacks direction.

Nondirectionality also renders suspect the claim that the resolution can be affirmed even as a philosophical statement. If examples of the resolution contradict each other in terms of their underlying values, the feasibility of endorsing the resolution is tenuous. The existence of conflicting examples suggests that the resolution is already functioning as a designated problem area, rather than as a statement meriting consideration in its own right.

To summarize: Resolutional advocacy is of limited utility in an activity that strives for realism and debatability (Rowland, 1986). Resolutions are so broadly worded that standards which critics might apply to test validity are arbitrary. Also, the use of the resolution to divide ground does not warrant the application of a test of topicality to negative counterplans. It is the affirmative choice of policy alternative that places substantive limits on discussion. If one rejects this formulation of the topicality burden in policy debate, the question of non-directionality of the resolution renders suspect the utility of imposing such a burden on the negative.

An additional problem with resolutional advocacy is that the need for precise language is decreased. For instance, in advancing the argument that a plan flaw is not intrinsic to the resolution, an affirmative can avoid the defense of a poorly developed plan. If, for example, an affirmative team chose an agent to enforce a policy who lacked the authority to do so, they might claim that such an error did not warrant rejection of the resolution. Creative argument against a thesis forwarded by the affirmative is discouraged if the negative is not rewarded for plan analysis.

Resolutional advocacy also holds affirmative teams accountable for ill-worded resolutions. The plan is far more representative of the thesis an affirmative wishes to defend than is the resolution. Plan emphasis maximizes advocates' choice of topic area. By focusing on the plan, rather than the resolution, an affirmative is responsible for its own interpretation of a resolution.[3]

Finally, to open discussion to the value of the resolution subjects debate to superficial analysis, including counterwarrants and the counterresolutional counterplan.[4] The problems entailed in the use of counterwarrants have been outlined by Keeshan and Ulrich (1980) and Ganer (1981). One problem with counterwarrants is that clash is reduced. The policy presented in first affirmative is eliminated as the focal point of discussion, and emphasis is placed upon generic disadvantages presented in second negative. Issue development is limited to the plan responses delivered in the first affirmative rebuttal and the answers provided in second negative rebuttal.

The counterresolutional counterplan is an argument with its own set of problems. This argument is based on the belief that a resolution represents a particular philosophy. The nondirectionality of a resolution renders this claim suspect. The resolution does not necessarily contain a unique philosophy that the negative may address. If a specific philosophy could be attributed to a resolution, the counterresolutional counterplan's competitiveness is based upon the legitimacy of philosophical competitiveness. The problems with this pseudo-standard have been addressed by Mancuso (1981).[5] These are but a few of the reasons why the practice of debate has moved from resolutional discussion to policy discussion.

The objection that division of argument ground is undermined by a topical counterplan does not stand up to close scrutiny. Once an affirmative has selected a particular policy to advocate, there is no further need for an assessment of the proposition's general validity. The research burdens remain limited, and the quality of policy comparison can in many instances be enhanced when a negative advocates a topical counterplan. In fact, our contention is that propositional debate can reduce the advocacy responsibility of an affirmative while encouraging superfluous argumentation.

A second major objection to the topical counterplan is that affirmative topicality and negative nontopicality must serve as absolute rules of the game. This convention has been translated into a revered tradition by proponents of resolutional advocacy (Corsi, 1986, p. 159). We agree with Jerome Corsi that policy debate can be enhanced if the activity frees itself from the traditional propositional format (Corsi, 1986, p. 160). One alternative would be the accceptance of the topic as a "problem area." From this perspective topicality would become a moot issue once the topicality of the affirmative policy is established. The perspective of topic as problem area maintains some discussion of jurisdictional limits while at the same time enhancing substantive discussion.

The final objection to the topical counterplan is that the negative could make minor alterations in the affirmative plan and defend a slightly amended policy. The claim is that the consideration of minor plan alterations would destroy the real world value of debate. However, such an illegitimate, insignificant counterplan can be dispensed with easily enough by a clever affirmative team. If the alteration presented by the negative does not compete with the example claimed in first affirmative, there is no reason why the affirmative could not incorporate it into the plan, or why both plans could not be considered together. Robert Rowland (1986) has made several suggestions that could be helpful in the reformulation of the plan. The affirmative could replan by incorporating portions of the negative policy while maintaining the resolutionally based mandate in the plan. The affirmative might also claim that only advantages that compete with the resolutional provisions of their plan serve as a rationale to vote for the negative (Rowland, 1986).

The affirmative could approach the problem of minor plan alteration in another fashion by detailing only the portions of the plan that respond to the charge of the particular resolution. Robert Rowland articulated the claims an affirmative may choose to make in this instance:

> At the same time, debate teams should be required to defend only those specific details of their policy position that are important. It is essential to know the important aspects of the policies advocated by the affirmative and negative, but as far as the educational function of debate is concerned, it is not important to know all the details of the administrative scheme under which the plan or counterplan would be implemented. (1986, p. 130)

Given a negative counterplan that is a minor alteration the affirmative can either incorporate the alteration when possible or forward arguments against the utility of discussing the policy's administrative scheme. This second option, claiming that administrative issues should not be discussed, is one that the negative may choose to dispute in a counterplan debate.

Also, if the alteration to the plan is trivial enough, it can readily be defeated on its own merits, or lack thereof. Reducing the number of board members in the plan from nine to seven seems to offer little contrast and no comparative advantage. On the other hand, if the negative is able to defend reasons why the apparently trivial alteration is beneficial and it competes with the affirmative plan, it may well be a substantive reason to reject the proposal, even though it appears minor at first. The framers of the Declaration of Independence would likely have considered a proposed amendment to change "all men are created equal" to "all persons are created equal" a nit-picking attempt to degrade the dignity of the issue at hand. In a later historical context, we can see a number of real reasons why one would want to include both halves of the human race in a landmark document of freedom. Such alterations entail much more than a minor wording change. This is not to predict or propose that topical counterplans focus on affirmative plan wording alone; we merely wish to point out that the triviality of this issue should be debated, rather than presumed.

The problem of determining what is significantly different policy is not one this negative strategy has forced upon debate. For many years, affirmative teams have proposed insignificant policy options and critics have not only established standards for evaluation, in many cases they have voted for them. In a debate in which a questionable counterplan is presented, the critic could stipulate that the counterplan must be substantially different from the affirmative plan or this standard could itself be a matter for debate.

The critic also has the option of voting on presumption in a debate when the alternatives are essentially the same. Traditionally presumption is always against the resolution; without the resolution on which to base presumption, the standard of presumption utilized in formal disputation could be applied to debate. Medieval disputation is, after all, the direct precursor of debate (Smith, 1948). In a disputation, an advocate defends a thesis in the face of objections and counter-arguments from an adversary (Rescher, 1977, p. 1). In disputation, presumption favors the most plausible alternative in order to vote on presumption (Rescher, 1977, pp. 37–38).

When utilized effectively the topical counterplan can enhance the quality of argument on regulatory issues. If an affirmative team used the strategy previously discussed, adopting the plan at the appropriate level with the appropriate agent, the negative may use a topical counterplan to force a debate on the validity of such a tactic. The negative argument would be that not only does such a position evade implementation discussion, it fails to reflect the way policymakers decide issues (Isaacson and Branham, 1980; Pressman and Wildavsky, 1984; Alexander, 1985; Davies and Hale, 1986; Marvel, 1982; O'Toole and Montjoy, 1984). The negative may be well served to make appropriate implementation arguments in some instances (Isaacson and Branham, 1980), especially when a topic does not isolate a specific agent. Often the affirmative tries to avoid discussion of implementation by claiming that the local, state, or national agents could enact the proposal. By providing the negative with the option of a topical counterplan, the affirmative may be forced to specify both agent and agency in the plan. The topical counterplan is a useful tool when the resolution is vague either at the level of agent of change or in the direction of policy change.

The topical counterplan calls into question the traditional belief that topicality should be a rule of the game applied to both affirmative and negative teams. Our position is that by requiring proof of topicality from the affirmative alone, adequate division of ground can be maintained and the quality of argumentation enhanced. As will be the norm with any alternate theoretical framework, the topical counterplan may be abused by those who take the underlying assumptions to their extreme. However, in the long run, the topical counterplan will provide the negative with an effective tool for advancement of substantive and implementation arguments derived from the affirmative policy option.

RATIONALE FOR THE TOPICAL COUNTERPLAN

As Keeshan and Ulrich have said, a theory that can enhance the quality of debate, promote the educational value of debate, and place both advocates on equal ground should gain adherence (Keeshan and Ulrich, 1980, p. 203). As we have pointed out throughout this essay, the topical counterplan meets all of these requirements.

The Quality of Debate

From the policymaking perspective the topical counterplan enhances the quality of debate. The topical counterplan substitutes in-depth argumentation on a policy for the shallower understanding of an expansive topic. A policy emphasis has the effect of crystalizing the issues to be discussed, whereas a focus on the topic as the area of discussion significantly reduces the likelihood of good on-point argumentation. The expansive scope of a debate resolution makes it more difficult for the negative to anticipate and prepare coherent argumentation. To present a competitive, topical counterplan, a negative team has to be well read on the substantive issues of the topic. The presentation of well-researched competitive positions highlights the important arguments early in the debate, and good clash usually ensues.

In considering the topical counterplan, we can see that one of its main contributions is to the quality of competitiveness argumentation. Without topicality serving as one of the standards for counterplan evaluation, a heavy emphasis will be placed upon counterplan competitiveness. In practice, for example, the speaker would spend more time on competitiveness if topicality was considered a moot issue. The topical counterplan might also have the effect of screening out weak competitiveness standards. For instance, the redundancy standard is exposed as an illegitimate one. Redundancy assumes that both the plan and the counterplan achieve the exact same significance, and the weight of presumption tips the scale towards the negative. Without a traditional notion of presumption to rest upon, the negative would be forced to claim a net benefit from counterplan adoption. A debate in which a topical counterplan is presented would focus the competition debate on the standards of mutual exclusivity and net benefits (Lichtman and Rohrer, 1980). Consider again a resolution on safety regulation of motor vehicles and the affirmative policy of installing air bags in autos. The negative team that counterplans with mandatory seatbelt use laws would claim that the topical counterplan is net beneficial. The critic would be asked to compare the life savings attributed to airbag use with the life savings attributed to seatbelt use laws and the financial risks associated with the installation of air bags. Allowing the negative to choose the policy that best competes with the affirmative plan without the artificial constraint of the resolution would facilitate argumentation on the substantive policy questions while crystalizing the debate over issues of policy competition.

Enhanced Educational Value

The topical counterplan clearly enhances the educational value of the activity. Initially, the topical counterplan moves debate in the direction of substantive disputation.

The affirmative team would defend its thesis, the plan, in face of objections made by the negative. This type of argumentation can be found elsewhere in the academy in the form of the degree candidate's oral examination (Rescher, 1977). When a candidate defends a thesis before a committee, one function the committee members serve is to provide opposition to the thesis with the intention of strengthening the quality of the claims made by the candidate (Rescher, 1977). In debate the topical counterplan would be a validating mechanism that tests the strength of the affirmative's claims. The topical counterplan allows the debaters to unpack the substantive issues in the topic area. For instance, the student can compare seatbelts and airbags and gain a better understanding of auto safety. The problem area of a debate resolution represents an important social issue that needs to be addressed by students. The topical counterplan effectively limits discussion to the substantial issues unique to that year's topics.

While there may be significant discussion concerning the legitimacy of a topical counterplan when it is first utilized in the debate community, we believe that in the long run topical counterplans will advance the quality of the substantive issues raised and the debate over counterplan competition. This assessment is based upon the debates we have seen where both sides accept the legitimacy of this strategy. By placing the discussion of procedural rules in the background, the substantive exchange between advocates is enhanced. The direct competition between thesis and counterargument builds up communal understanding. Such give and take is critical in the process of knowledge authentication (Rescher, 1977, pp. xi). In the long run a strong understanding of the policy issues found in the particular topic may be helpful in preparing students to confront real world problems. With a deep understanding of the problem area, the student will be better prepared to help in the process of social knowledge authentication.

A second educational benefit is the heightened understanding of the policymaking process. Direct policy competition and the question of which level of government should respond to a crisis are the stuff of which real world policy analysis is made. For instance, against an affirmative plan calling for a nationwide bottle bill, the negative could argue for nonreturnable cardboard containers (aseptics). The negative counterplan would claim to protect the quality of the environment while avoiding the financial hardships associated with a bottle bill. Aseptics are biodegradable and would not significantly affect the cost of the product at the supermaket (which some might argue would affect employment). This is a realistic policy option, especially when compared with a stragtegy proposed by Paulsen and Rhodes for the same case on the college debate topic, "RESOLVED: That the federal government should significantly strengthen the guarantee of consumer product safety required of manufacturers."

> They might suggest that past and proposed additions to general manufacturer liability for consumer products have resulted in a very dangerous state of affairs for the insurance industry. They could argue that Consumer Product Safety Commission actions have placed manufacturers in grave financial straits. They might suggest that safety requirements are

far too stringent for optimum innovation in pharmaceuticals. They could show that decision of the handgun controversy (in which the CPSC has been embroiled) in the direction indicated by the resolution would lead to massive citizen revolt, and so on ad infinitum. (Paulsen and Rhodes, 1979, p. 207)

Rather than forcing the negative to argue nonapplicable generics, the use of a topical counterplan allows the negative to defend a realistic and competitive option (aseptics). The students would compare two competitive, albeit topical, policy alternatives, aseptics and the bottle bill.

Equal Ground

An objection to the topical counterplan is that it violates the concept of equal ground. Such an objection is based on the belief that the resolution and not an affirmative policy determines ground. As pointed out earlier in this essay, such an assumption is fallacious.

In fact, the topical counterplan reestablishes negative ground. From the policy making perspective, the affirmative maintains ground because they still determine the specific problem area for discussion. Affirmative choice of ground is maintained and, in some instances, enhanced with the presentation of a topical counterplan.

As should be obvious, the topical counterplan expands negative ground. The negative is allowed to choose from a larger group of policy alternatives if they argue a topical position. If the affirmative anticipated a topical counterplan, the effect might also be an expansion of negative ground. The perception that a topical counterplan may be argued could force a usually hesitant affirmative into specifying the mandates and implementing agents of a plan. In the instances when a wide topic is being debated, it is critical to the negative that the affirmative detail a policy, for this may be the only way to ensure adequate negative ground. The use of a topical counterplan, or even the threatened use, would have the effect of expanding negative ground.

CONCLUSION

By presenting a topical counterplan, the negative may be presenting the most competitive alternative to an affirmative plan. If the emphasis in contemporary debate is on the plan and not the resolution, the advantages and disadvantages of a policy can best be understood if there is a comparison of policies. The topical counterplan simply expands the set of competing policy alternatives from which the negative can choose.

Notes

1. Assuming this theoretical perspective, a negative arguing a resolutional counterplan would lose the debate.
2. We are indebted to Dr. Robert J. Branham for this cogent example.
3. We appreciate the input of Dr. W. David Snowball on this issue.
4. The reasoning behind these positions can be found in Paulsen and Rhodes (1979), in Rhodes (1981), and in Mayer (1981).
5. One problem with philosophical competitiveness is that "such a standard, without requiring a disadvantage, would permit completely arbitrary philosophical distinctions to be advanced by the negative, making competitiveness a meaningless idea" (Mancuso, 1981, p. 8).

References

Alexander, E. R. (1985). "From Idea to Action: Notes for a Contingency Theory of the Policy Implementation Process." *Administration and Society* 16: 403–26.

Angeles, P. A. (1981). *Dictionary of Philosophy*. New York: Barnes and Nobles.

Copi, I. M. (1961). *Introduction to Logic*. 2nd ed. New York: Macmillan.

Corsi, J. (1986). "The Continuing Evolution of Policy Systems Debate: An Assessment and a Look Ahead." *Journal of the American Forensic Association* 22: 158–63.

Davies, T. R., and Hale, W. M. (1986). "Implementing a Policy and Planning for Managing State Use of Information Technology Resources." *Public Administration Review* 46: 516–21.

Ganer, P. M. (1981). Counterwarrants: An Idea Whose Time Has Not Yet Come." In G. Ziegelmueller and J. Rhodes, eds. *Dimensions of Argument: Proceedings of the Second Argumentation Conference*. Annandale, VA: SCA. 476–84.

Isaacson, T., and Branham, R. (1980). "Policy Fiat: Theoretical Battleground of the Eighties." *Speaker and Gavel* 17: 84–91.

Kaplow, L. (1981). "Rethinking Counterplans: A Reconciliation with Debate Theory." *Journal of the American Forensic Association* 17: 215–26.

Keeshan, M., and Ulrich, W. (1980). "A Critique of the Counterwarrant as a Negative Strategy." *Journal of the American Forensic Association* 16: 199–203.

Kneller, G. F. (1966). *Logic and the Language of Education*. New York: John Wiley and Sons.

Lichtman, A. J., and Rohrer, D. M. (1975). "A General Theory of the Counterplan." *Journal of the American Forensic Association* 12: 70–79.

Lichtman, A. J., and Rohrer, D. M (1980). "The Logic of Policy Dispute." *Journal of the American Forensic Association* 16: 236–47.

Madsen, A., and Louden, A. D. (1981). "Jurisdiction and the Evaluation of Topicality." *Journal of the American Forensic Association* 16: 73–83.

Mancuso, S. (1981). "Counterplans Must Be Competitive." In A. Louden and R. Solt, eds. *Alternatives in Education: Stagnation or Renewal?* Wake Forest, NC: Wake Forest University Press. 6–9.

Marcizewski, W. (1981). *Dictionary of Logic as Applied to the Study of Language*. The Hague: Martinus Nijhoff.

Marvel, M. K. (1982). "Implementation and Safety Regulation." *Administration & Society* 14: 15–33.

Mayer, M. (1981). "Extending Counterwarrants: The Counterresolutional Counterplan." *Journal of the American Forensic Association* 19: 122–27.

O'Toole, L. J., Jr., and Montjoy, R. (1984). "Interorganizational Policy Implementation: A Theoretical Perspective." *Public Administration Review* 44: 491–503.

Patterson, J. W., and Zarefsky, D. (1983). *Contemporary Debate*. Boston: Houghton Mifflin.

Paulsen, J. Q., and Rhodes, J. L. (1979). "The Counterwarrant as a Negative Strategy: A Modest Proposal." *Journal of the American Forensic Assocation* 15: 205–10.

Pressman, J. L., and Wildavsky, A. (1984). *Implementation*. Berkeley: University of California Press.

Rescher, N. (1977). *Dialectics: A Controversy-Oriented Approach to the Theory of Knowledge*. Albany: SUNY Press.

Rhodes, J. L. (1981). "A Defense of the Counterwarrant as Negative Argument." In G. Ziegelmueller and J. Rhodes eds. *Dimensions of Argument: Proceedings of the Second Argumentation Conference*. Annandale, VA: SCA. 485–93.

Rowland, R. C. (1986). "The Relationship Between Realism and Debatability in Policy Advocacy." *Journal of the American Forensic Association* 22: 125–34.

Simco, N. D., and James, G. G. (1976). *Elementary Logic*. Enrico, CA: Dickenson.

Smith, B. (1948). "Extracurricular Disputations: 1400–1650." *Quarterly Journal of Speech* 34: 473–76.

35

What Killed Schrodinger's Cat?

A Response to Panetta and Dolley

David M. Berube

Schrodinger's cat refers to a poor pussy locked in a box containing a Rube Goldberg device that will or will not emit cyanide gas depending on the outcome of a single quantum event—the radioactive discharge of an atom. The paradox is: Suppose that the cat is in the box for a period of time where the probability is 50 percent that the atom has discharged. If no one looks in the box, is the cat dead or alive? (Wolf, 1988, p. 50)

In a quantum sense, an observer cannot help but affect the reality of a phenomenon as a result of observing (the uncertainty principle). In a nonquantum parallel universe sense, that's not the case. Realities, often very different, can coexist. "In th[is] model, the cat is both alive and dead in separate but equal worlds" (Wolf, p. 50).

My working observation is that parametric topicality, defining the resolution as the case/plan, gives the affirmative a power of definition far beyond any priviledge or right traditionally associated with the initiator of an argument. When affirmative debaters look at the unfortunate kitty, they assign a corporeal value to the phenomenon, but that valuation is stipulative only, and does not deny the existence of other realities equally plausible and probable (the parallel-universe model). The resolution exists in parallel universes. It is both the affirmative case and not the affirmative case not only in separate debates, tournaments, and realities but also in the same debate with the affirmative resolutional world and the negative one.

When a nonpolicy debater, for example, is answering a charge from the negative that the case, and its proofs, are insufficient to prove the resolution true either because there is an entire or whole resolution,[1] which the affirmative proofs do not sufficiently constitute or because the affirmative proofs are hasty[2] and inadequate to justify the conclusion that should the affirmative proofs be true then the resolution is also true, she may be tempted to say "our case is the resolution." Her response suggests that after the first affirmative constructive speech, new parameters for the debate appear, consequently there is no entire or whole resolution beyond the affirmative proofs, the affirmative proofs become the substitute resolution. As a result, there is no resolution greater than the affirmative case/plan against which claims of sufficiency can be tested. This is parametric topicality, and this is a theoretical development that demands a notable proof burden.

As quantum physicists now feel compelled to rejustify their construction of what is real against the parallel universes model, so advocates of parametric topicality must justify the obliteration of the parallel universes of the resolution after the affirmative case/plan is introduced.

ORIGINS

The concept of parametric topicality can be gleaned from three articles. In 1973, Lichtman et al, defending the alternative justification case in policy debating, wrote: "It is not the responsibility of the affirmative to persuade the judge to accept all conceivable interpretations of the debate resolution" (p. 61). However, they added the caveat that "the plan represents one of the many proposals that are logically consistent with a reasonable interpretation of the resolution. No affirmative plan ever defines the resolution. . . . To assume that the proposals an affirmative chooses to debate defines the debate resolution is to assume some parts [necessarily] define the whole" (p. 63). Assuming such would be illogical. Proving such may be a different matter altogether, an issue tackled in the following.

In 1978, Dolley, discussing an "all-encompassing resolution," concluded differently. He wrote that all-encompassing (sometimes dual-directional) resolutions left "the negative no position to defend, if one accepts the assumption that the negative may not defend a topical position" (p. 8). His premise was that some resolutions may address all truth in some pragmatically known universe, consequently allowing the negative only nonresolutional positions may be problematical. Then, in 1989, Dolley joined with Panetta and straightforwardly defended the thesis that "the negative should have the option of presenting a topical counterplan" (p. 166), a conclusion Lichtman et al rejected in 1973 (p. 63). For Panetta and Dolley, the topical counterplan, which better defined the resolutional counterplan, involved a policy option that was not topical by affirmative standards of meaning yet still conceivably topical by other than affirmative standards in the debate instant. Panetta and Dolley's proofs for this thesis were "premised on the assumption that policy comparison, and not testing the validity of the resolution, is and should be the accepted practice in debate" (p. 167).

Debaters have cited predominantly pages 166 and 167 of the Panetta and Dolley article to justify parametric topicality. They seem to especially like paragraph six on page 166:

> It is important to note that the resolution as a concept—what Copi calls "the propositional function"—carries no intrinsic truth value standing alone. It is neither true nor false absent a specific substitution instance.

In this context, a substitution instance is "the result of substituting an individual variable (case with or without plan) into the proposition function (resolution)" (Copi, 1961, p. 305 and Panetta and Dolley, 1989, p. 166).

This practice has become particularly attractive in nonpolicy debate because Panetta and Dolley later claimed in their 1989 article that this viewpoint involves statements that "are not susceptible to the discovery of alternate instances, because such instances are irrelevant" (p. 168). Hence, no counterwarrants and no whole resolution debating. Also they claim, "Nor can there be hasty overgeneralization, because no generalization need be made to prove the argument true" (p. 168). Hence, no hasty gneralization.

PREMISE

The affirmative cannot be empowered to reshape the reality of a resolution. The affirmative may be assigned the privilege of inter- pretation, but that privilege does not carry the weight of imprimatur, and to deny the negative the probative opportunity to test an affirmative interpretation against the original text of the resolution is senseless. That opportunity becomes severely restricted when the affirmative begins adding existential quantifiers to a topic that in turn forecloses any comparisons of an affirmative instantiation to its source.

Panetta and Dolley's 1989 article showcases a practice in search of a theory and the logical foundation for their conclusions is nothing but a house of cards built with questionable scholarship. This essay will try to accomplish four things: First, an examination of existential instantiation as a substitute premise in propositional reasoning will be given (something Panetta and Dolley failed to do); second, the application of existential instantiation to debate will be tested; third, the utility of existential instantiation to discover meaning will be evaluated; and fourth, Panetta and Dolley's conclusions regarding resolutions, which they use to justify existential instantiation, will be reassessed and the misapplication by nonpolicy debaters of their conclusions about existential instantiation will be evidenced.

EXISTENTIAL INSTANTIATION RE-EXAMINED

When Popper wrestled with the dilemma that science was based upon induction, a system of logic that can never be valid in absolute terms (the argument of skeptics), he redefined the scientific method.

"The purpose of science is not verification but the *falsification* of theories. Propositional reasoning involves the use of rules of inference, but instead of having the probative force to verifty, it can *only* falsify. Falsification can be achieved by deduction [existential instantiation]. I can never absolutely prove the statement "All swans are white" to be true, but I only need to observe one black swan to prove that it is false" (Evans, 1982, p. 3).

Rules of inference in propositional reasoning, true to Popper's reconception of proof in science as a function of falsifiability, are as follows:

1. Assume the negative of what you wish to prove.
2. Deduce a logical contradiction.
3. Infer that your starting assumption is false (Evans, 1982, p. 116).

There are no equivalencies between what is demanded by rules of inference in propositional reasoning and what happens in debate, at least not like Panetta and Dolley intended. Recall, initially, that propositional reasoning in debate would begin with the affirmative, who cannot assume the negation of the resolution. If the affirmative attempted to insert some modifier to create the aresolution and then offered an existential instantiation that denied the aresolution, the only conclusion the affirmative could draw would be that the aresolution is false, but that doesn't say anything about the resolution per se. Though Panetta and Dolley claimed that "the resolution . . . is neither true nor false, absent a specific substantive instance" (p. 166), it would remain so even after existential instantiation by the affirmative if we are forced to follow rules of inference.

Furthermore, Panetta and Dolley's illustration is not correct. They argued: "The plan would be what logician Irving M. Copi defined as a *substitution instance*" (p. 166). For the premise "All humans are mortal," a substitution instance would allow the conclusion: "Socrates is mortal." A substitution instance is "the result of substituting an individual constant for the individual variable in that propositional function" (Copi, 1961, p. 305). In this example, it is "Socrates" for "All humans."

First, the subject term "Socrates" must meet the meaning of the subject term, "All humans," in the propositional function. Cocker spaniels and ALF as instantiations will not do. How to test whether a subject term is a substitute instance and meets the meaning of the subject term in the propositional function is mostly done observationally, either intuitively or inductively. Second, a substitute instance does not enable the logician to conclude that, should Socrates be human, all humans are mortals. Rather, as we know all too well, it only allows the conclusion that Socrates is mortal. This would mean that if the case/plan was a substitute instance, the only conclusion that can be drawn distances the case/plan from the resolution.

This is all highly problematical. Panetta and Dolley wrote: "By presenting a specific proposal in the form of a plan, the affirmative attempts to prove the resolution true by documenting the desirability of a specific topical instance" (p. 166). If the justification for this practice has something to do with the intrinsic failure of the resolution to embody truth, how can this misinterpretation of singular propositional logic compensate for this deficiency?

Next, Panetta and Dolley cited Copi, who wrote that "a propositional function will have some true substitution instances and some false substitution instances" (Copi, 1961, p. 305 and Panetta and Dolley, 1989, p. 166). Panetta and Dolley next wrote that "a plan must be topical to be a substitution instance" (p. 166). However, Panetta and Dolley left what constituted a topical substitution instance up for grabs, a problem I tackle in detail later. Nevertheless, it is my premise that Panetta and Dolley's definition of topicality in substitution logic is not black and white. Panetta and Dolley believed that "a *true* substitution instance must be topical and satisfy the requirements of the ubiquitous resolutional term *should*" (p. 166). For Copi, a *true* substitution term should conform to "ordinary grammar and traditional logic" (1961, p. 303). In singular propositional logic, a substitute subject term, Panetta and Dolley's vision of the plan or nonpolicy case, would need to satisfy the meaning of the subject term in the propositional function, Panetta and Dolley's resolution, for which it is being substituted. For me, the meaning in this setting would be a function of *representativeness*.

Next, Panetta and Dolley wrote that "a false substitution instance would be a topical plan that ought not to be adopted" (p. 166). Here,

Panetta and Dolley commit the fallacy of hasty generalization them-selves. While their statement is correct, false substitutions not only occur when the substitute subject term fails the predicate function, Panetta and Dolley's ubiquitous *should*, but also when the substitute subject term itself is unclear, not clearly discernible from the propositional function. Even in my previous example, a science fiction android and australopithecus are arguably substitute subject terms for humans, but their quality is a function of resemblance. Rather, fine and precise tests are used in analyzing substitute subject terms. Even if Panetta and Dolley insist on calling it *topicality*, it is not different from *representativeness*.

However, if the aforementioned isn't enough of a problem, consider that the negative *can* use existential instantiation to falsify the resolution. For purposes of the following, I will assume the resolution is a propositional function, and deduction is appropriate for analyzing the logical structure of natural language arguments (both of which I reject unequivocally later).

Using Evans' standards, the negative (1) assumes the resolution rather than their traditional a-resolution; (2) deduces a logical contra-diction, an existential instantiation, something like a counterresolu-tional counterplan, or even a counterwarrant, and (3) infers the resolution is false. But didn't Panetta and Dolley argue that the "counterresolutional counterplan is an argument with its own set of problems" (p. 171), and references Keeshan and Ulrich's (1980) and Ganer's (1981) reservations about counterwarrants?

My first remark, at this point, must be that some discussion about these issues has occurred since 1981.[3] Regardless, if we presume these indictments on counterresolutional counterplans and counterwarrants valid, then the option of existential instantiation is foreclosed for the negative as well as the affirmative. However, if Panetta and Dolley wish to make their case that existential instantiation is valid for affirming the resolution, they cannot simultaneously reject the same option for the negative, especially since existential instantiation is premised on falsi-fiability not verification.

The foundations for existential instantiation, whereby a case (with or without plan) becomes a substitute instance for the resolution, is a specter, and if debating resolutions can be done deductively, it will not be through propositional reasoning. However, Panetta and Dolley's problems do not stop here. When you borrow, you are responsible, and existential instantiation is groundless as a methodology in deciding debates.

EXISTENTIAL INSTANTIATION IS
INAPPLICABLE TO DEBATE

There are three reasons why existential instantiation is inapplicable: first, absolute truth in a debate resolution is not our goal, and, consequently, the skeptical fixation Panetta and Dolley have about absoluteness is misplaced; second, debate is not deductive in nature; and third, the resolution is not a proposition.

Panetta and Dolley believe that the resolution as a concept "carries no intrinsic truth value standing alone" (p. 166). They never defined truth in that statement. Debate truth is a special type of truth. It is neither essential nor intrinsic, it is relative or corresponding.

In discussing truth, we have generally embraced two theories. The *coherence theory of truth* defines fundamental truths. That is, a statement is true or false if "it coheres or fails to cohere with a system of other statements; that it is a member of a system whose elements are related to each other by ties of logical implication as the elements of pure mathematics are related" (White, 1967, p. 130). This deductive system is very inappropriate to debate. For example, Hallett observed the following: "Word meanings are not true or false, accurate or inaccurate. . . . Employing words in their established senses does not by itself guarantee truth. . . . Words can be used with identical senses to assert or deny the same theory" (1988, p. 122).

A second *correspondence theory of truth* is closer to what we do in debate. It sets the view that "truth consists in some form of correspondence between belief and fact" (Pryor, 1967, p. 238). Linguistic, and, in this case, rhetorical truth is consistent with Hallett's principle of relative similarilty:

> [F]or a statement of fact, or informative utterance, to be true, it suffices that its use of terms resemble more closely the established uses of those terms than it does those of rival, incompatible terms (1988, p. 91).

This interpretation seems sufficient given that it describes the use of extended arguments and documentation in debate, and that in assigning truth value to the resolution, the act has no significance or impact beyond itself: Nothing changes, it is a performative act only. As Kincade wrote, "Truth functions in speech rather like a nod of the head in gesture" (1958, p. 394). Ezorsky agreed:

> The question, "What does it mean to say that a statement is true?" seems properly answered by, "Just what the statement means and nothing more". . . . [M]y pronouncement that a move is correct or an act legal does not imply that I made the move or performed that act (1963, p. 114).

Copi's view of truth is unstated, but it can be discerned from his writing. Copi wrote that "validity depends upon the ways in which simple statements are truth-functionally combined into compound statements" (1961, p. 302). This statement reads like the correspondence view of truth. Consequently, Panetta and Dolley's skepticism is inappropriate.

Furthermore, when Copi introduced singular propositions in his textbook, he did so with the statement: "There are, however, *other* types of arguments to which the validity criteria of the two preceding chapters (symbolic logic and extended arguments) do not apply" (p. 302). But Copi, and others like him, never assumed that substitute instances were a prerequisite for establishing a propositional function true.

Issues relating to validity tests for propositional functions are germane to this discussion. In noncompound propositional functions, the simplest of which are singular propositions, according to Copi, "Validity depends rather upon the inner logical structure of the noncompound statements involved" (p. 303). Copi classified the pertinent tests of validity into two groups: universal instantiation and generalization (UI and UG) and existential instantiation and generalization (EI and EG).

UI and UG, and tests of singular propositions, are rejected by Panetta and Dolley's interpretation. UI means that "any substitute instance of a propositional function can validly be inferred from its universal quantification" (pp. 315–316). However, since Panetta and Dolley deny a universal quantifier for the propositional statement, their resolution, this test is irrelevant.

UG means, "Since *any* substitution is true, all substitution instances are true, and hence the universal generalization of that propositional function is true also" (p. 318). For Copi, the any substitution instance would be a singular instance chosen from all substitution instances that possess a certain property sufficient when combined with the predicate term to enable us to accept the conclusion. The property must be *definitional* such that the substitute instance defines the propositional function. Copi gave us the following example:

> A geometer, seeking to prove that all triangles possess a certain property, may begin with the words: "Let ABC be any arbitrarily selected triangle." Then the geometer begins to reason about the triangle ABC, and establishes that it has the property in question. From this he concludes that all triangles have that property. Now what justifies his final conclusion? Granted of the traingle ABC that *it* has the property, why doesn't it follow that all triangles do? (p. 317)

The problem for Panetta and Dolley is that defining their "any" substitute instance challenges the coexistence of the resolution. All they ask is: Is the cat alive or dead? The question is: Does the cat being alive or dead tell us anything about all cats? By deciding the cat is alive does not make all cats in a similar predicament alive. Panetta and Dolley obliterate the propositional function as soon as the substitute instance is made. As such, UG is another moot proof of validity for their purpose.

Let's consider the remaining two proofs of validity: EI and EG. The wisdom that an existential quantifier can be assumed where none exists is discussed later, but it remains a prerequisite to this entire discussion. We, therefore, momentarily throw caution to the wind and assume that when a resolution is unquantified an existential quantifier should be included.

EI is "the principle that from the existential quantification of a propositional function we may infer the truth of its constant" (Copi, 1961, pp. 320–321). This means, if the proposition reads, "For A or any X, we get Y," then the truth of $X_1 \ldots X_n$ can be inferred from the proposition. EG works the other way and reads, "Since the existential quantification of a propositional function is true if and only if it has at least one true instance, from any true substitution instance of a propositional function we may validly infer its existential quantification" (Copi, 1961, p. 321). Evidently, EG is the principle test embraced by Panetta and Dolley.

EG means: if I substitute "graduate schools in economics" for "U.S. higher education" in the 1983 CEDA topic on sacrificing quality for institutional survival, the first step must be to insert an existential quantifier. In addition to Madsen and Chandler's reservations regarding "filling-in" the "missing modifier" (1988, pp. 33–34), my view, evidenced in detail later, is that ambiguity caused by the absence of an explicit quantifier does not justify existentially instantive fill-ins. Furthermore, if any fill-ins occur, a universal quantifier is presumptive.

As a result, whoever inserts an existential quantifier accepts a proof burden, which is assumed by the affirmative or negative, depending on whether we are speaking about a squirrel case or a grotesque counterwarrant. That proof burden can only be met when we examine the understanding or knowledge character of the original propositional function. In nonpolicy debating, we have whole resolution and hasty generalization, both of which are premised on improving the level of understanding the resolution. While Panetta and Dolley's assertion that specificity increases thoroughness may implicate whole resolution, it ignores hasty generalization.

Absent a justification of the fill-in quantifier by the side making the instantiation, a justification intrinsic to the propositional function being examined (specific to the topic), EI and EG can only lead to the observation that *existential instantiation never can prove anything but itself true unless the propositional function from which it was drawn is written and understood as existentially quantified.*

Panetta and Dolley foresaw this universality conundrum, and they argued: "(N)ot every resolution is universally qualified. Many exist which are existentially quantified" (p. 167). As an example, they use a resolution engaging the indefinite article "a," which, of course, is existentially quantified. Then, to whet the devious appetites of some of their readers, they suggest that should we assume all resolutions are existentially quantified, then inductive overgeneralization is evaded. For resolutions, involving "some," "many," or even "a" or "an" as quantifiers, they are absolutely correct, but those are not prevalent in debate.

Panetta and Dolley dubbed resolutions without explicit quantifiers "propositional statements suffer(ing) from suppressed quantification" (p. 168). They further suggested that a particular quantifier such as "a" or "one" must be preferred over a universal, or near-universal quantifier, such as "all" or "most." Then, they forewarned us that "confusing universal and particular quantities [not qualities, a misprint in Panetta and Dolley] in an argument or inference" (Angeles, 1981, p. 233 and Panetta and Dolley, 1989, p. 168) risks the quantifier shift fallacy. Why this problem doesn't apply to assuming a nonuniversal, but does when you assume a universal or near-universal quantifier is never explained.

Earlier in Panetta and Dolley's article, they wrote that "academic debate theory has not thus far directly addressed the question of resolutional quantification" (p. 167). First, I suggest they read some of the scholarship in nonpolicy debate that has begun to do just that.[4] Regardless, that hardly excuses them from the blatant assertion that a case/plan examining a minority, if not a minutiae, of a resolution is logically justified. Nowhere do Panetta and Dolley give reasons why the focus of debate should not be on all, or at least most, of the resolution beyond the belabored dilemma about poorly worded resolutions embodying contradictory instances, the dual-directional resolution, an issue addressed later.

Panetta and Dolley worked from the premise: When in doubt, instantiate. However, there is at least one rule in quantification: "To make sense of quantification, the variables have to keep their references as we pass from the actual world to another, which is physically possible" (Follesdal, 1971, p. 58), hence the first problem: Instantiation reduces the range of the predicate function in the resolution. As an example, for the topic "poverty threatens political stability," once "some" is added before "poverty" or "among blacks" inserted after "poverty," "political stability" acquires a very specific context that may substantially alter the range of issues relevant to a discussion about political stability.

When confronted by suppressed quantification, universal quantification is always preferred to secure knowledge. "To *think* an object and to *know* an object are thus by no means the same thing" (Kant, 1934, p. 99). Regarding quantities, Kant left his viewpoint unambiguous. "If, on the other hand, we compare a singular with a universal judgment, merely as knowledge, in respect to quantity, the singular stands to the universal entity as unity to infinity, and is therefore in itself essentially different from the universal" (1934, p. 70). In categorical logic, universal quantification enables us to understand the interrelatedness of our environment. Studying all or none explains to us the material causes of things. That was one of Aristotle's arguments in *Metaphisica*.

Since instantiations drawn from words in the resolution are merely subsets of the universal and fail by agreement via parametric definition to stray outside of the universal, then interrelatedness is clearly less evident to the instantiator, while it may be unavoidable to the universalizor.

Furthermore, identity theory says that "interchangeability is the linguistic correlate of identity" (Wilson, 1959, p. 41). In discusssing the necessity of a definition of language, Wilson differentiated language from nonlanguage and developed criteria of adequacy, one of which maintains that a language can only be identical to itself if and only if "each expression of [its] common vocabulary has the same significance" (1959, p. 20). English is English when two speakers of English can meet and say "military intervention" and understand the concept as it relates to the beaches of Grenada, the skies over Baghdad, and the streets of Panama City. Instantiation denies this level of knowing and simply threatens language as effective communication since it de facto raises private meaning to the status of public meaning.

Finally, the quantifier may not be unintentionally suppressed in resolutions; it may be naive to assume the framers have no purpose behind leaving off a quantifier. Turbayne, in discussing metaphors, wrote: "Some things—very different this time—get the same name because, although they have very few things in common, either they may have a special likeness that someone is interested in or someone is interested in creating the likeness" (1962, p. 76). Maybe the ambiguous term was chosen for its ambiguity.

While Panetta and Dolley claimed specificity is preferred, they never can prove it is intentional by the framers and those people who vote for the NDT policy topic. While policy debate (NDT and NFL) may encourage instantiation as a competitive practice, nonpolicy debate (CEDA and LD) accepts instantiations if and only if they meet tests. For example, CEDA debate has stated its view clealy: The focus of debate in CEDA *is* the resolution (Walker, 1989), not any instantiation, unless that instantiation is sufficient to evade the fallacy of hasty generalization (Type II error).

My second major argument is that debate is not deductive, but existential instantiation is. The methodology is inapplicable. The inductive method in debate has been defended elsewhere, most recently in nonpolicy debate scholarship (see Berube 1983/1987, 1989 and McGee 1988), and their works will not be re-examined here.

Panetta and Dolley reject inductive methodology. As previously indicated, we do not search for absolute truth in debate, and Panetta and Dolley's and others' fixation with inductive skepticism must stop. "We constantly draw inferences and act on them. This kind of inference permeates all our empirical knowledge, all our actions, decisions and intentions" (Dilman, 1973, p. 30). As we will see later, it is through induction that subjunctive generalizations, policy resolutions, are fashioned. Stove put it clearest: "Skepticism about induction . . . stems from a certain *feeling*, a diffused or 'cosmic' feeling of insecurity" (1986, p. 106).

At this point, two additional arguments about induction seem justified. First, induction makes knowledge; deduction does not. "(I)n induction, our reasoning takes us beyond what we already know, it widens our knowledge. We can thus move from what we see to what we do not at the time see" (Dilman, 1973, p. 29). This is the working philosophy behind intercollegiate debating. It's why we change topics annually or semi-annually, and it's why Panetta and Dolley feel that increased specificity, variety in new ideas, increases thoroughness (p. 170). In comparison, Stove wrote that "after 2,500 years of hoping and searching . . . it can hardly be said that formal logic has been rich in positive results. . . . We didn't get where we are today by adopting . . . the Stone Age philosophy of cases rule" (1986, p. 131).

Second, induction cannot be more fallible than deduction because the premise-to-premise-to-conclusion leap in a traditional syllogism is nondeductively validated.

> [A philosopher] must either embrace inductive skepticism, or abandon deductivism. He must, that is, either affirm that a proposition about the observed is never a reason to believe a proposition about the unobserved; or he must admit that one proposition can be a reason to believe another, with the inference from the one to the other being valid (deductive). As the former alternative is scarcely compatible with sanity, most philosophers have sensibly preferred the latter. That is, they have abandoned deductivism, even if they have done so, in most cases, neither very consciously nor very enthusiastically. But to abandon deductivism is to acknowledge the existence of nondeductive logic (Dilman, 1973, pp. 132–133).

Assuming that any rival to deductivism must be a formal system, philosophers have searched for rules, rules they cannot find; since induction is based purely on confirmation, the same force makes inferences from one deductive premise to another on to a conclusion a sensible exercise in reasoning.

In debate, we are not searching for ultimate answers. The context must set the methodology. "Given the purpose for which we embark on [an explanation] and the kind of inquiry that is in question, our request, for further explanation will become pointless beyond a certain point, and the information they call for will cease to contribute to the understanding we all are seeking" (Dilman, 1973, p. 78).

My third major argument is that the resolution is not a proposition, but Panetta and Dolley treat it as such. "A proposition is a statement with truth value [and] in standard logic only two values are permitted: true and false" (Evans, 1982, p. 115). Panetta and Dolley, however, claim that "the resolution . . . carries *no* intrinsic truth value standing alone" (p. 166). Being the case, it must then be false. Deducing from a false premise may yield a valid argument, but the conclusion will be false. Accordingly, "a false substitution instance . . . ought not to be adopted" (Panetta and Dolley, p. 166). In nonpolicy debate it ought to be rejected. If the resolution is not a proposition, then maybe, propositional reasoning, which is deductive, cannot be assumed appropriate to analyze the logical structure of natural language arguments of the sort we find in debate.

EXISTENTIAL INSTANTIATION IS MEANINGLESS

Panetta and Dolley's theory deserves to be rejected on a semantic level as well, for existential instantiation in natural language arguments is meaningless.

First, existential instantiation is not implicitly meaningful. Labeling a young man Amos and studying Amos does not give us the full meaning of manness. Furthermore, this process would only enable people who have met Amos to know what manness means. Instantiation and indication simply do not constitute meaning. "If the definition explains the meaning of a word, surely it can't be essential that you should have heard the word before" (Wittgenstein, 1969, p. 2). Indeed, parametric definition necessitates illustration in terms of an existential instantiation. That explains nothing. "As soon as you think of replacing the mental image by, say, a painted one, and as soon as the image loses its occult character, it ceases to seem to impart any life to the sentence at all" (Wittgenstein, 1969, p. 5).

Don't we learn through illustration? Yes, but the process is much thicker. Consider a young father, Alfred, walking with his child, Sarah, in a city park. Sarah stops, bends down, and picks up a maple leaf. Alfred says, "That is a leaf." A few moments later, Sarah picks up a second leaf, an oak leaf. Alfred says, "That is a leaf." Sarah looks up to

Alfred, looks back at both leaves in her hands and says, "Leaf." What Sarah learned is the understanding of the general term "leaf." The particular leaves were only "a means to the end of producing 'in her' an idea which we imagine to be some kind of general image. . . . We are inclined to think that the general idea of a leaf is something like a visual image, but one which only contains what is common to all leaves" (Wittgenstein, 1969, p. 18) within that context. If Alfred pointed to a page of a book discarded on the ground flipping in the breeze and said, "leaf," if he pointed to a thin sheet of metal and said, "leaf," if he pointed to a hinged tabletop in a shop window and said, "leaf," or if he pointed to a discarded metal strip that was once part of a leaf spring and said, "leaf," the commonality necessary for establishing meaning of "leaf" as an organic thing is obfuscated, and Sarah would be confused.

This is metaphorical reasoning, a particularly inductive process, but if this process of discerning commonalities is to minimize error, *any* leaf will not do as *any* singular instantiation will not do. Copi's use of "singular" does not mean any are all equal or minimally sufficient. A singular proposition "asserts that a particular individual possessed a specified property" (Copi, 1961, p. 303). But, Copi goes on to write that "it is clear that one and the same subject term can occur in different singular propositions. . . . It is also clear that one and the same predicate terms can occur in different singular propositions" (p. 303). This being the case, we need to find instantiations that are near archetypal or at least representative, and to test that status we again are forced to return to *representativeness*.

Failure to do so results in what I wish to call the *fallacy of proparage*. Parametric definitions of a resolution are connected with the idea that the meaning of a word, phrase, clause, or sentence is an image, or a thing, a case with or without a per se plan, connected to the word—sentence. This roughly means we are looking at words—sentences as though they all were proper names, and we thus confuse the bearer of the name with the meaning of the name (see Wittgenstein, 1969, p. 18). On a simple level, conventional English differentiates proper from nonproper names by capitalizing the first letter of proper names. This procedure is used to minimize confusion. Parametric definition nullifies this convention and is unacceptable. Existential instantiation is unable to give meaning to a resolution absent an a priori requirement.

Secondly, existential instantiation is not explicity meaningful. Using a substitute instance to assign meaning to a resolution denies the function of topicality. Topicality in debate exists to test a proof to determine its pertinence. That test, in all forms, answers the question: Does the resolution mean the claim? My concern is that existential instantiation does not provide sufficient meaning to answer this question. Wittgenstein held that the proper way of understanding and resolving philosophical problems lies in arriving at a correct conception of language (McGinn, 1984, p. xi). McGinn took this view one step further. "We need to be clear about the nature of meaning before we can hope to be clear about anything else" (p. xi).

Wittgenstein defined what meaning is not. In *Philosophical Investigations*, he wrote:

> Meaning is as little an experience as intending. But what distinguishes an experience as intending? . . . . They have no experience–content. For the contents (images, for instance) which accompany and illustrate them are not the meaning or intending (1953, p. 217e).

Wittgenstein gave three reasons: First, understanding is a dispositional and not an occurrent condition of a person; second, a great variety of images may accompany understanding a particular word, either for the same person on different occasions or for different people; and third, there is no logical route from the intrinsic properties of an image to the meaning of the associated word (see McGinn, 1984, pp. 5–7).

When Panetta and Dolley engaged existential instantiation to indicate the resolution, they overclaimed the function of indicators as tools of meaning. "Indicators indicate what they indicate because an empirical correlation holds between their occurrence and the occurrence of the thing, fact, event, feature . . . indicated" (von Savigny, 1988, p. 5). If Panetta and Dolley viewed the relationship between the resolution and the instantiation as from resolution to instantiation (a quantum sense), they can only claim that the instantive proof is valid of and for the instantiation, as was discussed in the previous section. However, this thesis is somewhat at odds with their statement (p. 166) that instantiation may function to prove resolutions true, for when the relationship between a resolution and an instantiation can be probatively ambidirectional (a parallel universe sense), they not only tempt induction, which Panetta and Dolley reject, but also, as an indicator, the instantiation would need to meet some fundamental burdens, like representativeness.

For example, "An indicator cannot be used to indicate something unless it is discovered beforehand that it indicates the thing indicated" (von Savigny, 1988, p. 5). This would suggest that the relevance of an instantiation must be established a priori, and "discovering what indicators indicate means discovering the empirical correlations between the indicator and the thing indicated" (von Savigny, 1988, p. 5). How such a relationship can be established was examined by von Savigny.

> The degree of reliability depends on the form of the empirical correlation; the indicator is more reliable the higher the statistical probability of the thing indicated relative to the indicator (p. 6).

This bring us fully around to the rules of biased sample and biased statistics and back to hasty generalization unless Panetta and Dolley have discovered a methodology they've yet to reveal.

MISCONCEPTIONS AND MISCONCLUSIONS REVEALED

This section discusses two final issues: First, if we grant Panetta and Dolley's premises, are their conclusions applicable to nonpolicy debating; and second, is existential instantiation the proper conclusion for their premises.

First, policy and nonpolicy resolutions are sufficiently different such that Panetta and Dolley's conclusions regarding topical counterplans in policy debate have no analogue enabling the affirmative parametric definition in nonpolicy debate. Whether it justifies parametrics in policy debate will have to wait for another paper.

Theorists, including Matlon (1978), Zarefsky (1980), Warnick (1981) and, currently, Church and Wilbanks (1986), have gone through much trouble categorizing resolutions as policy, value, and fact, and all they seem to have managed to do has been to make statements about presumption and burden of proof that still do not enjoy consensus, and further subcategorize resolutions without deeply distinguishing their most fundamental difference: their mood.

What is mood? Mood "refers to verbal inflections or to syntactic contrasts that (1) denote by formal opposition the relations between one verb in the sentence and another verb structure; and (2) express a notional contrast that supposedly indicates the attitude of the speaker or writer toward the action or state of affairs expressed by the verb" (Harsh, 1968, pp. 12–13). In English, we utilize three moods, and we utilize each one "depending on whether the speaker or writer considers a syntactic structure as stating a fact (indicative mood), issuing a command (imperative mood), or expressing a nonfact or modification of fact (subjunctive mood)" (Harsh, 1968, p.13). We do not debate imperative statements per se, so the following examines the differences between the indicative (statement of fact and opinion) and the subjunctive (statement expressing a nonfact—what ought or ought not to be).

Policy resolutions, with or without that ubiquitous "should," are written in the subjunctive while most nonpolicy resolutions appear in the indicative. When that does not seem to occur, it is because sentence structure has been misshapen and upon its rewriting easily conforms to subjunctive form. Poutsma, in his discussion of modal categories in the subjunctive pattern, listed the auxiliaries "may, might, should, will, and would" (1926, pp. 13, 116–202) as used in forming the subjunctive. Notice the ubiquitous "should."

Some remarks about the consequent differences. First, policy resolutions are much broader and encompass far more instantiations that nonpolicy resolutions. James found it difficult to analyze subjunctive conditionals because its range "seems to overlap . . . with uses of the indicative" (1986, p. 6). He also discovered that the subjunctive had no temporal significance (p. 7). Semanticists define the subjunctive and its use as intentionally ambiguous, "which accounts for its many uses" (James, 1986, pp. 10–11). Since the claims made in indicative generalizations can be subsumed into the subjunctive universe of possibilities, the nonpolicy debater's job is more manageable by orders of magnitude.

Second, while subjunctive generalizations are ambiguous by nature, they can entail dual-directional realities. The indicative generalizations do not, short of misinterpretation. A fact or an opinion, by defintion, cannot be dual-directional. Facts are consensually sanctioned realities, and when two facts collide, they lose their factness and become beliefs. Statements of opinion are a bit trickier, nonetheless opinion that competes with itself only does so when certain additional or substitute variables interfere with the propositional function described in the indicative generalization.

The third difference is the best argument for Panetta and Dolley's theory. According to John Pollock, subjunctive conditionals, if absent a quantifier, should *not* be examined universally. Pollock has examined this thesis and concluded that "the attempt to analyze subjunctive generalizations . . . as universally quantified subjunctive conditionals is essentially bankrupt" (1976, p. 48); he claimed this to be true because a strict finding of truth for a subjunctive conditional would encourage the discoverer to consider even physically impossible objects.

However, Pollock's findings are suspect. His conclusions are highly modified by context; his illustrations are drawn from the natural sciences. His examples do not examine the problematic structures of natural language arguments. Though subjunctive conditionals should not be universally quantified, it does not mean they should, in turn, be all existentially quantified as one or any. Despite these reservations, Pollock's work is due a much deeper examination in resolving this issue than given here.

While Pollock's argument seems to support Panetta and Dolley's thesis, consider in conclusion here that he wrote subjunctive generalizations "start by confirming a number of generalizations inductively" (Pollock, 1976, p. 49). Oops! They are aggregated as a corpus of facts and opinion sufficient to suggest a conditional statement. Hence, we get a subjunctive generalization inductively. So, while Pollock believes universalizing a subjunctive conditional may be senseless, he would not find much solace in a process like Panetta and Dolley's instantiation, which is drawn from deductive method in analyzing a conditional that was constructed inductively.

In contrast, nonpolicy resolutions are distinctively different not only because they precede policy resolutions, but also because if Pollock's argument makes any sense, then subjunctive generalizations are built from instantiations. This would suggest that indicative generalizations are already instantiations. If they are universal instantiations, then they would need to be examined as a totality, but if they are, instead, existential instantiations, then applying Panetta and Dolley's theory to justify further instantiations threatens the Derridaen nightmare, an infinite regression.

Second, existential instantiation is not the proper conclusion for Panetta and Dolley's arguments about resolutional focus. Panetta and Dolley assume that resolutions cannot be the focus of debates, and commit a gross fallacy of sorts by presuming that all of the resolution would need to be defended by the affirmative in order for the resolution to remain the focus of debate. That simply is not the case (Berube, 1989). However, granting them this assumption, they found it necessary to engage existential instantiation as the mean to resolving the shortcomings of composing resolutions. This conclusion would be justified if and only if the solution for problematical resolutions would lie outside their composition, but that also cannot be the case. Panetta and Dolley believe "most resolutions are so broad that affirming them in their entirety is of little value" (p. 169). They believe that existential instantiation "is preferable to debating general resolutions" (p. 170). Further, they assert that "the more specific the [instantiation], the more thoroughly its desirability is assessed" (p. 170). Finally, they suggested that "the imposition of an arbitrary set of standards to assess its validity has very little real world application" (p. 169).

This argument fails for at least three reasons. First, granting that most rather than all resolutions are overly broad bespeaks to composing more limiting resolutions, obviously a task that has been accomplished on some occasions. This is an especially compelling conclusion to draw if we grant Panetta and Dolley their conclusion that increased specificity increases thoroughness.

Second, no rationale is given why infinitely regressive specificity increases thoroughness without exception. For that matter, overlimiting instantiations may sacrifice thoroughness for triviality and redundancy such that postulates repeated over and over again approach the status of axioms for little if any reason but their incessant repetition. Witness the spring CEDA handgun resolution. If specificity should not be assumed infinitely regressive in their argument, then where should we reach a barrier and how?

This bring some to a third objection. Panetta and Dolley assert that imposing a set of standards, such as tests of hasty generalization, is arbitrary. But why? (See Berube, 1989, for a discussion of standards of representativeness.) If Panetta and Dolley believed these standards, and others preceding and incorporated in them are arbitrary, then they should at least have rebutted them directly. Furthermore, Panetta and Dolley asserted that standards of this sort have little real world application, but failed to consider that these standards were drawn from the experimental method in science. If there is little real world application in drawing from the scientific method of Francis Bacon et al, maybe Panetta and Dolley's real world needs further examination because it is not the world shared by their peers.

Panetta and Dolley next argue that some resolutions embody dual-directionality. While this indictment may apply to some policy resolutions, it does not seem to relate to nonpolicy resolutions, which claim a subject-predicate relationship that articulates an effect rather than suggesting an effectuation.

Ignoring such, Panetta and Dolley claim that composing unidirectional resolutions is not the answer because "the framers cannot anticipate before the season begins the numerous (and sometimes devious) ways in which the directional terms in the topic can be construed to include the opposite" (p. 170). Why the element of discerning dual-directionality is exclusively the province of hindsight is never explained. Panetta and Dolley and others have been able to discover this phenomenon in retrospect, which more probably bespeaks the fanciful, if not incompetent, treatment of the composition of resolutions by framers other than themselves. If discussion and even debate by students after a resolution has been voted upon can discover dual-directionality, there is no reason why a similar process in the early compositional phases cannot produce the same discovery.

Panetta and Dolley furthermore, indict nondirectional resolutions, whatever they may happen to be. However, there is no reason why the only option is between dual-directional and nondirectional resolutions; the alternative of unidirectional ones remains.

Panetta and Dolley finally add that resolutional advocacy decreases the need for precise language, since in policy debates, affirmatives may replan as necessary to evade objections regarding flawed plans. Why this practice, one I choose not to defend here, does not improve our understanding of a resolution is never addressed by the writers, a burden their argument demands. Beyond their featureless claim that it "would destroy the real value of debate" (p. 172), a value they seem to believe is akin to a compulsive trek into triviality, Panetta and Dolley offer no rationale why discussing features should be preferred over discussing issues.

Next, when Panetta and Dolley describe case/plan selection as sometimes devious, they suggest that ill-wording may not be intrinsic to improperly worded resolutions at all, but rather to any resolution when the debaters are deviously motivated. Of course, if ill-wording has been peculiar to resolutions in the past, the solution would have been to improve the employment of more precise language in the composing process. If that is not possible, Panetta and Dolley need to make that case, but they did not.

Lastly, Panetta and Dolley rejected resolutional analysis because it encourages counterwarrants and counterresolutional counterplans. The logic of this claim was examined earlier in this essay.

CONCLUDING COMMENTS

Bile wrote way back in 1987 that "parametric focus makes [obscure examples] theoretically sound" (p. 8). We know that is true. What we do not need is a convoluted theory to justify a practice for the mere sake of its justification. It is my conclusion that parametric topicality has no sound theoretical basis, and this paper has tried to extend Rhodes' 1981 observation that the parametric function of a debate resolution "seems to have no real current underpinning" (p. 493).

While Panetta and Dolley test their contribution to debate theory by examining it against the three criteria of enhancing the quality of debate, enhancing its educational value, and ensuring equal ground (p. 174) (a series of conclusions that also need an examination beyond my passing reference in this paper), I feel that a fourth criterion, hinted at by Rhodes, needs to be added: Any contribution to debate theory must be logically sound lest we lose sight of what we're doing. We're educators first, and competitors second.

My concluding comment: There is a fertile middle ground between debating the entire resolution and existential instantiations; it is example analysis with controlling tests to reduce the inductive fallacy of hasty generalization. Analysis on this subject has been published elsewhere (Berube 1983/1987 and 1989).

Notes

1. The debate over whole resolution is over. While Bile (1987) may have inadvertently led readers to assume that he meant that affirmative should debate the entire resolution, that was never his intention. Debating the entire resolution is problematical; debating the whole resolution is not. For Bile and others, to debate the whole resolution is consistent with

Berube's (1983/1987 and 1989) position that examples may inductively enable the affirmative to make a truth statement about the resolution. Both Berube and Bile suggest that some examples are better than others. For Bile those examples would involve a sufficiently large subset of the resolution. For Berube those examples would need to be both representative and sufficiently large. For a summary of this observation, see Truesdale (1990).

2. Unrepresentative or insufficiently large subsets of the resolution commit the fallacies of biased statistics known as Type II error or hasty generalization.

3. See Rhodes (1981), Mayer (1982), Berube (1983, 1987), Simons (1984), Rhodes and Pfau (1985), Tolbert and Hunt (1985/1987), Rhodes and White (1986), Adams and Wilkins (1987), McGee (1988), and Berube (1989).

4. See Berube (1983/1987), Biggers (1985), Bile (1987), Madsen and Chandler (1988), and Berube (1989).

References

Adams, N. and Wilkins, T. (1987). "The Role of Justification in Topic Analysis." *CEDA Yearbook* 7: 21–26.

Angeles, P. A. (1981). *Dictionary of Philosophy*. New York: Barnes & Noble.

Berube, D. (1983/1987). "Debating Hasty Generalization." In D. Thomas and J. Hart, eds. *Advanced Debate: Readings in Theory, Practice, and Teaching.* Lincolnwood, IL: National Textbook Co. 483–89.

Berube, D. (1989). "Hasty Generalization Revisited, Part One: On Being Representative Examples." *CEDA Yearbook* 9: 43–53.

Biggers, T. (1985). "A Single Swallow and Other Leaps of Faith." *CEDA Yearbook* 6: 54–62.

Bile, J. (1987). "When the Whole is Greater Than the Sum of the Parts: The Implications of Holistic Resolutional Focus." *CEDA Yearbook* 8: 8–15.

Church, R. and Wilbanks, C. (1986). *Values and Policies in Controversy: An Introduction to Argumentation and Debate*. Scottsdale, AZ: Gorsuch Scarisbrick.

Copi, I. (1961). *Introduction to Logic*. 2nd ed. New York: MacMillan.

Dilman, I. (1973). *Induction and Deduction: A Study in Wittgenstein*. New York, Barnes & Noble.

Dolley, S. (1978). "Apocalypse When?: Determining and Comparing Catastrophic Risks." *Fertile Ground: Debater's Research Guide*. Winston-Salem, NC: Wake Forest University. 7–8.

Evans, J. St. B. T. (1982). *The Psychology of Deductive Reasoning*. London: Routledge & Kegan Paul.

Ezorsky, G. (1963). "Truth in Context," *The Journal of Philosophy* 6 (Feb.): 113–35.

Follesdal, D. (1971). "Quantification into Causal Contexts." In L. Linsky, ed. *Reference and Modality*. Oxford: Oxford University Press.

Ganer, P. M. (1981). "Counter-Warrant: An Idea Whose Time Has Not Yet Come." In G. Ziegelmueller and J. Rhodes, eds. *Argument in Transition: Proceedings of the Third Summer Conference on Argumentation*. Annandale, VA: Speech Communication Association. 476–84.

Hallett, G. (1988). *Language and Truth*. New Haven: Yale University Press.

Harsh, W. (1968). *The Subjunctive in English*. University, AL: University of Alabama Press.

James, F. (1986). *Semantics of the English Subjunctive.* Vancouver: University of British Columbia Press.

Kant, I. (1934). *Immanuel Kant's Critique of Pure Reason.* trans. N. Smith. New York: Macmillan.

Keeshan, M. and Ulrich, W. (1980). "The Counter-Warrant as a Negative Strategy." *Journal of the American Forensic Association* 16: 199.

Kincade, J. (1958). "On the Performatory Theory of Truth." *Mind* 60 (July): 394–98.

Lichtman, Allan J., Charles Garvin, and Jerome Corsi (1973). "The Alternative-Justification Affirmative: A New Case Form." *Journal of the American Forensic Association* 10 (Fall): 59–69.

Madsen, A. and Chandler, R. (1988). "When the Whole Becomes a Black Hole: Implications of the Holistic Perspective." *CEDA Yearbook* 9: 30–37.

Matlon, R. (1978). "Debating Propositions of Value." *Journal of the American Forensic Association* 14 (Spring): 194–204.

McGee, B. (1988). "Assessing Counterwarrants: Understanding Induction in Debate Practice." *CEDA Yearbook* 9: 63–70.

Mayer, M. (1982). "Extending Counterwarrants: The Counterresolutional Counterplan." *Journal of the American Forensic Association* 19: 122–27.

McGinn, C. (1984). *Wittgenstein on Meaning: An Interpretation and Evalution.* Oxford: Basil Blackwell.

Panetta, E. and Dolley, S. (1989). "The Topical Counterplan: A Competitive Policy Alternative." *Argumentation and Advocacy: Journal of the American Forensic Association* 25 (Winter): 165–77.

Pollock, J. (1967). *Subjunctive Reasoning.* Dordrecht: D. Riedel.

Poutsma, H. (1926). *A Grammar of Late Modern English.* Part II, sec. II. Groningen: P. Noordhoff.

Pryor, A. (1967). "Correspondence Theory of Truth." *Encyclopedia of Philosophy.* v. 2. New York: MacMillan. 223–32.

Rhodes, J. (1981). "A Defense of the Counterwarrant as Negative Argument." In G. Ziegelmueller and J. Rhodes, eds. *Argument in Transition: Proceedings of the Third Summer Conference on Argumentation.* Annandale, VA: Speech Communication Association. 822–36.

Rhodes, J. and Pfau, M. W. (1985). "Resolution or Example: A Reply to Herbeck and Katsulas." *Journal of the American Forensic Association* 21 (Winter): 146–49.

Rhodes, J. and White, A. C. (1986). "A Reply to Herbeck and Katsulas." *Journal of the American Forensic Association* 22 (Winter): 176–79.

Simon, R. (1984). "The Case Against Counter-Warrants in Value Debate." *CEDA Yearbook* 4: 49–53.

Stove, D. (1986). *The Rationality of Induction.* Oxford: Clarendon Press.

Tolbert, G. and Hunt, S. (1985). "Counterwarrants: A Method for Testing Topical Justification in CEDA Debate." *CEDA Yearbook* 5: 21–28.

Truesdale, M. (1990). "A Reappraisal of a Language-Based Justification for Holistic Resolutional Focus." Paper presented at the Speech Communication Association Convention, Chicago, Nov. 2, 1990.

Turbayne, C. (1962). *The Myth of Metaphor.* New Haven: Yale University Press.

von Savigny, E. (1988). *The Social Foundations of Meaning.* Berlin: Springer-Verlag.

Walker, G. (1989). "The Counterplan as Argument in Nonpolicy Debate." *Journal of the American Forensic Association* 25: 178–91.

Warnick, B. (1981). "Arguing Value Propositions." *Journal of the American Forensic Association* 18 (Fall): 109–19.

White, A. (1967). "Coherence Theory of Truth." *Encyclopedia of Philosophy*. v. 2. New York: MacMillan 130–33.

Wilson, N. (1959). *The Concept of Language*. Toronto: University of Toronto Press.

Wittgenstein, L. (1969). *The Blue and Brown Books*. Oxford: Basil Blackwell.

Wittgenstein, L. (1953). *Philosophical Investigations*. Oxford: Basil Blackwell.

Wolf, F. (1988). *Parallel Universes: The Search for Other Worlds*. New York: Touchstone Book.

Zarefsky, D. (1980). "Criteria for Evaluating Nonpolicy Argument." *CEDA Yearbook* 1: 9–16.

KEY TERMS

conditional counterplan
competitiveness
counterplan
fiat
mutual exclusivity

net benefits
parametrics
permutation
topical counterplan
utopian counterplan

DISCUSSION

1. Do you think Lichtman and Rohrer would agree with Herbeck's views on competitiveness? Why?

2. Do you think Lichtman and Rohrer would agree with Panetta on topicality? Why?

3. Some high school coaches urge their debaters not to run counterplans. Using judge adaptation and paradigm theory, explain why this could be a justifiable position.

4. Consider the 1991–92 high school policy debate topic—"RESOLVED: That the federal government should significantly increase social services to homeless individuals in the United States." Is a counterplan of reinstitutionalizing homeless mental patients competitive against any affirmative that offers homeless mental patients social services in the community setting?

5. Compare and contrast a stock issue, hypothesis testing, and a policy systems view of the basic counterplan burdens.

6. Against a topic that advocates federal government action, discuss the negative's ability to fiat an international agent counterplan.

7. What would Lichtman, et al., say concerning Panetta and Dolley's views on topical counterplans?

Part Eight

Theoretical Issues in Nonpolicy Debate

Although the status of publications in nonpolicy debate theory and practice is still in a relative catch-up phase when compared with the ongoing flow of policy-oriented text materials, the articles in this section demonstrate the increasing sophistication of nonpolicy debate theory. Most of the articles in the section are new to this edition, indicating not only that complexity has increased, but also that nonpolicy theory is undergoing a significant degree of upheaval.

One starting point for analyzing nonpolicy resolutions was the absence of the word "should." Another was the open-ended character of the subject matter. In most instances, resolutions chosen for debate did not specify or even imply any particular course of action. Upon what should a nonpolicy debate be based? How should a debate be initiated? What consititutes a prima facie case in the absence of any proposed plan? How does a debater go about proving a nonpolicy case? How does a judge determine who wins in a nonpolicy debate?

These and other questions called for answers which were not to be found readily in the most familiar debate textbooks and journals. Initially, nonpolicy resolutions were classified primarily as value resolutions, though not absolutely or purely so. (The premise leading to this classification assumes that there are only three categories of resolutions: fact, value, and policy. If no plan is entailed by the resolution, and "should" does not appear in the wording of the resolution, then the resolution cannot be a policy resolution. Thus, it must be either a fact resolution or a value resolution. The presence of vague and ambiguous modifiers, and implicit or explicit value judgments residing in a resolution, make it impossible to classify it as a factual statement. Thus, it must be a value resolution.) Searching for guidance in case analysis and case construction, debaters, coaches, and theorists searched the literature for discussions of values construction. Traditional rhetoric and argumentation offered few guidelines for nonpolicy debate. The quest led into disparate disciplines such as psychology, social psychology, sociology, philosophy, linguistics, political theory, ethics, and even aesthetics. Some investigators are now suggesting promising new leads may be found in religious studies, theology, popular culture, semiotics, literary criticism, mythology, and folklore.

It is significant to note that some of the earlier influential articles in nonpolicy debate were produced by leaders in policy debate. (This pattern of crossover versatility among debate theorists and writers continues today.) A common thread running through the earlier nonpolicy debate literature was its overt adaptation of the terminology and many of the concepts of policy debate theory. Yet nonpolicy debate theory and practice were different from their policy debate counterparts. As is true of many disciplines, some of the better theoretical work consisted of responses to earlier efforts. Just as CEDA itself grew out of dissatisfaction with policy debate practices in contests and tournaments, so did CEDA's theory arise out of the efforts of scholars and educators to correct and refine the most obviously inappropriate theories and practices that were then currently available.

Nonpolicy debate is difficult to judge, in large part because of the difficulty of identifying—and of applying—the appropriate standards, or criteria. Goulet and Bauer explore the practical application of criteria in debate, and offer some guidelines for their appropriate use (and cautions against inappropriate use).

Finally, the sticky question of *How?* is raised by O'Dor. In the final analysis can there be an intelligible method for weighing values? Regardless of the chosen standards or criteria, how can a fair and acceptable judgment be made by comparing the extent and degree to which the affirmative and negative meet the stipulated criteria? In a nonpolicy debate is it possible to quantify or weigh arguments? Do terms like "extent" and "degree" have any content? In a sophisticated discussion of measurement theory, O'Dor addresses these issues and others. First, he considers the theoretical basis for using quantitative measures in policy deliberations and shows the limitations that exist on both the suitability and the applicability of measurement theory in actual practice. In the absence of complete information for weighing costs and benefits, analysts use best indicators, which are most accessible. From there, O'Dor takes the next step to considering how, and in what manner, measurement theory can help the nonpolicy theorist and debater achieve the best approximation of meeting ideal criteria for decision.

Matlon's original essay on "Debating Questions of Value" established stock issues for value debate and was reprinted in our Third Edition. At the close of the past decade, Matlon was asked to reevaluate his ideas in light of what happened in the debate laboratory. His comments and recommendations may be surprising to those who have not already read them, and we are pleased to reprint his latest article here. One of Matlon's recommendations is that we consider debating questions of fact. Hart and McGee, in an essay written for this volume, attempt to identify where areas of status would appear in debates over a fact resolution. Ulrich discusses the nature of the nonpolicy topic.

Herbeck and Wong advocate the appropriateness of considering the policy implications of nonpolicy questions. Colbert and Thomas offer some stock issues in the development of offcase positions. Berube examines whether those same offcase positions need to be intrinsic to the resolution.

The most fierce theoretical controversy in nonpolicy debating flows from topicality argumentation: Though a plan is not required in nonpolicy debate, does it follow that the affirmative must necessarily debate the whole resolution? Is counterwarrant theory relevant to nonpolicy debate? Can the affirmative be permitted to justify the judge's commitment to a nonpolicy resolution on the basis of a single example? Can a value resolution be represented by a proposed new policy? Articles by Berube and by Bile are representative of the debate on these and other related questions.

36

The Role and Function of Affirmative Criteria

Andrew B. Goulet
Michael Bauer

Many articles have been written concerning the role and function of criteria in a debate round. Unfortunately, trends in recent CEDA debate clearly indicate that there are varying interpretations of how criteria can and should be used. After debating and judging life versus freedom criteria wars in recent semesters, we have concluded that there is a definitive need for a reexamination of criteria in CEDA.

Despite the amount of literature addressing criteria in CEDA, no one article provides debaters with clear guidelines for what they should be doing with the criteria part of their case. Affirmative teams generally make criteria the focal point of their first constructives, but few debaters understand what can be gained in this area of the debate. Debaters need to be clear about what they want to achieve with their criteria. Our intention is to update the practical utilization of criteria in the ever-changing CEDA debate circle. This article will give debaters some much-needed guidelines for clarifying the burdens that criteria necessarily must have in addition to the advantages that can be gained from advancing specific criteria.

A criterion by definition is "a standard, rule, or test by which something can be judged"[1]—in this case, the standards to judge a debate round. Thus, criteria in a debate round generally tell the judge how to filter the arguments advanced in the round. The use of criteria for judging debate has become paramount in CEDA. "Use of a criterion as a standard for judgment remains the most sound analytical basis for deciding nonpolicy controversies."[2]

Logically, the most important function of criteria is to provide clear and consistent standards for judging the debate round. Providing a way to measure the arguments in a debate round has become recognized as a prima facie burden. "First, a common principle for all nonpolicy topics is the need for a method of measurement."[3] The judge should have a concept of what the affirmative plans to accomplish with the remainder of their case and how the affirmative team intends to justify the resolution.

The criterion serves as the mechanism through which all arguments in the round are filtered. The affirmative needs to set a clear division of ground between their side and the negative. "It must be noted that this establishment of jurisdiction must not be self-fulfilling for either team."[4] Furthermore, the negative's path to gaining victory in the round should be clarified. This is not to say that the negative's ground cannot legitimately be considerably limited, but it should at least be clear. An affirmative would seem to have the right to limit the negative's ground as much as they can get away with without advancing a tautological criteria.

One of CEDA's attributes has been the wide variety of options each team has in developing positions. A CEDA resolution can be interpreted in an almost infinite number of ways. "The kind of debating which it [CEDA] wishes to sponsor is not clearly defined."[5] Thus, since just about anything is realistically possible, criteria should establish the boundaries for what the affirmative desires each side to argue.

For instance, affirmative criteria can serve to establish the type of resolution and to restrict argumentation in the round to this type. The 1991 spring CEDA topic, "RESOLVED: That the U.S. Supreme Court, on balance, has granted excessive power to law enforcement agencies," could be interpreted in numerous ways. The topic could be interpreted as a resolution of fact with the affirmative showing excess by proving that the power granted to law enforcement agencies has been greater than some individual right. The topic could be viewed as a value resolution with the affirmative showing that some important right, such as the right to privacy, is harmed when power has been granted. Notwithstanding, the topic could be defined as a resolution of quasi-policy with the affirmative arguing that had the U.S. Supreme Court chosen another option, the situation would be better.

It is important to note that the purpose of criteria differs depending on the resolutional interpretation. With topics viewed as value propositions, the criterion serves as the mechanism with which to determine what value is superior. "Criteria for judging values normally function as decision rules which indicate which values should be given preference in rendering a decision."[6] In quasi-policy debate, the criterion serves as the mechanism for making whatever normative claim the resolution calls for concerning the policy implied in the resolution. Moreover, criteria in a resolution of fact attempt to show on what level the statement in question will be proven to be true. "Criteria for judging facts, however, set debatable standards for determining what should constitute a fact."[7] In each case the criteria give the judge a concept of how the remainder of the affirmative case proves the resolution true.

Regardless of the interpretation, certain generalizations can be made about judging nonpolicy topics. "This sort of proposition would be judged according to two grounds: (1) What are the criteria for describing reality in the manner stated by the proposition? (2) Are these criteria satisfied?"[8] CEDA's evolution during the past few years indicates that criteria can and must go beyond what it did when CEDA was first created. As CEDA debate has grown more complex, so must its level of argumentation.

Criteria can be used not only to set up the affirmative warrant but to preempt negative attacks against the warrant. Whatever the interpretation, the affirmative would be wise to make their line of analysis clear in criteria in order to limit negative ground. The affirmative obviously chooses their case area because it gives them an inherent advantage. Many teams pick example cases because of the advantages they gain. "It gives the affirmative a competitive edge by restricting discussion to an area in which the affirmative is particularly competent, it reduces evidence abuse by discouraging the citation of nonreferent evidence, and it reduces uncertainty since examples give meaning to and draw meaning from regulations that are specific in application an[d] intent."[9] Thus, the affirmative would be well served to attemp to restrict debate to their example.

Restricting negative ground can be easily accomplished in criteria. For instance, the affirmative could restrict the argumentation in the round to their level of impacts. If the affirmative chooses to prove the resolution on a descriptive level, then the affirmative would indicate this in criteria. It would be counterproductive for an affirmative to allow the negative to beat them with normative impacts within their own criteria when they have no intention of justifying the resolution on a normative level in the first place. Thus, an affirmative would be justified in restricting the debate round's level of impacts to the level they choose.

CEDA affirmatives could include even more basic preempts within their criteria. Affirmatives advancing example cases could attempt to delegitimize counterwarrants as well as other generic argumentation. "Indeed, it is not uncommon for affirmatives in CEDA to allow negative teams to introduce counterwarrants without a word of protest at the theoretical level."[10] Affirmatives must remember that an example case is usually chosen for the aforementioned advantages; they might as well take full advantage of the situation.

Typical affirmatives today attempt to limit negative ground with theoretical positions tagged onto the bottom of case as underviews. This approach serves to muddle the round as the roles of the underviews become unclear when filtered within criteria. By putting these positions in their proper place, within criteria, the round thus becomes a little clearer. Since criteria set the parameters for what the judge can observe, theoretical discourse about what falls within negative ground would be included.

The dilemma arises as to how much leeway an affirmative should be allowed with their criteria. Since criteria arguments determine what the judge can look at in making his or her decision, they are vital to the outcome of the debate. "The selection and defense of criteria is critical to the debate."[11] The extent to which the affirmative must defend their criteria must be established. Judges currently have the option to decide which criteria is best. This usually implies accepting the affirmative's criterion if it is proven in the round to be reasonable. The question arises: If the affirmative's criteria are proven to be unreasonable or unacceptable, would this be enough to negate the resolution?

An affirmative has burdens to uphold when defending their criteria against negative attack, such as justifying the criteria they pick. "Mere assertion of a criterion is of little help."[12] Unfortunately, a significant number of CEDA affirmatives fail to provide any rationale for advancing their criteria. This article should serve as a reminder to debaters that there is a need to justify the criteria they are advancing. "Probably the most overlooked aspect of criteria argument is not the criteria themselves but the justification of criteria."[13]

While it seems logical that the affirmative right to define can be extended to allow them to offer their interpretation of the resolution as well, in the interests of fairness and tradition the negative has been allowed to offer their countercriteria. "The best" implies a choice between competing alternatives; as such, it is a part of both society and debate. A civil defendant is allowed to speak even if the plaintiff has established a reasonable case. Likewise, the best definition standard is widely accepted for topicality. There seems no reason to the present authors to accept affirmative criteria that are merely good if they have failed to provide the best in the round.

Often the last rebuttal concludes with reasonably good criteria positions from both sides and little hope for the judge to decide which one is better. At this point it seems logical to provide leeway to the affirmative which has successfully developed a reasonably good criteria. A judge would be justified in elevating the affirmative's criteria over the negative's countercriteria if the negative fails to show that the affirmative's is flawed or that the negative's is better.

Debaters can easily avoid putting the issue of which criteria to use in the judge's hands by providing reasons why their criteria are better in the round. While this seems to be a basic premise, it is too often overlooked in rounds. We suggest that the affirmative provide two further levels of analysis after outlining their criteria. First, the affirmative should provide reasons why their judging paradigm, decision rule, or value would supersede possible competitive judging paradigms, decision rules, or values. The second level of analysis concerns weighing mechanisms for competing criteria—standards for deciding which criterion is better.

A basic example would be an affirmative advancing the value of life as the filter for all arguments in the round. On one level, the affirmative would be wise to show not only that preserving life is good but why life is better than other values. The affirmative can recognize that other values such as freedom are important but are superseded by life. A possible line of argumentation would be for the affirmative to assert that life is the prerequisite for other values, which makes it the most important value. On the second level, the affirmative should then show why it is best, or at least acceptable, to prefer a value because it is a prerequisite to other values.

At this point some cynical CEDA debaters may be questioning how this framework would alter any of the existing life versus freedom clashes that permeate CEDA from time to time. By having a framework or a line of analysis to judge competing values, the debate over competing values would be raised to a higher level. At this point it would be irrelevant for the negative to advance a "freedom is good" position without first attacking the framework for judging competing values. While we do not claim to solve for all fruitless value clashes, it seems logical that debaters who are considering the framework for judging values will be arguing on a superior level than those debaters reading "life is great" and "freedom is fantastic" cards at each other.

Some CEDA philosophers feel that successful negative refutation of criteria can be a voting issue. "Because criteria are prima facie in nature, the negative can refute the affirmative criteria and thus justify a negative ballot."[14] This is true in very few circumstances. Even though the negative could prove the affirmative's criteria to be flawed, that does not mean that the criteria, at first glance, are not acceptable. The affirmative would still have met their prima facie burden of having criteria. The affirmative's criteria could be proven to be unreasonable in some manner, the criteria might be shown to be a tautology, for example; however, the contentions could still provide acceptable warrants for the resolution. If the premise that criteria provide the filters for the judge to weigh positions in the round is accepted, then a round with a defeated set of affirmative criteria would merely allow the judge to look at all arguments in the round without any kind of filter.

Criteria argumentation as a filter would be similar to topicality as a filter. "When the judge resolves the topicality dispute, the judge determines what the debate should be about. This does not mean that the negative team winning topicality will necessarily win the debate."[15] There is no logical justification for awarding the negative anything more than their countercriteria for merely defeating the affirmative's criteria. The affirmative meets its prima facie burden by providing criteria that, without negative argumentation, would allow for justification of the resolution.

CEDA's continuing evolution will most likely bring the need for futher reevaluation of criteria in coming years. Current CEDA debate needs better criteria analysis than most teams are providing. Our modest outline should make debaters think more about what benefits they are attempting to derive from their criteria. While many aspects of criteria argumentation may change, the need for affirmative teams to realize how best to gain the upper hand with their criteria will remain.

Notes

1. *Webster's New World Dictionary*, Second College Edition. (New York: Simon and Schuster, 1982), 336.
2. Ann M. Gill, "Catastrophe and Criterion: A Case For Justification," *1988 CEDA Yearbook*, p. 41.
3. Russell Taylor Church, "On Being Prima Facie—An Application to Nonpolicy Argument," *1986 CEDA Yearbook*, p. 31.
4. Mark A. Cole, Ronald G. Boggs, and Kevin M. Twohy, "The Function of Criteria in Nonpolicy Argumentation: Burdens and Approaches," *1986 CEDA Yearbook*, p. 38.
5. Ronald J. Matlon, "Debating Propositions of Value: An Idea Revisited," *1988 CEDA Yearbook*, p. 1.
6. John Hart and Brian R. McGee, "Propositions of Fact," *Advanced Debate*, 4th ed.
7. Hart and McGee.
8. David Zarefsky, "Criteria for Evaluating Nonpolicy Argument," *1980 CEDA Yearbook*, p. 11.
9. David M. Berube, "Debating Hasty Generalization," *1984 CEDA Yearbook*, p. 54.
10. Brian R. McGee, "Assessing Counterwarrants: Understanding Induction in Debate Practice," *1988 CEDA Yearbook*, p. 64.
11. Don Brownlee, "Approaches to the Evaluation of Criteria," *1987 CEDA Yearbook*, p. 63.
12. Gill, p. 41.
13. Cole, Boggs, and Twohy, p. 40.
14. Cole, Boggs, and Twohy, p. 41.
15. Walter Ulrich, "The Nature of the Topic in Value Debate," *1984 CEDA Yearbook*, p. 3.

37

It's About Time We Measure

Richard O'Dor

Numerous scholars criticize the practical and theoretical problems of nonpolicy debate. Gill (1986) argues, for example, that the practice of defining value-laden words, such as "detrimental" as abstract words offers no guidance for judgment. Bile (1987, 1989), Madsen and Chandler (1988), and Berube (1989) disagree regarding the benefits of debating the resolution from a holistic perspective. Other scholars, including Herbeck and Wong (1986), propose that debaters argue specific poilcy alternatives as a means of reducing the ambiguity of value issues. Essentially, all of the forenamed theorists are critical of the standards by which nonpolicy arguments are measured. Gill requests that definitional arguments provide a measurement for "detrimental." Bile, Madsen, and Chandler, and Berube differ on how holistic and subset interpretations affect measurement; while Herbeck and Wong simply eliminate value measurement by refocusing on policy measurement. If theorists wish to minimize the practical as well as the theoretical problems of nonpolicy debate, undoubtedly these theorists cannot continue to sidestep the concept of measurement. Thus, this essay examines measurement as an indispensable component of nonpolicy argumentation.

REVIEW OF NONPOLICY LITERATURE

Currently, only one writing (Church, 1986) in the Cross Examination Debate Association's (CEDA) Yearbooks examines measurement from a nonpolicy perspective. Because Church's primary purpose was identifing prima facie concepts of nonpolicy debate, the few paragraphs he writes on measurement provide only a cursory examination of the topic. However, the identification of measurement as a prima facie concept is a pivotal deviation from other nonpolicy essays on prima facie concepts (Matlon, 1981, 1988; Keefe, Harte, and Norton, 1982; Verch and Logue, 1982; Church and Wilbanks, 1986; Cole, Boggs, and Twohy, 1986; Leeman and Hamlett, 1989). Church claims that "a common principle for all nonpolicy topics is the need for a method of measurement" (p. 31). Without a method of measurement, Church suggests, a resolution cannot be debated in a meaningful way. Additionally, the essay indicates that the classification of the resolution as fact or value alters how measurement is argued. Church writes:

> For example, imagine advocates are debating a question of historical fact, such as "RESOLVED: That Lee Harvey Oswald killed John F. Kennedy." The measurement question becomes what is sufficient evidence to declare this assertion a fact (p. 31).

In contrast, measurement in a resolution of value requires the advocates to define the key evaluative term in a precise manner. Church explains:

> The most effective kinds of definitions are ones which contain explicit criteria. For example, if the term "desirable" was defined with a dictionary definition such as "worthwhile," then no measurement or evaluation would have been supplied. On the other hand, if the same term were defined conceptually in terms of cost/benefit analysis and a goal or value of disarmament, then the question of measurement or evaluation is much easier to resolve (p. 31).

Although these statements do not result in a definition of measurement, they suggest that the measurement question in a resolution of fact is limited to standards of evidence, while a measurement question in a resolution of value or judgment is restricted to evaluation. Nevertheless, a definition of "measurement" is critical in establishing methods for measuring standards of evidence and evaluation.

MEASUREMENT AND INDICATORS

Kerlinger (1977, p. 426) writes that "in its broadest sense, measurement is the assignment of numerals to objects or events according to rules." According to Kerlinger, the term "symbol" is interchangeable with "numeral." Measurement, therefore, does not necessarily require a quantitative meaning. For example, the symbols on the current CEDA ballot, such as "poor/needs improvement," possess no quantitative relation to speaker points. The ballot, in fact, stipulates that "the boxes do not have numerical significance." Thus, "symbols" and "numerals" impart no quantitative meaning unless these terms are assigned a numerical meaning.

If we accept that "numeral" and "symbol" have no quantitative meaning, how do we measure? We do not measure the object, event, or concept. We measure the indicants of the properties of the objects, events, or concepts. For example, Norrad identifies and monitors specific indicators in determining the risk of nuclear war as expressed in the five Defcon levels ranging from a low of five to an imminent nuclear war risk of one. Likewise, physicians monitor indicators in determining the likelihood of a specific illness; economists observe "key economic indicators" to determine the effectiveness of public policy decision-making; and even a grocery shopper examines the color and texture of fruit to discover its ripeness. All of these examples share the principle that the measurement of any object, event, or concept is determined by how it is operationalized by its indicators. This use of the term "operationalized" should not be confused with nonpolicy debaters' misuse of the same term for interpreting definitions (O'Dor, 1990).

Currently, debaters substitute one symbol for another instead of operationalizing an issue by its indicators. Sovereignty, national security, freedom, democracy, socialism, and other symbols become generic topics and are never operationalized. Ironically, arguing generic topics is inadvertently reinforced by argumentation scholars and by judges deciding debates on generic topics.

Scholars discuss the requirements of arguing value criterion in nonpolicy resolution of value. This discussion notwithstanding, none of their essays addresses Rokeach's (1979) request that values be operationalized. Instead, these theorists bestow a burden or subtopic perspective of advocacy. For instance, Cole, Boggs, and Twohy (1986) propose four subtopics for arguing a criterion: explicitness, threshold, probablity, and justification. All of these words imply measurement. In fact, Cole, Boggs, and Twohy even state that "an established standard for measurement is necessary to compare which is more important, democracy or capitalism" (p. 38). Regardless, these researchers never described the four burdens in terms of measuring a criterion.

Judges, voting for teams arguing generic topics, also inadvertently reinforce substitution. As a pinnacle of substitution, nuclear annihilation and other total destruction scenarios obscure the requirement to interrelate an issue to its corresponding indicators. Gill (1988) claims that catastrophe argumention mistakenly switches issues from the resolution to a topic of quantity. This claim misinterprets the problem. Substitution of topics does not materialize because "such debates become a game of quantity" (p. 39). It occurs because: (1) issues are not developed from a process perspective (O'Dor, 1990); (2) measurement is not an integral aspect of this process; and (3) topic substitution cloaks both debaters' and judges' inadequacies regarding measurement of issues. For example, Gill's solution of criteria justification disregards Cole, Boggs, and Twohy's statement, as do the writers themselves, that a "standard for measurement is necessary" to compare criteria. Gill claims that the judge chooses the best justification to adopt a criterion. Yet, Gill never identifies how the standard "best" is measured. The educational process of nonpolicy debate is stifled by subtopical requirements that never answer the question: How are conflicting nonpolicy issues measured in the decision-making process? Thus, it is not surprising that debaters argue "nth" degree scenarios that force an arbitrary measurement decision. Currently, all decisions regarding measurement are spurious.

The selection of indicators does not assign a numerical probability. As previously mentioned, measurement is a neutral concept; hence, the rule component of the definition guides how indicators are designated and evaluated.

RULES FOR MEASUREMENT

A rule is defined as "a guide, a method, a command that tells us what to do" (Kerlinger, p. 428). Thus, the definition includes "rule" because no measurement procedure is any better than its rules. Good rules provide sound measurement while bad rules impart poor measurement. To minimize measurement as a meaningless procedure, the rules of assignment, according to Kerlinger, must be tied to reality. Zeisel's (1985, p. xiv) claim that the "very complexity of social events requires a language of quantity" reaffirms the need to anchor measurement procedure to reality. As a measurement rule, the United States has assigned the numerals five through one to an enemy's actions according to how these specific actions threaten our immediate security. Furthermore, each numerical increase synchronizes with the United States' political and military actions. Indiscriminate assignments would unquestionably miscommunicate the probability of nuclear confrontation.

In an attempt to exclude actual indicators, a debater could argue that the documentation establishes an outcome measurement through probability phrases. However, these verbal probability phrases are inherently misleading (Woods, 1966; Lichtenstein and Newman, 1967; Bryant and Norman, 1980; Behn and Vaupel, 1982). For example, analyzing 163 students' numerical (0–100 percent) interpretation of twenty different probabilistic phrases, Behn and Vaupel discovered that the phrase "it is very probable that . . . " ranged from 1 to 80 with a median of 9, while "The probability of . . . is very high" extended from 71 to 100 with a median of 90. The divergency of these median scores highlights the inadequacies of probability phrases as measures. The debater's claim also disguises a request to substitute a single word-topic for a method of measuring. Behn and Vaupel suggest that "numerical— though still judgmental—probabilities have the advantage over such probability phrases, for they are much more specific and unambiguous" (p. 21).

According to Behn and Vaupel, "All analysis can be divided into two kinds: researched and quick analysis" (p. 3). Researched analysis encompasses a large statistical data base and includes mathematical modeling, computer simulation, game theory, cost/benefit analysis and other complex analytical tools. In contrast, quick analysis, developed by Behn and Vaupel, uses simplified decision trees (decision sapling with only a few branches), judgmental probabilities, and probability-preferences. These authors suggest that quick analysis is most helpful when data and time are extremely limited. These limitations also reflect the constraints of academic debate.

This essay also has constraints, therefore, readers should study Behn and Vaupel's text, *Quick Analysis for Busy Decision Makers*, for a comprehensive assessment. Hence, this essay will be limited to the three primary components of quick decision-making: decision saplings, judgmental, and preference-probabilities.

A decision tree depicts the various components in their proper relationship with each other. It is a schematic road map of the overall decision. According to Behn and Vaupel (p. 29), a decision tree has several advantages: (1) it is more precise than a verbal road; (2) it decomposes decision problems into more manageable components; (3) it forces the simplification of issues; (4) it requires specification of beliefs about uncertainty and preferences for outcomes; and (5) it presents the various factors in their proper relationship.

A decision tree is mapped left to right. The legends for the roadmap symbolize decision paths. A square decision node expresses the initial decision, triangular nodes depict terminal decisions and their corresponding outcomes, and circular nodes convey uncertainty junctures. Figure 1 illustrates a decision sapling for the dilemma of measurement. As illustrated, the initial decision, whether to measure, branches into two alternative choices, an upper decision (current practice) with a known outcome, and a lower decision (probability measurement) with an uncertain outcome. The current practice, although labeled "arbitrary for both teams," is riskless (its arbitrariness usually impacts both teams equally). The lower decision branch leads to a circular uncertainty node to which are attached two outcome branches and their consequences. The upper outcome branch (judge approves of probability measure-

Figure 1: Decision sapling for measuring

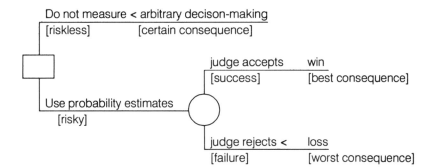

ment) provides the most desirable consequence (win). While the lower outcome branch (judge rejects) results in the least desirable consequence (loss). The forementioned advantages of a decision sapling become obvious if you compare this description of the sapling to Figure 1.

A decision tree illustrates the mutiple pathways of an issue and its decisions. However, the roadmap is incomplete until numerical probabilities are assigned to its symbols. Probabilities can be either empirical or judgmental assessments. An empirical probability predicts the relative frequency of a particular outcome based upon the ratio of the number of occurrences of the outcome (for example, hits) to the total number of uncertain events (at-bats). For instance, my children's softball batting averages of .870 and .840 suggest that the probability of a hit during their next at-bat is 87 and 84 percent (I am hopeful that the bases will be loaded for my daughters). AIDS testing, crime, nuclear alerts, and other events will repeat themselves. Their outcomes and consequences can be estimated by systematically assessing their historical outcomes and consequences. Because these outcomes consequences are expressed in probabilities, their results are not deterministic but based on a numerical assessment of their occurrence.

Judgmental probabilities are described by Behn and Vaupel as "an individual's degree of belief or degree of confidence that a particular event will occur" (p. 81). Although a 30 percent chance is an interpretation, it is unambiguous when compared to the probability phrase "it's possible." Behn and Vaupel suggest that "an ideal probability generator" be used to determine a probability. They explain,

> To think about how likely it is that the legislature will sustain a gubernatorial veto, it is helpful to compare this uncertain event with an easily comprehended but certain process that produces truly random outcomes. For example, if you think it is exactly as likely that the legislature will

sustain a veto as it is that a flipped coin will end up heads, then your judgmental probability of a veto being sustained is 0.5. It is possible to argue about what this judgmental probability should be, but its meaning is perfectly clear (p. 81).

An "ideal probability generator" can be a die, an urn randomly filled with different colored balls, or any other systematic number generator. Although Behn and Vaupel use the probability of 0.5 in the above description, they further argue that "assigning the probability 0.5 to a possible outcome is to confess complete ignorance about what the uncertain event even is" (p. 87). A 0.5 probability does not predict that A or B will occur. As Behn and Vaupel propose, "Clearly, anyone who says the probability of nuclear war occurring next year is 50 percent must be absolutely ignorant of what the event, nuclear war, really is" (p. 87).

As subdecisions, probability estimates are subjective although they are less questionable than probability phrases. If a measurement can only be understood by its indicators, then rules must guide how these estimates are determined. The following examples of rules should enhance the assignment of numerical estimates to the uncertainty of outcomes:

1. The highest degree of probability is the outcome occurring; all other estimates are less than 1.0 (100 percent probability is expressed as 1.0).
2. The numerical probability of an outcome is directly related to its indicators, historical prediction.
3. Independent indicators have more power of prediction than interdependent indicators.
4. Indicators with various potential outcomes have less predictability than indicators with one specific outcome.
5. The greater the outcome's destruction, the greater the need for specificity and corroboration of independent indicators.

To reduce any mathematical apprehension, these rules will be applied to an estimation of war between the United States and Iraq. The only perfect indicator of such a war is the war. However, Behn and Vaupel suggest that "the more information you have about what an uncertain outcome will be, the closer you will place the probability to 1 or 0" (p. 87). Predictions based on conflicts between the current political leaders, between the United States and Iraq, or between either the United States or Iraq and another country are the least risky estimate of a subsequent war. They are least risky because they historically approximate the current pattern. In contrast, a randomly assigned indicator would be the most risky indicator or have a probability of 0. Thus, if these comparable patterns resulted in armed conflict, especially for the same leaders, the closer the probability of war is 1.0.

Even a historical pattern is not a perfect indicator; therefore, its estimate must be reflected by other indicators. For example, the Iraqi evaluation of the outcome of conventional and nuclear war between Iraq and the United States may be underestimated based on previous United States military actions. If Iraq will withdraw because of a 0.8 probability of military action, the United States must refocus Iraq's estimate on current indicators of 0.8 or higher and uncouple the Iraqi estimate from previous U.S. military actions. In fact, George Bush (1990) reiterates that the Vietnam War cannot serve as an example for current U.S. military actions against Iraq. The United States' actions, other nation's military actions, and United Nations sanctions have more power of predicting war than U.S. actions independently have. Conversely, an indicator that suggests multiple outcomes only confuses an enemy.

Misled by the probability phrase "This plan has a fair chance of ultimate success" for the Bay of Pigs actions (Behn and Vaupel, p.77), Kennedy requested specificity and corroboration in estimating the risk of nuclear war during the Cuban missile crisis (Mueller, 1990). If an outcome's destruction is minimal, then the indicators can be fuzzy due to the limited effect of its occurrence. Thus, destruction that results from the use of chemical, biological, and nuclear weapons increases the need for specificity of indicators and reliance on independent indicators during the current crisis.

A preference-probability measures a decision maker's preference for a particular outcome. The higher the probability (closer to 1.0), the higher the decision maker's preference for that outcome. In contrast to pleas heard in a debate, Behn and Vaupel claim that "it is necessary to specify one's relative preference only for those outcomes that can possibly result from the decision" (p. 43). Figure 1 has three preferences: arbitrariness, a win, or a loss. The preference-probability for a riskless outcome (arbitrariness) is equal to its judgmental probability. Whereas the preference-probabilities for the two uncertainty outcomes (win/loss) sum to 1.0.

Probability measurements have indicators in reality. A preference-probability for nondiscrimination (0.75) should correspond to nondiscriminatory actions. While a person may state he or she does not discriminate, attitudes are more risky indicators than actions. Thus, a decision maker's values are operationalized by these indicators. As a measurement, the indicators must also comply with the five rules. Figure 2 illustrates a preference probability for the decision of whether to measure. The probability-preference for an affirmative team is 0.6 and for the negative team 0.4. These probabilities were selected based on the team's preference for affirmative in elimination rounds, the compatiblity between having the last speech and arbitrariness, and a somewhat liberal judging pool for typically progressive topics. The

Figure 2: Probability estimates for measuring

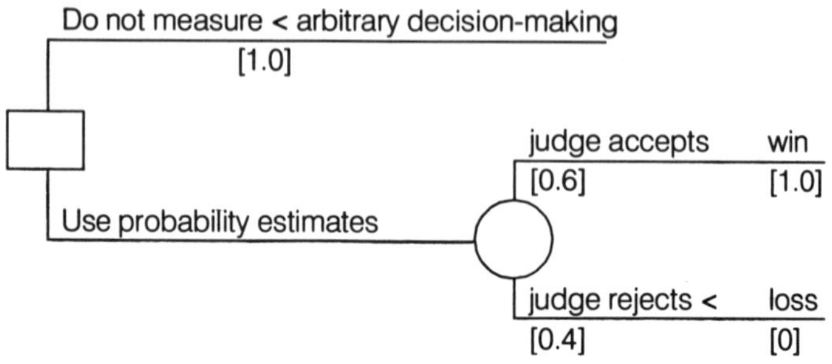

Do not measure < arbitrary decision-making
[1.0]

Use probability estimates

judge accepts   win
[0.6]   [1.0]

judge rejects <   loss
[0.4]   [0]

uncertainty preference probability is 1.0 for a win and 0 for a loss due to winning. These particular probabilities are also reflected in such actions as using win/loss records to justify budgets, to assign teams, or to select teams for specific tournaments.

In summary, measurement anchors the numerical assignment of meaning in an issue's indicators. Behn and Vaupel's methods for quick decision making demonstrate how numerical probabilities are assigned to the indicators of outcomes and their consequences. As previously mentioned, Church suggests that a resolution's classification as fact or value alters the measurement procedure. Thus, a complete discussion of any measurement procedure must include resolutional applications.

MEASURING RESOLUTIONS OF FACT

When debating a question of historical fact, such as "RESOLVED: That Lee Harvey Oswald killed John F. Kennedy," Church suggests, the measurement question becomes, "What is sufficient evidence to declare this assertion a fact" (p. 31). Although a tremendous number of researchers have investigated the Kennedy assassination, no clear measurement standard for sufficient evidence has ever been established. Unfortunately, legal probabilistic phrases are as ineffective as other probabilistic phrases. For instance, a survey of 347 judges reveals that their interpretation of the phrase "beyond a reasonable doubt" varies from 50 percent to a 100 percent chance (Behn and Vaupel, 1982). Nearly one-third of the judges interpreted it as 100 percent. This parallels my interactions with some debate judges that interpret a fact as a 100 percent chance occurrence. Claiming that one exception allows a judge to reject a resolution of fact, negative teams are betting that these judges are evaluating them.

One well-documented investigation of the Kennedy assassination (Lifton, 1980, 1988), uses the concept of best evidence to predict how Kennedy was assassinated. The body as the best evidence best determines the credibility of conflicting information regarding how Kennedy was assassinated. Thus, evidence not directly connected to observations of the body is relegated to secondary status.

Lifton's use of "best evidence" suggests an additional rule for resolutions of fact. However, instead of using "best evidence," this essay will use the term "best indicator." Lifton's use is more analogous to the early 18th century application of the term than the current application, which restricts "best evidence" to evaluating conflicts concerning production of original writing (Cleary, 1984). This new term could be substituted throughout Lifton's book without altering its outcome. "Best indicator" additionally minimizes any confusion between our two argumentation communities and reflects how the term "indicator" is used in other fields, for example economics. Thus, the following resolution of fact rule is proposed: The highest level of probability is always determined by the best indicators.

The inconsistencies between the doctors' immediate observations in Dallas and the doctors' observations during the autopsy would appear to nullify the forementioned rule. Although these patterns represent different stories and predictions, the body remains the best indicator even if it was altered. Analyzing all evidence linked to the body, Lifton concludes that the body was altered to depict a lone assassin.

Other indicators may corroborate this conclusion. For instance, it could be advocated that sound is the best indicator of the positions of assassins. (The predictability of other indicators would be lower than 0.5.) Sound would be selected because the probability of other indicators would be less due to restrictions of the visual field for witnesses or photographers.

Sound may be the best indicator of the number and locations of assassins, yet how it is examined could alter the specific judgmental probability. While people can interpret the direction of sound, a digital analysis increases the interpretation's probability estimate for identifying whether one or more assassins existed. In fact, digital audio analysis of the gunfire sounds, recorded from a motorcycle microphone, indicates that the gun sounds came from multiple directions (Lifton, 1988). The corroboration of these two indicators, the body and sound, increases the judgmental probability that the body was altered.

This concept of best indicator could also be applied to resolutions of values. Its application depends on the abstractness of each resolutional statement. The higher the level of abstraction, the higher a 0.5 probability is applied to a particular indicator. Unquestionably, an estimate of 0.5 conveys nothing about an indicator as a best indicator. Thus, abstract or vague resolutional statements necessitate multiple indicators.

MEASURING RESOLUTIONS OF VALUE

Because nuclear war has become the catastrophe of preference (Gill, 1988), this essay will focus on indicators of nuclear war as an example for other outcome arguments. Mueller (1990) disagrees with how the escalation metaphor corresponds to reality. According to Mueller a ladder is a more appropriate metaphor:

> Once on board an escalator, the riders are automatically lofted to the top unless thay make strenuous efforts to clamber back down. A more appropriate metaphor would be a ladder: The climber becomes more anxious with each upward step and finds that stopping or retreating requires less effort and is less frightening than continuing the ascent (p. 236).

The escalation metaphor is omnipresent no matter what specific resolution is being debated. The imagery it brings to mind has resulted in numerous decisions even though the ultimate outcome of a parade of horribles becomes unnecessary when the string of horribles is altered (Schlag and Skover, 1986).

Nuclear destruction scenarios are inevitably grounded in rhetoric and ignore reality. For example, Betts (1987) writes that the Cuban missile crisis was the only time the United States and the Soviet Union were on the brink of war. A debater could interpret Betts' statement as arguing that nuclear confrontations are extremely limited or as arguing that confrontation between the United States and the Soviet Union easily escalates to nuclear war. These interpretations use probability phrases as if they measure. Only probabilities phrases result in a single estimate projecting divergent measures.

Khrushchev's memoirs convey that the Soviets were trying to avoid war and would not have selected to retaliate even if the United States invaded Cuba. Mueller believes that the following actions authenticate Khrushchev's prediction: (1) the Soviet Union never sent out a demonstration alert; (2) the Soviet Union never reacted by creating trouble somewhere closer to home; (3) the United States limited its military actions to a naval blockade; and (4) the United States agreed to remove missiles in Italy and Turkey. Analyzing the transcripts of the United States' meetings, Welch and Blight (1987) demonstrate that the rhetoric of these meetings corresponded to these indicators. These analysts conclude that even if the Soviet Union had demanded an embarrassing compromise from the United States, the probability of war was next to zero. Thus, indicators of nuclear war would be actions promoting aggression rather than controlling aggression.

SUMMARY

The arbitrariness of nonmeasurable standards should be replaced by operationalizing measurements in their real world indicators. Decision saplings, judgmental probabilities, and preference-probabilities are offered as measurement tools for assigning estimates of outcomes and their consequences. Because rules determine if a measurement procedure is effective, five rules are offered as examples of how rules can be formulated to evaluate probability estimates. These measurement methods are then applied to resolutions of fact and value. Although the sketch of a decision tree is a laborious task, the schematic diagram of issues in a flow is its counterpart. These two diagrams could eventually be integrated into one, a measurement flow chart. Moreover, an aversion to quantification by either debaters or judges is absurd considering the use of numbers to measure the performance of debaters as speakers.

References

Berube, D. M. (1987). "Debating Hasty Generalizations." In D. Thomas and J. Hart, eds. *Advanced Debate*. Lincolnwood, IL: National Textbook Co. 483–89.

Berube, D. M. (1989). "Hasty Generalization Revisited, Part One: On Being Representative Examples." In W. Ulrich, ed. *CEDA Yearbook* 10: 8–15.

Betts, R. K. (1987). *Nuclear Blackmail and Nuclear Balance*. Washington: Brookings.

Behn, R. D. and Vaupel, J. W. (1982). *Quick Analysis for Busy Decision Makers*. New York: Basic Books.

Bile, J. T. (1987). "When the Whole Is Greater Than the Sum of the Parts: The Implications of Holistic Resolutional Focus." In B. J. Logue, ed. *CEDA Yearbook* 8: 8–15.

Bile, J. T. (1988). "Propositional Justification: Another View." In B. J. Logue, ed. *CEDA Yearbook* 9: 54–62.

Bryant, G. D. and Norman, G. R. (1980). "Expression of Probability Words and Numbers." *New England Journal of Medicine* 302. n7: 411.

Bush, G. (1990). Press interview, Nov. 22, 1990 from Saudi Arabia.

Church, R. T. (1986). "On Being 'Prima Facie'—An Application to Non-Policy Argument." B. J. Logue, ed. *CEDA Yearbook* 7: 29–35.

Church, R. T. and Wilbanks, G. (1986). *Values and Policies in Controversy: An Introduction to Argumentation and Debate*. Scottsdale, AZ: Gorsuch Scarisbrick.

Cleary, E. W. (1984). *McCormick on Evidence*. St. Paul: West Publishing Co.

Cole, M. A., Boggs, R. G., and Twohy, K. M. (1986). "The Function of Criteria in Non-Policy Argumentation: Burdens and Approaches." In B. J. Logue, ed. *CEDA Yearbook* 7: 36–42.

Gill, A. (1988). "Catastrophe and Criterion: A Case for Justification." In B. J. Logue, ed. *CEDA Yearbook* 9: 38–44.

Gill, A. (1986). "The Logic of Choice: A Model for Analysis of Propositions of Judgment." In B. J. Logue, ed. *CEDA Yearbook* 7: 1–13.

Herbeck, D. and Wong, K. (1986). "The Indivisibility of Value Claims from Policy Positions: An Argument for Policy in Value Debate." *CEDA Yearbook* 7: 14–28.

Keefe, C., Harte, T. B., and Norton, L. E. (1982). *Introduction to Debate*. New York: Macmillan.

Kerlinger, F. N. (1973). *Foundations of Behavioral Research*. 2nd ed. New York: Hotl, Rinehart and Winston.

Leeman, R. W. and Hamlett, R. A. (1989). "Calling a Counter-Warrant a Counter-Warrant: ,An Immodest Proposal." In W. Ulrich, ed. *CEDA Yearbook* 10: 54–66.

Lichtenstein, S. and Newman, J. R. (1967). "Empirical Scaling of Common Verbal Phrases Associated with Numerical Probabilities." *Psychonomic Science* 9: 563–64.

Lifton, D. S. (1980, 1988). *Best Evidence: Disguise and Deception in the Assassination of John F. Kennedy*. New York: Carrol and Graf Publishers.

Madsen, A. and Chandler, R. C. (1989). "When the Whole Becomes a Black Hole: Implications of the Holistic Perspective." In B. J. Logue ed. *CEDA Yearbook* 10: 30–37.

Matlon, R. J. (1981). "Propositions of Value: An Inquiry into Issue Analysis and the Locus of Presumption." In G. Ziegelmueller and J. Rhodes eds. *Dimensions of Argument: Proceedings of the Second Summer Conference on Argumentation*. Annandale, VA: Speech Communication Association. 496–98.

Matlon, R. J. (1988). "Debating Propositions of Value: An Idea Revisted." In B. J. Logue ed. *CEDA Yearbook* 9: 1–14.

Mueller, J. (1990). *Retreat from Doomsday: the Obsolescence of Major War*. New York: Basic Books.

O'Dor, R. (1990). "A Process Perspective of Definitional Arguments." On press.

Patterson, J. W. and Zarefsky, D. (1983). *Contemporary Debate*. Boston: Houghton Mifflin.

Rokeach, M. (1979). *Understanding Human Values: Individual and Society*. New York: Free Press.

Tolbert, G. and Hunt, S. (1985). "Counter-Warrants a Method for Testing Topical Justification in CEDA Debate." In D. Brownlee, ed. *CEDA Yearbook* 6: 21–28.

Ulrich, W. (1985). "The Legal System as a Source of Values." In D. Brownlee, ed. *CEDA Yearbook* 6: 7–13.

Verch, S. L. and Logue, B. J. (1982). "Increasing Value Clash: A Propositional and Structural Approach." In D. Brownlee, ed. *CEDA Yearbook* 3: 25–27.

Welch, D. A. and Blight, J. G. (1987). "The Eleventh Hour of the Cuban Missile Crisis: An Introduction to the Excomm Transcripts." *International Security* 12. 3 (Winter): 5–29.

Woods, D. H. "Improving Estimates that Involve Uncertainty." *Harvard Business Review* 44: 91–98.

38

Debating Propositions of Value

An Idea Revisited

Ronald J. Matlon

In the spring term of the 1974–75 debate year, CEDA chose its first value debate resolution, and "no one knew what to do!" (Tomlinson, 1983, p. 2). That proposition was, "RESOLVED: That American television has sacrificed quality for entertainment." Since the spring of 1975, the word "should" has never appeared in any official CEDA debate resolution. Hence, a grand experiment in value analysis was undertaken even though CEDA is not bound constitutionally or in any other way to debating only value propositions.

A decade has also passed since I wrote my first thoughts on debating value propositions (Matlon, 1978). I have been both amazed and gratified by the ongoing reactions to that manuscript as well as its companion piece (Matlon, 1981). The struggle over how to analyze and evaluate value proposition arguments has occupied considerable space and time in the literature of academic forensics as well as in the substance of several CEDA debate rounds.

Unfortunately, my impression, shared by many others, is that CEDA is not clear-cut value debate. Nor is it policy debate. Nor is it audience debate. Nor is it NDT debate. CEDA is an organization that has been very successful in sponsoring academic curricular debating and in producing a body of literature that makes it appear as the centerpiece of value debate activity, but the kind of debating it wishes to sponsor is not clearly defined, particularly in terms of helping coaches teach students the analytical skills necessary to perform well in rounds of CEDA competition. Anyone who claims she or he can identify a model

CEDA round is perpetuating a myth. That round may have been a demonstration of outstanding debate, but it cannot typify the mission of CEDA, since that mission is blurry. More will be said about the claims made in this paragraph later in the paper.

With this overview of CEDA debate in mind, I want you to know how pleased and complimented I am to be invited here to reflect on a decade of writing on and practice in CEDA debating, and to offer some thoughts about the future.[1] The nub of my remarks will focus on CEDA's mission. As already noted, I do not see a clear mission today, although the theory and practice erroneously indicate that the organization stands for the promotion of value debate. At this point, I simply want to point out that, in searching for a mission, CEDA leaders should being with the following question: "What is the most fundamental baseline information we can teach novice debaters who are being introduced to CEDA for the first time?" In other words, CEDA leaders need to go back to the beginning, to core knowledge and basic theory.

Nearly all of us begin teaching and coaching newcomers something about propositions and issue analysis. Textbooks in argumentation begin this way. Opening meetings with squads of newcomers begin this way. We like to identify with assurance that the proposition we are debating is one of fact, value, or policy (or similar nomenclature), and then proceed to explain the stock issues implicit in the chosen resolution. Stock issues are valuable teaching tools because they give our students a framework for building cases. My pedagogical philosophy is that a clear framework instills confidence in our students, especially the floundering beginners. Prescriptive formulas that are clear and sound produce students who are well educated in the fundamentals of debate analysis. Being well educated in the fundamentals is necessary before our students begin to engage in experimental analysis on their own. Therefore, as CEDA identifies its mission, it *must* focus on what fundamentals of the activity all of its students should be expected to know.

It is in this spirit that I write this paper, focusing on the propositions CEDA selects to debate and what can be taught to our novice debaters about how to approach those propositions. My impressions and suggestions will be organized around the following three topics: (1) how issue analysis theory for value propositions has developed to date; (2) problems in CEDA's approach to value debate; and (3) where do we go from here?

DEVELOPMENT OF ISSUE ANALYSIS THEORY FOR VALUE PROPOSITIONS

An abundance of refreshing and thoughtful theoretical dialogue has taken place as a result of the CEDA experiment in value analysis. The definitive and designative stock issue approach to analyzing value debate propositions (Matlon, 1978) has been impressively refined in the literature of academic debate over the past ten years. A number of authors have advanced the spirit of my objectivist approach to issue analysis. Four illustrations will suffice. First, Verch and Logue (1982) offer a five-step approach to analyzing propositions of value. Within the context of the definitive and designative issues, I take the liberty here to restructure their five-step approach into a four-step aproach as follows:

    I. *Definitive stock issue.* Justify the standard or measure to be used, whether criteria, a model, an ideal, or desirable aims or objectives.

        A. **Step One**. Identify the value to be affirmed and the value to be refuted (for instance, American jobs for American workers versus preserving good relations with foreign countries).

        B. **Step Two**. Present the criteria to be used to resolve the value conflict, and demonstrate why it is [they are] reasonable for resolving this conflict (for instance, how pervasive, recent, intense, and credible are the values noted in Step One).

    II. *Designative stock issue.* Determine whether the subject of the evaluation meets the criteria defined.

        A. **Step Three**. Apply the criteria to the value to be affirmed and show why the criteria are met (for instance, polls show unemployment in America is the most pressing national concern).

        B. **Step Four**: Demonstrate why winning this value conflict should resolve the conflict over winning the ballot (for instance, low domestic unemployment is a more pervasive, recent, intense, and credible value to the American public than any foreign policy issue).

    Second, Bartanen and Frank (1983) and Bartanen (1987) identify four steps that advance the definitive-designative stock issue framework. They utilize the audience's agenda as their paramount criterion. Again, taking the liberty of restructuring, their steps are outlined as follows:

    I. *Definitive stock issue.* Justify the standard or measure to be used, whether criteria, a model, an ideal, or desirable aims or objectives.

        A. **Step One**. Define the issues and values implied in the resolution (for instance, improved relations with the Soviet Union means increased agricultural sales and cultural exchanges).

        B. **Step Two**. Make assumptions about the audiences and

their value systems (for instance, the judge/critic in the immediate situation must believe that increased agricultural sales and cultural exchanges with the Soviet Union will result in improved relations with the United States and that improved Soviet-American relations is a desirable value).

II. *Designative stock issue*. Determine whether the subject of the evaluation meets the criterion defined.

    A. **Step Three**. Determine the significance of the exigence (for instance, the seriousness of the Soviet-American relationship problem for this audience and its relevance in terms of the judge/critic's value hierarchy).

    B. **Step Four**. Compare attention given to the germane problems and values of the immediate audience with potential competing problems and values (for instance, a comparison of improved Soviet-American relations with improved military preparedness, improved health care in America, and other concerns).

Third, Brownlee (1987) elaborated on the development of the definitive stock issue alone, particularly as it relates to the selection of criteria used as standards for a particular value judgment. Brownlee states that each chosen criterion should be clear, relevant, consistently applied, and supported by good reasons.

Fourth, Tuman (1987) says that a prima facie case for a proposition of value requires the establishment of four stock issues:

1. *Value identification*. (Recognize values explicity stated in the resolution, and others that may be implied. Using Rokeach's (1981) distinction, identify which values are instrumental and which are terminal.

2. *Criteria*. This stock issue combines the definitive and designative issues outlined by Matlon (1978).

3. *Value hierarchy and prioritization*. Compare different, competitive values. Adapt the comparison to the critic or audience.

4. *Topicality*. Justify the interpretation of the resolution as a correct interpretation.

These four stock issues appropriately broaden value proposition analysis beyond the definitive-designative model, and may serve as a formula for the future.

These four essays are only some of the ways in which theory has been advanced for determining appropriate issues for propositions of value. I am pleased to note that generically applied stock issues are still in the forefront of our thought, inasmuch as such issues have been useful for centuries in guiding our students in critical analysis. Unfortunately, all of this theory advancement has not led participants in CEDA into any commonly accepted ground regarding the model of ideal value debate.

PROBLEMS IN CEDA'S APPROACH
TO VALUE DEBATE

Two pervasive and interrelated issued analysis problems persist in CEDA debate rounds. These two problems seem to stem from a lack of a clear mission for CEDA and the myth that its current mission is to foster value debate.

First most CEDA debates on so-called propositions of value have actually become debates on propositions of quasi-policy. Even though I noted in 1978 that "value propositions are . . . intertwined with attitudes about policies insofar as they often *lead to or are embedded* in policy suggestions" (p. 195), I neither imagined nor wished that CEDA debate would focus on policy suggestions. Nevertheless, it has. On the surface, an "examination, of the terminology used in the activity would lead one to conclude that CEDA is actually value debate" (Shea, 1987, p. 3). However, debating about values "has rarely been the case in terms of the resolutions chosen or the debaters' approach to the resolutions" (Thomas, 1987, p. 448). The propositions selected are commonly referred to, not as value topics, but as quasi-policy resolutions, that is, resolutions that contain implicit plans or courses of action (Dixon and Leslie, 1984).

Let us look at some examples. "RESOLVED: That the United States is justified in providing military support to nondemocratic governments" caused CEDA debaters in 1985 to examine and evaluate past and current U.S. policy (Millsap and Millsap, 1985). "RESOLVED: That the American judicial system has overemphasized freedom of the press" in 1988 called for policy examples from affirmatives versus disadvantages of policy discontinuance from the negative. So-called pseudo-disadvantages or pseudo-counterwarrants to implied plans (Bartanen, 1982) are termed value manifestations (Vasilius, 1980) or value objections. Under the 1981 resolution that activism in politics by religious groups harms the American political process, negative teams examined the traditional policy stock issue of cost by citing future examples of value-induced behavior (for instance, religious groups would cease their positive contributions to civil rights, and race riots would develop) (Dempsey, 1984). Other times, analysis shifts to the policy stock issue of cure or workability (Bartanen and Frank, 1983). With the 1981 proposition that unauthorized immigration into the

United States is seriously detrimental to the United States, negatives were prompted to raise value (plan) objections such as the ineffectiveness of attempts to shut off borders (Bartanen, 1982). In addition, the policy stock issue of ill (significance of the problem) has become the affirmative's justification of the value (Zeuschner and Hill, 1981).

A clear line between value-oriented arguments and policy-oriented aguments is almost impossible to draw. And there is not much evidence anywhere that CEDA students will abandon their fascination with policy implications in value propositions (Dudczak, 1983). Several debate coaches in CEDA are encouraging their debaters to analytically approach value resolutions as debating propositions of quasi-policy.[2] Consider the following remarks:

> A debater confronting a value proposition need not begin in a state of confusion. Since value propositions are intricately woven into policy decisions, comparable issue analysis may be appropriate. The traditional policy stock issues of ill, blame, cure, and cost have an application ... (Brownlee, 1980, p. 44).

> Value benefits analysis ... is very similar to that which is already established in the policy debate arena. Quite simply, value benefits are to value-oriented debating like comparative advantages are to policies.... The value benefits analysis recognizes the legitimacy of paralleling comparative advantages as a clear, straightforward, and realistic/rational paradigm for seeking adherence to a value claim (Zeuschner, 1982, p. 16).

> Because value judgments are the basis for policy implementation, consideration of values is independent upon policy directions; thus a need exists to examine values in a conditional or hypothetical policy realm.... When arguing values in terms of action, the policy-making paradigm should be the only model used to debate value propositions (Jones and Crawford, 1984, pp. 11, 12).

> The proponents of value debate have been too hasty in rejecting the traditional stock issues. The questions contained in them apply not only to policy but also to the implied policy proposals found in value topics (Rowland, 1983, p. 828).

> We believe that a viable affirmative method of fulfilling its responsibilities is what we term the "policy implications" affirmative. Basically, the affirmative offers a prima facie case in support of a value or value system, consistent with that required by the resolution (the definitive stock issue). The justification for the value system, the designative stock issue, is grounded in the system's beneficial policy implications (Young and Gaske, 1984, p. 26).

> Attempts to separate value propositions from policy propositions created, at best, a limitation upon the advocate to the discovery of the full range of potential issues available to the consideration of the value in question.... Decision rules created by ... value arguments require a manifestation in policy in order to be meaningful (Dudczak, 1983, pp. 837, 838).

Two consequences are created by saying that CEDA is value debate, and then choosing propositions of quasi-policy. Both of these consequences hurt our ability to teach newcomers an analytical formula for success in CEDA debating. First, debaters are left in limbo as to how far they should go with their policy analysis in a quasi-policy/value debate. On one hand, several judges (especially those who either vigorously oppose anything that NDT practices or who want values debated only in the abstract with no hint of policy) punish debaters for making policy overtones. "The belief appears to exist among some judges of CEDA that value propositions and policy propositions are separable" (Dudczak, 1983, p. 838). On the other hand, as I will develop shortly, debating values in the abstract may be too difficult for most of our students. Policy analysis is a well-defined formula on which they can rely. The result is a tendency for many of the debaters to go into policy implications half-heartedly, while, at the same time, offering a watered-down analysis of values. More will be said about their analysis of values shortly.

Next, when CEDA propositions are debated in the abstract as pure value resolutions by one side, and debated as quasi-policy matters by the other side, a lack of clash ensues. With the 1983 CEDA proposition, "RESOLVED, that individual rights of privacy are more important than any other Constitutional right," some affirmative teams favorably weighed the value of this right along a value hierarchy, while some negative teams condemned specific actions such as bans on strip searches and inquiries into prior sexual history in rape trials (Dixon and Leslie, 1984). Two quite different lines of argumentation created confusion for all involved. In sum, the quasi-policy approach to value argumentation has created a loss of focus for the purpose of CEDA activity.

Second, there is no in-depth value analysis encouraged by debating quasi-policy topics. When I argued earlier for the adoption of value propositions (1978), I hoped that debaters would familiarize themselves with the works of philosophers, sociologists, and psychologists who wrote about values and value hierarchies. Landmark literature by Kluckhohn (1958), Parsons and Shils (1962), Williams (1970), and Rokeach (1981) serves as historical introduction to American values. In my 1981 essay, I argued that questions of ethics and morals would encourage our forensic students to chart new territory. I said that propositions such as "courage is not an admirable trait" and "people have no inalienable right to life, liberty, and the pursuit of happiness" were suitable resolutions to introduce our students to metaethics and value inquiry.

Others shared my view. Boggs (1987) posits that CEDA students must explore interdisciplinary literature to search for standards to resolve value conflict, standards such as social values, exigence and salience, anteriority, cost/benefit, and oughtness or normative value. Having debaters incorporate such standards of right and wrong into debate rounds would "increase the amount of value clash in nonpolicy debates" (Boggs, 1987, p. 32). Ulrich (1983) argues that "debaters should read Mill, Rawls, and Dworkin to develop a framework for analyzing values, and they should realize the implications of these theorists in debate rounds" (p. 25). He goes on to say that debaters should clearly outline the ethical, political, or social systems that they wish to defend, explaining what the system is and why the system is being used in a particular round. To do so effectively, the debaters must be knowledgeable in the history and philosophy of values.

Unfortunately, "it appears that all too few debaters have followed Matlon's advice, as most nonpolicy debaters include, at most, a superficial exposition and support of value comparison standards" (Boggs, 1987, p. 27). Too often, CEDA debaters "do little more than determine the relevant values implicit in the resolution and then proceed to argue which value sets are more important. The problem with this view is that it oversimplifies the nature of value controversies" (Herbeck and Wong, 1986, p. 18). There is little historical, philosophical, or theoretical understanding of value inquiry being displayed in rounds of CEDA debate.

As noted earlier, the problem stems from the wording of the propositions and the lack of a clearly defined mission for CEDA activity since the organization has not made a solid commitment to debating serious questions of ethics and morals. What, then, can be done about the mission of CEDA and the ongoing problems in debating quasi-policy topics instead of authentic value propositions? The answer to this question is addressed in the following section.

WHERE DO WE GO FROM HERE?

The centerpiece of this essay has been the debate proposition itself. Indeed, it is time for CEDA to closely examine its choice of propositions. At present, the proposition selections have placed CEDA activity in a sort of never-never land. Although I think a considerable amount of time and thought are needed to word clear-cut propositions of value, policy, or fact, and that some propositions never clearly fall into one of these three categories, I believe that this time-tested trichotomy still has merit. Therefore, I will use this classification scheme and argue that there are three possible paths to follow. They are:

1. attempt to debate authentic propositions of value
2. resume debating propositions of policy
3. begin debating propositions of fact

Let us consider each alternative in turn.

Should CEDA attempt to debate propositions of value? I am going to waffle in answering this question, although I lean toward a "probably not" reply. The theoretical essays discussed in the first section of the paper and the references on values noted in the second section of this paper hold promise that some day there can be a clear paradigm for teaching our students how to analyze and argue value resolutions. However, to be realistic, it may be unreasonable to expect novice debaters or even most experienced students of debate to understand that vast body of literature on values so they can be articulate value philosophers, sociologists, and psychologists. Perhaps this is the reason CEDA has been unable to make a wholehearted commitment to value debate on behalf of its student participants.

Even if our students could be taught how to analyze authentic value propositions, not quasi-policy topics, another serious problem with value resolutions exists. Presumption is nearly impossible to locate. Numerous writers, CEDA coaches, and students have groped with the slippery task of locating presumption in rounds of debate where genuine propositions of value are used, only to find the concept quite elusive. Because presumption is the yardstick debate judges should use to award a decision to an affirmative or a negative team, it is essential that the concept be clarified.[3] But, can this be done?

First, a jurisprudential definition of presumption (innocent until proven guilty) is inapplicable to values and countervalues. How can a value like democracy be innocent or guilty? Second, a status quo or existing institutions definition of presumption is nearly impossible to locate because of the shortcomings of public opinion polls and the vague notion of what constitutes prevailing popular or unpopular opinion. Third, the hypothesis-testing notion of presumption, which is the rule that it rests against the resolution (Podgurski, 1983), is arbitrary and artificial. Consider the spring 1984 CEDA proposition, "RESOLVED: That federal government censorship is justified to defend the national security of the United States." Does this not seem like a presumptive statement? Why should presumption be artificially placed against that statement? Fourth, the natural notion of presumption is that it can float from debate round to debate round. This definition affixes presumption in the mind of each judge. Unfortunately, this approach falsely assumes that debaters are able to know and understand each judge's value system prior to and during a debate. In a debate over abortion, does the judge in the back of the room hold a pro-life, pro-choice, or neutral view? Who knows? So, I am persuaded that floating (natural) presumption is equally unworkable for academic debate.

To summarize, "the overall impact on the conduct and critical evaluation of CEDA debate is lessened by the failure to attain agreement of what the locus of presumption is in value inquiry" (Young and Gaske, 1984, p. 25). Setting aside presumption entirely is a possible way out. But what do we have then? What rule or standard is used by judges to resolve a very close debate? Again, a dilemma ensues. On one hand, the concept of presumption cannot be used to break ties. On the other hand, no substitute concept or guideline has been offered.

The difficulties of probing the vast and difficult body of value literature and locating presumption with authentic propositions of value cause me to have reservations about making value debate the primary mission of CEDA at this time. Although attempting to debate authentic value propositions is not my preferred althernative, if such propositions are the focus of CEDA, they ought to be as far removed from quasi-policy wording as possible. Purer value propositions, such as "RESOLVED: That democracy is more important than life" or "RESOLVED: That courage is not an admirable trait," are superior from the standpoint of value analysis than adoption of a quasi-policy proposition, such as "RESOLVED: That the United States is justified in providing military support to nondemocratic governments."

Should CEDA resume debating propositions of policy? Yes, because that is essentially what is happening in CEDA now. Why hold back with quasi-policy, translated as "seeming to be" policy? Why not go all the way? We have a clear set of stock-issue guidelines for analyzing and evaluating policy debate. Furthermore, values can be debated within the context of policy resolutions. As Rowland (1983) correctly noted, "There is little need for an independent form of debate concerning values, because values are integral to policies" (p. 829). Policies can be evaluated rationally not only by examining their effects, but also by delving into their underlying values. Numerous authors, many of whom have been cited here, have given us guidelines for exploring value and value hierarchy analysis, which can be used to enrich policy argumentation. For example, affirmative debaters who build crucial comparative advantage issues or negative debaters who build crucial comparative disadvantage issues around the value of freedom can indeed use what has been written about values to deepen the philosophical under-pinnings of their claims.

Gross (1984), an advocate of CEDA adopting policy propositions, believes that CEDA's 1982 proposition, "RESOLVED: That a unilateral freeze by the United States on nuclear weapons production and development would be desirable," would have been a clearer topic if it had been worded, "RESOLVED: That the United States should adopt a unilateral freeze on the production and development of nuclear weapons." The latter wording "would have forced the affirmative team to commit itself to a particular program . . . [rather than taking] refuge in studied ambiguities about what it was they endorsed" (p. 8). It is through specific policy proposals that the concept of nuclear freeze takes on meaning.

Adopting policy propositions does not mean CEDA must abandon any commitment to advancing our knowledge about how to argue values. If CEDA moves in this direction, its concern must be with this question: "How can we get policy debaters to do more with underlying values?" The answer is found in wording policy propositions to contain clear value implications. Constitutional rights propositions are good. So are those that address some of these questions raised by Pfau, Thomas, and Ulrich (1987): "Is law and order more important than justice? Is the right to a fair trial more important than freedom of the press? Is the protection of the environment more important than economic growth?" (p. 24). Value inquiries such as these can lead to policy propositions such as "RESOLVED: That protection of the environment should take precedence over economic growth."

Not only can value analysis be encouraged by CEDA when carefully worded policy propositions are adopted, but many of the ambiguities created by debating value or quasi-policy questions can dissolve. For reasons cited earlier, debating concrete ideas is superior to debating abstract constructs. Therefore, the mission of CEDA might be to encourage debates over concrete and focused policy systems that are made more profound by in-depth considerations of underlying values and value hierarchies.

Should CEDA begin debating propositions of fact? Definitely. I ought to begin this discussion by identifying what a proposition of fact is. Propositions of fact help us discover what is or is not; whereas, propositions of value discover good and bad. The proposition of fact that "the cost of higher education is the major reason most people do not attend or drop out of college" measures is/existence or is not/nonexistence; the proposition of value that "it is wrong to charge students so much money for higher education" measures good/right or bad/wrong. The first of the two propositions above is a proposition of fact because it "describes a view of reality. . . . The purpose of the [proposition] . . . is to establish whether the stated description [of reality] is correct" (Patterson and Zarefsky, 1983, p. 16). The correctness of this view of reality can be measured and tested empirically. Meanwhile, while we may in part rely on empirical information to judge the right or wrong of something, empirical data alone will not suffice when examining values. The opinions of philosophers and an understanding of individual and societal wants and needs also matters.

Propositions of fact may examine the past, present, or future. Juries look at claims of past fact (what happened) when they consider propositions such as "John Doe is guilty of first degree murder." Economists argue claims of present fact (what is happening) when they consider propositions such as "The rate of inflation is increasing." People with political interests frequently debate claims of future fact (what will happen) when they consider propositions such as "Jesse Jackson will be elected president in 1996."

Many propositions of fact are also identified as historical or scientific in nature. "The historian attempts to interpret events within the framework of some explanation; the scientist, to interpret phenomena by reference to some theoretical structure" (Zarefsky, 1980, pp. 11–12). In these cases, historians and scientists are trying to discover meaning (what something means) with propositions like "RESOLVED: That Lyndon Johnson's War on Poverty exacerbated the problems of poverty in the United States" or "RESOLVED: That computers will alter the course of civilization." Notice, again, that the focus of these propositions is on is, was, or will be, not "good or bad."

If CEDA participants debated nonpolicy propositions of fact, many of the problems faced by debating propositions of value or quasi-policy might be overcome. In-depth fact analysis may be more within the reach of our students than in-depth value analysis. As one observer notes: "Propositions of fact . . . are often easy to understand since the advocate of the proposition needs only to demonstrate the existence of certain facts to prove her case to the audience" (Tuman, 1986, p. 86). Fact analysis requires empirical and authoritative validation; value analysis requires a comprehensive understanding of philosophy, sociology, and psychology. The former is more concrete; the latter is more abstract. Presumption may also be somewhat easier to locate with propositions of fact than propositions of value, especially if the framers of the propositions remain cognizant of what is generally presumed to be true.

In addition, debating propositions of fact may give us a fuller understanding of how the definitive and designative stock issues work. These two general and fundamental issues are certainly as endemic to fact resolutions as they are to value resolutions. With the definitive stock issue, we would ask: "What criteria are available to justify the fact (assess the degree of truth) claimed in the proposition?" With the designative stock issue, we would ask: "Does the fact claimed in the proposition conform to the criteria?"

Here are some examples:

Proposition: Sam is guilty of loitering.

Definitive Issue:	What constitutes loitering? (What criteria do we use to determine when loitering has taken place?)
Designative Issue:	Did Sam loiter? (Does Sam's action conform to the definition of loitering?)

Proposition: Capital punishment will deter crime.

Definitive Issue:	What constitutes a deterrence in crime?
Designative Issue:	Will capital punishment cause such a deterrence?

Proposition: The two-party system is dead in America.

Definitive Issue: What would make death an appropriate charac-
                             terization of the two-party system?
Designative Issue: Are these conditions satisfied (Zarefsky, 1980,
                             p. 14)?

Zarefsky (1980) shows how potential issues flow from these two stock issues with the following proposition, although I do not think this is a particularly well-balanced resolution:

Proposition: Jimmy Carter received stronger political support than Gerald Ford.
   Definitive Issue: What constitutes support?
   Potential Issues: 1. Number of voters
                       2. Intensity of partisan feeling
                       3. Independence of voters
                       4. Positive effect
                       5. Etc.
Designative Issue: Did Carter have stronger political support than Ford?
   Potential Issues: 1. Carter versus Ford regarding number of votes
                       2. Carter versus Ford regarding intensity of partisan feeling
                       3. Carter versus Ford regarding independence of voters
                       4. Carter versus Ford regarding positive effect
                       5. Etc.

Some of these potential issues may never be raised by either side in the debate; they become waived issues. Some of these potential issues may be introduced by one side and agreed to by the opposition; they become admitted issues. Some of these potential issues remain points of disagreement by the affirmative and the negative throughout the debate; they become actual issues or points of clash. For example, an affirmative team might say "intensity of partisan feeling constitutes political support," and the negative may admit to this issue. However, when the affirmative goes on to say that "Carter generated more intensity of partisan feeling among Democrats than Ford did among Republicans," the negative might disagree, and we have clash. Additional steps in the analysis of fact propositions are discussed in a variety of sources, one of which is found in Chapter 8 of Rybacki and Rybacki (1986).

Several propositions of fact for CEDA have already been suggested in this essay. Those propositions, as well as other possibilities for CEDA debate, are listed below:

> RESOLVED: That the cost of higher education is the major reason most people do not attend or drop out of college.
> RESOLVED: That "John Doe" (some accused and well-known person coming to trial after the debate season is over) is guilty of first degree murder.

RESOLVED: That the rate of inflation is increasing.

RESOLVED: That Jesse Jackson will be elected president in 1996.

RESOLVED: That Lyndon Johnson's War on Poverty exacerbated the problem of poverty in the United States.

RESOLVED: That computers will alter the course of civilization.

RESOLVED: That capital punishment deters crime.

RESOLVED: That the two-party system is dead in America.

RESOLVED: That flying saucers exist.

RESOLVED: That the American mass media is relatively free from government regulation.

RESOLVED: That granting tuition tax credits to the parents of children who attend private schools will perpetuate segregation.

RESOLVED: That violence on television causes violent behavior in children.

RESOLVED: That Lee Harvey Oswald killed President John Kennedy.

RESOLVED: That the stock market will collapse within a decade.

Numerous other possibilities exist. If CEDA wants to be in the forefront of generating theories of argument, its mission might be to turn to propositions of fact. Such a mission offers an exciting, yet realistic, challenge for coaches and debaters alike.

Of course, a fourth mission is always possible. CEDA could adopt the practice of debating propositions of fact, value, and policy on a rotational basis. This alternative has merit, too. It gives everyone some variety, and it permits needed growth and development in all three areas of argumentative analysis. If this course of action was followed, the CEDA topic committee would probably want to issue resolutional parameters indicating to the debaters and coaches what types of propositions are being offered. In any case, CEDA is at an important crossroads in its mission, and the focus of that mission ought to be on proposition designation.

In 1978, I and others urged that propositions of value be argued in academic forensics. CEDA attempted to pick up that challenge, and we have learned much about value analysis in the process. Unfortunately, in the process, CEDA lost its sense of direction by claiming to be the perpetrator of value debate, while resisting major changes away from policy debate. Now, the time has come for the leaders of CEDA to clearly articulate the purpose of the organization's existence. Now might be the ideal time to forge ahead by seeing if (a) value argument can be advanced within the context of a pure policy paradigm, and (b) we can refine our knowledge of the definitive and designative stock issues by debating propositions of fact. I believe that to embark on either or both missions could initiate a noteworthy dialog on debate theory and practice from which everyone in forensics can benefit. I look forward to another interesting decade ahead.

Notes

1. Sincere appreciation is expressed to my colleague, Brenda Logue, for valuable input into the preparation of this manuscript.
2. The National Forensic League adopted a Lincoln-Douglas format as a national high school tournament event in 1980. Unlike CEDA, the NFL established a rule that only value propositions could be debated, and the debaters could not use the policy stock issues for their analysis, although no alternative analytical approach was suggested.
3. The assumption here is that debates should be won by somebody. An alternative assumption, namely that nonpolicy debates can be judged as a tie, is offered by Thomas (1987).

References

Bartanen, M. (1987). "Application of the Issues-Agenda Paradigm to Speaker Duties and Stock Issues in Value Debates." *CEDA Yearbook* 8: 42–51.

Bartanen, M. (1982). "The Role of Values in Policy Controversies." *CEDA Yearbook* 3: 19–24.

Bartanen, M. and Frank, D. (1983). "Creating Procedural Distinctions Between Values and Policy Debate: The Issues-Agenda Model." *The Forensic of Pi Kappa Delta* 69: 1–9.

Boggs, R. (1987). "Comparing Values: A Review of Axiological Standards for Analytical Value Hierarchies." *CEDA Yearbook* 8: 27–32.

Brownlee, D. (1980). "Advocacy and Values." *CEDA Yearbook* 1: 43–47.

Brownlee, D. (1987). "Approaches to the Evaluation of Criteria." *CEDA Yearbook* 8: 59–63.

Dempsey, R. (1984). "The Theoretical Illegitimacy of Speculative Value Objections." *CEDA Yearbook* 5: 60–64.

Dixon, T. and Leslie, C. (1984). "Propositional Analysis: A Need for Focus in CEDA Debate." *CEDA Yearbook* 5: 16–23.

Dudczak, C. (1983). "Value Argument in a Competitive Setting: An Inhibition to Ordinary Language Use." In D. Zarefsky, M. Sillars, and J. Rhodes, eds. *Argument in Transition: Proceedings of the Third Summer Conference on Argumentation*. Annandale, VA: Speech Communication Association. 837–43.

Gross, B. (1984). "A Case for Debating Propositions of Policy." *CEDA Yearbook* 5: 7–10.

Herbeck, D. and Wong, K. (1986). "The Indivisibility of Value Claims from Policy Positions: An Argument for Policy in Value Debate." *CEDA Yearbook* 7: 14–28.

Jones, M. and Crawford, S. (1984). "Justification of Values in Terms of Action: A Rationale for a Modified Policy-Making Paradigm in Value Debate." *CEDA Yearbook* 5: 11–15.

Kluckhohn, C. (1985). *Mirror for Man*. New York: Whittlesey House.

Matlon, R. (1978). "Debating Propositions of Value." *Journal of the American Forensic Association* 14: 194–204.

Matlon, R. (1981). "Propositions of Value: An Inquiry into Issue Analysis and the Locus of Presumption." In G. Ziegelmueller and J. Rhodes, eds. *Dimensions of Argument: Proceedings of the Second Summer Conference on Argumentation*. Annandale, VA: Speech Communication Association. 494–512.

Millsap, S. and Millsap, S. (1985). "Reflections on Solvency in Quasi-Policy Propositions." *CEDA Yearbook* 6: 29–31.

Parsons, T. and Shils, E. (1962). *Toward a General Theory of Action*. Cambridge: Harvard University Press.

Patterson, J. and Zarefsky, D. (1983). *Contemporary Debate*. Boston: Houghton Mifflin.

Pfau, M., Thomas, D., and Ulrich, W. (1987). *Debate and Argument: A Systems Approach to Advocacy*. Glenview, IL: Scott, Foresman.

Podgurski, D. (1983). "Presumption in the Value Proposition Realm." *CEDA Yearbook* 4: 34–39.

Rokeach, M. (1981). *The Nature of Human Values*. London: Free Press.

Rowland, R. (1983). "The Philosophical Presuppositions of Value Debate." In D. Zarefsky, M. Sillars, and J. Rhodes, eds. *Argument in Transition: Proceedings of the Third Summer Conference on Argumentation*. Annandale, VA: Speech Communication Association. 822–36.

Rybacki, K. and Rybacki, D. (1986). *Advocacy and Opposition: An Introduction to Argumentation*. Englewood Cliffs: Prentice-Hall.

Shea, B. C. (1987). *The Language of CEDA*. Paper presented at the meeting of the Speech Communication Association, Boston, Nov.

Thomas, D. (1987). "Presumption in Non-Policy Debate: A Case for Natural Presumption Based on Current Non-Policy Paradigms." In D. Thomas and J. Hart, eds. *Advanced Debate: Readings in Theory, Practice, and Teaching*. Lincolnwood, IL: National Textbook Co. 448–68.

Tomlinson, J. (1983). "The Philosophy and Development of CEDA." *CEDA Yearbook* 4: 1–5.

Tuman, J. (1987). "Getting to First Base: Prima Facie Arguments for Propositions of Value." *Journal of the American Forensic Association* 24: 84–94.

Ulrich, W. (1983). "Philosophical Systems as Paradigms for Value Debate." *CEDA Yearbook* 4: 22–28.

Vasilius, J. (1980). "Value Proposition Debate: A Pragmatic Approach." *CEDA Yearbook* 1: 49–59.

Verch, S. and Logue, B. (1982). "Increasing Value Clash: A Propositional and Structural Approach." *CEDA Yearbook* 3: 25–28.

Williams, R. (1970). *American Society: A Sociological Interpretation*. New York: Alfred A. Knopf.

Young, G. and Gaske P. (1984). On Prima-Facie Value Argumentation: The Policy Implications Affirmative." *CEDA Yearbook* 5: 24–30.

Zarefsky, D. (1980). "Criteria for Evaluating Non-Policy Argument." *CEDA Yearbook* 1: 9–16.

Zeuschner, R. (1982). "Value Benefits Analysis as an Affirmative Paradigm." *CEDA Yearbook* 3: 16–18.

Zeuschner, R. and Hill, C. (1981). "Psychological Presumption: Its Place in Value Topic Debate." *CEDA Yearbook* 2: 20–24.

39

Propositions of Fact

John P. Hart
Brian R. McGee

Ronald Matlon's (1978) essay on value debate provided a basis for theoretical discussion in CEDA for the last decade. His most recent essay (Matlon, 1988) reevaluating those ideas should be equally influential in the decade to come. Matlon argues that propositions of value have proven too difficult for CEDA participants and theorists alike, resulting in CEDA debaters considering these questions a propositions of quasi-policy, a direction that has proven counterproductive. Our own experience is that many debates over quasi-policy have suffered from a *bad* ambiguity about the requirements of such a debate (solvency burdens and so on).

While Matlon's solution to this problems is to allow CEDA debating on straightforward questions of policy, he also advocates debating questions of fact. "If CEDA wants to be in the forefront of generating theories of argument, its mission might be to turn to propositions of fact" (Matlon, 1988, p. 12). Recent debate topics in CEDA, we believe, already have given debaters the opportunity to interpret those topics as propositions of fact. We will argue (1) that a theoretical basis for debating propositions of fact exists; and (2) that fact interpretations of current CEDA topics should be allowed, if these interpretations are well-supported by the debaters advancing them.

Gustav Bergmann (1951) defines statements of fact as those that say "something about the object or objects it mentions, and, depending only on the properties of these objects, ... is either true or false" (p. 206). Subsequent definitions in the literature appear to be drawn from this one. Alternate terms have been used for fact-inference, alleged fact, and judgment. All seem equally problematic; as long as we consider the fact debatable, the term is acceptable.

Since the turn of the century, argumentation theorists have made various distinctions between propositions of policy and other sorts of propositions (Terris, 1963). Many contemporary argumentation texts categorize propositions as propositions of fact, value, or policy. But until high school Lincoln-Douglas debate and collegiate CEDA debate developed, debaters could "be sure that a proposition of policy [would] be chosen for the national debate topic" (Wood, 1968, p. 12). One may legitimately ask whether CEDA provides a real alternative to NDT policy debate, however, if debaters are limited by judges, coaches, or their own high school training in policy debate to what Zarefsky (1980) has called "quasi-policy" interpretations of debate topics.[1] Whatever one's concern for a CEDA/NDT distinction, we believe that resolutional interpretation that favors debate over facts is not unfeasible or unjustifiable in many instances.

FACTS, VALUES, AND POLICIES UNDERSTOOD

Zeigelmueller, Kay, and Dause (1990) assert CEDA "believes that the proposition selected for debate plays a major role in determining the quality of the educational experience students receive" (pp. 161–162). CEDA certainly has been associated with value debate for many years (see Herbeck and Wong, 1986). But the variety of propositions selected for CEDA debate is not cut-and-dried. Sometimes debaters argue about what sort of topic they are debating. On the spring 1988 topic, "RESOLVED: That the American judicial system has overemphasized freedom of the press," for example, some affirmative debaters argued that the topic was a proposition of fact, while many negative debaters complained in response that "overemphasis" necessitates a value judgment. (As we will argue below, both of these assertions are correct.)

It seems counterintuitive to many members of the CEDA debate community that facts could be debated. Some have argued that facts either exist or don't exist. The existence or nonexistence of facts can be verified in a way that denies debate. Facts are objective rather than subjective. Propositions of value and policy, some argue, are the proper subject of academic debates.

The underlying premise of this argument is that facts are objective and undeniable. However, human beings make their own judgments about what constitutes fact, and human beings cannot divorce themselves from their own subjectivity to make objective decisions no matter how desperately they attempt to do so. We humans make judgments about the world in which we are situated, and often those judgments conflict with those made by other humans. As Spinelli (1989) concludes:

> To argue the case for a correct or incorrect interpretation of reality is highly misleading. Our conclusions are relative—based as they are upon a number of socio-cultural variables. Ours is a phenomenal reality, and as such, it remains open to a multiplicity of interpretations (p. 4).

We might follow Sartre and Burke in arguing that human beings are condemned to choose, but their choices may be quite different. Judgments regarding propositions of fact are quite subjective. Different persons may have quite different views of what is and is not fact.[2]

Some propositions of fact might indeed be difficult to dispute. "RESOLVED: That gravity exists" would be difficult for most college students, or physicists, to counter. One might even make the claim, as does Hicks (1980), that any topic or interpretation of a topic that denies the affirmative or the negative "room to argue" should be rejected. We believe, however, that in most instances, debate regarding a resolution interpreted as a proposition of fact can at least take place at the level of *criteria*. As Zarefsky (1980) argues, "Determining what would qualify as supporting evidence for a factual statement seldom is automatic" (pp. 14–15). Decisions regarding what constitutes a fact are normally made with the aid of certain methods of evaluation, which vary from person to person or debate to debate. As Zeigelmueller, Kay, and Dause (1990) observe, "A fact is established not by determining widespread acceptance but by applying relevant criteria or definitions" (p. 32).

In examining the proposition of fact, it is important to distinguish how judgments made regarding facts are separated from other sorts of judgments. All propositions require judgment regarding the extent to which they are true or correct, though the nature of the judgments involved may vary according to the wording of the specific proposition. A *fact judgment* is a judgment made about the conditions we discover in the world. Since we experience the world as individual humans with widely varying backgrounds and beliefs, judgments are made in accordance with our differing, unique perspectives on the world. These fact judgments may often be in conflict, but every human, as a result of her or his differing perspective, has her or his own set of facts. We describe the world and its contents as we believe they exist. We make no *normative* claims about those descriptions. The fact judgment is, of course, subjective but makes no claim regarding the goodness or badness of the fact.

A *value judgment*, in contrast, is a judgment made about what the conditions we discover in the world ought to be. We make a normative claim. Value judgments go beyond describing reality to judge the goodness or badness of reality. A *policy judgment* goes even further. In addition to describing reality and judging its goodness or badness, a policy judgment makes specific recommendations for change, which might, for example, be passed by a legislature. An alternative to the status quo is offered. One recently published debate text agrees with our explanation: "A proposition of fact requests that the audience affirm a particular state of affairs; a proposition of value asks the audience to affirm and evaluate; and a proposition of policy asks the audience to approve some action" (Lee and Lee, 1989, p. 48).

The divisions between fact, value, and policy are not rigid. The division of debate topics into different types of propositions serves a useful pedagogical purpose only if such a division helps students analyze and argue propositions more thoroughly. While we offer definitions of the different types of propositions and describe different means of analyzing facts, values, and policies, an ambiguity will always exist as to whether a debate topic fits one category or another. It is an ambiguity that persists when choosing between fact approaches versus value and policy approaches to affirming or negating the debate topic (and these different approaches to the topic might all be justifiable). Nevertheless, as we argue below, relatively clear burdens exist for those debaters who choose to interpret the resolution as a factual claim.

DEBATING FACTS

As many debaters in CEDA have perceived, it is difficult to distinguish between values and policies in practice. Affirmative debaters who make value judgments about current conditions are called utopian by negative debaters, who insist that the affirmative describe an alternative to the undesirable current state of affairs. This request by the negative is not inherently unreasonable. Few Americans would conceptually disagree with an affirmative term which argues that "the continued existence of poverty in the United States is unjustified." The difficulty is in judging what constitutes a justification for poverty. If all the policies that might ease or eradicate poverty present enormous disadvantages, the status quo, however unpleasant, might be justified. Many propositions that appear to address values may require an assessment of policies, as opponents fo the value approach insist that future conditions (alternatives to the status quo) be considered. The ambiguity between values and policies is explained by Cronkhite (1966):

> The only difference [between policy and value judgments] is that we have moved from judgment of a past and present policy to judgment of a future policy. Thus, it appears that a proposition of policy is merely a proposition of value extended into the future (p. 15).

The difficulty in practice of distinguishing between value and policy judgments is primarily caused by the normative character of these judgments. When one decides that some current state of affairs is bad, the defenders of the status quo will invariably ask that a superior alternative be presented and defended before the current state of affairs is rejected. If the current unpleasant reality is, nevertheless, the best option among many poor options, it is no longer a bad option.

Quasi-policy debate is often frustrating for judges and debaters because burdens of proof are uncertain. While relatively abstract propositions (for instance, "Equality is highly valued.") may not require alternative visions of the future, relatively concrete propositions (such as, "U.S. covert involvement in Central America is unjustified.") may demand specification of alternative policies. The degree to which quasi-policy debate necessitates traditional policy burdens or legitimizes the conventions of policy debate is unclear to both debaters and judges. As many negative debaters might complain, no experience is worse than finding out your opponent's plan in the second affirmative rebuttal!

In contrast, debate over resolutions interpreted as propositions of fact might allow a clearer delineation of affirmative and negative burdens. While normative value and policy claims are difficult to separate in practice, descriptive claims are more readily separated from normative claims. One may judge the nature of reality without judging whether reality is good or bad. Judgments about fact are prerequisites to value and policy judgments "since it is frequently essential to establish relevant facts before we can reach decisions about values or policies" (Freeley, 1990, p. 42). However, judgments about facts do not necessitate agreement on whether the facts are good or bad. Fact judgment is value-laden, since the criteria for fact determination may be judged good or bad, appropriate or inappropriate. But the fact itself need not be (and is not) judged good or bad. For example, on the hypothetical topic "RESOLVED: That the current method of electing the president of the United States is undemocratic," an enormous amount of debate might occur over the definition (and the value implications!) of the word "undemocratic." The goodness or badness of democracy itself, however, would not be relevant in determining whether or not the resolution is true.

We believe that this example illustrates one of our basic premises: A fact judgment does not imply a value judgment about the *fact* in the same way that a value judgment often implies a policy judgment about the *value*. We live in a world constituted by human subjectivity, but subjective humans must nevertheless choose some best descriptions of the world before productive group discussion of values and policies can exist. To find solutions, for example, to environmental problems, the fact of environmental problems must be recognized. However, agreement on the existence of certain facts, even though the value choices of those people involved helped determine what would be called the facts, nevertheless, does not imply value implications. In contrast, all but the most abstract of value propositions tend in practice to imply policy implications. Debate over propositions of fact is common, and the debate community can recognize this fact of human existence by showing a willingness to allow debate over facts.

One might argue, in response, that debates about facts "are inseparable from values." Terris (1963) is only the first of many theorists to argue that the test for propositions of fact and value is essentially the same, that is, establish criteria and demonstrate that the proposition meets the criteria. This argument does not, however, deny the possibility of debating resolutions of fact. Terris ignores a subtle but important difference between criteria for fact judgment and criteria for value judgment. Criteria for judging values normally function as decision rules that indicate which values should be given preference in rendering a decision. In contemporary debate practice, it is common to offer a value hierarchy as a criteria for value judgment. Criteria for judging facts, however, set debatable standards for determining what should constitute a fact. Such standards might include "the consensus viewpoints agreed upon by a group of individuals" (Spinelli, 1989, p. 5), or, on legal issues, agreement of the proposition with legal precedent (which is often not clear-cut). The standards for assessing fact may be unabashedly normative, and much debate might surround the values implicit or explicit in those standards. However, it is the extent to which the proposition correctly describes the world, rather than the normative implications of that proposition, with which we are concerned.

The spring 1988 "freedom of the press" topic was in our view a proposition of fact. However, the criteria for judging "overemphasis" was often normative. If the criteria for overemphasis was the consensus of American citizens, then the implication was that the opinion of the majority should matter (a normative claim). Even if the criteria for overemphasis was "no increased risk of nuclear waste," the proposition was still a proposition of fact. A value choice regarding criteria for overemphasis was required to affirm that topic, but the proposition nevertheless demanded a judgment about fact. The debate may ever center around the values implicit in the criteria for judging fact, but once the criteria is determined, it is the fact judgment of the proposition that is accepted or rejected by the judge. This example is consistent with Church and Wilbanks' (1986) observation that "the inclusion of a value in a proposition does not necessarily indicate that it is a proposition of value. Only when two values are compared do we have a proposition of value" (Church and Wilbanks, 1986, p. 40).

Many debaters and judges might wish for a series of stock issues, similar to those widely used in policy debate, with which one could evaluate propositions of fact. Potential for establishing a basis to debate questions of fact is found in Hultzen (1958). Hultzen's application of Quintilian's doctrine of *status* provides the potential for developing a criteria for evaluation of fact judgments. Hultzen noted three points of status: conjectural (an sit), definitive (quid sit), and qualitative (quale sit). Conjectural questions concern conjecture or existence of fact, definitive questions concern definition or classification, and qualitative questions deal with qualification or reservation (Hultzen, 1958, p. 98).

Applying these definitions to the freedom of press topic mentioned above, one might ask: (1) What does the American judicial system do? (2) Does that amount to overemphasis? and (3) Is it justified (are there reservations to that statement)? These three criteria are viewed by Hultzen as interdependent. The definitive question (Matlon's [1978] "definitive issue") concerns the establishment of a criteria by which the fact contained in the proposition is judged. The conjectural question (Matlon's [1978] "designative issue") concerns whether or not the proposition meets the established criteria. The qualitative question asks whether or not the criteria and the inference that the proposition meets the criteria are justified. In considering the freedom of press topic, negative debaters might primarily address the qualitative question by arguing that the affirmative's criteria is not a desirable one for judging overemphasis. If majoritarianism is a bad standard for determining facts (because the masses are poorly educated or irrational), then the criteria may not be justified.

Hultzen also covers some areas that are of importance in distinguishing questions of fact and policy and, more specifically, in delineating their implications in questions of fact. These are very important in that a review of literature indicates a gray area in differentiating questions of fact and policy. These issues are highly relevant for those wishing to determine how much policy implications should be considered in propositions of fact. Hultzen notes conjecture can exist in the deliberative as well as the forensic process (the term "forensic," in this case, meaning legal not debate). In deliberative analysis he theorizes that the issues of conjecture, definition, and quality can be considered by the issues of ill, reformability, remedy, and cost. These issues are synonymous with the stock issues in policy debate. Brownlee (1980) argued that propositions have value implications and, therefore, these stock issues can be used. However, a reading of Hultzen reveals the following reservations. First, he viewed questions of value as questions of fact, so Brownlee's thesis more precisely should read that questions of fact have policy implications (p. 101). Second, Hultzen notes that a forensic conjecture is only equivalent to certain conditions; therefore, the application is not always applicable. (It should be noted that he gives two reasons for this, the second of which, that the deliberative has no limit on time, is irrelevant to our discussion since this is not the case in the academic debate setting (p. 106).) Finally, he argues that there is a difference between questions of fact and policy (pp. 100, 123). (This position can be buttressed by interpreting Bergmann's definition as meaning exclusively the objects mentioned: not the word "only" in the definition.)

Those who seek to allow policy implications in questions of fact, as some of the literature indicated is acceptable, should note two items. First, Hultzen states the affirmative defines the ground (p. 113). This should indicate clash, as the affirmative would determine the ground on which policies are to be discussed. Such clash should answer the objection of those who view questions of fact as vague questions of policy. Second, Hultzen notes that the fourth stock issue of cost means that the difficulty that may be experienced during implementation of the policy should be considered (p. 114). This should help ground debating questions of fact in the real world as Hultzen's definition, combined with the absence of the term "should" in nonpolicy topics, could serve as a check on the advocacy of utopian positions that some have argued to be the bane of policy debate.

CONCLUSION

The following conclusions seem reasonable. First, the debate community has had difficulty, at both theoretical and practical levels, in coming to grips with propositions of value. More often value judgments become quasi-policy judgments, and confusion results. Second, some of these questions can, and perhaps ever more correctly, should be viewed as propositions of fact. Third, the potential for development of a theoretical basis for the consideration of propositions of fact exists. Fourth, depending on the wording of the debate topic, some sort of demarcation between propositions of fact and propositions of value and policy is possible. The distinction between facts and values may well be easier to make than the distinction between values and policies. Finally, values do enter into judgments about facts. In the end, however, the judge uses some criteria to make a judgment about the worth of the *description* contained by the proposition.

We believe that a strong rationale for debating propositions of fact exists. Debate over propositions of fact seems more clear-cut and less difficult than is debate over propositions of quasi-policy, where affirmative and negative burdens are often shrouded in uncertainty.

Perhaps the claim that debate had best focus on questions of policy is true. To definitively rebut that claim is not our purpose, although we do argue that allowing debaters to debate over the better resolutional interpretation (including factual interpretations) does not seem unreasonable. That is one of the reasons we have the forensic laboratory. We urge debaters to examine whether or not future resolutions can be interpreted as questions of fact, and then debate them accordingly.

Notes

1. We do not mean to argue that there *should* be a clear CEDA/NDT distinction, but we question whether such a differentiation exists in theory *or* practice. We so tend to believe that quasi-policy debate as currently practiced sometimes allows affirmatives to become moving targets, as we argue later in this essay. As Herbeck and Wong (1986) argue, "Our attempts to separate these interrelated issues [policies and values] have frequently led to ambiguous and unsatisfying argumentation" (p. 15).
2. Zarefsky (1980) distinguishes facts, which apparently are easily determined via some standard advanced within the proposition itself, from quasi-facts, which appear to be statements of fact but require some controversial and debatable determination of what constitutes adequate support of the correctness of the factual claim. A proposition of fact, for Zarefsky, might be "RESOLVED: The outdoor temperature is 60 degrees Fahrenheit," while a proposition of quasi-fact would be "RESOLVED: That the two-party system is dying in America" (p. 14). We find this distinction interesting, but we will continue to use the "fact" label to generically denote any proposition, debatable or not, that describes reality rather than makes a normative judgment about reality.

References

Bergmann, G. (1951). "Ideology." *Ethics* 61: 206.

Brownlee, D. (1980). "Advocacy and Values." *CEDA Yearbook* 1: 43–47.

Church, R. T. and Wilbanks, C. (1986). *Values and Policies in Controversy: An Introduction to Argumentation and Debate*. Scottsdale, AZ: Gorsuch Scarisbrick.

Cronkhite, G. (1966). "Propositions of Past and Future Fact and Value: A Proposed Classification." *Journal of the American Forensic Association* 3: 11–16.

Freeley, A. J. (1990). *Argumentation and Debate: Critical Thinking for Reasoned Decision Making*. 7th ed. Belmont, CA: Wadsworth.

Herbeck, D. and Wong, K. (1986). "The Indivisibility of Value Claims from Policy Positions: An Argument for Policy in Value Debate." *CEDA Yearbook* 7: 14–28.

Hicks, D. (1990). *Victimization in Criterial Argumentation: Moving from "Whine" to Argument*. Paper presented at the meeting of the Speech Communication Association, Chicago, Nov.

Hultzen, L. S. (1958). "Status in Deliberative Rhetoric." In D. C. Bryant, ed. *The Rhetorical Idiom: Essays in Rhetoric, Oratory, Language, and Drama*. New York: Russell & Russell.

Lee, R. E. and Lee, K. K. (1989). *Arguing Persuasively*. New York: Longman.

Matlon, R. J. (1978). "Debating Propositions of Value." *Journal of the American Forensic Association* 14: 194–204.

Matlon, R. J. (1988). "Debating Propositions of Value: An Idea Revisited." *CEDA Yearbook* 9: 1–14.

Spinelli, E. (1989). *The Interpreted World*. Beverly Hills, CA: Sage.

Terris, W. F. (1963). "The Classification of the Argumentative Proposition." *The Quarterly Journal of Speech* 49: 266–73.

Wood, R. V. (1968). *Strategic Debate*. 2nd ed. Lincolnwood, IL: National Textbook Co.

Zarefsky, D. (1980). "Criteria for Evaluative Non-Policy Argument." *CEDA Yearbook* 1: 9–16.

Zeigelmueller, G. W., Kay, J., and Dause, C. A. (1990). *Argumentation: Inquiry and Advocacy*. 2nd ed. Englewood Cliffs: Prentice-Hall.

40

Towards a Strategic Focus in Nonpolicy Debate

David J. Shipley[1]

A coherent strategy is essential to either team's success in competitive debate. As with any rhetorical actor, debaters must present "a plan of action, [or] a maneuver designed to overcome the obstacles in a particular rhetorical situation" (Campbell, 1982, p. 87). Strategy is this plan of action. Strategic debate is based on the relationship created between the various theoretical issues in a given debate.

THE ROLE OF THE CRITIC IN STRATEGIC DEBATE

The strategic focus relies on the debater's ability to analyze and synthesize issues. The strategic focus requires the teams to explain, justify, and relate arguments to the round as a whole. To accomplish this goal, critics must allow debaters the freedom to argue any theoretical position.

Nonintervention by critics allow debaters to increase their understanding of argumentation theory. Ulrich (1987) argues that by "requiring that debaters be able to defend argumentation theory, we require that they understand argument" (p. 186). For example, if a critic believes that topicality is always an absolute voting issue, debaters will be allowed to simply assert that topicality is a voting issue without explanation. This standard of proof differs from the standard employed in every other argument in a debate.

The rejection of theoretical arguments based on a critic's belief chills the development of theory. The application of a specific theoretical construct to a debate by a critic, regardless of the arguments advanced, destroys any incentive to argue or understand alternative theories. Ulrich (1987) argues that "encouraging debaters to argue theory in a round (which obviously cannot be done if the judge is rigid about theoretical issues) would expose debaters to a greater number of theories, as well as encourage them to develop modifications of existing theories" (p. 186). The discussion of theory in the debate round mirrors the discussion of theory outside of the debate round. Balthrop (1987) supports this position, stating that when "disagreement exists within the community over such issues . . . then such issues are likely to receive more discussion in debates because such issues are themselves now open for debate. At the same time, if practice does precede theory, it is equally probable that attacks upon widely accepted communal standards, generated for strategic reasons, may well bring those practices into question" (p. 176).

Intervention on theoretical issues reduces critical thinking. A critic, by making arguments for one side of a theoretical dispute, destroys incentive for either team to argue. There is no reason to argue if the critic's beliefs alone determine the outcome. A critic's unwillingness to accept any theoretical position reduces the debater's flexibility in the selection of arguments. Critics can promote quality argumentation by letting the debate be decided by the team that better explains and applies the theory in the context of the round. Balthrop (1987) argues that "the strength or persuasiveness of any argument in any given debate will emerge only through the interactions of the debaters themselves," since "no absolute, identifiable formula exists for evaluating any given argument" (p. 173). Ulrich (1987) states that the end result is better argumentation when critics require "that debaters discover weaknesses in argument and explain those weaknesses" before rejecting the argument (p. 187).

The use of a theory within a debate round allows the theory to be tested in the marketplace of debate. Oliver Wendell Holmes, Jr., dissenting in *Abrams v. United States* (1919), stated that "the ultimate good desired is better reached by free trade in ideas—that the best test of truth is the power of the thought to get itself accepted in the competition of the market" (Burton, 1979, p. 79). The marketplace of debate will reject impractical positions while allowing stronger positions to demonstrate a practical validity. Ulrich (1987) states that debate, like science, "can grow only by encouraging the development of new theories that, while they may seem initially to be weak, have the opportunity to prove themselves in the marketplace of ideas" (p. 185).

BURDENS UNDER THE STRATEGIC FOCUS

Beyond recognizing that "presumption and burden of proof are fundamental issues in argument," nonpolicy theory has not adequately explored the relation between presumption and the burden of proof (Church, 1986, p. 29). The concepts of burden of proof and presumption are not synonymous but confusingly interrelated. This confusion has been caused by the "common but misleading practice of using the terms 'presumption' and 'burden of proof' as if they were interchangeable" (Lichtman and Rohrer, 1987, p. 365).

In a legal setting there are two separate burdens, the burden of production and the burden of persuasion, to which "the term 'burden of proof' is occasionally but confusingly applied to" (Neuman, 1990, p. 214). According to *Black's Law Dictionary*, the "burden of proof is a term which describes two different concepts; first, the 'burden of persuasion,' which under traditional view never shifts from one party to the other at any stage in the proceeding, and second, the 'burden of going forward with the evidence' [or burden of production], which may shift back and forth between the parties as the trial progresses" (1990, p. 198, see also Dressler, 1987, pp. 45–56 and Neuman, 1990, pp. 213–215).

The burden of production determines which team must present which issues. In a criminal proceeding the "rule establishing the burden of production identifies the party at trial on whom is placed the initial obligation to provide factual evidence to support the particular legal claim in question" (Dressler, 1987, p. 46). In a criminal trial, the burden of production is not solely assigned to the prosecution. For example, in a murder trial, the prosecution must to provide evidence on the elements of the crime while the defense must provide evidence to support an affirmative defense of insanity or self-defense (Dressler, 1987, pp. 46–47). In debate, the burden of production is the same as the burden of presenting a prima facie case. Church (1986) argues that the "a priori question about argument is: 'Should we argue?' If the answer is yes, then a prima facie case must be put forth to justify the activity of arguing" (p. 29). Freeley (1986) defines prima facie as being "structurally and qualitatively strong enough to be logically self-sufficient" (p. 166).

To "justify the activity" or be "logically self-sufficient," the affirmative needs to discuss what the argument is about, how the argument will be evaluated, and how the evidence presented by the affirmative proves the probable truth of the argument. For example, if an individual wishes to initiate an argument on the proposition "rock music is bad," that individual must define the proposition. The individual must decide if rock music includes Willie Nelson, Sonny and Cher, and the Beatles; if rock music is limited to music that is played above a certain decibel level; or if rock music is music performed by people who wear leather and have long hair. After some limitation of the proposition has been achieved, the evaluative term must be defined. The term "bad" may be evaluated in terms of the effect of rock music on listeners' ear drums, the presence of satanic messages, or the propensity of listeners to commit suicide.

An assertion has been developed after the individual initiating the argument has limited the proposition and provided a means of evaluation. The assertion in the above hypothetical proposition could read "music that is played very loud is bad in terms of causing people to commit suicide." Since assertions have no inherent value in argumentation, the party initiating the argument needs to support the assertion by providing evidence such as testimony of parents, psychological studies, statistical studies, or judicial opinions. Once evidence to support the assertion is provided, the noninitiating party is able to respond. In the absence of an explanation of what the resolution is about (limitation) or how the resolution will be evaluated (evaluation), it is impossible to have a structured argument. If the affirmative does not give a reason why the premise is true (justification), there is no need for the negative to respond to an unsupported assertion. The affirmative's prima facie burden of presentation encompasses presenting a limitation, evaluation, and justification of the resolution.

The negative burden of presentation encompasses the introduction of new issues into the debate by the negative. This burden can be contrasted with the negative burden of rejoinder that requires the negative to respond to previously introduced arguments. The negative burden of presentation requires that counterwarrants, generic arguments, value-based disadvantages, and other offcase positions be introduced by the negative, if such positions are introduced at all. The burden of presentation also deals with theoretical positions such as whole resolution, hasty generalization, and subjustification or over-justification that bring in positions not included in the affirmative burden of presentation. The negative response to affirmative limitation (definitions), evaluation (criteria and decision rule), and justification (proof) are the only burdens of the negative that fall under the burden of rejoinder.

The burden of persuasion relates to the substantive issues that the affirmative must win to justify the resolution. *Black's Law Dictionary* (1990) defines the burden of persuasion as "the onus on the party with the burden of proof to convince the trier of fact of all the elements of his case" (p. 196). In law this burden relates to the amount of evidence needed to prove each element of a crime (Dressler, 1987).

This burden of persuasion has often been described in argument as the burden of presumption. For nonpolicy debate, in a strategic context, presumption is superseded by argumentation relating to the criteria and decision rule. All views of presumption require a level of significance to determine the amount of proof needed. This level of significance is determined by the arguments advanced in the context of a debate.

Traditional presumption in policy debate is placed against the advocate of a plan on the basis of an assumed risk of change. One flaw with the traditional rule is the failure to establish a degree of significance. Lichtman and Rohrer (1987) state that traditional presumption fails to address "how significant an advantage should be necessary to overcome an unfavorable prejudgment" (p. 349). Under traditional analysis, "Presumption can be assigned a mere feather's weight, toppling as soon as the affirmative shows any perceptible advantage. Or, it can impose a heavy burden of significance, upholding the present system until a large advantage to change is demonstrated" (p. 367).

Hypothesis testing places presumption against the resolution (hypothesis) to "assure a rigorous test of the proposition" (Zarefsky, 1987, p. 209). This placement of presumption mirrors the scientific method of testing, where the scientist must disprove the null hypothesis to establish the probable truth of the hypothesis. Vasilius (1980) argues for the application of hypothesis testing to nonpolicy debate.

In adapting the hypothesis-testing paradigm to nonpolicy debate, Scott and Wynn (1981) argue, the affirmative must sustain "enough proofs to overcome the false claim risk but also a preponderance of arguments, proofs, evidence, and reasoning over and above those advanced by the negative team" (p. 28). What constitutes enough proof is "situationally dependent on the arguments advanced by the affirmative and negative teams" (p. 28). Presumption is determined within the round based on the arguments made by the participants. Scott and Wynn (1981) further state that "significance burdens in debate rounds may vary accordingly, depending upon the arguments, criteria, and good reasons presented" (p. 29).

Thomas (1987) argues in favor of a natural presumption centered on the beliefs and attitudes of the audience. Natural presumption may invite intervention by critics who necessarily have a view of the validity of the resolution. An exaggerated use of natural presumption may yield undesirable results, but under most circumstances presumption would be determined "from the arguments put to [the critic] in the situation, not from any initial artificial presumption against the resolution" (Thomas, 1987, p. 451). Thomas further explains that "presumption must be appropriated by the debaters based on the arguments they bring to bear in the debate" (p. 451). This view of natural presumption allows the judge to decide from the arguments presented in a round which values to assign presumption.

Zeuschner and Hill (1981) argue in favor of a psychological presumption on the basis that "our opinions as a society are primarily based on our values as a society" (p. 22). This rule does not result in a random assignment of presumption against the affirmative. Due to different measures of societal opinion "the location of psychological presumption can always be at issue in a dispute between contending sides of an argument" (p. 22). This leads to the conclusion that the negative and affirmative are both "free to claim a presumption and communicate these claims to the audience" (p. 23).

All theories of presumption recognize the existence of a level of significance that must be overcome by the team that presumption is assigned against. Further, all of the above theories allow presumption to be determined within the round. In nonpolicy debate, this level of significance is found in the decision rule that accompanies criteria. This decision rule determines the level of persuasion that the affirmative must meet to establish the probable truth of the resolution. It is the decision rule, not presumption, that determines the level of persuasion required in nonpolicy debate.

LIMITATION OF THE RESOLUTION

In nonpolicy debate the affirmative limits and interprets the resolution through the presentation of definitions. Definitions determine what issues may be viewed to decide the validity of the resolution. Any issue that falls outside the bounds of the topic cannot be considered in evaluating the resolution. Definitions also determine affirmative prima-faciality, negative ground for topicality, and the scope of the terms in the resolution.

An affirmative failure to present a prima facie justification of the resolution, as delimited in the first affirmative, constitutes a failure to meet the affirmative burden of presentation. If the negative proves that the affirmative justification doesn't fall within the bounds set forth in the affirmative's definitions, the affirmative has not presented a warrant for the resolution. Since the negative has no warrant to respond to, the negative does not incur any burdens of presentation or rejoinder. There is no possibility of argument due to the affirmative failure, and as a result there is no substantive issue available to vote on. There is no reason to vote against the negative for not meeting nonexisting burdens. The critic can only vote against the affirmative for the failure to meet the prima facie affirmative burden of presentation.

For example, in debating the resolution "significantly stronger third parties in presidential elections would be beneficial to the United

States," many negative teams argued that the affirmative did not justify their own definition of "stronger." An affirmative may have defined stronger as relating to "vigor, durability, or power . . . " and provided analysis that the postfix "-er" was "used to form the comparative degree of adjectives" (American Heritage Dictionary, 1981, p. 1,277, p. 443). The negative argued that the affirmative only proved that *current* third parties were beneficial, where the resolution, as defined by the affirmative, required proof that comparatively more vigorous, durable, and powerful third parties would be beneficial. Since the affirmative did not meet their own definition of "stronger" as it modified "third parties," the affirmative failed to meet the burden of presentation in terms of justification.

While the negative must do no more than point out affirmative insufficiency to win the round under such circumstances, any further negative actions may relieve the affirmative of their burden of presentation. Any negative warrant against the resolution provides a justification for not adopting the resolution. The presence of this justification allows both teams to commence an argument. The ability to conduct an argument weakens the rationale for voting on a failure to meet the burden of presentation, since the critic is able to vote on a substantive issue.

While the affirmative's right to define and limit the topic is unquestioned, the negative has a corresponding right to challenge these definitions. The negative challenge of definitions is done through arguing topicality. To argue topicality the negative must establish standards to determine which definitions should delimit the resolution.

The negative should use a threshold standard when arguing that the affirmative has the burden of presenting a reasonable definition. A threshold standard sets a minimum level of reasonableness, below which any definition would be considered unreasonable. For example, in the resolution "the Supreme Court has granted excessive power to law enforcement agencies," many negatives argued that the affirmative definition of "granted" was not reasonable. Many affirmatives used *Black's Law Dictionary* to define grant as "to bestow or confer . . . a gift or bestowal by one having authority over it, as of land or money" (1990, p. 357). If a negative team sets a threshold standard that definitions must be in the proper context, the affirmative would violate this standard since the affirmative definition is drawn from the context of grants of land or money rather than grants of police power. The affirmative definition under such a standard would be unreasonable.

Once the negative proves that an affirmative definition is unreasonable, the negative is able to impact this violation in one of two ways. If the negative does not offer a counterdefinition, the critic could vote against the affirmative for a failure to properly limit the resolution (unless the affirmative could come up with a definition that meets the negative reasonability standard and makes the affirmative warrant topical). If the negative provides a counterdefinition that excludes the affirmative warrant from the topic, topicality would be a voting issue.

If the negative argues that the limitation of the resolution should be determined by the best definition, the negative must present a comparative standard that allows two definitions to be judged on a continuum. For example, if the negative argues that broad definitions are better, and presents a more inclusive definition than the affirmative's definition, the negative will have shown an affirmative violation of the broad definition standard. If the negative fails to present a counter-definition, the critic has no choice but to accept the flawed affirmative definition.

Topicality can become a significant issue when the negative argues counterwarrants that meet the negative definition. The critic can only look at arguments within the bounds of the topic. If the definitional argument renders the affirmative warrant nontopical, and the judge is only able to evaluate the negative warrant, the resolution will be disproven. While "topicality by itself would not be a voting issue, although tied with other issues (such as arguing that the resolution is untrue, given negative definitions) it can be a critical issue" (Ulrich, 1981, p. 3).

The negative is also able to attack the affirmative on the issue of underjustification. Affirmative definitions either permit a narrow inter-pretation or allow any number of interpretations to fall under the resolution. For example, under the resolution "the trend towards increasing foreign investment in the United States is detrimental to this nation," foreign investment was commonly defined to contain both direct investment (such as buildings) and portfolio investment (such as stocks and bonds). An affirmative case that defined foreign investment as both direct and portfolio investment and presented a justification only in terms of direct investment would have underjustified the resolution.

Whether underjustification is a voting issue by itself has been discussed extensively elsewhere (see Adams and Wilkins, 1987; Bile, 1988; Berube, 1987; and McGee, 1988). Under the strategic approach, complete justification is not a prima facie burden of presentation. It is unreasonable to hold an affirmative to this standard since there is a difference of opinion in the debate community as to the validity of underjustification as a voting issue. Underjustification falls under the negative burden of presentation due to the fact that underjustification assumes the affirmative has presented a valid warrant (thus meeting prima facie burdens) but attacks the resulting inference. It is illogical to hold the first affirmative to standards that are not introduced into the context of the round until the first negative speech. Total justification cannot be a prima facie burden, therefore the affirmative should be able to meet the negative standards in later speeches.

EVALUATION OF THE RESOLUTION

In nonpolicy debate the evaluation of the resolution is achieved through criteria and a decision rule. Gill (1988) states "criterion as a standard for judgment remains the most sound analytical basis for deciding nonpolicy controversies" (p. 87). A criterion is the operative definition of the key evaluative term or terms in the resolution (Church and Wilbanks, 1986, pp. 156–157). Criteria define the evaluative terms of a resolution by selecting a goal, value, or factual situation to evaluate the resolution. For example, in the resolution "the Supreme Court has granted excessive power to law enforcement agencies" the key evaluative term is "excessive." An affirmative may define excessive in terms of separation of powers (a goal), life (a value), or use a comparison between grants of power to law enforcement and grants of power to other agencies (a factual criterion).

Criteria function to focus the scope of the debate. A criterion limits debate to substantive arguments that impact the goal, value, or factual situation that defines the key evaluative term. If the negative runs an argument that does not impact on criteria, even if the result is catastrophe, the affirmative does not have to refute it (Gill, 1988). For example, under the law enforcement topic if an affirmative presents a value of due process, any impacts on life (such as a nuclear war) are not viewed in evaluating the resolution.

A decision rule is the standard by which criteria are measured or weighed. Zarefsky (1980) states the need for a measuring device since "each type of nonpolicy question requires judgment on the *standards* or *criteria* for decision—the decision rule. The means of resolving the dispute are themselves subject to argument" (p. 15). Like other standards, a decision rule can either provide a threshold or comparison. For a value-based criterion of privacy, a threshold decision rule would find the resolution to be true if the affirmative shows an increase in privacy, while a comparative decision rule would prove the resolution true if the affirmative shows an increase in privacy greater than the increase that would occur if the resolution was negated.

Decision rules can be stated or implied. If a decision rule is not explicit, it would be reasonable for the negative to infer a decision rule. For example, if the affirmative sets a criterion of freedom and maintains that freedom is good, a decision rule that instructs the critic to vote for the team that shows the most benefit or least harms to freedom can be implied. A decision rule is necessary, since to make a decision "a judgment must be made as to whether the circumstances in question satisfy the conditions stipulated in the decision rule" (Zarefsky, 1980, p. 15).

To indict affirmative criteria the negative must offer counter-criteria. The negative can attack the affirmative criteria by proving there is a higher or better value or proving the affirmative criterion is inherently bad. If the negative attacks the affirmative criterion on the basis that there is a better value (goal or factual situation), this infers a comparison with another value (goal or factual situation) presented by the negative.

If the negative attacks criteria by arguing that the value (goal or factual situation) chosen and advanced by the affirmative is inherently bad, a negative success has the effect of a turnaround on the affirmative criteria and decision rule. For example, a negative can argue that obtaining democracy is a bad value since it is impossible to attain perfect democracy, and it is not good to set an impossible goal. If the negative is successful then the effect of any increase in democracy by the affirmative would negate the resolution. The affirmative case would become a warrant against the resolution.

The negative may also target the decision rule for not fulfilling its function. A flawed decision rule does not measure or weigh criteria effectively. The negative must present an alternative decision rule to be successful in attacking a decision rule. If the affirmative presents a decision rule that is vague and difficult to measure criteria by, but the negative does not present an alternative, the round must be analyzed in terms of vague and fuzzy criteria. This evidences a preference to determine a round on a substantive judgment of the merits of the resolution rather than determining the outcome on a procedural issue.

The need for a counter-criteria is further justified in view of the burden of presentation. The affirmative has the burden of presentation in terms of evaluation (criteria and decision rule). The affirmative needs to present a method of evaluation, and then provide a warrant that justifies the resolution using that method of evaluation. The first affirmative cannot be expected to meet burdens and standards relating to what is necessary in criteria that are presented in the first negative speech.

THE CASE ATTACK

Under the strategic focus, if the negative refutes the affirmative case and does not offer any offcase positions, the negative will have disproven the resolution. The negative can refute the affirmative by either turning an impact or taking out a link.

By winning a turnaround on the affirmative case, the negative can disprove the resolution. For example, if an affirmative, under the resolution "violence is a justified response to political oppression," attempts to prove that violence brings attention to societal problems (supporting a criterion that values the politicization of problems), and the negative proves that violence actually detracts attention from societal problems, the negative has disproven the resolution. The affirmative case now becomes a warrant against the resolution. The critic must vote against the affirmative for not meeting their burden of persuasion.

If the negative takes out the links to the affirmative case, the negative has disproven the affirmative warrant for the resolution. Under the politicization of societal problems case as described above, if the negative proves that violence is used on behalf of known societal problems and does not cause any further politicization of societal problems, then the negative would disprove the affirmative warrant. Since the affirmative decision rule requires an increase in politicization to be shown to result from violence, and since the affirmative does not show an increase in violence, the affirmative has not met their burden of persuasion.

IN SEARCH OF THE CAREFUL GENERALIZATION

If the negative chooses to attack affirmative induction, the negative must address affirmative definitions, set standards to measure induction, and disprove the resolution with counterwarrants.

The negative must view definitions to determine how the affirmative has limited the scope of the resolution. If the affirmative's definitions narrow the resolution to the example presented, it is impossible to dispute the validity of the affirmative warrant on the basis of faulty induction. For example, under the violence topic some affirmatives defined political oppression as being the forcible rape of a woman. The affirmative case meets the whole of the resolution in terms of political oppression since rape is the only allowable example under the affirmative definitions. In such an instance, it is useless for the negative to attack affirmative induction without first attacking the narrow definition.

The distinction between broad definitions and narrow definitions is evident in assessing the topicality of counterwarrants. For example, if the negative ran a counterwarrant asserting that violence in Latin America is unjustified in response to the affirmative rape case, the counterwarrant would be nontopical, and the affirmative would not be required to refute the nontopical counterwarrant.

If the affirmative defines the resolutional terms broadly or the negative succeeds in substituting broad definitions by arguing topicality, the negative may attack affirmative induction and offer counterwarrants to disprove the resolution. The validity of counterwarrants and the fallacy of hasty generalization has been discussed thoroughly by other authors (see Paulsen and Rhodes, 1979; Berube, 1984; Simon, 1984; Ulrich, 1984; Tolbert and Hunt, 1985; Biggers, 1985; and McGee, 1988). McGee (1988) argued accurately that "current argumentation evaluation practices in CEDA are unacceptable when debaters utilize the argument from example. Inductive strength of the competing arguments from example, determined primarily by standards concerned with example germaneness and size, must be weighed before other assessments regarding those arguments are made" (p. 69). The strategic focus requires an analysis on the basis of germaneness and size and an explanation of how the example meets the standards by being representative and typical within the context of the round.

Arguing against affirmative induction requires clear and measurable standards. As stated above, it is not enough to provide a standard of typicality without showing how the affirmative is not typical. There is a need to compare the germaneness and size of the affirmative warrant with the negative counterwarrants. To show that the affirmative is not typical, the negative has to set standards of typicality relating to the words in the resolution and determine how to measure typicality. For example, in the resolution "RESOLVED: That increased foreign investment in the United States is detrimental to this nation," a negative's explanation of an attack on affirmative induction might be as follows:

> Affirmative violates typicality on the phrase "foreign investment." There are a number of different types of foreign investment, including portfolio or stock investment, the purchase of land, the purchase of government securities, and the purchase of factories. To be typical they must address a preponderance or 51 percent of foreign investment. Otherwise everyone is left in the dark about the majority of the resolution. According to negative evidence, the purchase of land is less than 5 percent. The affirmative fails to provide proof about 51 percent of the resolution. The impact of this argument is that in offcase the negative shows that the purchase of government securities and stock is beneficial, and we also show that securities and stock together represent around 70 percent of the total of foreign investment. Since the negative meets the standard of showing a preponderance of foreign investment is beneficial, a negative ballot is warranted.

The above analysis consists of five steps. The first step is to set the standard (in the example above, 51 percent), the second step is to justify the standard ("otherwise . . . left in the dark"), the third step is to prove the affirmative doesn't meet (land is only 5 percent), the fourth step is to show that the negative better meets the standard in terms of size (securities and stock is around 70 percent), and the fifth step is to show the impact of accepting the standard on the round (negative is more representative and shows the resolution to be false).

LOOKING FOR THE SUM OF THE PARTS

The need for the affirmative to present a holistic justification of the resolution has been debated in rounds and in academic journals (Bile, 1987; Madsen and Chandler 1988). Under a strategic context, if the negative proves that the affirmative does not support the whole resolution, they do not necessarily win the round. The affirmative does support part of the resolution. Only if the negative presents an offcase position that is relatively more generic to the resolution than the affirmative case should the negative win the ballot. Bile (1987) sets this standard in arguing that "the more generic an argument is to the resolution the greater its validity" (p. 13). If no support is given by the negative, the only inference of probable truth is the affirmative warrant. The critic has no choice but to vote for the partial warrant. Justification for a holistic focus not being a prima facie issue is provided above in the discussion of underjustification and hasty generalization. For a critic to weigh any generic argument within a strategic paradigm, the argument must fall within affirmative definitions and impact on either affirmative criteria or a negative counter-criteria.

CONCLUSION

K. Bartanan (1987) tells us that the way listeners choose between stories is in "examination of the completeness of the narrative elements presented and the relationships between the elements presented in support of a particular interpretation" (p. 420). A strategic focus, like a story, looks at the elements of a debate round in terms of the completeness of elements and the relationship between the elements. The result of a strategic focus increases the clash, clarity, and coherence of a debate.

The increase in clash does not come from addressing affirmative interpretation and case. In fact a strategic focus allows the negative to ignore case in some instances. If the negative chooses to ignore case, the negative must justify ignoring case and show an alternate view that disproves the resolution. This has the effect of introducing a larger number of issues into the debate and allows the negative to avoid making eight minutes of mindless topicality arguments and case presses. The affirmative, being denied the advantage of arguing on case, has two avenues of attack against the negative strategy. The affirmative can argue against the overview that justified the substantive position or against the substantive position itself.

While the multiple layers of analysis the negative may present can become confusing, the overall effect would be an increase in coherence. Often a theory argument is run without answering the question "So what?" In a strategic paradigm both teams are required to answer that question in terms of how specific arguments impact the decision as a whole. The negative must explain the relationship between the arguments so the critic can evaluate the arguments and reach a decision.

A strategic focus will increase education and critical thinking. Often debate is done in a vacuum. Whole resolution arguments are used in shells where they are not explained. Offcase positions are not related to anything, and the criteria often become moot by rebuttals. The strategic focus forces debaters to demonstrate a knowledge of how to apply the theories. A strategic focus asks debaters to go beyond stating the standards and asserting that the other team doesn't meet them. A strategic approach justifies, if not demands, making comparative judgments: Counterwarrants must compete against the affirmative warrants, negative interpretation must compete against the affirmative interpretation, and all arguments must be weighed through the decision rule. The strategic focus forces debaters to think, which will be more useful when they leave debate than knowing how to reach a nuclear war in four cards or less.[2]

This article represents an initial attempt to characterize a debate round as what it really is: an argument where the debaters are able to argue about how the argument is to be conducted. By limiting the prima facie burdens to presenting a limitation of the resolution, a method of evaluation of the resolution, and a justification in light of definitions and the decision rule, an attempt was made to give affirmative the greatest leeway to develop case approaches. By allowing the negative to introduce any theoretical argument to challenge the affirmative, the strategic focus allows the negative great leeway in argument selection. By limiting the availability of procedural issues for the critic to vote on, the strategic focus emphasizes the need for substantive arguments over a restrictive procedural posture that precludes an analysis of the issues.

Notes

1. While I take full responsibility for all ideas contained within this article, I am greatly indebted to Dr. David Thomas for his advice and encourage-

ment and to Andrew Goulet, who contributed to the initial draft of this article. This article is dedicated to the coaches from the University of Richmond who attempted to teach me how to debate strategically.

2. I hope this article is more coherent than those four-card nuclear war scenarios. The word "towards" is inserted in the title of this article to signify that the thoughts contained within are not completely developed. I would like nothing more than a scathing rebuttal to my ideas (no ad hominum attacks please) or a presentation of suggestions for modifications.

References

American Heritage Dictionary of the English Language (1981). Boston: Houghton Mifflin.

Adams, N. and Wilkins, T. (1987). "The Role of Justification in Topic Analysis." *CEDA Yearbook* 8: 21–26.

Balthrop, V. W. (1987). "Standards for Paradigm Evaluation." *Journal of the American Forensic Association* 18 (Winter): 133–40.

Bartanan, K. M. (1987). "Application of the Narrative Paradigm in CEDA Debate." In D. Thomas and J. Hart, eds. *Advanced Debate*. Lincolnwood, IL: National Textbook. 417–28.

Berube, D. M. (1984). "Debating Hasty Generalization." *CEDA Yearbook* 5: 54–59.

Biggers, T. (1985). "A Single Swallow and Other Leaps of Faith." *CEDA Yearbook* 6: 32–38.

Bile, J. T. (1987). "When the Whole Is Greater Than the Sum of the Parts: The Implications of Holistic Resolutional Focus." *CEDA Yearbook* 8: 8–15.

Bile, J. T. (1988). "Propositional Justification: Another View." *CEDA Yearbook* 9: 54–62.

Black's Law Dictionary (1990). St. Paul: West Publishing.

Burton, D. H. (1979). *Oliver Wendell Holmes Jr., What Manner of Liberal?* Huntington, NY: Krieger.

Church, R. T. (1986). "On Being 'Prima Facie'—An Application to Non-Policy Argument." *CEDA Yearbook* 7: 29–35.

Church and Wilbanks (1986). *Values and Policies in Controversy: An Introduction to Argumentation and Debate*. Scottsdale, AZ: Gorsuch Scarisbrick.

Dressler, J. (1987). *Understanding Criminal Law*. New York: Matthew Bender.

Freeley, A. J. (1986). *Argumentation and Debate: Reasoned Decision Making*. Belmont, CA: Wadsworth.

Gill, A. M. (1988). "Catastrophe and Criterion: A Case for Justification." *CEDA Yearbook* 9: 38–44.

Campbell, K. K. (1982). *The Rhetorical Act*. Belmont, CA: Wadsworth.

Lichtman and Rohrer (1987). "Decison Rules in Policy Debate." In D. Thomas and J. Hart, eds. *Advanced Debate*. Lincolnwood, IL: National Textbook. 347–72.

Madsen, A. and Chandler, R. C. (1988). "When the Whole Becomes a Black Hole: Implications of the Holistic Perspective." *CEDA Yearbook* 9: 30–37.

McGee, B. R. (1988). "Assessing Counter-Warrants: Understanding Induction in Debate Practice." *CEDA Yearbook* 9: 63–70.

Neuman, R. K. (1990). *Legal Reasoning and Legal Writing*. Boston: Little, Brown.

Paulsen, J. W. and Rhodes, J. (1979). "The Counter-Warrant as a Negative Strategy: A Modest Proposal." *Journal of the American Forensic Association* 21: 146–49.

Scott, R. J. and Wynn, T. (1981). "Avoidance of the False Claim: Some Considerations for Debating and Judging Proposition of Value." *Contributions on the Philosophy and Practice of CEDA* 2: 25–31.

Simon, R. (1984). "The Case Against Counterwarrants in Value Debate." *CEDA Yearbook* 5: 48–53.

Thomas, D. (1987). "Presumption in Non-Policy Debate: A Case for Natural Presumption Based on Current Non-Policy Paradigms." In D. Thomas and J. Hart, eds. *Advanced Debate*. 3rd ed. Lincolnwood, IL: National Textbook. 448–68.

Tolbert, G. and Hunt, S. (1985). "Counter-Warrants: A Method for Testing Topical Justification in CEDA Debate." *CEDA Yearbook* 6: 1–6.

Ulrich, W. (1984). "The Nature of the Topic in Value Debate." *CEDA Yearbook* 5: 1–6.

Ulrich, W. (1987). "In Search of Tabula Rasa." In D. Thomas and J. Hart, eds. *Advanced Debate*. Lincolnwood, IL: National Textbook. 183–90.

Vasilius, J. (1980). "Presumption, Presumption, Wherefore Art Thou Presumption?" *Perspective on Non-Policy Argument* 1: 33–42.

Zarefsky, D. (1987). "Argument as Hypothesis-Testing." In D. Thomas and J. Hart, eds. *Advanced Debate*. Lincolnwood, IL: National Textbook. 205–15.

Zarefsky, D. (1980). "Criteria for Evaluating Non-Policy Argument." *Perspective on Non-Policy Argument* 1: 9–16.

Zeuschner and Hill (1981). "Psychological Presumption: Its Place in Value Topic Debate." *Contributions on the Philosophy and Practice of CEDA* 2: 20–24.

41

The Indivisibility of Value Claims from Policy Positions

An Argument for Policy in Value Debate

Dale Herbeck
Kimball Wong

One of the traditional distinctions between debate as practiced by the National Debate Tournament (NDT) and the Cross Examination Debate Association (CEDA) has been the nature of the resolution being debated. While NDT has tended to focus almost exclusively on policy resolutions, CEDA has tended to focus on value resolutions.[1] In part, this difference in focus can be explained as an attempt to distinguish the different types of debate.

While the nature of the resolution distinguishes the two types of debate, CEDA's decision to focus on values can also be explained as a response to the perceived overemphasis on policy considerations. Marilyn Young made precisely this claim when she argued:

> For more than two decades, the competitive debate community has actively avoided a confrontation with that type of resolution popularly known as "the proposition of value. . . . The majority of the active debate community continues to push relentlessly toward policy debate based on quantitative (and, therefore, presumably more rational) analyses.[2]

CEDA's decision to debate value questions can be seen as an attempt to fill this void.[3] In the words of David Thomas and Maridell Fryar, "It is our intuitive feeling that one of the main reasons value resolutions are coming into vogue is to give students more experience in debating values, not facts, and in relating arguments to people, not to computers."[4] By providing a forum for debating questions of value, CEDA has provided such experience to contemporary debaters.[5]

CEDA has profitably debated such questions for the past eleven years (for the first three and a half years, CEDA debated policy topics). Over those years a line of thinking emerged that suggests such value debate is very different from traditional policy debate. This thinking has suggested that not only is the focus of value debate different from policy debate, but also that many of the theoretical constructs of policy debate are inapplicable in the value setting. It has been argued that the theoretical constructs of policy debate are of little use to students of policy debate. Consequently, there have been numerous appeals for improved value theory.[6]

Given the growth of CEDA, it is clear that value debating is a very viable activity. Still, despite this success we believe that an artifical bifurcation of value resolutions from policy considerations exists and has resulted in significant consequences. In particular, we believe this bifurcation has worked to the detriment of quality argumentation. We attempt to support this claim in the following sections. In the first section we argue that it is impossible to separate questions of value from policy considerations. In the second section we argue that our attempts to separate these interrelated issues have frequently led to ambiguous and unsatisfying argumentation. In the final section we argue that policy considerations should be allowed in value debate at the discretion of the affirmative.

THE INDIVISIBILITY OF VALUE AND POLICY QUESTIONS

Any attempt to neatly distinguish value and policy concerns is necessarily oversimplistic.[7] There is an inherent interrelationship between these types of questions. In distinguishing between different types of value resolutions, Ted Sheckels categorized them by equating them to the policy-making process. According to Sheckels, the "pre-new policy [proposition] offers a value judgment, which, if adopted, would lead one to perhaps then go a step further and advocate a new policy."[8] The second type of resolution is a "pre-present policy choice [proposition], which, if accepted, would lead one to go a step further and choose between two present policies."[9] The final type of resolution is the "pre-present policy rejection [proposition], which, if affirmed, would lead one to repudiate an existing policy choice."[10]

By defining value resolutions according to their implications in the policy-making process, Sheckels implicitly recognizes the inherent relationship between questions of value and policy. This is consistent with Matlon's claim that "value propositions are also intertwined with attitudes about policies insofar as they often *lead to or are embedded* in policy suggestions.[11] Thus, policy proposals frequently depend on value judgments.

At the same time, however, it should be remembered that many value questions frequently flow from policy problems. Depending on the nature and the scope of the policy being discussed, many different types of values can be involved. Frequently, slightly different policies will invoke an entirely different set of value considerations. By changing the nature of the policy being discussed, advocates can reorder their value claims. This is especially true in light of the fact that many value considerations flow from the application of broad principles to specific instances.

Despite the inherent indivisibility of value and policy questions, much of the current practice in value debate suggests that these issues are clearly separate and distinct. While policy debaters frequently make value claims, it is unusual for a value debater to make policy claims. Most policy claims are frequently dismissed in value debate precisely because they are policy claims. Unfortunately, the glib unwillingness to entertain policy arguments in value debates is not without consequence.

THE CONSEQUENCES OF BIFURCATING VALUE AND POLICY QUESTIONS

Because of the inherent interdependence between value and policy concerns, the artificial attempt by the forensic community to bifurcate these issues into discrete resolutions has had adverse consequences on value debate. These consequences are especially evident if one considers the way in which theorists suggest that value resolutions should be debated.

Working from a stock issues model, George Ziegelmueller and Charles Dause propose three questions that debaters should ask when considering value resolutions: "(1) Does the value really represent a good? (2) Is there a more important value? (3) Is the meaning of the value properly interpreted?"[12] Once the values have been identified, Ziegelmueller and Dause believe that the debaters should be able to compare the competing values to determine the more important value. Barbara Warnick suggested the following procedure for analyzing value topics:

Step 1.   Provide a definition for the evaluatum.
Step 2.   Locate the evaluatum within a field.

Step 3.   Establish the criteria or standards for evaluation.
Step 4.   Operationally clarify the standards or criteria by applying them to the evaluatum.[13]

This method is consistent with a five-step process proposed by Stephen
Verch and Brenda Logue in resolving value conflicts:

Step 1.   Identify the value to be affirmed and the value to be
refuted.
Step 2.   Present the criteria to be used to resolve the value
conflict, and demonstrate why [they are] reasonable for
resolving this conflict.
Step 3.   Apply the criteria to the value to be affirmed and show
why the criteria [are] met.
Step 4.   Apply the criteria to the value to be refuted and show
why the criteria, although reasonable, [are] not met.
Step 5.   Demonstrate why winning this value conflict should
resolve the conflict over winning the ballot.[14]

Although sympathetic to Verch and Logue, Diana Prentice and Jack
Kay complain that their process provides little guidance for determining
what criteria should be utilized to compare values.[15] Thus, they suggest
that a debater should begin with an "inquiry process" and then proceed
to the "advocacy process." This model suggests that debaters should
study the relevant value structure and then project this analysis into the
advocacy stage.

The problem with all these models for value debate is that they
work from an extremely simplistic understanding of the nature of value
questions. They assume that the debaters need do little more than
determine the relevant values implicit in the resolution and then
proceed to argue which value sets are more important. This view
oversimplifies the nature of value controversies. Admittedly, debaters
must identify the relevant importance of the competing values.
Nevertheless, their analysis must go one step further. To arrive at
informed decisions, debaters must measure the relevant significance of
the claim made upon any value. Simply put, an objective decision
requires debaters to consider the magnitude of the claim upon the value
and the importance of the value. Only then can the comparisons
required under most resolutions be made.

For example, most would agree that life is an important value.
Indeed, it might be argued that since life is necessary for all other
values, it is the single most important value. Consequently, it could be
claimed that if an affirmative team could lay claim on life as a value
upholding the resolution, they should necessarily win the debate.
However, we are also aware that all claims on life are not equal. A
governmental decision that results in 100,000 unjustified deaths is surely
more reprehensible than a governmental decision that results in but a

single unjustified death. Any decision that results in such wanton death is wrong, but in this instance it appears that one decision is certainly "more" wrong than the other.

This example suggests that to arrive at the proper conclusion it is necessary to consider more than the value. It is necessary to consider the degree of claim that an advocate can make on a value. According to George Kent, "Since there is no way to know in advance which particular values will serve to differentiate competing proposals, it is pointless to argue over the relative merits of different value hierarchies before developing concrete designs."[16] Absent such a design it is impossible to determine the relevant values and the extent of the claim that can be made upon those values.

A debate that merely identified the presence of competing values would be extremely unsatisfying. At the end of the debate the judege would undoubtedly be able to come to some sort of conclusion regarding which value or set of values was more important in the abstract sense. However, under such circumstances the judge would tend to arrive at a conclusion regarding the resolution based more upon subjective opinion than the argumentation in the debate. Unless debaters were able to link these values to the subjective conception of the resolution held by the judge, there would be no way that they could win the debate. Simply put, to argue a value proposition the advocates must do more than simply identify the relevant value or value sets. The advocates must identify the values and then link them to the resolution as perceived by the judges.

Unfortunately, this is where contemporary value debate breaks down. At present there is little theoretical understanding as to how to draw this objective linkage. There is no agreement on whether or not the affirmative must defend the whole resolution or whether the affirmative may defend some subset of the resolution. While policy debate has considered this issue at some length, there has been little consideration of this issue in value debate literature.[17] In particular, there is considerable ambiguity as to whether the affirmative may defend specific policy alternatives in value debate.

Consider for example the fall 1985 CEDA proposition: "RE-SOLVED: That restrictions on mass media coverage of terrorist activities in the United States are justified." The real controversy in these debates was what sort of restrictions were being discussed. In debate after debate we observed negative debaters argue that restrictions would violate the cherished First Amendment to the United States Constitution. In response, affirmatives would argue that the restrictions they advocated did not violate the First Amendment. Upon closer analysis we discovered that both teams were correct. Obtrusive restrictions (like prior restraints) on media coverage of terrorist activities clearly violated the First Amendment. But unobtrusive restrictions (such as access requirements), did not violate the First Amendment. Thus, the question became, which restrictions or collection of restrictions is the affirmative defending? Does the affirmative need to defend all possible restrictions on mass media coverage of terrorist activities? Can the affirmative defend some, but not all restrictions on media coverage of terrorist activities? Does the affirmative have the right to defend specific restrictions on media coverage of terrorist activities? Until we could ascertain which restrictions were being debated, it was impossible to determine if the First Amendment was being violated. And, absent some assessment of the degree of the impingement on the First Amendment, it was impossible to determine whether or not the resolution was justified.

Precisely the same problem occurred with the spring 1986 proposition, RESOLVED: That membership in the United Nations is no longer beneficial to the United States." Under this resolution affirmative teams frequently argued that membership in the United Nations was no longer beneficial to the United States. In response, negatives frequently charged that if the United States left the United Nations, then the United Nations would promptly collapse. Answering this argument, the affirmative argued that they were not actually advocating withdrawal from the United Nations. Rather, the affirmative would simply claim that they were advocating withdrawal from the undesirable portions of UN membership. Indeed, some affirmatives were so bold as to claim that the United States should actually commit more resources to the United Nations. Thus, the decision in the debate literally came down to how the judge viewed the resolution. If the judge viewed the resolution as being a precursor to policy, the affirmative team would lose. But if the judge viewed the resolution as being clearly distinct from policy, then the affirmative team would win. Obviously, the decision in the debate came down to the subjective interpretation held by the judge of the role that policy considerations hold in a value context.

Both of these examples demonstrate the problems that develop when value resolutions are considered as totally distinguishable from policy resolutions. There is more to comparing values than simply arguing the importance of the value. Rather, any reasoned comparison of values necessarily requires the debaters to measure the extent of the infringement on the relevant values. Unfortunately, the existing literature on the nature of value debate fails to recognize this problem.

ADVOCATING POLICY IN VALUE DEBATE

Given the adverse consequences associated with the artificial bifurcation of value and policy considerations, we propose that affirmatives be allowed the option of advocating specific policy alternatives within their constructive speeches. We emphasize that this be an option, and not a specific requirement that is placed on all affirmative teams. Allowing the affirmative such an option can be justified in several ways.

First, allowing affirmatives the option of including policy alternatives would minimize the ambiguity involved with value questions. Since the affirmative would be able to defend their position by designating value claims based on specific alternatives, it would be possible to determine the issues being debated. For example, in the previous section we explained the ambiguity that resulted under the topic calling for media restrictions on terrorism. In an effort to resolve this ambiguity and encourage more meaningful argumentation, the affirmative team could commit to a specific set of alternatives. For example, the affirmative could defend a specific set of restrictions limiting media access to ongoing terrorist events. Or, the affirmative could defend a specific scheme of prior restraints on media coverage of terrorist activities. In response to this strategy, the negative would need to develop arguments against these specific affirmative policy alternatives. Simply put, they would need to prove that these restrictions were unjustified. Presumably, the resulting debate would offer an intelligent consideration of these specific alternatives instead of the ambiguous debate that frequently resulted when there was no agreement on the specific alternative being debated.

By defending a specific policy alternative, the affirmative would have the ability to focus the debate on a specific proposal. This would allow both teams to adapt their argumentation to a definite idea instead of an abstract construct. Value debates will necessarily become much less abstract and more objectively suited for consistent decisions.

Second, allowing the affirmative the right to defend a specific set of policy alternatives would lead to more realistic debate. As presently conceived, the negative has every incentive to distort the resolution to the detriment of the affirmative. Under the terrorism topic, for example, the negative could argue that the government could simply prohibit mass media coverage of terrorist activities. Such a restriction would clearly be within the bounds of the resolution, and it would undoubtedly violate the First Amendment in a meaningful way. Even though no affirmative team would ever propose such an extreme restriction, this restriction still constituted a reason to reject the resolution. Debating such resolutions without allowing more specific focus encourages the negative team to propose absurd examples of the resolution.

In defense of debating only the value implications, critics might charge that negatives should only offer reasonable examples of the resolution. By offering the most obvious interpretations, they could claim, the negative could deny the resolution. While this is undoubtedly true, there is no reason why advocates would undertake the arduous task of proving that a mainstream interpretation was undesirable when they could undertake the much easier task of proving that an absurd interpretation of the resolution was undesirable. Moreover, what may be considered a mainstream interpretation by one judge may not be by another.

Third, allowing the affirmative to designate a specific policy alternative would allow for a more focused debate. To pretend that four debaters can definitively treat recent topics in a single hour is illogical. Arms sales, terrorism, and the United Nations (the three most recent CEDA topics) are problems that all defy easy answers. These issues are far too complex to be treated in the course of a single debate. Broad, unnecessarily abstract interpretations of value resolutions contribute to this problem. If the affirmative was able to limit the number of different ideas being discussed in the debate, it would be possible to debate a more manageable set of issues.

For these reasons, we believe that the affirmative should be allowed the option of defending a specific set of policy alternatives. Defining the specific policies being discussed will make it possible to determine the extent of the claim that the advocate can lay on the competing values. Furthermore, specification would allow for more realistic debate because it would absolve the affirmative of the need to defend absurd interpretations of the resolution. Finally, such a scheme would allow for a more focused and, therefore, more detailed debate.

While there are good reasons to allow the affirmative to defend specific policy alternatives, there will undoubtedly be those who are critical of this position. At face value, it might be charged that it may well prove impossible to offer specific policies under all value resolutions. For example, what if we were to debate the proposition "RESOLVED: That moral relativism has had a positive effect on America."[18] How could the affirmative defend examples of this resolution?

Admittedly, it might prove difficult for the affirmative to offer specific policies under specific value resolutions. However, this difficulty can be explained if one remembers the distinction between the different types of value resolutions as described by Sheckels. Obviously, under certain types of value resolutions it will be impossible to defend specific policies. However, this does not cut against our position. We are not arguing that values can never be discussed absent policy considerations. Rather, we are arguing that by their very nature certain value controversies are better considered in specific settings.

Moreover, we are not arguing that all affirmative teams should be forced to consider policy considerations. Instead, we are only arguing that under certain topics would it be theoretically legitimate for affirmatives to exercise that right if they chose to do so.

It might also be argued that allowing the affirmative to specify policy options would work to the detriment of the negative team. Since the affirmative could define ground so as to eliminate the most viable grounds, critics might charge that the negative would be placed at a competitive disadvantage. While such a result might be possible, we believe that it is preferable to the present situation. Under current practice, the negative frequently chooses the most absurd interpretations of the resolution to deny the affirmative case. Allowing the affirmative to defend only specific examples of the resolution would do little more than restore equity. Since the affirmative would be bound by their initial choices, they would be unable to gain any unfair advantage over the negative team.

Another criticism will come from those who believe that it is important to consider value questions. These critics will charge that allowing affirmatives to defend plans will transform value debate back into policy debate. This, according to the critics, would neatly circumvent the original goal of increasing discussion over values.

This criticism is not without merit. However, we believe that it can be discounted at several levels. First, allowing affirmatives to specify alternatives would reintroduce some policy considerations in CEDA debate. However, we see this as leading to improved value debate. Since it is impossible to separate values from policy considerations, we believe that allowing policy considerations will lead to more enlightened discussion of values. The previous examples illustrate this point. We believe there would be better discussion of values in a debate that considered the relative benefits of one specific restriction on media coverage than, in a debate in which all possible restrictions on media coverage were simultaneously advocated.

Second, we believe that there is already a great deal of policy argumentation in contemporary value debates. Given recent topics, the wording of the resolutions, and our desire to debate timely issues, the coummunity has already allowed policy questions to enter value debate.[19] Rather than complain about such crossover, we should recognize that such debates can still provide the meaningful discussion of values that led to the original attempt to debate only value questions.

Third, we believe that it would still be possible to encourage the detailed consideration of value questions. Debaters debate values when those issues are relevant to the topic. If we wish to avoid overemphasis on policy issues and encourage discussion of value issues, then we should select resolutions that lend themselves to value arguments. For example, if we selected a topic dealing with Fifth and Sixth Amendment rights, then we could reasonably expect there to be a good deal of debate over competing values. On the other hand, if we selected a topic that dealt with consumer products, then we could reasonably expect comparatively less discussion of values. By prudently framing and selecting the topic being discussed, we can continue to encourage debaters to focus on value questions.

One of the refreshing aspects of value debate is that there are no theoretical imperatives. Since the debate community is still creating a theoretical basis for value debate, we believe that it would be appropriate to recognize the inherent relationship between questions of value and policy alternatives. Toward that end we advocate that the affirmative be allowed the option of defending specific examples of the resolution should they believe that it would help to clarify the values being debated. This option will lead to a more realistic discussion, and finally, to more detailed argumentation.

Notes

1. NDT (or more correctly phrased, its precursors) has debated only one nonpolicy topic. In 1921–22, the proposition was "RESOLVED: That the principle of the closed shop is unjustifiable." Ronald J. Matlon, "Debating Propositions of Value," *Journal of the American Forensic Association* 14 (Spring 1978): 194.
2. Marilyn J. Young, "The Use of Evidence in Value Argument: A Suggestion," in *Proceedings of the Summer Conference on Argumentation*, ed. Jack Rhodes and Sara Newell (Annandale, VA: Speech Communication Association and the American Forensic Association, 1980), 287.
3. CEDA has debated a variety of different value resolutions. Although NDT has yet to debate a value resolution, there has been discussion of this idea. See, for example, William B. English, "Should the National Intercollegiate Debate Topic be a Nonpolicy Proposition? An Affirmative Answer," paper presented at the Speech Communication Association Convention, Houston, 1975.
4. David A. Thomas and Maridell Fryar, "Value Resolutions, Presumption, and Stock Issues," in *Dimensions of Argument: Proceedings of the Second Summer Conference on Argumentation*, ed. George Ziegelmueller and Jack Rhodes (Annandale, VA: Speech Communication Association, 1981), 529.
5. Theodore F. Sheckels, Jr., *Debating: Applied Rhetorical Theory* (New York: Longman, 1984), 80.
6. "Despite widespread recognition of the importance of value propositions . . . , scholars in argumentation have provided little guidance for the person caught up in arguing them." Joseph W. Wenzel and Dale J. Hample, "Categories and Dimensions of Value Propositions: Exploratory Studies," *Journal of the American Forensic Association* 11 (Winter 1975): 121.
7. See, for example, Lawrence E. Rothstein, "What about the Fact-Value Dichotomy: A Belated Reply," *Journal of Value Inquiry* 9 (1975): 307–11.
8. Sheckels, p. 80.
9. Sheckels, p. 81.
10. Sheckels, p. 81.
11. Matlon, p. 195. Emphasis in original.

12. George W. Ziegelmueller and Charles A. Dause, *Argumentation: Inquiry and Advocacy* (Englewood Cliffs: Prentice-Hall, 1975), 51.
13. These four steps are a summary of the procedure presented in Barbara Warnick, "Arguing Value Propositions," *Journal of the American Forensic Association* 18 (Fall 1981): 116–17.
14. Stephen L. Verch and Brenda J. Logue, "Increasing Value Clash: A Propositional and Structural Approach," *CEDA Yearbook*, ed. Don Brownlee (Cross Examination Debate Association, 1982), 27.
15. Diana Prentice and Jack Kay, *The Role of Values in Policy Debate* (Kansas City: National Federation of State High School Associations, 1985), 10–11.
16. George Kent, "Political Design," in *Planning Alternative World Futures: Values, Methods and Models*, ed. Louis Rene Beres and Harry R. Targ (New York: Praeger, 1975), 36.
17. In policy debate theory those who believe that the debate should focus on the entire resolution have argued for counterwarrants. A counterwarrant is an argument that justifies rejecting the resolution even though it might not justify rejecting the specific affirmative plan. For a defense of counterwarrants, see James W. Paulsen and Jack Rhodes, "The Counter-Warrant as a Negative Strategy," *Journal of the American Forensic Association* 15 (1980): 205–10; and Jack Rhodes, "A Defense of the Counter-Warrant as a Negative Strategy," in *Dimensions of Argument: Proceedings of the Second Summer Conference on Argumentation*, ed. George Ziegelmueller and Jack Rhodes (Annandale, VA: Speech Communication Association, 1981), 485–93. For a critique of counterwarrants, see Marjorie Keeshan and Walter Ulrich, "A Critique of the Counter-Warrant as a Negative Strategy," *Journal of the American Forensic Association* 16 (1980): 199–203; Pat Ganer, "Counter-Warrants: An Idea Whose Time Has Not Come," in *Dimensions of Argument: Proceedings of the Second Summer Conference on Argumentation*, ed. George Ziegelmueller and Jack Rhodes, (Annandale, VA: Speech Communication Association, 1981), 476–84; and Dale Herbeck and John P. Katsulas, "The Affirmative Topicality Burden: Any Reasonable Example of the Resolution," *Journal of the American Forensic Association* 21 (Winter 1985): 133–45.
18. This resolution is taken from English and is intended only as an illustration.
19. A graphic example of this occurred in the final round at the First National Championship of the Cross Examination Debate Association. In that debate the affirmative claimed that membership in the United Nations was no longer beneficial to the United States because the UN exacerbated conflict in the world. In defending the UN the negative argued (and prevailed by claiming) that U.S. membership was justified since the UN acted to decrease proliferation in the world. In this debate, both of the teams relied almost exclusively on policy claims to justify their respective positions.

42

Value Implications

Kent Colbert
David A. Thomas

The lack of universally accepted theory in nonpolicy debate has contributed to difficulty for debaters and judges alike (Wenzel and Hample, 1975; Brownlee, 1982; Colbert, 1987; and Cox and Jensen, 1988). The problem is especially apparent for second negative speakers in nonpolicy debates. Some of these debaters argue policy disadvantages when no policy is being advocated by the affirmative team. Others label offcase arguments "value objections" (VO) whether or not the affirmative supports values in their case. Ironically, the term "value objection," adopted primarily through convention, is not considered by many to be an accurate description of what second negatives in CEDA often do. Perella (1987) explains, "[A]lmost invariably the negative is not really objecting to the affirmative value, but proposing other applications" (p. 189–190).

Perella suggests the term "policy implication" may be more accurate in describing what many second negative debaters are attempting to accomplish. Indeed, in many situations he is right, but Perella's terminology correlates nonpolicy to traditional policy debate and suggests that pragmatic harms are weighed against affirmative values. In practice, many nonpolicy debaters attempt to consider values that conflict with endorsing the resolution. While it is clear that a consistent framework is needed by debaters to help delineate their speaker responsibilities, controversy over the direction and goals of nonpolicy debate style contributes to the confusion. This essay attempts to provide a more precise and specific method of developing a negative position on the affirmative value premise, which will be termed "value implications."

THE CONCEPT

Value implications (VI) should dispute the affirmative justification as a proper warrant for a resolution by making values the focus of an academic debate. Values are "broad modes of conduct.... When we express our values, we expess our own conceptions of worth or ideas about how something ought to be" (Warnick and Inch, 1989, p. 191). The implications of giving priority to one value over another is one approach to consider the values implied by many nonpolicy debate resolutions. Since we hold different valence for various values, the point of conflict sometimes involves prioritizing them. Prentice (1988) argues, "[V]alues are prioritized because they often cannot be achieved equally and simultaneously.... [T]he heart of clash in values debate is disagreement over the arrangement of value hierarchies" (p. 13). In this instance, the implications of prioritizing resolutional values should be the focus, not arguments labeled VOs that do not directly object to the affirmative's value justification.

The idea of hierarchy is just one of the qualities we assign to values; a more fundamental starting point is the root or foundational concept of a value. As such, values are the most abstract and non-empirical of these cognitive elements. They are benchmarks for us to use in interpreting the meanings of our beliefs, attributions of meaning, and motivations to act. Values are more or less irreducible major clusters of response sets. Before we speak of value hierarchy or priorities, we must recognize that all hold several different values.

Some of the values we hold are consistent with each other in a given situation, but some are inconsistent. Sensing a conflict between our attributions of meaning, and our motivations to action, flowing from the different values we hold, we are led to decide among competing impulses. The dissonance we feel leads us to justify our decisions and choices.

Until the situation arises, we do not ordinarily think of values being arranged hierarchically. We may believe in all values equally until we are required to apply them to an object. For instance, until we are required to cast a vote for or against a welfare program, we may not see any problem in believing in both equality and liberty. Likewise, we may believe a fetus is a human life, and could never imagine having an abortion for the usual reasons given. But we could simultaneously believe that it is better for a woman to be able to make that choice herself, for whatever reasons the choice raised to her. One can be a pro-lifer and a right-to-lifer at the same time, with no dissonance, until confronted with the need to believe somthing or take an action, such as the casting of a vote on a concrete issue.

The majority of nonpolicy debate resolutions offer a situation or scenario about which we can draw out the competing values pertinent to the choice. Sometimes nonpolicy resolutions frame conflicts between policy implications and value implications. The policy implication can involve a cost/benefit trade-off. However, a value implication looks beyond the good intentions or good motives of the actor or proponents when judging a resolution that requires a specific manifestation or expression of a value.

An implication of a value, or VI, can stem from analysis of any dimension, definitional parameter, component, or quality of the concept as a concept. The role of values in nonpolicy debates is in a quasi-policy setting such as the presidental election or the handgun issue—so values are always considered in an applied sense. A VI analyzes the option of applying one or another value to achieve a stated objective in the resolution. As such, values can be either pro- or anti-resolutional in the decision matrix, but provide implications one way or another.

CRITERIA

Several considerations should be made in formulating criteria for value implications. First, the situational context is essential in developing the implications of conflicting values. Our perception of values is influenced by cultural, social, contextual, and time factors. Church and Wilbanks (1986) observe, "Values cannot be judged in isolation. . . . Values cannot be debated unless they are compared with other values . . . We can only judge values within a context of specific behaviors when one value conflicts with another" (p. 39). Likewise, Smith and Hunsaker (1972) point out, "Values may conflict with each other; in wartime, the human life and the value of self-defense sometimes conflict with a value derived from a different drive; hunger conflicts with the value of a pleasant physical appearance. . . . " (p. 23). Since perceptions of values are not static, consideration of situational factors may be essential in developing VIs.

Another approach to formulating VIs is to prove that endorsing the resolution would create competing or conflicting values. In doing so, the negative associates a VI with endorsing the actions or values specified in a resolution. In this instance a VI considers if endorsement of the resolution or affirmative value leads to the demise of other values. The process of linking VIs is similar to linking disadvantages to specific operational plans, except VIs are associated with the acceptance of the values implicit in the resolution, definitional parameter, or component of the concept.

One useful perspective to link VIs may be found in the principle of necessity. Basically, the principle suggests that if X occurs, then Y is necessary or probable (usually the latter). When applying this principle to linking VIs, debaters can argue that endorsement of the affirmative value creates a stimulus that increases the probability of an adverse consequence. Littlejohn (1989) provides an excellent summary of causal, practical, and logical necessity that provides a useful perspective for linking VIs.

Causal necessity assumes a behavioral outcome. This approach treats values as a *force* over which man has no control. Values like success, freedom, or salvation, for example, can be affected by individual action, but a number of uncontrollable factors also strongly affect the outcome. Reordering values without considering these other forces can sometimes produce devastating results. One need only investigate the diffusion of innovations into primitive cultures to find numerous examples (Rogers, 1983). Although proving a cause relationship concerning values is difficult, this approach can be effective when argued persuasively.

Practical necessity explains events in terms of act and consequence. When applied to linking VIs this approach suggests some type of action or reaction is likely to result. If an affirmative value is endorsed, people may react in a way that either precludes the effects of endorsing the value or leads to consequences that harm other values. The popular New Right argument often uses a link of practical necessity. In this argument the negative suggests that reordering the affirmative values will lead to a consequence, such as enabling radical religious groups to enact private choice plans that effectively destroy public education. The impact of this VI doesn't occur because of uncontrollable forces. The link considers practical outcomes that produce harms. The major distinction in applying causal and practical involves the method that triggers the VI impact. The former involves direct effects ($X = Z$), whereas the latter occurs in a two-step flow ($X = Y$, which $= Z$).

Logical necessity is another fruitful perspective for developing VI links. It is the glue that holds the VI together and usually relies on internal consistency. Time links, for example, attempt to demonstrate that after, while, or since endorsing an affirmative value, harmful implications are likely. Because values change over time, providing time frames may sometimes be essential to establish logical necessity. Addition or contrast links, referred to as add-ons and turnarounds, tend to be constructed using logical necessity. Both accept a premise and reason that additional or contrary outcomes are likely. By identifying internally inconsistent definitions, criteria, or criteria that is not consistently supported by case justification are examples of using logical necessity to link VIs.

Although the principle of necessity has been overly simplified for purposes of this essay, it can provide a useful conceptual perspective to develop VI(s) links and should be further studied by debaters faced with this task. Incidentally, the principle of necessity is also useful for affirmative debaters attempting to link criterion and justification with the resolutional endorsement.

After the negative team links a VI to the acceptance of the resolution, the additional burden to indicate whether it occurs in a linear/incremental fashion, or after specific threshold/pressure points, is reached. Arguments like rights snowball, slippery slope, chilling effects, and domino theory suggest a linear progression of events that reach an ultimate impact. The impact increases as movement in a specific direction occurs.

Threshold impacts are different. There is no gradual building of the degree of impact—only the probability of occurrence. If the ICBM silos are emptied, the impact of the act reaches threshold when the warheads hit the earth. It is important to establish the type of impact (linear or threshold) being argued early enough in the debate so that differences between both teams may be carefully weighed for meaningful evaluation. In addition, debaters should establish if the impacts are reversible. Negative teams, therefore, should associate VIs to resolutional acceptance and demonstrate how their impacts outweigh the affirmative justification.

STANDARDS

At least three questions should be considered in formulating standards for value implications. (1) Has the negative team met their burden of proof in arguing an independent reason to reject the resolution? (2) Are the value implications unique to adopting the resolution? (3) Do the value implications provide typical and representative examples to justify rejecting the resolution?

First, has the negative met their burden of proof? Since the negative is essentially arguing that implications exist beyond what the affirmative case has suggested they must assume the burden to prove this to be the case. Biggers (1987) argues, "If the negative offers examples . . . [and] support the countergeneralization, then we would reject the affirmative generalization and accept the countergeneralization. In practical terms this would mean that we reject the truth of the resolution and accept its opposite or an alternative" (p. 494). The negative should be required to prove a sufficient countergeneralization. Perella (1987) says, "The negative may wish to introduce arguments which do not directly tie to the affirmative's case but which the judge should consider. . . . [I]t is important to know that on these [offcase] arguments the negative has the burden of proof . . . " (p. 81). Since the affirmative case must be representative and typical to inductively support the resolution, the negative team should have a similar burden in presenting VIs or countergeneralizations to independently reject the resolution. VIs should be typical and representative, or they would constitute a hasty generalization for rejecting the resolution. Hence, a standard of sufficient countergeneralization for VIs assists in providing equity between the affirmative and negative teams. Thus, when arguing VIs as an independent issue, the negative assumes the burden of proof.

When building VIs from a negative case perspective, it is important to establish whether the negative and affirmative values can coexist. If the VIs are mutually exclusive of and compete for existence with the affirmative justification, then a decision of which team best justifies the decision-making criterion can be reached. In this instance if the VI impact outweighs the affirmative justification, the negative team should win because the decision is limited to a choice between the two. However, if the VIs and the affirmative justification are not mutually exclusive, but still conflict, the degree of probability for each becomes important. How great are the risks of occurrence? Do the VIs have more probability of impact than the affirmative justification? A standard of probability or most likely outcome should be employed. Standards of possibility are seldom sufficient to reach a rational decision, and standards of certainty are seldom possible. A probability standard is useful to weigh competing values that are not mutually exclusive. Resolving disputes between the justification and implications is by no means an easy process; however, applying the concepts of mutual exclusiveness and probability can help to make the task less complicated.

A standard of uniqueness for VIs also seems appropriate. If the VIs occur, whether or not the resolution is accepted, there is no unique reason to reject the resolution. It would not be logical to weigh VI impacts if there is propensity for their occurrence independent of the resolution. Thus, VIs should be intrinsic and unique to accepting the resolution or affirmative value.

CONCLUSIONS

It is hoped the use of VIs, as defined in this essay, can assist debaters and debate judges when values become the focus of a nonpolicy debate. Certainly, a number of policy and value paradigms exist that may be more fruitful on some topics. However, when quasi-policy/value topics are used and teams attempt to focus on values implicit within a resolution, VIs can provide a structural framework from which negative teams may view a resolution.

In addition, several important cognitive exercises are encouraged when negative teams develop this approach. Debaters must consider the underlying assumptions of resolutions. Debaters must use inferential reasoning by calling for an inductive leap from VIs to the affirmative justification and ultimately the resolution. This is important because conceptual frameworks, in general, assist in honing critical thinking skills.

References

Biggers, T. (1987). "A Single Swallow and Other Leaps of Faith." In D. Thomas and J. Hart, eds. *Advanced Debate*. 3rd ed. Lincolnwood, IL: National Textbook. 490–95.

Bile, J. (1987). "When the Whole Is Greater Than the Sum of the Parts: The Implications of Holistic Resolutional Focus." *CEDA Yearbook* 8: 8–15.

Brownlee, D. (1982). "Debating Value Propositions." In C. Keefe, T. Harte, and L. Norton, eds. *Introduction to Debate*. New York: Macmillan.

Church, R. T. and Wilbanks, C. (1986). *Values and Policies in Controversy*. Scottsdale, AZ: Gorsuch Scarisbrick.

Colbert, K. R. (1987). *A Stock Issues Approach to CEDA Debate*. Paper presented at the annual meeting of the Speech Communication Association, Boston.

Cox, E. and Jensen, S. (1988). *An Alternative Method for Approaching Value Propositions*. Paper presented at the annual meeting of the Speech Communication Association, New Orleans.

Fadely, D. (1989). "Value Debating: Underlying Assumptions, Value Hierarchies, and Audience Analysis." *Debate Issues* 22: 4.

Littlejohn, S. (1989). *Theories of Human Communication*. 3rd ed. Belmont, CA: Wadsworth.

Patterson, J. and Zarefsky, D. (1983). *Contemporary Debate*. Boston: Houghton Mifflin.

Perella, J. (1987). *The Debate Method of Critical Thinking*. Dubuque: Kendall Hunt.

Pfau, M. (1987). "A Systematic Approach to Opposing Policy Change." In D. Thomas and J. Hart, eds. *Advanced Debate*. 3rd. ed. Lincolnwood, IL: National Textbook. 39–45.

Pierce, D. (1986). *The History of the Concept of Stasis*. Paper presented at the annual meeting of the Speech Communication Association, Chicago.

Prentice, D. (1988). "Political Debates and Their Application to the Teaching of Lincoln-Douglas Debate." *The Forensics Educator* 2: 13.

Rogers, E. (1983). *Diffusion of Innovations*. New York: Academic Free Press.

Rokeach, M. (1972). *Beliefs, Attitudes, and Values*. San Francisco: Jossey-Bass.

Smith, C. and Hunsaker, D. (1972). *The Bases of Argument: Ideas in Conflict*. New York: Bobbs Merrill.

Tolbert, G. and Hunt, S. (1987). In D. Thomas and J. Hart, eds. *Advanced Debate*. 3rd ed. Lincolnwood. IL: National Textbook.

Ulrich, W. (1985). "Debating Generic Disadvantages." *Debate Issues* 19: 10–14.

Warnick, B. and Inch E. (1989). *Critical Thinking and Communication: The Use of Reason in Argument*. New York: Macmillan.

Wenzel, J. and Hample, D. (1975). "Categories and Dimensions of Value Propositions: Exploratory Studies." *Journal of the American Forensics Association* 11: 121.

43

Hasty Generalization Revisited

David M. Berube

Hasty generalization has become a voguish issue in nonpolicy debating. Lacking evidence on a particular case, the negative debater searches for some way to convince the critic that the affirmative interpretation of the resolution should be rejected in spite of the paucity of negative issue clash. As affirmative debaters continue to turn to examples to prove nonpolicy resolutions true, the use of hasty generalization as a voting issue has become more prevalent.

The affirmative has chosen to debate examples of the resolution for many reasons: It gives the affirmative a competitive edge by restricting discussion to an area in which the affirmative is particularly competent, it reduces evidence abuse by discouraging the citation of nonreferent evidence, and it reduces uncertainty since examples give meaning to and draw meaning from regulations that are specific in application and intent.

Affirmative debaters cite Berube (1984) and others, who claim that value and policies are so closely related that debate about one cannot take place without a consideration of the other. Political and legal systems express the intentions as well as the structure of the status quo. Policies grow out of philosophical systems. As representative entities of greater ideational systems, policies are germane to any discussion of values. For some, philosophical systems may even be considered as pre-policy systems, which indicate the direction policymaking will take when confronted by significant social issues in the future. Consequently, to examine the primacy of a philosophical system, we tend to look at the policies that are extant and compare them to new policies that would grow out of an alternative political value system. The balancing process thereby provides debaters with an understanding of the true meanings and implications of shifts within a particular socio-political value infra-structure.

This approach, at least within the nonpolicy debate community, has become known as example analysis.

Paulsen and Rhodes (1979), Rhodes (1981), Rowland (1983), and Rhodes and Pfau (1985) argue that the focus of debate is the resolution. They say that nonpolicy topics have implied a broad set of policies, all of which must be defended for the affirmative to win. They ignore the process of logical analysis, which entails proving resolutions true by examples. They argue that debate is inductive but dent inductive reasoning, from example to rule, as justified for the affirmative. They argue that debate should be on the resolution but fail to explain how that is possible when a resolution entails contradictory examples. They argue that resolutional debate is preferred yet never provide a model of argument that can provide both depth and breadth of discussion in an activity which has speaking time restrictions.

Keeshan and Ulrich (1980) and Herbeck and Katsulas (1985), on the other hand, argue that the focus of debate is the example of the resolution and that the resolution exists only as a guide to assist in designating affirmative and negative territory.

These views are not mutually exclusive since the full set of the resolution envisaged by Rowland and Rhodes for nonpolicy debating is merely a large example of sorts. What is at issue is whether a subset example is less likely to produce probable truth than a full set example. We may tend to accept the generic approach to a resolution as more palatable since we presume that debating the full set of the resolution is more likely to demonstrate probable truth than arguing a subset. Yet, a subset of the resolution can be both argumentatively representative and sufficiently large to justify broad consensus about the acceptability of the resolutional statement. This is especially true when we define debate as argumentation to discern the *probable* truth of the resolution.

In addition, Rhodes' deductive system must be rejected for one simple reason—there is no alternative to induction. Sir Karl Popper assailed induction and rejected it, but he was unable to design a non-inductivist system. Ayer and others have concluded that "any successful policy must become an inductivist policy, since in order to be successful, it must correspond to some pattern in the events with which it deals; and the pattern must be projectible if the policy is to continue to succeed" (Ayer, 1968, p. 100). O'Hear explained:

> Any systematic counterinductivist policy presupposes some projectable pattern to events and is thus covertly inductivist and open to the objection that we are predicting what will happen on the basis—albeit in a com-

plicated way—of what has happened. It is precisely reasoning of this sort that Hume's objections to induction are designed to show we have no warrant for, and so a counterinductivist policy would be ruled out on the same grounds as an inductive policy (1980, p. 22).

Finally, there is no assurance that noninductivist systems are more reliable than inductivist ones. In truth, they may suffer from the same, or even more, damning fallacies.

COUNTERWARRANT THEORY

Regardless of the logical premises behind focus in debate, assume that Rhodes is correct and the focus is on the entire resolution. In response to unrepresentative and small examples introduced as typical plans in the NDT community, the counterwarrant surfaced as an attempt to prove that more typical examples of the resolution were disadvantageous. Counterwarrant theory is fueled by the belief that the focus of debate should be on the resolution. Arguing that debate is an inductive process and must adhere to the rigors of fundamental logic, Paulsen and Rhodes (1979) introduced hasty generalization as a mechanism to justify the use of the counterwarrant. Their thesis is that since the affirmative example is unrepresentative or insufficiently large, any generalization drawn from the affirmative example commits a Type II error, a hasty generalization. To offset this error, they suggest that the negative should present objections to the resolution, ignoring the affirmative warrant, in an effort to prove the resolution is probably not true. Regardless of the merits of the affirmative example (warrant), negative counterwarrants help to prove the resolution probably is not true.

INDICTING WHOLE RESOLUTIONAL FOCUS

The debate over resolutional focus has regressed into bickering over externalities. Responding to counterwarrants in nonpolicy debate, Bile (1987) argued that "the more generic arguments are, the greater their educational utility substantively promoting a more general education" (p. 9). Confusing whole-topic focus with holistic and synthetic thinking, with general education as both cause and characteristic, and with a liberal art curriculum, his criticism centers entirely upon the implications of whole resolutional focus. In reponse, though, Madsen and Chandler's article (1988) effectively rebutted that Bile's perspective "cannot be drawn from traditional educational theorists" for "critical to any theoretical position are the specific operationalizations of its assumptions and predictions," and though "a student can be taught theoretical knowledge, it is difficult to provide useful information to students without any application to the everyday world of existence" (p. 32). Madsen and Chandler also examine the consequences of whole resolutional focus without examining its intrinsic justification.

Furthermore, Bile asserted that students in nonpolicy debate are asked to make decisions regarding general concepts, and under the cloak of holism, he sententiously epigrammed that "the whole always exceeds that sum of its parts," presumably said to convince us that some greater truth is discoverable with a whole-istic method in debate. However, he failed to prove that some of the parts are not sufficient to reveal the truth of the whole.

Next, Bile unequivocally wrote that the "*only* way to encourage real breadth and depth is by focusing on the relatively generic topic" (p. 11). In defining "relatively," he suggested that debaters insert modifiers or quantifiers intuitively to redefine the resolution.

Lyons defined "quantifiers" as word-concepts used to "tell us how many entities or how much substance is beig referred to" (1977, p. 455). These terms have been "recently employed by linguists with reference to such words as *all, some, each, every*, and *any*" (p. 454). While each standard-form categorical proposition begins with one of these words, "some categorical propositions contain no words at all to indicate quantity [and] where there is no quantifier, what the sentence is intended to express may be doubtful," and linguists are near unanimous that "we can determine its meaning only by examining the context in which it occurs" (Copi, 1961, pp. 138, 205–206). Copi, unlike Bile, envisions a context beyond the debate round found instead in historical critical method.

Madsen and Chandler indicted Bile's quantification mandate as groundless. First it "assumed ordinary language and conversation between ordinary people. The appropriateness of these theories in the debate situation is unclear," especially since resolutions are not haphazardly constructed, they are "ontologically different than the imprecision and ambiguity of everyday language." Indeed, "modifiers may be intentionally left out in order to allow the implications of a single sentence to be debated" (p. 33). Second, "there are no standards to govern which specific modifiers in include" (p. 35). Since there is no such thing as the correct interpretation of a sentence (Lyons, 1977, p. 194), there is no place to turn for guidance. Third, "adding words to the topic also may increase the ambiguity inherent in the resolution, which would serve to counter the initial precision sought by the framers" (p. 35). The employment of parameters by NDT topic framers makes this observation painfully apparent. Of course, in a competitive setting it is unlikely that debaters can be trusted to work from an altruistic perspective, which leads to Madsen and Chandler's fourth and final argument against resolutional reconstruction. "As soon as debaters are encouraged to alter a resolution for educational reasons, the floodgates of addition would be opened" (p. 35). The implications might be ravaging and topicality arguments would become a deeper semantic quagmire.

Bile continued. "If the negative wins objections to the resolution (counterwarrants) more generic than the affirmative case, then it should win the debate even if the affirmative wins the case" (p. 12). This belief would completely invalidate the inductive nature of academic debate, would severely restrict affirmative privilege of definition, would skew negative bias beyond the negative block, would make clash unprofitable for the negative, and would figuratively billow the sails of those proverbial ships passing in the foggy night.

He also suggested that "until and unless such a proof [that one can infer a general truth from a specific example] is offered, a subset should be presumed to be nothing more" (p. 12). This belief not only assumes that any induction must be presumed fallacious on its face, but it weakly suggests that a resolutional subset is by difinition suspect, enabling the negative to argue that any affirmative proof minutely less than the full resolutional set, if that is discernible, is unacceptable. This is patently absurd.

Here are two additional reasons why whole resolutional focus is a pipedream and unlike the Bile and Madsen/Chandler polemic, these justifications are not drawn from the products of such a focus, they are found implicit to the character of a resolution.

First, absent the interjection of qualifiers, it is paradoxical to oblige the affirmative to defend the promulgation of human rights with both the threat of military intervention and disengagement (see the 1978–79 topic), the addition of health requirements, and cutting of the same, sacrificing educational quality (see the fall 1983 CEDA topic) (Church and Wilbanks, 1986, p. 337).

Second, there is *no* whole resolution for at least three reasons. First, no two things are identical. For Hume "an object is the same with itself" (Flew, 1961, p. 63). He found only formal identity statements "X is (is identical with, is the same as) X" as a truism. Non-Aristotelian semanticists like Korzybski define the concept of identity more precisely. For them, even formal identity statements, such as "$1 = 1$," are false by virtue of grammatical form: A subject cannot simultaneously serve as its own object (see 1958, pp. 194–195). For nonpolicy debating purposes, whole resolutional focus is more analogous to something called material identity statements: $X = Y$: An observation that, together with the aforementioned, confounds identity. "The function of material identity statements is precisely to assert of which appear to be, and thus could be taken to be, two things that in reality they are one thing," both informative and a posteriori, they "constitute the very backbone of thought and discourse" (Butchvarov, 1979, pp. 15 and 18). Discourse, of all sorts, demands the expansion and restriction of concepts; meaning is enhanced as parameters of a discussion are juggled.

Second, the implicit ambiguity of language precludes true material identity statements. In *Tractatus* 5.5303, Wittgenstein wrote: "Roughly speaking, to say of two things that they are identical is nonsense" (1961, p. 105). Why? Because all statements are inherently vague. "Vagueness isn't something provisional, to be eliminated later on by more precise knowledge, this is a characteristic of logical peculiarity" (Wittgenstein, 1975, p. 263). Of course, in order to keep debates interesting, vagueness may even become part of the framing process. Husserl, in surprising agreement with Wittgenstein, insisted that some concepts "are essentially and nonaccidentally inexact" (1962, p. 74). Merleau-Ponty (1952) put it best when he argued that demands for absolute self-evidence ironically lead to a declaration that the world is absurd. Immutable meaning feeds intellectual stagnation and converts searches for knowledge into an oxymoronic exercise.

Third, Cook (1975) found that trying to define things like the whole resolution produces an infinite regression. This is especially true since the topic is an open class, "one whose members could not be listed, because their number has no determinable limit" (Lyons, 1977, p. 155). The process is like a lottery official attempting to val a winner without knowing the winning numbers.

MASS TERMINOLOGY TESTS

In addition to the thesis of Paulsen and Rhodes, there are occasions when a linguistic approach has been used to force the affirmative to debate the entire resolution. This approach identifies mass terms in the resolution and claims that the affirmative must defend the entire set of items encompassed by a mass term in order to maintain the grammatical integrity of the resolutional statement. "Failure to deal with the entire set of the mass noun would make the affirmative warrant a hasty generalization" (Berube, 1986a, p. 6).

Very little has been written on mass terminology in resolutions. However, some grammatical standards are available to test whether a term is mass or not mass.

> 1. A mass term is distinct from a count term. Simply put, mass terms cannot be counted, such as one book, two books, five books.

2. A mass term cannot be pluralized.
3. A mass term cannot occur with a predeterminer. "Count nouns can occur with predeterminers like 'three,' 'seventeen,' 'a dozen,' 'many,' 'several,' 'few,' whereas mass nouns cannot" (Katz, 1972, p. 374). Mass nouns, for example, "are distinguished by amassives, words like 'much,' 'little,' and 'less'" (Ware, 1975, p. 379).
4. A mass term is sometimes individuated by a mass collective. A collective term in the resolution may transform a nonmass term into a mass term. This process of individuating syntactically converts simple nouns into mass nouns. For example, in the CEDA topic: "that membership in the United Nations is no longer beneficial to the United States," the term "United Nations" serves as a collective and individuates "membership" into a mass noun.

Since there are two means to debate hasty generalization, logical and grammatical, each of these set-ups for the counterwarrant is examined individually.

To determine massness, the debater runs a series of tests on the term in dispute.

To decide whether a term can be counted and, consequently, should not be considered a mass term, the debater demonstrates the term can be reasonably counted without changing the meaning of the term as discerned from its resolutional context.

To establish pluralizability, the debater again indicates that the term maintains contextually parallel meaning when it is pluralized.

To deny the mass feature of a term, a debater may try to demonstrate that it maintains meaning when it appears with a predeterminer.

Finally, a debater may want to demonstrate that the term at issue stands alone and is not contextually individuated by any other term in the resolution.

In every instance, testing for massness of a term requires that the hypothetical manipulation of the term does not prevent the employment of the term in a syntactically feasible sentence; the term must make sense when used in a sentence. In addition, the exercise cannot change the grammatical usage of the term as engaged in the resolution: nouns must remain as nouns.

INDUCTIVE FALLACY TESTS

Just any example will not do in inductively proving a resolution probably true. Those controls involve two fallacies within the genre of Type II errors.

1. One infers from an insufficently large or quantitatively un-representative sample to the whole population. We can call this the fallacy of small sample.
2. One infers from a peculiarly selected or qualitatively unrep-resentative sample to a whole population. We call this the *fallacy of biased statistics* (Carney and Scheer, 1975, p. 44).

To determine whether an affirmative example of the resolution is hasty, the following standards should be applied: Is the affirmative example representative, and is the affirmative example sufficiently large?

To establish representativeness, the affirmative must be able to demonstrate that the example shares fundamental characteristics with the resolution from which it is drawn. In other words, the affirmative subset is reasonably similar to the resolutional set. Negative counter-examples or counterwarrants must also share the same or better charac-teristics of the resolution in order to prove the resolution is probably not true.

To determine whether an affirmative example is sufficiently large, the affirmative should impose a simple formula that evaluates the number of actors affected times the gravity of harm. Size is a relative issue. While sample size in statistical sciences is discernible through a simple F test, which specifies minimal sample size necessary for signi-ficance in an experimental design, in rhetoric it is not as easy. The debate over resolving the fallacy of small sample appears elsewhere (see Bile 1987, 1988).

The *fallacy of biased statistics* requires that "the affirmative must be able to demonstrate that the examples share fundamental characteristics of the resolution from which it is drawn" (Berube, 1983/1987, p. 486). Biggers felt that the affirmative must somehow "establish the germane nature of the example used" (1985, p. 35). Initially, Berube argued that "the affirmative subset must be reasonably similar to the resolutional set from which it is drawn" (1986b, p. 10). However, both these viewpoints offered little guidance to the debater who must defend her examples against the negative claim of representativeness. Some tools may be found in the field of phenomenology.

Phenomenology is primarily concerned with determining the es-sences of things. "There are some properties that an object must have; if the object didn't have them, it wouldn't exist at all. These are the properties that an object has essentially" (Brody, 1980, p. 84). When Butchvarov discussed essence in an Aristotelian sense, he delineated three features: "a character, a content, [and] properties" (1979, p. 122). Though Bahm seemed correct when he asserted that "current mecha-nisms of resolutional interpretation have not offered clear means of combating multistability" (1988, p. 26), (perceptual objects very according to their context), an assertion that may be at the heart of determining representativeness, he also failed to present tools that can be applied for this purpose.

Bahm drew from phenomenology when he considered the intrinsicness argument in nonpolicy debate (1988). However, the process of optimal illustration also seems an appropriate perspective by which to determine the representativeness of the affirmative examples used in the inductive proof to prove the resolution probably true. Through reduction via perceptual variation, the affirmative may be able to demonstrate that their examples share characteristics from the resolution from which they were drawn and, consequently, evidence that their examples are not guilty of the fallacy of biased statistics.

Essence can be demonstrated in many ways, "arrived at by the comparison of many examples of a type of object and extracting from the descriptions of all these examples the common features by means of some kind of generalization" (Schmitt, 1967, p. 139). Husserl talked about a procedure that he called "free imaginative variation."

"Here we describe an example and then transform the description by adding or deleting one of the predicates contained in the description. With each addition or deletion, we ask whether the amended description can still be said to describe an example of the same kind of object as that which the example originally described was said to exemplify" (Schmitt, 1967, p. 41).

There are at least two ways to discern and defend against this type of representativeness argument.

First, *defining the necessary*. Butchvarov wrote that defining the necessary is "what is stated in the definition of the thing, a definition being understood as real rather than nominal (that is, not as a stipulation of linguistic usage)" (1979, p. 134). Using Aquinas, "the definition telling what a thing is signifies that by which a thing is located in its genus or species" (1968, p. 31). This process of definition centers a term or word within a certain group while maintaining its uniqueness. Branching from a genus to a species to a class is a linear process, which, though bidirectional, cannot accommodate identicalness between species or classes drawn along independent lines from a given genus. To consider definition in this context, "an essential statement classifies what it is about, subsumes it under a concept, establishes its place in conceptual space" (Butchvarov, 1979, p. 140). Butchvarov further explains that it involves the conception of "an entity in terms of its sort, for example, as a man or number, and this is why an entity's sort is usually a paradigm of a property it has necessarily, of one it cannot be conceived as not having" (1979, p. 132). Butchvarov, however, denied the use of definition by simile. Semi-automatic weapons are like handguns but are not handguns. Police are like civilians but they are not civilians. That's why, in turn, we call them semi-automatic weapons and police and not handguns and civilians. Since an essential statement will assert of an object that it is a certain entity, it expresses the relationship between an object and the entity the object is. "It is neither necessary nor sufficient that one recollect or single out in some other way a previously encountered thing" (p. 142). This process is a conceptual pursuit and not metaphysical sleight of hand. For example, on the handgun topic, necessary characteristics may include "controls" as *restrictions* versus "bans." Controls would be presumably on weapons that are hand held versus howitzers. Deeper analysis may require that handguns fire a projectile using an explosive charge. As illustration, though a vaccination gun used by a health professional is like a handgun and even shares some, if not most, of its essential characteristics, it is only near identical by simile or metaphor and has a fluid place in conceptual space, a nonplace. It is, consequently, not really, but nominally, defined, and not an essentially representative example from the class or resolutional set from which it is drawn.

Second, *defining the invariant*. Essences are "the necessary and invariant features of objects" (Schmitt, 1967, p. 139). Laycock considered a criterion of particular identity through time. "An object m at t1 is identical with an object n at t2 if m is spatiotemporally continuous with n between t1 and t2 under some covering concept F. A sub-task of the elucidation of this criterion, for any particular value of F, requires spelling out what changes can tolerate while remaining F—what are sometimes called the *persistence conditions* of Fs" (1972, p. 28). Butchvarov explained that "a necessarily true statement is one whose subject matter consists solely of nontemporal entities, or one that is an instantiation of a universal statement, which subject matter consists solely on nontemporal entities" (1979, pp. 128–129). This test insists that a good example is not time or scenario dependent. In order words, the reason the generalization that the resolution may be true based upon the observation that an example(s) is true is not due to an aberrant point in time or due to an improbable hypothetical reality. For example, magnet trigger locks on police firearms may be desirable in the present but not in a future scenario with police using nondeadly force like stunguns or with police functioning unarmed as in Great Britain. Also, handgun accidents in the home may justify restrictions on possession of handguns but not in a scenairo whereby gun locks, lock boxes, or gun education programs are common, a hardly implausible set of scenarios. This adding/deleting process involves predicates of the description that would naturally discredit the application of fanciful, trivial, and unrealistic assumptions.

THE ROLE OF HASTY GENERALIZATION ARGUMENTS IN DECISION MAKING

The cry of hasty generalization is not enough. The debate does not stop there for a subjective edict from the critic; the debate merely occurs on two levels: (1) testing of the examples as representative or size/significant or grammatically correct as a resolutional justification; and (2) testing of the issues as a justification to believe the resolution probably true.

Hasty generalization is not a voting issue per se unless the negative frames the debate within some sort of a hypothesis-testing paradigm. Zarefsky's (1976) hypothesis-testing paradigm would reject an affirmative warrant regardless of extrinsic reasonableness when the examples fail to be a good subset of the resolution. As such, hasty generalization may become an a priori issue. In nonpolicy debating, the a priori hasty generalization debate issue has become renamed subtopicality. And similar to policy debating, the negative argues the affirmative example as a jurisdictional issue and as such deserves primacy. The obvious affirmative response is to defend a nonhypothesis-testing paradigm that forces the negative to introduce and defend counterwarrants.

Nonpolicy debaters have been able to argue quite convincingly that debate is not hypothesis testing. The resolution is not written as a hypothesis. The resolution cannot be tested within the arbitrary time limits imposed on the activity. Debate is merely the demonstration of relative truth or probable truth of a resolutional statement. Debate is at best hypothesis building. It involves procedures whereby educated guesses are systematically excluded from a pool of reasonable guesses. Testing takes place subsequent to the debate.

Debate as a rhetorical activity deals with subjective fact finding. The determination of relative truth is based on authoritative yet opinionated statements rather than formal objective replicate research findings. Regardless, critics decide jurisdictional issues first. If hasty generalization is an a priori issue, this means that a critic evaluates the critieria issue setting up hasty generalization first and then tests the affirmative and negative examples against the criteria.

In order to demonstrate that the affirmative example is hasty and any subsequent generalization is unjustified, the negative should introduce the counterwarrant—an example of the resolutional set that proves the direction of the resolutional statement either inaccurate or undesirable or both.

The standards for a good counterwarrant must include the following:

    1. Use of the affirmative definitions or redefinition of the resolution using better definition standards.

2. Presentation of representative and sufficiently large counter examples of the resolution.
3. Proof that the affirmative examples to indicate probable truth of the resolution are deficient and the negative counterwarrants are superior.

Negative counterwarrants may suffer equally from the fallacy of hasty generalization if the counterwarrant examples are unrepresentative or insufficiently large to justify generalization. The affirmative can aruge that a single negative counterwarrant example results in poor generalization.

CONCLUSION

Arguing hasty generalization in nonpolicy debate will serve three purposes: (1) To improve issue selection and generally improve the student's learning experience based on topical analysis of a resolutional statement; (2) To decrease evidence-crammed nonanalytical debates and concentrate the debate on the inductive process intself; (3) To decrease hasty generalization as an issue. The more it is argued, the more the issue of hasty generalization will develop standards. Debaters will attempt to preempt hasty generalization debates by choosing better examples to prove the resolution is probably true.

For a critic of argument, hasty generalization debates can be resolved as follows:

1. Has the negative issued standards of representativeness or sample size or grammar for the claim of hasty generalization? Has the negative identified some fundamental characteristics of the resolution that the affirmative has not met?
2. Has the negative identified some superior actor–to–gravity size/significance relationship that the affirmative has not met?
3. Has the negative identified mass terms in the resolution that the affirmative has not wholly addressed?
4. In making the above arguments, has the negative issued an appropriate paradigm? The hypothesis-testing paradigm allows debates to be decided on hasty generalization alone. However, any alternate paradigm that requires the negative to present examples—counterwarrants—may also lend a rationale to reject an affirmative example as the sole basis for acceptance of the resolution.
5. Do the negative counterwarrants prove the resolution probably is not true better than the affirmative examples prove the resolution probably is true?

The role of the critic is to evaluate the performance of the debaters in each round, not to interject subjective judgments into the debates. If debaters insist on arguing hasty generalization and counterwarrants, they are obligated to present good argument. This article may serve to offer some basic guidelines to debaters and critics in the nonpolicy debate community.

References

Aquinas, T. (1968). *On Being and Essence*. 2nd ed. Trans. A. Maurer. Toronto: Pontifical Institute of Medieval Studies.

Ayer, A. (1968). *The Origins of Pragmatism*. London: Macmillan.

Bahm, K. (1988). "Intrinsic Justification: Meaning and Method." *CEDA Yearbook* 9: 23–29.

Berube, David (1986a). "Debating Mass and Collective Terms in Non-Policy Debate." *Starmakers* 3.2 (Spring): 5–6.

Berube, David (1986b). "Inductive Models in Argumentation." *Starmakers* 3.2 (Spring): 2–4.

Berube, D. (1984). "Non-Policy Debating and Affirmative Case Formats." Paper presented at the Western Speech Association Convention, University of Washington, Feb. 21.

Berube, David (1983). "Non-Policy Debating and Affirmative Case Formats." Paper presented at the WSCA Convention, Seattle, Feb. 21. (ERIC 1984).

Biggers, T. (1985). "A Single Swallow and Other Leaps of Faith." *CEDA Yearbook* 6: 32–38.

Bile, J. (1987). "When the Whole Is Greater Than the Sum of the Parts: The Implications of Holistic Resolutional Focus." *CEDA Yearbook* 8: 8–15.

Brody, B. (1980). *Identity and Essence*. Princeton: Princeton University Press.

Butchvarov, P. (1979). *Being Qua Being: A Theory of Identity, Existence, and Prediction*. Bloomington: Indiana University Press.

Carney, J. and Scheer, R. (1974). *Fundamentals of Logic*. 2nd ed. New York: Macmillan.

Church, R. and Wilbanks, C. (1986). *Values and Policies in Controversy: An Introduction to Argumentation and Debate*. Scottsdale, AZ: Gorsuch Scarisbrick.

Cook, K. (1975). "On the Usefulness of Quantities." *Synthese* 31: 443–57.

Copi, I. (1961). *Introduction to Logic*. 2nd ed. New York: Macmillan.

Flew, A. (1961). *Hume's Philosophy of Belief*. London: Routledge & Kegan Paul.

Herbeck, Dale A. and Katsulas, John P. (1985b). "A Response to Rhodes and Pfau." *Journal of the American Forensic Association* 21 (Spring): 240–43.

Husserl, E. (1962). *Ideas: General Introduction to Pure Phenomenology*. Trans. W. Boyce-Gibson. New York: Macmillan.

Katz, Jerold J. (1972). *Semantics*. New York: Harper & Row.

Keeshan, Marjorie and Ulrich, Walter (1980). "A Critique of the Counter-Warrant as Negative Strategy." *Journal of the American Forensic Association* 16 (Winter): 199–203.

Korzybski, A. (1958). *Science and Sanity: An Introduction to Non-Aristotelian Systems and General Semantics*. 4th ed. Clinton, MA: Colonial Press.

Laycock, H. (1972). "Some Questions of Ontology." *The Philosophical Review* 81: 3–42.

Lyons, J. (1977). *Semantics*. London: Cambridge University Press.

Madsen. A. and Chandler R. (1988). "When the Whole Becomes a Black Hole: Implications of the Holistic Perspective." *CEDA Yearbook* 9: 30–37.

Merleau-Ponty, N. (1952). *Phenomenology of Perception*. Trans. C. Smith. London: Routledge & Kegan Paul.

Paulsen, James W. and Rhodes, Jack (1979). "The Counter-Warrant as a Negative Strategy: A Modest Proposal." *Journal of the American Forensic Association* 15: 205–10.

Rhodes, Jack (1981). "A Defense of the Counter-Warrant as Negative Argument." *Dimensions of Argument: Proceedings of the Second Summer Conference on Argumentation*. Annandale, VA: SCA. 485–93.

Rhodes, Jack and Pfau, Michael W. (1985). "Resolution or Example: A Reply to Herbeck and Katsulas." *Journal of the American Forensic Association* 31 (Winter): 146–49.

Rowland, Robert (1983). "The Philosophical Predispositions of Value Debate." *Argument in Transition: Proceedings of the Third Summer Conference on Argumentation*. Annandale, VA: SCA. 822–36.

Schmitt, R. (1967). "Phenomenology." *Encyclopedia of Philosophy*. v. 6. New York: Macmillan. 135–51.

Ware, Robert X. (1975). "Some Bits and Pieces." *Syntheses* 31.

Wittgenstein, L. (1961). *Tractatus Logico-Philosophicus*. Trans. D. Pear and B. McGuinness. London: Routledge & Kegan Paul.

Wittgenstein, L. (1975). *Philosophical Remarks*. Trans. R. Hargreaves and R. White. Oxford: Blackwell.

44

When the Whole Is Greater Than the Sum of the Parts
The Implications of Holistic Resolutional Focus

Jeffrey T. Bile

Arguments based on an assumption of holistic resolutional focus are very much a part of contemporary academic debate. In a hypothetical debate on the topic "RESOLVED: That increased military preparedness is important," a negative utilizing a whole-resolution viewpoint and debating against an affirmative case that advocated a "1 percent increase in the number of M-16 rifles stockpiled" might argue something like this:

> The *whole resolution* should be the argumentative focus for this debate. There is a missing modifier in the topic that would quantify the amount of increase we should discuss. In absence of such a modifier, we should presume a qualifier of "generally" as opposed to "in certain specific cases," which has been implicitly inserted by the affirmative. While the affirmative might prove the need for a specific increase in M-16s, they do not prove the importance *on-balance* for generally "increased military preparedness." The affirmative does not meet its burden of proof. Attempts to use the affirmative case as an inductive proof for the resolution are flawed, given the general problems with induction and given that in this specific case such an inference would be invalid because of the logical problems with fallacy of composition and hasty generalization. Further, affirmative induction attempts would legitimize the same approach by the negative, and we could run counterwarrants. In conclusion, since the affirmative case is not *typical*, it is *sub-topical* and should be rejected.

This hypothetical is a hybrid of a number of arguments currently in use that are consonant with a holistic view of resolutional focus. The unstated premise in all these arguments—the linchpin upon which the rest of the argument depends—is the advocacy of whole resolution focus. Failure to make explicit the argument for holism, however, is often problematic since there is no agreement on whether or not debaters must argue the whole resolution (Herbeck and Wong, 1986).

The holistic view is one of two that currently dominate considerations regarding argumentative perspective in academic debate. The other approach, which I will refer to as the parametric approach, suggests that the resolution exists to place an outward boundary (or parameter) on advocacy and that as long as arguments selected fall within this jurisdiction, they are legitimate.

Traditionally, academic debaters argued the "totality of the resolution" (Kovalcheck, 1979, p. 31), and judges decided not on specifics but "on the general resolution" (Paulsen and Rhodes, 1979, p. 205). In fact, from "the beginning of the national resolution until about 1973–74, the entire resolution was normally thought to be debated.... The demarcation line approach is comparatively recent and seems to have no real theoretical underpinning other than current practice" (Rhodes, 1981, p. 493). The advent of the parametric view is a relatively recent phenomenon, which gained acceptance with the changing nature of topics (Kovalcheck, 1979; Pfau, 1979).

The shift toward the parametric approach has had significant effects on the debating process. An affirmative debating the "increased military" topic and utilizing parametric resolutional focus could, for example, legitimately advance a case discussing M-16s, the inadequacies of the Marine Corps Band, or the need for army boots. While these examples are obviously extreme, the reader should not miss the point that parametric focus makes these approaches theoretically (if not rhetorically) sound.

The situation becomes far more problematic when the debater combines parametric focus with a more persuasive example. Given the thousands of possible interpretations of most topics, it is not unlikely that hundreds would seem significant in a persuasive sense. The result is a significant increase in affirmative case possibilities. When parlayed with the affirmative right to define, the parametric approach usually means that the affirmative may select a case anywhere within the resolutional boundary and that the negative must debate only this case. The result for the negative is almost certainly a slow and painful death. The forensic community has had two main responses to this problem: the invention of counterwarrants (Paulsen and Rhodes, 1979) and a shift from NDT to CEDA, where holistic focus would presumedly prevail (Rowland, 1983; Tolbert and Hunt, 1985; Tomlinson, 1981; Ulrich, 1984).

THE MERITS OF HOLISTIC INTERPRETATION

Despite the wide appeal of whole-resolution focus within the CEDA community (Ulrich, 1984) and the exigency created by the drift of students away from it (Tolbert and Hunt, 1985), the rationales for holism are nevertheless poorly articulated in the literature. A number of authors, for example, discuss standards for induction or the legitimacy of counterwarrants (Berube, 1984; Biggers, 1985; Ganer, 1981; Rhodes, 1981; Simon, 1984; Tolbert and Hunt, 1985) but do so from a perspective that presupposes either the parametric or the holistic approach without critically defending that focus.

The lack of agreement and the paucity of justificatory literature create a need for whole-resolution advocacy. This author will offer two justifications for holistic focus. The first is that the more generic arguments are, the greater their educational utility. The second is that particularized interpretation legitimized by the parametric approach is inconsistent with rules for language interpretation developed in semantics and logic.

EDUCATIONAL JUSTIFICATION

Holistic resolutional focus is pedagogically preferable to the parametric approach. Academic debate is a powerful educational tool. In addition to the plethora of other process-based advantages, debaters are forced to learn a great deal substantively about significant contemporary topics in their world (Freeley, 1986). Once we accept that debaters will learn about the topics they debate, we must confront the question: "What is it that we want them to learn?" Holistic topic focus promotes a more general education than relatively narrow parametric sub-topics. This stands to reason since the research, preparation, presentation, and analysis of more general arguments are encouraged by a more general focus. The pedagogical question becomes: "Is a general or a specific educational focus pedagogically superior?" Murty (1963) argues that "unless a man is capable of thinking and planning for himself, and unless he is able to rise above the parochialism of his own time, race, and society . . . he cannot lead a full and integrated life. General education alone can enable everyone to do this" (p. 44). Murty lists holistic and synthetic thinking as well as recognition of pattern and perspective among the fruits of a general education. This author favors general education for a number of reasons.

Initially, general education enhances content relevance. Ulrich (1985) suggests that arguing generics can force the debater to understand issues common to a wide range of affairs. Sawhill (1979) concludes that general education has importance far beyond its immediate concern. This is intuitive. It is very unlikely that our students will ever be asked to decide the fate of a proposal for a 1 percent increase in M-16s; it is far more likely they will be asked to make decisions regarding the appropriate level of general military preparedness our nation should pursue.

Additionally, general education tends to have greater longevity (Goodlad, 1976) since theories tend to have more staying-power than facts. Educators argue, for example, that "liberal education provides a general background which makes reorientation easier. By stressing the theory of a subject matter, it avoids imprisonment in the narrow applications which may soon be obsolete" (Eastman, 1981, p. 30). The general intellectual skills associated with a broad-based education are quite valuable. Bisconti's research (1976) found that only 8 percent of graduates listed specific knowledge as the most important aspect of their education and that the number decreased as their careers progressed.

> Instead, they reported that general concepts of their majors, general learning in college, and the study experience itself were more valuable. These results suggest that, over time, the value of specific knowledge declines while the importance of general intellectual skills associated with liberal education grows.

For example, understanding the specifics of Reagan's military policies had less relevance after 1989; understanding the merits of military preparedness, however, will have utility for as long as there are militaries. General education is preferable, therefore, since it enhances the relevance and longevity of learning.

It is significant that both Eastman and Bisconti equate general education with liberal education. This should not be surprising. While the term has been used in a number of different senses, "in contemporary nonphilosophic usage, any education accepted as relatively broad and general rather than narrow and specialized" is termed liberal education (Good, 1959, p. 318). Ever since Dewey (1925) argued that what made an education liberal was its breadth or generality, liberal education "can best be expressed as that of an education directed toward developing not specific skills and abilities but the general capacities" (Hirst, 1971). Dejnozka and Kapel (1982) agree that liberal education is "currently defined as a form of education that is broad and general as opposed to being specialized" (p. 301). Page and Thomas (1977) define the liberal arts as those academic disciplines "that are broader in their range and scope ... they are presumed to develop general intellectual ability and a wide cultural background of knowledge." Liberal education has consistently been equated with broad and general education and contrasted with narrow or specialized education

(Blishen, 1969; Carpenter, 1960; Dejnozka and Kapel, 1982; Dressel, Mayhew and McGrath, 1959; Greene, 1953; Gordon, 1963; Hirst, 1971; Mayhew, 1960; Menon, 1963; Murty, 1963; Page and Thomas, 1977; Simons, 1963;Venkataraman, 1963; Wegener, 1978).

Little wonder that Averill (1983) argues that holism is a term "which distinguishes the consensus about liberal learning, and it points to the range of competencies students must be assisted to achieve. By holism I understand, for one thing, a rejection of unidimensional pre-occupations. . . " (p. 10). He concludes by noting that "liberal education is, by its very nature, pervasive and holistic" (p. 74).

This author would suggest, therefore, that to the extent that holistic resolutional focus promotes holistic education, it is in line with the best of the liberal arts tradition. But is a liberal education valuable? Fortunately, this question has already been investigated by educational philosophers and researchers. Their conclusion? General, holistic, broad-based, and theoretical liberal education is preferable to specific, fragmented, narrowly focused, and factual specialized education. Research suggests that the more liberal education is, the more students achieve. Reporting the results of their research, Winter and colleagues (1978) note that:

> For more than 2,000 years a liberal education has been the ideal of the West. . . . The tradition goes back to Plato. . . . Our findings suggest that liberal education does in fact change students more or less as Plato envisioned. . . . [It] appears to promote increases in conceptual and socio-emotional sophistication. . . . Students trained in the liberal arts are better able to form valid concepts, analyze arguments, define themselves, and orient themselves maturely to their world (p. 69).

It is not this writer's intention to imply that the parametrical approach has no educational value. Debating specifics does not make it impossible to form valid concepts, analyze arguments, or to orient oneself to the world. Everything else being equal, however, the more general education is, the more one can expect such sophistications. Since a holistic topic focus produces relatively more generic learning than a relatively specific sub-topic, it should be viewed as pedagogically desirable.

Some have suggested that debating a number of specifics will add up to the same education as debating generics. It is this author's contention that debating a large number of sub-topics only adds up to the sum of *some* of the parts, nothing greater than the sum of the parts, and certainly not the whole. There were literally thousands of possible sub-topics on the "military preparedness" topic for example, but no debater was involved in more than 200 debates on this topic. Debating 200 different sub-topics provides a fraction of the depth of debating a single generic topic 200 times. In addition, debating 200 different sub-topics is not truly broad but rather *repetitively narrow*, in that some sub-topics are never examined and some boundaries are never explored. By encouraging the development of generic, holistic, integrative frameworks, the whole always exceeds the sum of the parts. The only way to encourage real breadth and depth—a true general education—is by focusing on the relatively generic topic rather than more specific sub-topics.

LANGUAGE JUSTIFICATION

The second rationale for holistic focus is that generic interpretation is most compatible with rules of interpretation in light of a missing modifier. Most of us would consider the proposition "birds can fly" as true even though we are aware of some that can't, because we intuitively insert the generic modifier "most" in front of "birds" or "typically/ generally" in front of "fly." This intuition is semantically correct. Linguist John Lyons (1981) argues:

> What is meant by "generic" may be seen by considering such sets of sentences as the following: (1) The lion is a friendly beast. (2) A lion is a friendly beast. (3) Lions are friendly beasts. Each of these sentences may be used to assert a generic proposition: this is, a proposition which says something, not about this or that group of lions or about any particular individual lion, but about the class of lions as such . . . " (p. 193).

Lyons continues by indicating that the "kind of adverbial modifier that suggests itself for insertion" is one "that approximates in meaning to 'generally,' 'typically,' 'characteristically,' or 'normally' " (p. 195). While semantic rules support generic interpretation, the field of logic provides additional supportive rules. Logicians tend to interpret indesignate form propositions with missing quantification modifiers as universal or as expressing group tendency (Barnstable, 1975). Van Der Auwera (1985, p. 188) argues that when choosing "between the generic or the non-generic or particular" reading of the statement "A whale lives in the sea, " that in most contexts, the preferred interpretation is generic. He further argues that while interpretation should be guided by context, there "are some cases, however, where the choice is independent of context." He gives the statement: "Kangaroos have no tails" as one which is always generic. Logical conventions would certainly reject a particularized topic rendering.

Clearly, linguistic and logical conventions support generic interpretation. It is not this author's intent to imply that the academic debate must be bound by the conventions of ordinary language, but rather to suggest that an interpretation which is intuitively, semantically, and logically correct should have some presumption until arguments are established that reject generic interpretation.

ARGUMENTATIVE IMPLICATIONS OF HOLISTIC FOCUS

Despite the rationales for generic interpretation, some have objected to the whole-resolution perspective. These objections are most frequently based on a misunderstanding of the implications of resolutional focus. Holistic focus does not: (1) eliminate all discussion of specific examples; (2) eliminate the affirmative right to define; (3) require the affirmative to prove each and every example true; (4) justify counterwarrants; (5) unduly encourage example stacking; or (6) favor the negative. Biggers (1985) states this author's position when he argues that most objections to holistic focus "are logically unsupportable" (p. 32).

Accepting a whole-resolution focus does, however, have several implications for the evaluation of the probative force of arguments. The first implication is that generic arguments should take precedence. If the purpose of debate is to establish the probable truth of the whole resolution, then arguments that are more generic to the resolution should have greater weight than those less generic. If, for example, the negative wins objections to the resolution more generic than the affirmative case, then it should win the debate even if the affirmative wins its case, as the negative arguments would offer a more valid generalization about the truth of the resolution.

The second implication is that arguments from subset are not prima facie. By this I mean that a part is not, on its face, logically self-sufficient to prove the whole. Subsets do not necessarily support the larger claim. Tolbert and Hunt (1985) argue that:

> An area of argumentation related to hasty generalization is topical justification. Topical justification suggests that, should an affirmative present and win an example of the resolution, it still might not prove the resolution true. Rather, the affirmative example only would have been proven to be true and some subcategory of the resolution only might be true. In other words, the case could well be sub-topical (p. 23).

This does not mean that examples cannot be used. What it does mean is that he who asserts that one can infer the general from a specific example should be required to prove the reasonability of that inference. Until and unless such proof is offered, a subset should be presumed to be nothing more. How might an advocate establish the reasonability of his or her inference? Biggers (1985) suggested several requirements for advancing a valid inductive argument:

The argument consists of evidence (examples from a particular class about which a particular conclusion can be made), a warrant (a statement to the effect that what is true of a sample from the class is also true of the class as a whole), support for the warrant (a belief that the examples in the evidence are germane to the claim, adequate in number and fairly selected), reservations (any instances that reduce our faith in the probability of the conclusion), and a conclusion (the idea that what is true of the examples is also true of the class as a whole) (Toulmin, 1958). Each element in this chain of reasoning is critical and must be supported if the argument as a whole is to be accepted (p. 33).

Biggers continued by noting that "even if the warrant can be supported" in this way, the argument should be defeated if the opposition "offers examples that better meet the criteria outlined above and that support the countergeneralization" (p. 36). That is, once the debater attempts to prove an argument from example, she or he opens the door to the opponent using the same inductive approach to disprove the argument. Hence, if one side utilizes example analysis, they legitimize the other side's use of the counterwarrant.

A third potential implication of resolutional focus is for what has been called the "intrinsicness" argument (Bryant, 1982). This argument suggests that an opponent's claim does not justify the affirmation or negation of the resolution unless the claim is unique to that side of the resolution (or its absence intrinsic to the other). In policy debate, counterplans are a pragmatic implication of this theoretical standard. CEDA debaters have suggested that the same theoretical basis justifies intrinsicness arguments in nonpolicy debate.

It is further argued that to disallow intrinsicness arguments shifts the focus of nonpolicy debates from inherent worth of values to the coincidence of current policies. On the fall 1986 topic, for example, some debaters argued that the disadvantages of underground nuclear testing did not disprove the value of military preparedness, since these disadvantages were not intrinsic to military preparedness. Military preparedness could, after all, be increased without increasing underground testing. Holistic-resolution focus buttresses this intrinsicness argument in cases where an advocate utilizes a relatively narrow temporal, spatial, or political context when the resolution makes no such limitation. The "Republican Senate" argument, for example, held that military preparedness was uniquely valuable in the weeks preceding the 1986 elections but, as no such temporal limitation was mentioned in the topic, this argument may well have been a hasty generalization.

CONCLUSION

Academic debates traditionally utilized the whole resolution as their point of departure. While holistic focus is still explicitly espoused and implicitly embraced in many arguments, it has recently been challenged by a parametric view of topic interpretation. This trend has resulted in a relative shift from generic argumentation to more narrow intellectual pursuits. This development is unfortunate for at least two reasons. The first is that the more generic arguments are, the greater their educational utility. The second is that particularized interpretation legitimized by the parametric approach is inconsistent with rules for language interpretation developed in semantics and logic. While some have objected to resolutional holism, the complaints are most often based on misunderstandings of its implications. The adoption of the holistic perspective does have three implications for the probative force of an argument. First, the more generic an argument is to the resolution the greater its value. Second, arguments from subset example do not have self-evident strength. Finally, arguments that are not intrinsic to resolutional conditions should be seen as inductively weak.

The rationales for resolutional focus have received insufficient attention. This author has suggested that knowing the rules is more useful than knowing an exception to them. It is hoped that this effort can serve as a springboard for further discussions in debate rounds, in the literature, and within the topic selection process regarding the appropriate role of the resolution in academic debate.

References

Averill, L. (1983). *Learning to Be Human: A Vision for the Liberal Arts*. Port Washington, NY: Associated Faculty Press.

Barnstable, P. K. (1975). *Logic: Depth Grammar of Rationality*. Dublin: Gill and Macmillan.

Berube, D. M. (1984). "Debating Hasty Generalization." *CEDA Yearbook* 5: 54–59.

Biggers, T. (1985). "A Single Swallow and Other Leaps of Faith." *CEDA Yearbook* 6: 32–38.

Bisconti, A. S. and Soloman, L. C. (1976). *College Education on the Job—The Graduates Viewpoints*. Bethlehem, PA: The CPC Foundation.

Blishen, E., ed. (1969). *Blonde's Encyclopedia of Education*. London: Blonde Educational Ltd.

Brademas, J. (1986). *Washington, D.C. to Washington Square*. New York: Weidenfield and Nicolson.

Bryant, M. (1982). *An Examination of Resolution Focus*. Paper presented at the annual convention of the Speech Communication Association, Louisville, Nov.

Carpenter, M. (1960). "The Humanities Program at Stephens College." In J. A.

Fisher, ed. *The Humanities in General Education*. Dubuque: Wm. C. Brown. 79–91.

Dejnozka, E. L. and Kapel, D. E. (1982). *American Educators' Encyclopedia*. Westport: Greenwood Press.

Dewey, J. (1925). *Democracy and Education: An Introduction to the Philosophy of Education*. New York: Macmillan.

Dressel, P. L., Mayhem, L. B., and McGrath, E. J. (1959). *The Liberal Arts*. New York: Columbia.

Eastman, R. M. (1981). "Five Great Powers of a Free Liberal Arts Education." *Vital Speeches* 47: 29–32.

Freeley, A. J. (1986). *Argumentation and Debate: Reasoned Decision Making*. Belmont, CA: Wadsworth.

Ganer, P. M. (1981). "Counter-Warrants: An Idea Whose Times Has Not Come." In G. Ziegelmueller and J. Rhodes, eds. *Dimensions of Argument: Proceedings of the Second Summer Conference on Argumentation*. Annandale, VA: Speech Communication Association. 476–84.

Good, C. V., ed. (1959). *Dictionary of Education*. New York: McGraw-Hill.

Goodlad, S. (1976). *Conflict and Consensus in Higher Education*. London: Hodder and Stroughton.

Gordon, D. (1963). "General Education and the Unity of Knowledge." In K. S. Murty, ed. *General Education Reconsidered*. New York: Asia Publishing. 54–63.

Greene, T. M. (1953). *Liberal Education Reconsidered*. Cambridge: Harvard University Press.

Herbeck, D. and Wong, K. (1986). "The Indivisibility of Value Claims from Policy Positions: An Argument for Policy in Value Debate." *CEDA Yearbook* 7: 14–28.

Hirst, P. H. (1971). "Liberal Education." In L. Deighton, ed. *The Encyclopedia of Education*. New York: Macmillan and Free Press. 505–9.

Kelley, B. M. (1982). "An Alternative to NDT Debate." *Philosophy and Practice of CEDA* 3: 8–14.

Kovalcheck, K. (1979). "Retrospective: Forensics in the 1970s." *Speaker and Gavel* 17 (Fall): 31–33.

Lippincott, W. T. (1979). "Why Higher Education Continues to Fail." *Journal of Chemical Education* 56: 69.

Lyons, J. (1981). *Semantics*. Cambridge: Cambridge University Press.

Mayhew, L. B. (1960). *General Education*. New York: Harper and Brothers.

Menon, L. N. (1963). "General Education: Integrated Purposeful Education." In K. S. Murty, ed. *General Education Reconsidered*. New York: Asia Publishing. 17–23.

Murty, K. S. (1963). "Education for Free Men." In K. S. Murty, ed. *General Education Reconsidered*. New York: Asia Publishing. 40–46.

Page, G. T. and Thomas, J. B. (1977). *International Dictionary of Education*. New York: Nichols Publishing.

Paulsen, J. W. and Rhodes, J. (1979). "The Counter-Warrant as Negative Strategy: A Modest Proposal." *Journal of the American Forensic Association* 15: 205–10.

Pfau, M. (1979). "The 1970s: A Decade of Change." *Speaker and Gavel* 17 (Fall): 46–47.

Rhodes, J. (1981). "A Defense of the Counter-Warrant as Negative Argument." In G. Ziegelmueller and J. Rhodes, eds. *Dimensions of Argument: Proceedings of the Second Summer Conference on Argumentation*. Annandale, VA: Speech Communication Association. 485–93.

Rowland, R. (1983). "The Philosophical Perspectives of Value Debate." In D. Zarefsky, M. Sillars, and J. Rhodes, eds. *Argument in Transition: Proceedings of the Third Summer Conference on Argumentation*. Annandale, VA: Speech Communication Association. 822–36.

Sawhill, J. C. (1979). "The Unlettered University." *The Modern Language Journal* 63: 281–85.

Simon, R. (1984). "The Case Against Counter-Warrants in Value Debate." *CEDA Yearbook* 5: 48–53.

Simons, K. (1963). "The Meaning of General Education." In K. S. Murty, ed. *General Education Reconsidered*. New York: Asia Publishing. 24–32.

Tolbert, G. and Hunt, S. (1985). "Counter-Warrants: A Method for Testing Topical Justification in CEDA Debate." *CEDA Yearbook* 6: 21–28.

Tomlinson, J. (1981). "CEDA as an Alternative." *The Forensic* (Fall): 14–16.

Ulrich, W. (1985). Debating Generic Disadvantages." *Debate Issues* (Feb.): 14.

Ulrich, W. (1984). "The Nature of the Topic in Value Debate." *CEDA Yearbook* 5: 1–6.

Van de Auwera, J. (1985). *Language and Logic: A Speculative and Condition-Theoretic Study*. Amsterdam: John Benjamins Publishing.

Venkataraman, S. (1963). "The Nature and Scope of General Education." In K. S. Murty, ed. *General Education Reconsidered*. New York: Asia Publishing. 33–39.

Wegener, C. (1978). *Liberal Education and the Modern University*. Chicago: University of Chicago Press.

Winter, D. G., Stewart, A. J., and McClelland, D. C. (1978). "Grading the Effects of a Liberal Arts Education." *Psychology Today* (Sept.): 69–106.

45

Debating Impacts
Intrinsicness Argumentation in Nonpolicy Debating

David M. Berube

As critics, we find ourselves evaluating whether the availability of Mark Twain's *Huckleberry Finn* would demobilize a racial war, whether the extension of First Amendment protections to four artists of homoerotica will sufficiently accelerate efforts to find a cure for AIDS, or, given the possibility that municipalities may begin to face public buildings with materials allowing graffiti artists a more permanent canvas for their social criticism, the American neo-conservative movement will become so incensed that it will force the election of a Republican House of Representatives, which will vote funding for Bush's Strategic Defense Initiative and prompt a Soviet first strike.

These arguments are fairly absurd. If Toulmin examined them, he would suggest that something is seriously missing, that something being qualifiers.

There are two ways to force arguers to engage qualifiers in extended arguments. Judges can intervene directly into the debates forbidding such arguments, or we can attempt to develop a calculus that will allow us to analyze these types of arguments to reveal their shortcomings.

Judge intervention must be rejected. It is frightening to hear debate critics argue that their peers "should treat overused positions and old briefs the same way performance (interpretation) critics treat programs of overused literature (such as *The Glass Menagerie*), namely, by assigning low speaker points and (in debate), if necessary, a loss" (Preston, 1989, p. 21). My first remark must be that Tennessee Williams' *Menagerie* is excellent literature, but I remember that I learned it was excellent by reading it myself, and to discourage anyone from investigating its beauty for themselves is fascist. Preston's reasoning violates the educational process of discovery.

In 1966, Dennis Day wrote that "if personal conviction on a particular subject has a preponderance of truth in its favor, it will prevail over other views even when all views are fully presented" (p. 8). Day and others have called for a hearing that will decide rationally rather than dogmatically. To choose to ban certain issues smacks of censorship and has no place in academic debating. Critical thinking cannot be learned if some subjects become taboo. Furthermore, knowledge is never served when tyranny substitutes for discourse and reasoned judgement. "[T]he ethics of democratic discourse do not allow a prejudgment of the reasonableness of discourse as a condition of its expression" (Day, 1966, p. 10).

Of course, there are bad and tired generic arguments. However, the solution rests with enabling a working calculus that will allow us to discover their faults and reject them as bad arguments rather than as bad ideas.

Argumentatively, there are two approaches that can be used to analyze extended arguments that include generics. First, we can insist that debaters analyze the risks associated with whatever impact scenario they are designing. Second, we can consider embracing the countercase, not a counterplan but a test of qualification.

Regarding the first option: There is sufficient scholarship elsewhere addressing risk analysis. Follert wrote on subjective expected utility in 1981, and Dolley on scenarios in 1986 and 1988. The only observation I wish to make is that when dealing with the extended argument, the longer the argument chain, the greater the percentage of error associated with the occurrence of the anterior and the posterior events. The probability of error functions along this chain geometrically. As a result, a small input may relate to a large outcome, but that relationship may be infinitesimal and unquantifiable.

The only thing missing from this calculus is a standard for deciding when risk is insufficient to serve as a reason in deciding whether something is probably true or probably the correct thing to do. These issues need to be discussed. However, the remainder of this paper will address the second alternative.

THE BEGINNING

We begin with a reexamination of justification, traditionally a negative policy argument. A negative debater would claim that the plan is not justified as a solution for the problem posed by the case.

Sklansky (1979) wrote that "the affirmative team could be accused of not justifying their plan" if "there may be better or simpler ways of gaining the affirmative advantages" (p. 81). Originally, to use Sklansky's description, "a justification argument . . . is simply a threat of a counter-plan" (p. 81). The argument usually took the form of "why the plan—why not something like . . . "

Sklansky charged that forcing the affirmative to attack phantom counterplans was an impossible task. This hollow observation ignores what obligations the affirmative may have in case and plan selection, a process which when carefully undertaken would make the justification argument irrelevant. Instead, Sklansky placed blame solely on the negative when bad debating most generally begins with a poor affirmative selection of ground. Next, he suggested that since two policies—the affirmative and the status quo—are available for evaluation, and as a result, policy choices are available, the justification argument has no home in policy debate. Evidently, these indictments are mostly inappropriate to the nonpolicy model. Justification as a negative strategy in nonpolicy debate has simply yet to be assailed.

The problem in nonpolicy debate, in general, and the extended argument, in particular, is overjustification. Turner (1979) defined over-justification in policy debate. It occurs when "the reason for change warrants *more* than the plan implements" (p. 78). Here the affirmative overclaims the impact of a modest reform.

In both policy and nonpolicy debating, this phenomenon is not exclusively an affirmatively instigated problem. This practice has also found a home in case impact flips, value objections, disadvantages, policy implications, and counterplan advantages; and it's becoming more and more popular. The extended argument can be most often found in the generic.

The generic is quintessentially overjustification. It is "a genre of argument that seeks to link a particular aspect of one position to a . . . substantial impact" (Brewster, 1984, p. 14). Walker and Congalton examined this argument form in 1987.

> Generic arguments are not ephemeral debate curiosities. The generic argument is a frequently occurring and oft-rewarded debate position. Generic arguments can become credible-relevant arguments. Generic argument constitutes good debate practice when it reflects a grounding in argumentation theory and meets critieria for argumentative excellence (p. 126).

They found generic arguments legitimized when (1) they are linked to the argument fields of the debate resolution; (2) they meet appropriate standards of design and appraisal; and (3) they are field/resolution dependent (p. 134).

Many nonpolicy arguments have begun to be impacted by Armageddon and ecocide generics. Their appearance reflects two phenomena: (1) the enormous post-war information explosion with the accelerated rise of the personal computer and efficient, widely available photocopying; and (2) the cycling of evidence especially from backfiles and debate handbooks (Dolley, 1988, p. 3).

The emergence of generics owes much to these phenomena, but to fault ill-conceived arguments is not to condemn the sources or to demand their banishment. Instead, generic arguments are completely reasonable when they provide us with a better understanding of the debate resolutional field. Unfortunately, though Armageddon and ecocide are important, they are simply not webbed into every resolution.

This brings us to a metaphor, a metaphor that will help us visualize the overjustification issue. Impacts function as a web. At the center is heinous and egregious harm and leading to that central point are many filaments of reasoning, some stronger than others, and many bisected and trisected by intersecting filaments. The problem with contemporary impacting is that we have been led to assume that all filaments are of equal strength and that the intersecting filaments are irrelevant. In reality, the intersecting filaments are very relevant; they represent alternative routes toward and away from the midpoint. They illustrate the countercase.

DEFINITION

The countercase is an argument that insists that the relationship between the data and claim, the warrant, of a second argument is not enough to accept the second argument as minimally sufficient. This argument is designed to force an adversary making the overclaim to accept a qualifier to her claim, which makes her case unacceptably insufficient.

AN ANALOGUE

The countercase formalizes the intrinsicness argument of policy debating. Since in nonpolicy debating, nothing is adopted, this type of test is more at home here than in policy debating.

Traditionally, in policy debating, the affirmative has argued that a disadvantage can be prevented by the present system absent plan adoption. The debater engaging the traditional intrinsicness argument "is saying that the avoidance of the disadvantage does not require the rejection of the affirmative plan" (Brewster, 1984, p. 15). The debater is arguing that policy is not adopted in a vacuum—the present system engages reform and simultaneously compensates for drawbacks the reform may cause or aggravate by making systemic adjustments. The affirmative does not necessarily amend her plan to stimulate these levels of systemic compensation, but merely argues that the present system is sufficiently rational and will act when called upon to do so by the exigencies of the situation. Example: If the extension of most favored nation trading status to the People's Democratic Republic of Korea would provoke the Republic of Korea to close down its markets to Japanese exports in retribution, with all its consequent mega-issues, then the United States upon granting most favored nation status to the PDRK would consider confidence building in its relationship with the ROK or might even compensate the ROK such that its knee-jerk reaction would be mitigated.

Policy debaters have also used intrinsicness arguments against certain counterplan advantages. An extracompetitive counterplan advantage refers to reasons why the counterplan should be adopted that are derived from action beyond that which is directly competitive with the affirmative significance claim and mutually exclusive with the affirmative plan. Here, the affirmative argues that there is no reason to adopt the counterplan to produce the extracompetitive advantage, rather the plan should be adopted and other action (topical or nontopical) could be adopted to produce the counterplan advantage in question. Example: The affirmative argues to ban the electoral college and use the popular vote to select the president. The negative wants to adopt a socialist form of government, which they argue would better speak in the people's interests. The negative also claims that socialism reduces the risk of nuclear exchange between the superpowers. The affirmative responds that the deterrence advantage is extracompetitive. If we wanted to reduce the probability of a nuclear exchange, we might consider serious arms negotiations.

The underlying premise of the intrinsicness argument is found in incremental decision-making. Morello explained in 1982 that "the present system is not a static entity. Rather, any present system moves, changes and adapts itself to new conditions." He discovered that the present system alters itself "in an incremental fashion," a sort of "self-correcting feedback" (p. 115).

Confronted with a problem, our natural tendency is not to scrap everything and adapt a radical alternative. Whether we are policymakers or homemakers, we evaluate our condition and then make fine modifications in our emotional, social, and physical environments in order to reduce the unpleasantness of the situation. It is absurd to believe that our choices are only between radical alternatives: Feed the hungry and starve millions in the next generation, or starve the hungry and kill millions today. So it is with mega-issue extended arguments. The intrinsicness argument, therefore, attempts to reintroduce the incremental nature of decision-making into the debate context.

Intrinsicness and the countercase may have a home in nonpolicy debate. Not only have generic and extended arguments with improbable linkages become regular occurrences in nonpolicy debate, but in nonpolicy debating, we would also see the countercase used in many more settings. It would be used to take out case impact flips and value objections, disadvantages and policy implications, and concomitant advantages, and cases that describe only accidental features of the resolution. In general, it could be used to explain away exaggerated linkage. Presumably, by forcing a reasoned discussion on necessary causes of a phenomenon, we get not only a better argument why something is true or ought to be done, but also a better understanding of the issue. These countercases, alternative explanations, force a redefinition of the intuited phenomenon until all peripheral and associated characteristics become stripped away, approaching a point whereby we are defining the essence of the thing.

GROUNDS

The prevalent paradigms accommodate this argument form. First, *hypothesis testing*. Brewster argued in support of the traditional hypothesis-testing model that "the debate can be viewed as a *test of the resolution*. If various programs can serve to eliminate the problems attendant to the resolution, the problem fails to serve as a reason to reject the resolution" (1984, p. 15). Intrinsicness arguments are tests.

Second, *policy making*. Systems, philosophical or otherwise, examined in debate are dynamic. According to Madsen (1989), "[W]hen analyzing competing policies through a system's lens, the focus would not isolate the specifics of the policies but would rather consider the two options as shaped and influenced by their relevant surrounding environments" (p. 73). It is simply inane to remove issues from their context, especially since the context is often inescapably interwoven into the issue. Remove the issue from its environment and the issue loses perspective and valuation. Intrinsicness arguments demand a more context-focused analysis.

Third, *gaming*. In all games, scenario alternatives are evaluated. Snider (1984) found that "gaming attempts to speculate about the future by setting up "What if?" situations. A series of scenarios can be developed describing different actions, and then individuals can act out a number of roles within the scenarios" (p. 166). The free-forming intuiting nature of the intrinsicness argument may assist us in studying alternative futures, whether as competing policies or philosophies.

Fourth, *narrative*. All good narratives accommodate subplots and reversals as long as coherence isn't sacrificed. As K. Bartanen (1985) maintained, "Good stories are those which pass the tests of narrative probability and narrative fidelity. Narrative probability demands that stories be coherent, that their parts be orderly and logically related in such a way as to make the events they recount and account for comprehensible" (p. 3). Hollihan et al (1987), defining narrative probability explained, "Most audiences do not enjoy a book, play, or film that does not hang together and make some kind of sense. Complex plots are enjoyable as long as we can follow them..." (p. 188). Instrinsicness arguments help us tie up all the loose ends by forcing a *thick* analysis of the causes and effects of the phenomenon being examined.

APPLICATIONS OF THE THEORY

Case Impact Flips and Value Objections

The affirmative impacts their case with some value. With the first genre of value objection, the negative argues a value flip: The affirmative-specified value is not only not desirable but undesirable. These are value turnarounds and generally "go against the grain of accepted beliefs precisely because the opponent has taken an unusual position in order to surprise the other team" (Hollihan, 1985, p. 51). Example: The affirmative maintains that artistic expression liberates the human spirit, parodizing the empowered, rejecting the entrenched power wielders. The negative responds that art is patriarchal, extinguishing a superior feminist spirit. The negative argument flips the affirmative's and objects to the value the affirmative seeks to uphold. That's the case impact flip. The affirmative, upon examining the negative's feminist mindset position, may discover means to arrive at feminist goals without suppressing artistic expression per se. In other words, the values of criticism via artistic expression and feminist mandates may be able to coexist— patriarchal art criticizing from within while women develop a genre of artistic expression of their own. For that matter, only when the art of men is publicly ridiculed by strong feminist voices will the agenda of the women's movement be confronted. The countercase, in this situation, functions like the counterplan permutation test of mutual exclusivity— have both. Rather than maligning the negative turnaround because it is exotic, the countercase allows the affirmative to dismiss the claim on firmer argumentative ground.

A second type of value objection is associated with the affirmative criteria for evaluating affirmative and negative claims. Example: The affirmative suggests that rights are absolute. The negative counterclaims that viewing any value as absolute is unacceptable. Rigid imperatives are insensitive and unaccommodating to the exigencies of living in a complex world.

Another example: The affirmative argues a hierarchy of values whereby some things are more important than others. The negative may counterclaim that hierarchies are destructive such that calculating vertically or horizontally ignores heterarchies that are more realistic in our growing interdependent, holistic, and interwoven society.

The negative, in these debates, may claim that the criteria of the affirmative are void and must be rejected, consequently availing the negative the option of offering their own criteria, either those implicit to standardized language rules or those of their choosing.

In response, the affirmative countercase may seek to minimize the shortcomings of an imperative or a hierarchy by suggesting an option to accommodate minority concerns in the world of absolutes, such as the renegotiation of a new imperative, or by suggesting options to compensate for interrelated needs by more flexible hierarchies, double hierarchies, or even hierarchies nested within others.

Disadvantages and Policy Implications

Whether we call them disadvantages or policy implications is a semantic shell game. They are similarly structured—linked and impacted. What seems to appall nonpolicy critics and many of their policy colleagues is the trend toward improbable risk linkages and mega-issues scenarios. This is particularly troublesome for the affirmative in nonpolicy debate because "[w]ithout a plan, the affirmative is open to attack against every form of behavior associated with their value position the negative may choose to project" (Dempsey, 1984, p. 62). The affirmative adopts nothing and consequently is unable to design a plan that mitigates the link or impact of the policy implication. As a result, the negative claims that the affirmative value becomes concretized into disastrous policies.

The affirmative can always argue that nothing is adopted and there are no implications. However, most negatives are well versed in debating the intimate connection between values and policy. Another means is needed to discourage this practice beyond the whine. That may be the countercase argument. Example: The affirmative helps the U.S. economy, which increases domestic growth. The negative argues growth devastates the world via misguided consumption. Of course, nearly everything we do causes growth, but beyond this uniqueness response, demanding that the relationship is a necessary one, the affirmative may argue that the present system would never accept or reject policy recommendations on the grounds that it causes growth. If, indeed, it included growth in its policy-deciding matrix, the present system would adopt the recommended policy and then compensate for bad growth by tightening the money supply or even aiding groups and regions that were disaffected. A very recent example: The affirmative argues that allowing copyright exceptions for montage productions will insure individual rights of expression. The negative claims that individual rights snowball and may delay the transition to Miller's benign eco-communitarianism. The affirmative responds with extending individual rights of expression while simultaneously suggesting the restriction of property rights. In both of these situations, the effect is mitigated by tracing cross-linkages to other causes.

Concomitant Advantages

While policy debate has traditionally allowed affirmatives to specify ancillary features of the plan that are reasonably necessary for the plan's operation, it has mostly denied the affirmative the option of adding plan planks that produce advantages not exclusive to the part of the plan mandated by the resolution. Those advantages are extratopical.

The extratopical advantage has an evil twin. Concomitant advantages are advantages that may be the product of the plan. They are not the direct result of the plan, however, but the outcome of an extended argument chain. Deciding to adopt a policy based on a concomitant advantage would entail action that on its face seems irrelevant to the claim being made.

Flaningham (1981) found that "resolutions are sufficient conditions for the production of concomitant advantages but are not necessary preconditions for their attainment" (p. 2). These are nonresolutional advantages, advantages that are any and all benefits coming from the adoption of a topical plan.

> Since concomitant adantages are co-incidental effects of the resolution, they can be created both by the resolutional and by nonresolutional systems. Not requiring changes in the essential properties of systems which are alternatives to the resolution, concomitant advantages could be created by existent systems or nonresolutional counterplans (p. 5).

In effect, Flaningham was demanding "that benefits flow from essential differences between the resolution and logical alternatives to the resolution" (p. 3).

Concomitant advantages return us to a study of justification and a review of inherency.

First, regarding *justification*. Adams and Wilkins explained the problem in 1987: "Teams present broad, sweeping ideological truths and claims, of which the resolution may be only a fragment of the argument" (p. 23). They believed that when "the resolution is overjustified, the debate becomes blurred on resolutional issues and comes to focus on issues of less significance to the topic" (p. 23). We have two topics each year in CEDA and five in high school Lincoln-Douglas debating. One of the reasons is to prevent large programs with enormous research capabilities from outstripping the smaller programs. However, absent a tool like the countercase to stymie the concomitant justification, this is all useless, since topic wording is becoming less and less relevant when the debaters continue to link different issues to the same scenarios and impacts. Some refocusing may be necessary.

Second, regarding *inherency*. Kruger (1965a) discussed the role of inherency as protections against post hoc reasoning (p. 80). In response, Newman (1965) defended a bifurcation of defects associated with a faulty present system into functional, or contingent, and organic, or inherent, faults (p. 67). Newman was convinced that there are cases when a policy can be described as a syndrome such that arguing what could be done is fanciful at best. Kruger (1965b) defended his position claiming that "the therapeutic action should be fitted to the nature of the ailment" (1965b, p. 113).

Newman felt that Kruger's preoccupation with *essential character* was a vestige of Platonism (p. 69). Kruger traded insults by placing Newman's arguments among those of "pragmatists and their philosophical brethren, the operationalists and logical positivists" (p. 113). However, beyond the ad hominems, Kruger felt essences were "tremendously important in enabling us to organize knowledge, to get hold of the enormous variety of the world, for they are the basis upon which we make significant classifications" (1965b, p. 114). Returning to Aristotle's theory of the predictables, Kruger argued simply that if a claim is introduced, drawn from an essential characteristic of the phenomenon being examined, then the arguer has demonstrated a need for change, or a statement of wrongness. By proximating data and claim, the arguer's proof suggests a logically testable premise. Kruger understood that as the distance between data and claim increases so does our problematical reliance upon authoritative warrants.

Dudczak (1988) set inherency in a nonpolicy setting: "Inherency asks the question whether an element has a necessary, intrinsic, or essential relationship within a larger system. . . . Something is inherent because it bears some constant relationship to another thing" (p. 15). He sees its importance in terms of whether an arguer can sustain each part in a reasoning chain (p. 20). While his conclusion merely demands that the arguer maintains consistent descriptions as "a prerequisite to alleging correspondence between the evidence grounds and the assumed warrant for the claim" (pp. 20–21), others, especially Bahm, developed the implications even further.

Bahm (1988) advocated a test "to reveal and invalidate contingent arguments.... [T]ests which [would] reveal and invalidate an opponent's narrow and contingent claims" (p. 28). Bahm draws from phenomenology in making his case for the intrinsic counterplan and counterwarrants, and seems to have lost most of the debate community in the process. While I find his work important in defining the representative characteristics of a proof, there are simpler ways to approach the tortured concomitant advantage.

Countercases are means to dejustify the concomitant affirmative warrant for the resolution. Whereas, in policy debate, the person initiating the intrinsicness arguments is, in essence, counterplanning away the disadvantage impact, in CEDA, the debater initiating the countercase is suggesting that the link from the affirmative data to claim is not good or simple. The debater is arguing that the qualifier is less than minimally sufficient to conclude that a good reason to accept the affirmative proof can be found in the associated claim.

Resolutional Ground

Bahm wrote that "the argument from intrinsicness states that the benefits or harms claimed by one side must flow intrinsically (necessarily or essentially) from that side's resolutional ground" (p. 23). Example: Since censorship implies some prior restraint, the reasons why the infringement is undesirable must be associated with the act of suppression, a rights issue, and not based upon some hypothetical discussion of a consciousness shift emanating from public viewing of the artifact. Suppression is an essential property of censorship; audience consciousness raising is accidental or contingent. Why? Because consciousness raising can be the cause or effect of an enormous range of phenomena other than censorship. Suppression, on the other hand, is fundamental to an understanding of censorship.

Two pages later, Bahm referred to Zarefsky in rebutting Dudczak's understanding of inherency and found in Zarefsky a study of inherency (1977) wherein answers regarding resolutional ground begin to emerge. While Lagrave (1979) and others attempted to establish dimension of proof (cause, permanence, and reform) implicit to an inherency, Zarefsky (1977) offered an operational definition steeped in the language of phenomenology.

> The advocate mentally should divide the universe of relevant options other than those embraced in the propositions into characteristics that are *essential* to its nonpropositional nature and those which merely are *incidental* futures—a division, that is, into core and periphery (p. 184).

Next, he suggested that whether claims can be made to establish both the how-possibility and why-necessarily can be tested to identify core motives (p. 186). He concluded that this testing for cause would "permit control over events through understanding them. . . . Without the use of causal argument, how can one adjudicate conflicting interpretations of *fact*? What reason could be cited to favor one view over another? Indeed, not to insist upon good reasons in response to causal questions is to deny the role of reason in questions of value or policy" (p. 189). Causality testing will help discover the characteristics of the sociopolitical system in which we function. Multiple causation (a number of conditions, all occurring simultaneously, contributing to a complex causal relationship), equifinality (a variety of independent causes producing similar effects), and multiple effects (any one change in a system will have impact on other relationships within the system, on behavior of a number of other systems, and with action relating to a number of different goals) need to be revealed in order to produce self-contained and consistent value systems (Newton, 1979). Even more importantly, causal testing helps answer the question Zarefsky posited in 1977: "Why do presumably good people tolerate evil?" Without answering that question, we learn nothing about who we really are, what this world has really become, and what can be done about it.

Bile (1987, p. 13) and Bahm (1988, p. 26) and Berube (1989) fundamentally agree. The focus should be on the resolution. Subsets are acceptable subjects as resolutional proofs if they are representative and a test of representativeness is found via intuiting essences. However, intuiting essences has a role to play beyond jurisdictional disputes. The countercase can help for the affirmative arguing a subset of the resolution to select and defend an example addressing the central nature and essential characteristics of the resolution being debated. After the inductive fallacy is resolved, the affirmative is still obligated to test the essential features of the resolution via the examples they have selected, and it may be the countercase that helps keep them honest.

GENERALIZATIONS AND BURDENS

Bahm's approach, reduction and variation (pp. 26–28), begins to justify the countercase. He boldly legitimizes imaginative counterplanning (p. 27) not merely as a negative response to a twisted affirmative proof, but as a tool for delinking a policy implication for disadvantage in a situation "which presumes a particular manner of affirming the resolution, and as such is not intrinsic" (p. 28).

I merely want to liberalize his position such that free imaginative countercasing can serve to:

1. delink, initially or internally, a case impact flip or a value objection;
2. delink, initially or internally, a disadvantage or policy implication;
3. delink, initially or internally, a concomitant advantage;
4. reveal and delink cases from the resolution when that case functions from an accidental or contingent property of the resolution.

Since the affirmative and the negative in nonpolicy debating do not initiate change with countercases but merely design a solvent counterscenario, the countercase, unlike the counterplan, does not need to be competitive. It merely functions to dejustify the claim. The countercase must merely be (1) better, most usually a function of proximity (reduced probability of error, or lessened confoundness), and (2) simpler, less likely to be baffled by indirectness (vagaries of private meaning, hidden assumptions, or phantom agendas).

Permutations—irrelevant. Do both! Do what? Nothing is done. However, if we are searching for reasons why a phenomenon is true, right, just, correct, fair, or even ought to be done, we would invest decision costs in the most prudent explanation, that envisaged in the countercase. Countercases, consequently, finally give form and meaning to the much-maligned justification argument.

Though the countercase does not need to be competitive per se, it cannot be topical. The countercase cannot serve as an alternative affirmative warrant. If the affirmative has chosen to define their proofs in any way but parametrically (our case is the resolution), then the affirmative can legitimately capture the countercase as an additional, or even substitute, claim for believing that the resolution is probably true.

In policy debating, this discussion focuses on the permutation as a test to determine the germaneness of the intrinsicness argument. But in nonpolicy debate, the focus is on whether the intrinsicness argument, the countercase, is resolutional.

DRAWBACKS

There are at least three serious indictments of this approach. First, the debate process may make the form of introspection discussed above problematical. We have imposed time limits and other informal rules into the debating process. These may not accommodate the type of analysis that encourages free imaginative thinking. This cynical condemnation, however, has been appended to every new and difficult study— we don't have time, we don't know how to indulge its demands, and so on. The answer is three-fold: (1) do not focus on discerning the final or ultimate essence of the phenomenon under study, but use the calculus as a metaphor or paradigm; (2) merely attempt to get closest to the essence of the phenomenon, as debate is adversarial and relative success should be awarded; and (3) consider changing the formal and informal rules.

Second, debate resolutions and even generic extended arguments are designed with complex word phrases that may not have an identifiable essence per se. This is a more difficult problem to resolve. If we examine each word to isolate its separate essence and then begin reattaching the word-essences to produce a likeness of the resolution or generic, we may create a beast very unlike its progenitor. The key to this level of essencing is to begin with a mental reconstruction of the sentence and then test it after that point. The standards for reconstruction will be ruled by topicality and other jurisdictional concerns and the narrative that is produced can then be studied like we probe an interpretation of a classical piece of literature by rereading and reconstructing a textually driven analysis.

Third, countercases tend to substitute for risk analysis and lead to superficial discussion of solvency. This problem is easier to solve. First, there is no reason why risk analysis and countercasing cannot function productively together. Moreover, the problems associated with discussing probability and valences of extended arguments when performing risk analysis could be clarified with a better understanding of cause and essence of the impact scenarios. Second, the countercase, like the case, needs to be solvent. The countercase will need to prove that his or her suggested counterscenario is solvent. This theory is not grounded in formal scientific methodology per se. Burdens are assumed by the initiator and one of those is solvency.

CONCLUSION

This brief paper has been an attempt to standardize and legitimize arguments of justification and inherency in nonpolicy debating. While intrinsicness arguments may have some procedural problems in policy debating, their utility in the form of the countercase in nonpolicy debate has yet to be fully investigated. My hope is that this paper will examine the aforementioned points in greater detail and provoke thoughtful rebuttal.

References

Adams, N. and Wilkins, T. (1987). "The Role of Justification in Topic Analysis." *CEDA Handbook* 8: 21–26.

Bahm, K. (1988). "Intrinsic Justification: Meaning and Method." *CEDA Handbook* 9: 23–29.

Bartanen, K. (1985). "Application of the Narrative Paradigm to CEDA Debate." Paper presented at the Speech Communication Association Annual Convention in Denver, Nov. 9.

Berube, D. (1989). "Hasty Generalization Revisited, Part One: On Being Representative Examples." *CEDA Yearbook* 9: 43–53.

Bile, J. (1987). "When the Whole is Greater Than the Sum of the Parts: The Implications of Holistic Resolutional Focus." *CEDA Handbook* 8: 8–15.

Brewster, B. (1984). "Analysis of Disadvantages: Scenarios and Intrinsicness." Winston-Salem, NC: Debater's Research Guide, Wake Forest University. 14–16.

Day, D. (1966). "The Ethics of Democratic Debate." *Central States Speech Journal* 17 (Feb.): 5–14.

Dempsey, R. (1984). "The Theoretical Illegitimacy of Speculative Value Objections." *CEDA Yearbook* 5: 60–64.

Dolley, S. (1986). "Apocalypse When? Determining and Comparing Catastrophic Risks." Winston-Salem, NC: Debater's Research Guide, Wake Forest University. 2–6.

Dolley, S. (1988). "Scenario-Building and the Ethics of Multiple-Source Generics." Paper presented at the Speech Communication Association Annual Convention in New Orleans, Nov. 5.

Dudczak, C. (1988). "Inherency as a Stock Issue in Non-Policy Propositions." *CEDA Handbook* 9: 15–22.

Flaningham, C. (1981). "Concomitant vs. Comparative Advantages: Sufficient vs. Necessary Conditions." *Journal of the American Forensic Association* 18 (Summer): 1–8.

Follert, V. (1981). "Risk Analysis: Its Application to Argumentation and Decision Making." *Journal of the American Forensic Association* 18 (Fall): 99–108.

Hollihan, T. (1985). "The Use of 'Turnarounds' in Academic Debate: A Theoretical Rationale and Standards for Their Evaluation." *Speaker and Gavel* 22: 45–51.

Hollihan, T., et al. (1987). "Debaters as Storytellers: The Narrative Perspective in Academic Debate." *Journal of the American Forensic Association* 23 (Spring): 184–93.

Kruger, A. (1965a). "The Underlying Assumptions of Policy Questions: III. Inherent Evil." *Speaker and Gavel* 2 (March): 79–82.

Kruger, A. (1965b). "The Inherent Need: Further Clarification." *Journal of the American Forensic Association* 2 (Sept.): 109–19.

Lagrave, C. (1979). "Inherency: An Historical View." In D. Thomas, ed. *Advanced Debate*. Lincolnwood, IL: National Textbook. 97–104.

Madsen, A. (1989). "General Systems Theory and Counterplan Competition." *Argumentation and Advocacy* 26 (Fall): 71–82.

Morello, J. (1982). "Defending the Present System's Capacity for Incremental Changes." *Journal of the American Forensic Association* 19 (Fall) 115–21.

Newman, R. (1965). "The Inherent and Compelling Need." *Journal of the American Forensic Association* 2 (May): 66–71.

Newton, K. (1979). "The Present System as System: A Defense." in D. Thomas, ed. *Advanced Debate*. Lincolnwood, IL: National Textbook. 183–87.

Preston, C. (1989). "The Use and Misuse of Generic Argumentation in Cross Examination Debate Association Debate." Paper presented at the Speech Communication Association convention, San Francisco, Nov. 19.

Sklansky, D. (1979). "Response to Justification." in D. Thomas, ed. *Adanced Debate*. Lincolnwood, IL: National Textbook. 80–82.

Snider, A. (1984). "Games Without Frontiers: A Design for Communication Scholars and Forensic Educators." *Journal of the American Forensic Association* 20 (Winter): 162–70.

Turner, G. (1979). "Justification." In D. Thomas, ed. *Advanced Debate*. Lincolnwood, IL: National Textbook. 78–80.

Walker, G. and J. Congalton. (1987). "Generic Arguments and Argument Fields." *Journal of the American Forensic Association* 23 (Winter): 125–35.

Zarefsky, D. (1977). "The Role of Causal Argument in Policy Controversies." *Journal of the American Forensic Association* 13 (Spring): 179–91.

KEY TERMS

clarity	hierarchy	propositions of fact
consistency	indicator	propositions of value
countercriteria	intrinsicness	relevance
criteria	measurement	rules
decision sapling	operationalize	subjectivity
decision tree	quantification	value criteria
filter	quasi-policy	value implication
generic	preference	value objection
good reasons	priority	whole resolution
hasty generalization	probability	

DISCUSSION

1. What is the most important function of a set of criteria, according to Goulet and Bauer's article?
2. What do Goulet and Bauer mean by their comment that criteria argumentation can "serve as a filter"?
3. What does O'Dor say is the relationship between measurement and indicators?
4. What is a decision tree? A decision sapling?
5. How can decision rules be applied to fact resolutions? To value resolutions?
6. Can running a whole resolution position and a hasty generalization position on the negative be potentially contradictory? Why?
7. How do stock issues in questions of fact differ from questions of policy?

8. What is the relevance of the Berube article in Part Seven to non-policy debate?
9. What does Matlon claim are the stock issues of a question of value?
10. What are the stock issues in the construction of a value implication?
11. Compare and contrast the concept of intrinsicness in questions of nonpolicy with the concept of inherency in questions of policy.
12. Consider the spring 1991 CEDA topic—"RESOLVED: That the United States Supreme Court, on balance, has granted excessive power to law enforcement agencies." Is this a question of fact or value?
13. Using the above example, would counterwarrants be justified under this topic?

Appendix A

Author Directory

V. William Balthrop
Chair and Associate Professor
University of North Carolina
Chapel Hill, North Carolina

John Bart
Assistant Professor and Director
of Forensics
Augustana College
Sioux Falls, South Dakota

Kristine M. Bartanen
Chair and Associate Professor
University of Puget Sound
Tacoma, Washington

Michael Bauer
Debate Coach
University of Richmond
Richmond, Virginia

David M. Berube
Assistant Professor
University of South Carolina
Columbia, South Carolina

Thompson Biggers
Assistant Professor
University of Miami
Coral Gables, Florida

Jeffrey Bile
Instructor and Director
of Forensics
Southern Illinois University
Carbondale, Illinois

Gloria Cabada
Graduate Student
Duke University
Durham, North Carolina

Kent Colbert
Associate Professor
University of Pacific
Stockton, California

Jerome Corsi
Consultant
Portland, Oregon

E. Sam Cox
Assistant Professor and Director
of Forensics
Central Missouri State University
Warrensburg, Missouri

Steven Dolley
Assistant Director of Debate
University of Vermont
Burlington, Vermont

Craig Dudczak
Associate Professor
Syracuse University
Syracuse, New York

Robert H. Gass, Jr.
Associate Professor
California State University
Fullerton, California

Andrew B. Goulet
Debater
University of Richmond
Richmond, Virginia

J. Cinder Griffin
Graduate Student
Bryn Mawr College
Bryn Mawr, Pennsylvania

Dave Harris
Attorney
St. Louis, Missouri

John P. Hart
Assistant Professor and Director
of Forensics
Northeast Missouri State
University
Kirksville, Missouri

Dwaine Hemphill
Former Director of Forensics
Kansas State University
Manhattan, Kansas

Dale A. Herbeck
Assistant Professor and Director
of Forensics
Boston College
Chestnut Hill, Massachusetts

John P. Katsulas
Assistant Debate Coach
Boston College
Chestnut Hill, Massachusetts

Tim Lee
Attorney
Houston, Texas

Allan J. Lichtman
Professor of History
American University
Washington, D.C.

Ronald J. Matlon
Chair and Professor
Towson State University
Towson, Maryland

Brian McGee
Instructor and Director of
Forensics
Northeast Louisiana University
Monroe, Louisiana

Richard O'Dor
Director of Forensics
Duke University
Durham, North Carolina

Edward Panetta
Assistant Professor
University of Georgia
Athens, Georgia

Donn W. Parson
Professor
University of Kansas
Lawrence, Kansas

James W. Paulsen
Attorney
Salt Lake City, Vermont

Michael Pfau
Chair and Professor
Augustana College
Sioux Falls, South Dakota

Kendall R. Phillips
Central Missouri State University
Warrensburg, Missouri

Diana Prentice
Assistant Professor
University of Kansas
Lawrence, Kansas

Holly Raider
Graduate Student
Columbia University
New York, New York

Jack Rhodes
Associate Professor and Director
of Forensics
Miami University
Oxford, Ohio

Daniel M. Rohrer
Former Director of Forensics
Boston College
Chestnut Hill, Massachusetts

David J. Shipley
Law Student
Wake Forest University
Winston Salem, North Carolina

A. C. Snider
Associate Professor and Director
of Forensics
University of Vermont
Burlington, Vermont

Roger Solt
Debate Coach
University of Kentucky
Lexington, Kentucky

David A. Thomas
Associate Professor and Director
of Forensics
University of Richmond
Richmond, Virginia

Walter Ulrich
Assistant Professor and Debate
Coach
University of Northern Iowa
Cedar Falls, Iowa

James J. Unger
Director
National Forensics Institute
Washington, D.C.

Kimball Wong
Former Debater
Boston College
Chestnut Hill, Massachusetts

David Zarefsky
Dean and Professor
Northwestern University
Evanston, Illinois

George Ziegelmueller
Professor and Director of
Forensics
Wayne State University
Detroit, Michigan

Appendix B

Source Notes

Part One: Overview of the Discipline

1. **Colbert and Biggers**, "Why Should We Support Debate?" *Journal of the American Forensic Association* 21 (Spring 1985): 237–40. This article appeared in *Advanced Debate*, 3rd ed., pp. 2–6.

2. **Griffin and Raider**, "Women in Debate." This article originally appeared as "Women in High School Debate," in R. E. Solt, ed., *Punishment and Paradigms: Pros and Cons* (Winston-Salem. NC: Debaters Research Guide, 1989), 2–5. Reprinted by permission. Edited for this anthology.

3. **Snider**, "Ethics in Debate: A Gaming Perspective." *The National Forensic Journal* 2 (Fall 1984): 119–34. Reprinted by permission. Edited for this anthology.

Part Two: Advanced Debate Practices

4. **Lichtman, Rohrer, and Corsi**, "Affirmative Case Approaches." This article appeared in *Advanced Debate*, 2nd ed., pp. 173–82 and *Advanced Debate*, 3rd ed., pp. 31–38. Edited for this edition.

5. **Pfau**, "A Systematic Approach to Opposing Policy Change." This article appeared in *Advanced Debate*, 2nd ed., under the title, "A Systematic Approach to Debating the Second Negative," pp. 188–99, and *Advanced Debate*, 3rd ed., pp. 39–45. Edited for this edition.

6. **Hemphill**, "A Reevaluation of Negative Division of Duties." This article was originally published under the title "First Negative Strategies: A Reevaluation of Negative Division of Duties," *Argument in Transition: Proceedings of the Third Summer Conference on Argumentation*, David Zarefsky, Malcolm Sillars, and Jack Rhodes, eds. (Annandale, VA: Speech Communication Association, 1983), 883–92. Reprinted by permission. This article appeared in *Advanced Debate*, 3rd ed., pp. 46–55.

7. **Ziegelmueller**, "Cross-Examination Reexamined." This article was originally published in *Argument in Transition: Proceedings of the Third Summer Conference on Argumentation*, David Zarefsky, Malcolm O. Sillars, and Jack Rhodes, eds. (Annandale, VA: Speech Communication Association, 1983), 893–903. This article appeared in *Advanced Debate*, 3rd ed., pp. 66–74. Reprinted by permission.

8. **Cabada**, "Preparation Time." This article originally appeared as "Prep Time: Maximizing a Valuable Resource," in *Retirement Security: Shuffleboard on the Titanic* (Winston-Salem, NC: Debaters Research Guide, 1988), 2–6. Reprinted by permission. Edited for this edition.

9. **Ulrich**, "A Theory of the Turnaround." *Speaker and Gavel* 16 (Summer 1979): 73–76. This article appeared in *Advanced Debate*, 3rd ed., pp. 84–89.

10. **Prentice**, "Strategic Considerations in Lincoln-Douglas Debate." Written for this edition.

11. **Cox and Phillips**, "Strategic Consideration in Parliamentary Debate." Paper presented at the Speech Communication Association at Chicago, Nov. 3, 1990. Originally titled "Impact and Implications of Parliamentary Format on American Debate."

12. **Lee, Harris, and Dudczak**, "The Use of Empirical Studies in Debate." This article appeared in *Advanced Debate*, 2nd ed., pp. 251–71 and *Advanced Debate*, 3rd ed., pp. 321–30. The original title was "Empirical Studies and Their Use in Debate."

13. **Zarefsky**, "The Role of Causal Argument in Policy Controversies." *Journal of the American Forensic Association* 13 (Spring 1977): 179–92. Reprinted by permission. This article appeared in *Advanced Debate*, 2nd ed., pp. 105–21, and *Advanced Debate*, 3rd ed., pp. 331–46.

Part Three: Resolutional Considerations

14. **Lichtman, Rohrer, and Corsi**, "The Debate Resolution." This article appeared in *Advanced Debate*, 2nd ed., pp. 83–88, and *Advanced Debate*, 3rd ed., pp. 126–29.

15. **Unger**, "Topicality: Why Not the Best?" This article originally appeared in *The Rostrum* 56 (Oct. 1981): 4–9. It appeared in *Advanced Debate*, 3rd ed., pp. 139–43.

16. **Parson and Bart**, "On Being Reasonable: The Last Refuge of Scoundrels: Part II, The Scoundrels Strike Back." This article was written especially for this anthology. It originally appeared in *Advanced Debate*, 3rd ed., pp. 130–38.

17. **Herbeck and Katsulas**, "The Affirmative Topicality Burden: Any Reasonable Example." *Journal of the American Forensic Association* 21 (Winter 1985): 133–45. Reprinted by permission. It appeared in *Advanced Debate*, 3rd ed., pp. 144–55. Edited for this edition.

18. **Paulsen and Rhodes**, "The Counterwarrant as a Negative Strategy: A Modest Proposal." *Journal of the American Forensic Association* 15 (Spring 1979): 205–10. It appeared in *Advanced Debate*, 3rd ed., pp. 156–64.

Part Four: Decision Rules

19. **Lichtman and Rohrer**, "Decision Rules in Policy Debate: Presumption and Burden of Proof." This article originally appeared in two parts in *Issues* (Feb. and Dec. 1974). Reprinted by permission. This article appeared in *Advanced Debate*, 2nd ed., pp. 42–69, and *Advanced Debate*, 3rd ed., pp. 347–72.

20. **Hart**, "Presumption in Policy Systems." This is a revision of a paper entitled "Towards a Nonstatic Theory of Presumption in Resolving Policy Controversy," presented to the Speech Communication Association Convention, Chicago, Nov. 1984. It appeared in *Advanced Debate*, 3rd ed., pp. 373–84.

21. **Thomas**, "Presumption in Nonpolicy Debate: A Case for Natural Presumption Based on Current Nonpolicy Paradigms." This article was

written especially for this anthology. It appeared in *Advanced Debate*, 3rd ed., pp. 448–68.

Part Five: Models of the Debate Process

22. Ulrich, "Stock Issues." Originally written as Chapter 2, *Debating Paradigms* (San Francisco: Griffin Research, in press). Used by permission. Edited for this edition.

23. Zarefsky, "Argument as Hypothesis Testing." This article appeared in *Advanced Debate*, 2nd ed., pp. 375–90, and *Advanced Debate*, 3rd ed., pp. 205–15. Edited for this edition.

24. Lichtman, Rohrer, and Corsi, "Policy Systems Analysis in Debate." This article appeared in *Advanced Debate*, 3rd ed., pp. 216–30.

25. Lichtman, Rohrer, and Hart, "Policy Systems Revisited." Parts of this article appeared in the *Journal of the American Forensic Association*. See Allan J. Lichtman, "Competing Models of the Debate Process," *JAFA* 22, (Winter 1986): 147–51. Revised and expanded by John Hart (in consultation with Lichtman) for this anthology. It appeared in *Advanced Debate*, 3rd ed., pp. 231–40.

Part Six: Judging Stances

26. Balthrop, "The Debate Judge as 'Critic of Argument.'" *Journal of the American Forensic Association* 20 (Summer 1983): 1–15. Reprinted by permission. It appeared in *Advanced Debate*, 3rd ed., pp. 166–82.

27. Ulrich, "In Search of *Tabula Rasa*." Paper presented to the Speech Communication Association Convention, Anaheim, Nov. 1981. It appeared in *Advanced Debate*, 3rd ed., pp. 183–91.

28. Snider, "Game Theory." Written for this edition.

29. K. Bartanen, "Application of the Narrative Paradigm in CEDA Debate." Paper presented to the Central States Speech Communication Association Convention at Denver, Nov. 1985. It appeared in *Advanced Debate*, 3rd ed., pp. 417–28.

30. Gass, "The Narrative Perspective on Academic Debate: A Critique." *Journal of the American Forensic Association* 25 (Fall 1988): 78–92. Used by permission.

Part Seven: Theoretical Issues in Policy Debate

31. Lichtman and Rohrer, "A General Theory of the Counterplan." *Journal of the American Forensic Association* 12 (Fall 1975): 70–79. Reprinted by permission. This article appeared in *Advanced Debate*, 2nd ed., pp. 200–12, and *Advanced Debate*, 3rd ed., pp. 243–53.

32. Herbeck, "A Permutation Standard of Competitiveness." *Journal of the American Forensic Association* 22 (Summer 1985): 12–19. It appeared in *Advanced Debate*, 3rd ed., pp. 254–63.

33. Solt, "Fiat: Resolving the Ambiguities of 'Should.'" *Journal of the American Forensic Association* 25 (Winter 1989): 117+. Used by permission.

34. Panetta and Dolley, "Topical Counterplans." Originally appeared as "The Topical Counterplan: A Competitive Policy Alternative," *Journal of the American Forensic Association* 25 (Winter 1989): 165–76. Used by permission.

35. Berube, "Parametric Topicality: A Response to Panetta and Dolley." Written for this edition.

Part Eight: Theoretical Issues in Nonpolicy Debate

36. Goulet and Bauer, "The Role and Function of Affirmative Criteria." Written for this anthology.

37. O'Dor, "It's About Time We Measure." Written for this anthology.

38. Matlon, "Debating Propositions of Value: An Idea Revisited." *CEDA Yearbook* 9 (1988): 1–14. Used by permission.

39. Hart and McGee, "Propositions of Fact." Written for this anthology.

40. Shipley, "Towards a Stategic Focus in Nonpolicy Debate." Written for this anthology.

41. Herbeck and Wong, "The Indivisibility of Value Claims from Policy Positions: An Argument for Policy in Value Debate." *CEDA Yearbook* (1986): 14–28. Used by permission.

42. Colbert and Thomas, "Value Implications." Written for this anthology. An earlier verison appeared as "Value Implications for Lincoln-Douglas Debate," *The Forensic Educator* 4 (1989/1990): 12–16.

43. Berube, "Hasty Generalization Revisited." This article appeared in *Advanced Debate*, 3rd ed., pp. 483–89. The author has rewritten the article for this edition.

44. Bile, "When the Whole Is Greater Than the Sum of the Parts: The Implications of Holistic Resolutional Focus." *CEDA Yearbook* 8 (1987): pp. 6–15. Used by permission.

45. Berube, "Debating Impacts: Intrinsicness Argumentation In Nonpolicy Debating." Written for this anthology.

NTC DEBATE AND SPEECH BOOKS

Debate
ADVANCED DEBATE, ed. Thomas & Hart
BASIC DEBATE, Fryar, Thomas, & Goodnight
COACHING AND DIRECTING FORENSICS, Klopf
CROSS-EXAMINATION IN DEBATE, Copeland
DICTIONARY OF DEBATE, Hanson
FORENSIC TOURNAMENTS: PLANNING AND ADMINISTRATION, Goodnight & Zarefsky
GETTING STARTED IN DEBATE, Goodnight
JUDGING ACADEMIC DEBATE, Ulrich
MODERN DEBATE CASE TECHNIQUES, Terry et al.
MOVING FROM POLICY TO VALUE DEBATE, Richards
STRATEGIC DEBATE, Wood & Goodnight
STUDENT CONGRESS & LINCOLN-DOUGLAS DEBATE, Giertz & Mezzera

Speech Communication
ACTIVITIES FOR EFFECTIVE COMMUNICATION, LiSacchi
THE BASICS OF SPEECH, Galvin, Cooper, & Gordon
CONTEMPORARY SPEECH, HopKins & Whitaker
CREATIVE SPEAKING, Buys et al.
DYNAMICS OF SPEECH, Myers & Herndon
GETTING STARTED IN PUBLIC SPEAKING, Prentice & Payne
LISTENING BY DOING, Galvin
LITERATURE ALIVE! Gamble & Gamble
MEETINGS: RULES & PROCEDURES, Pohl
PERSON TO PERSON, Galvin & Book
PUBLIC SPEAKING TODAY! Prentice & Payne
SELF-AWARENESS, Ratliffe & Herman
SPEAKING BY DOING, Buys, Sill, & Beck

For a current catalog and information about our complete line
of language arts books, write:
National Textbook Company,
a division of NTC Publishing Group
4255 West Touhy Avenue
Lincolnwood (Chicago), Illinois 60646-1975 U.S.A.